LIFT

TAKE YOUR STUDYING
TO THE NEXT LEVEL.

This book comes with 1-year digital access to the
Examples & Explanations for this course.

Step 1: Go to www.CasebookConnect.com/LIFT and redeem your access code to get started.

Access Code:  EEST230487976480

Step 2: Go to your BOOKSHELF and select your online *Examples & Explanations* to start reading, highlighting, and taking notes in the margins of your e-book.

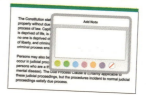

Step 3: Select the STUDY tab in your toolbar to access the questions from your book in interactive format, designed to give you extra practice and help you master the course material.

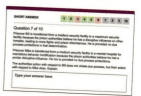

Is this a used casebook? Access code already scratched off?

You can purchase the online *Examples & Explanations* and still access all of the powerful tools listed above. Please visit CasebookConnect.com/Catalog to learn more about Connected Study Aids.

PLEASE NOTE: Each access code provides 12 month access and can only be used once. This code will also expire one year after the discontinuation of the corresponding print title and must be redeemed before then. CCH reserves the right to discontinue this program at any time for any business reason. For further details, please see the Casebook Connect End User Agreement.

PIN: 9111149619

02001

Secured Transactions

ASPEN CASEBOOK SERIES

Secured Transactions
A Systems Approach

Eighth Edition

Lynn M. LoPucki
Security Pacific Bank Distinguished Professor of Law
UCLA Law School

Elizabeth Warren
Leo E. Gottlieb Professor of Law Emeritus
Harvard University

Robert M. Lawless
Max L. Rowe Professor of Law
University of Illinois College of Law

 Wolters Kluwer

Published by Wolters Kluwer in New York.

Wolters Kluwer serves customers worldwide with CCH, Aspen Publishers, and Kluwer Law International products. (www.wolterskluwerlb.com)

To contact Customer Service, e-mail customer.service@wolterskluwer.com, call 1-800-234-1660, fax 1-800-901-9075, or mail correspondence to:

Wolters Kluwer
Attn: Order Department
PO Box 990
Frederick, MD 21705

Printed in the United States of America.

3 4 5 6 7 8 9 0

ISBN 978-1-4548-5793-8

Library of Congress Cataloging-in-Publication Data

LoPucki, Lynn M., author.
  [Secured credit]
  Secured transactions : a systems approach / Lynn M. LoPucki, Security Pacific Bank Distinguished Professor of Law, UCLA Law School; Elizabeth Warren, Leo E. Gottlieb Professor of Law Emeritus, Harvard University; Robert M. Lawless, Max L. Rowe Professor of Law, University of Illinois College of Law. — Eighth edition.
     pages cm. — (Aspen casebook series)
   ISBN 978-1-4548-5793-8
   1. Debtor and creditor--United States . 2. Security (Law) — United States. 3. Bankruptcy — United States . I. Warren, Elizabeth, author. II. Lawless, Robert M., 1964- author. III. Title.

KF1501.L65 2016
346.7307'7 — dc23
                                                         2015033561

About Wolters Kluwer Law & Business

Wolters Kluwer Law & Business is a leading global provider of intelligent information and digital solutions for legal and business professionals in key specialty areas, and respected educational resources for professors and law students. Wolters Kluwer Law & Business connects legal and business professionals as well as those in the education market with timely, specialized authoritative content and information-enabled solutions to support success through productivity, accuracy and mobility.

Serving customers worldwide, Wolters Kluwer Law & Business products include those under the Aspen Publishers, CCH, Kluwer Law International, Loislaw, ftwilliam.com and MediRegs family of products.

CCH products have been a trusted resource since 1913, and are highly regarded resources for legal, securities, antitrust and trade regulation, government contracting, banking, pension, payroll, employment and labor, and healthcare reimbursement and compliance professionals.

Aspen Publishers products provide essential information to attorneys, business professionals and law students. Written by preeminent authorities, the product line offers analytical and practical information in a range of specialty practice areas from securities law and intellectual property to mergers and acquisitions and pension/benefits. Aspen's trusted legal education resources provide professors and students with high-quality, up-to-date and effective resources for successful instruction and study in all areas of the law.

Kluwer Law International products provide the global business community with reliable international legal information in English. Legal practitioners, corporate counsel and business executives around the world rely on Kluwer Law journals, looseleafs, books, and electronic products for comprehensive information in many areas of international legal practice.

Loislaw is a comprehensive online legal research product providing legal content to law firm practitioners of various specializations. Loislaw provides attorneys with the ability to quickly and efficiently find the necessary legal information they need, when and where they need it, by facilitating access to primary law as well as state-specific law, records, forms and treatises.

ftwilliam.com offers employee benefits professionals the highest quality plan documents (retirement, welfare and non-qualified) and government forms (5500/PBGC, 1099 and IRS) software at highly competitive prices.

MediRegs products provide integrated health care compliance content and software solutions for professionals in healthcare, higher education and life sciences, including professionals in accounting, law and consulting.

Wolters Kluwer Law & Business, a division of Wolters Kluwer, is headquartered in New York. Wolters Kluwer is a market-leading global information services company focused on professionals.

For Walter O. Weyrauch
—L.M.L.

For Allan Axelrod
—E.W.

For J. Martin Lawless
—R.M.L.

Summary of Contents

Contents

Acknowledgments

We are deeply indebted to Jay L. Westbrook, University of Texas School of Law, for his intellectual contributions to this book. Jay deserves credit as a codeveloper of what we here call "the systems approach." Many of our colleagues contributed to this edition by making comments on earlier editions. They include:

Allan Axelrod, Rutgers-Newark Center for Law & Justice (deceased)
John D. Ayer, University of California, Davis School of Law
Roger Bernhardt, Golden Gate University School of Law
Nicholas Brannick, Ohio State University College of Law
Beth Buckley, SUNY Buffalo School of Law
Scott J. Burnham, University of Montana School of Law
Amy C. Bushaw, Lewis & Clark Law School
Jonathon S. Byington, University of Montana School of Law
Robert Chapman, Willamette University College of Law
Wendy Gerwick Couture, University of Idaho College of Law
Jeffrey T. Ferriell, Capital University Law School
Wilson Freyermuth, University of Missouri-Columbia School of Law
Michael D. Guttentag, Loyola Law School, Los Angeles
Russell Hakes, Widener University School of Law
Jim Hawkins, University of Houston Law Center
Kathryn R. Heidt, University of Pittsburgh Law School (deceased)
Paul Hoffman, UMKC School of Law
Margaret Howard, Washington and Lee University School of Law
Sarah Jane Hughes, Indiana University School of Law-Bloomington
Melissa B. Jacoby, University of North Carolina School of Law
Edward Janger, Brooklyn Law School
Phyllis M. Jones, University of Arkansas at Little Rock School of Law
Andrew Kaufman, Harvard Law School
Daniel L. Keating, Washington University School of Law
Kenneth C. Kettering, New York Law School
Jason J. Kilborn, The John Marshall Law School
Charles Lincoln Knapp, University of California, Hastings College of the Law
F. Stephen Knippenberg, University of Oklahoma Law Center
Michael M. Korybut, Saint Louis University School of Law
Adam J. Levitin, Georgetown University Law Center
Angela K. Littwin, University of Texas School of Law
Ronald J. Mann, Columbia Law School
Bruce Markell, Northwestern University School of Law
Colin P. Marks, St. Mary's University School of Law

Nathalie D. Martin, University of New Mexico School of Law

Jeffrey M. McFarland, Florida Coastal School of Law

Gary Neustadter, Santa Clara University School of Law

Katherine Porter, University of California, Irvine School of Law

John A.E. Pottow, University of Michigan Law School

C. Scott Pryor, Regent University School of Law

Marc Roark, Savannah Law School

Arnold Rosenberg, Thomas Jefferson School of Law

Steven L. Sepinuck, Gonzaga University School of Law

Paul M. Shupack, Yeshiva University, Cardozo School of Law

Joshua M. Silverstein, University of Arkansas at Little Rock School of Law

Lars S. Smith, University of Louisville School of Law

David Snyder, American University, Washington College of Law

Charles J. Tabb, University of Illinois College of Law

Catherine Tinker, University of South Dakota School of Law

Stephen J. Ware, University of Kansas School of Law

G. Ray Warner, St. John's University School of Law

Elaine Ann Welle, University of Wyoming College of Law

Zipporah B. Wiseman, University of Texas School of Law

William J. Woodard, Jr., Temple University School of Law

We are indebted to them, their students, and our own students at the University of Pennsylvania, Harvard, Washington University, the University of Wisconsin, Cornell, UCLA, and the University of Illinois for putting up with our errors, both substantive and typographical, and for helping us improve the book.

Numerous people who work in the secured credit system were kind enough to answer our questions about the system and otherwise provide information. They include Naran U. Burchinow, General Counsel for Deutsche Financial Services; Carl Ernst, President of UCC Filing Guide, Inc.; Jerry Grossman, at Heller, Erhman, White, and McAuliffe, San Francisco, California; and Ed Hand, UCC Filing and Search Services, Tallahassee, Florida. Joanne Margherita and Karen Mathews served as desktop publishers and manuscript organizers. Barbara Smith, Bill Cobb, Cathy Stites, Eric Aguilara, and Heather Suve provided valuable assistance with research. While our work was in progress, Peter Benvenutti's bankruptcy department at Heller, Erhman, White, and McAuliffe sheltered one of the authors from the dark, bitter cold of two Wisconsin winters under the rubric "Scholar-in-Residence" and made available the resources of the firm.

The following have granted permission to reprint:

North American Syndicate for special permission to reprint the Dunagin's People cartoon that appears in Assignment 35.

The Virginia Law Review for permission to reprint portions of Lynn M. LoPucki, The Unsecured Creditor's Bargain, 80 Va. L. Rev. 1887 (1994).

Deutsche Financial Services for permission to reprint portions of the Security Agreement and Floorplan Agreement that appear in Assignment 15.

Matthew Bender & Co. for permission to reprint the security agreement default provisions from Howard Ruda, Asset-Based Financing. Copyright © 2015 Matthew Bender & Company, Inc., a LexisNexis company. All rights reserved.

Anthony B. Kronman, Fred B. Rothman & Company, and the Yale Law Journal for permission to reprint portions of Thomas H. Jackson and Anthony Kronman, Secured Financing and Priorities Among Creditors, 88 Yale L.J. 1143,1147-1148 (1979).

Robert E. Scott and the Columbia Law Review for permission to reprint portions of Robert E. Scott, A Relational Theory of Secured Financing, 86 Colum. L. Rev. 901, 904-911 (1986).

Steven L. Harris, Charles W. Mooney, Jr., Fred B. Rothman & Company and the Virginia Law Review for permission to reprint portions of Steven L. Harris and Charles W. Mooney, Jr., A Property-Based Theory of Security Interests: Taking Debtor's Choices Seriously, 80 Va. L. Rev. 2021, 2021-2023, 2047-2053 (1994).

Donald B. Dowart for permission to reprint Donald B. Dowart, Memorandum: Priorities of Maritime Lien and Preferred Ship Mortgages, Feb. 9, 1993.

The Cornell Law Review for permission to reprint Elizabeth Warren, Making Policy with Imperfect Information: The Article 9 Full Priority Debates, 81 Cornell L. Rev. 1373 (1997).

Fred B. Rothman & Company and the Yale Law Journal for permission to reprint portions of Lynn M. LoPucki, The Death of Liability, 106 Yale L.J. 1 (1996).

Ronald J. Mann and the Georgetown Law Journal for permission to reprint portions of Ronald J. Mann, The Role of Secured Credit in Small-Business Lending, 86 Geo. L.J. 1 (1997).

Arvin I. Abraham, and Bernd P. Delahaye for permission to reprint a portion of Lynn M. LoPucki, Arvin I. Abraham, and Bernd P. Delahaye, Optimizing English and American Security Interests, 88 Notre Dame L. Rev. 1785 (2013).

INTRODUCTION

In the movie *Wall Street*, the neophyte stockbroker is concerned that what Gordon Gekko proposes is insider trading. Gekko responds, "Either you're *inside,* or you're *outside.*" That is the way it is with credit. Either you're *secured* or you're *unsecured.*

You may already have some sense of the difference. We usually describe secured loans by reference to the collateral. We talk about home loans, car loans, inventory loans, and farm crop loans, to mention just a few. Among the credit extensions usually made on an unsecured basis are credit cards, bonds issued to investors by large companies, student loans, loans between friends, trade credit (a business's purchase of inventory on credit), and many loans by commercial banks and insurance companies.

Secured status comes in essentially three forms: security interests created by contracts, liens created by statutes, and liens created by judicial acts. Each security interest or lien is a relationship between a debt and property that serves as collateral. The debt can be almost any kind of contractual promise or legal obligation. Collateral can be nearly anything of value, real or personal, tangible or intangible. The security interest or lien is the right, in the event that the debt is not paid when due, to force a sale of the collateral and have the proceeds applied to pay the debt.

Secured creditors have "priority" over unsecured creditors. Priority is the right to be paid from the value of the collateral, up to the full amount of the debt, in preference to competing claimants.

A security interest can prioritize not only a debt, but any legal right that carries a damage remedy. That is, unilaterally granting a security interest to the holder of one right gives that holder priority over the holders of all other rights. As a result, security interests and liens are fundamental to all deal making, from divorce settlements to corporate mergers. By determining whose legal rights have priority, security determines who has privilege and power. Security's effects are present even if the obligation is never in default. Anyone who has taken out a mortgage on a home or signed a security agreement to finance a car will know what we mean.

Most secured creditors obtain their rights by contract. Those private contracts—*security agreements*—bind the parties who sign them. In addition to establishing the legal rights of the debtor and creditor, the security agreement is effective against third parties. For example, Uniform Commercial Code §9-201 provides that "Except as otherwise provided in the Uniform Commercial Code, a security agreement is effective according to its terms between the parties, against purchasers of the collateral, and against creditors." Security is an agreement between A and B that C take nothing.

The idea of a private contract that binds non-parties is, for most of us, startling. Defenders analogize security agreements to real estate conveyances. They argue that, by granting a security interest, the debtor conditionally sells the collateral to the extent of the secured obligation. (Quite a mouthful, isn't it?) They also note that the Uniform Commercial Code requires the parties, in most instances, to provide "notice to the world" of the agreement's existence by making a UCC filing. (What? You've never heard of the UCC filing system? Your legal rights have been affected by this system since before you were born. When you make certain purchases, you are charged with the knowledge that the system would have provided — if only you had known to look.)

The concept of security permeates the law. This book explores the use of that concept across numerous bodies of law, but the emphasis is on Article 9 of the Uniform Commercial Code. We have tried to write this book so that its five major topics can be covered in any order. Those topics are (1) remedies, (2) creation of security interests, (3) default, (4) perfection, and (5) priority. Regardless of the order in which you cover them, we think you will find the following overview helpful.

The book has two parts. Part One deals with the relationships between a debtor and a secured creditor. Part Two deals with competitions among secured creditors and a variety of other parties who may claim collateral.

Part One begins with remedies — the consequences of secured credit. Under state law, secured creditors have the right to force sale of the debtor's property after default and have the sale proceeds applied to the obligation. Debtors generally remain liable for any unpaid balances — called "deficiencies" — remaining after application of the sale proceeds.

An unsecured creditor can become a secured creditor by obtaining a judgment on the debt, obtaining a writ of execution based on the judgment, and then levying on specific property of the debtor. From the moment of levy, such a creditor is referred to as a "lien creditor." Becoming a lien creditor by levy is a relatively ineffective remedy because (1) creditors who obtained secured status by contract when they loaned money to the debtor will have established their rights earlier and have priority over the lien creditor, (2) some creditors who obtained secured status by contract have self-help repossession rights not available to unsecured or lien creditors, and (3) the rights of lien creditors, but not those of creditors who obtained secured status by contract, are subject to exemption laws.

Because foreclosure and execution sale procedures are often antiquated and ineffective, property often sells for substantially less than it is worth. Article 9 takes a different approach. It authorizes the secured creditor to conduct the sale. Instead of specifying procedures for sale, Article 9 requires that every aspect of the sale be commercially reasonable and leaves it to the secured creditors to devise the procedures.

When a debtor files bankruptcy, creditors are automatically stayed (enjoined) from exercising their remedies. Secured creditors are entitled to adequate protection against decline in the value of their collateral during the bankruptcy case and to relief from the stay if the debtor can't provide adequate protection. Ultimately, secured creditors are entitled to the value of their collateral, up to the full amount the debtor owes them. Unsecured creditors are not entitled to adequate protection of their expectancies or to relief from the automatic stay. Instead, they receive a pro-rata share of what remains after provision for or payment of secured creditors.

Part One then turns to the creation of security interests. The debtor and the creditor create a security interest by entering into a "security agreement." A security interest is said to "attach" to the collateral after the last of three events has occurred: (1) the debtor has signed or "authenticated" a security agreement that provides a description of the collateral, (2) the secured creditor has given "value," usually by disbursing loan proceeds, and (3) the debtor has acquired rights in the collateral.

When a debtor sells or otherwise disposes of collateral, two important rules apply. First, a security interest granted by that debtor-seller generally continues in the collateral in the hands of the buyer. Second, the security interest attaches to the sale proceeds.

The first rule has numerous exceptions. The most important is that a buyer in the ordinary course of the seller's business takes free of any security interest the seller created. For example, someone who buys restaurant equipment from a restaurant equipment dealer takes free of a security interest in favor of the dealer's inventory lender, but someone who buys restaurant equipment from a restaurant does not take free of a security interest in favor of the restaurant's equipment lender.

A security interest granted by the debtor-seller attaches to the proceeds in either type of sale. To illustrate, if a restaurant sold unneeded restaurant equipment for $90,000 in cash, the restaurant's bank lender might have a security interest in both the equipment in the hands of the buyer and the $90,000 in the hands of the seller.

A security agreement may provide that property acquired in the future will be collateral. Such an "after acquired property" clause will cease to be effective when the debtor files bankruptcy. But even during bankruptcy, security interests continue to attach to proceeds.

Bankruptcy courts have the authority to limit a secured creditor's proceeds "based on the equities of the case." A classic example of the equities-of-the-case exception occurs in inventory lending. Suppose a restaurant equipment dealer is in bankruptcy. The dealer buys equipment wholesale for $50,000 and sells it at retail for $90,000. A bankruptcy court might use the exception to limit the inventory lender's interest in the $90,000 of proceeds to $50,000. The court might reason that the $40,000 difference represents the debtor's contribution of value by advertising the equipment for sale, paying the salesperson's wages, providing the retail floor space, and paying other expenses of the sale.

Law and policy limit the types of property that may be collateral. Excluded items include individuals' future earnings, pension rights, some kinds of licenses and franchises, and certain low-value consumer goods.

The last topic in Part One is default. Generally, a creditor may exercise remedies only when the debtor is in default. After default, if the loan agreement so provides, the creditor may "accelerate" installment payments by declaring future payments immediately due and payable. Under state law, a debtor can cure a default, but cannot reverse an acceleration. Under bankruptcy law, a debtor may be able to reverse an acceleration by proposing and obtaining court confirmation of a repayment plan.

Part Two of the book begins with a simple description of priority. Priority is a right to be provided for, or paid from, the value of the collateral before other creditors are paid anything at all. Generally speaking, the first creditor to "perfect" its security interest or lien by giving puplic notice in a manner authorized by law has priority.

The most commonly authorized manner for giving notice of a security interest or lien is to file the notice in the appropriate filing system. Future lenders can discover the existence of prior liens by searching the appropriate filing system before making their loans. After the debtor repays the obligation, the notice can be cancelled by filing a satisfaction or termination statement.

If the notice is in a form authorized by Article 9, the notice is called a "financing statement." For most kinds of collateral, financing statements are effective for only five years, but can be extended by filing "continuation statements."

Filing and searching in the Article 9 filing systems are by debtor's name. Filings are ineffective unless made in the debtor's correct name or a name sufficiently similar that the filings will show up in a search under the correct name. Article 9 filings also include the parties' addresses and a description of the collateral to make it easier for searchers to recognize relevant filings. Filing and searching in other filing systems may be by the debtor's name or by a number — such as a real estate tract number or the VIN number that identifies an automobile.

Secured parties can use two other methods of perfection: taking possession of tangible collateral or taking "control" of intangible collateral. For some types of collateral, these methods are merely permitted, while for other types they are required. In addition, some security interests and liens are automatically perfected without the secured party providing any notice to future lenders.

Security interests in real property — called "mortgages" or "deeds of trust" — are perfected by recording in county filing systems. Mortgages encumber not just land and buildings, but also property affixed to land or buildings ("fixtures"). Security interests in fixtures can also be perfected by filing Article 9 financing statements in the real estate or Article 9 filing systems.

The appropriate manner of perfection may depend on the type of collateral, the manner in which it is used, the name of the owner, the location of the debtor, or the location of the collateral. If these conditions change between the time of filing and the time of searching, a searcher may be unable to discover a prior lender's notice. In response to some condition changes, the prior lender must conform its notice to the changed condition by some statutory deadline. In response to others, the later lender must discover the change on its own.

The last subject covered is priority. Creditors with differing priorities in the same collateral may foreclose in any order. They may do so against all or any portion of their collateral, unless their choice would unfairly damage a subordinate lien holder. Any creditor's sale discharges the lien under which the sale is held and all subordinate liens. The proceeds of a sale are distributed to the lien under which the sale is held and all subordinate liens. Prior liens continue to encumber the collateral in the hands of the buyer.

Bankruptcy can alter three key principles of the secured credit system. First, bankruptcy's "automatic stay" can delay foreclosures by senior liens to protect the interests of junior liens and unsecured creditors. Second, the bankruptcy courts can sell collateral free and clear of liens in some circumstances. The proceeds of sale are distributed in accord with nonbankruptcy priorities. Third, the bankruptcy courts can grant new liens with priority over existing liens, conditioned on "adequate protection" of the existing lienors' interests. In addition, if a preexisting creditor improves its priority position in the period immediately prior to bankruptcy, either by becoming secured, or if already secured, by receiving additional collateral, the trustee in bankruptcy or debtor in possession can avoid the improvement.

The remainder of this book examines the competitions among particular kinds of liens and interests in collateral. They include Article 9 security interests, purchase-money security interests, future advances, real estate mortgages, execution liens, trustees in bankruptcy, sellers, buyers, and statutory liens including federal tax liens. The rules that determine priority between parties in these categories are spread among several different bodies of law. Most operate by assigning a priority date to each of two contestants based on the circumstances of the particular case and awarding priority to the one with the earlier date.

We have written this book with an attitude. Legal education has a way of taking simple things and making them seem complex. In this book we have made every effort to do the opposite—to make this complex, technical subject as simple as possible. This is a course for second- and third-year students who have already mastered reading cases. The threshold intellectual task here is to read statutes; the ultimate intellectual task is to see how law functions together with other elements as a law-related system. Someone who masters that task can see law with new eyes—can see better whom law helps, whom it hurts, what implications it has for planning and transactional work, and how it can be manipulated, for better or for worse, to produce unexpected outcomes.

To make the whole more understandable, we have throughout this book regarded secured credit as a system, with subsystems that work together to accomplish the system's principal goal. That goal is to facilitate credit extensions and deal-making without sanctioning injustice.

To the extent the system succeeds in doing that, it does so in two ways. First, it provides secured creditors with a coercive remedy—repossession and resale of collateral—that does not destroy too much of the value of the collateral in the process. The existence of a coercive remedy encourages debtors to pay voluntarily. The principal subsystems that provide this remedy are:

1. *Procedures for creating security interests.* This subsystem consists of laws, forms, and (dare we say it?) rituals used by debtors and their creditors to elevate claims to secured status.
2. *Rules authorizing self-help.* UCC §§9-607 and 9-609 authorize secured creditors to repossess collateral and redirect their debtor's incoming payments to themselves, all without judicial process.
3. *State remedies system.* State governments provide systems by which government officials declare foreclosures, repossess collateral, and sell the

collateral for the benefit of secured creditors. All of this is accomplished pursuant to judicial orders and procedures established by law.

4. *Bankruptcy system.* The federal government provides a bankruptcy system in which bankruptcy judges, bankruptcy trustees, and other officials ensure the preservation of secured creditors' collateral while the debtor continues to use the collateral or the bankruptcy officials liquidate it. While these bankruptcy procedures overlap and duplicate those of the older state remedies system, they are less rigid and therefore more effective than those of the state remedies system.

The second manner in which the secured credit system facilitates credit extension is by letting lenders know, before they commit, what priority or rights in the collateral they will have against third parties in the event of default. Here, three subsystems are at work:

1. *Public record systems.* Federal, state, and local governments operate thousands of public record systems in which various kinds of secured parties are required to "file" or "record" their interests in order to perfect them. The records in these systems are indexed by public officials and then searched by later lenders who seek to discover the security interests, if any, that will have priority over the ones they themselves plan to take.

2. *Rules of priority.* State law, including Article 9 of the Uniform Commercial Code and thousands of statutory lien laws, contains rules intended to govern priority in competitions between particular kinds of claimants to collateral. Federal law provides additional rules of priority in the areas of bankruptcy, taxation, patents, trademarks, copyrights, admiralty, and others. These rules are interpreted, reconciled, and enforced in state, federal, and bankruptcy courts and, of course, in private negotiations between competing parties.

3. *Bankruptcy lien avoidance.* Secured creditors frequently fail to satisfy the complex technical requirements to perfect their interests. These failures result in relatively few challenges by competing creditors. Bankruptcy law fills the gap by appointing a person to serve as "trustee" in the bankruptcy case, arming that person with the rights of a hypothetical aggrieved lien creditor and providing incentives for the trustee to challenge any security interest that may be vulnerable. From a systems perspective, the effect is to greatly increase the level of enforcement and contentiousness in the system. That in turn increases the incentives for secured creditors to comply with the technicalities of the system, as well as providing jobs for lawyers.

As may already be apparent, the systems approach we employ in this book looks at more than just law. Law is one of the many elements that together constitute the secured credit system. To teach the law without teaching the system in which it is embedded would deprive the law of much of its meaning and make it more difficult to understand. But to teach the whole system requires discussion of institutions, people, and other things that are not "law." Among them are sheriffs, bankruptcy trustees, filing systems, security agreements, financing statements, search companies, Vehicle Identification Numbers, closing practices, collateral repurchase agreements, and a variety of other commercial and legal practices. Together with law from a variety of sources, these things constitute the system we know as secured credit and the subject of this course. If you would like to know more about the systems approach, see Lynn M. LoPucki, The Systems Approach to Law, 82 Cornell L. Rev. 479 (1997).

Article 9 of the Uniform Commercial Code (the UCC) constitutes much of secured transactions law. The Uniform Law Commission collaborates with the American Law Institute to produce the UCC. The Official Text of the UCC is just a recommendation to the states. The UCC does not become the law of a state until the state adopts it. All 50 states have adopted the UCC, but some states have also adopted nonuniform amendments. Because these amendments can be outcome determinative, lawyers generally work not with the UCC, but with the version or versions adopted by the relevant state or states.

The Uniform Law Commission revised Article 9 extensively in 1998, effective in 2001. All 50 states adopted that revision. The Commission promulgated additional changes in 2010, effective in 2013. As of this writing, all states except Oklahoma have adopted the 2010 amendments.

We have heavily edited the cases in the book. To ease readability, we have not marked our omissions with ellipses. In each instance we have tried to be faithful to both the letter and spirit of the original.

We have tried to include in each assignment all of the information needed to answer the problems at the end. The problems in a set are presented roughly in the order of their difficulty. The most difficult problems are in practice settings. Many of them are sufficiently complex to challenge even lawyers who have been practicing commercial law for many years. Our assumption is that each member of the class, working alone or perhaps with one or two others, will find a satisfying solution to each problem before class. In class, students will present and discuss a variety of solutions and then attempt to settle on one or two that seem best. The process is not unlike that followed in most large law firms when several lawyers meet to brainstorm and formulate case strategy. Like most lawyers, we think that such sessions are the most challenging, intellectually exciting, and fun parts of law practice.

Lynn M. LoPucki
Elizabeth Warren
Robert M. Lawless

September 2015

I don't know as I want a Lawyer to tell me what I cannot do.
I hire him to tell me how to do what I want to do.

—J. P. Morgan

Secured Transactions

Part One
The Creditor-Debtor Relationship

Chapter 1.   Creditors' Remedies Under State Law

Assignment 1:   Remedies of Unsecured Creditors Under State Law

A.   Who Is an Unsecured Creditor?

The legal concepts of debtor and creditor apply to a wide variety of human relationships. The archetype is the relationship between the borrower and lender of money. But anyone who is owed a legal obligation that can be reduced to a money judgment is a creditor of the party owing the obligation. At the instant one car slides into another, the victim of a car accident becomes a creditor. Similarly, the company with a valid patent infringement claim, the consumer with a defective product still covered by a warranty, and the child who is the beneficiary of a noncustodial parent's court-imposed support obligation are all creditors. The obligations owed to them can be reduced to money obligations. The company that infringed the patent, the manufacturer or seller of the goods, and the noncustodial parent are their debtors.

Many debtor-creditor relationships are entered into voluntarily, as when a creditor has lent money to a debtor. But many others are entered into involuntarily. The soon-to-be debtor's first contact with the soon-to-be creditor may be when their cars occupy the same space in the road simultaneously. The parties may meet on a happy occasion, such as the cash purchase of a product covered by a warranty. Until the product fails they may not even realize that they are not just buyer and seller, but also debtor and creditor. Or a party may be wary about the credit relationship—a child's representative may be acutely aware of the depressing statistics on support compliance—but have no reasonable alternative to becoming a creditor.

Unless a creditor contracts with the debtor for secured status or is granted it by statute, the creditor will be *unsecured*. Unsecured creditors are the *general creditors* or *ordinary creditors* that populate state collection proceedings. They include creditors who contracted for unsecured status, but also creditors such as the tort victims mentioned above, who got their creditor status in circumstances that do not permit prior negotiations. They also include incautious creditors, uninformed creditors, and creditors who were unable for any number of reasons to negotiate for security. If the unsecured creditor has already obtained a court judgment to establish liability, the creditor is a *judgment creditor*, but the mere grant of a judgment does not alter the creditor's unsecured status.

In this assignment, we examine the legal remedies available to all creditors. These are the minimum rights guaranteed to anyone owed an obligation that can be reduced to a money judgment. In later assignments, we will use these remedies as a baseline for comparing and understanding the enhanced collection rights that only secured creditors enjoy.

Much of law is about liability and the determination of damages. But winning a money judgment for a breach of contract, a tort, a treble-damage antitrust suit, or some other kind of case may be only the beginning of the story. One of the authors of this book worked hard on the liability issues of her first trial (a rousing traffic accident in Rockaway, New Jersey, in 1977). At the conclusion of the trial in Hill v. Pyser (unreported), the judge awarded her client full damages — $147.58. The defendants left the courtroom sullen and unhappy. The plaintiffs were ebullient — justice had prevailed! But once the courtroom had cleared and smiles and handshakes had been exchanged all around, the client paused and, with evident embarrassment, asked the truly critical question: "Uh, how do we get paid?" A long, painful silence followed. The clever coauthor-to-be did not have the faintest idea. Because the defendants did not whip out their checkbooks and pay up, it seemed that still more legal process might be necessary.

Liability may be hotly disputed and parties may litigate vigorously, as they did in the Rockaway car accident. Or liability may be undisputed, as often happens when a debtor borrows money and is simply unable to repay. Either way, if no payment follows, the party owed an obligation may find that even after judgment has become "final," there can be a long and sometimes tortuous process ahead before any money changes hands.

Nothing in this discussion should be taken to imply that debtors seldom pay their unsecured debts. How often debtors actually repay is an empirical question. The evidence suggests that debtors pay voluntarily in the overwhelming majority of cases. Even when debtors would like to escape their obligations, their unsecured creditors typically can muster enough leverage, legal and otherwise, to compel repayment. But these are not the situations most attorneys are likely to encounter in their practices. Unsecured creditors bring lawyers into the tough cases, when the debtors are likely to be resistant and the availability of assets is uncertain. The lawyer who seeks to collect on a judgment on an unsecured debt usually faces a stiff challenge.

B.   How Do Unsecured Creditors Compel Payment?

The unsecured creditor's path to collection is narrow. Not only does the law provide procedures for the collection of unsecured debts, it regulates or bars outright many alternatives. Among the remedies prohibited to unsecured creditors is self-help seizure of the debtor's property. (This rule does not prevent the creditor from "setting off" a debt owing to its debtor against a debt owing from its debtor; it merely prohibits the creditor from seizing property for the purpose of creating such a setoff.) In most instances, a prohibited seizure of a debtor's property will constitute the tort of conversion.

> Conversion is the wrongful exercise of dominion and control over another's property in denial of or inconsistent with his rights. . . . A plaintiff need not establish that the defendant acted with a wrongful intent. The intent required is not necessarily a matter of conscious wrongdoing. It is rather an intent to exercise a dominion or control over the goods which is in fact inconsistent with the plaintiff's rights. Winkle Chevy-Olds-Pontiac, Inc. v. Condon, 830 S.W.2d 740 (Tex. App. 1992).

Additionally, the creditor that wrongfully takes possession of property of the debtor may be charged with larceny, even though the value of the property taken is less than the amount owed. Finally, although the creditor has the right to demand payment from the debtor, if the creditor does so in an unreasonable manner, the creditor may incur liability for wrongful collection practices. The creditor is entitled to coerce payment of the debt only through the judicial processes specified by the state. Although these processes are fundamentally the same in all states, there are differences in the language used to describe the processes and the myriad ways they are implemented. These differences in language and method of implementation can make it difficult to see the common system structure. In this assignment we try to focus on that common system structure.

The first step in the debt collection process is to file a complaint with an appropriate court, and serve process on the debtor-defendant. If the complaint is filed with a small claims court, the next step may be a hearing in which the court will resolve the entire case by entering a final judgment. If the debt exceeds the jurisdiction of the local small claims court, the procedure is the one you saw in your first year course on civil procedure. The debtor may file motions in response to the complaint, and need not answer it until those motions are resolved. Once the answer is filed the case may be set for trial months in the future. (If the facts are not in dispute, it may be resolved earlier on summary judgment.) If the debtor does not defend the case, a default judgment may be entered in as little as 30 or 40 days. But even without a substantial defense, a debtor-defendant can usually drag the case out for six months to a year before the court enters judgment.

The story in the following case begins where this description ends — with the entry of a judgment. After judgment, the creditor's attorney spent countless hours trying to collect. We include the case not so much for its exposition of the law governing execution, levy, and the obscure remedy of amercement, as for what it shows about the system by which execution is made. The story of Jeffrey Israelow's tenacious pursuit of $6,317 conveys something of the enormity of the unsecured creditor's task when facing a recalcitrant debtor.

The basis for the plaintiff's judgment against Hotel California is briefly alluded to in the first footnote of the case. The judgment was only one milestone on a long, tortuous route to collection. The opinion is a catalog of the kinds of problems that plaintiffs encounter in attempting to collect an unsecured judgment against a stubborn debtor. What is extraordinary about this case is that the court did something about these problems and published a lengthy opinion.

Vitale v. Hotel California, Inc.

446 A.2d 880 (N.J. Super. Ct. Law 1982)

STALLER, J.S.C.

Plaintiff David J. Vitale, Jr. brings this motion pursuant to N.J.S.A. 40A:9-109 to amerce, that is, hold liable the Sheriff of Monmouth County, William Lanzaro, for failing to execute a writ based on a judgment against defendant Hotel California, Inc. (California). [A]mercement of a sheriff has not been the topic of any reported decision in New Jersey since 1907, and [has been] infrequently reported elsewhere.

The chronology of events is as follows: Vitale obtained a final judgment against California in the amount of $6,317 plus costs on August 12, 1980,[2] and thereafter learned that California held the liquor license for "The Fast Lane," a bar featuring "punk rock" entertainers, located in Asbury Park, New Jersey. A writ of execution issued on June 23, 1981, and on July 9 the sheriff received the writ along with a cover letter from plaintiff instructing him to levy upon all monies and personal property at The Fast Lane. A check to cover the sheriff's costs up to $50 was enclosed.

Then began plaintiff's travail with the sheriff's office which gave rise to this proceeding. On July 27 the office indicated to plaintiff's attorney, Jeffrey K. Israelow, that a levy was not possible since the bar was only open late in the evening, from about 10 P.M. to 2 A.M., and that the writ would be returned unsatisfied. Israelow thereupon advised a deputy sheriff that it was absolutely necessary to proceed to make the levy during the open hours.

The writ was turned over to a deputy sheriff by the name of Guinan whom Israelow persuaded to make the levy during those late weekend hours when the bar was primarily open for business. Guinan reported to Israelow that he went to The Fast Lane on July 31 accompanied by an Asbury Park police officer, identified himself and announced his purpose at the door, but was denied access by the bar's "bouncers." Fearing that violence might ensue, the officers left. Lanzaro confirmed this fact by a letter dated August 3 in which he asked plaintiff for further instructions. Israelow then advised Guinan to make the levy and arrest anyone interfering with execution, pursuant to the officer's authority under N.J.S.A. 2C:29-1 and other statutes. After conferring with his superiors, Guinan informed Israelow that a court order would be necessary to gain access to the establishment!

On August 5, on plaintiff's application reciting the above facts, this court ordered that the sheriff be permitted access to the bar and to arrest anyone who interfered with the levy to show cause before the court why such person should not be held in contempt of the order. Israelow immediately transmitted the order to the sheriff's office with a letter instructing him to levy first

---

2. In the principal action, Vitale v. Hotel California, Inc., plaintiff obtained a default judgment based on the claim that defendant's wrongful refusal to verify that plaintiff was an employee of defendant at the time of an automobile accident deprived him of income continuation benefits under an insurance policy.

upon the cash registers or places where cash might be held and advising him to be accompanied by sufficient personnel to effectuate any arrests that might become necessary. Guinan then went to the bar on the weekend of August 8, but found it had closed early. After speaking with Israelow he again went on the morning of August 15 and was able to seize $714 in cash and other personal property. Guinan reported back to Israelow the same day and indicated his belief that additional money may have been secreted before he was able to levy upon it. When Israelow instructed Guinan to make further levies until the writ was satisfied, Guinan told Israelow that he would have to consult with his superiors before taking further action.

On or about August 17 or 18 Israelow again instructed the sheriff's office to make successive levies and then was informed of the sheriff's contention that only one levy need be made under a writ of execution. After telephoning but not getting through to Lanzaro, Israelow forwarded him a letter dated August 19 and a mailgram dated August 20, again requesting the additional levies. Lanzaro telephoned Israelow on August 21 to tell him that he would consult with Monmouth County counsel, Richard O'Connor. Later that day, O'Connor's office informed Israelow that the sheriff had been instructed not to make any additional levies under the writ.

Unable to reach O'Connor by phone, Israelow wrote a letter to him on August 24 detailing plaintiff's position and threatening to seek amercement. On August 31 Israelow made good the threat by filing this motion. The hearing on the motion was continued several times until January 14, 1982 at the request of the parties who were trying to negotiate a solution.

The sheriff does not refute the facts outlined above but maintains that it is unreasonable to expect any sheriff to command his officers or deputies "to go forth on an unknown number of occasions, at an unreasonable hour, to seize proceeds of an establishment such as The Fast Lane." The sheriff suggests that plaintiff pursue other "reasonable, speedy and inexpensive measures" to satisfy the judgment, to wit, obtaining an order that defendant pay over proceeds of the operation, conducting proceedings to determine where the proceeds are deposited, or locating and seizing other assets of the judgment debtor.

At argument Israelow described his difficulty in collecting the judgment debt: The personal property levied on at The Fast Lane on August 15 was verified as belonging to the landlord of the establishment. Upon this discovery, that California was only a tenant, a scheduled sheriff's sale was necessarily canceled. Also, California's president made a complete disclosure of assets after she had been arrested on an order to show cause, but an attempted levy on the corporate bank account was unsuccessful because the account was overdrawn.

The sheriff further argues that upon seizure of money on August 15 the writ of execution was satisfied and should have been returned, although no return in fact was ever made within the three-month life of the writ. Lack of proof as to loss or damage to plaintiff resulting from the sheriff's [in]action is also raised as a defense. Lastly, the sheriff maintains that the pleading is deficient for failure to specifically state the basis for amercement.

Three basic, interrelated questions are presented for resolution. (1) Are successive levies possible under one writ of execution? (2) When may a sheriff refuse to levy as instructed by a plaintiff, on the basis that the request is unreasonable or onerous? (3) Was the conduct of Sheriff Lanzaro and his office in respect to the writ such as to subject him to amercement?

Before proceeding to answer the first question, a brief overview of execution procedure would be beneficial. A successful plaintiff who obtains a judgment against a defendant may cause the personal property of the defendant/judgment debtor to be seized and sold and the proceeds applied to the judgment and costs by way of execution. To do this, plaintiff obtains a writ of execution, directing the sheriff to levy and make a return within three months after the date of issuance. A "return" is the physical return of the original writ to the court clerk, indorsed with the executing officer's brief description of what was done. In addition, the officer must file a verified statement of when and how much money was collected and the balance due on execution fees or costs.

The writ must be promptly executed upon and returned. The writ may be returned before the return date if, notwithstanding diligent effort, the judgment cannot be satisfied any further. Once an execution has been returned, a sheriff cannot thereafter levy upon any property under the writ. Nor can a valid levy be made after the return date. Successive executions upon the same judgment are possible. Therefore, if the first seizure is insufficient, the creditor may seek an alias writ for levy upon other goods. Thereafter, the plaintiff may seek an unlimited number of pluries writs until the judgment is satisfied. The proceeds from the sheriff's sale of seized property are paid to the judgment creditor or to his or her attorney or to the court clerk.

Throughout the process plaintiff plays a crucial role. Plaintiff must prepare the writ, have it entered by the court clerk and see that it is delivered to the sheriff with instructions as to levying. If necessary, plaintiff should conduct discovery to locate and identify property to be levied upon. Complementary to plaintiff's responsibility is the sheriff's duty to execute the writ according to the plaintiff's instructions. The writ is in the "exclusive control" of the judgment creditor; the sheriff must follow the creditor's reasonable instructions regarding the time and manner of making the levy and must abide by special instructions to make an immediate levy, if practicable, when plaintiff demonstrates necessity.

I.   SUCCESSIVE LEVIES UNDER ONE WRIT

The first question presented, whether successive levies can be made under one writ, can be simply answered—"yes." The rule that further levies under one writ are authorized under the same writ before the return day if the initial levy does not satisfy the judgment is recognized universally.

II.   REASONABLENESS OF REQUESTED LEVIES

That brings us to the second question, whether the sheriff rightly refused to honor an unreasonable request to levy. The particular elements of the request perceived as unreasonable must be reviewed.

The sheriff first objects to the "unknown number of occasions" that he and his deputies would have to go forth to attempt levy in order to comply with plaintiff's wishes. Since there is no limit to the number of executions that conceivably could issue within 20 years after a judgment was entered until the judgment is satisfied, there is technically no limit to the number of times that a sheriff might be required to levy. Nevertheless, practical, operational considerations of a sheriff's office impose an obligation on a plaintiff not to request inordinately frequent and numerous levies. The one successful levy netting $714 on August 15 can be used to project what was entailed by plaintiff's request for levies on successive weekend nights. By extrapolation, the sheriff might have had to levy approximately nine times in the space of one to two months to comply with the request. This many potential levies under one judgment may be unusual but is not in itself unreasonable and, under the circumstances, was not excessive since the bar was basically a summer operation. Furthermore, seizure of several hundred dollars at one time demonstrated the effectiveness of this mode of levying.

There was also some indication of irregularity in the days of the week that The Fast Lane was open for business. Sheriff's counsel acknowledged, however, that local newspaper advertisements for The Fast Lane could be consulted to remove uncertainty about operating hours. Plaintiff, moreover, expressed a willingness to facilitate the execution in any way, and no doubt would have relayed the necessary information if lack thereof had actually presented a stumbling block.

The objection as to the unreasonably late hour requested for the levy cannot be sustained either. The bar was open for business, mostly on weekends, from about 10 P.M. to 2 A.M. Israelow directed that service be made during those hours; the sheriff avers that the instruction was to levy at 2 A.M. Whatever the precise instruction was, levy was to be made at some time during those nighttime hours—levying at 2 A.M. would probably find the cash registers near their fullest and thus minimize the number of additional levies required. Levy under a writ of execution may be made at any hour of the day; there is no issue of privacy here that might dictate otherwise. The Fast Lane's late open hours impelled the late-at-night levy. Like police officers, sheriffs and their deputies may be obliged to work at times of the day and week when the rest of the populace sleep or recreate.

The threat of violence engendered by attempting the levy goes to the heart of the sheriff's objections. "[T]o seize proceeds of an establishment *such as The Fast Lane*" uncamouflages what may have been the most unappetizing aspect of the requested levy. (Emphasis supplied.) On July 31, fearing violence, the deputy sheriff and an Asbury Park police officer allowed themselves to be turned away by bouncers at the door. At that juncture, at the sheriff's instigation and upon plaintiff's application, this court ordered, under what it considered as its inherent powers, that anyone interfering with the execution be arrested and brought before the court to show good cause. Armed with the order, the sheriff successfully levied on August 15. Nevertheless, the refusal to make further levies implies that a conscious decision may have been made to risk amercement rather than further confrontations at the bar.

When is physical force appropriate in making a levy? The general rule is that:

> [an] officer may force an entry into any enclosure except the dwelling house of the judgment debtor in order to levy a fieri facias on the debtor's goods and even in the case of the debtor's home, when the officer is once inside, he may break open inner doors or trunks to come at the goods. . . .

[A]ccording to Lanzaro's recital, on July 31 The Fast Lane bouncers did in fact obstruct the officer from "performing an official function by means of intimidation," N.J.S.A. 2C:29-1, giving the officers probable cause to arrest them. Their resistance to the lawful process might have been a basis for criminal conviction. Although the officers did not believe themselves to be in a position to use physical force, they apparently did not summon back-up help to effectuate the levy or make arrests incidental thereto.

Are sheriffs' deputies to be faulted for not using physical force in a nonemergency situation? The nature of law is to physically force people, if need be, to do things or refrain from doing things that they would be free to do or not do in the "natural state"; the hope is that the benefit to society will more than compensate for the loss of individual freedom. Sheriff's officers act as the physical extension of the power of the court, and thus, of the law and the will of the people. Necessarily, then, the privilege of such civil service occasionally demands risking bodily harm to oneself. Only in this way will the lawless be kept from becoming the de facto law makers. Philosophy aside, the record is barren of facts showing any imminent harm to the sheriff's officers on July 31 other than the vague averment that attempting to carry out the levy may have triggered a violent reaction. I find this unembellished defense insufficient to justify not making the levy.

III.   AMERCEMENT

Consequently, by concluding that the sheriff failed to abide by plaintiff's proper requests to levy, I reach the question of amercement.

By proceeding in amercement, a judgment creditor may hold a sheriff liable for failing to properly execute against a judgment debtor.

I conclude that plaintiff was denied the benefit of the writ and that the consequential loss amounts to the judgment debt of $6,317 less any amounts heretofore collected. The speculation that The Fast Lane will operate again this summer is not cognizable in mitigation of the amercement but would suggest that the sheriff pursue whatever civil remedy may be available against the judgment debtor for indemnification.

The difficult, distasteful aspects of executing writs demand that sheriffs be dealt with fairly, with an eye to the practicalities of their job. My reluctance to amerce a sheriff beset with such unpleasant tasks is only overcome by the convincing proof that Sheriff Lanzaro owed and breached a duty to plaintiff to make the successive levies as requested. In short, by invoking the remedy of amercement, I choose to satisfy plaintiff's debt where the sheriff has not.

_____

In describing its ruling as a choice to "satisfy" plaintiff's debt, the court exaggerates only slightly. The sheriff will almost certainly write a check to Mr. Vitale. (If you have considered the possibility that the sheriff might not do so, you already have caught the spirit of our subject.) If the sheriff chooses to return to The Fast Lane, the next time it will be to collect for the sheriff's own account.

Vitale shows the highly technical nature of the legal process for collection of a judgment. The steps may be many. At any one of them, the judgment creditor may make a mistake or be frustrated by the mistakes of others. Even the creditor who makes no mistakes, encounters no legal anomalies, and enjoys the full cooperation of officials may find the path difficult. Mr. Vitale was an employee of Hotel California before he became its creditor. He may have known its legal structure and may have had some idea what assets the corporation had. Many creditors will start with far less information.

Even the information known to Mr. Vitale proved inadequate at several points. Recall that earlier in Mr. Vitale's collection efforts, California's president had been arrested on an order to show cause. She was apparently released only after she had made a complete disclosure of assets, including the existence of a bank account. But before Mr. Vitale could get the sheriff to levy on the bank account, the debtor evidently withdrew the money. Also recall that Vitale levied on the personal property in The Fast Lane, probably assuming that the property (tables, chairs, and sound equipment) belonged to the judgment debtor. Vitale began the steps necessary to schedule a sheriff's sale, only to discover that the property belonged to the landlord. If the landlord and the judgment debtor were corporate cousins, kissing cousins, or some other kin or conspirators, Vitale *may* have had legal grounds to challenge the separate ownership. But that challenge itself would have increased the expense of collection and perhaps also slowed collection. Notice also that the court's opinion mentions earlier collection attempts only incidentally to the decision at hand; Vitale may have made other efforts to collect this debt. Moreover, note that while The Fast Lane was no ordinary business, it at least had a regular trade in a stable location and generated hard cash on a daily basis. Had the debtor been mobile or able to hide its assets the plaintiff's task might have been much harder.

The *Vitale* case illustrates the power of the judgment creditor ultimately to coerce payment. In *Vitale*, the coercion was through the remedy of levy under writ of execution. Other remedies are available as well. For example, if a third party is in possession of property of the debtor or owes money to the debtor, the creditor can cause the sheriff to serve a writ of garnishment on the third party. The effect of the writ is to require the third party to pay the judgment creditor rather than the debtor. Garnishment and other remedies of unsecured creditors are covered in more detail in the debtor-creditor course.

One side note on the *Vitale* case: We find ourselves speculating on how many attorney hours (and consequent fees) went into this little collection story to net $6,317. Law is not free — a point that may be driven home with more force in collection law than almost anywhere else.

The *Vitale* case is highly unusual in its award of a remedy against the sheriff. The case that follows reaches the far more common result. What the two cases share in common is that the unsecured creditor plaintiffs have difficulty getting the relevant officials to act when quick action is necessary. In both cases, the debtors' attorneys did everything they could to get the sheriff's attention, directed the sheriff to valuable assets, and stressed the need for urgency. In both cases, the sheriffs' delays prevented recovery. The need to work through government officials is a substantial barrier to unsecured creditors' collection efforts.

Common w/ Ellerbee

Ellerbee v. County of Los Angeles

187 Cal. App. 4th 1206, 114 Cal. Rptr. 3d 756
(Cal. App. 2d 2010)

JOHNSON, J.

Ellerbee is the holder of an August 2001 Superior Court judgment against Todd Anthony Shaw, aka "Too Short," arising out of the death of Ellerbee's son, for which Shaw is responsible. The judgment was amended on June 14, 2007 to add several additional joint debtors. As of June 18 the unpaid principal and accrued interest on the outstanding judgment was $1,091,380.40. On June 18 the Superior Court issued a writ of execution to, among others, defendant Lee Baca, Sheriff of the County of Los Angeles.

On June 21, Ellerbee's attorney, Montie Day, delivered the writ to the Sheriff's Department. The writ was accompanied by the payment of appropriate fees and Day's written instructions noting that new debtors had been added to an existing judgment, and that the debtors were "being paid royalties on an ongoing basis." Day "requested that the service of the writ be expedited," and effected "as soon as possible." The Sheriff received the instructions on June 28.

On July 5, Day contacted the Sheriff's Department to confirm its receipt of the writ and instructions. He stressed the importance of prompt service of the writ on Sony BMG, as Sony Records was in the process of making a new release for Shaw (an entertainer/rapper). The Sheriff's Department advised Day the writ would be served forthwith. The Sheriff's Department served the writ on Sony BMG on August 14. Meanwhile, on July 19, Sony BMG paid $10,000 to Shaw.

On September 5, after learning that Shaw was beginning an appearance on a weekly show on MTV Networks (MTV), Ellerbee sent "supplemental instructions" by overnight mail to the Sheriff's Department. Ellerbee was concerned that Shaw's show, a live "reality show," could be terminated at any time. In his instructions to the Sheriff's Department, Ellerbee's attorney explained the debtor was currently being paid on a weekly basis, and requested the writ be served on MTV, "as soon as possible." The Sheriff's Department received Ellerbee's supplemental instructions on September 6 and, on that day, advised Ellerbee's attorney it would promptly process the levy and garnishment. On September 24 Day wrote to the Sheriff's Department to ascertain the status of the service of the writ. He stressed that "time . . . was . . . of the essence" because monies owed Ellerbee may have been paid to Shaw by third parties, and urged the Sheriff to take "PROMPT" action to ensure that Sony BMG and MTV were served. The Sheriff's Department served MTV on October 12. Between September 6 and October 16, MTV paid Shaw a total of $56,799.30, of which Ellerbee claims $53,953.82 should have gone to him.

Ellerbee's judgment remains unpaid. Shaw, who owes federal taxes of over $1 million, and has declared bankruptcy, is not able to satisfy the judgment.

After exhausting his administrative remedies, Ellerbee filed this action against the County and the Sheriff for negligence. Ellerbee alleged the Sheriff breached an unspecified statutory duty of care by failing promptly to serve the writ on Sony BMG and MTV and that, as a result, he suffered damages of $65,952.83.

The California Supreme Court discussed the rigid requirements for imposition of governmental liability under Government Code section 815.6 in Haggis v. City of Los Angeles (2000) 22 Cal. 4th 490, 93 Cal. Rptr. 2d 327, 993 P.2d 983:

> First and foremost, application of section 815.6 requires that the enactment at issue be *obligatory,* rather than merely discretionary or permissive, in its directions to the public entity; it must *require,* rather than merely authorize or permit, that a particular action be taken or not taken. It is not enough, moreover, that the public entity or officer have been under an obligation to perform a function if the function itself involves the exercise of discretion. Whether an enactment creates a mandatory duty is a question of law: Whether a particular statute is intended to impose a mandatory duty, rather than a mere obligation to perform a discretionary function, is a question of statutory interpretation for the courts. Second, but equally important, section 815.6 requires that the mandatory duty be designed to protect against the particular kind of injury the plaintiff suffered. The plaintiff must show the injury is one of the consequences which the [enacting body] sought to prevent through imposing the alleged mandatory duty.

This action founders on the first prong.

Here, the only "mandatory" statutory duty is that the governmental entity or employee act "in accordance with the written instructions" provided by the judgment creditor. (Code Civ. Proc., § 687.010, subd. (b).) The statute makes no reference to any duty to comply with deadlines or timing requests contained in the judgment creditor's instructions. Thus, as here, a creditor's private instructions to act "promptly," or to serve a writ "as soon as possible" do not impose a mandatory obligation on the Sheriff. It is not enough that the public entity or employee have a duty to perform a function if that function itself involves the exercise of discretion. The Sheriff retains complete discretion to determine how and when it is feasible to allocate departmental resources to effect service, constrained only by the parameters that it be done prior to the writ's expiration. In this case there is no dispute that the writs were ultimately served within the 180 day period. No mandatory statutory duty was alleged or violated, and the trial court erred when it denied the County's motion for judgment on the pleadings and allowed the action to proceed to trial on a theory of common law negligence.

▶ Half Assignment Ends

C.   Limitations on Compelling Payment

Vitale also illustrates a number of procedural and practical limitations on the exercise of the judgment creditor's power. For example, the creditor must do whatever discovery is necessary to identify property subject to seizure, and then instruct the sheriff on where to go and what to seize. The risk of error is even greater than is apparent from the court's opinion in *Vitale*. If the property seized turns out to belong to a third party, the judgment creditor may be liable for any damages caused to the third party. Worse yet, the wrongful exercise of dominion and control over the property of another constitutes the tort of conversion. The third party can refuse to accept return of the property and instead recover its value from the judgment creditor. Even if the judgment creditor is willing to take the risk of a wrongful execution, creditors have no right to conduct fishing expeditions by simply showing up at the debtor's home or place of business with a cooperative law enforcement officer.

While a judgment creditor has the right to obtain information about the judgment debtor's assets through discovery, the process can be long and painful. The judgment creditor must find the judgment debtor and force him or her to sit for examination. The judgment debtor may be less than forthcoming in discovery. Debtors may not keep their assets in predictable forms. As a result, questions about assets must be carefully framed. Any attorney with a few years in practice can tell stories about carefully caged answers and tiny verbal loopholes that permitted determined debtors to conceal their assets without crossing the line to criminal fraud or provable perjury.

Even if the judgment creditor discovers the location of the assets, the assets may not remain stationary. The debtor compelled to reveal their location may move them before the judgment creditor can get the sheriff to respond. Recall that the money in The Fast Lane's checking account disappeared just one step ahead of the sheriff. Debtors who plan in advance can transfer title to others, move assets out of the jurisdiction, or consume them. All states have adopted laws authorizing the courts to void debtors' "fraudulent transfers" in actions brought by creditors. Beyond the brief discussion in Section D below, the study of these laws is beyond the scope of this book, but it is enough to know that use of these laws is expensive and the laws themselves are relatively ineffective. If, for example, a debtor sells its property to a bona fide purchaser for value and disperses the proceeds in numerous transactions, that value is probably beyond the creditor's reach.

A creditor who has filed suit against the debtor to collect an unsecured debt may be eligible for a "provisional remedy" even before obtaining a judgment. If, for example, the debtor is fraudulently disposing of its property during the lawsuit, the creditor may have the right to an immediate "attachment" of whatever property the debtor still has. But access to this remedy is sharply limited by the constitutional requirements of due process and, in most states, by statutory prerequisites to issuance of a prejudgment writ of attachment.

When debtors refuse to answer questions during discovery, they can be subject to contempt sanctions. If they lie, they can be charged with perjury. But few creditors consider it worth the expense to pursue these remedies and many prosecutors are reluctant to employ them against debtors anyway.

To employ any of the remedies discussed here, creditors typically face many of the information and control problems previously discussed. And the practical problems of finding the debtor or the debtor's property can be overwhelming. When the debtor disappears and the creditor discovers that the assets it has been chasing were the subject of a wire transfer of money to a corporation in an offshore haven, that is probably the end of the game.

Even if the debtor does not deliberately attempt to defeat the creditor's collection effort, the creditor's task may be complex. The creditor may obtain a judgment and begin enforcement procedures only to discover that the debtor has moved to another state. Because a money judgment can be enforced only in the state where rendered, the creditor must establish the judgment in the destination state before invoking the enforcement procedures of that state. If the debtor moves out of the United States, the creditor's task may be even more difficult.

[Handwritten margin note: Money judgment only enforced in state where rendered]

Until the sheriff arrives to levy on a debtor's assets, the debtor can continue to transact business. Without violating any law, the debtor may lose the assets in business operations, exchange them for other assets of reasonably equivalent value, or apply them to the payment of other bona fide debts. It is not fraudulent for a debtor to pay one of its creditors, even if the effect is to leave nothing for others, so long as the debtor does not make the payment for the purpose of defrauding the others. Such a payment is referred to as a *preference*. Absent the filing of a bankruptcy case, once such a payment is made, it is irreversible.

Exemption statutes may provide yet another impediment to collection of the judgment debt. These statutes, which exist in all 50 states, prevent the sheriff from seizing certain property under a writ of execution. The property is said to be *exempt* from the remedies available to unsecured creditors.

[Handwritten margin note: Exemption Statutes]

The content of the statutes varies from state to state. The general idea is to ensure that collection does not leave a debtor destitute. Many of the recurring themes are present in the Wisconsin statutes that follow.

Wisconsin Statutes Annotated

(2015)

§815.18   PROPERTY EXEMPT FROM EXECUTION

(1) This section shall be construed to secure its full benefit to debtors and to advance the humane purpose of preserving to debtors and their dependents the means of obtaining a livelihood, the enjoyment of property necessary to sustain life and the opportunity to avoid becoming public charges.

(2) In this section:

(c) "Debtor" means an individual. "Debtor" does not include an association, a corporation, a partnership, a cooperative, an unincorporated cooperative association, or a political body. . . .

(e) "Depository account" means [an] account maintained with a bank, credit union, insurance company, savings bank, . . . or like organization.

(f) "Equipment" means goods used or bought for use primarily in a business, including farming and a profession. . . .

(h) "Exempt" means free from any lien obtained by judicial proceedings and is not liable to seizure or sale on execution or on any provisional or final process issued from any court, or any proceedings in aid of court process. . . .

(3) The debtor's interest in or right to receive the following property is exempt. . . .

(a) *Provisions for burial.* Cemetery lots, aboveground burial facilities, burial monuments, tombstones, coffins or other articles for the burial of the dead owned by the debtor and intended for the burial of the debtor or the debtor's family.

(b) *Business and farm property.* 1. Equipment, inventory, farm products, and professional books used in the business of the debtor or the business of a dependent of the debtor, not to exceed $15,000 in aggregate value.

2. If the debtor does not claim an exemption under subd. 1., any interest of the debtor, not to exceed $15,000 in aggregate value, in a closely held business that employs the debtor or in whose business the debtor is actively involved. . . .

(d) *Consumer goods.* Household goods and furnishings, wearing apparel, keepsakes, jewelry and other articles of personal adornment, appliances, books, musical instruments, firearms, sporting goods, animals or other tangible personal property held primarily for the personal, family or household use of the debtor or a dependent of the debtor, not to exceed $12,000 in aggregate value. . . .

(g) *Motor vehicles.* Motor vehicles not to exceed $4,000 in aggregate value. Any unused amount of the aggregate value from paragraph (d) may be added to this exemption to increase the aggregate exempt value of motor vehicles under this paragraph.

(h) *Net income.* Seventy-five percent of the debtor's net income for each one week pay period. The benefits of this exemption are limited to the extent reasonably necessary for the support of the debtor and the debtor's dependents, but to not less than 30 times the greater of the state or federal minimum wage. . . .

(k) *Depository accounts.* Depository accounts in the aggregate value of $5,000. . . .

(6)(a) A debtor shall affirmatively claim an exemption or select specific property in which to claim an exemption. The debtor may make the claim at the time of seizure of property or within a reasonable time after the seizure, but shall make the claim prior to the disposition of the property by sale or by court order. . . . The debtor or a person acting on the debtor's behalf shall make any required affirmative claim, either orally or in writing, to the creditor, the creditor's attorney or the officer seeking to impose a lien by court action upon the property in which the exemption is claimed. A debtor waives his or her exemption rights by failing to follow the procedure under this paragraph. A contractual waiver of exemption rights by any debtor before judgment on the claim is void. . . .

(9) In the case of property that is partially exempt, the debtor or any person acting on the debtor's behalf is entitled to claim the exempt portion of property. The exempt portion claimed shall be set apart for the debtor . . . and the nonexempt portion shall be subject to a creditor's claim. If partially exempt property is indivisible, the property may be sold and the exempt value of the property paid to the debtor. . . .

(12) Limitations on exemptions. No property otherwise exempt may be claimed as exempt in any proceeding brought by any person to recover the whole or part of the purchase price of the property or against the claim or interest of a holder

of a security interest, . . . condominium or homeowners association assessment or maintenance lien or both, mortgage or any consensual or statutory lien.

§815.20   HOMESTEAD EXEMPTION DEFINITION

(1) An exempt homestead as defined in §990.01(14) selected by a resident owner and occupied by him or her shall be exempt from execution, from the lien of every judgment and from liability for the debts of the owner to the amount of $75,000, except mortgages, laborers', mechanics' and purchase money liens and taxes and except as otherwise provided.

§990.01

(14) "Exempt homestead" means the dwelling, including a building, condominium, mobile home, house trailer or cooperative . . . and so much of the land surrounding it as is reasonably necessary for its use as a home, but not less than 0.25 acre, if available, and not exceeding 40 acres, within the limitation as to value under §815.20. . . .

———————

A few states recognize homestead exemptions without dollar limitation, with the result that houses and the surrounding land worth millions of dollars can qualify. Some recognize no homestead exemption at all. Most, like Wisconsin, recognize a homestead exemption, but impose a dollar limit.

Both state and federal law protect debtors' wages. Federal statutes provide that a minimum of 75 percent of debtors' earnings from personal services will generally be exempt in all states. 15 U.S.C.A. §1671. Some states exempt a greater percentage of earnings from personal services, and a few, including Florida (for the head of a household only), Texas, and Pennsylvania, exempt all earnings from personal services. State and federal laws exempt most pensions and retirement accounts.

In short, exemption laws prevent creditors from taking many of the most valuable and easy-to-locate assets that debtors own. Such laws also protect individual debtors, in part by keeping households intact and preventing some debtors from becoming charges of the state. The course on debtors' and creditors' rights examines exemption laws in more detail.

D.   Voidable Transfers

There are some limits on what a debtor can do in resisting collection. All 50 states have laws that permit creditors to set aside their debtor's voidable transfers and recover the property transferred. Those laws declare several types of transfers voidable, but two types are particularly important.

First, any transfer made "with actual intent to hinder, delay, or defraud any creditor" is voidable. Uniform Voidable Transactions Act (UVTA) §4(a). (This law was called the Uniform Fraudulent Transfer Act (UFTA) until 2014.) Because this provision has only a single element—bad intent—it can reach and reverse any transfer that a scheming debtor can conceive. The principal difficulty, of course, is in proving the intent. The statute helps out a little by listing several acts from which "actual intent" can be inferred, such as a transfer that is hidden or made to an insider. UVTA §4(b). Even with the list, actual intent is still tough to prove.

Second, any transfer made "without receiving a reasonably equivalent value in exchange for the transfer" is voidable if the debtor was insolvent at the time of the transfer. UVTA §5(a). This provision conceives of the debtor's estate as having some value. The debtor can continue to do business or transact its affairs. In the process, the debtor can exchange its assets for other assets—provided that the other assets have approximately the same value. The debtor cannot make gifts or sell assets for less than reasonably equivalent value. A debtor is "insolvent" if "the sum of the debtor's debts is greater than all of the debtor's [unencumbered, non-exempt] assets." UVTA §2(a), 1(2). No proof of fraudulent intent is required. A transfer made in good faith with no wrongful intent is voidable if the elements of this provision are present.

Despite its breadth, voidable transfer law is largely impotent. Transfers are easy to make and difficult to discover and avoid. By the time a creditor discovers the voidable transfer, the transferee may have retransferred the property to a bona fide purchaser for value. The creditor's remedy is then limited to the debtor and the initial transferee—as an unsecured creditor.

E.   Is the Law Serious About Collecting Unsecured Debts?

The law governing the enforcement of unsecured legal obligations affects a wide spectrum of rights. In contract law, tort law, antitrust law, and a long list of other areas, rights and liabilities are enforced only through the imposition of civil liability in the form of unsecured money judgments. Yet, as we have seen, the mechanisms for the enforcement of civil judgments for money damages are often ineffective.

Legal mechanisms are available for the enforcement of obligations that the law takes seriously. Courts can order those who are subject to their jurisdiction to meet their legal obligations and can imprison them if they refuse to comply. The law authorizes courts to do so in regard to many obligations, including the obligation to pay alimony or child support, the obligation not to trespass or steal, and the obligation to perform under a contract to sell real property. But they do not include judgments for personal injuries, the wages of working people, or the breaches of most kinds of contracts. The availability of effective remedies to enforce particular rights reflects to some degree the relative values society places on those rights. Whether enforcement of a particular right is civil or criminal, monetary or equitable, summary or with great delay, is an important measure of the right itself. It is not surprising to observe that criminal remedies are reserved for violation of rights we hold dearer than mere money obligations. It may be somewhat more surprising, however, to discover that some creditors have collection rights superior to those of others. Such differences provide insight into the social values reflected in law.

Problem Set 1

1.1.   A year ago, the local Fun Furniture Outlet was having a liquidation sale. Lisa Charney wanted to buy some redwood lawn furniture but didn't have the cash. Her friend and neighbor, Jeffrey Reed, lent $1,000 to Lisa. Jeff and Lisa were good friends, and Lisa said she would pay him back in a couple of months. When she did not, Jeff's reminders became increasingly acrimonious. Now Lisa and Jeff haven't spoken for two months, and she still hasn't paid anything.

Jeff is a journeyman electrician whose union has legal insurance entitling Jeff to four free hours of consultation a year with your firm. The firm charges a reduced rate of $160 an hour for services other than consultation or hours in excess of four. Jeff came in today, showed you Lisa's signed "I.O.U." for the loan, and asked if he could just go over and take the lawn furniture Lisa had purchased with his money. The furniture is in Lisa's backyard. Jeff says he likes it and would be satisfied to have it in payment. Jeff is sure the furniture is worth less than the amount Lisa owes him. What do you tell him?

1.2.   Karen Benning is a successful dentist who was approached last year to lend money to a day care center that wanted to expand. She checked into the center thoroughly and saw that they had a good location, a friendly staff, few outstanding debts, and reasonable profit projections. They had substantial capital assets, including an elaborate network of teaching computers and child-sized exercise equipment. She made a $50,000 loan to the owner, Nathalie Martin, repayable in quarterly installments over five years, at prime plus five percentage points.

The center has not missed a quarterly payment. But Benning has heard some very bad reports from a friend who used to have a child in the center, so she renewed her investigations. Benning sees that the center has moved to a new, more "upscale" location that is far more expensive. Their prices are higher, forcing out more than a third of their old customers. Because the new location is farther away from public transportation, many of their old employees have left. Many of the new employees are temps, resulting in high turnover rates and low employee morale. The person now in charge is the brother of the owner, a foul-tempered man who barks orders and frightens the children. Martin sold the best of the computers and exercise equipment to finance the move and to pay herself and her brother during the start-up phase at the new location. The business is much deeper in debt and is behind on rent and utility payments. Benning is unsure whether the business will even survive, much less whether it will pay her.

Benning consults you for help. She feels sure the business could make a profit if it were properly run. She has heard that the old manager whom Martin fired to make room for her brother would be pleased to return. Benning wants to be repaid in full and she is worried. What do you advise?

1.3.   Six months have passed since the preceding problem. The day care center folded and Benning has a default judgment against its owner, Nathalie Martin, for more than $60,000 in past due interest and principal on Benning's loan. Benning wants to know when she will be paid. What do *you* need to know to answer her question? What are the possible sources of that information? If Martin doesn't pay the judgment, how will you collect it? What do you think of Benning's suggestion that you send the sheriff to levy on the day care center's equipment?

▶ Half Assignment Ends

1.4.   The following debt collection story appeared in David Margolick's *New York Times* column, "At the Bar":

Jonesport, Me. . . .

Earlier this summer Bert S. Look, whose family has been catching crustaceans out of this sleepy fishing village on the eastern end of the Maine coast since 1910, was the picture of frustration. For months, he has since explained, a local seafood wholesaler named John Kostandin had owed him nearly $30,000, and he was powerless to make him pay. The usual legal remedies, he believed, were worthless.

"I could have gone through nine million district attorneys and nine million lawyers and I wouldn't have gotten anything," Mr. Look said. "I was willing to try anything nonviolent." So, in the best tradition of Maine lobstermen, who cut the lines on the traps of their disreputable competitors, he resorted to self-help. Actually, he had one helper: a self-styled professional prankster known only as "Deep Homard." (Homard is French for lobster.)

In June, Homard, posing as a friend of [horror novelist Stephen King], called Mr. Kostandin. He said that the novelist, who lives nearby in Bangor, needed three-and-a-half tons of lobsters for his annual lobster bake. Of course, the lobsters would end up with Mr. Look rather than Mr. King; at slightly more than $4 a pound, they would neatly cover Mr. Kostandin's tab to Mr. Look. . . .

Apparently enticed by meeting Mr. King — and the prospect of catering future King shindigs — Mr. Kostandin, accompanied by his wife and 78 crates of live lobsters, drove to Dysart's Truck Stop in Hermon, where they were told, Mr. King would meet them. Told there that the novelist had been detained, Mr. Kostandin left the lobsters behind and headed, via a limousine provided by Mr. Look, for a purported rendezvous with the author at the Panda Garden, a Chinese restaurant in Bangor. By the time he deduced that he had been had, Mr. Look had the lobsters, which he promptly sold.

David Margolick, At the Bar, N.Y. Times, Sept. 17, 1993, at B8 col. 1. Mr. Look got only $19,000 for the lobsters. He comes to you for legal representation in collecting the rest. Your first call was to Stephen King. Although the conversation was very scary, it is clear that King doesn't want to be involved. What do we do next?

1.5.   Assume now that Nathalie Martin is living in Wisconsin. During her deposition, Martin testifies that she owns the following property, all free and clear of liens or security interests:

a.   A four-year-old Toyota automobile worth $15,000.
b.   A house that she recently inherited from her mother, estimated to be worth about $275,000 and subject to a mortgage in the amount of $225,000.
c.   The equipment from the day care center, which has a resale value of about $25,000.
d.   A bank account with a current balance of $12,265.92.

What can the sheriff take from her to satisfy your judgment? Is there any hurry in getting the sheriff to do that? Can you move fast enough?

■ End of Default Problem Set

1.6.   During a deposition in aid of execution, you, as Benning's lawyer, asked Martin whether anyone owed her (Martin) any money. Martin hesitated briefly in a way that made you suspicious, and then answered "Not that I can remember." You'd like to jog her memory, or maybe even set up a perjury charge, by following up with some questions that suggest specific kinds of debts that might be owing to her. What questions might you ask? If she does remember a debt, such as a bank account, how and when will you pursue that asset further?

Assignment 2:   Security and Foreclosure

The law provides for enforcement of money obligations. But, as should be apparent from Assignment 1, the legal remedies of unsecured creditors are cumbersome, expensive, and problematic in terms of what they will yield. The financial institutions that make car loans, home loans, and most business loans can and do insist on having a set of collection rights considerably more effective than the baseline set discussed in the preceding assignment.

This more effective set is known as a *lien*. The Bankruptcy Code accurately describes a lien as "a charge against or an interest in property to secure payment of a debt or performance of an obligation." Bankr. Code §101 (definition of "lien"). Thus, a lien is a relationship between particular property (the *collateral*) and a particular debt or obligation. The general nature of the relationship is that if the debt is not paid when due, the creditor can compel the application of the value of the collateral to payment of the debt. The process by which the creditor compels application is called *foreclosure*.

The most important type of lien is the *security interest*. Used in its broadest sense, that term encompasses any lien created by contract between debtor and creditor. It includes real estate mortgages and deeds of trust as well as the security interests in personal property created under Article 9 of the Uniform Commercial Code. See Bankr. Code §101 (definitions of "security agreement," "security interest," and "lien"; Internal Revenue Code §6323(h)(1)).

Although security interests will be our primary focus in the remainder of this book, you will also encounter two types of nonconsensual liens: (1) liens granted by statute, such as mechanic's liens (*statutory liens*) or by common law (*common law liens*) and (2) liens obtained by unsecured creditors through judicial process (*judicial liens*).

In Part One of this book, we discuss security interests in the simplest situations — that is, where only the interests of a debtor and a single creditor are involved. We look first at the remedies available to a secured creditor, and then we turn to what a creditor must do to become secured. Later, in Part Two, we will take up the question of priorities — the relative rights of multiple creditors competing for the same collateral.

What property will serve as collateral for a security interest depends on custom and the needs of the particular parties. When a car dealer lends the money to purchase a car, the car will usually be the collateral. When a business borrows, it might grant a security interest in its equipment, its inventory, its accounts receivable or any or all other property it may own. Virtually anything recognized as property can serve as collateral. (Spouses and children won't work, but your dog or your parakeet will.) The usefulness of property as collateral will ultimately depend on (1) how much value the creditor can extract from it after default (will it bring anything at resale?), and (2) how much leverage the creditor can derive from its ability to deprive the debtor of the property (how much will the debtor be willing and able to pay to keep it?).

The agreement that creates the security interest may impose obligations on the debtor that apply even in the absence of default. (For the curious, there is an example of a security agreement in Assignment 15 of this book.) The security interest itself has a direct effect only in the event of the debtor's default. The default may be a failure to pay the debt or a failure to comply with some other provision of the security agreement. Because the rights of the holder of a security interest are principally rights that take effect after default, a security interest can be described as a right in property that is contingent on nonpayment of a debt. That is, the right to enforce the debt against the property that serves as collateral is contingent upon the occurrence of a default. The typical methods of enforcement lead to a sale of the collateral and application of as much of the proceeds of sale as necessary to payment of the debt.

The recognition of enhanced collection rights for secured creditors necessarily diminishes the effectiveness of the collection rights of general unsecured creditors. For example, if Creditor A has a security interest in the debtor's car that exceeds the entire value of the car, the value of the car will not be available to satisfy unsecured Creditor B's execution. The ease with which a debtor can grant security interests virtually assures that by the time a debtor is in serious financial difficulty, an unsecured creditor will have difficulty finding property to sell to satisfy its debt. In essence, unsecured creditors get only what is left after provisions have been made for secured creditors. In contested cases, that is usually nothing. Having security—or lacking it—is usually the difference between collecting or not collecting the debt.

Considering the disadvantages inherent in being an unsecured creditor, one might wonder why anyone assumes that role. Some creditors may prefer unsecured status because they are compensated by receiving a higher rate of interest. (This is the standard explanation given by economists.) But many, such as the victim of a car accident or an employee with an action for wrongful discharge, do not choose the role of unsecured creditor; they are thrown into it without the opportunity to negotiate. Some unsecured creditors agree to a contract that leaves them unsecured without realizing that fact or without recognizing its importance. For example, if you have ever prepaid rent on an apartment or paid for an airline ticket (even if you charged it to your credit card), you agreed to accept unsecured status in the event the landlord did not provide the apartment or the airline did not provide the flight. Lots of people have discovered their unsecured status when an airline stopped flying or a landlord went broke.

Others may understand the implications of assuming unsecured status, but be constrained by business custom and practice from seeking secured status. Consider, for example, the law student who accepts a job with a large law firm. Along with the job, the student accepts the status of an unsecured creditor for wages, accrued benefits, and other obligations. To request security for those obligations would be an egregious social error. The problem is not just that the law student lacks bargaining leverage; the inability to negotiate for security applies even to the law student who is in great demand, and the inability persists even if the student were willing to accept a much lower salary. In fact, even if the law firm *wanted* to accede to a job applicant's demand for security, to do so probably would breach the firm's contracts with its bank lenders. Who gets security is as much a matter of established custom as of economics.

A. The Necessity of Foreclosure

Why does the law permit a debtor to grant one creditor collection rights that are superior to those of another? There are a number of competing economic explanations for this harsh inequality, as well as some explanations rooted in custom and long-standing business practice. We think one reason is the tremendous complexity the law would have encountered if it had attempted to ban security. Were security banned, debtors temporarily short of cash still would have been able to sell their property to get the cash they needed. They still would have been able to buy it back later when they had the cash. At the same time, debtors would have been unable to grant a lesser right — a right in the buyer/secured creditor to keep the property contingent on the debtor's nonpayment of a debt. The following story isn't exactly true, but it does explain the strange language and practice of foreclosure.

The Invention of Security: A Pseudo History

The place is England. The time is the Middle Ages. Existing legal concepts include the ownership of property, the ability to transfer it, and the ability to contract for such transfers.

Debord is the owner of Blackacre and is in need of a loan. His neighbor, Creech, is willing to make the $100 loan, but wants to be *certain* he* will be repaid. Debord and Creech intend to create what we today call a security interest, but our story opens before the courts recognized such a device.

To maximize the likelihood that the courts would give effect to their intention without a recognized legal device, Creech and Debord expressed their deal using legal concepts that were familiar to the courts. Their deal had three parts:

True intent of Debord and Creech	*Legal form they adopted*
1. Debord grants Creech a security interest in Blackacre	1. Debord sells and deeds Blackacre to Creech
2. Creech lends $100 to Debord	2. Creech pays $100 purchase price for Blackacre
3. Debord agrees to repay the loan with $10 interest, on March 1	3. Creech grants Debord an option to purchase Blackacre from Creech on March 1 for $110

*At that time in history, only men were allowed to engage in these transactions.

Because Blackacre was worth $500, once this transaction was in place Creech could be "secure" in the knowledge that the loan would almost certainly be repaid. Even if it were not, Creech would have something even more valuable, the ownership of Blackacre. Assuming he repaid the loan on time, it cost Debord nothing to provide Creech with this security. The result was to enable the two of them to get together on a loan that might otherwise not have been made.

The first time they made this deal, matters went smoothly. Debord repaid the loan on time and Creech reconveyed Blackacre. But the second time they did it, Debord was late with the payment. When he tendered the money on March 15, Creech refused to take it and refused to reconvey Blackacre. "You breached the deal, and I'm keeping the land," he said with some delight. The law governing the form in which they had put their transaction was on Creech's side. "Time was of the essence" in an option contract, and if the buyer did not pay the purchase price at the agreed time, the buyer lost the right to purchase.

With no remedy at law, Debord went to the chancellor for equity. He explained the true intention of the deal he had made with Creech and the position Creech was now taking. He emphasized that unless the chancellor granted relief, his $500 property would be forfeited for failure to repay a $100 loan. Although the documents supported Creech's position, the chancellor granted relief. Reciting the maxims (maxims were very big in the Middle Ages) that "Equity abhors a forfeiture" and "Equity looks to substance over form," he ordered that Debord could "redeem" Blackacre by repaying the loan with interest and compensating Creech for any damages sustained by the delay. Debord did so, and never did business with Creech again.

Despite Creech's loss before the chancellor, his experience with secured lending to this point had not been all that bad. True, the chancellor had dashed his dream of picking up Blackacre for $100. In Debord v. Creech the chancellor had established that even slow-paying debtors had an equitable right to redeem their property. But the chancellor had conditioned this "equity of redemption" on payment in full, including Creech's interest and attorneys fees. Security worked.

Creech continued to make loans and continued to put them in the form of a "deed absolute" combined with an option to purchase. Inevitably, he ran into a problem. Davenport, another of Creech's borrowers, failed to repay a loan secured by Greenacre. Months passed. Creech had possession of Greenacre and wanted to spruce it up and sell it to another buyer. But what if Davenport later exercised his equity of redemption? How long did Creech have to wait for his title to Greenacre to be clear of the equity of redemption? Creech asked his lawyer. "No way to know," the lawyer said, "short of asking the chancellor." The lawyer prepared a petition asking the chancellor to "foreclose" Davenport's equity of redemption. That petition was the first mortgage foreclosure.

When Creech and his lawyer went before the chancellor, Davenport was there. Davenport made the usual arguments about forfeiture and told the same old stories about how he was just about to come up with the money to redeem. By today's standards, the chancellor was a bleeding-heart liberal. He gave Davenport a continuance, reset the hearing for a date two months away, and expressed his hope that Davenport would redeem before then. Knowing the chancellor, Creech's lawyer feared a string of continuances unless he could persuade the chancellor that Creech's interests were in greater jeopardy than Davenport's.

At the continued hearing, Creech's lawyer presented expert testimony that the value of Greenacre was no greater than the amount of the loan. Even if the chancellor cut off the equity of redemption today, Creech would take a loss. Davenport had no "equity" in Greenacre to protect, said Creech's lawyer, picking up the language the court of equity used to refer to the amount by which the value of the property exceeded the amount of the loans against it. Because of the accruing interest, the lawyer continued, Creech's potential loss grew greater with every passing day. After Creech's lawyer had finished his presentation, Davenport, in a voice choked with emotion, spoke of his many happy years on Greenacre, the little knoll where his dog was buried, and his expert appraisals showing that Greenacre was worth "at least five times" the amount owing on the loan.

The chancellor reflected on the issues and concluded that where the equities now lay depended on the value of Greenacre. Despite his generally liberal beliefs, the chancellor, a very early Renaissance man, was also a staunch believer in markets. Based on that belief, he devised what he considered a very clever "market-based" solution. The issue of value would be resolved by offering Greenacre for sale. To ensure that the sale was fair and open, the chancellor would have a notice posted in the town square, and the sheriff would conduct the sale of Greenacre on the courthouse steps. The highest bidder would get the land free of Davenport's right to redeem. As the chancellor put it, the sale would "cut off the equitable right of redemption." The proceeds from the sale would be used first to repay Creech's loan, thus ensuring that Creech would recover whatever value there was in the property, up to the amount of the loan. If the property brought less than the amount owing to Creech, Creech would have to bring his action for the *deficiency* on the law side. If the property brought more, the *surplus* would go to Davenport on the equity side. Because Davenport would get the market value of the property less the amount he owed on the debt, he would suffer no forfeiture.

The sale was held, and Creech v. Davenport was entered in the Year Book. Unfortunately, the amount of the sale price was not recorded. The entries were, however, sufficient to show that the remedies of the parties to a secured transaction had assumed the form they would retain for a millennium.

This story makes several important points. First, the right to redeem is the debtor's right to pay the secured debt even after default and retain ownership of the collateral. "From the time the full obligation secured by a mortgage becomes due and payable until the mortgage is foreclosed, a mortgagor has the right to redeem the real estate from the mortgage." Restatement (Third) of Property: Mortgages §3.1(a) (1997). UCC §9-623 provides a right to redeem Article 9 collateral.

Second, it illustrates that parties who wish to do so can easily construct the security relationship using the everyday conventions of sale and option to purchase. (Indeed, it might be difficult to permit a debtor like Debord to transfer ownership of property yet prohibit him from transferring mere collection rights relating to the same property.) If the chancellor had refused to recognize the special nature of the sale from Debord to Creech, the sale and option to repurchase would have been valid. Debord could still have entered into this "secured" transaction, but he would not have been protected against forfeiture. To *prevent* these transactions would have required both the chancellor's recognition of the special nature of this sale and some more aggressive action such as, for example, forfeiting the *creditor's* interest.

Third, the story shows that in the hands of clever parties, or their clever lawyers, existing legal forms can be employed in ways unanticipated by the lawmakers. Using nothing but existing concepts of sale and option, Creech and Debord invented security. Such resourcefulness in structuring transactions is common in commercial law. As the lawyers invent new devices, the courts must consider whether to recognize and give effect to them, or whether to deny recognition and wrestle with the consequences. In making their decisions about whether to recognize new devices, courts are often constrained by the practicalities of enforcing the rules they think most desirable from a policy standpoint. Thus the judges are not entirely in control; lawyers play an active role in shaping the law.

Fourth, in determining which transactions are in the nature of security and must be foreclosed, one cannot rely on the documents. A transaction is in the nature of security if the intent is to provide one party with an interest in the property of another, which interest is contingent upon the nonpayment of a debt. Even if the only document in existence labels the transaction as a sale, the relationship created may be a security interest. It is truly the substance that matters, not the form.

B. Transactions Intended as Security

The third lesson from Creech v. Debord is subtle and complex. Foreclosure by any procedure is technical, time-consuming, and expensive. Lawyers and their clients wish to avoid it whenever possible. The irony is that if the intent of the parties is to relieve a secured creditor of the necessity to foreclose, the attempt will fail. Regardless of the form in which the parties choose to cast their deal, if the deal is security, the law will recast it as security. The concept is not an easy one to grasp. As in the following case, commercial lawyers frequently embarrass themselves by making deals that run afoul of the "intended as security" doctrine.

Basile v. Erhal Holding Corporation

538 N.Y.S.2d 831 (N.Y. App. Div. 1989)

JUDGES: MOLLEN, P.J., THOMPSON, RUBIN AND SPATT, JJ., concur. . . .

In 1982, the plaintiff, the owner of property located at 244 Morris Avenue in Peekskill, mortgaged the property to the Erhal Holding Corp. (hereinafter Erhal) in return for a loan at an alleged usurious rate. The plaintiff instituted this action, inter alia, to declare the mortgage null and void on the ground of usury. On June 2, 1986, and June 6, 1986, while the matter was awaiting trial, the parties entered into a stipulation of settlement in open court whereby the plaintiff agreed to execute a mortgage to Erhal in the sum of $101,303.59 together with a deed "in lieu of foreclosure" which would not be recorded by Erhal as long as the plaintiff fulfilled her obligations under the terms and conditions of the mortgage. The mortgage provided, inter alia, that the plaintiff would pay monthly interest payments on the mortgage amount at a rate of 12% per annum for a one-year period; at the end of that period, the entire balance was to become due. The mortgage agreement also included the following provision; "The mortgagor herein has simultaneously executed a deed in lieu of foreclosure which may be recorded by the mortgagee for any default herein."

During the settlement colloquy, the trial court questioned the plaintiff regarding her understanding of the terms of the settlement. At that time, the plaintiff indicated that she understood that if she violated the terms of the mortgage agreement, Erhal could record the deed and become the owner of the subject premises.

The plaintiff subsequently defaulted in several mortgage payments and failed to pay the real estate taxes and fire insurance premiums for the demised premises as provided for in the mortgage agreement. As a result of the plaintiff's default, Erhal recorded the deed in lieu of foreclosure in December 1986. Thereafter, Erhal moved, by order to show cause, for an order declaring that the plaintiff's right of redemption with respect to the property was waived when the mortgage and deed in lieu of foreclosure were executed in June 1986. The plaintiff cross-moved, inter alia, for an order directing Erhal to accept a check in the sum of $101,303.59 plus interest tendered by the plaintiff and to deliver to the plaintiff a satisfaction of mortgage and a deed for the premises, free and clear of all encumbrances.

The Supreme Court granted Erhal's motion and declared that "the plaintiff no longer has any right of redemption of the subject property." The plaintiff's cross motion was denied.

We conclude that the Supreme Court erred in declaring that the plaintiff waived her right of redemption in the demised premises. A deed conveying real property, although absolute on its face, will be considered to be a mortgage when the instrument is executed as security for a debt. The purpose behind this rule was explained in Peugh v. Davis (96 U.S. 332, 336-337):

> It is an established doctrine that a court of equity will treat a deed, absolute in form, as a mortgage, when it is executed as a security for a loan of money. That court looks beyond the terms of the instrument to the real transaction; and when that is shown to be one of security, and not of sale, it will give effect to the actual contract of the parties. It is also an established doctrine that an equity of redemption is inseparably connected with a mortgage; that is to say, so long as the instrument is one of security, the borrower has in a court of equity a right to redeem the property upon payment of the loan. This right cannot be waived or abandoned by any stipulation of the parties made at the time, even if embodied in the mortgage. This is a doctrine from which a court of equity never deviates (see also Maher v. Alma Realty Co., 70 A.D.2d 931 ["plaintiffs cannot waive their right of redemption even by stipulation in open court"]).

In this case, it is clear that the deed in lieu of foreclosure executed by the plaintiff with the $101,303.59 mortgage was not intended as an absolute conveyance or sale of the property by the plaintiff but rather was intended to be security for the plaintiff's $101,303.59 debt to Erhal. As such, the deed constituted a mortgage and the attempted waiver of the plaintiff's right of redemption in the property in the in-court stipulation of settlement as well as the mortgage agreement was ineffective. Erhal's sole remedy is to institute an action in foreclosure. The plaintiff will have a right to redeem the property at any time prior to the actual sale of the premises by tendering to Erhal the principal and interest due on the mortgage.

The "intended as security" doctrine applies to personal property transactions as well as those involving real property. UCC §9-109(a)(1) provides that Article 9 applies to "any transaction, regardless of its form, that creates a security interest in personal property." Comment 2 to that section elaborates: "When a security interest is created, this Article applies regardless of the form of the transaction or the name that parties have given to it. Likewise, the subjective intention of the parties with respect to the legal characterization of their transaction is irrelevant to whether this article applies." The situations where the "intended as security" doctrine could possibly apply are limited only by lawyers' creativity in structuring new transactions, but the doctrine commonly applies in the following kinds of transactions.

1. Conditional Sales

Owners who intend to sell goods on credit sometimes seek to retain title to the goods until the buyer has finished paying for the goods. Consistent with the intended as security doctrine, however, UCC §2-401(1) provides that "Any retention or reservation by the seller of the title (property) in goods shipped or delivered to the buyer is limited in effect to a reservation of a security interest." The consequence is that the buyer becomes the owner of the goods and the seller becomes a secured creditor for the price of the goods.

For example, assume that Smyrna wants to sell her Buick Skylark to Brodsky. Brodsky wants to take delivery of the car now and pay for it in monthly payments over the course of a year. Smyrna doesn't mind receiving her payments over the course of the year, but neither does she want to be troubled with the formalities of secured credit. Smyrna and Brodsky strike the following deal: Smyrna agrees to sell her car to Brodsky one year from today. The agreement is contingent on Brodsky's paying the purchase price in equal monthly payments over the year. Until Brodsky has finished paying, Smyrna will remain the owner of the Skylark and keep the title in her name. So long as he is current on his payments, Brodsky will have the right to use it. Once he finishes paying, Smyrna will transfer title to him.

Smyrna and Brodsky may think they have invented an ingenious substitute for security. They have not. What they have done is to reinvent security — just as the lawyers and parties in *Basile* did. Article 9 will apply to the transaction. UCC §9-109(a)(1). For the purpose of applying the rules in Article 9, Brodsky is the owner of the Skylark, Smyrna is a secured party, and the contract they have entered into is a security agreement. If Smyrna fails to comply with the Article 9 rules governing their transaction, she will suffer the consequences.

2.   Leases Intended as Security Interests

A seller's attempt to retain ownership as security for payment of the purchase price sometimes takes the form of a lease. (Federal income tax savings are often an additional motivation for characterizing the transaction as a lease.) If the term of the lease extends for the entire remaining economic life of the collateral, the economic effect of the lease on the parties (taxes aside) may be identical to the economic effect of a sale with a security interest back for the purchase price. To illustrate, assume that Space Corporation owns a satellite that will circle the earth for five years and then enter the atmosphere and vaporize. Space Corporation wants to sell the satellite for $500 million, payable with interest at 7 percent per year in 60 equal monthly installments of $9.9 million. For a variety of reasons, the parties may prefer to characterize the transaction as a lease. The lease could provide for 60 monthly rental payments of $9.9 million. Either way, Communications, Inc. pays, and Space Corporation receives, $9.9 million a month for 60 months. Either way, Space Corporation will repossess if Communications, Inc. doesn't make the payments. Either way, neither owns anything at the end of five years. A sale, combined with a security interest securing payment of the purchase price, has precisely the same economic impact on the parties as a lease for the entire economic life of the property.

Notice also that this transaction, regardless of which form the parties choose, meets the definition of a security interest. Space Corporation's interest in the satellite is entirely contingent on the nonpayment of a debt. In one case it is a debt for the purchase price; in the other case it is a debt for rental payments. The transaction is a security interest and Article 9 applies to it. UCC §9-109(a)(1). Space Corporation is the secured party and Communications, Inc. is the debtor.

We used the example of an asset with a highly predictable economic life in order to make the example as simple as possible. Assume instead that the property is an automobile. The parties may expect that this type of automobile could wear out in two or three years or could remain in service for ten or twenty. They also expect that when it finally breaks down and is too expensive to repair, it will have no value. Finally, they expect, on average, that this automobile will remain in service for seven years. If the parties agree to lease this automobile for seven years, the lease is a security interest. UCC §1-203. The same is true if the parties agree to lease this automobile for four years and the lessee has an option to buy it at the end of the lease for $100. On the other hand, if the parties lease the automobile for only three years, or lease it for seven years and give the lessee the option to terminate the lease at three years and pay no more rent, the lease is a "true" lease and not a security interest. The reason is that the contract transferred only part of the anticipated economic life of the automobile to the lessee.

Parties frequently intend a transaction that is in essence a sale, but seek to have it treated as a lease for tax purposes. Because the tax treatment is so valuable, they are often willing to distort the substantive economic terms in order to acquire it. The distortion is typically to shorten the period of the lease to less than the economic life of the property, and require or induce the lessee to buy the lessor's reversion for its market value at the end of the lease. What minimum distortion is sufficient to qualify the transaction as a lease is a constantly recurring legal issue that is frequently opined on and litigated by commercial lawyers. We will return to the lease/sale topic in Assignment 21.

3.   *Sales of Accounts*

Many businesses sell their products or services on unsecured credit. For example, an auto parts manufacturer might give its dealers 30 days to pay for merchandise shipped to them. While outstanding, the debt is an "account payable" of the dealer-debtor and an "account receivable" of the creditor-manufacturer. Article 9 refers to accounts receivable as "accounts." UCC §9-102(a)(2). The person who owes an account is called an "account debtor." UCC §9-102(a)(3).

   Although each separate account may be small and remain outstanding for only a short period of time, a business that sells on credit will typically have many of them. In the aggregate, the accounts of such a business may have substantial value over a long time. In our example, at any given time the auto parts manufacturer might be owed hundreds of thousands of dollars by its dealers.

   An auto parts manufacturer that is short of cash might solve its problem either of two ways. First, it might sell the accounts at a discount. "Factors" are businesses that specialize in buying accounts. If, for example, Auto Parts Corporation generates $1 million in accounts receivable each month and the accounts remain outstanding for an average of 120 days, Factor might buy those accounts for $950,000, and collect $1 million from them. Ignoring expenses, Auto Parts Corporation receives $950,000 at the time of the transaction instead of $1 million at the time the accounts are later collected.

   Auto Parts Corporation might achieve exactly the same thing by using the accounts as collateral to borrow $950,000 from a bank. If Auto Parts collects $1 million from the accounts, and pays $950,000 in principal and $50,000 of interest to the bank, the loan transaction has essentially the same effect as the sale transaction. Ignoring expenses, Auto Parts Corporation receives $950,000 at the time of the loan transaction instead of $1 million at the time the accounts are later collected.

   These two transactions are in substance the same. If the law seeks to characterize the transactions according to their substance, whom should the law treat as the owner of the accounts? Usually, we consider the person who stands to gain from increases in the value and lose from decreases in the value of a financial asset to be the owner. That suggests we consider a fact not given in these examples: Who bears the risk that some or all of the accounts will not be collected? If Factor will bear the loss, the sale is a true sale. If, on the other hand, Auto Parts Corporation has agreed to pay any deficiency so that Factor still receives $1 million in total, the first transaction is merely a security interest disguised as a sale.

   Unfortunately, the courts have not consistently made this distinction. Contracts for the sale of accounts frequently give the purchaser a "right of recourse" against the seller with respect to unpaid accounts. That is, if the account debtor does not pay, the deal is that the seller will buy the account back for the initial sale price. The effect is to guarantee the "purchaser" the full face amount of the accounts. A sale of accounts with recourse is in substance a secured loan, but numerous courts have held otherwise.

To finesse the problem, Article 9 provides that "this article applies to . . . a sale of accounts" as well as "a security interest in accounts." UCC §9-109(a)(3). Comment 4 explains that "[t]his approach generally has been successful in avoiding difficult problems of distinguishing between transactions in which a receivable secures an obligation and those in which the receivable has been sold outright. In many commercial financing transactions the distinction is blurred." This solution is, however, incomplete. Article 9 does not ignore the distinction between true sales of accounts and security interests in accounts in all circumstances. Sometimes the courts must still distinguish the two.

4.   Asset Securitization

To "securitize" an asset is to divide ownership of its value into large numbers of identical shares. For example, the owner of a business can "securitize" the business by forming a new corporation, transferring ownership of the business to the corporation, and having the corporation issue 10,000 shares of stock. To own a share is to indirectly own one ten-thousandth of the value of the business.

Although any kind of asset can be securitized, pools of mortgages and accounts (particularly accounts arising out of the use of credit cards) are the types of assets most commonly securitized. The owner of the accounts, referred to as the "originator," sells the accounts to a separate entity referred to as the "special purpose vehicle" (SPV). The SPV is most frequently a trust, but can be any type of entity that has limited liability and is capable of issuing tradable securities. The securities issued are mostly debt instruments referred to as "certificates." The SPV issues the certificates in "tranches." A tranche is a priority level. If the account debtors' payments are insufficient to pay all of the certificates, the SPV pays them to the first tranche, pro rata in proportion to their shares, until the first tranche certificates are paid in full. The SPV pays the excess, if any, to the second tranche in the same manner. The SPV repeats the process for each successive tranche, until the money is exhausted.

Like any other sale of accounts, a securitization of accounts can be with or without recourse. If it is with recourse, the originator has agreed to buy back uncollected accounts or, more commonly, to substitute new accounts for any uncollected accounts.

Like the parties to a lease, the parties to an asset securitization often seek to disguise one kind of transaction as another. Specifically, the investors who buy certificates typically want to be guaranteed a fixed return. They do not want the risks of true ownership of the accounts. Thus the transactions are with recourse. This means that the SPV is actually a lender.

The parties do not, however, want one of the consequences of lender status. If the originator files bankruptcy, the SPV, as a lender, will be involved. Thus the parties seek in their documents to combine the substance of lending with the appearance of sale. We will return to the subject of asset securitization in Assignment 21.

▶ Half Assignment Ends

C.   Foreclosure Procedure

A foreclosure process is referred to as *judicial* if it is accomplished by the entry of a court order. The procedures for judicial foreclosure differ widely from state to state and with the type of collateral involved. Article 9 provides a nonjudicial procedure for personal property foreclosure, but Article 9 also permits secured parties to use judicial foreclosure methods if they prefer.

As you read the following material, be sure to distinguish the foreclosure of a security interest from the taking of possession of collateral. Foreclosure is a process that operates on the ownership of collateral. It transfers ownership from the debtor to the purchaser at the foreclosure sale and cuts off the debtor's right to redeem the collateral. This change in ownership is typically accompanied by a transfer of possession. But the transfer of possession can occur before, during, or after foreclosure. In some cases, it may not occur at all. For example, the secured creditor may foreclose against collateral, purchase it at the foreclosure sale, and lease it back to the debtor who has been in possession all along. Assignment 3 will discuss the secured creditor's right to possession and the means by which the secured creditor can get it. Foreclosure operates on ownership, not possession.

1.   *Judicial Foreclosure*

A foreclosure process is referred to as *judicial* if it is accomplished by the entry of a court order. Procedures by which secured creditors can sue for such orders are available in every state. In a judicial foreclosure, a creditor holding a mortgage or security interest typically files a civil action against the debtor. In the complaint, the creditor details the terms of the loan and the nature of the default, and requests that the equity of redemption be "foreclosed." The complaint is served on the debtor and any subordinate lien holders, who then have a period of time (usually 20 days) in which to raise defenses.

Only in rare cases will the debtor have a defense that would preclude foreclosure altogether. But a debtor who seeks a delay can often find some technical defect in the complaint (such as an erroneous calculation of interest) that will at least require amendment and at most require that the case be placed on a trial calendar that is months or years long. Once any such issues have been resolved and the plaintiff has established that it is entitled to foreclose, the court will enter a *final judgment of foreclosure.*

As part of the judgment, the court usually sets a date for the foreclosure sale. The procedures for sale are the subject of Assignment 4. The sheriff sells the collateral, collects the proceeds of sale, and holds them until the foreclosing creditor obtains an order confirming the sale. In most states, that order extinguishes the equity of redemption and authorizes the sheriff to disburse the proceeds.

Ordinarily, the debtor will remain in possession of the collateral until the sale has been confirmed by the court. The purchaser is then entitled to possession. If the debtor will not surrender the premises, the purchaser is entitled to a *writ of assistance*, which in some states is known as a *writ of possession*. The writ of assistance directs the sheriff to put the purchaser in possession. The process is much like that for a levy under a writ of execution.

The large majority of foreclosures are unopposed, and the debtors often surrender possession before the sheriff comes. But a substantial minority of debtors resist at some or all stages of the proceedings.

Amir Efrati, The Court House: How One Family Fought Foreclosure

Wall Street Journal, Dec. 28, 2007, at A1

BEACHWOOD, Ohio—Faced with the threat of foreclosure, many homeowners give up and abandon their homes. Then there's Richard Davet.

He and his wife, Lynn, lived in a six-bedroom home in this Cleveland suburb for nearly 20 years when, in 1996, he was served with a foreclosure lawsuit. Rather than turn over the keys, he hit the law books. Flooding the courts with papers, Mr. Davet staved off foreclosure for 11 years, until this past January, when a county sheriff's deputy evicted the couple and changed the locks. They didn't make a mortgage payment the entire time.

"Our four Scottish terriers are buried there," says the 63-year-old Mr. Davet. "It was heaven on earth, an unbelievable property, and they took it from us like candy from a baby."

Foreclosure actions are generally routine, typically taking from a few months to a couple of years to get the borrower out of the home. Companies turn the work over to so-called foreclosure-mill law firms, and generally cases are uncontested.

These days, more homeowners are digging in their heels. They delay foreclosures by filing for bankruptcy on the eve of a court-ordered sale of the property, or by refusing to answer the door when the plaintiff tries to "serve" them with a foreclosure lawsuit. They pay lawyers a few hundred dollars to file a motion that can buy them a little more time.

But few are as dogged as Mr. Davet. And his fight may not be over yet. Though ousted from his home for nearly a year now, he is trying to get the charming 1940s house back, plus damages. He's relying on the legal argument—currently making headlines—that a financial institution can only file a foreclosure action if it can prove it actually owns and holds the mortgage and promissory note.

[The Davets] made their mortgage payments, but on one loan, they allegedly made payments late—90 times, according to NationsBanc Mortgage Corp., which assessed the couple some $4,000 in late fees. After the Davets for two years refused demands to pay the late fees, during which NationsBanc began refusing to accept their regular mortgage payments, the company sued for foreclosure. . . . Mr. Davet insists the late fees were erroneous—he points to a deposition in which a NationsBanc employee conceded that the company couldn't back up its claims for a chunk of the fees.

He started with the help of lawyers, but those arrangements didn't last. . . . On his own, as a "pro se" litigant, Mr. Davet was undeterred. "Mr. Davet has litigated these same issues over and over again . . . and in each instance the courts have dismissed his claims," said NationsBanc.

Statutes in some states mandate delays or waiting periods in addition to those the debtor can gain by defending the action. For example, a Wisconsin statute provides that residential mortgage foreclosure sales may not be held until twelve months after the date on which the judgment is entered. If the foreclosing creditor elects to waive its right to a deficiency judgment, the period is shortened to six months.

The existence of statutes such as these demonstrates that the delay in the procedure for judicial foreclosure is not entirely inadvertent. Particularly in farming regions of the United States, there is a strong populist tradition in which the image of the foreclosing lender is that of the cold, calculating bank seeking a windfall through the debtor's default, while the image of the defending debtor is that of the victim struggling to keep a home and often a means of livelihood. Although it would be easy to make mortgage foreclosure more efficient, for those who make the laws in many states, the perceived fairness of the system is of greater concern.

With the cooperation of the debtor after default, a secured creditor may be able to avoid the necessity to foreclose. If there are no other liens or interests in the collateral, the debtor can simply transfer the property to the creditor by means of a *deed in lieu of foreclosure*. Such a deed does not "clog the equity of redemption" if it immediately extinguishes the mortgage and the underlying mortgage debt. Creditors sometimes persuade the debtor to grant a deed in lieu of foreclosure by persuading the debtor that it is better to lose the house now and have no further liability than to lose the house later and be liable for a deficiency. In some cases, creditors persuade debtors to surrender the property by paying the debtors an additional sum of money — in effect, purchasing the debtors' equity of redemption.

2. *Real Property Power of Sale Foreclosure*

About 25 states permit the mortgage lender and borrower to opt for a quicker, simpler method of foreclosure against real property. The lender and borrower do so by including in the security agreement a *power of sale*. In some of these states, the security agreement will be in the traditional form of a *mortgage*; in others, including California, it will be in the form of a *deed of trust*. The deed of trust states in essence that the collateral will be held in trust by the creditor or a third party such as a bank or title company. The borrower agrees that in the event of default, the trustee can sell the property and pay the loan from the proceeds of sale. Because the purpose of this arrangement is to secure payment of the loan, the law regards it not as an actual trust but as simply another form of security interest.

Foreclosure is still necessary when the creditor has a power of sale, but it can be accomplished through a procedure that does not include filing a lawsuit. For example, under California law, upon default under a mortgage or deed of trust containing a power of sale, the creditor can file in the public records a notice setting forth the nature of the debtor's default and the creditor's election to sell the property. If the debtor does not cure the default within 90 days, the creditor can set a time and place for sale, advertise it for 20 days, and then sell the property at auction. Pursuant to the power of sale contained in the deed of trust, the trustee conveys title to the purchaser at auction. The sale forecloses the debtor's right to redeem.

The primary purpose for permitting power of sale as an alternative means of foreclosure is to avoid the expense and delay of litigation. But even a power-of-sale foreclosure may end up in court. If the debtor refuses to surrender possession after the sale, the purchaser must sue for it. The cause of action may be for unlawful detainer, ejectment, or eviction. The debtor who has defenses to the foreclosure can defend that action or bring its own action to enjoin the sale or, if it has already been held, to set it aside. In some states the debtor can also bring a tort action for *wrongful sale*. In some states the secured creditor can sue for a deficiency judgment after the sale has been held, but others prohibit deficiency judgments when the foreclosure is by power of sale.

3.   UCC Foreclosure by Sale

The process by which a secured creditor forecloses a security interest in personal property is much simpler than the process for real property. The difference results largely from historical accident. The law and traditions of real estate foreclosure developed at an earlier time, when the lending of money was considered not quite so respectable as it is today and the most valuable assets were real estate. Restrictions placed on real estate foreclosure during that era have survived, but those restrictions were not extended to the later-developing process of personal property foreclosure.

Article 9 of the Uniform Commercial Code governs the foreclosure of security interests in personal property. It provides that after default, the secured party may sell, lease, license, or otherwise dispose of any or all of the collateral. UCC §9-610(a). That sale or disposition itself forecloses the debtor's right to redeem the property. UCC §9-623. It extinguishes the creditor's security interest in the collateral and transfers to the purchaser all of the debtor's rights in the collateral. UCC §9-617(a). Alternatively, if the creditor so chooses, it may foreclose by any available judicial procedure. UCC §9-601(a).

Problem Set 2

2.1. In a parallel universe, you are again pursuing Nathalie Martin from Problem 1.5 in Wisconsin to recover Karen Benning's $50,000. This time, however, Benning had the foresight to get Martin to sign a security agreement taking the property listed below as security. As in Problem 1.5, Martin owns the property free and clear of any liens or security interests other than Benning's.

a. Which of the following items can Benning reach through foreclosure of her security interest? See Wisconsin Statutes §815.18, §815.20, and §990.01(14), reproduced in Assignment 1.

1. A four-year-old Toyota automobile worth $15,000.
2. A house that Martin recently inherited from her mother, estimated to be worth about $275,000 and subject to a mortgage in the amount of $225,000.
3. Martin still owns the equipment from the day care center, which has a resale value of about $25,000.
4. A bank account containing $12,265.92.

b. "Waiver" is the voluntary relinquishment of a known right. Is Karen's security interest void as a waiver of exemptions under Wis. Stat. §815.18(6)(a)?

2.2. Bonnie Brezhnev runs a used-car lot in a low-income neighborhood. Even with cheap prices and low payments, she ends up repossessing a lot of cars. To ease the administrative burden, Bonnie plans to begin leasing the cars rather than selling them. That is, on a car she currently would sell for $5,000, no money down, with interest at 18 percent per annum, the payments would be $180.77 for three years. Instead, Bonnie proposes to lease the same car for $180.77 per month and offer the lessee an option to buy the car at the end of that period for $10. The lease will provide that, on default, Bonnie has the right to terminate the lease and the option to buy. "I will remain the owner of the car. If a lessee defaults, I'll just repossess the car and put it back on the lot instead of having to go through all that Article 9 rigmarole," Bonnie says. What advice do you give Bonnie about this plan? UCC §9-109(a)(1), Comment 2 to §9-109, and UCC §§1-201(b)(35) first and last sentences, 1-203.

2.3. Your client is a bank that makes home loans. The client has noticed that the market for *Sharia*-compliant lending is expanding, and the client wants to enter it. Under Islamic law, a transaction is *Sharia*-compliant only if the bank does not charge interest and shares in the transaction's risks. The bank proposes to meet those requirements by entering into partnerships with home buyers rather than making loans to home buyers. To illustrate, the bank ordinarily would lend $800,000 to a customer to purchase a $1 million home. Principal and interest (at the rate of 6 percent per year) would be repayable over 30 years in equal monthly installments of $5,995.51. In the *Sharia*-compliant transaction, the bank would form a partnership with the customer. The bank would contribute $800,000 for an 80 percent interest in the partnership; the customer would contribute $200,000 for a 20 percent interest. The partnership agreement would entitle the customer to live in the home and require the customer to purchase the bank's interest for $2,158,381.89, payable without interest, in equal monthly payments of $5,995.51 over 30 years. The money comes out exactly the same, but no "interest" is charged.

An Islamic finance expert is advising the bank on whether this transaction is *Sharia*-compliant. But the bank wants your advice on how these transactions will be treated in the event of default. Assume that all loans will be made in the United States and that U.S. law will apply. What do you tell the client's board of directors? UCC §9-109(a)(1).

▶ HALF ASSIGNMENT ENDS

2.4. The statutes of the state in which you are practicing authorize foreclosure against real property only by judicial process. Your firm is on retainer for the asset recovery department of Enterprise State Bank, and your case load includes more than a dozen foreclosures that are now in process for ESB. The cases are averaging about a year in the courts, producing substantial fees for the firm and good billables for you. Last week, Hiri Mashimoto, your contact at the bank, sent you yet another file, a residential foreclosure against John and Linda O'Hurley. You wrote the usual letter detailing the defaults under the mortgage documents and exercising the bank's right to accelerate.

a.   Much to your surprise, Linda O'Hurley came to see you today. She explained that about a year ago her husband was diagnosed as having cancer. He has been undergoing both chemical and radiation therapy. Given the level of the family's noninsured medical expenses and his reduced workload, the O'Hurleys realize that they can no longer afford the house. She says the house is still worth more than the balance owing on the loan, but her efforts to sell it in a slow market have been unsuccessful. She and her husband are willing to turn the house over to the bank, but they don't want to be sued or to have "a foreclosure on [their] record." O'Hurley said she is not represented by an attorney, but she would like you to draw up the necessary papers. What do you tell her?

> **Model Rule of Professional Conduct 4.3.** In dealing on behalf of a client with a person who is not represented by counsel, a lawyer shall not state or imply that the lawyer is disinterested. When the lawyer knows or reasonably should know that the unrepresented person misunderstands the lawyer's role in the matter, the lawyer shall make reasonable efforts to correct the misunderstanding. The lawyer shall not give legal advice to an unrepresented person, other than the advice to secure counsel, if the lawyer knows or reasonably should know that the interests of such a person are or have a reasonable possibility of being in conflict with the interests of the client.

b.   Mr. Mashimoto wants to know if there are any "legal problems" with Mrs. O'Hurley's offer. Are there?

c.   What if the O'Hurleys execute the deed today, with an understanding that you will give it back to them if they make up the back payments within 60 days, but that otherwise you will record it?

2.5. Your discussions of the O'Hurley plans got Mr. Mashimoto thinking about other ways to escape the delay and expense of foreclosure. He is back in your office today with an idea for "getting around this foreclosure thing." He proposes that when the bank makes a real estate loan, the bank will require that the borrower sign an irrevocable power of attorney authorizing another bank (the borrower can select the "trustee bank" from an approved list) to execute and deliver a deed in lieu of foreclosure in the event that (1) the debtor is in default under the mortgage and (2) the default continues for a period of 90 days. Mr. Mashimoto realizes that the trustee bank won't sign the deed if the debtor contests the default in any way, and he would still have to foreclose in such case. But he hopes that "at least this will eliminate the expense and delay in the clear cases." Will it? How does Mashimoto's proposal differ from a California deed of trust?

2.6.   Mr. Mashimoto has yet another idea. Many of the bank's commercial loans are made to corporate debtors. He proposes that at the time such a loan is made, in addition to the mortgage against the real estate owned by the corporation, the bank take a security interest in the stock of the corporation and take possession of the share certificates. If there is a default, the bank will foreclose on the stock by giving ten days' notice, UCC §9-612(b), and selling it pursuant to UCC §§9-610(a), (b), and (c), and 9-604(a)(1). In that sale, the bank can buy the stock for a modest price. (The value of the stock will be the value of the corporation's equity in the real estate — probably very little when the property is in foreclosure.) The bank will then elect its own employees as directors of the corporation, and the employees as directors will cause the corporation to execute a deed in lieu of foreclosure on the defaulted mortgage. You know that all of this can be done under the corporation law of the state, and someone else in your firm will tend to the securities law issues, but will it work from the debtor-creditor angle? UCC §§9-610(a), (b), and (c), 9-623.

■ End of Default Problem Set

2.7.   You are on the staff of state Senator Candy Rowsey. Rowsey sees herself as an activist reformer, and she is concerned about the high cost and excessive litigation involved in mortgage foreclosure. The state currently permits only judicial foreclosure, and the statute has no mandatory waiting periods. But debtors struggling to save their homes or businesses often raise petty issues in the hopes of obtaining delays, much like what happened in the Davet story. Because Rowsey gets her campaign money from the banks and her votes from the farmers, she doesn't want to do anything that will harm either interest, but she is appalled at the waste of money and judicial effort as the parties fight over issues of no real importance. She wants you to come up with something that will be neutral in its effect but more efficient. Any ideas?

2.8.   Arakaki, a general contractor, subcontracted work to C&S Electric. C&S subcontracted part of the work to Consolidated. Consolidated, C&S, and Arakaki also entered into a joint check agreement. The agreement provided that Arakaki would pay Consolidated's invoices by checks made payable jointly to C&S and Consolidated. (The effect of making a check payable to two payees is that neither of them can collect the check until the other indorses the check.) Arakaki promised to deliver the checks to Consolidated, and C&S agreed to indorse them to Consolidated. The agreement stated that its sole purpose was to provide for payment of Consolidated's invoices and that the agreement did not constitute an assignment of funds. Does this agreement constitute a security interest in favor of Consolidated in the corresponding accounts owing from Arakaki to C&S? UCC §§1-201(b)(35), 9-109(a)(1) and Comment 2.

Assignment 3: Repossession of Collateral

A. The Importance of Possession Pending Foreclosure

The period of time from the debtor's default until the equity of redemption is foreclosed may be negligible or extend for years. This Assignment addresses the issue of who will have possession of the collateral during that time.

Who will have possession is important for at least five reasons. First, the party in possession probably will capture the use value of the collateral. If the collateral is a house, the debtor can live in it or the creditor can rent it out. Second, only the party in possession may have access to the property to evaluate it before it is sold, which confers an advantage in bidding. Third, the creditor's gain of possession may interrupt the debtor's use. For example, if the collateral is the inventory and equipment of a business, a shift of possession may make it impossible for the business to continue. Fourth, by determining who is physically in a position to maintain or destroy the collateral, possession may determine whether and how the collateral is preserved. Lastly, possession — or the right to obtain it — provides bargaining leverage. The debtor who still has possession of the automobile has what amounts to a hostage that the debtor may be able to exchange for a reduction in the amount of the debt. Similarly, the creditor who holds a right to possession that, if exercised, would close the debtor's business may instead be able to extract changes in the terms of the loan.

Many security agreements provide that the creditor has the right to possession immediately upon default. Such a provision, however, is only the starting point for legal analysis. Whether courts will enforce such a provision depends on the circumstances. Even if the secured creditor obtains the *right* to possession from such a provision, the jurisdiction may require that the secured creditor follow particular procedures to obtain that possession. Because the rules for possession of real estate and personal property differ sharply, we discuss them separately.

B. The Right to Possession Pending Foreclosure — Personal Property

Article 9 of the Uniform Commercial Code governs nearly all security interests in personal property. On the issue of possession pending foreclosure, it favors the secured creditor in the strongest terms. Unless otherwise agreed, UCC §9-609 gives the secured party the right to take possession immediately on default. The secured party need not involve courts or public officials if the secured party can get possession without a breach of the peace. But if the debtor resists repossession, the secured party must obtain a court order for possession and have the sheriff take possession from the debtor. The easiest way to obtain such an order is by filing an action for replevin.

The replevin action is a direct descendant of the common law "writ of replevin" commonly used to recover possession of wandering cattle and other tangible personal property. Generally speaking, any party entitled to possession of tangible personal property is entitled to the writ. The writ directs the sheriff to take possession of the property from the defendant and give it to the plaintiff. By far the most common users of replevin today are secured creditors entitled to possession of collateral pursuant to UCC §9-609.

To obtain the remedy, the secured creditor files a civil action against the debtor. Immediately upon filing, the creditor can move for an order granting immediate temporary possession pending the outcome of the case. Typically, the plaintiff can obtain a hearing on the motion in no more than 10 to 20 days. In most states, the plaintiff must give notice of the hearing to the debtor, but in some, the hearing can be held and the temporary writ of replevin issued before the debtor is even aware that the case has been filed. If the secured creditor establishes at the hearing that it is likely to prevail in the action, the court issues the temporary writ of replevin. Issuance of the writ is usually conditioned on the creditor's posting a bond to protect the debtor in the event that the debtor ultimately prevails in the replevin action. (A bond is either a cash deposit with the clerk of the court or the written commitment of an insurance company to pay the debtor's damages from loss of possession if the debtor ultimately prevails.) The debtor can regain possession by posting a similar bond in favor of the creditor. But if the debtor is in financial difficulty (as is usually the case in a replevin action), the debtor will probably be unable to do so.

Once the writ has been issued and possession of the collateral transferred to the secured creditor, most debtors have no reason to defend the replevin action. Judgment is entered by default. The effect is that after default, a secured creditor usually can obtain possession of collateral that is tangible personal property through judicial procedure within two or three weeks. The creditor can then complete the foreclosure by selling the collateral in a commercially reasonable manner. UCC §9-610(a) and (b).

In Del's Big Saver Foods, Inc. v. Carpenter Cook, Inc., 603 F. Supp. 1071 (W.D. Wis. 1985), a secured creditor explored the limits of this powerful remedy. The debtors in that case, Burdell and Janice Robish, operated a retail grocery store. The secured creditor, Carpenter Cook, held a security interest in all of the Robishes' equipment and inventory. When the Robishes allegedly defaulted in making payments on the secured debt, Carpenter Cook filed an action for replevin.

Without notice of any kind to the Robishes, Carpenter Cook immediately asked a judge to issue a temporary writ of replevin. Carpenter Cook made no allegations of fraud or special circumstances. It merely filed an affidavit stating that the Robishes were in default and asserting that "the collateral would deteriorate in the hands of the Robishes," and posted a $100,000 bond. The judge issued the writ of temporary replevin on the same day Carpenter Cook filed the complaint. The writ directed the sheriff to take the equipment and inventory from the Robishes and give possession to Carpenter Cook. Later that day, writ in hand, Carpenter Cook gave the Robishes their first notice that the replevin action had been filed. Carpenter Cook demanded that the Robishes turn over the store and threatened that if they did not do so Carpenter Cook would have the sheriff "remove [them] bodily." The Robishes surrendered possession of the store.

Later, the Robishes sued Carpenter Cook and its lawyers in federal court, alleging that Wisconsin's procedure for temporary possession denied the Robishes due process of law. The court held Wisconsin's procedure constitutional because it complied with a series of decisions by the Supreme Court on the limits of replevin procedure. Despite the lack of any prior notice or opportunity to be heard *before* the court took its property, the Wisconsin procedure gave the Robishes the right "to seek an immediate post-seizure hearing." That is all due process requires. Thus, in a state with a replevin statute like Wisconsin's, any secured creditor can obtain a writ of temporary replevin and have the sheriff seize its collateral with no prior notice to the debtor and no prior opportunity to be heard.

What would have happened if the Robishes had refused to surrender possession to the sheriff? In most states, the sheriff is authorized to use force to take possession. Recall the New Jersey statute in the *Vitale* case that authorized the sheriff to "force an entry into any enclosure except the dwelling house of the judgment debtor in order to levy." Statutes vary widely on the subject.

Wisconsin Statutes

(2015)

§810.09   PROPERTY IN BUILDING, HOW TAKEN

If the property or any part thereof is in a building or enclosure the sheriff may demand its delivery. If the property is not delivered the sheriff shall advise the plaintiff of the refusal of the delivery. The plaintiff may then apply to the court for a warrant upon a sufficient showing of probable cause that the property is contained in the building or enclosure and upon delivery of the warrant of the judicial officer to the sheriff the sheriff may then enter and take the property.

12 Oklahoma Statutes

(2015)

§1582.   OFFICER MAY BREAK INTO BUILDINGS

The sheriff . . . , in the execution of the order for delivery, may break open any building or inclosure in which the property claimed, or any part thereof, is concealed, but not until he has been refused an entrance into said building or inclosure and the delivery of the property, after having demanded the same.

C.   The Article 9 Right to Self-Help Repossession

Probably most secured creditors would like to avoid the hassle and expenses of working through courts and sheriffs to obtain possession of their collateral. But many have no choice. Judicial procedures are often mandatory.

The principal exception is that a creditor with an Article 9 security interest in tangible, personal property can bypass the courts and the sheriff and do its own repossessing. The creditor's reason for doing so is usually to save time, effort, and money. The right to "self-help repossession" is derived from UCC §9-609. That section provides that after default a secured party may take possession of the collateral.

Security agreements typically require that the debtor surrender possession upon default, and some debtors actually do just that. A debtor who is behind on payments on his car loan may simply drive the car to the bank and hand over the keys. But most debtors do not surrender so easily. They ignore the bank's demands for possession and keep on driving. Some try to get together enough money to make up the back payments in the hope that they can renew their relationship with the bank. Others plan to deal with the problem when necessary by filing bankruptcy. Still others simply try to get as much use out of the car as they can before it is taken from them. Many debtors have no plan at all—they just wait to see what tomorrow brings. The secured creditor who wants the car from any of these debtors must take the initiative.

The secured creditor can file a replevin action against the debtor, obtain judicial recognition of its right to possession, and send the sheriff out to take the car. But the secured creditor can move even faster without judicial process. For example, if the car buyer is behind on the payments and the car is parked in a public place, unlocked, with the keys in it, the secured creditor, or its agent, is entitled to hop in and drive the car away.

Finding the car with the keys is a neat story, but repossession is seldom so easy. In many cases, the secured creditor will have difficulty locating its collateral. The car may be kept on private property, inside a fence, or in a locked garage. The car itself may be locked or inoperable. And the neighbors may want to know what somebody skulking in the back lot with a picklock is up to.

A small, somewhat disreputable industry specializes in solving these kinds of problems for secured lenders. For a few hundred dollars, these collection or repossession ("repo") agencies will find an item of collateral, take it from the debtor, and turn it over to the secured creditor. Much can go wrong in the process. Repossessors may invade the property of third parties in search of their collateral or they may repossess the wrong goods. Debtors may defend their possession with harsh words, fists, or guns. The courts generally hold that the duty to refrain from breach of the peace during repossession is nondelegable, making the secured creditors liable for the consequences of illegal repossessions by their independent contractors. E.g., Robinson v. Citicorp National Services, Inc., 921 S.W.2d 52 (Mo. App. 1996) (holding secured creditor potentially liable for debtor's death by heart attack during a wrongful repossession).

UCC §9-609(a)(2) gives the creditor the option to leave "equipment" temporarily in the possession of the debtor but render it unusable. In the ordinary application of that provision, the collateral is a large piece of equipment, such as a factory machine, for which removal to a warehouse would be difficult and costly. The creditor might remove key parts from the machine so that it cannot be used pending sale.

D.   The Limits of Self-Help: Breach of the Peace

repossess
w/o breach
of peace

The right to repossess collateral is not a license to engage in any behavior necessary to get it. The UCC permits self-help repossession only if the secured creditor can repossess without breach of the peace. UCC §9-609(b)(2). Not surprisingly, most lawsuits involving a creditor's self-help repossession — and much planning advice about self-help — turn on what constitutes a breach of the peace.

Duke v. Garcia
2014 WL 1318646 (D.N.M. 2014)

BALDOCK, Circuit Judge.

Gustavo Soto owns and operates Access Auto Recovery, LLC, a New Mexico business specializing in the repossession of motor vehicles. Plaintiff Tiar Duke sued Soto and Access Auto, among other Defendants, on a number of claims involving the April 2011 repossession of her car.

I.

The relevant, undisputed facts are as follows. On April 15, 2011, Defendant Soto drove his Access Auto tow truck to Plaintiff's home in Rio Rancho, New Mexico, intending to repossess her Dodge Charger due to her failure to make payments. With Soto was Jerome Baca, an Access Auto employee. At Plaintiff's home, the duo spotted the Charger, and Plaintiff spotted the duo. Baca then exited the truck and approached Plaintiff's garage. A confrontation ensued, the details of which are fiercely disputed. Most significantly for purposes here, Soto testified he saw Plaintiff push Baca several times, whereas Plaintiff testified it was in fact Baca who pushed her several times. At some point during this fracas, Soto left his truck and approached Plaintiff and Baca. Minutes later, Plaintiff and Soto each called 9-1-1. While waiting for the police, Soto and Baca did not leave Plaintiff's property. Several Rio Rancho police officers eventually arrived, separated the parties, interviewed them, and then coordinated Soto and Baca's repossession of the vehicle.

III. TRESPASS TO LAND & UNIFORM COMMERCIAL CODE

Plaintiff first claims Defendants Soto and Access Auto trespassed on her land. This is a state-law claim brought under 28 U.S.C. §1367, so the Court applies

New Mexico statutory law and common law. "Trespassing, both at common law and by statute, is the entry onto another's property without permission of the owner." State v. Tower, 59 P.3d 1264 (N.M. App. 2002). Both sides agree Soto and Baca's initial entry onto Plaintiff's property was *not* a trespass to land because it was privileged under N.M. Stat. Ann. §55-9-609. This statute, which copies UCC §9-609 verbatim, authorizes a secured party to take possession of a collateral "without judicial process, if it proceeds without a breach of the peace." No one disputes Access Auto and Soto were pursuing a collateral on behalf of Defendant Automobile Acceptance Corp., a secured party. So Plaintiff's trespass claim is actually that Defendants failed to leave her land *after* they lost their UCC-based privilege to be there because of a breach of the peace. Plaintiff's second claim—closely related to the first—is brought under the UCC directly, which "supports the recovery of actual damages for committing a breach of the peace in violation of Section 9-609." [UCC §9-625 cmt. 3.] In short, Plaintiff asserts Soto and Baca violated [UCC §9-609] by repossessing her car after a breach of the peace.

The parties agree a breach of the peace occurs when a debtor orally protests repossession. Plaintiff asserts she breached the peace by orally protesting Soto and Baca's repossession efforts. Defendants, on the other hand, assert Plaintiff never told Soto and Baca to leave her property. The Court disagrees, at least in regard to Baca, and by extension, Access Auto. On the record presented, a reasonable jury would have no choice but to conclude Plaintiff demanded Baca leave her property. Indeed, evidence indicates Plaintiff made *numerous* such demands. In deposition, Plaintiff testified her first words to Baca were "Get out of my garage." Plaintiff also testified she told Baca "if he didn't leave, I was going to call the police." Furthermore, Officer Benjamin Sanchez, himself a Defendant, testified when he arrived at the scene Plaintiff was "irate" and repeatedly screaming "I want them off my property!" Officer Adrian Garcia, also a Defendant, similarly stated he heard Plaintiff "in an escalated voice speaking to Mr. Sanchez that she wanted them off her property." Finally, the transcript of Plaintiff's three 9-1-1 calls leaves zero doubt—an oral demand was made: [Editors: This is one of the three transcripts in the court's opinion.]

Track 3
(telephone ringing)
[*Operator*]: Sandoval County 911. What is the address of the emergency?
[*Duke*]: Yes. Is someone coming to 1629?
[*Operator*]: Yes. We have three officers on the way.
[*Duke*]: Okay. How much longer do we have to wait? I mean this is an emergency.
[*Operator*]: They are on their way, Ma'am. We have three officers on their way. What's going on right now?
[*Duke*]: Okay. These guys—*They won't leave*—
[*Operator*]: Oh.
[*Duke*]: He's here standing in my—he's blocking—he has his hands on my damn garage. He's blocking me from pulling it down. *And he don't need to be in my garage.*
[*Operator*]: Okay. The male is?
[*Duke*]: Yes. The guy. *He is standing right here and won't move.*

Male voice: _____ [presumably inaudible]
[*Duke*]: Okay, *then move so I can let this down. He will not get out of my garage.*
[*Operator*]: Is he inside your garage?
[*Duke*]: He is. He is.
[*Operator*]: How many—how many people are out there? How many males?
[*Duke*]: There is two. . . . And I am a female.
[*Operator*]: Okay. And where is the other male?
[*Duke*]: He's right here also.
[*Operator*]: Is he in the garage as well?
[*Duke*]: No. He is just _____ [presumably inaudible].
Male voice: Tell her why we are here. To repossess your car.
End of Track

These calls document *nine* different times where Plaintiff directly tells a man attempting to repossess her car to either leave her property or get out of her garage. An additional *six* times Plaintiff tells the operator she wants this man to leave. Access Auto and Soto do not contest the transcript's authenticity. Nor do they argue the operator's (highly questionable) assurance that the repossession was lawful affects the analysis. Rather, they first assert Plaintiff's statements, in the recording and otherwise, are self-serving.

Soto . . . testified he saw Plaintiff shove Baca almost immediately after Baca entered her property. Similarly, in his 9-1-1 call, Soto stated Plaintiff was "pushing [Baca] because she is trying to shut the garage." Pushing is physical violence, and actual violence means a breach of the peace has occurred, regardless of who initiated it.

In response, Access Auto and Soto contend Plaintiff's "crazy" and "bizarre behavior when she pushed Baca" did not revoke the privilege to be on her land because she gave no indication she was opposed to the repossession. Again, this is undeniably false in regard to Baca. As to Soto, Defendants cite his testimony that Plaintiff did not "act like she was opposed" to the taking of the vehicle because she "told us that she had it worked out with the bank." Soto's testimony is self-contradictory, as pushing someone who enters your property to repossess your car is almost the definition of opposing repossession. We could reject Soto's testimony because of this contradiction and the fact that the rest of the evidence here—most importantly, the 9-1-1 tapes and Sanchez and Garcia's testimony—renders it utterly implausible. Regardless, Soto himself *admits* he viewed the push as a breach of the peace, and he has cited no case law where physical violence occurred and a court nevertheless declined to find breach of the peace as a matter of law. At the end of the day, Soto witnessed a breach of the peace and yet did not leave Plaintiff's property until he repossessed her car.

Two additional arguments raised by Access Auto and Soto should be addressed. First, they argue, seemingly in the alternative, that they cannot be liable for trespass to land or violation of [UCC §9-609] because they abandoned repossession once Plaintiff called the police, and the subsequent repossession was a separate attempt to which Plaintiff voluntarily agreed. Access Auto and Soto again rely on Soto's deposition, where he disclaimed any intent or hope to repossess the vehicle after the police were called. Said Soto, "We stopped for the cops. . . . [I]f it wasn't going to happen to get [the] vehicle, we were—you know, that was it."

As above, this narrative is utterly implausible. Even if accepted as true, however, Access Auto and Soto would still be liable on the claims here as a matter of law. Soto's testimony would not affect the trespass to land claim because it is undisputed Soto and Baca never left Plaintiff's property while waiting for the police, even though the breach of peace unquestionably terminated their privilege to be there. This was a trespass to land. And in regard to [UCC §9-609], not only did Soto testify the police were present during the eventual repossession, but he essentially concedes they controlled the process. "[Attorney]: Who told you that [Plaintiff] was giving up the vehicle for repossession? [Soto]: The cops. . . . [Attorney]: Did you overhear any conversations that [led] you to understand what it was that [led] Ms. Duke to decide to give up the vehicle voluntarily? [Soto]: No." According to the New Mexico Supreme Court, a non-judicial repossession is automatically wrongful when "a repossessor is . . . assisted by law enforcement officials in order to prevent a breach of the peace. . . . [T]he imprimatur of the state evinced by the presence of a law enforcement official, without judicial process, removes a repossession from the ambit of [the previous version of UCC §9-609]." Waisner v. Jones, 755 P.2d 598, 602 (N.M. 1988). As such, even if Access Auto and Soto totally abandoned their first repossession attempt, their later, successful effort did not comply with [UCC §9-609]. Thus, they are directly liable under the UCC, in addition to being liable for trespass to land.

Second, Access Auto and Soto argue Plaintiff's motion should be denied even if they lose on these issues. To reach this fanciful conclusion, Access Auto and Soto assert a judicial resolution at this juncture would not streamline litigation because a trial on damages would cover the same territory as a trial on the merits. Defendants cite no binding or even remotely persuasive law for this wishful thinking, so the Court declines to exercise its discretion in such a manner.

In summary, the Court finds as a matter of law that Defendants Access Auto and Soto intentionally trespassed on Plaintiff's land when they repossessed her vehicle, and that Access Auto violated [UCC §9-609] when Soto and Baca continued with the repossession after a breach of the peace. We therefore grant Plaintiff summary judgment on these claims. [Editors: The court also granted summary judgment to the plaintiff on her claims under New Mexico's Unfair Practices Act.]

Not surprisingly, there is considerable dispute over precisely what kind of facts constitute a breach of the peace. Here is a sampling of cases holding that there was a breach of the peace:

1. The repossessor alerted the police and three police cars arrived at the scene ahead of the repossessor. The debtor's mother told the police that there was an ongoing dispute regarding the financing. A police officer advised the debtor's mother that the repossession was inevitable, and also stated that "it's a civil issue, it's not a criminal issue. You've got to get a hold of an attorney if you want to fight the repossession and everything else." At the officer's request, the debtor gave him the keys to her vehicle. The court held the repossession illegal because the officer assisted in the repossession rather than merely being present to

maintain order. Anderson v. City of Oak Park, 2014 WL 4415956 (E.D. Mich. 2014).

2.   The first time the repossessor attempted to take a heavy-duty rotary mower from the debtor's home, the debtor ordered him off the premises. Almost a month later, the repossessor came back with two more men. The debtor was not home, but the debtor's son told the men they should not take the mower and "protested" its removal. But "surrounded" by the three, he did nothing further to stop them because he "was afraid of being beaten." The court held that "when [the secured creditor's] agents were physically confronted by [the debtor's] representative, disregarded his request to desist their efforts at repossession and refused to depart from the private premises upon which the collateral was kept, they committed a breach of the peace within the meaning of [UCC §9-609], lost the protective application of that section, and thereafter stood as would any other person who unlawfully refuses to depart from the land of another." Morris v. First National Bank & Trust Co. of Ravenna, Ohio, 254 N.E.2d 683 (Ohio 1970).

3.   During the repossession of a car, the Marcuses "argued loudly" with the repossessor. The repossessor beckoned a nearby police officer to the scene. Both sides argued with the officer and the Marcuses tried to unhook the car from the repossessor's wrecker. When the officer told the Marcuses to "keep [their] mouths shut, go back in the house, or [they] would indeed go to jail that day," the Marcuses let the repossession occur. The appeals court said

> officers are not state actors during a private repossession if they act only to keep the peace, but they cross the line if they affirmatively intervene to aid the repossessor. . . . The plaintiff's resistance to the taking of his property need not be strong. The general rule is that a debtor's request for the financer to leave the car alone must be obeyed. Even polite repossessors breach the peace if they meet resistance from the debtor. If a breach of peace occurs, self-help repossession is statutorily precluded.

Marcus v. McCollum, 394 F.3d 813 (10th Cir. 2004).

4.   To repossess a bulldozer, the repossessors cut a chain used to lock a fence. Because that was done after the end of the work day, it left plaintiff's heavy equipment storage area containing approximately $350,000 worth of equipment unsecured and unprotected. Citing a case in which the repossessor's having broken a window to unlock a door to a debtor's residence and repossess a piano was a breach of the peace, the court held that cutting the chain was improper. Laurel Coal Co. v. Walter E. Heller & Co., Inc., 539 F. Supp. 1006 (W.D. Pa. 1982).

5.   The repossessor backed a tow truck into the driveway and "began to hook the vehicle up." The family asked the repossessors what they were doing. Told the vehicle was being repossessed, the debtor and one of her daughters jumped into the car. The repossessors towed the vehicle out of the driveway and into the street, with the debtor's family and neighbors yelling at the repossessors to stop towing the vehicle with individuals in the vehicle. The police arrived and told the repossessors

to stop. The court held these allegations sufficient to state a claim for breach of the peace because nothing in UCC §9-609 "suggests that the fault for any breach must lie solely with the party doing the repossessing." Smith v. AFS Acceptance, LLC, 2012 WL 1969415 (N.D. Ill. 2012).

Cases holding that there was not a breach of the peace:

1. The debtor's complaint for wrongful repossession alleged that the repossessor followed him to Big Stone Gap, Virginia, where he was staying with his daughter. About 2:00 A.M., the repossessor entered plaintiff's truck, started it, raced the engine, and "barrel[ed] out of the lot and down the street." The debtor said he and his daughter "did not know what was happening and were in fear." The court held that the complaint failed to state a cause of action. The court considered the "stealthy manner" in which the repossession was effected as "calculated to avoid a breach of the peace because the prospect of a confrontation with the plaintiff was less at 2 A.M. than it would have been in the daylight hours or in the early evening." Even though the repossession may have violated some traffic ordinance, it was not "an incitement to violence or to break the peace." That the repossessor was an off-duty deputy sheriff also did not matter, because the plaintiff did not know that while the repossession was in progress. Wallace v. Chrysler Credit Corp., 743 F. Supp. 1228 (W.D. Va. 1990).

2. Two repossessors used a wrecker to repossess a woman's automobile from her driveway. Awakened by the noise, she ran outside to stop them and "hollered at them" as they were driving away. The two men stopped. They told her they were repossessing the car. She explained that she had been attempting to bring the past payments up to date and informed the men that the car contained personal items belonging to a third person. The men "stepped between her and the car" when she attempted to retrieve them, gave her the personal items, and drove off with her car "without further complaint from [her]." She admitted that the men were polite throughout the encounter and did not make any threats toward her or do anything that caused her to fear any physical harm. The dissent noted that plaintiff was a single parent living with her two small children and observed that "facing the wrecking crew in the dead of night, [plaintiff] did everything she could to stop them short of introducing physical force," but the majority said the repossession was proper. Williams v. Ford Motor Credit Co., 674 F.2d 717 (8th Cir. 1982).

3. On the secured creditor's first attempt to repossess her car, the debtor successfully ordered the repossessor off the premises. The debtor claimed that she had a gun in the house and would use it if he came back. She later called the repossessor's office and threatened that "if she caught anyone on her property again trying to take her car, [she] would leave him laying right where [she] saw him." Thirty days later, the intrepid repossessor took the car from the debtor's driveway,

awakening her with the sound of "burning rubber." No confrontation occurred. The debtor did not know the car was being taken until the repossessor had safely departed with it. The court held that despite the "potential for violence" the debtor had previously communicated, the repossession had not breached the peace. Wade v. Ford Motor Credit Co., 668 P.2d 183 (Kan. Ct. App. 1983).

4. The collateral was a bus located in the debtor's business premises. The repossessor cut a lock to enter property marked "No Trespassing" to get the bus. The court held that this repossession was not a breach of the peace because the security agreement signed by the debtor permitted the creditor to "enter any premises . . . without liability for trespass." Wombles Charters, Inc. v. Orix Credit Alliance, Inc., 39 UCC Rep. Serv. 2d 599 (S.D.N.Y. 1999).

5. The two truck rigs that served as collateral were in the possession of a truck equipment dealer. The repossessor obtained possession of the rigs by fraudulently misrepresenting to the truck equipment dealer that the debtor had given him permission to repossess. The court ruled that the misrepresentation was not a breach of the peace because it did not "support a potential for immediate violence." K.B. Oil Co. v. Ford Motor Credit Co., Inc., 811 F.2d 310 (6th Cir. 1987).

6. The repossessing team had hooked the plaintiff's car to the tow truck and had started driving away when the plaintiff voiced an objection to the repossession and started moving toward the car. The car had already been moved from its parking spot when the plaintiff began objecting to the repossession. A third person restrained the plaintiff, and the car was successfully repossessed. The court said "once a repossession agent has gained sufficient dominion over collateral to control it, the repossession has been completed." Clark v. Auto Recovery Bureau Conn., Inc., 889 F. Supp. 543 (D. Conn. 1994).

7. The repossessor towed the wrong car from a public street, not knowing that the debtor's two children were inside. When he later discovered the children, he "immediately" and "peaceably" returned both the children and the car. The court held there was no breach of the peace because "there is no evidence that [the repossessor] proceeded with the attempted repossession over an objection communicated to him at, near, or incident to the seizure of the property." Chapa v. Traciers & Associates, 267 S.W.3d 386 (Tex. App. 2008).

▶ Half Assignment Ends

E.   Self-Help Against Accounts as Collateral

In the event of default, UCC §§9-607 and 9-406(a) provide a self-help remedy to the party holding a security interest in accounts. Under §9-607, the secured creditor who knows the identity of the account debtors can simply send them written notices to pay directly to the secured creditor. The account debtor who receives such a notice can discharge its obligation only by paying the secured party. UCC §9-406(a). An account debtor who is concerned whether the person sending the notice is actually entitled to the money can request proof of the assignment. UCC §9-406(c). Ultimately, the account debtor, at its own risk, must determine whom to pay.

For example, in Marine National Bank v. Airco, Inc., 389 F. Supp. 231 (W.D. Pa. 1975), Midland National Bank made loans to Craneways that were secured by various collateral of Craneways, including its accounts receivable. In June of 1971, Craneways' president notified the bank that it had a contract with Airco to reconstruct a crane. Once the work was complete, Airco owed Craneways $23,000. On July 19, 1971, the bank sent, and Airco acknowledged receiving, a registered letter notifying Airco that the bank held a security agreement covering all of Craneways' accounts receivable. The letter demanded that Airco pay any sums due Craneways to the bank. In August 1971, Craneways delivered the crane. Airco then paid $18,000 of the balance owing to Craneways. Craneways endorsed the check to the IRS to pay its taxes. In the bank's lawsuit against Airco, the court entered judgment in favor of the bank for $13,000, the remaining amount Craneways owed to the bank.

Marine National demonstrates how powerful the self-help remedy against accounts can be. The bank was able to recover its collateral — the account — even though that required the account debtor, Airco, to pay more than it owed. Airco theoretically had the right to recover its erroneous payment from Craneways, but by the time Marine National sued Airco, Craneways was out of business and the debt was uncollectible.

In some respects, accounts make good collateral. The self-help remedy is easy to employ and accounts are by their nature readily converted to cash. But there are serious practical problems that render them less than ideal as collateral. A secured creditor's exercise of its right to notify account debtors can have devastating effects. Account debtors are motivated to pay their debts in part by their desire to keep doing business with the debtor and in part by the fear of legal action. For example, audio dealers will generally continue to pay the audio manufacturer, absent notice from the bank, because they know that if they don't, the manufacturer will stop shipping equipment to them and may bring suit against them.

If, however, the manufacturer's bank has taken over the account, both motives may be undermined. The takeover signals to the dealers that the bank has lost confidence in the manufacturer's ability to meet its obligations and may suggest that the manufacturer will soon be out of business. The dealers may decide to withhold payment of the accounts to protect themselves against the manufacturer's future failure to provide service or honor warranties. Knowing that debtors in financial difficulty lack credibility, dealers may be more likely to complain about the manufacturer's products or to question the manufacturer's accounting. Worse yet, the dealers may realize that if the manufacturer's business fails, it may be difficult for either the manufacturer or the bank to sue them on the unpaid account. The bank financing the manufacturer may not have the information necessary to prove the account obligation to a judge or jury, and the failed debtor may be unwilling to assist. As a result,

the accounts can be expensive to collect or may become completely uncollectible. To avoid these problems, account lenders often choose to leave the
debtors in control of the accounts and to aid the debtors in their collection.

F.   The Right to Possession Pending
Foreclosure — Real Property

1.   The Debtor's Right to Possession During Foreclosure

The general rule is that mortgagees never become entitled to possession of
mortgaged real property in their capacity as mortgagees. The debtor remains
owner of the property and is entitled to possession of it until the court forecloses the debtor's equity of redemption and the sheriff sells the property.
Only the purchaser at the foreclosure sale (who may, of course, be the same
person as the mortgagee) is entitled to dispossess the debtor.

The remedies by which purchasers at foreclosure sales obtain possession
from mortgagors who do not vacate voluntarily vary from state to state. In
some jurisdictions, the purchaser must file an action for eviction or ejectment
and obtain a court order for removal. In others, the court can issue a writ of
possession or writ of assistance on motion by the purchaser. In either event,
the purchaser can probably have the sheriff on the scene with badge and gun
in no more than 10 to 20 days after the purchase.

2.   Appointment of a Receiver

While a foreclosure case is pending, any interested party can apply for the
appointment of a *receiver* to preserve the value of the collateral. To illustrate,
assume that the collateral is an apartment building. Although some of the
apartments are occupied by rent-paying tenants, the total rents have been
insufficient to enable the debtor to make its mortgage payment. The
debtor-landlord has fallen behind in its mortgage payments, and the mortgagee has filed a complaint for foreclosure. The debtor currently sees no way
it can redeem the property, but also knows that foreclosure will take several
months. The debtor continues to collect the rents from the existing tenants
but does not pay anything to the mortgagee. It spends no money on necessary
maintenance for the apartment building. Tenants begin to complain about
the appearance of the property and its poor state of repair. Some move out,
further reducing the flow of rents and impairing the value of the collateral. In
circumstances such as these, the court may grant temporary relief to the mortgagee in the form of the appointment of a receiver.

The receiver will be an officer of the court with fiduciary obligations to all
who have an interest in the property. He or she will have the right to collect
the rents and use the money to maintain the building, as well as the authority

to rent the apartments. Typically, the receiver will retain any rents collected in excess of the amounts necessary to maintain the property, pending the outcome of the mortgage foreclosure action.

On the facts of this illustration, appointment of the receiver will temporarily cut off the debtor's cash flow from the collateral until the judgment of foreclosure cuts it off permanently. The mortgagee does not get access to the cash flow directly, but the cash flow will be used in part to maintain the value of the collateral—in effect giving the mortgagee the benefit of it.

A foreclosing mortgagee does not always succeed in winning the appointment of a receiver. Courts rarely appoint receivers unless the terms of the mortgages provide for such appointments. Even when the mortgages so provide, appointment is an equitable remedy that remains in the sound discretion of the court. The creditor must show that under the circumstances of the particular case its remedy at law (foreclosure alone) is inadequate. That usually will be true only when the value of the property is inadequate to satisfy the mortgage debt and the mortgagor is insolvent so that any deficiency judgment will be uncollectible. Only in rare and extreme circumstances do the courts appoint receivers to take possession of owner-occupied residential real estate; a defaulting debtor can nearly always count on retaining possession of the family home while the debtor struggles to save it from foreclosure. Receivers are appointed to take possession of owner-occupied commercial real estate somewhat more often, but the courts are understandably reluctant to dispossess a debtor who is operating its business from the mortgaged premises.

Many states have statutes governing the appointment of receivers in mortgage foreclosure cases. Typically these statutes mention a few of the factors of concern to the courts in determining whether to appoint a receiver, but do not prohibit consideration of other factors. The factors mentioned in this statute are typical of the statutes generally.

California Code of Civil Procedure

Cal. Civ. Proc. Code §564(b) (2015)

[A] receiver may be appointed by the court in which an action or proceeding is pending, or by a judge thereof, in the following cases: . . .

> 2. In an action by a secured lender for the foreclosure of the deed of trust or mortgage and sale of the property . . . where it appears that the property is in danger of being lost, removed, or materially injured, or that the condition of the deed of trust or mortgage has not been performed, and that the property is probably insufficient to discharge the deed of trust or mortgage debt.

———————

The receiver typically takes possession of the collateral during the foreclosure case and delivers possession directly to the purchaser at the foreclosure sale.

An Illinois statute illustrates another approach to the possession issue. It authorizes the court to give possession to the secured creditor—before the debtor has had its day in court.

Illinois Mortgage Foreclosure Law

735 Ill. Comp. Stat. 5/15-1701(b)(2) (2015)

Nonresidential real property

[In cases involving nonresidential real property,] if (i) the mortgagee is so authorized by the terms of the mortgage or other written instrument, and (ii) the court is satisfied that there is a reasonable probability that the mortgagee will prevail on a final hearing of the cause, the mortgagee shall upon request be placed in possession of the real estate, except that if the mortgagor shall object and show good cause, the court shall allow the mortgagor to remain in possession.

---

3. Assignments of Rents

If the parties contemplate that the debtor will rent the collateral to others during the term of the mortgage, the mortgage is likely to include a provision by which the debtor assigns the rents from the property to the mortgagee as additional security. The provision gives the mortgagee the right to collect the rents directly from the tenants in the event of default under the mortgage. Because collecting the rents from mortgaged property that has been rented to third parties, like appointing a receiver, is functionally the equivalent of taking possession, some courts are reluctant to give effect to the assignment of rents clause. But other courts hold that a mortgagee who declares a default, notifies the tenants to pay the rent to it, and proceeds to collect the rent without foreclosing is acting within its rights.

Problem Set 3

3.1. Look back at Problem 1.1. Now assume that Jeffrey produced a second paper at your meeting with him. He explained that he had gone to an office supply store and picked up a form titled "Personal Property Security Agreement" and he had Lisa sign it. You look it over and decide it is a perfectly enforceable security agreement designating the lawn furniture as collateral. Does your advice change? UCC §§9-102(a)(73) and (74), 9-609.

3.2. Melissa Jacoby is the head of the collections department at Commercial Finance, a valued, long-time client of your firm. CF frequently has occasion to repossess equipment from building construction sites in several states. CF's usual practice is to obtain judicial process and then have the sheriff do the actual repossession. When the judicial process is too slow or the sheriff too inflexible, Jacoby hires local repo people to effect a self-help repossession. To make sure they act responsibly and effectively, she personally goes with them and "calls the shots." CF can't afford to bring counsel along every time they repossess property, so Jacoby has asked you to work out some guidelines on "how far she can go" in attempting a repossession.

Jacoby explains the circumstances she usually encounters: The borrower typically is a general contractor or a subcontractor who is responsible for some specific aspect of construction, such as excavation or the concrete work. The general contractor deals with the owner and provides safety and security for the site. Larger sites are fenced; some, but not all, have guards on the premises during the night. Some equipment is left on the construction site overnight, while the rest is typically under heavier security at the debtor's place of business. Some of the repossession targets are motor vehicles, but most are heavy equipment such as bulldozers or power generators that must be carried by truck.

Outline your advice to Jacoby. Focus on the situation where the collateral is a bulldozer owned by a subcontractor, the site is owned by a developer, and fences and security are provided by the general contractor. Consider each of these situations:

a. Sites where there is neither a guard nor a fence.
b. Sites where there is a fence but no guard.
c. Sites where there is a guard.
d. The debtor keeps the bulldozer in a locked, steel building on the debtor's own property.
e. As CF's regular counsel, you should also consider whether there is anything that should be in CF's security agreements about repossession that might make Jacoby's job easier.

See UCC §§9-609, 9-201, 9-602(6), 9-603.

3.3. Salvatore Ferragamo is the sole owner of Ferragamo Construction Company. Your firm has worked with Sal for 16 years, doing all the legal work for his company from incorporation through the negotiation of its insurance contracts. Terrible weather and late deliveries by suppliers have put the company behind in its work schedule and consequently in what it can collect from its customers. The company has missed its third monthly payment to ITT Finance, which provides financing secured by Ferragamo's equipment. Sal says he needs just a week or two of uninterrupted operations to turn the corner financially.

This morning Sal received a letter by registered mail from ITT declaring the loan in default and directing him to assemble the collateral and make it available to ITT for repossession. Even though his security agreement with ITT provides that he will do precisely that, Sal has decided not to comply. Instead, he wants to know what he can do, short of bankruptcy, to resist repossession.

Rule 1.2 of the ABA Model Rules of Professional Conduct provides in part:

(d) A lawyer shall not counsel a client to engage, or assist a client, in conduct that the lawyer knows is criminal or fraudulent, but a lawyer may discuss the legal consequences of any proposed course of conduct with a client and may counsel or assist a client to make a good faith effort to determine the validity, scope, meaning or application of the law.

a.   If the ITT people come for the equipment, how should he handle the situation?

b.   How should he handle the situation if the repossessors bring the police with them?

c.   What if the sheriff is with them and they have a writ of replevin?

d.   If they don't bring the police, should Sal call the police?

e.   Should Sal hide the equipment where the repossessors can't find it? Assume that the state has a statute identical to Wis. Stat. §943.84, which provides that "[w]hoever, with intent to defraud, . . . conceals any personal property in which he knows another has a security interest . . . is guilty of a Class E felony."

3.4.   If ITT's lawyers gave ITT the same advice you gave Commercial Finance in Problem 3.2, would they be able to repossess Sal's equipment through self-help? In other words, if both the debtor and the creditor have the best legal advice regarding self-help repossession and follow it carefully, who "wins"?

▶ HALF ASSIGNMENT ENDS

3.5.   Deare Distributors sells farming equipment to retail farming supply stores. Firstbank and Deare have a working arrangement under which Firstbank lends an amount equal to 60 percent of Deare's accounts receivable, secured by the accounts. When Deare makes a sale, it sends a copy of the invoice to Firstbank. The bank deposits an amount equal to 60 percent of the invoice to Deare's bank account. When the supply store pays the invoice, Deare is required to apply 60 percent of the proceeds to repay the loan immediately.

Deare has requested that Firstbank's interest in the accounts not be made known to the account debtors "because it might make them nervous." Firstbank is considering honoring that request in the absence of default, but it consults with you to ask about the risks of this arrangement. You want to consider why Deare might cheat and how it could do so. Is there any way to discover such cheating without contacting Deare's customers?

3.6.   A year after the preceding problem, Firstbank is back with additional questions. Deare ultimately defaulted on the loan, and two months ago Firstbank notified the account debtors to pay Firstbank directly.

a.   Horne's Feed and Seed, one of Deare's account debtors, claims that it paid Deare in full last month and refuses to pay Firstbank. Can Firstbank collect from Horne's? UCC §§9-406(a), 9-607(a).

b.   Another account debtor, Wilson's Farming Goods, has refused to pay anything, claiming that although they received $42,000 in equipment, they have untended warranty claims amounting to $19,000. What can Firstbank collect from Wilson's? UCC §9-404(a).

■ END OF DEFAULT PROBLEM SET

3.7.   As you were cleaning the sludge from your spam filter, your eye caught an email with the subject "Notice of Assignment of Account." The notice instructed you to pay your MasterCard bill to American Financial Corporation at a post office box in Phoenix, Arizona. As you stretched your finger toward the Delete key, you noticed that the email contained the last four digits of your MasterCard account number.

a.   Is it possible that this is an effective notification to pay an assignee pursuant to UCC §9-406(a) and (b)? UCC §1-202(e).

b.   What should you do next? UCC §9-406(c) and Comment 4 to §9-406.

3.8.   You have been counsel for Ronald Silber, the owner of Sound Emporium, for several years. Silber tells you that the business is experiencing some temporary cash-flow problems and he would like your advice on how to deal with them. You elicit the following list of problems:

a.   The business owes Southern Savings about $520,000 against the business premises, which are worth about $600,000. The mortgage is at 9 percent, and payments are $4,182 a month. Silber is two payments in arrears, and a third one is due next week. He received a notice from Southern's lawyers stating that if the payments are not brought up to date within ten days, Southern will foreclose. Assume that, under the law of the state, if the mortgage is accelerated, the acceleration can later be reversed by paying the arrearage at any time "before foreclosure."

[handwritten margin note: secured thru Go thru with foreclosure]

b.   The business owes about $180,000 to Citizen's Bank. The loan is secured by the trade fixtures and equipment of the business. The loan is at 11 percent per year and the quarterly interest payment in the amount of $5,150 is 45 days past due. The loan officer says it must be brought current or "legal action will be taken."

[handwritten margin note: secured will have to turn over]

c.   The utility bill is almost two months past due. The total amount owing for the two-month period is about $2,400. Silber has received the standard form notice that unless payment is made within ten days, utility service will be cut off.

[handwritten margin note: unsecured payment arrangement]

d.   Two suppliers are hounding Silber to pay invoices that are now more than 120 days old. Silber owes each about $40,000. One supplier has a security interest in the inventory it sold to Sound Emporium; the other does not. Both suppliers have hired local attorneys and are threatening immediate legal action. Silber says he could purchase similar inventory elsewhere, but he would have to pay cash.

[handwritten margin note: secured Will have to TURN over equip]

There are several other creditors, but none are really pushing for immediate payment. Silber wants desperately to keep the doors open because he thinks that in four to six months he can turn the business around. But over the next two or three months, he will have only about $8,000 a month to devote to the payments listed above. Silber says bankruptcy is "absolutely out of the question," and, from the way he says it, you know he means it (at least for now). Instead, he wants your opinion on how to allocate the money among these creditors and he also wants to know "what they can do if they don't get paid." What are your questions for Silber? What do you need to know about the law of your state? Based on what you now know and assuming your state's law is in accord with the majority, what's your advice? See UCC §9-609.

[handwritten margin note: $8,000]

[handwritten note at bottom: How much money are you making currently. Utility - payment arrangement. Why did you wait so long? Have you been communicating with creditors? Any way you can make agreement now.]

Model Rules of Professional Conduct, Rule 3.2: Expediting Litigation—A lawyer shall make reasonable efforts to expedite litigation consistent with the interest of the client.

Official Comment: Dilatory practices bring the administration of justice into disrepute. . . . Nor will a failure to expedite be reasonable if done for the purpose of frustrating an opposing party's attempt to obtain rightful redress or repose. It is not a justification that similar conduct is often tolerated by the bench and bar. The question is whether a competent lawyer acting in good faith would regard the course of action as having *some substantial purpose other than delay*. Realizing financial or other benefit from otherwise improper delay in litigation is not a legitimate interest of the client. (Emphasis added.)

In light of these provisions, can you counsel Silber at all?

3.9. Your firm represents Stanley Zabriskie and Zabriskie Autos. When Zabriskie sells a car, he arranges financing. The loans are made by a separate financing company. When the buyer defaults, Zabriskie usually has to buy the loan back from the finance company and enforce it himself. (This procedure is known as *recourse financing*.) After a default and repurchase, Zabriskie typically refers the matter to Auto Repossessors (AR). If AR can get possession of the car peacefully, Zabriskie pays them $300; if not, Zabriskie refers the matter to Tyler & Yin (T & Y), a law firm that specializes in small collection cases. T & Y will file an action for replevin and, as permitted under local law, obtain the writ of possession without prior notice to the debtor. Provided that the debtor does not defend the replevin action, they charge a flat $600 for the case; otherwise they charge on an hourly basis.

Five months ago, Zabriskie Autos sold a car to Sandra Evans. Evans made the first two payments, then missed the next three. On the few occasions that Stanley Zabriskie has been able to contact her, she has complained about the quality of the car, the representations the salesperson made to her, and the financing Zabriskie obtained for her. Stanley Zabriskie thinks her complaints are just an excuse to keep him from repossessing, but when you press him, he admits there may be some truth to her claims. He'd like to "run this one through the regular procedure." As corporate counsel, what's your advice? UCC §9-609.

3.10. Your client, Rudy Russo, sells used cars to customers with bad credit. After encountering all sorts of problems with repossessions, he has found a technical solution. He wants to install a GPS device and a starter interrupt mechanism in each car he sells on credit. The technology will allow Russo to remotely disable the ignition of a car owned by any person who falls behind on his or her payments. If working correctly, the interrupt mechanism will not disable the car while it is moving, but a borrower could be left stranded in a remote location. If the borrower pays up, Russo can re-activate the car. If not, the GPS will tell Russo's employees where the car is located. Rudy wants to know if his idea would be legal under the UCC. Do you have any advice for him? UCC §§9-102(a)(33), 1-302(a) and (b), 9-602, 9-603(b), 9-609(a) and (b).

Assignment 4: Judicial Sale and Deficiency

After a judgment has been entered in a judicial foreclosure, a public official sells the collateral. The purpose of the sale is to convert the value of property to cash, so that all or part of that value can be used to pay the debt. The proceeds of sale are applied first to the expenses of sale, and then to the payment of the secured debt. Any remaining proceeds—referred to as the *surplus*—go to the debtor. If the proceeds are insufficient to pay the expenses of sale and the secured debt in full, the debtor may remain liable for the *deficiency*.

A foreclosure sale is rarely a simple conversion of value. For reasons we discuss further below, collateral frequently sells for much less than its value. But for most purposes, the law clings to the legal fiction that the price paid in an auction foreclosure sale is the collateral's value. As the Supreme Court put it: "We deem, as the law has always deemed, that a fair and proper price, or a 'reasonably equivalent value,' for foreclosed property, is the price in fact received at the foreclosure sale, so long as all the requirements of the State's foreclosure law have been complied with." BFP v. Resolution Trust Corp., 511 U.S. 531 (1994).

The requirement that collateral be exposed to public sale as part of the foreclosure process generally cannot be varied by contract. Even if the mortgage specifically provides for the secured creditor to become the owner of the collateral in the event of default and foreclosure, the public sale must still be held. Without the sale, the possibility always remains that the creditor has picked up the property at too great a bargain, or, to reverse the focus and put it in the language of the courts, the debtor has suffered a forfeiture. Recall that foreclosures originated in equity, and "equity," the maxim goes, "abhors a forfeiture."

As you read this assignment, keep in mind that Article 9 security interests can be foreclosed judicially, see UCC §9-601(a)(1), but seldom are. Assignment 5 discusses the sale procedure commonly employed in nonjudicial foreclosure under UCC §§9-610(a) and (b).

A. Strict Foreclosure

Strict foreclosure is foreclosure that does not result in a sale. Strict foreclosure cuts off the debtor's equity of redemption, and the secured creditor becomes the owner of the collateral. Strict foreclosure of real estate mortgages is the norm in Vermont and is available in some circumstances in Connecticut. It is available for contracts for deed or installment land contracts in the large majority of states.

✳ Contracts for deed are contracts for the sale of real property that provide for payment of the purchase price in installments with delivery of the deed only after the last payment is made. Contract for deed sellers must foreclose through court process. But the foreclosure does not lead to sale. Instead, the court forfeits the debtor's interest in the property and title remains with the seller.

Contracts for deed are used primarily in sales of real estate of relatively small value on small down payments. Their strict foreclosure occasionally forfeits a substantial equity that a buyer has built up over several years, a result that has prompted serious policy concerns and some protective legislation. However, strict foreclosure is not in sufficiently wide use to warrant detailed coverage in this book. Throughout the remainder of this assignment, we focus on the typical judicial foreclosure procedures that require public sale of the collateral.

B.   Foreclosure Sale Procedure

In most states, statutes specify the manner in which a foreclosure sale must be held. A typical statute might provide that all foreclosure sales within the county are to be held by auction sale on the steps of the courthouse between the hours of 10:00 A.M. and 2:00 P.M. on the first and third Tuesdays of the month, with the property going to the highest bidder for cash. Judicial foreclosure sales are nearly always conducted by a public official, usually the sheriff, the clerk of the court, or a court commissioner. Anyone may bid at the sale. For reasons that will become apparent in the next section, the creditor who brings the foreclosure case is typically the highest bidder at the sale.

The court that orders a foreclosure sale may have discretion to determine some aspects of the manner in which the sale is held, such as the period of advertising, the manner in which bidders identify themselves, and the minimum increments for bidding. When the last bid is made, the officer conducting the sale identifies the highest bidder. Typically, that bidder must immediately make a deposit of a portion of the purchase price in cash or by cashier's check. Under most procedures the balance of the purchase price must be paid within a few hours or days. If the high bidder does not make good on its bid, the applicable procedure may require either that the property then be sold to the second highest bidder or that a new sale be scheduled. The high bidder who did not perform may forfeit its deposit and may also be liable in contract for damages.

In most foreclosure procedures, the court must review the circumstances under which the sale was held and *confirm* the sale before the sale can be consummated. The debtor, or other parties in interest, may object to the sale on the grounds that the officer did not conduct the sale in accord with the law or the judgment of foreclosure, or that the sale price was inadequate. If the court does not confirm the sale, it will schedule a resale. If it confirms the sale, the officer who conducted the sale will execute a deed or bill of sale conveying the property to the purchaser.

Once a sale has been confirmed, the official disburses the sale proceeds. The money goes first to reimburse the foreclosing creditor for the expenses of sale. Next, the proceeds are distributed to the foreclosing creditor up to the amount of the debt secured by the foreclosed lien. Assuming there are no other liens, any remaining surplus goes to the debtor. If the proceeds of sale are insufficient to pay the full amount of the debt secured by the foreclosed lien, the foreclosing creditor may ask the court to enter a judgment for the deficiency. The circumstances under which courts grant deficiency judgments are discussed in section D, below. If the deficiency judgment is granted, the foreclosing creditor can collect it in the same manner as any other judgment on an unsecured debt.

While the foreclosure is in progress, the mortgage debtor has the right to redeem the property from the mortgage by paying the full amount due under the mortgage, including interest and attorneys fees. This *common law* right to redeem is typically cut off (*foreclosed*, in the legal parlance) as of the time of the sale. In a minority of states, the debtor also has a *statutory* right to redeem the collateral from the buyer after the sale. Statutory rights to redeem range in length from about six months to three years, with one year being the most common period. Except when the court appoints a receiver, the debtor usually remains in possession during the statutory period for redemption. Redemption is accomplished by paying the purchaser the amount the purchaser paid at the sale. Under some procedures, the redemption price will also include interest on the sale price and other expenses incurred by the purchaser in connection with the sale. But the redemption price typically does not include the purchaser's costs of maintaining or improving the property during the period, if any, that it was in the purchaser's possession.

Rights of redemption are freely transferable. As a consequence, debtors who cannot afford to exercise their rights of redemption can sell those rights to others who can exercise them. The greater the discount at which a debtor's property is sold in the judicial sale, the greater is the value of the statutory right to redeem it. The debtor can recapture some of that discount by selling the right to redeem.

When the buyer of a statutory right to redeem exercises it after the sale, the auction purchaser is reimbursed for the price it paid, but loses the property. Some courts hold that the redeemer who reimburses the purchaser takes the property free and clear of the lien that forced the sale. That is, the redeemer steps into the shoes of the purchaser. Others hold that the redeemer takes the property subject to the unpaid lien. Under the latter rule, the redeemer must pay the balance to own the property free of the lien.

C.   Problems with Foreclosure Sale Procedure

Foreclosure sale prices are often shockingly low. If the court is shocked by a price, the court can set the sale aside. But as the following case illustrates, the courts are not easy to shock. If the court sets the sale aside (or, under the procedures in some states, refuses to confirm it) the court will order another auction.

In the following case, the debtor tries a different route — let the sale stand, but limit the deficiency to the difference between the amount of the debt and the market value of the property. The court, however, is not willing to go along.

First Bank v. Fischer & Frichtel, Inc.

364 S.W.3d 216 (Mo. 2012)

LAURA DENVIR STITH, JUDGE.

First Bank is a privately owned company that provides both retail and commercial banking services to its clients. Fischer & Frichtel is a real-estate developer with more than sixty years of experience in the industry. From 2005 to the beginning of 2008, Fischer & Frichtel had hundreds of millions of dollars in revenue and earned tens of millions of dollars in profit. Among its business deals in June 2000 was the purchase of 21 lots in Franklin County for a residential development.

To finance the acquisition, Fischer & Frichtel borrowed $2,576,000 from First Bank, in favor of which it executed a deed of trust pledging the lots as collateral for the loan. When the loan matured on September 1, 2008, Fischer & Frichtel was contractually obligated to pay First Bank the remaining principal on the loan, $1,133,875. Fischer & Frichtel chose instead to default on the loan, and First Bank foreclosed on the nine lots remaining unsold that were subject to the deed of trust. The foreclosure sale was held in December 2008, and First Bank acquired the nine unsold lots after making the sole bid of $466,000. Fischer & Frichtel did not bid and does not claim that the foreclosure sale was not properly noticed or conducted.

In November 2008, just prior to the foreclosure sale, First Bank filed suit against Fischer & Frichtel seeking to recover the unpaid principal and interest on the loan. At the trial in January 2010, Fischer & Frichtel presented expert testimony from an appraiser that, although First Bank paid only $466,000, the fair market value of the nine lots at the time of the foreclosure was nearly double that, $918,000. It also showed that internal First Bank documents valued the property at $1,134,000 at the time of the default in September 2008.

[T]he jury found that the fair market value of the lots was $918,000, the value testified to by Fischer & Frichtel's expert, and that Fischer & Frichtel therefore owed First Bank $215,875 (the difference between the amount of unpaid principal on the loan and the fair market value of the property at the time of the foreclosure sale) plus $37,500 in interest.

Missouri and many of the other states in which the method of measuring deficiencies is governed by the common law traditionally require a debtor to pay as a deficiency the full difference between the debt and the foreclosure sale price. They do not permit a debtor to attack the sufficiency of the foreclosure sale price as part of the deficiency proceeding even if the debtor believes that the foreclosure sale price was inadequate.

This does not mean Missouri does not give a debtor a mechanism for attacking an inadequate foreclosure sale price. Rather, a debtor who believes that the foreclosure sale price was inadequate can bring an action to void the foreclosure sale itself.

Missouri permits the debtor to void a properly noticed and carried out foreclosure sale only by showing that "the inadequacy . . . [of the sale price is] so gross that it shocks the conscience . . . and is in itself evidence of fraud." Cockrell v. Taylor, 347 Mo. 1, 145 S.W.2d 416, 422 (1940). This is the predominant standard used by courts in determining whether to void the foreclosure sale, but what is sufficient to "shock the conscience" of a court seems to vary greatly. Some states, such as Oregon and Wisconsin, have found sale prices of more than half the fair market value sufficient to shock the conscience and set aside the sale, while others uphold sales for less than 40 percent of the fair market value. Missouri's standard for proving that a foreclosure sale "shocks the conscience" is among the strictest in the country; more than one Missouri case has refused to set aside a sale that was only 20 to 30 percent of the fair market value because of Missouri's historical practice of requiring an inference of fraud in addition to a sale price that "shocks the conscience."

Fischer & Frichtel argues that this standard for setting aside a foreclosure sale is so high that it is only an illusory remedy for an unfairly low sale price and that because the foreclosure process inherently produces artificially low sale prices, it almost inevitably leads to windfalls for lenders. Fischer & Frichtel suggests that the foreclosure process is unfair in part because cash must be offered for the property by the bidder. This is a problem for the ordinary bidder, particularly a homeowner or small business owner, because the statutory minimum time period between notice of foreclosure and the actual sale is often less than a month, an insufficient amount of time to allow potential bidders to secure financing.

Fischer & Frichtel notes that the lender does not have this financing problem, as it does not have to pay with cash, but instead simply may deduct the purchase price from the amount of principal the borrower owes. Because realistically the lender often will be the sole bidder, it can buy the foreclosed property for far less than market value, sell the property at a profit and then collect a deficiency from the borrower based on the below-market value it paid for the property. The lender receives both the benefit of buying the property for less than fair market value and also of only having to reduce the deficiency it is entitled to by the below fair market price paid at the foreclosure sale.

Here, the public policy reasons that form the basis of Fischer & Frichtel's argument for modification of the more than century-old practice of using the foreclosure sale price have no application to a sophisticated debtor such as it. While the foreclosure sale price was barely more than 50 percent of the fair market value later determined by the jury, the lender gave cogent reasons for its lower bid due to the depressed real estate market and the bulk nature of the sale, as of trial the lender had not been able to sell the property, and Fischer & Frichtel has not argued it could not have purchased the property at the foreclosure sale (or indeed thereafter while the property was still on the market for $675,000, a good deal less than Fischer & Frichtel says is its fair market value).

This is not a case, therefore, in which to consider a modification of the standard for setting aside a foreclosure sale solely due to inadequacy of price or whether a change should be made in the manner of determining a deficiency where the foreclosure price is less than the fair market value.

RICHARD B. TEITELMAN, CHIEF JUSTICE, dissenting.

I respectfully dissent. The purpose of a damage award is to make the injured party whole without creating a windfall. Accordingly, in nearly every context in which a party sustains damage to or the loss of a property or business interest, Missouri law measures damages by reference to fair market value. Yet in the foreclosure context, Missouri law ignores the fair market value of the foreclosed property and, instead, measures the lender's damages with reference to the foreclosure sale price. Rather than making the injured party whole, this anomaly in the law of damages, in many cases, will require the defaulting party to subsidize a substantial windfall to the lender. Aside from the fact that this anomaly long has been a part of Missouri law, there is no other compelling reason for continued adherence to a measure of damages that too often enriches one party at the expense of another. Consequently, I would hold that damages in a deficiency action should be measured by reference to the fair market value of the foreclosed property.

The underlying deficiency judgment is nothing more than a means of calculating First Bank's damages for Fischer & Fritchel's breach of a contract that was secured by the foreclosed property. The issue is simply assigning a value to the foreclosed property to calculate First Bank's actual damages fairly.

———————

The point that sale can result in substantial forfeiture has never been illustrated better than in Amalgamated Bank v. Superior Court, 149 Cal. App. 4th 1003 (2007). The court gave this description of the facts:

> As judgment creditor, PTF requested that the Sacramento County Sheriff issue a writ of sale to execute upon parcel 007 and sell it to the highest bidder. A public auction was scheduled for February 24, 2004, at 10:00 A.M. Palmbaum arrived there with $10 million in available funds. The property was worth approximately $6.5 million, and PTF intended to place an opening bid of $6 million.
>
> The sheriff commenced the sale around 10:00 A.M. (the exact time is the subject of intense dispute) and Palmbaum submitted an opening bid of $2,000. Palmbaum's bid turned out to be the only bid because PTF's designated bidders got stuck in traffic on the morning of February 24 on their way from the Bay Area to Sacramento, arriving at the auction room sometime after 10:00 A.M. After the sheriff's gavel fell confirming a sale to Palmbaum for $2,000, the late-arriving bidders vociferously objected, demanding that the sale be rescinded. The officer replied that bidding was closed and the property had been sold to Palmbaum.

PTF sued to set the sale aside for irregularities. The trial court held that the applicable statute gave only the debtor the right to set the sale aside for irregularities, and granted summary judgment for Palmbaum. The appellate court affirmed, and Palmbaum got the $6.5 million property for $2,000. Subsequent litigation revealed more about what had delayed PTF's bidders. They went to the wrong courthouse, where one of them was detained by security for possessing a penknife on a keychain.

A number of aspects of foreclosure sale procedure contribute to its frequent failure to bring reasonable prices for the property that is sold: (1) The sales are poorly advertised. (2) Prospective buyers are given little opportunity to inspect the property before the bidding, but they must accept the property "as is." (3) The rule of caveat emptor applies with regard to the state of the title. (4) The sale often takes place in a hostile environment, making it difficult for the prospective bidder to get information about the property. (5) The buyer may be unable to use the property until the statutory redemption period expires. These five aspects are considered separately.

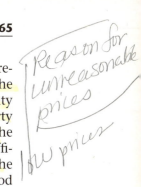

1. Advertising

An owner who wants to sell property usually advertises for buyers. If the property is a house, for example, the owner may hire a real estate broker to find buyers or will, at the very least, run an ad in a newspaper. The owner will try to describe the house in a way that will both encourage readers to respond and help them decide whether the house is suitable to their needs. Owners who want to sell their property advertise in a manner calculated to attract potential buyers.

The way a foreclosure sale is advertised may be fixed by statute or the judgment of foreclosure. The following procedure is probably a bit more modern than most:

Wisconsin Statutes Annotated
(2015)

§815.31 NOTICE OF SALE OF REALTY; MANNER; ADJOURNMENT

(1) The time and place of holding any sale of real estate on execution shall be publicly advertised by posting a written notice describing the real estate to be sold with reasonable certainty in one public place in the town or municipality where such real estate is to be sold and, if the county where such real estate is to be sold maintains a Web site, by posting a notice on the Web site, at least 3 weeks prior to the date of sale; and also in one public place of the town or municipality in which the real estate is situated, if it is not in the town or municipality where the sale is to be held and, if the county where such real estate is situated maintains a Web site, also posting a notice on the Web site. If the town or municipality where such real estate is situated or is to be sold maintains a Web site, the town or municipality may also post a notice on its Web site.

(2) A copy of the notice of sale shall be printed each week for 3 successive weeks in a newspaper of the county prior to the date of sale.

The officer conducting the sale is rarely concerned with the price the sale will bring. Because debtors sometimes attempt to have sales set aside on the basis that they were not conducted strictly in accord with formal legal requirements, the officer's primary concern is usually to comply with those requirements. The result is sale notices like the one in Figure 1. The figure is a faithful reproduction (including the misspelling of "trustee") of a notice that appeared in a Wisconsin newspaper pursuant to the statute quoted above.

The sheriffs, lawyers, or parties who place legal notices often select newspapers of limited circulation because the cost of running the ad is lower. Major newspapers segregate legal notices from the advertisements placed by owners and realtors. Either way, the legal notices rarely attract buyers interested in owning the property. To the extent they bring in bidders at all, the bidders are usually professional bargain hunters who plan to buy low and resell the property at a profit.

2. Inspection

As we discussed in Assignment 3, under most foreclosure sale procedures the debtor is entitled to remain in possession of the property until after the sale is held. The mortgage contract usually grants the foreclosing creditor the right to inspect the collateral in preparation for bidding at the sale. Such a provision ordinarily will be specifically enforced. Others who wish to bid at the sale can observe the property from adjacent public places, but they have no right to enter in order to inspect. The consequences can be unexpected.

STATE OF WISCONSIN, CIRCUIT COURT,
DODGE COUNTY
Case No. 12 CV 467

Ocwen Loan Servicing, LLC as servicer for Deutsche Bank National Trust Company as trestee for Morgan Stanley ABS Capital I Inc. Trust 2007-NC2 Mortgage Pass-through Certificates, Series 2007-NC2

Plaintiff,

VS

JOSEPH D. FOLK, et al.

Defendant(s)

NOTICE OF SHERIFF'S SALE

PLEASE TAKE NOTICE that by virtue of a judgment of foreclosure entered on August13, 2013 in the amount of $101,835.81 the Sheriff will sell the described premises at public auction as follows:

TIME: July 8, 2015 at 10:00AM

TERMS: By bidding at the sheriff sale, prospective buyer is consenting to be bound by the following terms: 1) 10% down in cash or money order at the time of sale; balance due within 10 days of confirmation of sale; failure to pay balance due will result in forfeit of deposit to plaintiff. 2) Sold "as is" and subject to all legal liens and encumbrances. 3) Plaintiff opens bidding on the property, either in person or via fax and as recited by the sheriff department in the event that no opening bid is offered, plaintiff retains the right to request the sale be declared as invalid as the sale if fatally defective.

PLACE: in the lobby of the Dodge County Law Enforcement Center located at 124 West Street, Juneau, Wisconsin

DESCRIPTION: 305 of the City of Juneau's Assessor's Plat No. 3, Dodge County, Wisconsin

PROPERTY ADDRESS: 241 North Depot Street, Juneau, WI 53039

TAX KEY NO.: 241-1115-2223-045

Dated this 29th day of May, 2015.
/s/ Sheriff Patricia M. Ninmann
Dodge County Sheriff

Scott D. Nabke
J Peterman Legal Group Ltd.
State Bar No. 1037979165
Bishops Way, Suite 100
Brookfield, WI
53005262-790-5719

Please go to www.jpetermanlegalgroup.com to obtain the bid for this sale.

J Peterman Legal Group Ltd. is the creditor's attorney and is attempting to collect a debt on its behalf. Any information obtained will be used for that purpose.

PUB. Daily Cttizen 6-12-15 6-19-15
6-26-15
#232823

FIGURE 1.   Notice of Foreclosure Sale

Homebuyer Finds Remains of Owner

Associated Press, November 21, 2000

TOLEDO, Ohio (AP)—A man making his first visit to a house he bought at a sheriff's auction found skeletal remains believed to be those of the former owner. Police said there was no evidence of foul play, but the county coroner was to examine the remains. Authorities said the man may have been dead more than two years. Police said the remains apparently were those of Eugene Bearringer, who would have been 50. The skeleton was found on the living room floor Monday by William Houttekier of Temperance, Mich.

The house was sold last week at auction because taxes weren't paid on the property for several years. County authorities had tried to contact Bearringer and out-of-state relatives through mailings. County Auditor Larry Kaczala said that when the property is foreclosed and goes up for sale, no one from the county ever sets foot in it. "The government would have no right to go onto that property, because we don't own it. We just sell it for the back taxes," he said.

Dean Nowakowski, 33, who lives two houses away, said the last time he saw Bearringer was more than two years ago. "I always wondered what happened to that dude," he said. "It got awful quiet over there."

The "dead body in house" scenario happened again in 2014 to a purchaser at a Cape Coral, Florida, tax sale. In *Wells Fargo v. Tamis*, an unreported 2007 New Jersey case, a man bought his neighbor's house at a foreclosure sale for $2.6 million. Despite the representation of the neighbor (who continued to live in the house and refused to permit inspection) that everything was "fine" inside, the house turned out to be inhabited by over 140 dogs and cats, many of them long deceased. The house had to be demolished. These cases together make the point that it is difficult to place a value on a house without being able to see what is inside. That is, however, precisely what most bidders at foreclosure sales must do.

3.   Title and Condition

Judicial sales are one of the few situations in which the rule of caveat emptor still applies. As the case that follows illustrates, buyers take subject to any defects in the title that they could have discovered through a search of the public records or an inspection of the property. Mr. Marino might have had a reasonable chance in an action against the seller in an ordinary private sale, but he discovered that in a judicial foreclosure sale he was without remedy.

Marino v. United Bank of Illinois, N.A.

484 N.E.2d 935 (Ill. App. Ct. 1985)

SCHNAKE, J.

Lawrence Marino, plaintiff, successfully bid at a sheriff's sale which took place on November 22, 1983. The property was being sold after United Bank of Illinois filed a complaint to foreclose a mortgage executed by Kenneth and Elizabeth Vosberg on January 9, 1981. After purchasing the property plaintiff attempted, in the instant action, to vacate the sale and to have his purchase money returned, on the basis of misrepresentations alleged to have been made by Linda Kream, an attorney who was sent to bid at the sale as representative of Theodore Liebovich, the attorney for the mortgagee. On May 30, 1984, the trial court ordered the sale vacated. However, on defendant's motion to reconsider, the trial court reversed its earlier order and confirmed the sale. Plaintiff Marino appeals from that order.

On November 22, 1983, the sheriff's sale of the property was held. According to plaintiff, Lawrence Marino, he intended to find out about the property and then make a decision as to whether to bid. He did not examine the records of the Winnebago County recorder's office to check the title, nor did he consult an attorney prior to submitting a bid. He attempted to obtain information through talking with Deputy Sheriff Claytor before the sale. Plaintiff asked Claytor about liens and encumbrances on the property, and Claytor told him that there was a mortgage of $8,800, $2,000 in attorney fees, $2,100 in taxes owed, and other miscellaneous liens, the total of which amounted to $14,327. Claytor told plaintiff to check with Liebovich, the attorney who was handling the case. Plaintiff then talked with attorney Linda Kream, who told him that she was attending the sale in place of Liebovich. According to plaintiff, he asked Linda Kream whether there were any encumbrances on the property. Before replying, Kream looked through a file and replied, "Well there's none that I can see," and then said, "This isn't my case, so I wouldn't know." Kream indicated to Marino that it was Liebovich's case, but that he was not available that day.

Linda Kream testified that she was an associate attorney with the firm of Liebovich and Gaziano and that Liebovich had asked her to appear at the sale and bid on behalf of the United Bank of Illinois. She had a foreclosure file and a cashier's check in an amount over $13,000. Kream testified that she was unfamiliar with the file as she had not been handling the case. Before the sale, plaintiff approached her and asked her how much she was going to bid. After telling him, plaintiff indicated that he would bid $1 more. Kream testified that plaintiff then asked her if there were any liens ahead of the bank's, and that she replied that it was not her case, so she would only know what was contained in the file. Plaintiff asked if she would look through the file, and she did. She then told plaintiff that there did not appear to be any other liens, but that she was not sure and she would not want him to rely on that. On cross-examination, Kream indicated that there was a title policy on file, but that she did not examine it.

Plaintiff successfully bid $13,541 for the property and the court approved the sale on December 12, 1983. On April 6, 1984, plaintiff sought to vacate the sale, alleging that Kream had informed him that no other liens or encumbrances existed on the property, and that he relied on her statement and thereafter purchased the property. He further asserted that he had since been joined as a defendant in an action by First Federal Savings and Loan of Rockford, and that it was at that time that he first became aware of liens and encumbrances superior to his interest. Marino's complaint alleged that United Bank of Illinois had a duty to join all parties with liens on the property, and asked that the sale be vacated and his money returned.

In response, United Bank of Illinois contended that plaintiff was not entitled to set aside the sale unless he could show fraud or misrepresentation, there were no statements made to induce plaintiff to purchase the property, and that plaintiff could not reasonably have relied on any statements that were made. In an affidavit, Kream stated that at the time of the sheriff's sale, she did not have knowledge of the liens which were listed in plaintiff's motion to vacate.

The court found no fraud, but ordered the sale vacated because of Marino's reliance on Kream's unintentional misrepresentation. The court ordered United Bank of Illinois to reimburse Marino for the amount of money it received from the sale. United Bank of Illinois moved for reconsideration, alleging that Marino failed to prove that an assertion of fact was made to him on which he was entitled to rely, that plaintiff failed to prove the existence of the liens, and that there was no cause of action for an unintentional misrepresentation. The court granted defendant's motion to reconsider, vacated its prior order, and confirmed the sheriff's sale of November 22, 1983. Notice of appeal was timely filed.

Generally the doctrine of caveat emptor applies to judicial sales, and the risk of a mistake or defect of title is to be borne by the purchaser unless there is fraud, misrepresentation, or mistake of fact. In this case, plaintiff Marino alleges that because there was a misrepresentation by Kream, equity requires that the sale be vacated.

To establish fraudulent misrepresentation, plaintiff must show a false statement of material fact made by defendant, defendant's knowledge or belief that the statement was false, defendant's intent to induce plaintiff to act, an action by plaintiff in justifiable reliance on that statement, and damage to plaintiff resulting from such reliance. These elements must be proved for a charge of fraud, whether in a suit at law or in equity.

Examining these elements, it is clear that plaintiff failed to prove a fraudulent misrepresentation by attorney Kream. To begin with, plaintiff failed to prove a false statement of material fact. Matters of fact are to be distinguished from expressions of opinion, which cannot form the basis of an action of fraud. A representation is one of opinion rather than fact if it only expresses the speaker's belief, without certainty, as to the existence of a fact. By both plaintiff's and Kream's account, Kream indicated that from the information in the file there did not appear to be any liens or encumbrances, but she expressly told plaintiff that she was not sure of that fact because it was not her case. Her statement would appear to be an opinion since it was only her belief, stated without certainty, as to the existence of a fact. In his brief, plaintiff argues that due to Kream's status as an attorney, she can be said to have held herself out to have "special knowledge" such that there was an implied assertion of fact. In view of her expressed disclaimer of knowledge of any facts of the case, plaintiff's argument is not persuasive.

There was also no evidence that the statement made was known to be false, and the lack of certainty expressed by Kream would not support a finding that she made the statement with the intent to induce plaintiff to act. In determining whether there was justified reliance, it is necessary to consider all of the facts in plaintiff's actual knowledge as well as those which he could have discovered by the exercise of ordinary prudence. While a person may rely on a statement without investigation if the party making the statement creates a false sense of security or blocks further inquiry, it must be determined whether the facts were such as to put a reasonable man on inquiry. In this case, the lack of certainty of Kream's statement was sufficient to put a reasonable person on inquiry, and plaintiff was not justified in relying on that statement without taking appropriate steps to check the title. . . .

Plaintiff contends that it was incumbent upon defendant to search for liens and encumbrances and join all parties having subsequent liens, and that, in foreclosure, the mortgagee should search for intervening transfers or liens and should join record owners as parties defendant. However, in Baldi v. Chicago Title & Trust Co. (1983), 13 Ill. App. 3d 29, 31-33, 446 N.E.2d 1205, 1207-1208, the court rejected an argument that a junior mortgagee should be a necessary party to a foreclosure of a senior encumbrance. While defendant could have joined those parties with subsequent liens on the property, it had no duty to do so.

The judgment of the circuit court of Winnebago County is therefore affirmed.

The court notes that there are "liens and encumbrances" on the property that the bank's foreclosure did not extinguish. Neither their nature, nor the precise reason that the foreclosure did not extinguish them, matters. Whatever the liens are, Marino takes subject to them because he is a purchaser at a foreclosure sale. As the court makes clear, finding out what liens survive foreclosure is the responsibility of the foreclosure sale bidder. Caveat emptor!

The risks to a bidder at a judicial sale extend beyond the state of the title. In Horicon State Bank v. Kant Lumber Co., Inc., 478 N.W.2d 26 (Wis. Ct. App. 1991), the bank foreclosed its mortgage against property owned by the lumber company. In preparation for the sale, the bank hired an appraiser who examined the property and appraised it as worth $6,000. The bank was the only bidder at the sale. It bid $10,000 to be sure the court would confirm the sale. When the bank attempted to resell the property, it discovered that the property was environmentally contaminated and that clean-up costs would be from $5,000 to $13,500 and perhaps more. On the bank's application, the court refused to set aside the sale, saying that the bank's appraiser should have seen evidence of the pollution when the appraiser inspected the property and "the bank should have had the [environmental] evaluation made before the sale." The court concluded, "[We] will not intervene if an overbid at a sheriff's sale results from the bidder's ignorance."

As Marino and Horicon illustrate, a person who would like to bid at a sale may have to incur substantial expense in preparation. Yet many of the judicial sales that are advertised never take place. The debtor finds the money to redeem the property, makes peace with the foreclosing creditor, or files bankruptcy. Persons who have invested time and money preparing to bid at those sales simply lose their investments.

4. Hostile Situation

Need to know a good deal about property

To make an intelligent purchase of a parcel of real estate, particularly if it includes a building, the buyer must know a good deal about it. Most sales of real property occur between willing buyers and sellers. The buyers get most of the information they need by refusing to purchase unless the seller furnishes it. Because sellers want to sell, they are usually willing to furnish needed information and provide access to the property.

Many foreclosure sales, on the other hand, take place in a hostile environment. Often there is no one with either a motive or an obligation to furnish information to prospective purchasers. In fact, a debtor's strategy for retaining its property often calls for preventing third parties from obtaining the information they need to bid. Foreclosing creditors may not be able to furnish information because they do not themselves have access to it. In many cases, the creditors prefer to purchase the property at the judicial sale, evaluate it, and then resell it. As a result, the price at the first sale is of little consequence to them. They are satisfied with a low-price sale, followed by another sale for an amount approaching a market price.

Can't get info on foreclosure

The officer who conducts the sale is rarely a good source of information, either. Typically the officer has no obligation or incentive to furnish information, but the officer may have liability for furnishing incorrect information. As a result, most have little to say about the condition of the property or the terms of the sale.

Often the debtor's best strategy is to provoke some procedural irregularity in the sale and litigate over it as a means of obtaining delay. For example, the debtor may encourage judgment-proof friends or relatives to make the highest bid at the sale and then not pay the purchase price. The high bidder at a judicial sale must consider the possibility that it will become entangled in litigation over the validity of the sale. Finally, there is always the possibility that after the bidding is concluded, but before the buyer can be put into possession, the debtor will destroy the property.

5. The Statutory Right to Redeem

As we noted above, a debtor who has the right to redeem the property after sale usually also remains entitled to possession. The high bidder at the sale may have to wait months or even years for possession. Even if the bidder can obtain possession, if the right to redeem is later exercised, the bidder may be unable to recover money spent to preserve or improve the property during the bidder's time of possession. That may discourage the successful bidder from making improvements necessary to return the property to productive use until the statutory redemption period runs. That in turn may reduce the amounts that bidders are willing to pay for property at a judicial sale.

With all these problems, it is hardly surprising that there are few bidders at most judicial sales and that, except for credit bids by foreclosing creditors, the bidding usually stops far short of the market value of the property.

Once the creditor's collateral has been sold at a judicial sale, the balance of the debt is often uncollectible. An antideficiency statute may bar the creditor from obtaining a deficiency judgment. Even if the creditor gets a judgment, the creditor may be unable to collect because the debtor is bankrupt or judgment-proof. In such cases, the creditor loses nothing by bidding the full amount of its debt at the foreclosure sale, even if the bid is far in excess of the value of the collateral.

Assume that a creditor has forced a sale of collateral and knows that it will not be able to collect a deficiency. Such a creditor has little reason not to bid the full amount of its debt. The reason may be clearer from an example. Assume that the debtor owes the creditor $1 million, secured by collateral worth $200,000. If the creditor buys the property for $200,000 at the foreclosure sale, its total recovery on the debt will be the $200,000 it obtains from resale of the property. If, instead, the creditor bids $1 million at the sale, the outcome would be the same. The creditor need not pay the $1 million purchase price to the sheriff; the creditor is entitled to a credit for the amount of its bid. In this scenario too, the creditor's total recovery on the debt is the $200,000 it obtains from resale.

The creditor who makes a high credit bid gains several advantages. The creditor minimizes the likelihood that the sale will be set aside for inadequacy of price. The creditor also minimizes the likelihood that the debtor will exercise its statutory right to redeem the property. Most statutory redemption is for the amount of the sale price. If the debtor in our example wanted to redeem its $200,000 property, the debtor would have to pay $1 million — a highly unlikely event. The foreclosing creditor who is willing to credit bid the entire amount of its secured debt need not incur the expense of evaluating the collateral prior to the sale. If the creditor is outbid, the creditor will recover the full amount of the secured debt; if it is not outbid, it will have the property to inspect, evaluate, improve, and resell at its leisure.

A creditor who buys its collateral at the sale always runs some risk that the sale will be set aside or the property redeemed. Notwithstanding that risk, the creditor-purchaser is completely free to seek a profit on resale. That profit on resale will belong to the creditor, not the debtor.

In fact, purchase by the foreclosing creditor for later resale is by far the dominant pattern in mortgage foreclosures. One of our students recently studied 100 randomly selected mortgage foreclosures in Minnesota and found that the mortgagee purchased the property in 98 percent of the cases. All of the creditors were banks or commercial lenders who would have to resell the collateral.

In effect, this means that the mortgage foreclosure process, in its most common manifestation, is a two-sale process: The first sale, the judicial one, is not so much a real exposure of the collateral to the market as a symbolic formality that cuts off the debtor's right to redeem or at least starts the redemption period running. The resale for market price that will return the property to productive use occurs some time later. Notice what happens to the debtor's equity in the property when the first sale is for only the amount of the foreclosed lien. The buyer at the first sale (usually the lien holder) gets the property for the amount of the lien and resells it for a price approaching market value, thereby capturing the debtor's equity.

F.   Judicial Sale Procedure: A Functional Analysis

As we noted at the beginning of this assignment, some commentators see the judicial sale process as a method for valuing the collateral. By fixing the collateral's value, the process determines the amount of the deficiency judgment or, if the debtor has an equity in the property, it ensures that the equity will not be forfeited. But if that is the intent, the process does not accomplish it. Except in those cases in which foreclosing creditors credit bid the amounts of their debts, the bids at foreclosure and other judicial sales bring only a fraction of the value of the property sold. While credit bids are often near or even in excess of the market value of the property sold, they are hardly a sign that the process is working. To the contrary, the purpose of a credit bid is usually to avoid reliance on the judicial sale process.

Although the judicial sale process does a poor job of valuing the collateral, it has important side effects that some see as its virtue. If the debtor has an equity in the property, a judicial sale threatens to forfeit it. Some commentators suggest that this motivates knowledgeable debtors to liquidate their property before that occurs. If the debtor owes more than the property is likely to bring at the sale, forced sale at an inadequate price may threaten to result in a deficiency judgment in an excessive amount. That in turn motivates knowledgeable debtors to attempt to come to terms with the foreclosing creditor. It would be wrong, however, to conclude that these side effects render the grossly inefficient procedures for foreclosure sale either elegant or efficient. Threatening to blow the property to bits would accomplish as much, and the explosives might be less expensive.

Problem Set 4

4.1.   You represent Commercial Bank with regard to an upcoming judicial foreclosure sale. The balance owing on the mortgage is $530,000. Commercial estimates that the house is worth between $400,000 and $450,000. Under the law of your state, Commercial will not be able to obtain a judgment for any deficiency remaining after the sale. Commercial wants to know how much they should bid at the sale. Consider these possibilities as you map out your strategy:

a.   Commercial is the only bidder present at the sale. For what amount should they buy the property?

b.   A third party has bid $531,000. Should Commercial go higher?

c.   A third party has bid $440,000. Should Commercial go higher?

4.2.   As part of your firm's pro bono program, you represent Sallie Hudson. Sallie fell three payments behind on her mortgage. First Savings, the mortgage

lender, accelerated, filed for foreclosure, and obtained a judgment. The foreclosure sale is set for a date four weeks from now. The judgment is for $530,000.
Sallie would like to keep the house, but she doesn't have the money to redeem
it. She also has more than $100,000 in unsecured credit card debt that she can-
not pay. She asks whether she should be doing anything in preparation for the
sale? Assume you are in a jurisdiction where the grant of a deficiency is within
the discretion of the court, based on the equities of the case. In this situation,
the practical effect is that neither you nor First Savings can be certain whether
the court will grant a deficiency judgment.

a. If the house has a fair market value of $400,000 to $450,000, what is
your advice?

b. If the house has a fair market value of $700,000 to $750,000, what is
your advice?

c. Sallie's brother-in-law deals in real estate and has the financial ability to
buy this house. He is willing to do so and let Sallie keep living in it. How does
that change your answers to (a) and (b)? If Sallie's brother-in-law succeeds in
buying the house for $531,000, is that a voidable transfer? UVTA. §§3(b), 4(a)
(1), 5(a), 8(a).

4.3. In a parallel universe in which you've never met Sallie Hudson, you are
interested in buying a house. The neighborhood you like best is Spring Green. In
scanning the legal notices this morning, you saw that a house in Spring Green
is scheduled for a judicial foreclosure sale in four weeks. The notice shows that
First Savings and Loan is plaintiff in the foreclosure case, Sallie Hudson is the
defendant, and the case number is 09-1263. The notice does not indicate the
balance owing on the mortgage. It does give the address and legal description
of the property and the name of the creditor's attorney, Jason Kovan. You'd like
to try to buy this house, particularly if you can get a bargain on it. What information will you need to formulate a bid? Where will you get it? Will Hudson be
willing to help? Kovan? First Savings? The sheriff who will conduct the sale?

4.4. You represent American Insurance Company. They have asked you to
prepare a bidding strategy for an upcoming foreclosure sale. American holds
the first mortgage, in the amount of $40 million, against an apartment build-
ing that is under construction and unoccupied. They estimate that the building is worth about $36 million as is. The debtor is a corporation that owns no
other assets, but payment of the loan has been guaranteed by four wealthy
individuals who are the owners of the corporation. So long as there are no
problems with the foreclosure sale and the deficiency is in the range of about
five to ten million dollars, American anticipates that they probably will be able
to recover most or all of it from the four guarantors. The law of your state provides for no statutory right to redeem. In planning your strategy, consider the
following possibilities:

a. American is the only bidder present at the sale. For what amount should
it buy the property?

b. A lawyer representing a corporation you have never heard of appears
at the sale and bids $40 million. You doubt that the mysterious bidder actu-
ally has $40 million, but under the law of your state, the successful bidder
who makes a $2,000 deposit will have four hours to increase the deposit to
one-third of the bid price. The officer conducting the sale tells you that if the

bidder does not increase the deposit within that time, the court probably will reschedule the sale for a date about a month from now. Should American bid higher?

    c.   Under the law of your state, if the high bidder at a public sale fails to purchase the property, the officer conducting the sale must sell to the second highest bidder. Does this change your initial bidding strategy? What if there are two strangers at your sale, and one bids $24 million and the second immediately bids $50 million. What should you do?

■ End of Default Problem Set

    4.5.   You received a call from Paul Tosci, a senior lending officer for Seal Rock Bank. The bank has been approached by a shopping center developer, Margo Marshak, who would like a $2.5 million standby commitment to enable her to bid on a shopping center that is to be sold at a judicial foreclosure sale. On the basis of recent sales of roughly comparable shopping centers, Tosci estimates the value of this one to be $5.1 million. He explains that Marshak will pay a $25,000 nonrefundable fee for the bank's legally binding commitment to lend $2.5 million against the shopping center in the event that the developer wins the bid. The bank will also earn the market rate of interest on the loan if the bank is called on to make it. Marshak will provide title insurance at her own expense and invest at least $500,000 of her own money in the shopping center. What advice do you give Tosci? Is this likely to be good business for Seal Rock? What problems do you foresee? Would you feel better about the deal if (1) Marshak was the one who originally developed the shopping center and her brother-in-law is the debtor being foreclosed against, or (2) Marshak is an outsider with no prior ties to the shopping center?

    4.6.   You continue in your job as chief legislative aide to state Senator Candy Rowsey. A recent state supreme court decision has ruled that creditors can recover deficiency judgments from their debtors following any kind of foreclosure sale. Several newspaper editorials have decried this result, focusing on hapless homeowners caught in a real estate market downturn. Senator Rowsey chairs the judiciary committee, and she wants a recommendation from you on whether she should propose legislation to restrict deficiency judgments. Give her an outline of your point of view, including the kinds of restrictions you would choose if some proposal to limit deficiency judgments went forward.

Assignment 5:   Article 9 Sale and Deficiency

Sales under Article 9 of the Uniform Commercial Code serve essentially the same purposes as judicial sales. They determine the value of the collateral and convert that value into cash. If the debtor has equity in the collateral, conversion to cash makes it possible for the secured creditor to pay itself from the proceeds of sale and send the surplus to the debtor. If the sale is for less than the amount of the debt, that determination of value provides the basis for a court to later decide how much of the debt remains owing.

As with real property foreclosures, the requirement that the collateral be offered for sale as part of the personal property foreclosure process cannot be waived or varied in the initial lending contract. UCC §§9-602(7) and (10), 9-620. For example, a provision in a car loan agreement that, in the event of default and repossession, the secured creditor can retain the car in satisfaction of the debt is unenforceable. The sale is an essential feature of the foreclosure process, and the debtor has a right to have the collateral sold regardless of the contractual language.

A.   Acceptance of Collateral

Acceptance of collateral under UCC §9-620 is roughly analogous to acceptance of a deed in lieu of foreclosure under real estate law, but stated more elaborately. After a default has occurred, the debtor can consent to the secured party retaining the collateral in full or in *partial satisfaction* of the obligation it secures. "Partial satisfaction" means that the debtor receives credit against the debt in some amount but continues to owe the remainder.

While a right to consent sounds harmless enough, in most instances the consent will not be real. UCC §9-620(c)(2) implies consent if the secured party sends the debtor a proposal for retention of the collateral in full satisfaction of the debt and does not receive a notification of objection to the proposal within 20 days. An oral objection is insufficient. As the following case illustrates, debtors who do nothing, perhaps because they are confused by the procedures, are deemed to have consented.

McDonald v. Yarchenko
81 UCC Rep. Serv. 2d 165 (D. Or. 2013)

HERNÁNDEZ, DISTRICT JUDGE:

McDonald and Yarchenko are both members of David Hill LLC (the "LLC"), a member-managed Oregon limited liability company. McDonald's declaration states that in 2007 he made a number of loans to Yarchenko so that Yarchenko could make his 2007 capital contribution to the LLC. The Promissory Note shows that McDonald lent Yarchenko $22,000 and that Yarchenko pledged his one-sixth interest in the LLC as security for the loan.

According to the terms of the Promissory Note, the outstanding balance of the loan and accrued interest was due on July 1, 2009. Yarchenko, however, did not pay off the outstanding balance and the accrued interest as he had agreed pursuant to the Promissory Note. On October 29, 2010, McDonald sent Yarchenko a Demand Notice which stated that Yarchenko was in default of the Promissory Note and that if Yarchenko did not pay the loan, McDonald would "take possession of [Yarchenko's] interest in [the LLC]" pursuant to the terms of the Promissory Note. Yarchenko did not respond to the Demand Notice.

McDonald followed the Demand Notice with a letter dated January 3, 2011, in which he proposed that Yarchenko "sign over [his] shares of [the LLC] in exchange for cancellation of all [of Yarchenko's] debt . . . both secured and unsecured." Attached to the letter was a proposed amendment to the Operating Agreement, which shows McDonald's membership interest as 33.34%—McDonald's previous membership interest of 16.67% plus Yarchenko's membership interest of 16.67%—and which effectively shows Yarchenko as no longer being a member of the LLC. Yarchenko did not respond to McDonald's January 3, 2011, letter.

On July 27, 2011, McDonald's previous attorney, Frederick Carman, sent another letter to Yarchenko reiterating that Yarchenko had not paid off the Promissory Note. Carman's July 27, 2011, letter also made the "unconditional" proposal that McDonald would accept Yarchenko's 16.67% interest in the LLC "in full satisfaction" of the Promissory Note. Yarchenko did not respond to McDonald's July 27, 2011, letter, and as of today, the June 22, 2007, loan remains unpaid. At oral argument on July 12, 2013, the parties agreed that Yarchenko's membership interest is worth at least $407,335.41.

McDonald contends that he followed the procedure set forth in [UCC §9-620] and thus has properly foreclosed on Yarchenko's membership interest in the LLC. Yarchenko's briefings on this issue apply the wrong statute. Yarchenko asserts that McDonald failed to dispose of the collateral in a commercially reasonable manner under [UCC §9-610] and failed to properly notify Yarchenko of his alleged disposition of the collateral under [UCC §9-611]. Neither of those statutes applies to the actions taken by McDonald, who was operating under [UCC §9-620]. Comment 1 to UCC §9-620, which is incorporated into Oregon law at [UCC §9-620], states:

> [UCC §9-620] and the two sections following deal with strict foreclosure, a procedure by which the secured party acquires the debtor's interest in the collateral without the need for a sale or other disposition under §9-610. . . . [S]trict foreclosures should be encouraged and often will produce better results than a disposition for all concerned.

UCC §9-620 cmt. 1 (2010). Comment 1 clarifies that strict foreclosure is encouraged and is not governed by the other requirements for disposition under [UCC §9-610] or [§9-611], the sections on which Yarchenko relies.

Applying [UCC §9-620], I conclude that McDonald properly foreclosed on Yarchenko's collateral in full satisfaction of the obligation. Under [UCC §9-620], "A debtor consents to an acceptance of collateral in full satisfaction of the obligation it secures" if the secured party:

> (A) Sends to the debtor after default a proposal that is unconditional or subject only to a condition that collateral not in the possession of the secured party be preserved or maintained;
> (B) In the proposal, proposes to accept collateral in full satisfaction of the obligation it secures; and
> (C) Does not receive a notification of objection authenticated by the debtor within 20 days after the proposal is sent.

[UCC §9-620(c)(2)(A)-(C)]. Here, McDonald sent Yarchenko an unconditional proposal after Yarchenko had defaulted on his loan, proposing to accept Yarchenko's membership interest in the LLC in full satisfaction of the Promissory Note and the unsecured loans Yarchenko owed to McDonald. The record shows that on July 27, 2011, McDonald sent a letter stating, "Mr. McDonald proposes to accept the collateral securing the note which consists of a 16.67% interest in David Hill Development LLC in full satisfaction of the secured promissory note. This proposal is unconditional. You do not have to take any action in order to accept this proposal." Yarchenko did not respond to that letter, let alone respond within 20 days as required under [UCC §9-620(c)(2)(C)]. In other words, the July 27, 2011, letter and Yarchenko's failure to object constituted acceptance of Yarchenko's membership interest in the LLC as full satisfaction of the Promissory Note under [UCC §9-620].

Yarchenko argues this award, "which is worth approximately $1.6 million, would be a windfall for Plaintiff and an unjust and devastating loss for Mr. Yarchenko, especially considering that Mr. Yarchenko only barrowed [sic] $22,000 from Plaintiff and has repaid $10,000." The Official Comments to the UCC allude to this issue in the context of the obligation of good faith, stating:

> [I]n the normal case proposals and acceptances should be not second-guessed on the basis of the "value" of the collateral involved. Disputes about valuation or even a clear excess of collateral value over the amount of obligations satisfied do not necessarily demonstrate the absence of good faith.

UCC § 9-620 cmt. 11 (2010). That McDonald's strict foreclosure may result in a windfall does not, by itself, amount to bad faith or otherwise render the foreclosure improper under UCC §9-620. *See* Eddy v. Glen Devore Pers. Trust, 131 Wash. App. 1015 (Wash. App. 2006) (unpublished) (rejecting the argument that "the transaction was unconscionable because tendering a $90,000 promissory note for a $5,000 debt is unconscionable on its face and strict foreclosure resulted in a windfall for the Trust" under the same section of the UCC).

––––––––––––

The UCC §9-620 no-objection process is confusing because most people — probably even most lawyers — assume that a "proposal" must be affirmatively accepted to have any effect. In this case, the confusion enabled McDonald to "accept" Yarchenko's $407,000 interest in David Hill LLC for a debt of $22,000.

This right to consent is subject to four conditions. First, there must be no objection from others holding liens against the collateral. UCC §9-620(a)(2). Second, acceptance in partial satisfaction is not permitted in a consumer transaction, making sale an absolute prerequisite to a deficiency judgment. UCC §9-620(g). Third, if the collateral is consumer goods, the debtor can consent, in writing or by silence, to strict foreclosure only after repossession. UCC §9-620(a). Fourth, strict foreclosure is not permitted if the debtor has paid 60 percent of the cash price of consumer goods purchased on credit or 60 percent of the loan against other consumer goods. The debtor can waive this requirement, but only in an agreement to that effect entered into and authenticated after default. UCC §9-624(a).

The fourth condition is directed against the unscrupulous practice of forfeiting debtors' equities in property when the debtors have nearly completed payment. If the debtor has paid 60 percent of the cash price or original loan amount, the likelihood that the debtor has an equity in the property is high. UCC §9-620(e) was drafted to protect debtors against loss of such equities. What is perhaps more remarkable about the provision is its narrowness: It provides no protection to consumers who have paid less than 60 percent and no protection to nonconsumers, regardless of how much the nonconsumers have paid. The implicit assumptions seem to be that consumers who have paid less than 60 percent don't have an equity, and anyone other than a consumer will be sophisticated enough to protect its equity by making the objection described in UCC §9-620(c).

B. Sale Procedure Under Article 9

When Article 9 applies, UCC §9-610 governs the procedure for sale of the collateral. The most important difference from the judicial sale procedure studied in the previous assignment is that the secured creditor, not a public official, conducts the sale and distributes the sale proceeds. UCC §9-610 gives the creditor broad latitude to determine the method and timing of the sale. Depending on the circumstances, the creditor may be able to sell the property by auction, by setting a fixed price and finding a buyer who will pay that price, or by negotiating with interested parties.

This does not mean a foreclosing creditor can sell the collateral however it pleases. The foreclosing creditor has a duty to the debtor to choose a procedure for sale that is commercially reasonable. In fact, "every aspect of the disposition, including the method, manner, time, place and terms must be commercially reasonable." UCC §9-610(b). To a much greater degree than most judicial sale procedures, the UCC sale procedure is directed at getting a good price for the collateral. Under many judicial sale procedures, for example, shares of stock in Microsoft would have to be sold at a sheriff's sale after foreclosure; under the provisions of Article 9, they can be sold on a stock exchange.

Section 9-611(c)(1) also requires that the creditor give the debtor prior notice of the sale. The purpose of notice is to enable the debtor to observe the sale, participate in it, or otherwise protect its rights. One thing the debtor might do, if it learns of the sale in time, is seek out additional persons to bid.

UCC §9-623 codifies the common law right to redeem. Under its provisions, redemption is accomplished by paying the full amount of the debt, including the secured creditor's attorneys fees and expenses of sale. As we explored in Assignment 4, judicial sales are often subject to an additional statutory right to redeem that continues after the sale. No additional statutory right to redeem exists after an Article 9 sale. At the moment the creditor enters into a contract for disposition of the collateral, it is too late for the debtor to redeem it.

Failure to comply with the requirements of Article 9 or even a court order governing a sale is not grounds to set the sale aside. The only ground on which an Article 9 sale can be set aside is lack of good faith on the part of the buyer. UCC §9-617(b). This rule encourages third parties to buy at Article 9 sales, by assuring them that they can keep whatever they buy. If the collateral is consumer goods, the debtor may be entitled to recover a statutory penalty from a secured party who violates the procedures of Article 9. If the collateral is not consumer goods, the debtor is limited to an action against the secured creditor for actual damages.

Sales under Article 9 are governed by these procedures even if the creditor obtained possession of the collateral by filing a replevin case rather than using a UCC self-help remedy. The court that granted the judgment of replevin does not supervise the sale process or confirm the sale after it has occurred.

When collateral is sold for an insufficient price, the injury to the debtor may come in either of two forms. The first type of injury is loss of all or part of the debtor's equity. In fact, few debtors sue for such a loss. Many debtors have no equity to lose. For example, the balance owing on a car loan often exceeds the resale value of the car during the early part of the loan repayment period (when debtors are most likely to default). The debtor who has lost an equity may not have the financial resources necessary to bring suit. Finally, even if the debtor can afford to bring suit, it may not be worth it. The cost of the suit may exceed the amount that could be recovered.

The second type of injury to debtors from an insufficient sale price is the entry of a deficiency judgment in an amount larger than is appropriate. UCC §9-615(d) states the general rule that the obligor on a secured debt is liable for any deficiency remaining after application of the sale proceeds. Two antideficiency statutes limit that rule. UCC §9-615(f) applies when the secured party buys the collateral at the sale. In calculating the deficiency under it, the amount that would have been realized in a complying sale to a third party is treated as if it were the actual sale price. UCC §9-626(a)(3) applies when the sale does not comply with the requirements of Article 9. In calculating the deficiency under it, the amount that would have been realized in a complying sale is treated as if it were the actual sale price.

Litigation over deficiencies is more common than litigation over a debtor's loss of equity. One reason is that the deficiency litigation is initiated by the creditors, who can usually better afford it, both because they are in better financial condition and because they tend to be repeat players who can make this kind of litigation part of their business routine. Nonetheless, important disincentives to suing for deficiencies exist, especially against debtors who resist. The UCC standard of a "commercially reasonable sale" is so vague that such a debtor can nearly always find something to complain about. By investing a relatively small amount to defend against the creditor's action for a deficiency, the debtor can put the creditor to substantial legal expense. If the debtor shows any inclination to resist, the creditor will find it difficult to justify the expense of continuing. Even creditors who win deficiency judgments seldom collect them.

Debtors commonly defend actions for deficiency judgments by asserting that the creditor retained the collateral instead of conducting a sale, that the creditor did not give proper notice of the sale, or that the creditor conducted the sale in a manner that was not commercially reasonable. Each of these defenses is considered below.

C. Problems with Article 9 Sale Procedure

1. Failure to Sell the Collateral

UCC §9-610(a) provides that a secured party *may* sell the collateral after default. But there is no express requirement that the secured party *must* sell the collateral after default and, aside from the narrow exception for some consumer goods in §9-620(f), no time fixed within which any sale must occur. A secured party who obtains possession of the collateral after default may prefer to keep it and use it. Even a secured creditor who plans to sell the collateral eventually may want to keep it temporarily while waiting to see if the repossession itself spurs the debtor or a guarantor to come up with the money. In some cases a secured party might be unable to sell the collateral because a law or regulation prohibits resale or because the collateral has been destroyed or become worthless (for example, a secured party might repossess alcoholic beverages but not have a license to sell them). Finally, a secured party who intends to sell repossessed collateral may simply procrastinate. Should any of these cases come before a court, the first issue would be whether the secured party was attempting to accept collateral without complying with the UCC §9-620 restrictions on acceptance of collateral. If the court concluded that the secured party was attempting an improper acceptance, the court could order a sale or award damages for noncompliance. UCC §9-625(a) and (b). If the court concluded that the secured party was proceeding to sale, the second issue would be whether the secured party was doing so at a commercially reasonable pace.

While the secured party has possession of the collateral, it may decline in value. That alone entitles the debtor to no remedy. But if the secured creditor's delay in selling is commercially unreasonable, the secured creditor's deficiency will be limited to the amount that would have been left owing if the sale had been commercially reasonable. See UCC §9-626(a).

2.   The Requirement of Notice of Sale

UCC §9-611 requires that the secured party send notice to the debtor, guarantors, and some lienors. To identify the lienors, the secured party may have to conduct a search of the public records. The failure to give this notice does not invalidate the sale, UCC §9-617, but it is a defect that can have the effect of reducing the amount of the deficiency the secured party can recover or, as the following case illustrates, eliminating the deficiency altogether.

In re Downing

286 B.R. 900 (Bankr. W.D. Mo. 2002)

ARTHUR B. FEDERMAN, CHIEF BANKRUPTCY JUDGE.

FACTUAL BACKGROUND

On September 25, 2000, Mr. Downing purchased a 1999 BMW 528i from BMW, and granted BMW a lien on the car. On March 27, 2002 Mr. Downing surrendered the vehicle to BMW. On April 4, 2002, BMW notified Mr. Downing that it intended to sell the car, as allowed under state law, no sooner than 10 days after the date of the notice. On August 1, 2002, BMW sold the car at a commercial auction in Milwaukee, Wisconsin. After the sale, BMW filed an unsecured deficiency claim in this case in the amount of $18,517.24. Mr. Downing objected to the claim, on the grounds that BMW did not provide him with proper notice of the sale as required by Missouri's version of Article 9 of the Uniform Commercial Code (the UCC).

DISCUSSION

In Missouri, compliance with the notice provisions of Article 9 is a prerequisite to the recovery of a deficiency following the sale of repossessed collateral. As the court in *McKesson Corporation* stated, "strict compliance is required because deficiency judgments after repossession of collateral are in derogation of common law . . . in other words, since deficiency judgments were unheard of in common law, the right to a deficiency judgment accrues only after strict compliance with a relevant statute." McKesson Corp. v. Colman's Grant Village, Inc., 938 S.W.2d 631, 633 (Mo. Ct. App. 1997). The party seeking the deficiency judgment has the burden of proving the sufficiency of the notice. Any doubt as to what constitutes strict compliance with the statutory requirements must be resolved in favor of the debtor.

The parties agree that the adequacy of the notice is governed by [UCC §§9-613 and 9-614]. [UCC §9-613] provides the contents and form of notification prior to the disposition of non-consumer goods.

Except in a consumer-goods transaction, the following rules apply:
(1) The contents of a notification of disposition are sufficient if the notification:
    (A) Describes the debtor and the secured party;
    (B) Describes the collateral that is the subject of the intended disposition;
    (C) States the method of intended disposition;
    (D) States that the debtor is entitled to an accounting of the unpaid indebtedness and states the charge, if any, for an accounting; and
    (E) States the time and place of a public sale or the time after which any other disposition is to be made.

[UCC §9-614] applies those same requirements to consumer-goods dispositions. In addition, when disposing of consumer goods, the creditor must provide a "description of any liability for a deficiency of the person to which the notification is sent," and a "telephone number from which the amount that must be paid to the secured party to redeem the collateral under [UCC §9-623] is available." The pertinent distinction between the two provisions is that in nonconsumer-goods dispositions, the question of whether the contents of a notification that lacks any of the required information are nevertheless sufficient is a question of fact. Since an automobile is a consumer good, however, the sufficiency of the notice sent by BMW must be evaluated pursuant to both [UCC §§9-613 and 9-614].

The notice sent by BMW was in the form of a letter dated April 4, 2002. The letter identified the debtor as Steven L. Downing, the creditor as BMW, and the collateral as a 1999 BMW 528i, WBADP5340XBR95304. It then stated as follows:

> This letter confirms you have rejected and/or terminated your loan due to the filing of bankruptcy. BMW Financial Services NA, LLC has taken possession of the Vehicle.
>
> You are notified that BMW Financial Services NA, LLC intends to sell the vehicle as allowed under state law, but no sooner than 10 days after the date of this letter. . . .
>
> Should you have any questions, call us at the number referenced below, Monday through Friday, 9:00 A.M. to 5:00 P.M. ET or at either address listed below.

At the hearing, BMW represented that it sold the 1999 BMW at a commercial auction in Milwaukee, Wisconsin attended only by automobile dealers. As such, BMW argues that the sale was a private sale to commercial buyers, therefore, it was not required to provide Mr. Downing with the exact time and place of the auction. While BMW offered no support for this contention, in fact, other courts have held that a dealers-only auction is not public in character. Professor Barkley Clark, likewise, posits that where a sale is open only to automobile dealers, it is closed to some aspect of the market; therefore, it is a private sale. Nonetheless, the UCC clearly required BMW to inform Mr. Downing as to whether it would sell the car at either a private sale or public sale. Mr. Downing rightly points out in his brief that the notice sent by BMW did not inform him of the type of sale contemplated, or that he would be responsible for any deficiency. It also failed to inform Mr. Downing of his right to an accounting of the exact amount of his indebtedness, or what BMW claimed the indebtedness to be at the time of the sale. The burden of proof is on BMW to demonstrate that it has in all respects complied with the notice provisions of the UCC. By the express terms of the statute, that includes

[handwritten margin notes: "Comply with Notice provision" / "private Sale - Not required to provide Downing w/ exact time and place of auction" / "No Rt to accting"]

the method of disposition. BMW did not specify the nature of the sale, it did not inform Mr. Downing of his potential liability, and it did not inform him of his right to an accounting. For all of these reasons, I find that the notice did not strictly comply with the requirements of [UCC §9-613] as made applicable to consumer-goods transactions by [UCC §9-614].

BMW also argues that since the Downings' plan provided that Mr. Downing intended to surrender the vehicle, Missouri law does not require it to advise him of his right to redeem the vehicle. But that is not the sole purpose served by the notice. If a debtor is given the terms of the private sale, he has the opportunity to offer better terms. If a debtor is told the time and place of a public sale, he has an opportunity to appear at the sale, or have someone appear on his behalf, and bid. In any event, Missouri has long held that the right to a deficiency exists only if the creditor strictly complies with the statutory requirements of the UCC, regardless of whether there was any resulting harm to the debtor from the failed notice.

The notification was not sufficient, therefore, under Missouri law, BMW loses its right to a deficiency judgment. Debtors' objection to the claim of BMW will be sustained.

Failure to send a required notice of sale may have other consequences. UCC §9-625(b) makes the creditor liable for actual damages. If the collateral is consumer goods, UCC §9-625(c) also makes the creditor liable for a statutory penalty in "an amount not less than the credit service charge plus 10 percent of the principal amount of the obligation or the time-price differential plus 10 percent of the cash price." The "credit service charge" and the "time-price differential" are different ways of describing the total amount of interest the creditor is charging on the loan, so the penalties can be substantial.

3. The Requirement of a Commercially Reasonable Sale

The provision of UCC §9-610(b) requiring that "[e]very aspect of a disposition of collateral, including the method, manner, time, place, and other terms, must be commercially reasonable" is deliberately vague. The purpose is to bring the knowledge and ingenuity of the secured party to bear in determining a reasonable way to dispose of the particular kind of collateral. The underlying assumption is that what methods, manners, times, or places are reasonable will differ with the type of collateral, and perhaps with other circumstances. Procedures that are reasonable to dispose of a few hundred dollars worth of office furniture may not be reasonable for disposing of millions of dollars worth of laboratory equipment. In each case, the secured creditor should discover a reasonable method of disposition and use it. Ordinarily that will be a method that reasonable owners of the particular type of property would use if their own money were at stake.

In most cases in which the commercial reasonableness of a sale is challenged, a close factual inquiry is required. In the following case the applicable law was the Connecticut version of the UCC

General Electric Capital Corp. v. Nichols

2011 WL 1638048 (D. Conn. 2011)

Janet C. Hall, District Judge.

On December 14, 2007, General Electric and Nichols Equipment entered into a contract in which General Electric agreed to finance Nichols Equipment's purchase of six Mack trucks, each bearing a concrete pump manufactured by Schwing. The promissory note executed by the parties was secured by the trucks themselves, and amounted, in principal, to $3,306,542.17.

As further security, Gary Nichols signed an Individual Guaranty, also dated December 14, 2007. In the Guaranty, Nichols agreed to pay any sum which became due under the loan agreement, whether the amount due represented "principal, interest, rent, late charges, indemnities, an original balance, an accelerated balance, liquidated damages, a balance reduced by partial payment . . . or any other type of sum of any kind whatsoever."

Beginning in April 2009, Nichols Equipment failed to make its required payments. By letters dated April 23 and 27, 2009, General Electric notified Nichols of Nichols Equipment's default and demanded payment under the Guaranty. On May 8, 2009, General Electric filed the present action, to recover payment from Nichols pursuant to the Guaranty.

On August 10, 2009, in an action against Nichols Equipment, an Alabama Circuit Judge ordered the surrender of the six trucks, which General Electric obtained at some point that same month. Shortly after receiving the trucks, General Electric began preparations to sell them. At General Electric's direction, Value Centers, LLC ("Value Centers") took possession of the trucks from Nichols Equipment. Value Centers inspected the trucks and estimated a total value of $1,095,000. This comported with General Electric's internal valuation of the trucks of $985,000.

Value Centers placed advertisements on their website and in the paper and internet versions of two periodicals, Truck Paper and Machinery Trader. General Electric does not indicate when these advertisements were placed or for how long. The only dated documentation is from an issue of Truck Paper dated October 9, 2009. Value Centers also made several telephone calls to "existing contacts in the construction industry" to see if they were interested in the trucks. No further description of these contacts is in the record before the court.

Value Centers received "a number of inquiries and offers." Among these were an offer from a buyer based in the Middle East and an inquiry by a man named Pat from Pioneer Concrete Pumping Services, Inc. In September 2009, Value Centers received an offer from Pumpcrete, a company based in Toronto, to purchase three of the trucks for a total of $700,000. Value Centers, at General Electric's direction, counter-offered $730,000. When Pumpcrete refused to accept the counter offer, General Electric directed Value Centers to accept the $700,000 offer. Pumpcrete purchased the three trucks on September 29, 2009.

A few weeks later, Value Centers located another buyer for one of the remaining trucks. On October 14, 2009, Caselridge Concrete, also from Toronto, purchased the truck for $200,000. Finally, on October 27, 2009, Pumpcrete purchased the two remaining trucks for $400,000. Pumpcrete had initially offered $300,000 for the trucks, but, after a series of negotiations, Pumpcrete agreed to the final number.

In total, General Electric sold the six trucks for $1,300,000. After deducting Value Centers' commission from this figure, General Electric netted $1,196,000. According to General Electric, after subtracting this sum from the total due under the Guaranty, Nichols still owes General Electric an amount not less than $2,490,451.26, plus "interest . . . , costs, expenses, and future attorney's fees, all of which continue to accrue."

Nichols argues, in Opposition to General Electric's Motion, that General Electric conducted its sales in a manner contrary to Connecticut law. In support of this contention, Nichols cites to a Report prepared at his request by James Bodeker. In this Report, Bodeker opines that the trucks were not sold, valued, or marketed in a commercially reasonable manner.

Bodeker is the Vice President of Sales and Marketing at Pioneer Concrete Pumping Service, Inc. He has been in the concrete pumping industry, in both sales and marketing, since 1994. He has conducted or supervised the sale of over 1000 concrete pumps.

Based on his review of the record in this case, including Value Centers' inspection reports, Bodeker concluded that the six Mack trucks and their attached pumps were substantially undervalued. According to Bodeker, the trucks were, in the aggregate, worth $2,300,000. Bodeker believed the difference in appraisals resulted from General Electric's calculations based on the year the trucks were manufactured (2007), as opposed to the year the concrete pumps were manufactured (2008), and the failure to take into account add-ons and specialized options. Further, Bodeker concluded that the time frame between acquiring the trucks in August 2009 and the sale of the trucks in October 2009 was an unreasonably short period of time.

Bodeker additionally disparaged General Electric's marketing techniques. He stated that there was no indication that General Electric contacted any of the major distributors of concrete pumps to help determine values, purchase the trucks, or remarket them. Further, he noted that Truck Paper and Machinary Trader were "not reliable or standard resources for the sale of specialty equipment like concrete pumps."

In light of the undisputed fact that Nichols Equipment defaulted on its debt obligations to General Electric, the only remaining question is what, if anything, does Nichols owe to General Electric pursuant to his guaranty. This question, then, hinges on the disposition of the six Mack trucks used as collateral. Under Connecticut law, if General Electric failed to act in a commercially reasonable manner when it disposed of these trucks, then it may be entitled to substantially less or even no recovery from Nichols. However, if General Electric can prove that it acted in a commercially reasonable manner, then it is entitled to full recovery (less the net value it received from the sale of the trucks).

For the following reasons, the court denies General Electric's Motion to Preclude Bodeker's testimony. In light of this holding, the court concludes that there remain material issues of fact, and, thus, the court denies plaintiff's Motion for Summary Judgment.

As an initial matter, Bodeker appears well-qualified to render an opinion in this case. He has spent sixteen years in the concrete pumping industry, primarily in sales but also in marketing. Bodeker has sold or supervised the sale of over 1000 concrete pumps. He has trained at a sales and service school operated by Schwing (the manufacturer of the concrete pumps in question), and he has managed as many as thirteen different concrete pump stores.

General Electric makes much of the fact that Bodeker is not a certified appraiser and not aware of the Uniform Standard of Professional Appraisers Practice. While such credentials might well lend weight to his assessment, the court finds that Bodeker's substantial sales experience in the relevant industry is more than sufficient to qualify him to testify as to the valuation of the concrete pumps in question.

In Chavers v. Frazier, 93 B.R. 366 (Bankr. M.D. Tenn. 1989), the court held the sale of a private jet not to be commercially reasonable. Cases like *Chavers* and *Nichols* contrast starkly with judicial sale cases. The expert in *Nichols* is poised to testify that two months is an inadequate time in which to advertise the sale of trucks with concrete pumps. But judicial sale procedures would rarely allow that much time. The *Chavers* court was disappointed in advertising that ran only briefly in the *Wall Street Journal* and *Trade-A-Plane*, and the *Nichols* court expressed similar disappointment in advertising that ran in *Truck Paper* and *Machinery Trader*. But under most judicial sale procedures, the ads might have run only in the legal notices column of a local newspaper. The *Chavers* court complained that the secured creditor had not performed certain maintenance on the aircraft before sale. But in a judicial sale, the sheriff could have sold the Lear jet in exactly the condition in which it was repossessed. Finally, in *Nichols* and *Chavers*, the sale prices were just below 60 percent of the asserted fair market value — prices that would easily have passed muster in most judicial sale procedures.

If the secured party fails to give notice of sale or to conduct the sale in a commercially reasonable manner, there is a rebuttable presumption that the value of the collateral was at least equal to the amount of the debt. UCC §9-626(a)(4). As a result, the secured creditor can recover a deficiency only by rebutting the presumption. It does that by proving that the collateral was worth some amount less than the amount of the debt. In that event, the secured creditor is entitled to a deficiency in an amount equal to the amount by which the debt exceeds the value of the collateral. Notice that the overall effect of this rebuttable presumption rule is that the court must determine the value of the collateral. See UCC §§9-626(a)(3) and (4).

To illustrate, assume that Paul owes Carson $250,000, and that when Paul defaults, Carson repossesses equipment that is subject to Carson's security agreement. The equipment is worth $120,000, but Carson sells it in a commercially unreasonable manner and receives only $80,000. Carson sues for the deficiency. Provided that Carson carries his burden of proving that the collateral is worth only $120,000, Carson can recover a $130,000 deficiency judgment.

Article 9 excepts consumer transactions from the rebuttable presumption rule and leaves to "the court the determination of the proper rules in consumer transactions." UCC §9-626(b). The established approaches are essentially two. The majority rule is the rebuttable presumption rule. The minority rule, which you saw applied in *Downing*, is that failure to comply with the procedural requirements of Article 9 forfeits any right the secured creditor may have to a deficiency judgment. The latter rule relieves the court of the necessity to guess what the price would have been absent the sale defect.

To illustrate the difference between these views, assume that Consumer Paul owes Carson $250,000, and that when Paul defaults, Carson repossesses the yacht that is subject to Carson's security agreement. The yacht is worth $120,000, but Carson sells it in a commercially unreasonable manner and recovers only $80,000. Carson then sues Paul for the $170,000 deficiency. In a jurisdiction that followed the minority rule, the court would not grant a deficiency judgment. In a court that followed the rebuttable presumption rule, the court would begin with a presumption that the collateral was worth the full amount of the debt, $250,000, and no deficiency judgment should be granted. But if Carson proved that the value of the collateral was in fact $120,000, Carson still could recover a $130,000 deficiency judgment.

D.   Article 9 Sale Procedure: A Functional Analysis

The secured creditor's incentives in an Article 9 sale largely depend on what it believes the collateral is worth and whether it can collect a deficiency. If the secured creditor believes it can collect a deficiency judgment from the debtor or a guarantor, the secured creditor may find it profitable to skimp on advertising the sale and buy the collateral cheaply for less than its resale value. The creditor then can get a double recovery by reselling the collateral and suing the debtor for a deficiency. The secured creditor's risk in pursuing the strategy is minimal. If a court concludes that the sale price was less than would have been recovered in a commercially reasonable sale, the debtor's only remedy is to be credited for the difference between the actual price and the would-have-been-recovered price. The creditor is no worse off than if it had not pursued the strategy.

Similarly, if the secured creditor believes that the collateral is worth more than the amount owing, the secured creditor may find it profitable to advertise the sale poorly, buy the collateral for the amount owing at the Article 9 sale, sell the collateral for its fair market value, and then wait to see whether the debtor sues for the surplus.

In many cases, however, the collateral will be worth less than the amount owing and the secured creditor will have little or no chance of collecting a deficiency judgment. The secured creditor's recovery will be only what it receives for the collateral. In those circumstances, the secured creditor gains nothing by buying at the sale. Its incentive is to sell the collateral in the Article 9 sale for as much as it can get.

Ultimately, these kinds of speculations are incapable of discovering the true level of effectiveness of the Article 9 sale system. What is needed is empirical evidence on the frequency with which the different fact patterns present themselves. How often do debtors have equity in repossessed collateral? How common is it for creditors to buy at Article 9 sales? How likely are debtors to defend against the entry of deficiency judgments? Unfortunately, little of this kind of evidence is available.

In part, the dearth of data results from the fact that Article 9 has created a partially secret sale system. Public Article 9 sales are conducted in public, but private Article 9 sales can take place behind closed doors with no notice to anyone of the time and place at which they will occur. Neither kind of sale routinely generates a public record, making even the public sales difficult to study.

Problem Set 5

5.1. The bank repossessed Maxwell's silver Hummer and sent him notification that the bank would sell it in a private sale "after ten days from this notice." The balance owing on the loan, including principal, interest, attorneys fees, and expenses of sale is $100,000.

a.   If the fair market value of the car is $80,000, but it sells for $70,000 in a commercially reasonable sale, what is the proper amount for the court to award as a deficiency? UCC §§9-615(d), 9-626(a)(3), (b), and 9-627(a).

b.   How much would Maxwell have to pay to redeem the car? UCC §9-623. When must he pay it?

c.   If Maxwell has enough money to redeem the car, would you recommend that he do so or that he purchase another car just like it for $80,000?

d.   At Maxwell's prompting, a friend of his offers $80,000 for the car. The bank refuses the offer because they follow a policy of selling all the cars they repossess through auto auctions. The friend can't go to the auction, because it is only open to dealers. At the auction, the car sells for $70,000. Now how much should the deficiency be? UCC §§9-626, 9-627(a) and (b) including Comment 4.

5.2. Your firm represents Wewoka State Bank, which recently repossessed and sold the inventory and equipment of an auto parts store. The debt secured by the collateral was in the principal amount of $57,345, plus interest to the date of the sale in the amount of $3,541. The security agreement provides that in the event of default, the debtor will pay the bank's reasonable attorneys fees incurred in collecting the debt. Your fees are in the amount of $3,000 for replevy of the collateral and $650 for preparing for sale; you intend to charge an additional $350 for your opinion on distribution of the proceeds of sale. The bank also spent $1,500 preserving the collateral while it was in their possession and an additional $750 advertising the sale. The debtor has numerous other creditors, none of whom has a lien or security interest against the inventory and equipment. One of those creditors, Auto Parts Depot, holds a money judgment against debtor, heard about the auction, and sent the bank a letter demanding that their $4,200 judgment be paid out of the proceeds of sale. (If you need to know what the security agreement says to answer these questions, use the security agreement in Assignment 15, below.)

a. The highest bid at the auction was $47,136, which was bid by a third party. That money is now in your possession. To whom should you pay it? (That is, indicate to whom you would make the checks out, and in what amounts.) How much is the deficiency? See UCC §§9-615(a).

b. If the highest bid at the auction had been $75,000, to whom should you pay the money? Is the bank either required or permitted to pay Auto Parts Depot from the proceeds?

5.3. East Bank does a steady business in the repossession of automobiles. They sell the automobiles through a "dealers-only" auction. Over the years they have had numerous problems with sending notices of sale to the debtors whose cars are being sold. Notices have been sent in improper form or with typographical errors or have been returned because the debtor has changed addresses. Debtors have occasionally challenged the length of notice (East Bank gives five days' notice, but tries to send it at least ten days before the sale). The ten-day delay runs up the storage costs on the automobiles and the bank gets stuck for most of them in the end. The people at the bank think the notice requirement is rather silly anyway, given that the debtors can't get into the auto auction.

East Bank would like you to look into whether there is any way to dispense with the notices. They are sure that none of their borrowers would object to a waiver contained in the security agreement, even if it were specifically pointed out to them.

a. Does East Bank have to send these notices? See UCC §§9-602(7), 9-603(a), 9-611(b), (c)(1), and (d), 9-612, 9-613, 9-614, and 9-624(a); Comment 9 to §9-610; Comment 7 to §9-611.

b. Is it ethical to advise the client not to send the notices?

c. What will happen if the client doesn't send them? UCC §9-625(a), (b), and (c).

d. Can East Bank dispense with selling a repossessed automobile if East Bank and the debtor agree on a deficiency amount? UCC §9-620(c)(1) and (g).

5.4. Your client, Grizzly Bear Bank, is on a run of bad luck. The bank recently repossessed what should have been a $345,000 helicopter, only to find that the engine and all of the electronics had been removed by the debtor (in violation of the security agreement), leaving a hull with no resale value. The amount of the debt is currently $345,000. Fortunately, the debt is personally guaranteed by four wealthy individuals.

Grizzly would like to know if it is all right to throw the hull away. If not, what is the bank supposed to do with it? See UCC §§9-610(a), 9-620, 9-626, and Comment 4 to §9-610.

5.5. Your client, Pedro Perez-Ortiz, bought a retail store from Lamp Fair, Inc. for $50,000 down and a promissory note in the amount of $277,000. The note was secured by a security interest in the store. Pedro couldn't make the payments on the debt, so he gave Lamp Fair the keys. Lamp Fair resumed operation of the store and sent Pedro a bill for $131,000, which the company said was the excess of what Pedro owed after crediting him for the value of the store. Pedro refused to pay, and Lamp Fair has now sued him for the $131,000. When you told Lamp Fair's lawyer that Lamp Fair couldn't sue for a deficiency without selling the store first, she snapped "where does it say that in Article 9?" UCC §§9-610(a), 9-615(d)(2), 9-620, 9-626.

5.6.   *Law Abiding Citizen* is a 2009 thriller starring Jamie Foxx and Gerard Butler. The film did over $70 million at the box office and was released on DVD and Blu-ray in February 2011. *The Rebound* is a 2009 romantic comedy starring Catherine Zeta-Jones and Justin Bartha.

LEGAL NOTICES

NOTICE OF PUBLIC SALE OF COLLATERAL

PLEASE TAKE NOTICE that pursuant to Section 9-610 of the Uniform Commercial Code in effect in the State of New York, FC Holding (FilmII) LLC ("Agent"), as successor collateral agent and secured party of record for itself and other holders ("Holders") of certain Secured Second Lien Notes ("Notes") issued by The Film Department LLC, and pursuant to a certain Guaranty and Security Agreement (together with the Notes and the related financing and security agreements, the "Agreements") with the Film Department LLC, The Film Department Holdings LLC, TFD Literary Acquisitions, LLC, TFD Music, LLC, Film Department Music, LLC, AF Productions, Inc., BD Productions, LLC, Rebound Distribution LLC, LAC Films, LLC and The Film Department International, LLC (Collectively, the "Debtor"), shall on June 22, 2011 at 10:00 a.m.(Pacific Time) sell to the qualified highest bidder, for cash or on otherwise acceptable terms (as determined by Agent in accordance with its Bid and Sale Procedures) all personal property of Debtor consisting of, and relating to: (a) the motion pictures (I)"The Rebound" and (II)"Law Abiding Citizen," including all underlying rights with respect thereto and any and all other productions based thereon, including sequels, prequels, television productions and remakes thereof and all ancillary rights related thereto to the extent held by the Debtor and (b) all rights of the Debtor in certain motion picture projects in development (collectively, the "Collateral").

Agent reserves the right to postpone and re-notice the time and date of the auction. If competing offers with different terms and conditions are submitted, Agent will determine which offer will be accepted, and its decision in this regard will be final. Agent reserves the right to adjourn the sale pending such determination.

This sale shall be made on an AS-IS, WHERE-IS basis, without recourse, covenants, representations or warranties (express or implied) by Agent. Agent does not make any representations or warranties as to the Collateral and the sale is specifically subject to all taxes, liens (other than those of the Agent under the Agreements), claims, assessments, liabilities and encumbrances that may exist against the Collateral. Without limiting the foregoing, the Agent expressly disclaims all representations and warranties with regard to the Collateral including without limitation those relating to the condition of title to, the completeness or accuracy of any description of, or the rights and liabilities that accompany the Collateral.

The sale will be made to satisfy the current indebtedness and obligations of the Debtor to Agent and the other Holders under the Agreements, which indebtedness have been accelerated following the occurrence of certain defaults by the Debtor under the Agreements.

The sale shall take place at the offices of Manatt, Phelps & Phillips, LLP at 11355 West Olympic Blvd., Los Angeles, CA 90064 subject to the terms and conditions of Agent's Bid and Sale Procedures (as the same may be amended or modified at any time prior to the sale). Agent reserves the right to postpone and renotice the time and date of the sale. Please contact Lindsay Conner, Esq. at (310)312-4229 with any questions regarding the sale, to obtain a copy of Agent's Bid and Sale Procedures or to make an appointment to review the materials relating to the Collateral. Agent reserves the right to require any person requesting additional information regarding this sale to disclose the person or entity upon whose behalf such information is being sought and to require the execution and delivery of a confidentiality agreement with Agent as a precondition to the receipt of or access to any confidential or sensitive information concerning Agent, the sale or this Collateral.

This ad — actual size — ran three times in *Variety*, the leading movie industry publication, starting June 6, 2011. The ad announced an Article 9 sale of the two films by public auction on June 22, 2011. It was the only print advertising for the sale. The secured creditor also hired two former principals of the debtor to identify and contact potential bidders. Manatt, Phelps & Phillips, the firm that handled the foreclosure, is a highly regarded law firm with a substantial intellectual property practice.

    a.   The rights to be sold are worth millions of dollars. Does this look to you like a commercially reasonable sale? UCC §§9-610(b), 9-627(a) and (b).

    b.   What's the penalty if it isn't? UCC §§9-625(a), (b), and (d), 9-626(a).

    c.   What do you think is going on? UCC §9-617(b).

■ End of Default Problem Set

5.7.   You represent the Chavers, who have repossessed a Learjet from the Frazier Group, Inc. The debtor is insolvent. Even if a deficiency judgment is entered, it will be uncollectible. The Chavers estimate that the jet is worth about $800,000. The debt is about $850,000. The Chavers would like to avoid the expenses of sale and just keep the jet for their personal use.

a.   What should they do? UCC §§9-610, 9-611, 9-620, 9-621.

b.   What if the debtor objects to their retention of the collateral and they simply ignore the objection? See UCC §§9-619, 9-622. Will they have a title problem if they later decide to sell or encumber the plane? Model Rules of Professional Conduct Rule 1.16 provides: "[A] lawyer shall not represent a client or, where representation has commenced, shall withdraw from the representation of a client if: (1) the representation will result in violation of the rules of professional conduct or other law."

c.   What if the Chavers simply announce that they have sold the jet to themselves for $800,000? UCC §§9-610(c), 9-617.

5.8.   Assume that on the facts of Problem 5.4, Grizzly Bear Bank throws the hull away and sues the guarantors for the full amount of the debt. Through expert testimony, the guarantors prove that if Grizzly had spent $245,000 to install an engine and electronics in the hull, the helicopter would have sold for $345,000. To what deficiency judgment, if any, would Grizzly have been entitled? UCC §§9-102(a)(64), 9-626(a)(3).

Chapter 2. Creditors' Remedies in Bankruptcy

How bankruptcy filing can interrupt collection actions

Assignment 6: Bankruptcy and the Automatic Stay

A. The Federal Bankruptcy System

The preceding assignments assumed that the parties resolved their differences without resort to bankruptcy. But debtors that are in financial difficulty often file bankruptcy petitions. (Or, in rare circumstances, one or more of their creditors may file petitions against them.) In 2014 alone, there were over 900,000 bankruptcy filings. A bankruptcy filing stays further collection action, except through the bankruptcy court.

Under the supremacy doctrine, once a case is filed, federal bankruptcy laws, rights, and procedures supersede state collection laws, rights, and procedures. Bankruptcy law is the ultimate arbiter of the parties' right.

fed law Rts supercede State collection laws

The substitution is, however, far from complete. Bankruptcy law defers to state collection laws in numerous respects. For the most part, bankruptcy law continues to recognize the property rights that existed prior to bankruptcy. For the most part, secured creditors continue to be secured. Property exempt from state remedies is probably also exempt from bankruptcy remedies.

Perhaps the biggest difference between state and bankruptcy remedies is that state remedies cannot discharge debt. The Constitution reserves to the federal government the power to establish "uniform laws on bankruptcy." The essence of that power is the ability to discharge — essentially extinguish — debt obligations. States can, and have, legislated the existence of collective procedures to coordinate resolution of distressed debtors' financial problems. But because the states lack the power to discharge debt, those procedures are only faint shadows of bankruptcy.

state remedies cannot discharge debt

While only a small percentage of all debt is ultimately resolved in bankruptcy, the bankruptcy system has an important impact on debtor-creditor relationships. When a debtor is in financial difficulty, the shadow of a possible bankruptcy falls across all the debtor's dealings. Sophisticated lenders are aware of bankruptcy's possibility, both at the beginning of the relationship and with greater intensity as the debtor's financial condition worsens. They may plan to pursue their remedies under state law if their debtors should default, but they understand that their right to do so can be preempted at any time if the debtor files for bankruptcy. Through their impact on strategic planning, bankruptcy laws affect the collection system more than the number of actual bankruptcy filings would suggest.

creditor's Right to do so can be preempted at anytime if the debtor files for bankrupcy

It is not possible to teach the entire bankruptcy system in a course on secured credit, and we do not attempt to do so here. Nonetheless, it is also impossible to understand the secured credit system without understanding the role that bankruptcy plays in it. In this assignment we give a brief overview of bankruptcy and discuss how a bankruptcy filing can interrupt the collection actions you studied in prior assignments. In Assignment 7 we explore how creditors collect claims in bankruptcy and how much they can expect to receive. In both assignments, our focus is on the sharp differences in the rights of secured and unsecured creditors.

B.   Filing a Bankruptcy Case

A bankruptcy case can be initiated by either a debtor or its creditors. Well over 99 percent, however, are "voluntary," meaning that they are initiated by the debtor. The proportion of involuntary filings is considerably higher in business cases. In a 1994 study, Professors Warren and Westbrook found that about 3 percent of business bankruptcies were filed by the creditors. Professor Lynn M. LoPucki's Bankruptcy Research Database shows about that same portion of involuntary filings among large, public companies. http://lopucki.law.ucla.edu.

A "voluntary" petition may not be entirely voluntary: many debtors walk the plank to the bankruptcy clerk's office with the creditors' swords at their backs, the creditors having made clear what they will do unless the debtor files. In this assignment we focus on the typical debtor who files a petition with the bankruptcy court—even if that debtor is only a few steps ahead of the creditors.

To file a bankruptcy case, the debtor, usually with the assistance of an attorney, fills out forms making extensive disclosures of the debtor's assets, debts, income, and financial history. The debtor's attorney files the forms electronically with the bankruptcy court through the PACER system. http://www .pacer.gov. At the instant of filing, two things happen: A bankruptcy estate, which consists of all the property of the debtor, is automatically created, and a stay against any collection activities is automatically imposed. Bankr. Code §§362(a), 541(a)(1). Both events occur by operation of law without any action by the court.

Because the debtor's property is now a part of a bankruptcy estate, the debtor cannot use it to pay prepetition debts. Nor is any prepetition creditor allowed to collect anything from this estate until the case is resolved. From this moment forward, the payments and collections must be made according to bankruptcy procedures.

Bankruptcy cases proceed differently, depending on the chapter of the Bankruptcy Code under which the debtor files. The three chapters most commonly used are Chapters 7, 11, and 13. Each of these chapters is, in essence, a deal that the bankruptcy system offers to any debtor eligible for relief under that chapter.

The Chapter 7 deal is that the debtor surrenders all of the debtor's non-exempt assets to a bankruptcy trustee and, in exchange, receives a discharge of all of the debtor's dischargeable debt. In most states, the property that is exempt is the same property that is exempt from execution under state law. In some states, the debtor is permitted to choose between those state law exemptions and the list of exemptions contained in Bankruptcy Code §522(d). Debts excluded from discharge include domestic support obligations, most taxes, debts incurred through fraud, student loans, and a miscellany of others. Debtors who want to keep their collateral have essentially three options for dealing with the secured creditors. First, the debtor can "reaffirm" all or part of the debt in a written agreement with the secured creditor. Reaffirmation agreements must be disclosed to the bankruptcy courts and are highly regulated. Bankr. Code §524(c). Second, if the collateral is tangible personal property such as an automobile, the debtor can redeem the collateral by paying its fair market value in cash. Third, many debtors continue making their payments without entering into a reaffirmation agreement, in the hope that either the secured creditor won't try to foreclose after bankruptcy or won't be successful in doing so.

Chpt 7 surrenders all Non exempt Assets

Corporate and partnership debtors cannot get discharges in Chapter 7. As a result, Chapter 7 is useful mostly to human debtors (referred to as "individuals"), including those who are sole proprietors.

The Chapter 11 deal is that the debtor nearly always remains in possession of the property of the estate during the pendency of the case. The debtor can continue to operate its business and to manage its financial affairs. The debtor proposes a plan to restructure its debt. To "restructure" debt is to reduce the amount owing, change the terms of repayment, or both. Creditors are entitled to vote on the plan, but even if they vote no, the court may "cram down" the plan against creditors. Cramdown is authorized only if the plan respects the priority rights among creditors and shareholders (creditors come ahead of shareholders, and some creditor groups come ahead of others) and the plan promises that the debtor will pay each creditor at least as much as that creditor would receive under Chapter 7. If the court confirms the plan, the debtor's obligations under the plan replace the debtor's prepetition obligations under state law. The remainder of the debt is discharged.

Chpt 11 Reduce amount owing change terms of owing or both

Individuals may file under Chapter 11. Their cases proceed under both the general rules applicable in Chapter 11 cases and special rules applicable only to individual debtors. Those special rules resemble Chapter 13 procedure.

The Chapter 13 deal is available only to individual debtors whose unsecured debts are less than $383,175 and whose secured debts are less than $1,149,525. (The amounts are adjusted automatically for inflation.) The debtor proposes a plan to pay all of the debtor's disposable income, if any, to unsecured creditors over a period of three to five years if the debtor's income is below the state median, or for five years if the debtor's income is above the state median. Disposable income is the income remaining after various allowances for living expenses, including payments to secured creditors for homes and automobiles. The value of the proposed payments to each creditor must be at least as great as the amount of the dividend the creditor would have received in Chapter 7. The court confirms the plan if it meets the statutory requirements. Creditors do not vote. If the debtor makes the required plan payments, the debtor receives a discharge of the debtor's dischargeable debts and keeps all property, not just exempt property.

plan to pay all with disposable income

C.   The Automatic Stay

Once the debtor has filed for bankruptcy, unsecured creditors (*general creditors*, in bankruptcy parlance) can file their claims and have disputes regarding them resolved in the bankruptcy case, but they have few other specific rights as the case moves toward resolution. If the debtor violates the provisions of the Bankruptcy Code, the creditor or the trustee may complain in court. Barring that, there is little that an individual unsecured creditor can do. For unsecured creditors, bankruptcy is a collective — and largely passive — proceeding.

The creditors as a group benefit from collective action. Even if the debtor does not reorganize, a single trustee liquidating the debtor's property in a single proceeding is more efficient than individual creditors competing to liquidate the debtor's property in numerous proceedings. The costs of the

Differences among the Basic Types of Bankruptcy Cases

	Chapter 7	Corporate Chapter 11	Individual Chapter 11	Chapter 13
Eligibility to file	Individuals and corporations	Corporations	Individuals	Individuals who meet debt limits
Nature of case	Liquidation	Debtor proposes and court confirms a debt restructuring plan	Debtor proposes and court confirms a debt restructuring plan	Debtor proposes and court confirms a debt restructuring plan
Duration of the plan	Not applicable	No limit	No limit	Three to five years
Who is in possession of the bankruptcy estate?	Trustee	Debtor, but in rare cases, court may appoint a trustee	Debtor, but in rare cases, court may appoint a trustee	Debtor
Creditor involvement	Minimal	Creditors may form committees, vote on plan, and object to plan	Creditors may form committees, vote on plan, and object to plan	Creditors may object to plan
Time discharge is granted	About 90 days after filing	At plan confirmation	Upon completion of payments	Upon completion of payments
Filing fee	$335	$1,717	$1,717	$310

unified proceeding are paid from the estate, so their impact is distributed pro rata among the creditors. The least aggressive creditors reap the most benefit, because they would have lost the race for the assets under state law.

The most aggressive creditors are generally worse off in bankruptcy than they would have been under state collection law. Bankruptcy requires that they share pro rata with other creditors any debtor's assets they discover.

In the absence of bankruptcy, an aggressive unsecured creditor can disrupt the debtor's business, employment, and financial affairs by seizing assets. The leverage generated by these activities can sometimes be so great that the debtor will do whatever is necessary to pay the debt, even if sale of its assets would yield nothing for the aggressive creditor. Once bankruptcy is filed, even an aggressive unsecured creditor cannot generate much leverage. And at the end of the bankruptcy process, the creditor's claims may be discharged entirely, eliminating any right to collect from the debtor.

Bankruptcy courts take stay violations seriously. They usually hold deliberate violators in contempt of court and impose fines sufficient to make them regret their transgressions. In some circumstances, individuals injured by stay violations can sue for damages. See Bankr. Code §362(k). Actions taken in violation of the stay are either void or voidable, and many courts impose on even the innocent violator of the stay the obligation to undo the violation by returning property or correcting public records. As a result, few lawyers or parties deliberately violate the automatic stay.

The reasons for the creation of the estate and imposition of the automatic stay are both practical and theoretical. By stopping all payments and collections, bankruptcy provides an opportunity to account for all the assets in the estate and all the charges against the estate. In a sense, the automatic stay locks up the estate temporarily so that an accurate count and an orderly distribution can be made. The stay also gives the debtor breathing room either to make an orderly liquidation of assets or to construct a plan of reorganization. Imposing a stay halts ongoing litigation in the state system and substitutes what is often a more abbreviated and efficient set of bankruptcy procedures for resolving disputes over outstanding debts. Perhaps most critical from the general creditor's point of view, the stay freezes the relative rights of creditors as of the moment of the bankruptcy filing. The race of diligence fostered by state procedures is over; creditors can take no additional action to improve their own chances of recovery at the expense of others. Instead, all further actions by unsecured creditors against the debtor must be collective actions taken on behalf of *all* the creditors. The stay illustrates, and other Code provisions reinforce, that for general, unsecured creditors, bankruptcy is a collective proceeding.

The language of the Bankruptcy Code fixing the scope of the automatic stay is broad. It provides that a stay is "applicable to all entities" against "any act" to collect a prepetition debt. Bankr. Code §362(a). The stay protects the debtor personally as well as the property of the estate. The stay applies both to direct collection attempts (e.g., levying against the debtor's property), as well as more indirect attempts (e.g., initiating a lawsuit to establish the debtor's liability on a debt as a prerequisite to eventual collection).

While the stay is broad, it is not unlimited. Only actions to collect pre-filing obligations are stayed. The Bankruptcy Code does not halt criminal

[handwritten margin notes: "→ stay protects" and "pre-filing obligations are stayed"]

proceedings against the debtor. If the debtor is under criminal indictment, for example, filing a bankruptcy petition will not stay the trial. Bankr. Code §362(b)(1). (This is not a surprising provision, lest every criminal defendant make a quick stop at the bankruptcy desk on the way to trial.) Debtors can file for bankruptcy and receive at least temporary relief from the government's attempts to collect fines and penalties for past violations of government regulations, but they remain subject to government actions to abate continuing violations. Bankr. Code §362(b)(4). (Again, it is not a big surprise that airlines must follow FAA safety restrictions and oil drillers must comply with pollution regulations, even if they are flying or drilling after they have filed for Chapter 11.)

With regard to unsecured creditors, the automatic stay generally remains in effect until the conclusion of the bankruptcy case. See Bankr. Code §362(c)(1) and (2). Unsecured creditors rarely have grounds to lift the stay; they must rely on the operation of the bankruptcy process to collect the debts owed to them. In effect, unsecured creditors are on board for the ride through bankruptcy. They can monitor the process to make certain the rules are followed, or they can rely on the bankruptcy trustee or debtor in possession, but they have only collective rights and they must await disposition of the case to get any money. An unsecured creditor's best course is usually to file a proof of claim, hope for the best, and expect the worst.

D.   Lifting the Stay for Secured Creditors

Secured creditors fare better than unsecured creditors. Bankruptcy recognizes and generally gives effect to secured creditors' priority rights. Bankruptcy may delay secured creditors' enforcement of those rights, but bankruptcy still promises secured creditors eventual access either to their collateral or to property or money of equivalent value. A secured creditor is assured of recovering the amount of its debt or the value of its collateral, whichever is less. Unsecured creditors (including secured creditors claiming for the unsecured portions of their claims) have only the right to share pro rata in whatever is left after paying the secured creditors and the expenses of the bankruptcy case.

Because each secured creditor is usually secured by different collateral, the interests of any two secured creditors are rarely precisely the same. For example, the holder of an over secured first mortgage on the debtor's home may suffer only minor inconvenience from the automatic stay, while the holder of a second security interest in accounts receivable may stand to lose everything if the account is not collected efficiently. Secured creditors, each claiming different collateral or different priority in the same collateral, stand in sharp contrast to unsecured creditors who share pro rata in whatever is available after provisions have been made for the payment to secured creditors of the value of their collateral.

Bankruptcy procedure affords secured creditors a number of ways in which they can monitor their collateral and participate individually in the bankruptcy case. Both their greater substantive rights and the fact of their participation give them greater ability to influence the course of the bankruptcy case.

When a bankruptcy case is filed, the collection actions of a secured creditor, like those of an unsecured creditor, are immediately interrupted. But for the secured creditor, imposition of the automatic stay is often only the beginning of a new game. The secured creditor retains its lien and may be able to get the stay lifted and continue with its nonbankruptcy collection efforts.

The grounds for lifting the stay are set forth in Bankruptcy Code §362(d)(1) and (2). To summarize, the court must always lift the stay if the trustee or debtor does not provide the creditor with adequate protection. But even if the trustee or debtor provides adequate protection, the court must nevertheless lift the stay if (1) there is no equity in the collateral that the trustee or debtor might realize for unsecured creditors and (2) the collateral is not necessary to an effective reorganization. (Two other bases for lifting the stay are not discussed here. The first applies only to a narrow range of "single asset real estate" cases; the second applies only if the petition was part of a scheme to delay, hinder, and defraud a real property secured creditor.) This complex combination of requirements may seem a jumble at first, but it sorts out rather sensibly once one understands two reasons why the bankruptcy system might want to commandeer a secured creditor's collateral over the secured creditor's objection.

The first is that the collateral may be worth more than the debt secured by it, and the estate's equity in the collateral may be available to the debtor and other creditors only through bankruptcy procedure. For example, if Dubchek files under Chapter 7 owing $30,000 to Salman and the debt is secured by a nonexempt Buick LaCrosse worth $40,000, the estate has a $10,000 equity in it. If the stay is left in place, the trustee can sell the LaCrosse for $40,000 and pay the secured creditor $30,000, leaving $10,000 (less the expenses of sale) to pay unsecured creditors. The fear apparently motivating bankruptcy policy in this regard is that if the stay is lifted, Salman will foreclose and the LaCrosse will be sold for less than its value, leaving little or nothing for the unsecured creditors. That is, bankruptcy policy is based on the realization that state sale procedures often fail to yield reasonably equivalent value. Even if the LaCrosse were sold for its full value under nonbankruptcy law, the net proceeds after payment of the secured creditor and the expenses of sale would have been turned over to the debtor, not the unsecured creditors. The unsecured creditors might have had a difficult time reaching the proceeds through garnishment or execution.

The second reason for commandeering a secured creditor's collateral is to enable the debtor to reorganize—that is, to remain in business or keep a job, make money, and pay some of the debts. For example, if Dubchek had no equity in the LaCrosse, but could not continue her profitable Donut Delivery Service without it, the LaCrosse might be "necessary to an effective reorganization." Bankr. Code §362(d)(2). Without it, Dubchek might have no income and be unable to pay anything to unsecured creditors. (On the other hand, if Dubchek had two cars and the Donut Delivery Service could carry on just as well with either one, retention of the LaCrosse would not be necessary for an effective reorganization.) In the remainder of our discussion of the stay, we will refer to these two reasons for retaining collateral—that the debtor has an equity in it or that it is necessary to an effective reorganization—as *bankruptcy purposes*. To be entitled to retain the secured creditor's collateral, the debtor or trustee must show at a minimum that its retention of the collateral serves a bankruptcy purpose. In the absence of such justification, the secured creditor can demand that the stay be lifted.

To appreciate fully the importance of these bankruptcy purposes, it is critical to realize how effective the bankruptcy system can sometimes be in realizing the full value of the debtor's assets or income-earning potential. In re 26 Trumbull Street, 77 B.R. 374 (Bankr. D. Conn. 1987), illustrates. Before bankruptcy, the debtor closed the restaurant it had been operating in leased premises. The bankruptcy estate contained two items of property: the restaurant equipment and the restaurant's interest in its lease. The parties agreed that if the restaurant equipment were removed from the leased premises, the equipment would have been worth only $21,500, but sold together with the lease, it was worth $90,000. The case did not explain why the difference was so great. Most likely, it was because the equipment was suited for use with the leased premises. It fit the space and might even have been damaged through removal. In place, the equipment and lease constituted a restaurant; removed, the equipment was a difficult marketing problem. Nevertheless, if a creditor with a debt of $21,500 (or less) that was secured by the equipment could have repossessed the equipment and sold it separate from the lease for $21,500, the secured creditor would have had little reason not to do so immediately. The estate—and the other creditors—would have lost the additional $68,500 value. Only by leaving the stay in effect could the bankruptcy court prevent the loss.

Even if the estate's retention of the collateral would serve a bankruptcy purpose, that alone is not sufficient to defeat a secured creditor's motion to lift the stay. The debtor also must protect the secured creditor against loss as a result of the delay in foreclosure that is caused by the stay. Bankr. Code §362(d)(1). The debtor must furnish *adequate protection*, a term of art defined only by example in Bankruptcy Code §361. Generally speaking, a secured creditor's interest is adequately protected when provisions that the court considers adequate have been made to protect the secured creditor from loss as a result of a decline in the value of the secured creditor's collateral during the time the creditor is immobilized by the automatic stay. If the debtor cannot provide what the court considers adequate protection, the court must lift the stay and allow the creditor to foreclose.

To continue with our earlier example, assume that Dubchek owes $50,000 to Salman and that the LaCrosse is worth $40,000 when the automatic stay is imposed. Based on these numbers, Dubchek has no equity in the LaCrosse. But assume further that retention of the LaCrosse is necessary to Dubchek's reorganization. The court should not lift the stay pursuant to Bankruptcy Code §362(d)(2) because the property is necessary for an effective reorganization. But Salman is not through. Salman can move to lift the stay for lack of adequate protection pursuant to Bankruptcy Code §362(d)(1). Under these circumstances, Dubchek must furnish adequate protection against postfiling decline in the value of the car or lose it.

The bankruptcy court decides what constitutes adequate protection. Based on experience with the depreciation of similar automobiles, the parties may show that the decline in the value of the LaCrosse is likely to be about $12,000 during the year Dubchek will be in bankruptcy, so the value of the car will go from $40,000 to $28,000. If this $12,000 decline in fact occurs, the resulting loss imposed on Salman would be a result of the delay imposed by the automatic stay. That is, were it not for the automatic stay, Salman could foreclose now and recover $40,000. If the stay prevents Salman from foreclosing for a year and the value of the collateral drops to $28,000, Salman might recover only $28,000, losing the additional $12,000 he would have enjoyed in an early foreclosure. In these circumstances, the bankruptcy court will require Dubchek to protect Salman against this anticipated $12,000 loss.

Salman's adequate protection may come in any of several forms. Dubchek might pay Salman $1,000 each month as the car declines in value. Or Dubchek might grant Salman an additional lien against property worth at least $12,000. There are few limits on the form the protection may take, so long as it is "adequate" in the eyes of the bankruptcy judge. But if Dubchek cannot or does not furnish adequate protection to Salman, Salman will be entitled to have the stay lifted. Dubchek's potentially profitable Donut Delivery Service will be history.

Notice that if the car in the preceding example had been worth $100,000, Salman would have been in no real danger of loss from ordinary depreciation. Even if the value of the car fell to $70,000 during bankruptcy, it would have remained easily sufficient to cover the balance on the loan, plus accruing interest and attorneys fees. Such an excess of collateral value over loan amount is referred to in bankruptcy parlance as a *cushion of equity*. The bankruptcy courts recognize that a cushion of equity of sufficient size may alone adequately protect a secured creditor against loss. If such a cushion already provides adequate protection to the secured creditor, the secured creditor has no right to additional protection in the form of periodic payments or additional collateral.

Exactly how large the cushion of equity must be to provide protection depends on the circumstances. Key circumstances include (1) the nature of the factors that might change the value of the collateral, (2) the volatility of the market in which the creditor might have to sell it, and (3) the rate at which the secured debt is likely to increase in amount. Of course, the apparent size of the cushion of equity depends on the value the court assigns to the collateral. The question of how large a cushion exists often becomes intertwined with the question of how large a cushion is necessary, giving the court considerable flexibility to do what it thinks best.

While secured creditors are entitled to adequate protection against loss from a decline in the value of their collateral, they are not entitled to protection against other losses resulting from imposition of the automatic stay. United Savings of Texas v. Timbers of Inwood Forest Associates, 484 U.S. 365 (1988). To illustrate, assume that the LaCrosse is worth $40,000, Salman's lien against it is in the same amount, and that the value of the LaCrosse is not expected to decline during the one-year bankruptcy. On these facts, Dubchek need do nothing to provide adequate protection. One result will be that Salman will lose the time value of his $40,000 in this scenario. But for the stay, Salman could have invested his $40,000 and earned interest during the year. With the money stuck in a bankruptcy case, he could not. Bankruptcy affords no protection for the time value of money in these circumstances.

In the following case, the Craddock-Terry Shoe Corporation was attempting to reorganize in Chapter 11. Two of its secured creditors, Lincoln and

Westinghouse, sought to lift the stay, raising issues under both prongs of Bankruptcy Code §362(d)(1) and (2). The court addressed whether the stay should be lifted under either, providing us with a look at how the two sections are used in tandem by many undersecured creditors. In order to decide any of the legal issues, however, the court first had to resolve the threshold question of the value of the property. If the court had assigned the property a different value, the outcome might have been different as well.

In re Craddock-Terry Shoe Corporation
98 B.R. 250 (Bankr. W.D. Va. 1988)

WILLIAM E. ANDERSON, UNITED STATES BANKRUPTCY JUDGE

The plaintiffs, Lincoln National Life Insurance Company ("Lincoln") and Westinghouse Credit Corporation ("Westinghouse"), have moved the Court to lift the automatic stay imposed by section 362(a) of the Bankruptcy Code, 11 U.S.C. §362(a), or in the alternative, to provide Lincoln and Westinghouse adequate protection for certain collateral in which they have a security interest. The collateral at issue is the customer mailing lists, catalogues, and certain trademarks of Hill Brothers, a division of Craddock-Terry Shoe Corporation ("Craddock-Terry"), the debtor.

BACKGROUND FACTS

On April 30, 1986, the plaintiffs, Lincoln and Westinghouse, loaned the debtor, Craddock-Terry, $9,000,000. As security for that loan, Lincoln and Westinghouse obtained a security interest in the mailing list, customer list, catalogues, and four trademarks ("the collateral") of Hill Brothers, a mail-order division of Craddock-Terry. Debtor's Chapter 11 petition was filed on October 21, 1987. Craddock-Terry has shut down all its operations, except for Hill Brothers.

As of the petition date, debtor owed Lincoln and Westinghouse $9,587,812.50. The debtor does not dispute that Lincoln and Westinghouse have a valid and perfected lien on the mailing list, customer list, catalogues, and trademarks of Hill Brothers. The collateral is worth less than the amount owed Lincoln and Westinghouse. In fact, the debtor had on the petition date, and still has, no equity in the collateral.

Concerned that the value of their collateral appeared to be seriously declining, Lincoln and Westinghouse originally filed their motion for relief from stay on March 1, 1988. The hearing on the motion, originally scheduled for April 21, 1988, was continued to May 4, 1988, and final arguments were heard on May 10, 1988.

The evidence introduced at the hearing indicates that, during the Chapter 11 case, Hill Brothers has experienced a serious cash flow problem which has reduced the number of orders which can be filled (the fill rate), cut in half the number of spring catalogues planned to be mailed, and reduced the rate at which new names are added to the Hill Brothers mailing list. In addition, returns of merchandise have increased. These factors have resulted in a serious decline in the value of the collateral.

The plaintiffs presented evidence that on the date the debtor's petition was filed, before the adverse impact of the cash flow problems and the list management problems, the value of the mailing list in place and in use at Hill Brothers was $8.7 million, but that its value on April 30, 1988, was $5.7 million. Their expert at trial had used the same valuation method as that used by an accounting firm whose earlier appraisal the debtor had used to obtain the loans. He testified that he had used a method appropriate for valuing a mailing list in use by a company, known as the discounted cash flow method. The resulting value is the value to the business which is using the list. A mailing list is carefully built up over the years by adding names each year and developing an active list of persons who like and buy the particular product of the company. Its value in place to the company using it is necessarily much greater than to an outside buyer or renter.

The debtor presented its own expert testimony from an individual heavily involved in the direct marketing industry. The debtor's expert stated that the fair market value of the list, if sold to other companies, was $700,000 on the petition date and $330,000 as of the hearing date. He utilized a model containing twelve factors from which he calculated the value of the list. These factors included expected revenues and expenses, customer attrition, rental income, comparison to outside lists, and customer affinity for the debtor's product.

DISCUSSION

Bankruptcy Code section 362(d)(1) and (2) provide relief from the stay imposed by section 362(a) in either of two circumstances. The stay will be lifted "for cause, including the lack of adequate protection of an interest in property of [a] party in interest." 11 U.S.C. §362(d)(1). The stay will also be lifted "with respect to a stay of an act against property under subsection (a) of this section, if (A) the debtor does not have an equity in such property; and (B) such property is not necessary to an effective reorganization." 11 U.S.C. §362(d)(2). Lincoln and Westinghouse have asserted that they are entitled to relief under either part of section 362(d). The debtor claims to the contrary that its mailing list is vital to its reorganization and that it has offered adequate protection for any decline in the collateral's value. The court will consider sections 362(d)(1) and 362(d)(2) in reverse order.

I.   Section 362(D)(2)

Neither party disputes that Craddock-Terry has no equity in the collateral. The debt secured by the collateral is greater than $9,000,000, and although the parties have widely divergent views of the value of the collateral for purposes of this motion, each places a lower value on it than the amount of the debt. "Equity" is defined as the amount by which the value of the collateral exceeds the debt it secures. Thus, the debtor has no equity in the collateral and the first requirement of section 362(d)(2) is met.

Each party also agrees that if the debtor can possibly reorganize, this collateral is essential to its survival. Lincoln and Westinghouse claim, however, that even if the debtor retains and uses the collateral, no effective reorganization is possible.

In short, Lincoln and Westinghouse have no faith in the debtor's proposed plan for reorganization or its proposed business plan. They point to reduced catalog mailings and the reduced fill rate for customers' orders since the initiation of bankruptcy proceedings, both of which have caused the decline in value of the mailing list and, therefore, of the business itself.

The debtor, on the other hand, while admitting that its fill rate and catalog mailings have decreased, introduced evidence that the intrinsic value of the mailing list has not been irreparably harmed. The debtor's expert testified that an infusion of capital appropriately applied to the mailing list could revive the list's value, and that he had in fact seen this occur in a similar situation. The debtor's own representative testified that approximately $4,000,000 would be available to the debtor from the recent sale of the bulk of the company's assets to The Old Time Gospel Hour and to T/W Properties. He further testified that $900,000 of this influx of cash was designated for revitalization of the mailing list, and thereby, the company.

Since the filing of the debtor's petition the general theme of this reorganization has been to sell most of the company's assets and use the proceeds to reorganize the company's Hill Brothers division into a viable entity. The debtor has finally reached the point where it will have capital with which to effect those plans. The law is clear that a court "should not precipitously sound the death knell for a debtor by prematurely determining that the debtor's prospects for economic revival are poor." In re Shockley Forest Indus., Inc., 5 B.R. 160 (Bankr. M.D. Tenn. 1980). The evidence before the court as yet gives no basis for a conclusion that this reorganization is no longer in prospect, and therefore the court finds that the collateral at issue here is necessary to an effective reorganization. Consequently, the automatic stay will not be lifted pursuant to section 362(d)(2).

II. SECTION 362(D)(1)

Lincoln and Westinghouse are entitled to relief from the stay, however, if the debtor cannot satisfy section 362(d)(1) by providing adequate protection for the interest of Lincoln and Westinghouse in the collateral. The debtor has offered replacement liens in all its assets, which it claims will provide adequate protection either from the date of the motion or, if necessary, from the date of the petition. The parties agree that the value of the collateral has declined since the date the petition was filed and also since the date the motion was filed. They disagree as to the amount of decline in value and as to the date from which adequate protection is necessary.

The major focus of the parties during the hearing on this motion and in their final arguments was on the proper value to assign to the collateral at the various stages herein. The Bankruptcy Code provides no specific guidance as to the standard to be used to value property for purposes of providing creditors adequate protection with respect to section 362(d). Section 361 establishes three non-exclusive methods of providing adequate protection of a creditor's interest in property, but specifies no means for valuing that interest. Section 506(a) states that the value of a creditor's interest in the estate's interest in property "shall be determined in light of the purpose of the valuation and of the proposed disposition or use of such property, and in conjunction with any hearing on such disposition or use or on a plan affecting such creditor's interest," 11 U.S.C. §506(a), but gives no other insight into how such value should be determined.

Consequently courts have looked to the legislative history behind these two sections to find reasonable and proper methods of valuation. The legislative history of section 506(a) establishes that valuation methods should not be rigid:

> "value" does not necessarily contemplate forced sale or liquidation value of collateral; nor does it always imply a full going concern value. Courts will have to determine value on a case-by-case basis, taking into account the facts of each case and the competing interests in the case.

H.R. Rep. No. 95–595, 95th Cong., 1st Sess. 356 (1977).

In order to determine the most commercially reasonable disposition practicable, the court must follow the directive of section 506 and consider the purpose of the valuation. The purpose of adequate protection "as stated in the legislative history [of section 361] is to insure that the secured creditor receives in value essentially what he bargained for." In re Ram Mfg., Inc., 32 B.R. 969, 971 (Bankr. E.D. Pa. 1983). Therefore "adequate protection for a secured creditor means that the creditor must receive the same *measure* of protection in bankruptcy that he could have had outside of bankruptcy although the *type* of protection may differ from the bargain initially struck between the parties." Id. at 972. (quoting In re Winslow Center Assoc., 32 B.R. 685, 688 (Bankr. E.D. Pa. 1983)) (emphasis in original). In other words, the value of the interest of Lincoln and Westinghouse in the collateral is equivalent to what they could have recovered through foreclosure, had the debtor defaulted but not filed its petition for Chapter 11 relief. The benefit initially bargained for, and to be protected under sections 361 and 362, was the value obtainable from the most commercially reasonable disposition of the collateral within the context of foreclosure proceedings.

A customer list, as an asset, is a strange hybrid. Although actually represented by a physical asset (the list), its worth is basically as an intangible. The utility of the list results both from Craddock-Terry's established reputation and service, and from the inclination of the particular consumers on the list to purchase shoes, of the kind and quality which Craddock-Terry sells, from Craddock-Terry. The testimony indicated that the value of the list is far greater to Craddock-Terry than to anyone else. The debtor's expert testified that even competitors in the shoe business would not value the list as highly as Craddock-Terry for various reasons, including the fact that crossover with their own lists could be as high as fifty percent.

The debtor did introduce evidence of the value of the list if sold through an arm's-length transaction. The debtor's expert testified that this was not a "fire-sale" value, but indeed the fair market value. He used a model which is widely used in the direct marketing industry to determine mailing list values for third parties. His analysis took into account a variety of factors including not only list maintenance expenses and revenues, but also customer attrition, customer affinity for Craddock-Terry, and replacement cost, among others. His appraisal indicated that the collateral had a fair market value of not more than $700,000 as of the petition date, not more than $500,000 as of February 1988, and not more than $330,000 as of the hearing date. The Court finds this evidence to be credible and, as to the

[handwritten margin note: purpose of adequate protection]

insufficient to satisfy the discharged nonrecourse debt, the secured creditor cannot obtain a deficiency judgment against the debtor because the debtor no longer owes the debt.

Under Article 9 of the Uniform Commercial Code, the special collection rights of a personal property secured creditor are referred to as a *security interest.* The special collection rights of a previously unsecured creditor who has levied against property of the debtor are referred to as a *lien.* See, e.g., UCC §9–102(a)(52), defining *lien creditor.* The special collection rights of a creditor consensually secured by an interest in real estate are typically referred to as a *mortgage.* UCC §9–102(a)(55). In some states, those rights might be in the form of a *deed of trust,* a device that, despite its difference in form, has much the same effect as a mortgage.

The Bankruptcy Code, §101(51), like the Internal Revenue Code, §6323(h)(1), groups Article 9 security interests together with real estate mortgages and deeds of trust under the term *security interest.* The Bankruptcy Code then lumps security interests together with all other secured statuses, including judicial and statutory liens, under the term *lien.* Bankr. Code §101(37). Thus, an Article 9 security interest, a real estate mortgage, a deed of trust, and the rights of a lien creditor are all liens within the contemplation of the Bankruptcy Code.

A creditor's *claim* in bankruptcy is, in essence, the amount of the debt owed to the creditor under nonbankruptcy law at the time the bankruptcy case is filed. Bankr. Code §§101(5) and (12). Notice that the amount of the claim is the amount actually owed. In this respect, the word *claim* does not have its ordinary meaning when used in bankruptcy. Absent bankruptcy, to say that a party "claims" something implies that the claim may not be correct; the same implication does not inhere in the use of "claim" in bankruptcy.

Only claims that are *allowed* are eligible to share in the distributions made in the bankruptcy case. Bankruptcy Code §502(b) contains a list of the kinds of claims that are not allowed, but the exceptions are not relevant for our purposes. Because the difference between a claim and an allowed claim is so slight, bankruptcy lawyers often speak of "claims" when they mean "allowed claims." We often do the same here.

Because the amount of the debt and the amount of the corresponding claim are determined under different rules, they can diverge as the bankruptcy case continues. In determining the creditor's rights in the bankruptcy case, it is usually the amount of the *claim* that is important. In determining the creditor's rights in a nonbankruptcy forum after the stay has been lifted or the bankruptcy case has been dismissed, it is usually the amount of the *debt* that is important. So, for example, interest may not be accruing on the *claim* even though it is accruing on the *debt.* If the case is dismissed from bankruptcy without a discharge for the debtor, the creditor might reassert its collection rights at state law. In such a case, the creditor would seek payment of the debt, including all the interest due from the inception of the loan, rather than simply the claim that would have been allowed in the bankruptcy case.

B.   The Claims Process

How much creditors are paid from a bankruptcy estate depends on how much the various creditors are owed, the creditors' relative priorities in the estate, and the value available with which to pay them. How the bankruptcy system determines these three variables and combines them to yield a set of distributions for a particular case is the subject of the remainder of this assignment.

To guide you through it, we provide this quick overview. Through a claims process, the bankruptcy system determines the Bankruptcy Code §502 amounts of all creditors' claims — that is, the amounts those creditors were owed under nonbankruptcy law as of the date of bankruptcy. Some claims are permitted to grow through the accrual of interest and collection costs during the bankruptcy case while others are not. The amounts available for distribution may be determined by actually selling the assets, through negotiations, or by court decision. A reorganization plan allocates the projected amounts available for distribution among the claimants, based on the claimants' priorities and other sources of negotiating leverage.

Absent bankruptcy, in order to establish the amount owed to it, an unsecured creditor has to bring a lawsuit, usually in state court, alleging the facts that establish the underlying liability as well as the amount owed. Even a secured creditor that is unable to gain possession by self-help must bring an action in court. If the debtor contests the action, the secured creditor must prove the existence of the debt and the amount owing.

Once a bankruptcy has been filed, the automatic stay bars creditors from taking those steps. Bankruptcy substitutes a much cheaper, easier system for a creditor to establish its claim. The creditor files a one-page form called a *proof of claim*, describing the debt and stating that it remains outstanding. Bankr. Code §501(a). If the claim is based on a written contract or other document, the contract or document must be attached. If no one objects to the claim, the claim is deemed "allowed" in the bankruptcy process. Bankr. Code §502(a). In Chapter 11 cases, the process is even easier. The debtor must file "schedules" that list its creditors with the amounts owing to each. If the debtor schedules a debt in the correct amount, and does not indicate that the debt is disputed, contingent, or unliquidated, the creditor need not file a proof of claim. Bankr. Code §1111(a).

Under nonbankruptcy procedures, debtors often have a substantial incentive to dispute collection claims. Absent a dispute, a creditor can obtain a quick judgment and enforce it by seizing the debtor's assets. If the debtor disputes all or part of the debt, the creditor typically has no remedy until the dispute is resolved. In the meantime, the debtor can remain in business and continue to use its assets. It should not be surprising that in the absence of bankruptcy, many debtors stall for time by disputing debts on the flimsiest of grounds.

In bankruptcy, however, a determination that the debt is owed does not lead to seizure of the debtor's assets. Whether the debtor retains possession of the property does not turn on whether the money is owed. Thus the principal incentive for the debtor to raise disputes is eliminated. In addition, most of the disputes that are raised in a bankruptcy proceeding are easier to resolve because the parties realize that the estate will pay only a small percentage of whatever is ultimately determined to be owed. For example, if the debtor will pay ten cents on the dollar of allowed claims, a dispute over whether the debtor owed the creditor $10,000 at the time the debtor filed the petition is actually a dispute over $1,000. Neither side will be as inclined to fight it. For both these reasons, objections to claims in bankruptcy cases are uncommon. Most claims are simply filed by the creditors and deemed allowed by operation of law.

Claims against the estate are accelerated as a consequence of the bankruptcy filing. Bankr. Code §502(b)(1). If, for example, the debtor owes the creditor $10,000 payable in monthly installments of $1,000 each month over the next ten months and only one payment is currently due, the claim in bankruptcy is the total amount owed, not just the current payment. The creditor will file a claim for $10,000, the full, accelerated debt. And the whole debt, not just the payments currently due, will be resolved during the bankruptcy case.

If a claim is disputed, bankruptcy law provides for a quicker resolution of the dispute than is generally available under state law. While complex disputes may be subject to a full-scale trial after both sides have had an opportunity for discovery, most objections to claims are resolved in a single evidentiary hearing. If the ultimate resolution of a claim threatens to delay the bankruptcy case or distribution, the bankruptcy court can estimate the amount of a claim, allow it in the estimated amount, and proceed. Bankr. Code §502(c). In either a hearing on an objection to a claim or in a claims estimation proceeding, a creditor might show, for example, that it had sold the debtor equipment, the agreed price of the equipment, and the payments received by the time of the filing. The debtor might then bring in evidence that the equipment had failed to operate as promised, giving the debtor a contract law right to set off damages against the amount owed. The debtor might claim that nothing is owed or that a reduced sum is appropriate. If the debtor outside bankruptcy had a legal defense to payment, the bankruptcy estate will have the same defense. Bankr. Code §558. But if the bankruptcy court determines that the full amount is owed, the claim will be allowed in full. The court would typically consider the evidence proffered and rule on the amount of the claim.

Different creditors may have different bases for their claims. A department store, for example, might have a claim for the charges made by a debtor and not yet paid. An employee might have a claim for past wages. A tort victim might have a claim for injuries. Taxing authorities might have claims for back taxes due. Utilities may have claims for unpaid services. Landlords may have claims for unpaid rents, and hospitals may have claims for services provided. Sellers of goods may have claims for the purchase price of goods sold to the debtor. Buyers of goods may have warranty claims against their sellers. Some creditors may even have claims contingent on events that have not yet occurred (e.g., a potential claim against a debtor's guarantor when the debtor is not yet in default), or claims that are not yet fixed in amount (e.g., claims for personal injuries that have not yet been heard by a jury). The list is as long and varied as the number of ways one can become obligated to pay money. Unless the holders of these claims had obtained liens before the filing of the bankruptcy case, their claims will all be unsecured in the bankruptcy case and the amounts owed will be determined through the routine claims procedure. Bankruptcy law gives some groups of unsecured creditors priority over others, see Bankr. Code §507(a), but of the unsecured creditors listed in this paragraph, all but the taxing authorities and the employee would share pro rata with each other.

The procedure for claims estimation is itself remarkable. In re Apex Oil Co., 92 B.R. 843 (Bankr. E.D. Mo. 1988), illustrates the point: A $1.4 billion dispute between the debtor oil company and the U.S. Department of Energy had gone on for years, with no resolution in sight. Within a short time after the debtor filed bankruptcy, the bankruptcy court established procedures for resolving the dispute and scheduled two days of court hearings on the amount of the claim. The parties quickly settled the claim, and the company, which had been spending enormous resources on trying to resolve this dispute, returned to its primary business functions. Such accelerated procedures are necessary for achieving the rapid resolution of financial problems that bankruptcy contemplates. Of course, it should also be apparent that as procedures are abbreviated and parties are hurried toward a compromise, some rough justice may be dispensed along the way.

C.   Calculating Claim Amounts

1.   Unsecured Claims

Most debts listed (*scheduled*, in bankruptcy parlance) in a bankruptcy case are undisputed. The debtor owes the money and has no defense. Even so, calculating the amounts in which the various claims should be allowed and from that the amounts appropriate for distribution on each can require considerable knowledge of bankruptcy law.

Bankruptcy Code §502(b) provides essentially that the amount of an unsecured claim in a bankruptcy case is the amount owing under nonbankruptcy law as of the date of the filing of the petition. If the creditor's contract with the debtor provides for the debtor to pay the attorneys fees of the creditor or to reimburse the creditor for other fees, those amounts are included in the claim, provided that they were incurred prior to the time the bankruptcy case was filed. Bankr. Code §502(b)(1).

The amount of the unsecured claim does not grow with the accrual of interest during the bankruptcy case. This conclusion is derived from the restriction that an unsecured creditor's claim may not include "unmatured interest." Bankr. Code §502(b)(2). The reason for disallowing postpetition interest lies in the collective nature of bankruptcy. To understand it, consider that in the vast majority of bankruptcy cases, estate assets will be sufficient to pay only a portion of the claims. As of the moment of the filing of the petition, each unsecured creditor is entitled to a pro rata share of a fixed pool of assets. To allow interest to accrue on the claims between the filing of the case and the ultimate distribution would not increase the value of the pool. If unsecured creditors were allowed to accrue interest on their claims at the rates specified in their contracts, the only effect would be to shift some of the recovery from low interest creditors to high interest creditors. While some might argue that is the bargain initially struck among the creditors, that is not the policy reflected in the Bankruptcy Code. Instead, for the purposes of accruing postpetition interest, all the unsecured creditors are equal, even if their initial contracts were different.

Traditionally, the courts have declined to permit unsecured creditors to include postpetition attorneys fees in the amounts of their claims. Dicta in a Supreme Court case threw this never quite-settled rule into doubt. Travelers Cas. & Surety Co. v. Pacific Gas & Elec. Co., 549 U.S. 443 (2007). The lower courts are now split on the issue, with the weight of authority in favor of allowing post-petition attorneys fees on unsecured claims.

To illustrate the calculation of the amount of an unsecured claim, assume that Maggie purchased computer paper from John on June 1 at an agreed price of $5,000 payable in three months at 12 percent interest, and that Maggie filed for bankruptcy on September 1. John would file a claim for $5,150 ($5,000 principal and $150 accrued interest). If Maggie filed bankruptcy on July 15 instead, the claim would be for $5,075 ($5,000 plus $75 accrued interest). If Maggie made no payments but delayed filing until the following June 1, John would have to consult the contract and applicable contract law to determine the amount of his claim: If his contract entitled him to accrue interest after default at the same contract rate, he would have a claim for $5,600; if the contract provided for a higher rate of interest after the default (sometimes referred to as a *default rate*), as many contracts do, he could claim that higher amount. In addition, if John spent $1,000 in collection costs before the bankruptcy filing, and the contract provided for reimbursement of these costs, he could add that amount to his claim. But John could not claim any amount he would not be entitled to under nonbankruptcy law as of the moment of filing, with the possible exception for attorneys fees mentioned in the preceding paragraph.

If the estate had sufficient assets to pay 10 percent of the claims against it, John's claim of $5,600 (June 1 filing) would yield a check for $560. The remaining $5,040 would be uncollectible. Absent extraordinary circumstances, the bankruptcy court would discharge Maggie from liability for it. If the claim had been larger, including $1,000 in prefiling collection costs and another $500 in default interest, John's claim would have grown to $7,100, and his actual recovery would have risen to $710.

2.   Secured Claims

Calculating the amount of a creditor's secured claim begins with a determination of the amount owing under nonbankruptcy law, as indicated in Bankruptcy Code §502. This step is the same for a secured claim as for an unsecured claim.

The next step is to bifurcate the claim as required under Bankruptcy Code §506(a)(1). That section provides that the claim of a secured creditor can be a *secured claim* only to the extent of the value of the collateral. The remainder of the creditor's claim is an *unsecured claim.* Bankr. Code §506(a)(1). If the value of the collateral is less than the Bankruptcy Code §502 amount of the secured creditor's claim, the effect will be to divide the secured creditor's claim into two claims: One will be a secured claim in an amount equal to the value of the collateral, and the other will be an unsecured claim for the deficiency.

To illustrate this bifurcation of claims, consider an example. If Bonnie Kraemer owes First National Bank $40,000 secured by a boat worth $50,000, First National has a $40,000 allowed secured claim. If the boat were worth only $35,000, First National would have a $35,000 secured claim and a $5,000 unsecured claim. The bank's unsecured claim would be treated just like any other unsecured claim. The treatment of its secured claim is the primary subject of the remainder of this chapter.

The next step in determining the amount of the secured claim is to determine whether the creditor is entitled to accrue postpetition interest, attorneys fees, or costs on its claim. As previously noted, unsecured creditors generally cannot accrue such postpetition charges, even if they were entitled to these charges under their contract and under nonbankruptcy law. Bankruptcy Code §506(b) entitles the holder of a secured claim to accrue postfiling interest, attorneys fees, and costs on its claim when three conditions are met: (1) the attorneys fees and costs must be "reasonable"; (2) payment of the attorneys fees and costs by the debtor must be "provided for under the agreement or state statute under which [the] claim arose"; (3) interest, attorneys fees, and costs can be accrued only to the extent that the value of the collateral exceeds the amount of the claim secured by it. (Bankruptcy lawyers and judges refer to such a claim as being *over secured.*)

Therefore, to continue with the example, if Bonnie Kraemer's debt of $40,000 is secured by a boat worth $50,000 at the time the bankruptcy case is filed, the claim could grow as interest, attorneys fees, and other costs accrue during the bankruptcy case, up to an additional $10,000. The entire secured claim could not exceed the value of the collateral, $50,000. If, on the other hand, the collateral were worth only $35,000, First National's $40,000 claim would be bifurcated into a secured claim of $35,000 and an unsecured claim of $5,000, and neither claim would be permitted to grow. (Bankruptcy lawyers and judges would refer to the $40,000 claim as *undersecured.*) Keep in mind that these rules that prevent interest, attorneys fees, and costs from accruing on a *claim* do not prevent them from accruing on the underlying *debt.*

D. Payments on Unsecured Claims

How much do unsecured creditors typically receive in a bankruptcy? There have been only a handful of empirical studies of recoveries through the bankruptcy system. In the leading study of Chapter 7 recoveries, Professor Dalie Jimenez wrote:

Chapter 7 continues to be the most used chapter of the Bankruptcy Code, accounting for about two out of every three consumer bankruptcies. All of the data reported about asset cases indicate that they are rare, irrespective of whether the filer is a corporate entity or an individual. This Article confirms those findings. Only 7% (169) of the 2,500 individual Chapter 7 cases examined were asset cases. In the median asset case, the trustee captured assets worth $3,411.

Dalie Jimenez, *The Distribution of Assets in Consumer Chapter 7 Bankruptcy Cases*, 83 American Bankruptcy Law Journal 795, 800 (2009). Professor Jimenez reports median total debt in those cases of $61,916. Thus, unsecured creditors get nothing at all in 93 percent of cases, and only a few pennies on the dollar in the remaining 7 percent.

Chapter 11 and Chapter 13 cases yield more. In a multidistrict study conducted by two of us, there was great variation by district, but the average Chapter 13 plan promised a 28 percent recovery to unsecured creditors. Eighteen percent of the Chapter 13 debtors promised full repayment, and another 23 percent promised to repay more than half of their outstanding debts. Of course, this means only that the debtors promised to pay, not that the creditors actually got the money—an important distinction in the debtor–creditor biz.

In a study of large, public company debtors who confirmed Chapter 11 plans from 1991 through 1996, Professor LoPucki found that plans provided 100 percent repayment to general unsecured creditors in 44 of 78 reorganization cases (56 percent). *The Myth of the Residual Owner*, 82 Washington University Law Quarterly 1341 (2004). Bankruptcy Research Database data for the period since 1996 shows that plans provided 100 percent repayment to unsecured creditors in only 6 of 86 cases (7 percent). In most instances these were not just paper recoveries. The distributions were made in stocks, bonds, and promissory notes that the creditors could immediately sell for cash.

The data from these studies lead to two conclusions, both of which must be kept in mind when evaluating the prospects for recovery in a particular case. First, the fate of most unsecured creditors in bankruptcy is not a happy one. The vast majority face discharge of the debts owing to them, with no, or at best, nominal, payment. Second, there are many cases in which unsecured creditors manage a substantial or even a full recovery. Sophisticated unsecured creditors understand that to know what they will get from a bankruptcy case, they need to know the circumstances of the particular case.

E.   Bankruptcy Sales

1.   The Sale Process

As we discussed in the preceding assignment, one purpose of bankruptcy procedure is to maximize the creditors' recovery by maximizing the sale price of the debtors' property. As we saw in Assignment 4, judicial sale procedures are often grossly ineffective in that regard. Chapter 7 provides a sale procedure *types of Chpt 7 Sales*

541(a)

that is generally much more effective. Under the supervision of the bank-ruptcy court, the trustee sells the property in whatever manner the trustee thinks will maximize the net proceeds. The broad leeway given to the trustee permits alternative forms of sale, such as going-out-of-business sales at the business sites, sales in already established markets, or sales through brokers, to name just a few.

When the trustee liquidates the property of the estate, the trustee ordinarily sells only the debtor's equity in property subject to a security interest, because that is all the estate has succeeded to under Bankruptcy Code §541(a). The trustee does that by making the sale "subject to" the secured creditor's lien. For example, if Bonnie Kraemer's boat were worth $50,000 and the only lien against it was the $40,000 security interest of First National Bank, the trustee would sell the estate's interest for $10,000. The buyer would take the boat subject to the bank's $40,000 lien and the trustee would distribute the $10,000 purchase price to the unsecured creditors, as set forth in Bankruptcy Code §726(a).

The sale in this example would terminate the automatic stay with regard to the boat. Bankr. Code §362(c)(1). The bankruptcy case might continue, but the boat would no longer be part of it. First National Bank would be free to foreclose its lien, just as if there had not been a bankruptcy. As a practical matter, foreclosure probably would not be necessary. The buyer probably bought with full knowledge of First National's lien and its ability to foreclose it, and had already set aside $40,000 to pay First National.

If the boat were worth $35,000 instead of $50,000, the debtor's interest (bare ownership) would have become property of the estate. But that interest would have been of inconsequential value to the estate: The trustee would have a difficult time finding a responsible buyer for a $35,000 boat that was subject to a $40,000 lien. In fact, ownership of such a boat probably would have been a financial burden on the trustee to fulfill its minimal obligation to the secured creditor. The trustee would have had to incur storage charges. Section 554(a) of the Bankruptcy Code authorizes the trustee to *abandon* property of the estate that is burdensome or of inconsequential value to the estate. When a trustee abandons property, it ceases to be property of the estate and ownership reverts to the debtor. Because the automatic stay protects the debtor as well as the estate, Bankr. Code §362(a)(5), the secured creditor must still move to lift the stay before continuing with foreclosure.

One other disposition of collateral is common in bankruptcy. Under some circumstances, the trustee can sell the collateral "free and clear of liens." Bankr. Code §363(f). For example, assume again that Bonnie Kraemer's boat was worth only $35,000, but the circumstances were such that the trustee was entitled to sell it free and clear of liens. The trustee presumably would sell it for $35,000 in cash. The sale would transfer First National's lien from the boat to the proceeds of sale. The amount of First National's secured claim would then be limited not by the value of the boat, *approximately* $35,000, but by the value of the proceeds, *exactly* $35,000. A secured creditor may also see a trustee's greater flexibility in conducting a sale as likely to yield more money on liquidation and may ask the trustee to conduct the sale.

If the sale of the boat free and clear of liens brought $50,000 instead, First National's entire claim would be secured. The trustee would pay $40,000 to First National and $10,000 would remain in the estate. The circumstances under which a trustee can sell collateral free and clear of liens will be considered in greater detail in Assignment 27.

2.   Who Pays the Sale Expenses?

The preceding example makes little mention of the expenses that would have been incurred by the trustee in storing or selling the boat. Yet some expenses will be incurred almost any time a trustee sells property. Initially, the trustee will incur them, by, for example, contracting for the services of a real estate broker. When the trustee sells property subject to a security interest, can these expenses be passed along to the secured creditor by deducting them from the secured creditor's proceeds of sale? Or must the estate bear the expenses? In some situations, the resolution of this issue will be critical. Consider, for example, a house that probably can be sold for $1,000,000, but only through a real estate broker who will charge a $60,000 fee. If the mortgage against this house is $920,000, the estate's interest might be worth $20,000 or $80,000, depending on who must bear the expenses of sale.

Resolution of this issue is found in Bankruptcy Code §506(c), which authorizes a trustee who has incurred "reasonable, necessary costs and expenses of preserving, or disposing of" property securing an allowed secured claim to recover them from the property. That language is ambiguous, however, as to whether the trustee deducts the costs and expenses from the secured creditor's share of the proceeds, from the debtor's share of the proceeds, or from some combination of the two. The ambiguity is at least partially resolved by the language limiting the trustee's right to deduct from the proceeds "to the extent of any benefit to [the secured creditor]." That is, absent benefit to the secured creditor from the trustee's expenditures, the trustee cannot deduct anything from the proceeds of sale.

Some ambiguity remains: "benefit" in comparison to what? Selling through a broker instead of selling without a broker? Paying for a security service instead of letting the property be destroyed by vandals? If this were the comparison, trustees would virtually always be able to charge their costs and expenses to the collateral. In *In re Wine Boutique, Inc.,* 117 B.R. 506 (Bankr. W.D. Mo. 1990), the court answered the "In comparison to what?" question in a manner that cost the secured creditor in that case but would favor the secured creditors in many other cases. In that case, the debtor in possession (a "trustee") hired a real estate broker to sell its liquor store. The agent sold the store for $338,000, which all agreed was a fair price. Twin City State Bank held a lien against the store for an amount in excess of $338,000. The trustee nevertheless sought to deduct the $21,000 fee it paid the broker from the proceeds of sale before turning them over to Twin City. Having identified the issue as whether Twin City "benefitted from the sale," the Court answered the question in the affirmative—and stuck Twin City with the costs:

[In bankruptcy] Twin City did not have to foreclose on the property and incur the financial burdens, and time burdens, that are usually associated with such action. Instead, Twin City was freed from these problems by virtue of the broker's prompt disposition of the property. Further, had *Twin City lifted the stay and taken possession of the realty and the personalty, it would have had to sell same and pay its broker a commission also.* [Emphasis added.] 117 B.R. 506 (Bankr. W.D. Mo. 1990).

Notice the comparison employed by the court to answer the "benefit" question. The court compares what actually happened with what would have happened if the stay had been lifted and the secured creditor had dealt with the problem on its own.

Apply this reasoning to the hypothetical in which the trustee incurs $60,000 of selling expense to sell property subject to a $920,000 lien for a gross price of $1,000,000. The result is that the trustee cannot recover the $60,000 expenditure from the secured creditor's $920,000 share of the proceeds. The $60,000 selling expenses will be paid from the estate's share, leaving only $20,000 for distribution to unsecured creditors. The reason is that the secured creditor did not benefit from the trustee's expenditure of the brokerage fee. Had the secured creditor lifted the stay and taken possession of the house in this example, it would most likely have had to sell the house and pay its broker a commission as well. But unlike *Wine Boutique*, the loss here would not have come to rest on the secured creditor: In this hypothetical, the secured creditor is protected by an equity in the property, so the secured creditor could have, under state law, added the costs of foreclosure to the amount of its secured debt, and still recovered the entire debt from the proceeds of sale. The secured creditor does not "benefit" from the trustee's costs and expenses because even if the secured creditor incurred those expenses itself, it would have been reimbursed from the sale of the collateral.

The result is that a trustee's sale of an *undersecured* creditor's collateral will ordinarily benefit that creditor and be deducted from its recovery. But the trustee's sale of property when the debt is sufficiently *over secured* will not. The actual outcome often depends on a complex analysis of what would have happened if the stay had been lifted and the secured creditor had been permitted to liquidate the collateral.

F.   Secured Creditor Entitlements

1.   General Rules

In reorganization cases, the debtor typically seeks to keep the collateral and to continue using it. The collateral may be anything from a car or wedding ring in a Chapter 13 to millions of dollars' worth of factory equipment or a hotel or office building in a Chapter 11. The debtor's plan may be to reduce the amount of the secured debt, to reschedule payment over a longer period of time, or both. The debtor can accomplish these things over the objection of the secured creditor, if at all, only through confirmation of a Chapter 11 plan or a Chapter 13 plan.

The confirmation of a corporate debtor's Chapter 11 plan discharges the old secured debts and payment schedules and substitutes new ones. Bankr. Code §1141(d)(1)(A). The plan must specify that the creditor retain its lien under Bankruptcy Code §1129(b)(2)(A)(i)(I), but after confirmation, the lien secures only the new debt. The confirmation of a plan to which the creditor has not agreed is graphically referred to by bankruptcy lawyers and judges as a *cramdown*.

Individual debtors under Chapter 11 or Chapter 13 receive a discharge only after the debtor completes all the payments under the plan, which is materially different from the discharge at confirmation for corporate debtors under Chapter 11. Bankr. Code §§1141(d)(5) and 1328(a). The general rule is that once the individual debtor completes plan payments to unsecured creditors, the secured debts will be similarly stripped down to the value of the collateral by entry of the discharge. Exceptions to the general rule exist in Chapters 11 and 13 for the mortgage on the debtor's principal residence and in Chapter 13 for any lien on an automobile the debtor purchased in the 2½ years before bankruptcy. Bankr. Code §§1123(b)(5), 1322(b)(5), 1325(a)(5). Because a principal residence and automobiles are likely to be an individual debtor's most substantial assets, it might be said that the "exception" in this instance is really the general rule.

Debtors and their secured creditors often agree on the treatment to be accorded the secured creditors under plans, but the negotiations take place in the shadow of what the court would do in the absence of agreement. The terms agreed upon are usually just the parties' best estimate of what the court would impose. For that reason, we examine the statutory standards for cramdown with an eye to determining the minimum repayment that the court will consider "fair and equitable," which is the amount the plan proponent will therefore be entitled to cram down. The minimums are basically the same under both Chapter 11 and Chapter 13. Compare Bankruptcy Code §1129(b)(2)(A) with Bankruptcy Code §1325(a)(5). The rules are most clearly stated in the latter section. Under that section, unless the secured creditor accepts (agrees to its treatment under) the plan, the debtor must either:

1. surrender the collateral to the secured creditor in satisfaction of the secured claim, or
2. distribute to the creditor, on account of the secured claim, property with a value as of the effective date of the plan that is not less than the amount of the allowed secured claim.

The first alternative is clear and is one most debtors want to avoid. The second requires some explanation. It essentially establishes a three-step process for testing the adequacy of the proposed distribution to a secured creditor. The first step is to determine the amount of the allowed secured claim. The second is to determine the value of the proposed distribution. The final step is to determine that the latter is at least equal to the former.

Although the secured claim must be paid in full, the payment promised under the plan need not be immediate or in cash. The debtor need only promise the creditor property that has a value at least as great as the amount of the secured claim. Theoretically, the property handed over might be an automobile or an elephant. When it is real estate, the lawyers refer to them as "eat dirt plans." But nearly always the property is a promise of future payments. The payments are usually regular monthly, quarterly, or annual payments (although an occasional case may provide for a balloon payment at some specified time in the future). Chapter 13 generally requires equal monthly payments to secured creditors, Bankr. Code §1325(a)(5)(B)(iii)(I). Thus a Chapter 13 debtor, for example, might propose to pay $300 per month for three years on her car loan. A Chapter 11 debtor might propose irregular payments that reflect the odd times when the debtor expects to have cash available. A farmer, for example, might propose to pay $30,000 of the secured claim on the effective date of the plan and the balance in a lump sum when the debtor sells the wheat crop next August.

2. Valuing Future Payments

It is not sufficient that the payments total the *amount* of the allowed secured claim. They must have a *value* as of the effective date of the plan of that amount. (The "effective date of the plan" is nowhere defined in the Bankruptcy Code, but it is generally understood to be a date, specified in the plan, about 10 to 30 days after confirmation.) Of course, a payment of $1,000 made on the effective date of the plan has a value of $1,000 as of that date. But a promissory note, delivered on the effective date of the plan, promising to pay $1,000, without interest, one year after the effective date, will have a value lower than $1,000.

Effective date of the plan [handwritten margin note]

This concept — that money is worth more to a person if the person gets it sooner — is generally referred to as the *time value of money.* To illustrate the concept, assume that the market rate of interest is 10 percent. In the market in which that rate was fixed, some parties (lenders) are agreeing to pay $100 now in return for the agreement of other parties (borrowers) to pay back $110 one year later. If both lenders and borrowers are acting voluntarily (in some sense at least), this market is telling us that $100 now is the equivalent in value of $110 a year from now.

It follows that the amount of money that must be paid at some later time to have a present value of $X as of the effective date of the plan is $X plus interest at the market rate from the effective date of the plan to the date of payment. So, for example, if a creditor's allowed secured claim is $100, any plan that proposes to pay the creditor at least $100 plus interest at the market rate from the effective date of the plan to the date of payment will meet the "value" requirement. The promise of future payments will have a *present value,* as of the effective date of the plan, of at least $100.

In establishing a market rate of interest, the participants in a market consider a number of factors. They estimate the effects of inflation and the likelihood that $100 paid back in a year will not purchase as much as would $100 today. They also consider the risk that this particular borrower or borrowers of this type will not repay the loan or will not repay it in full. The greater the par-

oversecured 506 [handwritten margin note]

ties' assessments of both inflation and risk, the higher the charge for the use of the creditor's money and the higher the interest rate for the loan.

The term *market rate of interest* is necessarily ambiguous. At any given time, money is being borrowed and lent at many different rates of interest in many different "markets." For example, a bank may be borrowing money from the Federal Reserve at 6.5 percent and paying interest on short-term deposits at 7 percent and long-term deposits at 8 percent, while at the same time it is lending money on home loans at 8.5 percent, on commercial loans at rates from 9 percent to 12 percent, and charging 19 percent on outstanding credit card balances. If there is such a thing as a market rate of interest, each of these rates must represent a different market. To which market should the court look to fulfill the objectives of the Bankruptcy Code provisions regarding cramdown? In the following case, the Supreme Court faced precisely that question.

Till v. SCS Credit Corporation

541 U.S. 465 (2004)

STEVENS, J.,

On October 2, 1998, petitioners Lee and Amy Till, residents of Kokomo, Indiana, purchased a used truck from Instant Auto Finance for $6,395 plus $330.75 in fees and taxes. They made a $300 down payment and financed the balance of the purchase price by entering into a retail installment contract that Instant Auto immediately assigned to respondent, SCS Credit Corporation. Petitioners' initial indebtedness amounted to $8,285.24—the $6,425.75 balance of the truck purchase plus a finance charge of 21% per year for 136 weeks, or $1,859.49. Under the contract, petitioners agreed to make 68 biweekly payments to cover this debt; Instant Auto—and subsequently respondent—retained a purchase money security interest that gave it the right to repossess the truck if petitioners defaulted under the contract.

On October 25, 1999, petitioners, by then in default on their payments to respondent, filed a joint petition for relief under Chapter 13 of the Bankruptcy Code. At the time of the filing, respondent's outstanding claim amounted to $4,894.89, but the parties agreed that the truck securing the claim was worth only $4,000. In accordance with the Bankruptcy Code, therefore, respondent's secured claim was limited to $4,000, and the $894.89 balance was unsecured.

The proposed plan also provided that petitioners would pay interest on the secured portion of respondent's claim at a rate of 9.5% per year. Petitioners arrived at this "prime-plus" or "formula rate" by augmenting the national prime rate of approximately 8% (applied by banks when making low-risk loans) to account for the risk of nonpayment posed by borrowers in their financial position.

11 U.S.C. §1325(a)(5)(B) does not mention the term "discount rate" or the word "interest." Rather, it simply requires bankruptcy courts to ensure that the property to be distributed to a particular secured creditor over the life of a bankruptcy plan has a total "value, as of the effective date of the plan," that equals or exceeds the value of the creditor's allowed secured claim—in this case, $4,000.

That command is easily satisfied when the plan provides for a lump-sum payment to the creditor. Matters are not so simple, however, when the debt is to be discharged by a series of payments over time. A debtor's promise of future payments is worth less than an immediate payment of the same total amount because the creditor cannot use the money right away, inflation may cause the value of the dollar to decline before the debtor pays, and there is always some risk of nonpayment. The challenge for bankruptcy courts reviewing such repayment schemes, therefore, is to choose an interest rate sufficient to compensate the creditor for these concerns.

Although §1325(a)(5)(B) entitles the creditor to property whose present value objectively equals or exceeds the value of the collateral, it does not require that the terms of the cram down loan match the terms to which the debtor and creditor agreed prebankruptcy, nor does it require that the cram down terms make the creditor subjectively indifferent between present foreclosure and future payment. Indeed, the very idea of a "cram down" loan precludes the latter result: By definition, a creditor forced to accept such a loan would prefer instead to foreclose. Thus, a court choosing a cram down interest rate need not consider the creditor's individual circumstances, such as its prebankruptcy dealings with the debtor or the alternative loans it could make if permitted to foreclose. Rather, the court should aim to treat similarly situated creditors similarly, and to ensure that an objective economic analysis would suggest the debtor's interest payments will adequately compensate all such creditors for the time value of their money and the risk of default.

Taking its cue from ordinary lending practices, the [formula] approach begins by looking to the national prime rate, reported daily in the press, which reflects the financial market's estimate of the amount a commercial bank should charge a creditworthy commercial borrower to compensate for the opportunity costs of the loan, the risk of inflation, and the relatively slight risk of default. Because bankrupt debtors typically pose a greater risk of nonpayment than solvent commercial borrowers, the approach then requires a bankruptcy court to adjust the prime rate accordingly. The appropriate size of that risk adjustment depends, of course, on such factors as the circumstances of the estate, the nature of the security, and the duration and feasibility of the reorganization plan.

We do not decide the proper scale for the risk adjustment, as the issue is not before us. The Bankruptcy Court in this case approved a risk adjustment of 1.5%, and other courts have generally approved adjustments of 1% to 3%. Respondent's core argument is that a risk adjustment in this range is entirely inadequate to compensate a creditor for the real risk that the plan will fail. There is some dispute about the true scale of that risk—respondent claims that more than 60% of Chapter 13 plans fail, but petitioners argue that the failure rate for approved Chapter 13 plans is much lower. We need not resolve that dispute. It is sufficient for our purposes to note that, under 11 U.S.C. §1325(a)(6), a court may not approve a plan unless, after considering all creditors' objections and receiving the advice of the trustee, the judge is persuaded that "the debtor will be able to make all payments under the plan and to comply with the plan." Together with the cram down provision, this requirement obligates the court to select a rate high enough to compensate the creditor for its risk but not so high as to doom the plan. If the court determines that the likelihood of default is so high as to necessitate an "eye-popping" interest rate, 301 F.3d at 593 (Rovner, J., dissenting), the plan probably should not be confirmed.

————————

Till is a Chapter 13 case about the interest rate on a $4,000 automobile loan. The amount in issue was only a few hundred dollars. But to a debtor struggling to get by, that might be a large amount of money. In a large Chapter 11 case, the loans might be hundreds of millions or even billions of dollars. In those cases, the significance of the plan's rate of interest should be obvious. If the parties cannot agree on a rate of interest, the bankruptcy court will determine one. The courts are split on whether *Till*'s "prime plus" formula applies in Chapter 11 cases, with some courts using *Till* and others using different formulas to simulate a "market rate of interest."

Problem Set 7

7.1.   You are still counsel to CompuSoft (see Problem 6.1). CFO Martha Ertman wants you to go over the calculation of a claim so that they can file one correctly when a debtor files for bankruptcy. Ertman has picked out one of the outstanding debts—$30,000 worth of repair work done for Argossy, Inc. The contract provides for interest at 18 percent per year for all accounts, beginning at billing. The market rate of interest is 12 percent. The work was done on February 15 and the bill was sent to Argossy on March 15. Argossy didn't pay, and it filed for bankruptcy on September 15. The bankruptcy case is still pending on December 15, when you consult with Ertman. You also note that you spent two hours working on the case in August, for which you billed CompuSoft $400, but the contract between Argossy and CompuSoft says nothing about who will pay collection costs. How much is the claim in the Argossy case? Explain to Ertman how you arrived at the calculation. Bankr. Code §502(b).

7.2.   Several months after the meeting in Problem 7.1, Ertman called you to say that she just received the trustee's Final Report and Account showing that after payment of the expenses of administration and the other priority debt, there will be $59,575 available for distribution to general unsecured creditors in the Chapter 7 case. Unsecured claims (including CompuSoft's) total $1,191,500. She wants to know what that means for CompuSoft.

7.3.   Another of your firm's most active clients is Commercial Investors (CI), a consortium of private investors that places high-risk loans with small businesses. Today Andrea Wu, the vice-president for the Workouts department, asks you to file a proof of claim against Speedo Printing, a small company that filed for Chapter 11 three months ago. According to CI's records, at the time Speedo filed, it owed CI $340,000 plus six months of interest at 12 percent per year. The loan was secured by an interest in Speedo's printing equipment, which was appraised a couple of months ago at $400,000.

a. Assuming that collateral value holds up in bankruptcy court, how much is CI's claim? Bankr. Code §§502, 506.

b. If the court also used a 12 percent interest rate for the pending bankruptcy, how much should CI expect to be paid under a plan of reorganization that is confirmed today? Bankr. Code §1129(b)(2)(A)(i)(II).

c. How much should CI expect to be paid if the reorganization plan is not confirmed for another year?

7.4. Wu is back in your office about a week later. She had the property reappraised, and it seems that the fair market value is more like $325,000. (The earlier appraisal was wrong.) She has also learned that the debtor estimates that there will be sufficient assets to pay the unsecured creditors about 10 percent of their outstanding claims.

a. Describe CI's claim now. Bankr. Code §§502, 506.

b. What should CI expect to be paid under a plan of reorganization?

c. Does it matter to CI whether the plan is confirmed today or a year from today?

7.5. Another week passes and Wu is back again. At your request, she had been searching her records for a copy of the security agreement. She has finally come to the conclusion that no security agreement was ever signed.

a. Now what is the nature of CI's claim? Bankr. Code §§502, 506.

b. If the 10 percent payout for unsecured creditors persists, what should CI expect under a plan of reorganization?

7.6. As a member of the U.S. Panel of Trustees, you have been appointed to serve as trustee in a number of Chapter 7 cases. One assigned today is the case of Tonia Perez, whose summer house is in the estate. The summer house is encumbered by a mortgage to First Capital. The amount currently owing on the mortgage is $850,000, which includes interest accrued to date at the contract rate of 10 percent per annum. You talked with the real estate broker you ordinarily use in such cases. She told you that she thought she could get $1,000,000 for the summer house. But the market is slow, and she estimates that there is only about a 50 percent chance that the sale would take place in the next six months. As usual, she would discount her commission from the 7 percent that most brokers charge to the 6 percent she charges you. She estimates your share of the other costs of sale and the prorations, including $7,000 in property taxes, at $10,000.

a. If you are able to sell this house in exactly six months, how much money will the sale produce for the estate? Bankr. Code §541(a)(1).

b. How does that amount vary if you sell at an earlier or later time? Is trying to sell the house the right thing to do? See Bankr. Code §§506(b) and (c).

c. Can First Capital prevent you from trying to sell? Bankr. Code §§362(d)(1), 554(b).

7.7. Martin O'Keefe recently filed under Chapter 7, and you were appointed trustee. After you approved O'Keefe's exemptions, abandoned property that would be worthless to the estate, gathered and liquidated the remaining nonexempt property, and made allowance for payment of your own fees, you have the following:

Proceeds from sale of Piper aircraft	$214,000
Proceeds from sale of coin collection	26,000
Proceeds from turnover of cash in bank account	2,200
Total	$242,200

O'Keefe has only one secured creditor, Friendly Credit, who is owed $150,000 against the Piper aircraft.

    a.   If O'Keefe owes $300,000 to other creditors, all unsecured, what distributions do you make? What is the percentage paid to the unsecured creditors?

    b.   If Friendly Credit's security interest was in the coin collection instead of the Piper aircraft, what would your distributions be? What would the percentage paid to the unsecured creditors be?

Chapter 3.   Creation and Scope of Security Interests

Assignment 8:   Formalities for Attachment

In earlier assignments we compared secured creditors' collection rights with unsecured creditors' collection rights. We saw that secured creditors' rights are more powerful. As a result, secured creditors are more likely to collect the amounts owing to them.

In this assignment we turn to the question of how someone becomes a secured creditor. As in earlier assignments, our focus continues to be on security interests created under Article 9 and, for comparison purposes, on mortgages and deeds of trust created under real estate law.

Creditors taking security interests under Article 9 or real estate law have one key characteristic in common: They obtain their status by contract with the debtor. Article 9 secured creditors and real estate mortgagees are, by definition, consensual creditors. They have enhanced collection rights because, at an earlier time in the relationship, their debtors consented to those rights. In this assignment we explore that agreement between debtor and creditor.

A.   A Prototypical Secured Transaction

Most security interests are created as part of transactions in which money is lent or property is sold. When a bank lends money to a corporation, for example, it may insist, as a condition of the loan, that the corporation grant it a security interest in some or all of the corporation's assets. Similarly, an automobile dealer who sells on credit will nearly always require the buyer to give a security interest in the automobile purchased.

The story that follows describes an ordinary secured transaction: a debtor who borrows money from a bank to buy a business.

Fisherman's Pier: A Prototypical Secured Transaction

Kenneth Kettering is a celebrity chef with his own television show called "Mr. Chef." For several years, he has worked at Fisherman's Pier, a restaurant owned by Stella Parker. Stella recently decided to sell Fisherman's Pier and retire. When Kenneth heard the news, he went to talk to her about buying the business. In a series of meetings, Kenneth and Stella worked out the terms of sale. Stella would sell Fisherman's Pier, including the kitchen equipment, furniture, fixtures, furnishings, building lease, and goodwill to Kenneth for $1,000,000 in cash.

Kenneth did not have $1,000,000, but he had family and friends lined up to invest in his venture. He could raise enough money to provide working capital for the business, and to apply about $400,000 toward the purchase price. The rest would have to be borrowed. Kenneth retained attorney Ellen Bartell to draft an "Agreement for Purchase and Sale," which he and Stella signed. The agreement was contingent on Kenneth getting a $600,000 bank loan to complete the purchase. That is, if Kenneth could not get the loan, neither party would be bound by the contract.

Kenneth made an appointment to see Maura Sun in the Commercial Loan Department of First National Bank. In their first meeting, they talked about Kenneth's television show, the restaurant business, Kenneth's business experience, the Agreement for Purchase and Sale, and some of the key terms on which First National makes commercial loans. Before Kenneth left, Sun gave him a copy of the bank's loan application form.

The application form asked for essentially four kinds of information. The first was personal information about Kenneth. What was his date of birth? His social security number? Where had he lived during what periods of time? Was he married? The second was information about his financial condition. What did he own? What debts did he owe? What had his income been over the past several years? The form required that he attach copies of his income tax returns for the past two years. The third was information about his credit history. From whom had he borrowed money in the past? What credit cards did he have? Had he ever filed for bankruptcy? Been foreclosed against? The last part of the form was a description of the collateral he could offer for the loan. Kenneth completed the application in a couple of days and returned it to Maura Sun. Sun told Kenneth that it "looked like everything was in order" and she thought there would be no problems with the loan. Sun said she would get back to Kenneth within about a week.

Sun ordered a credit check on Kenneth from a credit reporting agency, personally called three of Kenneth's credit references, and scheduled Kenneth's application for a meeting of the bank's loan committee. Both the report and the references were good. Sun presented the loan application to the committee and it was approved, contingent on an appraisal of the restaurant at a value of at least $1,000,000. The bank's appraiser visited the restaurant, looked at the equipment, measured the square footage of the building, checked the business receipts for the past year, collected information on some comparable sales, and appraised the restaurant as having a "market value" of $1,000,000.

Sun then called Kenneth and told him the good news. The loan had been approved and Scott Pryor, the bank's lawyer, would "handle the closing." The lawyers scheduled the loan closing for a date about three weeks away and began preparing the documents and gathering the information they would need.

At the bank's request, Kenneth signed an authorization for Sun to file a financing statement. Pryor drafted a financing statement on the official form set forth in UCC §9-521 and sent it to the Secretary of State for filing in the UCC filing system. The financing statement would provide public notice of the bank's security interest in Fisherman's Pier. Pryor also ordered a search of the UCC filing system for other financing statements filed against Stella Parker or Fisherman's Pier and a search of the county real estate records for mortgages filed against them. The bank wanted a security interest in the assets ahead of all others; only through such a search would Pryor know whether there were already other security interests against those assets. The search results showed no relevant filings in the real estate recording system and only one financing statement other than First National's. It was in favor of Valley State Bank, which had lent money to Stella using the restaurant as collateral. Pryor sent an email to Valley State Bank, advising Valley State that Stella was selling the restaurant and requesting that Valley State advise him of the exact amount necessary to pay off the loan. He also asked that Valley State authorize the filing of a "termination statement" in the UCC records.

The closing was held as scheduled at Ellen Bartell's office. Kenneth signed a promissory note for $600,000 and a Security Agreement (a copy of a security agreement appears in Assignment 15). Stella delivered a bill of sale for the restaurant property, an assignment of her rights under the lease, and the keys to the restaurant. Pryor delivered First National Bank's check to an employee from Valley State Bank. The check was for $388,390, the exact balance outstanding on the Valley State loan, with interest computed up to the day of the closing. The Valley State employee gave Pryor the signed Authorization to File Termination Statement. Then he delivered a check for the balance of the $600,000 loan (after deducting the expenses, including Pryor's attorneys fees) to Stella. Kenneth paid the balance of the purchase price with a cashier's check he obtained that morning with money from his investors and from his own savings. At that point Stella had her $1,000,000 sale price, less the amount paid to Valley State. Kenneth had his restaurant, subject to a $600,000 security interest in favor of First National. First National had Kenneth's promissory note for $600,000, secured by a first security interest in the restaurant assets. First National could be reasonably confident that if the loan was not paid when due, it would have the right to take possession of the restaurant and sell it to satisfy the outstanding debt. The parties all shook hands and agreed among themselves that the closing was complete.

_400000_
equity

Secured transactions vary in detail and complexity. As the hundreds of published cases each year attest, some are less than orderly. Nonetheless, the transaction described here is typical of many commercial credit transactions.

Two aspects of the Fisherman's Pier story require some additional explanation. First, as you were reading about the closing, you may have wondered what would have happened if one of the checks or documents had been missing. Most closings are conducted on the implicit understanding that unless all of the contemplated checks and documents are exchanged, none that are exchanged should be taken from the room or be of any effect. If one or more are missing, the parties will select one member of the group to hold the checks and documents currently available until all the contemplated checks and documents are available. Only then is the person selected as escrow agent authorized to deliver any of them and only then do they take effect.

Second, while the bank in this story filed a financing statement, it is important to realize that this step was not necessary to create a security interest enforceable against Kenneth. UCC §9-203(b). That a security interest is *enforceable* against the debtor means that, in the event of default, the secured party

_9-203(b)_

[margin note: perfect]

can foreclose on the collateral. By contrast, for a security interest to have priority over some other creditors, such as another secured party who lends against the same collateral, the creditor must *perfect* the interest by having the debtor authorize a financing statement and filing that statement in the public records.

The subject of priority is reserved for Part Two of this book. We mention the financing statement here only because nearly all creditors who create a security interest choose to take the additional step of perfecting it against third parties. Not to mention the financing statement would have made the story unrealistic.

As parties create security interests, they themselves sometimes confuse the formalities necessary to create a security interest with those necessary to perfect it. As you read the following section about the formalities necessary to create a security interest, the reasons for this confusion should become clearer.

B.   Formalities for Article 9 Security Interests

[margin note: Security interest attach]

UCC §9-203(b) lists three formalities required for the creation of a security interest enforceable against the debtor: (1) Either the collateral must be in the possession of the secured creditor or the debtor must have "authenticated a security agreement which contains a description of the collateral"; (2) value must have been given; (3) the debtor must have rights in the collateral. Only when all three of these requirements have been met does the security interest *attach* to the collateral and become enforceable against the debtor. UCC §§9-203(a) and (b).

1.   *Possession or Authenticated Security Agreement*

[margin note: Authenticated can be email or oral NOT just written]

Article 9 authorizes two different kinds of security agreements. Most agreements are authenticated records, UCC §9-102(a)(70). Usually "authenticated record" is just a fancy way of saying a signed writing. The term is generic, however, to allow for other possible ways to document the agreement, such as email. Instead of an authenticated record, the secured creditor may create a security interest by taking possession of the goods pursuant to an oral agreement to create the interest. UCC §9-203(b)(3)(B).

[margin note: oral agreement 9-203(b)(3)(B)]

Pawns are perhaps the most familiar example of security agreements made effective by possession. In a typical pawn, the debtor goes into the pawnshop with some valuable item. (In B-movies of the 1930s and 1940s, a down-and-out musician brings in his instrument to signify that he has reached the end of the line both financially and spiritually. This usually happens in the opening scene, before he meets the woman who saves his life, and so on. It is usually drizzling rain when he approaches the pawnshop.) The pawnshop offers to lend some amount against the goods, typically for 30 days. It holds the goods for the agreed period, during which time the debtor (if fortunes reverse quickly) can come in to pay off the loan and reclaim the collateral. If the debtor does not redeem the property by paying the loan, the pawnbroker sells the collateral and — pursuant to pawnbroker statutes that supersede Article 9 — keeps the proceeds of sale. As a bankruptcy judge, now-Professor Bruce Markell noted:

[handwritten margin note: pawnbroker statutes supersede article 9]

> Pawning one's goods differs from borrowing against them; in a typical pawn, a debtor deposits goods with the pawnbroker, and receives money in return. If the customer does not "redeem" his pawn within a specified time, tradition has it that the power to sell the goods deposited automatically passes to the pawnbroker. If the pawnbroker's subsequent sale of the goods does not cover the loan, the pawnbroker takes the loss; conversely, if the pawnbroker sells the goods for more than the money lent, custom allows the pawnbroker to keep the surplus. Another way to characterize the transaction is as a nonrecourse loan by the pawnbroker to the customer, with agreed strict foreclosure on the redemption date. . . .
>
> *[handwritten margin note: Non recourse loan]*
>
> Despite its venerable history, pawnbroking has lately experienced something of a public relations crisis. Pawnbrokers are regulated in a manner designed to deter personal property theft, and often are found in low-income neighborhoods on the fringe of respectability. Despite efforts to improve this image, "the negative portrait lingers; pawnshops continue to be cast as nuisance businesses, in the company of tattoo shops and massage parlors, and somewhere in rank between liquor stores and houses of prostitution." Jarret C. Oeltjen, Florida Pawnbroking: An Industry in Transition, 23 Fla. St. U. L. Rev. 995, 996 (1966).

In re Schwalb, 347 B.R. 726 (Bankr. D. Nev. 2006).

Pawnshops aside, possessory secured lending is rare. Most debtors who borrow against their property want to keep and use the property while they repay the loan. Those who incur debt to buy a home, an automobile, or production machinery typically are unwilling to defer possession until the debt is paid. Most of the time their creditors don't want possession anyway. Commercial financiers realize that they would be more secure if they took possession of the pigs or packing emulsion against which they lend because they wouldn't have to worry about the collateral's physical disappearance. But the added safety is in most cases insufficient to justify the inconvenience. Even more important, in a commercial context most debtors use the collateral to produce the income to pay the loan. To accommodate them, lenders have devised methods (referred to as *field warehousing*) for taking possession of collateral while at the same time allowing debtors to use it. But even these methods add expense and complexity that most lenders consider unwarranted in most situations. Hence, the most common arrangement is to rely on a written security arrangement and leave the debtor in possession of the collateral.

The prototypical secured transaction is based on a writing. The debtor signs a document called a *security agreement*, which typically contains a description of the collateral, a description of the obligations secured, and other provisions. Those other provisions may define default, specify the rights of the secured creditor on default, require that the debtor care for the collateral and keep it insured, and impose other obligations on the debtor. (Recall that an example of such an agreement appears in Assignment 15.) When the debtor has signed such an agreement, the UCC §9-203(b)(3)(A) requirement of an authenticated security agreement is fulfilled. See UCC §9-102(a)(7).

A third kind of security agreement that is neither oral nor written can also fulfill the requirement of UCC §9-203(b)(3). This third kind must be inscribed on some "medium" on which it can be stored and from which it can be retrieved. An example would be a security agreement typed on a computer and saved to disk, but never printed or signed by hand. Information so inscribed is referred to as a "record." See UCC §9-102(a)(70). To constitute a security agreement of the third kind, the debtor must "with present intention to adopt or accept" the record "attach . . . an electronic sound, symbol or process" to the record or logically associate it with the record. UCC §9-102(a)(7)(B). The language is sufficiently obscure to provide little clue as to the boundaries of the doctrine, but the drafters' intention to validate entirely electronic security agreements is clear. If Kenneth Kettering borrows money from First National Bank, and in the course of that transaction the bank sends Kenneth an email containing an offer of security agreement terms and Kenneth sends an email reply accepting those terms, Kenneth and First National have a security agreement of the third kind—without a writing or a signature.

Although the authenticated security agreement requirement is easy to comply with, in a surprising number of cases the parties manage to get it wrong. Either no security agreement is authenticated by the debtor or the one that is authenticated has no description of the collateral. When that occurs, the secured creditor often attempts to rely on other documents that, although not intended as a security agreement, nevertheless meet the skeletal requirements of UCC §9-203(b)(3). In these cases, the courts are often asked to decide what minimum record will suffice.

In re Schwalb

347 B.R. 726 (Bankr. D. Nev. 2006)

Bruce A. Markell, Bankruptcy Judge.

Ms. Schwalb and her father initially approached Pioneer [Loan and Jewelry, a pawnbroker] in June of 2004. Mr. Schwalb had done business with Pioneer and, at that time, enjoyed some goodwill with it. Ms. Schwalb's Infiniti QX4 Sport Utility Vehicle was offered as collateral, and Pioneer advanced $4,000 against possession of the certificate of title for the vehicle. The parties testified that Ms. Schwalb gave Pioneer her certificate of title after she signed it as seller. The buyer's name was left blank.

When she received the $4,000 in loan proceeds, Ms. Schwalb signed a document referred to by the parties as a pawn ticket. The pawn ticket is a preprinted form used by Pioneer in its pawnbroker business. It is a simple 5-inch-by-8-inch form, with text front and back. Among other things, the front has blanks for describing the property pawned, for the amount of the loan and for the repayment date.

On Ms. Schwalb's pawn ticket, the parties designated the property pawned as an Infiniti QX4 Sport Utility Vehicle, and included its Vehicle Identification Number (VIN). The ticket also contained the loan terms. Ms. Schwalb was to repay the $4,000 in 120 days, plus $1,605 interest. The disclosed annual interest rate was 122.04%. If Ms. Schwalb did not "redeem" the pawn and pay the loan within the 120 days, the pawn ticket indicated that "you shall . . . forfeit all right and interest in the pawned property to the pawnbroker who shall hereby acquire an absolute title to the same." Just before the blank on the pawn ticket in which the parties inserted the description of the Infiniti and its VIN, the pawn ticket indicated, in very small five-point type, "You are giving a security interest in the following property:" Pioneer did not retain possession of the vehicle. Ms. Schwalb drove off in it with her $4,000. Pioneer put the signed certificate of title in a safe on its premises.

1. ATTACHMENT GENERALLY

The initial consequence of Article 9's applicability is that the creation and status of Pioneer's interest is governed by a combination of the common law of contract law and the statutory provisions of Article 9. For an Article 9 security interest to be enforceable, it must "attach." UCC §9-203.

Attachment, in turn, has three requirements: (1) value has to have been given; (2) the debtor must have rights in the collateral; and (3) either (a) the debtor has authenticated a security agreement that provides a description of the collateral, or (b) the secured party possesses the collateral pursuant to a security agreement. UCC §9-203(b)(1)-(3).

Value is present in the form of the loans extended by Pioneer to Ms. Schwalb. [UCC §1-204 (formerly §1-201(44)]. Similarly, there is no doubt that, at the time of each transaction, Ms. Schwalb's ownership rights in the vehicles were sufficient "rights in the collateral" for a security interest to attach.

The issue thus boils down to whether the "debtor authenticated a security agreement that provides a description of the collateral," or whether the collateral was "in the possession of the secured party under UCC §9-313 pursuant to the debtor's security agreement."

A. Authenticated Agreement

Ms. Schwalb contends that the pawn ticket is legally insufficient as a security agreement. At trial, she testified that she did not know what she was signing at the time she received each of the two loans. Each pawn ticket used, however, contained the following preprinted language just before a description of the automobile involved as well as its VIN: "You are giving a security interest in the following property:"

Thus, the only question is whether the agreement also included collateral as security for repayment of the loan. Each pawn ticket definitively described the vehicle at issue, by make, model and VIN. The issue is thus whether the words "[y]ou are giving" adequately "create[] or provide[]" for a security interest in the vehicles. The safest and traditional words to accomplish this task are words of grant or assignment, such as "I hereby grant a security interest in X to secure repayment of my debt to you" or "I assign this property to you to secure what I owe you."

In these phrases, the operative verbs—grant, assign, etc.—are in the present tense and indicate a present act. But the word used by the pawn ticket—"giving"—is not in the present tense but instead is the present participle of the verb "to give." Ms. Schwalb contends that use of the participle "giving" can only be read to refer to Pioneer's description of what Pioneer thought Ms. Schwalb had done or was doing—not as Ms. Schwalb's acknowledgment that she was engaging in a legally significant act. The analogy would be to something like noting that the statement "You are falling" describes an action taken by another rather than separately constituting the act of falling.

But this is a quibble. While a description may not be the act it describes, by signing the pawn ticket Ms. Schwalb acknowledged and adopted the act it described—giving a security interest. Moreover, the statutory verbs are "creates" or "provides." Even if the language did not "create" the security interest as Ms. Schwalb contends, it certainly did provide for "giving" one.

The insistence on formal words of grant or transfer is inconsistent with the structure and intent of Article 9. As the Idaho Supreme Court noted with respect to the original version of Article 9:

> Courts have often repeated that no magic words are necessary to create a security interest and that the agreement itself need not even contain the term "security interest." This is in keeping with the policy of the code that form should not prevail over substance and that, whenever possible, effect should be given to the parties' intent.

Simplot v. Owens, 119 Idaho 243 (1990).

The proper policy considerations are well stated by a leading commentator on Article 9: "There is no requirement for words of grant. In fact, such a requirement smacks of the antiquated formalism the drafters were trying to avoid." 1 CLARK & CLARK, at ¶ 2.02[1][c].

Ms. Schwalb's further argument that she did not understand the import of the words she subscribed to is also unavailing. Even though they appear in tiny five-point type, the words are discernable as an integral part of the pawn ticket. It has long been the common law rule that signing a document authenticates and adopts the words it contains, even if there was a lack of subjective understanding of the words or their legal effect. In essence, people are presumed to be bound by what they sign.

For those who worry—or just wonder—about the people who traipse across our stage, Renee Schwalb, after a few defaults along the way, completed the payments under her Chapter 13 plan. Over four years, she paid a total of $34,288.70 to the trustee. The trustee paid $11,356.88 of that amount to Schwalb's attorney, $3,408.81 to herself for her fees, and $19,523.01 to Pioneer Loan as principal and interest on the $4,000 secured debt. Four years of payments, and the unsecured creditors got nothing.

In *Schwalb*, the court found all of the elements of a security agreement in a single sentence. In other cases, the courts have found those elements spread through two or more documents.

In re Giaimo
440 B.R. 761 (6th Cir. BAP 2010)

ARTHUR I. HARRIS, Bankruptcy Judge.

The issue presented by this appeal is whether an application for certificate of title to a motor vehicle and a certificate of title, both identifying the lienholder, are sufficient under Ohio law to create a security interest in a vehicle.

On June 11, 2009, Evonne M. Giaimo ("Debtor") filed a voluntary petition for relief under chapter 7 of the Bankruptcy Code. Listed on the Debtor's schedules of assets was a 2008 Toyota RAV 4. The Debtor purchased the vehicle in February 2008, with an interest free loan from her grandmother, Veronica O'Keefe ("O'Keefe"). The Debtor and O'Keefe did not execute any formal loan documents.

William Todd Drown ("Trustee") was appointed chapter 7 trustee of the Debtor's bankruptcy estate. The Debtor provided the Trustee with the Application for the Certificate of Title prepared by the dealership where the vehicle was purchased. The application contained a description of the vehicle, identified O'Keefe as the lienholder, and was signed by the Debtor. The Debtor also provided the Trustee with the Ohio Certificate of Title to the vehicle which also identified O'Keefe as lienholder. At the meeting of creditors, the Debtor testified that these are the only documents regarding O'Keefe's lien and security interest in the vehicle. Apart from these two documents, there is no evidence of a written security agreement between the Debtor and O'Keefe.

The term "security agreement" is defined as "an agreement that creates or provides for a security interest." [UCC §9-102(a)(73)]. It has been well established that while no specific words or formalized documents are necessarily required to create a security interest, there must be some written documentation that indicates the parties' intent to create a security interest.

> It thus appears that no special form of words is required to give rise to a security interest. It is, however, necessary that an intent to grant or to create a security interest be manifested. It would be sufficient if the parties use language which leads to the conclusion that it was the intention of the parties that a security interest be created.

Silver Creek Supply v. Powell, 521 N.E.2d 828, 833 (Ohio App. 1987). In their treatise on the UCC, Professors White and Summers comment on how easily a secured party can create an enforceable Article 9 security interest under Section 9-203:

> Consider how little suffices to bind the debtor. For example, it is enough for the debtor to write on the back of an envelope, "I hereby grant bank a security interest in my cattle, John Jones." If the bank makes a loan and the debtor owns the cattle, the parties created a valid security interest despite its informality.

4 White & Summers, *Uniform Commercial Code,* §31-2 (6th ed. 2010). White and Summers further note:

> [UCC §]9-203 does not require more [than a showing that parties intended a security interest] for as [Official] comment 3 [to 9-203] states, the writing requirement is a formal requisite "in the nature of a statute of frauds." A statute of frauds requirement on the model of 2-201 merely contemplates objective indicia of the possibility of an underlying actual agreement—here an agreement for security.

Id. at §31-3.

Rather than requiring one single document evidencing [intent to create a security interest], courts typically "review all the documents between the parties to determine whether a sufficient *written* foundation has been established for the creation of a security interest." *Silver Creek,* 521 N.E.2d at 832 (emphasis in original).

This approach, often referred to as the "composite documents approach," "examines all the documents executed between a debtor and a creditor to determine, if taken together, whether the 'writing or writings, regardless of label, adequately describes the collateral, carries the signature of the debtor, and establishes that in fact a security interest was agreed upon.'" *Belfance v. Buonpane (In re Omega Door Co., Inc.),* 399 B.R. 295, 306 (6th Cir. BAP 2009). Official Comment 3 to [UCC §9-203] explains that the requirement of a writing is "in the nature of a Statute of Frauds."

In *Silver Creek,* the only document available that purported to establish a security agreement was a standardized financing statement. The court concluded that while some financing statements may contain language sufficient to evidence an agreement, "the financing statement herein fails to adequately evidence that the parties manifested, in writing, an intent to create a security interest." In doing so, the court distinguished the facts of the case before it from those in other cases where a security interest was created, including *In re McCormick,* where an application for a certificate of title and issuance of the certificate satisfied the requirement for a security agreement under Michigan's version of UCC §9-203. See *Silver Creek,* 521 N.E.2d at 833.

Another instructive decision is the bankruptcy court's decision in Yoppolo v. Trombley (In re De Vincent), 238 B.R. 722 (Bankr. N.D. Ohio 1999). In *De Vincent,* the debtor owned a vehicle financed by her sister. The debtor and her sister both signed a promissory note, and the debtor's sister was identified as the lienholder on the certificate of title. The promissory note simply identified the parties, the vehicle, the total purchase price, and the monthly payments to be made, but said nothing about a security interest in the vehicle. When the debtor filed for chapter 7 relief, the trustee sought to avoid the sister's security interest and lien on the grounds that the promissory note lacked the necessary language to create a security interest in the vehicle. The debtor's sister asserted that her lien was perfected by virtue of the promissory note and the lien noted on the certificate of title.

The court looked to Article 9 of the UCC, as enacted by Ohio in chapter 1309, to determine whether the sister had a valid security interest in the vehicle. *In re De Vincent,* 238 B.R. at 725-26. Like the case at hand, the only element of [UCC §9-203] at issue was whether there was a valid security agreement. The debtor's sister argued that the promissory note in conjunction with the notation on the certificate of title that listed her as a lienholder demonstrated the necessary intent to create a security interest under the "composite documents" approach. In rejecting the defendant's argument, the court explained that because neither a financing statement, the equivalent of a vehicle's certificate of title, alone, nor a promissory note alone, exhibit the requisite intent to create a security interest, it could not find that the two documents standing together, under the circumstances of the case, demonstrated that the debtor and the defendant intended to create a security interest in the vehicle at issue.

In this case, however, in keeping with the liberal policies of the UCC, we hold, and we believe the Ohio Supreme Court would similarly hold, that the application for certificate of title, a document which was not presented in *De Vincent,* and the certificate of title itself, taken together, constitute a security agreement within the meaning of [UCC §9-203]. While we are aware that other courts have come to the opposite conclusion, we are also in the company of many courts which have reached the same conclusion.

In the present case, the application for a certificate of title is a writing signed by the Debtor and sworn to and subscribed in the presence of a notary. The application specifically identifies the collateral, the Toyota RAV 4 with its vehicle identification number, and instructs the State of Ohio to issue a title showing O'Keefe as lienholder. The application includes the following printed language regarding liens on the motor vehicle:

> The following is a full statement of all liens on said motor vehicle. *If no lien, state "none"*. If more than one lien, attach statement of all additional liens.

In handwriting following the words "Lienholder" and "Address" are: "VERONICA OKEEFE" and "21626 N. 156 DR. Sun City W AZ 85375" respectively. Unlike simple financing statements, which are often filed in anticipation of a *possible* loan and security agreement, an application for a certificate of title is not completed unless there is an actual purchase or transfer of a motor vehicle. When the Debtor signed the application for certificate of title, the form required her to list "a full statement of all liens on said motor vehicle." We can fathom no reason why the Debtor would have signed the application for certificate of title identifying O'Keefe as the lienholder if she did not intend to grant a security interest to O'Keefe in the vehicle.

We therefore hold that the Debtor's application for certificate of title and certificate of title indicate that the parties intended to create a security interest and that the written application for certificate of title constitutes a security agreement within the meaning of [UCC §9-203]. To find otherwise would place undue emphasis on formalism and be contrary to the general principle that the UCC be "liberally construed and applied to promote [its] underlying purposes and policies[,]" including simplification and modernization of "the law governing commercial transactions." [UCC §1-103(a)].

In *Giaimo*, the court applied the "composite document approach," which is also referred to as the "composite document rule" or the "composite document theory." "The composite document rule provides that there need not be a separate document labeled 'security agreement,' but that all relevant loan documents may be examined to determine whether a security agreement exists." In re Wyatt, 338 B.R. 76, 82 (Bankr. W.D. Mo. 2006). The large majority of states recognize the rule's existence, but there are substantial differences in its application.

The differences are principally in what documents courts will consider. Some say they will consider "all the documents executed between a debtor and a creditor." In re Omega Door Co., Inc., 399 B.R. 295, 306 (6th Cir. B.A.P. 2009). Most courts limit consideration to documents created as part of the original loan transaction. For example, the Seventh Circuit refused to consider a document signed by the debtor three years after the loan transaction, saying that "it indicates only that S Coal believed that it had created a security interest at that earlier time." Caterpillar Fin. Services Corp. v. Peoples National Bank, N.A., 710 F.3d 691, 697 (7th Cir. 2013). A few courts have, however, considered documents created after the initial loan transaction.

Some courts require that the documents not be inconsistent with one another. Some go further, requiring "some internal connection with one another" or that there be a "reference" in one document to the other. Most courts will consider documents not signed by the debtor, provided that the debtor did sign at least one document.

Courts rarely consider a financing statement alone to satisfy the documentation requirement, but they frequently consider them along with other documents. Financing statements are weak evidence of the intention to enter into a security agreement because (1) they rarely contain grant language, (2) they frequently describe collateral more expansively than the accompanying security agreements do, (3) they are not signed by the debtor, and (4) they are frequently authorized and filed before the parties have decided to enter into the transaction. See UCC §9-502(d) ("A financing statement may be filed before a security agreement is made or a security interest otherwise attaches.") As one court noted, the debtor may not even have known that the financing statement was filed.

In *Giaimo*, the court pointed out the crucial difference between consideration of a financing statement and consideration of an application for a certificate of title. The financing statement is often filed in anticipation of a *possible* security agreement, while the application for a certificate of title is not completed unless there is an *actual* sale transaction. One must understand the context in which a document was created and the document's function before one can determine what a court should properly infer from its creation.

The consequence of failing to obtain an authenticated security agreement is that the creditor has no security interest. The creditor is, therefore, unsecured.

When the parties intended to create a security agreement and thought they had succeeded, the remedy is surprisingly harsh. Of course, for those who remember covering the Statute of Frauds in first-year contract law, the remedy of nonenforcement even in the face of clear intent of the parties should be familiar.

The competing policy—that written security agreements should *not* be required in every case—is expressed in the doctrine of equitable mortgages. Under that doctrine, the courts can enforce oral security agreements where doing so would be "equitable." The doctrine is impliedly repudiated in the text of UCC §9-203(b)(3). Widows and orphans who want the special collection rights of the Article 9 secured creditor must jump through the hoops like everyone else.

In a common scenario, the debtor signs a security agreement that does not contain a description of collateral. The place in the security agreement for the description may be left blank, or the security agreement may refer to an attached exhibit that is not attached or may not yet even be in existence. On these facts, the courts hold the security agreement to be invalid. In a common variant on these facts, the debtor authorizes the secured creditor to complete the agreement later, and the secured creditor does so. That is, the secured creditor fills in the blank on the security agreement in the intended manner or attaches the intended exhibit. The courts are divided on this variant. A majority hold that the order in which the security agreement is assembled does not matter. In re O & G Leasing, LLC, 456 B.R. 652 (Bankr. S.D. Miss. 2011). But a substantial minority hold that a secured creditor that does not have a valid security agreement cannot create one later, even if authorized to do so. In re Spivey, 1998 WL 34066138 (Bankr. S.D. Ga. 1998).

It is useful to look closely at UCC §9-203(b)(3)(A) to see what it says about the fill-in-the-blanks-later problem. Does that provision require that the description of collateral be in the agreement at the time the agreement is authenticated?

2. Value Has Been Given

A security interest is not enforceable until "value has been given." The drafters of the UCC defined "value" in §1-204 so broadly that the requirement is virtually always met in a commercial transaction. As a result, it is difficult to discern any policy reason for the inclusion of the *value* requirement in UCC §9-203(b)(1). Although the section does not say who must give value, the assumption seems to be that it is the creditor.

In most security agreements the debtors assume numerous obligations (pay the debt, keep the collateral insured, notify the creditor of any change of address, etc.). The debtor's promises clearly constitute value. But the secured creditor may assume few or no obligations. In fact, some forms of security agreements do not even have a place for the secured party's signature. Nevertheless, the creditor typically will have lent money, sold property to the debtor on credit, or promised to do one or the other in reliance on the debtor's grant or promise of a security interest. After all, that's usually why the debtor signed the agreement. It is true that a debtor might sign a security agreement with neither a loan nor the promise of a loan. But in that case, the debtor does not need a "no value given" defense. If the creditor hasn't made a loan, the debtor's defense to any collection effort—whether or not a security interest exists—is that the debtor doesn't owe anything to the creditor.

The definition of "value" used in Article 9 not only encompasses all forms of consideration that would support an ordinary contract, it even includes one form of consideration that does not pass muster in common law contracts: past consideration. UCC §1-204 provides that "a person gives value for rights (the security interest) if he acquires them . . . (2) as security for . . . a pre-existing claim." This means that even in situations where the debtor grants a security interest to secure an already outstanding debt and the creditor neither gives nor promises anything new in return, the creditor has given value under the Code definitions.

It is worth noting the ease with which an unsecured debt can become a secured debt at any time in the debtor-creditor relationship. While the typical transaction includes the grant of security at the time the debt is incurred, a significant portion of commercial transactions involve credit relationships that start out unsecured and become secured later. Some trade creditors ordinarily extend credit on an unsecured basis, but insist on a security agreement if the debtor does not pay within a reasonable time. Or a creditor may have a judgment stemming from a tort action or contract breach, but recognize that the pursuit of state collection remedies might be expensive. Instead of enforcing the judgment immediately, the creditor might agree to take payment of the outstanding obligation over time, secured by an interest in some property of the debtor. The Code provides such parties with an easy, enforceable mechanism to change the debtor-creditor relationship to include a security interest.

A situation in which the secured creditor did not give value at all is unlikely to lead to litigation for the simple reason that the secured creditor won't be injured by whatever happened. Nonetheless, the value requirement has not become entirely irrelevant to commercial transactions. For reasons we explain in later chapters, it may matter *when* the secured creditor gave value because only then did the security interest attach. A delay in giving value can sometimes lead to surprising results.

3.   *The Debtor Has Rights in the Collateral*

It may seem to go without saying that a person cannot grant a security interest in someone else's property. Despite that, and the fact that the drafters of Article 9 were not getting paid by the word, they chose to address the matter anyway, in UCC §9-203(b)(2).

The courts have read at least three significant subtexts into this rule. First, they read it to mean that if the debtor owns a limited interest in property and grants a security interest in the property, the security interest will generally attach to only that limited interest. See Comment 6 to UCC §9-203. For example, Wilson Leasing owns machinery and leases it to Darby Construction. Darby grants a security interest in the machinery to CreditLine Investors. CreditLine will have a security interest only in what Darby owns, which is a leasehold. CreditLine will not have a security interest in the machinery. (Of course, CreditLine may have a cause of action against Darby for breach of covenants in the security agreement, and Darby may also have violated its agreement with Wilson Leasing as well.) To lend more dignity to this simple rule that a debtor can't grant a security interest in someone else's property, lawyers sometimes translate it into Latin (*nemo dat non habet*) and then back into old English (He who hath not, cannot give). In oral argument or negotiations, the effect is much more powerful than saying it in ordinary English.

Parties sometimes deliberately create security interests in property in which the debtor has something less than outright ownership. The debtor may, for example, be the lessee under a favorable long-term lease of an aircraft. The right to use an aircraft that today would rent for $8,000 a month, but to pay only the $5,000-a-month rent specified in the lease signed five years ago, may be a valuable right indeed, particularly if many years remain on the lease term. The lessee's rights under such a lease may be a valuable asset. The lessee can grant a security interest in the lease, and if the debtor-lessee defaults under the secured loan, the secured creditor can foreclose on the lessee's rights under the lease and sell them to the highest bidder. Similarly, a debtor may have no more than a contract to purchase property, but if the contract is favorable and enforceable, the contract may have significant value. If it does, someone may be willing to lend against it. Once again, Article 9 is written expansively to encompass the creation of security interests in nearly anything that has value, if the parties choose to create them.

The second subtext the courts read into the rule may seem virtually a contradiction of the first. Some "owners" who acquired their rights in property by fraud have the power to transfer to bona fide purchasers ownership rights they themselves do not have. See UCC §2-403. In the same analytic vein, such "owners" can also grant security interests in the rights they do not have. The subject is subtle, complex, and peripheral to an understanding of the basic concepts of security, so we do not address it until nearly the end of this book. For now, it is safe to ignore it.

The third subtext the courts read into the rule relates to the *time* at which the security interest becomes enforceable. For example, assume that Alice owns a hot air balloon that she plans to sell to Harris. Harris grants Credit Corp. a security interest in the balloon. At this instant, Credit Corp.'s security interest is not enforceable because Harris has no rights in the collateral. If Harris later purchases the balloon from Alice, Credit Corp.'s security interest becomes enforceable at the precise instant Harris first acquires rights in the property. In later assignments, it will become clear why parties want their security interests to arise at the instant their debtors acquire the collateral. For now, we note that this provision makes that possible.

C.   Formalities for Real Estate Mortgages

Like virtually every other aspect of real estate law, the formalities for the creation of real estate mortgages that are enforceable against the debtor differ from state to state. Most states require that the mortgage be in writing and signed by the debtor in the presence of one or more witnesses. Some, as in the Ohio statute that follows, require acknowledgment (essentially notarization) although most require that step only as a prerequisite to recording the mortgage.

Ohio Revised Code Ann.

(2015)

§5301.01   ACKNOWLEDGMENT OF DEEDS, MORTGAGES, LAND CONTRACTS, AND LEASES

(A) A deed, mortgage, land contract . . . or lease of any interest in real property . . . shall be signed by the grantor, mortgagor, vendor, or lessor. . . . The signing shall be acknowledged by the grantor, mortgagor, vendor, or lessor. . . . The signing shall be acknowledged by the grantor, mortgagor, vendor, or lessor . . . before a judge or clerk of a court of record in this state, or a county auditor, county engineer, notary public, or mayor, who shall certify the acknowledgement and subscribe the official's name to the certificate of the acknowledgement.

———————

While real estate law generally requires more formality to create an enforceable security interest than does Article 9, real estate law is probably also more flexible in dealing with extreme cases. For example, in Wolf v. Schumacher, 477 N.W.2d 827 (N.D. 1991), the court found that an oral mortgage was excepted from the Statute of Frauds on the basis of partial performance. Had the case been governed by the UCC, it is unlikely that the security agreement would have been upheld. Notwithstanding an occasional case that saves a careless creditor, real estate practice is known for its obsessive adherence to the details of conveyancing, and the field abounds with stories of millions of dollars that were lost because someone failed to execute some particular paper in the required ritualized form. Real estate conveyancing is not a good place for free spirits.

Problem Set 8

8.1. a. Your client, First State Bank, loaned $150,000 to Coyote Laboratories, Inc. Coyote fell on hard times and filed bankruptcy. R.K. Maroon, the bank's president, told you that the loan was to be secured by certain laboratory equipment, and the only documentation is this email:

First State Bank

———————

From:	Coyote, Wile E. <wecoyote@coyotelabs.com>
Sent:	Thursday, February 12, 2015 4:35 PM
To:	R.K. Maroon, President
Subject:	Loan Collateral

Thank you for the delightful lunch today. As we discussed, I grant to First State Bank a first security interest in our laboratory equipment to secure the bank's $150,000 loan.

You filed a secured proof of claim in the bankruptcy case, and attached a printed copy of the email. The bankruptcy trustee objected to your proof of claim, citing "(1) the complete lack of any security agreement, (2) the lack of a signature, and (3) the lack of a description of collateral." The case is likely to pay ten cents on the dollar to unsecured creditors. Maroon wants to know whether you think it is worth contesting this objection. What do you tell him? UCC §§9-102(a)(7), (a)(70), (a)(74), 9-203(b).
    b. If instead of sending the email, Coyote had called Maroon and told him exactly the same thing, would First State have a security interest in the equipment?
    c. What if Coyote had been unable to reach Maroon and left a voicemail message saying exactly the same thing? Does it matter if Maroon deleted the voicemail message immediately after listening to it?

8.2.   You are working as a law clerk for Judge Heather Clifford. Judge Clifford has given you the exhibits from a recently completed bench trial and asked you "whether they meet the authenticated security agreement requirement of UCC §9-203(b)(3)(A)." The first is a promissory note for $50,000 that was signed by the debtor but not by the secured party. The note recites that it is "secured by collateral described in a security agreement bearing the same date as this note." The second is a financing statement that describes the collateral as "all of the inventory and equipment of [the debtor's] business." Although the financing statement was not signed, it was accompanied by another writing that was signed by the debtor: an authorization for the secured party to file such financing statements and amendments as the secured party may deem necessary or expedient to protect its existing and future rights in collateral. The third is a letter from the debtor's attorney to the creditor that states, "Enclosed are the promissory note and financing statement which give you a security interest in my client's inventory and equipment." No other writings were introduced. What do you tell the judge? Is this a question that can be answered from the documents alone, or do you need to read the testimony? UCC §9-102(a)(7).

[handwritten margin note: debtor intend to enter security agreement?]

8.3.   You recently joined the legal department at First National Bank and work under the direct supervision of Scott Pryor. To begin your training, Pryor takes you to the Kettering closing described in the first few pages of this assignment. While you are driving back to the bank from the closing, Pryor asks you at precisely what point in time First National Bank's security interest attached to the Fisherman's Pier restaurant. What do you tell him? See UCC §§1-204, 9-203(b)(3)(A), 2-501(1).

8.4.   When you arrived at the Kettering closing, you pulled from your file the security agreement you had prepared. The description of collateral read: "The restaurant equipment described on the attached list." No list was attached. Ellen Bartell had promised to bring the list of equipment to the closing so it could be attached, but by the time you arrived at the closing, both of you had forgotten. Without realizing the error, the parties signed the security agreement without the list attached. The closing was completed and the loan proceeds were disbursed.

a.   Did the bank, at that moment, have a security interest enforceable against Kenneth?

b.   Two weeks later, Ellen Bartell remembered the list. She mailed it to Pryor with a letter of apology. When he received it, he immediately stapled it to the security agreement. He then asked you whether you thought the agreement was enforceable. What should your reply be?

c.   Would it have made any difference if Bartell had discovered the omission two years later and the parties did the same thing?

d. What if she discovered it after Kenneth filed for bankruptcy and the parties did the same thing? See Bankr. Code §362(a)(4) and (5).

8.5.   Early in your second year of solo practice, things seem to have gotten out of control. Although the work is incredibly interesting and you're making really good money, there never seems to be enough time to get everything done. Several months ago, you represented Porter Equipment on a deal for Porter to sell earthmoving equipment (essentially, an oversized bulldozer) to Winfield Construction Company. At the closing, Porter took $800,000 of the purchase price in the form of a promissory note secured by an interest in the bulldozer. A few weeks ago, Winfield filed for bankruptcy. Today, the trustee called and asked that you forward a copy of the security agreement.

When you checked the file, you noted that the financing statement on file with the Secretary of State describes the collateral as "earth moving equipment," but the description of the collateral in the security agreement is simply blank. You noted the sick, breathless feeling that seemed to come from the pit of your stomach, but, since you began practicing law, you had learned to recognize as an adrenaline-induced palpitation of the heart (generally not life-threatening). By rummaging around in the file you were able to jog your memory as to what had happened. Katie Porter had promised you a description of the bulldozer a few days before the closing, but she hadn't sent it. At the closing, you had explained to the president of Winfield that the description of the bulldozer was forthcoming. He signed the security agreement with the description blank and orally authorized you to fill it in when you got the description. Porter emailed you the description a few weeks later when you were especially busy. The email said "Here is the description I promised." You printed the email and stuck it in the file, meaning to come back to it later, but it slipped your mind.

Your first thought was self-loathing. How could *you*, who always had it together better than your law school classmates, have committed malpractice? Your thoughts turned darker yet when you realized that even if Porter got most of her $800,000 out of your tight-fisted malpractice carrier (more likely, she'd net about $200,000 to $300,000 after her attorneys fees—after all, she too was negligent, right?), you were going to be humiliated in the process, she was never going to trust you again, and you would probably never be able to pay even the balance of her loss. Eventually, you settle down to think about what really mattered. What do you do now?

Assume that your state has adopted the Model Rules of Professional Conduct. Those rules provide in relevant part:

Rule 1.4
   (b) A lawyer shall explain a matter to the extent reasonably necessary to permit the client to make informed decisions regarding the representation.
Rule 1.6
   (a) A lawyer shall not reveal information relating to the representation of a client unless the client gives informed consent, the disclosure is impliedly authorized in order to carry out the representation or the disclosure is permitted by paragraph (b).
   (b) A lawyer may reveal information relating to the representation of a client to the extent the lawyer reasonably believes necessary: . . .
      (2) to prevent the client from committing a crime or fraud that is reasonably certain to result in substantial injury to the financial interests or property of another and in furtherance of which the client has used or is using the lawyer's services;
      (3) to prevent, mitigate or rectify substantial injury to the financial interests or property of another that is reasonably certain to result or has resulted from the client's commission of a crime or fraud in furtherance of which the client has used the lawyer's services. . . .

Rule 1.9

(c) A lawyer who has formerly represented a client in a matter or whose present or former firm has formerly represented a client in a matter shall not thereafter:

(1) use information relating to the representation to the disadvantage of the former client except as these Rules would permit or require with respect to a client, or when the information has become generally known; or

(2) reveal information relating to the representation except as these Rules would permit or require with respect to a client.

Rule 1.16

(b) . . . [A] lawyer may withdraw from representing a client if:

(1) withdrawal can be accomplished without material adverse effect on the interests of the client;

(2) the client persists in a course of action involving the lawyer's services that the lawyer reasonably believes is criminal or fraudulent; [or]

(4) the client insists upon taking action that the lawyer considers repugnant or with which the lawyer has a fundamental disagreement. . . .

Rule 3.3

(a) A lawyer shall not knowingly:

(1) make a false statement of fact or law to a tribunal or fail to correct a false statement of material fact or law previously made to the tribunal by the lawyer;

(3) offer evidence that the lawyer knows to be false. If a lawyer, the lawyer's client, or a witness called by the lawyer, has offered material evidence and the lawyer comes to know of its falsity, the lawyer shall take reasonable remedial measures, including, if necessary, disclosure to the tribunal. . . .

Rule 4.1

. . . [A] lawyer shall not knowingly make a false statement of material fact . . . to a third person. [The comment to this rule provides that a lawyer "generally has no affirmative duty to inform an opposing party of relevant facts."]

Rule 8.4

It is professional misconduct for a lawyer to . . . engage in conduct involving dishonesty, fraud, deceit or misrepresentation.

Terminology

"Fraud" or "fraudulent" denotes conduct having a purpose to deceive and not merely negligent misrepresentation or failure to apprise another of relevant information.

So what do you do?

8.6.   Assume that in the previous problem you finally turned the matter over to the client and withdrew. About five months later, you arrived at the bankruptcy court early for a scheduled hearing in another case and decided to listen in on the case then before the court. By coincidence, it was the trustee's case against Porter Equipment. Porter's new lawyer, Harold Silver, was examining Katie Porter, the company president, on direct. Porter testified that the signature on the security agreement was her own, that the agreement was "genuine" and that it expressed the agreement between the parties. Porter was not asked, and did not say, anything about the description of collateral. Silver offered the agreement in evidence. The trustee did not object and the court admitted it. What do you do now?

Assignment 9: Which Collateral and Obligations Are Covered?

A security interest is, in essence, the right to apply the value of the collateral to the holder's debt. To apply the value of collateral, one must first determine the identity of the collateral. Courts and parties identify collateral by reading, and if necessary, interpreting the descriptions of collateral.

This assignment first discusses the legal principles that govern the interpretation of security agreements generally. Then we apply those principles to the interpretation of security agreement descriptions of collateral. From the previous assignment, you know that every security agreement contains a description of the collateral. Each also contains a description of the obligations secured. These descriptions determine what will be covered (unless they conflict with some specific provision of law). In this assignment we consider the possibility that a description will be so vague or indefinite that it will be legally insufficient. We discuss the circumstances that determine whether after-acquired property is included in descriptions and briefly describe the law governing descriptions of collateral in real estate mortgages. We close with a brief discussion of the law governing what obligations are secured.

As you read, keep in mind that in most secured transactions there will be at least two descriptions of collateral: one in the security agreement that is the contract between the parties and one in the financing statement that will be filed in the public records. In keeping with our focus in Part One of this book on the relationship between the debtor and the creditor, we examine only the security agreement description here. Financing statement descriptions serve different functions. We address them in Assignment 18.

A. Interpreting Security Agreements

1. Debtor Against Creditor

A security agreement is, among other things, a contract between debtor and creditor. UCC §9-102(a)(74). The rules that govern the interpretation of contracts generally apply to security agreements as well. See UCC §§9-201(a), 1-201(b)(3), and 1-303. Generally, the court will try to determine the intention of the parties as objectively expressed in the written security agreement. Where the agreement is ambiguous, parol evidence may be introduced; where the writing results from mutual mistake, the security agreement can be reformed. For example, in In re Schutz, 241 B.R. 646 (Bankr. W.D. Mo. 1999), the debtor

[handwritten margin note: Security Agreement 9-102(a)(74)]

purchased a "Sunshine-382" mobile home on credit, but the security agreement misdescribed it as a "1996 Titan Home, Model S-382." The bankruptcy court held the creditor's claim secured nevertheless, explaining that "an error on the part of a scrivener that results in a mutual mistake as to the intent of the parties at the time they negotiated the contract justifies reformation of the contract to reflect the intent of the parties."

Some courts have held that the filing of bankruptcy precludes reformation. Reasoning that the bankruptcy estate represents the interests of unsecured creditors who were not parties to the bargain and not responsible for the mistake, the court in In re Duckworth, 776 F.3d 453 (7th Cir. 2014), refused to reform a security agreement that referred to the secured obligation as a promissory note dated "December 13, 2008." The only note executed between the parties was dated "December 15, 2008." The court held the bank to be unsecured.

2.   Creditor Against Third Party

Although a security agreement is a contract between the debtor and creditor, it also binds purchasers of the collateral and creditors. UCC §9-201(a). This should strike you as remarkable. We know of no other law that gives A and B the right to enter into an agreement that is binding on C. The effect of this provision is often that the secured party takes collateral that the other creditors were counting on for collection. Not surprisingly, when the courts are called upon to construe the meaning of security agreements in cases involving such a third party, the courts are likely to interpret them more literally than in accord with the intention of the debtor and secured party. That includes the provisions of a security agreement that state what collateral is covered by the agreement.

3.   Interpreting Descriptions of Collateral

Article 9 defines many types of collateral, including "accounts" (UCC §9-102(a)(2)), "equipment" (UCC §9-102(a)(33)), "inventory" (UCC §9-102(a)(48)), "instruments" (UCC §9-102(a)(47)), "consumer goods" (UCC §9-102(a)(23)), and "general intangibles" (UCC §9-102(a)(42)). Some of the definitions are not in accord with the common meanings of the defined terms. For example, the grant of a security interest in all of the debtor's *accounts* might be intended to include bank accounts, but UCC §9-102(a)(2) defines "accounts" in such a manner that bank accounts are not included. Similarly, UCC §9-102(a)(33) defines "equipment" much more broadly than does the common usage of that term. Only a person who has read the definition would be likely to guess that racehorses might be included. See In re Bob Schwermer & Assoc., Inc., 27 B.R. 304 (Bankr. N.D. Ill. 1983). The paintings hanging in a law firm's lobby are "equipment" because they are neither inventory, farm products, or consumer goods. UCC §9-102(a)(33). The owner of a restaurant could easily sign a security agreement with boilerplate language granting a security interest in its "general intangibles" without realizing that its liquor license would be included. See, e.g., In re Genuario, 10

UCC2d 978 (Bankr. R.I. 1989) (grant of a security interest in debtor's "general intangibles" includes liquor license).

When parties use a UCC-defined term in a security agreement, the courts usually (but not always) give the term its Article 9 meaning rather than its common meaning. We think the courts are often wrong in doing so; the results can easily be contrary to the intention of parties who were not even aware of the Article 9 definitions of the words they were using. We believe the better view is that words used in a security agreement, like words used in any other agreement, should be assigned the meaning that the parties intended in using them. The definitions of those same words under Article 9 are only one indication of what the parties might have intended by using them.

B.   Sufficiency of Description: Article 9 Security Agreements

The primary function of the description of collateral in a security agreement is to enable interested parties to identify the collateral. Those parties certainly include the debtor and creditor. They may also include other creditors disadvantaged by the grant of security, trustees in bankruptcy, or courts that must decide cases brought by any of them. To identify the collateral means to determine that a particular item of property is or is not included.

In re Murphy
80 UCC Rep. Serv. 2d 764 (Bankr. D. Kan. 2013)

DALE L. SOMERS, UNITED STATES BANKRUPTCY JUDGE.

Debtor filed her motion asserting that four items of personal property are not subject to a purchase money security interest (PMSI) as claimed by creditor Capital One. The property is four items of electronics purchased from Best Buy using a Best Buy credit card. According to Debtor, there is no PMSI because the description of the collateral in the alleged security agreement is not sufficiently specific.

The Best Buy credit Application, signed by Debtor, provides: "You grant the Bank a purchase money security interest in the goods purchased on your Account." It also provides: "you agree to the terms and conditions of the Cardholder Agreement and Disclosure Statement which shall be sent to you with the Card." That Cardholder Agreement includes a full paragraph about security, which includes the statement, "you grant us a purchase money security interest in the goods purchased with your Card. . . ." Capital One has provided copies of the sales receipts for the four items, but they do not incorporate the terms of the Application or the Cardholder Agreement. There is no security agreement provision on the receipts.

The question is whether the security interest attached to the four items. The condition for attachment which is in issue requires that the Debtor has authenticated a security agreement that provides a description of the collateral. The sufficiency of descriptions of collateral is addressed by [UCC §9-108].

Debtor contends that describing the collateral as "goods purchased on your Account" does not comply with [UCC §9-108]. The argument is that since the sale was a consumer transaction, subsection (e)(2) applies and was violated because it prohibits description by type of collateral and, in the Debtor's view, "goods purchased" is a type of collateral. Debtor contends that the security agreement must describe the specific goods purchased, such as TV or VCR.

Debtor's proposed construction of [UCC §9-108(e)(2)] is not correct. The "description by type" not permitted for consumer goods is the "types" of collateral defined in the UCC, such as accounts, chattel paper, consumer goods, deposit accounts equipment, general intangibles, and so forth. "Goods purchased on your Account" is not a "type of collateral defined in the uniform commercial code." The purpose of the collateral description in the security agreement is to define the security interest as between the parties; unlike a financing statement, the purpose of a security agreement is not to give notice to third parties. The description "goods purchased on your Account" adequately defines the collateral between the Debtor and the holder of the account.

Retailers often try to take security interests in the goods they sell to consumers and describe the collateral with some variant of the language used in *Murphy*. The view expressed in *Murphy*—that the description need be no more specific than "merchandise" or "goods" "purchased on the account"—is the majority view. It is consistent with both the language of Article 9 and the case law from the commercial context. But a substantial number of courts bridle at the use of security interests in consumer transactions and are quick to find fault with the descriptions used. For example, In re Shirel, 251 B.R. 157 (Bankr. W.D. Okla. 2000), found a description of all "merchandise purchased with the credit card" to be inadequate, because it did not "sufficiently describe the collateral so that a third party could reasonably identify the items." The court said that the description "must at least identify the type or class of collateral" and said that "a sufficient description might have been merely 'a refrigerator.'"

Whether a description actually enables "third parties" to identify collateral depends on who the third parties are, what information they start with, and what obligations can be placed on them to gather additional information. The courts routinely hold descriptions effective, even though a third party looking at the security agreement alone would have no idea what was included.

The same is true of descriptions that use terms of art that would have no meaning to most third parties. For example, in In re Schmidt, 1987 U.S. Dist. LEXIS (W.D. Okla. 1987), the security agreement described the collateral as "crops . . . growing on the real estate described by ASCS Farm Serial Numbers . . . J-528, J-552, J-557 & J-572." People dealing in agricultural finance would generally know what these numbers mean and how they could use them to look up the descriptions of the land in other records. The parcels described by the ASCS numbers included both land not farmed by the Schmidts and land farmed by them. The court held the description adequate.

UCC §9-108(c) provides that "A description of collateral as 'all the debtor's assets' or 'all the debtor's personal property' or using words of similar import does not reasonably identify collateral." The drafters chose not to state their reasons for adopting this provision. Based on prior case law, the probable reason was that the drafters feared that use of such descriptions would make it too easy to grant a security interest in all of one's property without realizing one was doing so. There is no indication that the provision was intended—or will be interpreted—to prevent a debtor from giving a security interest in all of the debtor's assets by describing them individually or by categories.

▶ HALF ASSIGNMENT ENDS

C. Describing After-Acquired Property

After-acquired property is a term used to refer to property that a debtor acquires after the security agreement is authenticated or the security interest is otherwise created. Consider the example of an equipment manufacturer that gives its dealers 30 days in which to pay for equipment the manufacturer delivers to them. The dealers' obligations to pay are accounts receivable ("accounts") owned by the manufacturer. Manufacturers often borrow money from a lender that takes a security interest in the manufacturers' accounts.

With the passage of time, dealers will pay the accounts owing on the date the parties signed the security agreement. In a typical business, nearly all of them will be paid in about 60 to 120 days, and the ones that are not may never be paid. During that period, new accounts will arise from additional deliveries of equipment. The new accounts are after-acquired property. If the secured lender has a security interest in the after-acquired accounts, the secured lender will have approximately the same collateral it had at the time it made the loan. If the secured lender does not have a security interest in the after-acquired accounts, the secured lender may have hardly any collateral at all.

Under some of the laws that preceded Article 9, it was impossible to grant a security interest in after-acquired property. The law required that the collateral be in existence when the parties signed the security agreement. Parties who wanted after-acquired property to secure an obligation had to execute a security agreement each time the debtor acquired additional property. At the time, that was a staggering inconvenience with collateral such as accounts. The drafters of Article 9 addressed the problem by validating provisions in security agreements that extend the description of collateral to after-acquired property. UCC §9-204(a). Such descriptions commonly include the words "after-acquired property," but descriptions can use other words and, as is discussed in the case below, the inclusion of after-acquired property can even be implied in compelling circumstances.

Article 9 deems after-acquired property clauses ineffective with respect to two kinds of collateral. The first kind is consumer goods that the debtor acquires more than 10 days after the secured party gives value. This limitation is part of a general policy against taking security interests in consumer goods unless those interests secure the purchase price of the collateral. In the 1960s and 1970s, small loan companies took blanket security interests in debtors' household goods. After default, they threatened to take the debtors' furniture, clothing, family photographs, and other items. Those items would net little or nothing at sale, but taking them imposed lots of pain on the debtors. UCC §9-204(b)(1) made that unsavory practice a little more difficult.

The second kind is commercial tort claims. Here the concern is that even sophisticated business debtors would be surprised by the consequences of such a grant. Consider the example of a business debtor that grants a security interest in every UCC category of collateral — including commercial tort claims — except inventory. A third party tortiously destroys the debtor's inventory. This debtor would probably be quite surprised to realize that the security interest covers the debtor's tort claim for loss of the inventory.

With those specific exceptions, after-acquired property clauses remain in common use. With computerization of the American economy, however, the necessity for them is declining. A computer can be programmed to grant a security interest in each account as it is created. Some department stores include a security agreement on the receipt for each credit purchase. Similarly, there is no reason why the record of the sale of a case of toothpaste from a distributor to a retail drugstore cannot contain the grant of a security interest. But in the latter illustration, the individual grant of a security interest offers no obvious advantage over an after-acquired property clause and so seems unlikely to replace it.

In the following case, the court discusses the differing views on the necessity for a specific provision in the security agreement to grant after-acquired collateral as security.

Stoumbos v. Kilimnik

988 F.2d 949 (9th Cir. 1993)

FLETCHER, CIRCUIT JUDGE:

[On May 1, 1982, Kilimnik sold a business to AAM, retaining a security interest. The description of collateral was obscure and scattered through several documents, but the court held it to be the equivalent of "inventory and equipment." The security agreement did use "after acquired" language with respect to accounts receivable. When the buyer defaulted in October 1985, Kilimnik seized all of the inventory and equipment then in the possession of the buyer, including inventory and equipment acquired by the buyer after May 1, 1982. The buyer filed bankruptcy and the trustee, Stoumbos, sued Kilimnik for return of the after-acquired inventory and equipment.]

Kilimnik, however, argues that, where a creditor acquires a security interest in equipment and inventory, the court should find that this interest automatically extends to after-acquired inventory and equipment. There is substantial support for the proposition that, where a financing statement or security agreement provides for a security interest in "all inventory" (or uses similar broad language), the document incorporates after-acquired inventory. The rationale is that inventory is constantly turning over, and no creditor could reasonably agree to be secured by an asset that would vanish in a short time in the normal course of business. The position that no express language is required is described as the "majority" view, *American Family Marketing*, 92 B.R. at 953, or the "modern trend," *Sims Office Supply*, 83 B.R. at 72. There is, however, contrary authority, which reasons that "the [UCC] contemplates that a security agreement should clearly spell out any claims to after acquired collateral." Covey v. First Nat'l Bank (In re Balcain Equip. Co., Inc.), 80 B.R. 461, 462 (Bankr. C.D. Ill. 1987).

No Washington or Ninth Circuit cases appear to be directly on point. We conclude that we need not decide whether to adopt the "majority" view in this case since the Purchase Agreement does not contain the usual language granting a security interest in "all inventory" or "inventory," but only in the items specifically described in paragraph 1 as "inventory . . . on hand at May 1, 1982."

In addition, the rationale of the "automatic" security interest cases does not apply to after-acquired equipment. Those cases discuss cyclically depleted and replenished assets such as inventory or accounts receivable. Unlike inventory, equipment is not normally subject to frequent turnover.

We are aware that the financing statement mentions after-acquired equipment, suggesting that the parties intended Kilimnik's security interest would extend this far. Yet we must look to the entire circumstances under which the purchase agreement was made to ascertain its meaning. Under Washington law, a contract is interpreted by reference to many contextual factors, including the subject matter of the transaction, the subsequent conduct of the parties and the reasonableness of their interpretations.

The trustee here advances the more reasonable interpretation: Kilimnik took a kind of "purchase money" interest in the equipment he sold to AAM, but he did not get the additional security of a blanket interest in all equipment the company ever acquired after the sale. The subject matter of the transaction also supports this conclusion.

Kilimnik would not have had a clear reason to want after-acquired equipment covered by the purchase agreement. As we have seen, equipment, unlike inventory, is not normally subject to frequent turnover. Even if limited to the equipment on hand at the time of the sale, his interest would have been secure.

In summary, we conclude that Kilimnik's security interest was limited to equipment and inventory owned by AAM on May 1, 1982.

Stoumbos characterizes the view that no express language is required to include after acquired inventory as collateral as the "majority" view. The court puts "majority" in quotation marks because there are not two views, but many different, fact-dependent ones. Ultimately, the intention of the parties, as objectively expressed, is supposed to control. Comment 3 to UCC §9-108 states:

Much litigation has arisen over whether a description in a security agreement is sufficient to include after-acquired collateral if the agreement does not explicitly so provide. This question is one of contract interpretation and is not susceptible to a statutory rule. Accordingly, this section contains no reference to descriptions of after-acquired property.

After-acquired property clauses enable security interests to "float" on collateral. That is, the precise items that constitute the collateral constantly change as the debtor buys new items and sells the old ones. But the collateral, as a whole, remains relatively stable in identity and value, much like the accounts example we used to introduce this idea.

After-acquired property clauses are not unusual when creditors take interests in broad categories of collateral such as equipment, farm products, or general intangibles. With regard to each, a particular debtor is likely to be disposing of some items and acquiring others over time, so that it makes more sense to think of the collateral as the category rather than as the individual items within it at any given time. After-acquired property clauses make it possible for the parties to a long-term financing relationship to do that. Such a security interest is sometimes referred to as a *floating lien.*

Lending contracts often link the total value of the collateral, including after-acquired collateral, to the total amount of the loan. A bank, for example, may agree to lend 65 percent of the purchase price of all inventory owned by the debtor. When inventory is sold, the debtor must pay down the loan; when new inventory arrives, the bank advances a portion of the purchase price. But after-acquired property clauses are not always linked to agreements to make additional loans. Under some arrangements, additional acquisitions of collateral covered by the after-acquired property clause are simply a windfall to the creditor. Perhaps for this reason, after-acquired property clauses become ineffective upon the filing of a bankruptcy case. Bankr. Code §552(a). We explore this subject in more detail in Assignment 11.

D.   Which Obligations Are Secured?

The general rules regarding interpretation of security agreements apply to provisions specifying what obligations are secured. Virtually any obligation can be secured if the parties make their intention clear. In Pawtucket Institution for Savings v. Gagnon, 475 A.2d 1028 (R.I. 1984), the mortgage secured a promise by the debtor to build a building. That is, if the debtor did not build the building, the debtor would owe a debt for the resulting damages and the mortgage against already existing real property would secure it. In indicating what obligations are secured, no particular form is required. If the security agreement states that it secures a certain debt in the amount of $25,000 and such a debt exists, it is secured.

A security interest can also secure a debt that does not yet exist but which the parties contemplate will come into existence in the future. If the future obligation will come into existence as the result of an additional extension of credit by the secured creditor, it is referred to as a *future advance.* UCC §9-204(c) provides that "A security agreement may provide that collateral secures . . . future advances. . . ."

Debtors often execute agreements that purport to secure every obligation to the secured creditor of any kind that may come into existence in the future. If the creditor later lends additional money, a security agreement with such a future-advance clause will ensure that the subsequent loan is secured from its inception. Such provisions are often referred to as dragnet clauses. They are valid when contained in Article 9 security agreements. The comment to UCC §9-204 states that "the parties are free to agree that a security interest secures any obligation whatsoever. Determining the obligations secured by collateral is solely a matter of construing the parties' agreement under applicable law. This Article rejects the holdings of cases decided under former Article 9 that applied other tests. . . ." For an example of a very simple, straightforward dragnet clause, see paragraph 3 of the Agreement for Wholesale Financing in Assignment 15.

Security agreements usually provide that, in the event of default, the debtor will pay the creditor's attorneys fees and other expenses of collection. They authorize the creditor to add these amounts to the secured indebtedness. These provisions are considered valid and effective in both personal property and real estate security agreements, and, as you have already seen in Assignment 7, in bankruptcy. In recent years, courts have begun to refer to them as "nonadvance" provisions, because the creditor does not advance the amount secured by them to the debtor. Interest that accrues on a secured obligation is also included in the nonadvance category. Between debtor and secured creditor, provisions securing nonadvances are of equal validity and effect with those securing advances.

E.   Real Estate Mortgages

While the rules regarding descriptions of collateral in real estate mortgages are controlled by a separate body of law, they are remarkably similar to the rules under Article 9. The description in a mortgage must describe the land sufficiently to identify it. But the description may refer to separate documents, such as maps or plats for that purpose. A description may be so vague as to render the mortgage void. But if the description is merely ambiguous, parol evidence may be used to explain its meaning. Broad descriptions such as "all grantor's property in the county" are generally good as between the mortgagor and mortgagee. (Real estate lawyers refer to these as "Mother Hubbard clauses," presumably because the cupboard will be bare when the next creditor arrives.)

The physical nature of real estate makes it easier to identify than many kinds of personal property. While older descriptions of land, particularly in the northeastern United States, may describe it by reference to "monuments" such as trees, rocks, and streams that are later difficult to identify or that are less than permanent, in most parts of the United States descriptions are by reference to maps or plats that are ultimately located by reference to monuments (iron stakes) placed by government survey. The stakes are carefully maintained as reference points for surveyors. As a result, a well-written description of real property can identify it with virtually no uncertainty.

In real estate practice, the debtor executes a separate mortgage document each time the debtor adds land to the secured creditor's collateral. Real estate law recognizes a doctrine of *after-acquired title* that applies to mortgages and permits an earlier mortgage document to convey a security interest in land later acquired by the mortgagor. See United Oklahoma Bank v. Moss, 793 P.2d 1359 (Okla. 1990). But, in contrast to the situation with respect to personal property, where after-acquired property clauses are common, there seems to be little need for the doctrine with respect to real estate transactions and correspondingly little use of it.

Permanent buildings become part of the real estate, as do other structures permanently affixed to land, such as fences or sidewalks (known as *fixtures*). They are automatically included in a description that refers only to the land. The rule applies whether they are affixed to the real estate before or after the mortgage is executed. Thus, in a sense, every real estate mortgage automatically reaches "after-affixed" property. In later assignments we will discuss property affixed to real estate in greater detail.

Future-advance clauses can be included in real estate mortgages. The typical construction mortgage, under which the lender agrees to make advances each time construction reaches designated stages of completion, is an example. There are, however, some limitations on the use of future-advance clauses in real estate mortgages. First, some states disfavor the use of dragnet clauses by demanding strict proof that the later advance is one that was in the contemplation of the parties at the time they executed the real estate mortgage. In those states the mortgagee will want to describe the future debt as specifically as possible at the time the mortgage is granted and refer to the mortgage in the documentation for the future debt when it is incurred. Second, some states require that a recorded mortgage indicate a maximum amount of indebtedness to be secured; the mortgage cannot effectively secure more than the amount indicated in it. For example, a $75,000 home mortgage in such a state might recite that it secures a loan in the initial amount of $75,000, that future advances are contemplated, but the mortgage will not secure obligations exceeding $90,000. See, e.g., Fla. Stat. §697.04. Finally, in some states real property cannot secure obligations that cannot be reduced to money. Fluctuating accounts, contingent debts, or promises to build a building can each be reduced to a specific dollar amount at the time of foreclosure. But an obligation to provide future support for a living person might be much more difficult to value and as a result might not be considered a proper subject of security.

Problem Set 9

9.1. Which of the following is a sufficient description of collateral? UCC§9-108.

a. "All equipment and inventory." UCC §9-102(a)(33) and (48).

b. "All items purchased with the card" in an agreement signed at the time the debtor obtained a credit card from a department store.

c. "Restaurant equipment located at 123 Main Street." The debtor is a restaurant chain that has a store at that location.

[margin notes: A S   can't use/insufficient   B(3)]

d. "All of the debtor's consumer goods." The debtor signed the security agreement to borrow $5,000 from Household Finance in order to purchase tickets on a cruise ship.

e. "All goods other than consumer goods." UCC §9-102(a)(44).

9.2. You are practicing with a firm in Oklahoma that does all the legal work for Walter's Department Store (Walter's). Walter's practice has been to take a security interest in everything that a credit card holder purchases on his or her account. While they do not repossess clothing or other items without resale value, they do repossess many kinds of appliances and household goods. They make the decision after default. Under the reasoning in *Murphy*, they think they have enforceable security interests in everything they sell, based on this language in the application for a Walter's credit card: "Cardholder grants Walter's a security interest in all items purchased on the account." Walter's does business in several jurisdictions, so they expect to encounter bankruptcy judges who follow the *Murphy* line of decisions and others who follow the *Shirel* line of decisions. Can you think of a way for Walter's to take security interests that would be good even under *Shirel*'s reasoning? UCC §§9-203(b)(3)(A), 9-102(a)(23), 9-108(e).

Oh, and be careful not to violate 16 C.F.R. 444.2, which provides that "it is an unfair act or practice . . . for a lender . . . to take or receive from a consumer an obligation that . . . constitutes or contains a nonpossessory security interest in household goods other than a purchase money security interest."

9.3. Abbye Atkinson is a hard-headed bank loan officer, always on the lookout to make operations more efficient. Instead of taking the time to make long lists of collateral—and the risk of leaving something out or mis-describing something—she suggests that in cases in which the bank is essentially locking up everything, that it switch to describing the collateral as "all the debtor's property." The UCC clearly prohibits this, but Abbye wants to understand why. How do you explain the underlying policy? Is there any room to move in the direction Abbye wants?

▶ Half Assignment Ends

9.4. Robert and Mary Gillam have come to see you about their financial problems. For the past seven years, they have made their living farming. When they started, they borrowed $350,000 from the First National Bank of Frenville and granted a security interest in "crops growing on the debtor's farm in Osprey County, about 14 miles from Tilanook" and most of their farm equipment. (The location information is correct and the debtors own only a single farm.) The Gillams have paid that loan down to $190,000. It is now the middle of the growing season and the Gillams don't have enough cash to get them through the harvest. They would like to borrow against their current crop, but First National won't lend them any more money. The second lender they approached, Production Credit Association (PCA), told them that the current crop was unacceptable as collateral because "First National already has it, and we don't make crop loans in second position." This upset the Gillams, because they had assumed that their current crop was not covered by First National's security interest.

[margin note: After acquired/floating lien is not included]

a.   Who is right on the point of law?

b.   What should the Gillams do? UCC §§9-108(a), (b), 9-203(b)(3)(A), 9-204.

9.5.   Ace Bank lends against the "fixtures and equipment" of a bar. Six years later the owner absconds, taking all of the fixtures and equipment in the bar with him. The bank takes possession of the bar and finds no personal property whatsoever, and bare wires where the light fixtures used to be. When apprehended for the crime of removing collateral from the state in violation of the security agreement, the debtor admits to taking all of the fixture and equipment from the bar, but says he has taken no collateral. The prosecutor agrees. The chief loan officer for Ace is pounding on your desk, asking how this can be so. How could it? (This problem is based on a true story.)

9.6.   Richard Cohen, a client of your firm, asked Sandra Bernhard, the partner for whom you work, for an opinion on a "situation" in which he is involved. Because it is a very small matter, Bernhard has asked you to look into it, tell her what the arguments will be on each side, and evaluate them. You have learned that Cohen lent $300,000 to Aircraft Video Marketing, Inc. (AVMI) four years ago and entered into a security agreement that listed the collateral as

> "All of Debtor's equipment, including replacement parts, additions, repairs, and accessories incorporated therein or affixed thereto. Without limitation the term 'equipment' includes all items used in recording, processing, playing back, or broadcasting moving or still pictures, by whatever process."

AVMI owned certain video equipment at the time the security agreement was signed and acquired additional video equipment of a similar nature later. Like the original equipment, the additional equipment was used in AVMI's business for playing back motion pictures. When AVMI defaulted, another creditor of AVMI's, First National Bank of Omaha, claimed the equipment. After Cohen established that his security interest predated First National's, they dropped their claim to the original equipment. But they continue to claim the equipment AVMI bought later, saying that it is not covered by the terms of Cohen's security agreement. What's your assessment? UCC §9-201(a).

■ END OF DEFAULT PROBLEM SET

9.7.   The Gillams are also raising sheep on the property. They sell the wool and sometimes the cuddly little lambs themselves. (You've heard of lamb chops, right?) They would like your written opinion that the sheep are not covered by First Bank's security interest. With the opinion letter, they say that PCA will make a loan against the sheep. Can you give it? UCC §9-102(a)(34) and Comment 4.a to UCC §9-102.

9.8.   Draft the document necessary to create a security interest in an object that your teacher will bring to class if this problem is assigned. You will be the secured party. Your teacher will be the debtor. You may assume that your teacher owns the object. The document you prepare should be one that, if you advanced $1000 to the teacher as a loan and the teacher signed the document, would create a valid, legally enforceable security interest in the object. Omit from the document all provisions not necessary to achieve validity and legal (not practical) enforceability. Do not take a security interest in anything other than the object.

Assignment 10:   Proceeds, Products, and Other Value-Tracing Concepts

In the previous assignment, you learned that when a debtor and creditor contract for a security interest, they must describe the collateral. Once they have done so, they typically put the documents away. They are likely to refer to the documents again only when some difficulty arises in their relationship, by which time it is often too late to make changes.

In the meantime, items of collateral may go through transformations that take them outside the description of collateral in the security agreement. Oil may become plastic, and then plastic may become shipping containers. Individual cattle in a herd may die, but only after they have produced an even larger number of offspring. Inventory that serves as collateral may be sold on credit. The account debtors who purchased the inventory may pay their accounts with checks, and the debtor may deposit those checks into a bank account.

When a debtor and creditor anticipate such transformations, they usually choose to have the security interest continue in the collateral as it changes form or, if the debtor disposes of it to a third party, to have the security interest attach to whatever the debtor receives in return.

The source of this preference lies in the nature of the secured creditor's relationship to the collateral. Secured creditors look to collateral for repayment. Although they care about the form their collateral takes, they care more about what it is worth. When the debtor transforms the value of an item of collateral to some other type of asset, the secured creditor usually wants and expects the security interest to follow. If security interests did not follow value, a debtor could unilaterally deprive the creditor of that value merely by transferring the collateral.

At the time they negotiate their security agreements, debtors too may be thinking in terms of value and may be willing to permit security interests to follow value. By giving their secured creditors interests that "float" from one item to another as the value is transformed, debtors make transformations less threatening to their secured creditors. The result is that the secured creditors are more willing to give debtors the freedom to make transformations.

One way to ensure that a security interest will follow the value is to include express language in the description of the collateral in the security agreement that covers all forms the value is likely to take. For example, a bank that lends against inventory can easily anticipate that the inventory will be sold, resulting in accounts, negotiable instruments, or money. If the description of collateral is "inventory, accounts, instruments, money, and bank accounts," transformation of the value from one of these forms of collateral to another will not reduce the value of the bank's security. Similarly, if the parties contemplate the possibility that the collateral will be destroyed by accident but the loss will be insured, they can provide that any payment from an insurance company for loss of the inventory also will serve as collateral.

Secured creditors cannot always anticipate the transformations their collateral might undergo or the nature of the property for which it may be exchanged. An alternative might be to encumber all of the debtor's property. But either approach may unduly restrict a debtor. Consider, for example, the debtor who is financing not the entire business, but only a single piece of equipment. If that debtor grants a security interest in the equipment and every other form that value might later take, the debtor might not be able to obtain inventory financing or other equipment financing. And all the secured creditors would want a first claim on the debtor's accounts, instruments, money, and bank accounts.

A more practical solution is to employ what we call *value-tracing concepts*—terms of art that indicate that in certain kinds of transformations of the collateral the security interest should follow the value in prescribed ways.

The value-tracing concepts most commonly employed are *proceeds,* *products, rents, profits,* and *offspring*. Debtors and creditors use these terms of art in security agreements and legislatures use them in statutes. In theory, each of these terms identifies a particular set of tracing rules, although, as is usual in law, neither the parties that use the terms, nor the courts that interpret them, always agree on what the rules are. We begin with the most important of these concepts.

A. Proceeds

1. Definition

Read the definition of "proceeds" in UCC §9-102(a)(64). Under this definition, a security interest will follow the value of collateral through some transformations but not others. If the debtor sells the collateral, the security interest will attach to the price paid, whether it is in the form of an account, a promissory note, or cash. If the debtor leases the collateral, the security interest will attach to the rents received. If the debtor merely uses the collateral in its business, the revenues of the business are not proceeds. For example, in 1st Source Bank v. Wilson Bank & Trust, 735 F.3d 500 (6th Cir. 2013), the court held that the revenues of a trucking company were not the proceeds of its fleet of trucks.

UCC §9-102(a)(64)(C), providing that "rights arising out of the collateral" are proceeds, was added in 2001. The drafters of Article 9—great champions of the secured creditor—inserted it without explanation. In *1st Source Bank*, the court placed an important limit on the new provision, stating that "for rights to 'arise out of' collateral, they must have been obtained as a result of some loss or dispossession of the party's interest in that collateral, not simply by its use."

In re Wiersma, 283 B.R. 294 (Bankr. D. Idaho 2002), was the first case to interpret the new provision. Through the negligence of Geitzen, an electrician, the debtors' dairy cows were subjected to electrical shocks and became sick or died. When the debtors settled their $6 million lawsuit for $2.5 million, their secured creditor bank claimed the settlement as "proceeds" of its collateral: the herd and the milk it produced. The court said:

> Debtors argue that some of the components of their damages do not represent proceeds of cows and milk serving as collateral and should not, therefore, be subject to UCB's security interest. For example, their complaint includes a reservation of a right to amend the complaint to request punitive damages. Because Gietzens' insurer is offering to settle all claims, including potential punitive damage claims which are not attributable to any particular item of UCB's collateral, Debtors contend the settlement represents some damages not directly related to the loss of collateral.
>
> In this instance, though, the legislature has spoken. The UCC definition of "proceeds" includes within its scope whatever is acquired upon disposition of collateral, all rights arising out of collateral, and includes all claims arising out of the loss of, or damage to, collateral. [UCC §9-102(64).] All of the categories listed in Debtors' damage analysis stem from either damage to Debtors' cows or from the loss of milk and cows. Even the "miscellaneous" and "labor" categories arise from damage to or loss of cows and milk because they represent expenses such as veterinarian bills and the Debtors' extra labor costs associated with dealing with the electrical problem affecting the cows. The same is true with respect to Debtors' claim for punitive damages. Thus, given these facts, the Court concludes Debtors' claims against Gietzen arose out of the loss of, and damage to, UCB's collateral, the cows and milk.

In other words, it doesn't matter whether the settlement paid was for damage to the collateral or for other damages. It is all proceeds because the court believes the claim "arose out of" the collateral.

In Helms v. Certified Packaging Corp., 551 F.3d 675 (7th Cir. 2008), the court interpreted the phrase "claims arising out of the loss . . . of . . . the collateral" in accord with a value-tracing approach. In that case, Rothschild negligently failed to obtain business-loss insurance for the debtor. The debtor's business, and the collateral, were damaged by fire. The debtor sued Rothschild and the secured creditor claimed the lawsuit as its collateral. The court said:

> [I]f Rothschild . . . had failed to obtain insurance coverage for damage to the physical assets that secured LaSalle's loan, the claim against the broker rather than for loss of business would be a claim to proceeds of collateral. But the claim against Rothschild was for failure to obtain business-loss insurance, and we do not see how compensation for that failure can be considered proceeds of collateral. The usual proceeds of collateral are the money obtained from selling it. By a modest extension, as we have just seen, they are money obtained in compensation for a diminution in the value of the collateral. But replacing a business loss is not restoring the value of damaged collateral. There is no necessary relation between the value of collateral and a business loss that results from its being destroyed or damaged—as this case illustrates: the business losses exceeded the impairment of the value of the collateral ninefold. The claim of a secured creditor to the proceeds of collateral

[handwritten margin note: proceeds cannot exceed value of the collateral 9-102(a)(64)(D)(E)]

cannot exceed the value of the collateral. UCC § 9-102(a)(64)(D), (E). Recall the qualification in the definition of proceeds in UCC § 9-102(a)(64)(D): "to the extent of the value of collateral."

Despite such limitations in phrasing, some of the language in UCC §9-102(a)(64) clearly does give secured creditors more than they would be entitled to under a strict value-tracing analysis. For example, the secured creditor is able to claim all of the proceeds of a sale or rental, even though a substantial part of that value does not flow from the collateral, but is instead contributed by the debtor. Consider the specific case of a bank that finances the inventory of a furniture store. The store buys an item of furniture wholesale for $500 and sells it retail for $1,000. To accomplish that, the debtor must maintain a place of business, advertise, provide a salesperson to assist the customer, and make delivery. But the entire $1,000 is proceeds because it was "acquired upon the sale . . . of collateral." Before the sale, the bank has only $500 of collateral. After the sale, it has $1,000 of collateral. That is no mere value tracing. Yet it is the typical sale of collateral.

Perhaps because the consequence of finding that collateral has been disposed of is so severe—the secured party gets whatever was acquired in the transaction—some courts are reluctant to make that finding. In cases where the value of the collateral disposed of is small in relation to what is received, these courts ignore the disposition of collateral and hold that none of the property received is proceeds. For example, if you buy food and drink in a hotel and charge it to your room, some courts may not consider the obligation to pay for it to be proceeds of the hotel's food and drink inventory. The reasoning is that most of the obligation is not for the food and drink but for the services of preparing and serving them. The rest, these courts assume, should be ignored as *de minimis*. In a similar vein, courts have held that a corn crop is not proceeds of the seed from which it was grown, Searcy Farm Supply, LLC v. Merchants and Planters Bank, 369 Ark. 487 (2007), and that hogs are not the proceeds of the feed they consume, Farmers Cooperative Elevator Co. v. Union State Bank, 409 N.W.2d 178 (Iowa 1987).

Proceeds is thus an all-or-nothing concept. Courts may quibble about what was acquired upon the exchange of collateral. If the debtor sells strawberries that are collateral and charges the buyer the purchase price of the strawberries plus $36,000 for shipping, the $36,000 may not be acquired upon the exchange of the strawberries, and therefore not become proceeds. But if the the debtor sells the same strawberries for a "delivered price" that includes the shipping charges, the entire price received probably is proceeds. Johanson Transportation Service v. Rich Pik'd Rite Inc., 164 Cal. App. 3d 583 (1995). UCC §9-102(a)(64)(D) and (E) provide rules for dividing litigation or insurance proceeds into proceeds and non-proceeds and courts will sometimes talk about deposit accounts as proceeds to a particular dollar amount. But whether the putative proceeds are goods or cash-for-goods, the courts treat them as entirely proceeds or not proceeds at all.

When the parties have done a poor job of expressing their desire that the security interest follow the value of the collateral, some courts are quick to infer it, even if the inference does violence to the definition of the terms used.

For example, in McLemore, Trustee v. Mid-South Agri-Chemical Corp., 41 B.R. 369 (Bankr. M.D. Tenn. 1984), one creditor's security agreement provided an interest in the debtor's "corn crop" and "proceeds" of the corn crop and another's provided an interest in "all crops, annual and perennial, and other plant products now planted, growing or grown, or which are hereafter planted or otherwise become growing crops or other plant products" and "proceeds" from these crops. Later, the debtor joined the PIK Diversion Program, a government subsidy program in which the debtor contracted with the U.S. government not to grow crops on the property. The debtor received a substantial cash payment for *not* growing crops on the land identified. The court held that the PIK payments were proceeds of the crops that were never planted. The court reconciled its decision with the definition in UCC §9-102(a)(64) by stating that "Participation in the PIK program 'disposes' of the debtor's corn crops by precluding their cultivation." But the assertion that a debtor disposed of something that never came into existence is at best a legal fiction. The *McLemore* court focused on the economic equivalence of the crops and the payments; the existence of one precluded the existence of the other. While the court did not mention value tracing, that is what it did. Not all courts, however, have taken this route with regard to PIK payments. Some have stuck with the plain meaning of UCC §9-102(a)(64), ruling that the payments are not proceeds of the crop. But the *McLemore* case is important as an illustration of the impetus in some courts to translate "proceeds" into a concept of economic equivalence.

"Proceeds" are "collateral" within the definition of the latter term in UCC §9-102(a)(12). As a result, when proceeds are disposed of or rights arise out of them, whatever is received is "proceeds." Thus the proceeds of proceeds are proceeds. To illustrate, assume ZBank has a security interest in the inventory of Billie's Toy Shop. Billie's Toy Shop sells some toys to Marjorie Venutti and Venutti writes a check for the $250 purchase price. We already know that the check is proceeds. Now assume that Billie's Toy Shop deposits the check to its bank account and the check is collected. The money in the account is now proceeds of the toys because it was received in exchange for proceeds of the toys. If Billie's Toy Shop uses the money to buy more toys, the new toys will be the proceeds of the old toys.

Even without using the concept of proceeds or tracing the value from the old toys into the new ones, the new toys would be subject to ZBank's security interest as "after-acquired property." See *Stoumbos v. Kilimnik*, in Assignment 9. The concepts of proceeds and after-acquired property frequently overlap, but the former is a value-tracing concept, while the latter is not. We will say more about this later.

Even if the security agreement makes no mention of proceeds, a security interest automatically covers them. This rule derives from UCC §§9-203(f) and 9-315(a). To illustrate, assume that the ZBank's security agreement with Billie's Toy Shop describes the collateral as "inventory and equipment" but does not mention the proceeds of inventory and equipment. ZBank's security interest nevertheless extends to the proceeds of inventory and equipment.

2. *Termination of Security Interest in the Collateral After Authorized Disposition*

Secured creditors sometimes authorize their debtors to dispose of the collateral free of the security interest. This authorization might be contained in the security agreement, as when the inventory lender to a department store agrees that the store can sell inventory to customers free of the security interest. Alternatively, this authorization might be expressed by the secured creditor at some later time, as when the bank that financed an automobile approves the owner's plan to sell it free of the security interest. Finally, this authorization might be implied from the circumstances or conduct of the parties, as when the security agreement between an inventory lender and a department store is silent on the matter of sale of collateral or where the bank that financed a herd of cattle knows that the debtor has been selling cattle from the herd to buyers who do not think they are taking subject to a security interest and the bank has not objected to the sales. In any of these instances, UCC §9-315(a)(1) gives effect to the authorization: The buyer takes free of the security interest and the secured creditor can look only to the debtor and the proceeds.

implied from circumstances or conduct of parties
9-315(a)(1)

3. *Continuation of Security Interest in the Collateral After Unauthorized Disposition*

In some secured financing arrangements, the parties contemplate that the debtor will sell the collateral only pursuant to further arrangements. For example, the security agreement may require that the secured creditor authorize sales to particular customers. This arrangement is often used in the financing of expensive items of collateral. For example, the bank that finances an airplane dealer may require that the dealer obtain authorization each time it sells an airplane. When the dealer finds a buyer for one of its planes, it makes the contract contingent on the approval of its financing bank and forwards the contract to the bank. One reason for such an arrangement is to allow the bank to pass on the nature and adequacy of the consideration the dealer will receive from the sale. Another is to alert the bank that the consideration is about to be paid, so the bank can be involved in determining what portion should be applied to the secured debt and what portion should remain with the dealer.

The language of many security agreements prohibits sale of the collateral. For example, the following provision appears in the Wisconsin Bankers Association standard form for a Motor Vehicle Consumer Security Agreement: "[The debtor] shall . . . not sell, lease or otherwise dispose of [the automobile] except as specifically authorized in this Agreement or in writing by the Seller." The agreement does not authorize any sales by the debtor. Of course, such a clause does not mean that the buyer cannot sell the car at all. A security interest is only a contingent right to the collateral in the event that the debtor does not pay the secured obligation. When the debtor pays, the security interest terminates and the debtor is free to sell. The true meaning of such a clause is that the debtor must pay the debt in full in order to have the right to sell the collateral.

To understand how this might work in practice, assume that Arthur Dent purchased a Ford Prefect with financing from ZBank, under a security agreement that contained the provision set forth in the preceding paragraph and ZBank did not otherwise authorize sale. Arthur owes $12,000 against the car, and wants to sell it to Trillian McWilliams for $10,000. If Arthur has $12,000 in cash, he can pay ZBank, terminate its lien, and then sell the car.

Similarly, if Arthur has $2,000 and Trillian is willing to pay in advance, Arthur can do the same. But it would be foolish for a person in Trillian's position to do so. If Arthur got Trillian's money, but for some reason could not (or did not) deliver the car, Trillian might be only an unsecured creditor of Arthur's. Just as ZBank won't give up its security interest until it gets its money, Trillian should not give up her money until she gets clear title to the car.

The solution is to arrange for a simultaneous exchange of the security interest, the car, and the money. Arthur, Trillian, and ZBank will agree that someone will be escrowee or trustee for the transaction. In this example, the parties are likely to select ZBank. (Even with the nasty things some banks have done in recent decades, most people still trust banks more than they trust each other.) ZBank will wear two hats in the transaction: that of secured party and that of trustee or escrowee. Arthur and Trillian will pay their money to ZBank in trust, Arthur will authorize transfer of title to Trillian, and ZBank will execute the document terminating its lien. The terms of the trust are that if ZBank receives all the money, the transfer authorization, and the termination statement by an agreed date, ZBank can "close" the transaction by filing the termination statement and the transfer authorization with the Department of Motor Vehicles and disbursing the $12,000 from its trust account to its operating account. If ZBank does not receive the money and the documents, ZBank must return what it did receive and the nonbreaching party may then seek appropriate legal remedies against the breaching party.

If Arthur doesn't have $2,000, he cannot close. He may then be in a position where he can neither make his payments on the car, nor sell it without ZBank's consent. A sale that will produce proceeds less than necessary to satisfy the secured debt is commonly referred to as a "short" sale. If ZBank does not consent to this short sale, Arthur might need to seek relief in bankruptcy.

Of course, if Arthur owed less than the sale price of the car, he could have closed and walked away with some cash. For example, if he owed $12,000 and Trillian were buying for $14,000, the parties would still need the escrow arrangement to protect themselves, but the sale would go through and Arthur could get the $2,000 difference between the loan amount and the contract price.

Despite their contracts not to sell collateral without their secured party's consent, debtors often do so. Some even go a step further by collecting the purchase price and spending it without paying the secured loan. Many states have enacted statutes making such conduct criminal. For example, Illinois added the section set forth below to its version of UCC §9-315. Notice that this statute does not make every unauthorized sale a crime—only those in which the debtor willfully and wrongfully fails to pay the proceeds to the secured party.

Illinois Compiled Statutes

810 Ill. Comp. Stat. 5/9-315.01 (2015)

It is unlawful for a debtor under the terms of a security agreement (a) who has no right of sale or other disposition of the collateral or (b) who has a right of sale or other disposition of the collateral and is to account to the secured party for the proceeds of any sale or other disposition of the collateral, to sell or otherwise dispose of the collateral and willfully and wrongfully to fail to pay the secured party the amount of said proceeds due under the security agreement. Failure to pay such proceeds to the secured party within 10 days after the sale or other disposition of the collateral is prima facie evidence of a willful and wanton failure to pay. [Such conduct is a Class 3 felony, punishable by two to five years in prison.]

New York goes a step further, making it a crime merely to sell collateral in violation of a security agreement that prohibits sale.

New York Penal Law

§185.05 (2015)

A person is guilty of fraud involving a security interest when, having executed a security agreement creating a security interest in personal property securing a monetary obligation owed to a secured party, and . . . [h]aving under the security agreement no right of sale or other disposition of the property, he knowingly secretes, withholds or disposes of such property in violation of the security agreement. Fraud involving a security interest is a Class A misdemeanor.

Even if the security agreement expressly prohibits sale of the collateral, the debtor has the power under UCC §9-401 to transfer ownership to a buyer. (The transfer will be a breach of the security agreement.) To understand the effect of UCC §9-401, you must read it together with UCC §9-315(a)(1), which provides that a security interest "continues in collateral notwithstanding sale." The result is that after a sale that the secured party has not authorized to be free of the security interest, the buyer will own the collateral subject to the security interest. The buyer may or may not know of that interest. (In Assignment 36, we will examine UCC §9-320(a), which protects buyers in the ordinary course of business against security interests created by their sellers, but for now you should assume that the sales we talk about are not in the ordinary course of business.)

Unless the secured party has authorized the debtor to sell the collateral free of the security interest, the security interest continues in the original collateral and also in the proceeds. UCC §9-315(a). This is no mere tracing of the value of the collateral; it is potentially a multiplication of the value in favor of the secured creditor. Probably the rationale is that when the debtor sells without authorization, the secured creditor needs additional protection. The original collateral, the proceeds, or both are likely to be in jeopardy. Indeed, a common scenario is that the debtor sells the collateral to obtain cash, which it desperately needs to meet other obligations. By the time the secured party learns of the sale, the debtor has spent the money and the collateral itself is in the hands of a bona fide purchaser or somewhere the secured creditor cannot find it.

[handwritten margin note: bona fide purchase — doesn't know of security interest]

Nevertheless, the multiplication of collateral that can result from the rules of UCC §§9-102(a)(12) and (64) and 9-315(a) is striking. Assume, for example, that ZBank has a security interest in Jack's cow. Without authorization from ZBank, Jack sells the cow to Barbara for $2,000. ZBank's security interest continues in the collateral (the cow) and also in the identifiable proceeds of that sale (the $2,000). If Jack then uses the $2,000 of proceeds to buy some beans, the beans will also be proceeds under UCC §9-102(a)(64) (recall that the proceeds of proceeds are proceeds) and ZBank's security interest will continue in the beans under UCC §9-315(a). ZBank can foreclose against the cow and the beans, and collect its money where it can. Whether ZBank can also collect from the cash in the hands of the bean seller is considered in the next section.

Now assume that before ZBank forecloses, Barbara resells the cow for $2,500. Under UCC §9-315(a), ZBank's security interest continues in the cow despite the resale. (Notice that UCC §9-315(a) does not say that the sale must be by the obligor.) The $2,500 Barbara received for the cow is also proceeds of ZBank's collateral because it was acquired upon disposition of the cow that was collateral. This example illustrates that unauthorized sales of collateral can cause it to multiply dramatically. Just as the monster in the old B-movie, *The Blob*, absorbed everything it came in contact with and grew constantly larger, the secured creditor's collateral absorbs everything for which it is exchanged and grows larger also. (If you decide to do outside research on this one, be sure to see the original film, starring Steve McQueen. The concept was entirely botched in the remake.)

Associated Industries v. Keystone General Inc. (In re Keystone General Inc.), 135 B.R. 275 (Bankr. S.D. Ohio 1991), gives an example of how collateral can proliferate through unauthorized disposition. Star Bank financed Keystone General's inventory under a security agreement that extended to after-acquired property. Keystone General bought $1.9 million of inventory from Associated, failed to pay for it, and later returned it to Associated. But because Keystone General had rights in the collateral in the interim, Star Bank's security interest attached. When Keystone General returned the inventory to Associated in exchange for a credit to Keystone's account — without Star Bank's authorization to do so free of Star Bank's lien — Star Bank's security interest continued in the inventory pursuant to UCC §9-315(a). Star Bank ended up with a security interest in electronic components that its debtor hadn't paid for and no longer owned or possessed.

Secured creditors who insist on security agreement provisions restricting the sale of their collateral often intend to enforce the restriction only if their relationship with the debtor sours. So long as the relationship remains good, they allow the debtor to sell portions of the collateral and ignore the restrictions. When the relationship does sour, these creditors often find that the courts will not enforce the restrictions. Instead, the courts may hold that the creditor waived the conditions on sale by its course of performance with the debtor and that the sale to the third party was therefore authorized. UCC §1-303(a), (f).

These waiver cases usually seem to arise in the context of sales of livestock, where sales by debtors are pretty much continuous and the buyers are not protected by UCC §9-320(a). For example, in Gretna State Bank v. Cornbelt Livestock Co., 463 N.W.2d 975 (Neb. 1990), the security agreement prohibited sale of the dairy cows that served as collateral except with the express written permission of the bank. The bank knew, however, that the debtor had been selling cows without the bank's express written permission in violation of the security agreement and had not objected. Later, when the bank sued a livestock market that had participated in the sales, the court directed a verdict against the bank on the ground that it had waived the prohibition on sales.

4. Limitations on the Secured Creditor's Ability to Trace Collateral

In *The Blob* it quickly became apparent to Steve McQueen that if his proceeds-like adversary went unchecked, it would eventually absorb everything. What keeps a secured creditor's collateral from doing the same? To answer this question completely, you will need some concepts that we do not discuss until Part Two of this book. The short version is that sales of collateral in the ordinary course of business often strip liens from the collateral. The stripping, however, is far from complete. The cereal you ate for breakfast this morning was probably covered with security interests. Yuck!

One limitation we can discuss here is that a security interest continues to encumber proceeds only so long as the proceeds remain "identifiable." See UCC §9-315(a)(2). To figure out what this means, begin by distinguishing the concepts of *commingling* and *identifiability*. To commingle collateral is to put it together in one mass with identical noncollateral so that no one can tell which is *actually* which. When Farmer Brown puts her wheat in a storage silo in Oklahoma, the grain will become commingled with that of lots of other Okie farmers. No one could pick out which grains were Brown's. Nevertheless, such commingled grain may be legally identifiable: that is, the law may provide a rule that arbitrarily designates a particular part of the mass as the collateral. Such a tracing rule enables the court to tell which grain is *legally* which.

Tracing is most often required when the debtor commingles cash proceeds with other money in a bank account. The secured creditor may be quick on the debtor's heels but fail to arrive until after the debtor has written checks on the account disbursing some of the money to payees from whom it cannot be recovered. The secured creditor, of course, would like to claim that the money remaining in the account is its collateral and, if necessary, that the money paid out was someone else's. Other parties (typically other creditors and the bank in which the funds were deposited) will probably want to make the opposite claim: The secured creditor's collateral was used to make payments and the money remaining in the account is theirs. UCC §9-315(b) provides that the secured party can prevail by identifying the funds remaining in the bank account as its collateral by "a method of tracing, including application of equitable principles" that is permitted under non-UCC law with respect to the type of collateral. Comment 3 to that section refers to the "equitable principle" most commonly employed: the *lowest intermediate balance rule*. That rule provides that the amount of the secured creditor's collateral remaining in a bank account after the deposit of proceeds and subsequent transactions is the lowest balance of all funds in the account from the time of the deposit to the completion of the transactions. To put it another way, in calculating the amount of proceeds remaining in the account, the debtor is presumed to spend first from the debtor's own funds; whatever remains is proceeds.

The table below illustrates application of the rule. Arthur Dent sells his encumbered Ford Prefect for $20,000, which he receives in payments of $12,000 and $8,000. Arthur deposits the two checks to his bank account, which already contains $3,000. At the end of the month, Arthur's bank statement reveals the following transactions:

Description	Deposits	Withdrawals	Balance
Opening balance			$3,000
Sale of Prefect (1)	$12,000		15,000
Tuition payment		$11,000	4,000
Sale of Prefect (2)	8,000		12,000
Books		7,000	5,000
Student loan	6,000		11,000

The amount of identifiable proceeds remaining in the account after the tuition payment was $4,000. The amount of identifiable proceeds grew to $12,000 with the second deposit of proceeds, fell to $5,000 after the payment for books (the lowest intermediate balance), and remained at that number until the end of the month.

If a bank account contains the proceeds of more than one secured creditor's collateral, each is entitled to a pro rata share based on the amount it contributed. Restatement (Third) of Restitution and Unjust Enrichment §59 comment f. Thus, for example, if secured party one traced $30,000 into a bank account and secured party two traced $60,000 into that same account, but the debtor dissipated $69,000, leaving only $21,000 in the bank account, secured party one is entitled to $7,000 and secured party two is entitled to $14,000.

In the case that follows, the court held that a secured creditor could not trace its collateral. As you read the case, try to imagine the evidence that would have satisfied the court.

In re Oriental Rug Warehouse Club, Inc.

205 B.R. 407 (Bankr. D. Minn. 1997)

NANCY C. DREHER, UNITED STATES BANKRUPTCY JUDGE.

1. The Debtor is a Minnesota corporation engaged in the business of selling oriental rugs and carpets at retail. On April 29, 1993, the Debtor and Yashar entered into a "consignment agreement," whereby Debtor took possession of several of Yashar's rugs for the purpose of reselling them in its business. Debtor agreed to pay Yashar a total consignment price of $106,073.00 for the rugs, and agreed to apply the proceeds received from resale to the outstanding amount owed to Yashar.

3. Debtor sold a portion of the consigned rugs but failed to remit the proceeds from the sales to Yashar as provided by their agreement. Instead, the Debtor invested the proceeds from the sale of Yashar's rugs into the purchase of replacement rug inventory or otherwise retained the proceeds. On or around May of 1995, the brother of the president of Yashar went to the Debtor's place of business and repossessed all of the consigned rugs which were still in the Debtor's possession and which had not yet been sold. Although the Debtor currently has rugs in its inventory, the Debtor no longer possesses rugs that were supplied by Yashar.

4. On April 15, 1996, Debtor filed a petition for relief under Chapter 11 of the United States Bankruptcy Code. On August 20, 1996, Yashar filed a proof of secured claim in the amount of $64,243.00, representing the outstanding amount still owed to Yashar for the rugs which had been sold by the Debtor without remitting the proceeds. Pursuant to 11 U.S.C. §502, the Debtor has objected to Yashar's secured claim.

CONCLUSIONS OF LAW

In this case, the objective characteristics of the agreement between the Debtor and Yashar indicate that the parties did not intend to create a true consignment, but instead intended to grant Yashar a security interest in the consigned rugs. Therefore, instead of creating a true consignment relationship whereby the consignee acts as agent to sell the property of the consignor, the parties to the present case created a standard "floor plan" arrangement whereby Yashar agreed to finance the Debtor's inventory in exchange for a security interest in the consigned rugs. As a secured financing arrangement, therefore, the transaction between the Debtor and Yashar is governed by the provisions of Article 9 of the UCC.

II.   SECURITY INTERESTS IN PROCEEDS UNDER [UCC §9-315(A)]

Although the originally consigned rugs no longer remain in the Debtor's possession, Yashar argues that the Debtor's current inventory constitutes "proceeds" from the Debtor's sale of the consigned rugs, and that Yashar is therefore entitled to a security interest in the Debtor's remaining inventory. Section [9-315] of the Uniform Commercial Code governs the continuation and perfection of a security interest in proceeds. Therefore, before addressing the merits of the arguments of counsel, it is appropriate to address the provisions of [§9-315] in some detail.

A.   Continuation of a Security Interest in Proceeds: §9-315(a)

Section [9-102(a)(64)] of the UCC defines the term "proceeds" to include "whatever is received upon the sale, exchange, collection or other disposition of collateral or proceeds." [UCC §9-102(a)(64)]. Section [9-315(a)], in turn, provides that, upon the sale of collateral, a security interest in that collateral "continues in any *identifiable proceeds* including collections received by the debtor." [UCC §9-315(a)] (emphasis added). The secured party has the burden of establishing that something constitutes identifiable proceeds from the sale or disposition of the secured party's collateral. To do this, the secured party must "trace" the claimed proceeds back to the original collateral; in other words, the secured party must establish that the alleged proceeds "arose directly from the sale or other disposition of the collateral and that these alleged proceeds cannot have arisen from any other source." [C.O. Funk & Son v. Sullivan Equipment], 415 N.E.2d at 1313.

Special tracing problems arise where cash proceeds are commingled with other deposits in a single bank account. Because of the fungible nature of cash proceeds, there is some authority that cash proceeds are no longer identifiable once they are commingled with other funds. The majority of courts, however, have utilized equitable principles borrowed from the law of trusts to identify whether commingled funds constitute proceeds received from an earlier disposition of collateral. In particular, these courts have utilized the "intermediate balance rule," which creates a presumption that the proceeds of the disposition of collateral remain in a commingled account as long as the account balance is equal to or exceeds the amounts of the proceeds. Therefore, the intermediate balance rule presumes that a debtor who spends money from a commingled account spends first from his own funds. Once the balance of the commingled account drops below the amount of the deposited proceeds, then the secured creditor's interest in the proceeds abates accordingly.

Intermediate balance rule presumes [handwritten margin note]

III.   Yashar's Claim

In this case, Yashar alleges that the Debtor sold its collateral in exchange for cash proceeds, deposited the cash proceeds into the Debtor's general checking account, and then reinvested the cash proceeds to buy more rug inventory. Therefore, to succeed in its claim under the UCC, Yashar must show that: 1) the Debtor's current assets constitute "identifiable proceeds" arising from the disposition of its original collateral under [§9-315(a)]; and 2) the proceeds were properly perfected under [§§9-315(c) and(d)]. Yashar has not argued that it can trace the Debtor's current rug inventory to the sale of its collateral, however. In fact, Yashar has conceded that "it is impossible to reconstruct exactly what the Debtor did with the proceeds of the sale of Yashar's consigned inventory." Instead, Yashar argues that, although a secured creditor claiming an interest in proceeds has the burden of tracing proceeds when it litigates against other secured creditors, a secured creditor should not bear the burden of tracing when it litigates against the debtor. In suits between a debtor and a secured creditor, Yashar asserts, it is unfair to place the burden of tracing proceeds on the secured creditor, who has no ability to control the debtor's books and record keeping procedures.

Yashar's argument simply has no support in either the case law or in the UCC. Although Yashar may think it unfair to place the burden of tracing proceeds squarely on the shoulders of the party claiming the security interest, both the case law and the leading commentaries are clear in this regard. Where a creditor wishes to claim a security interest in proceeds under [§9-315], the burden is on the party claiming the security interest to identify the proceeds. In this situation, Yashar should have protected itself by carefully monitoring the Debtor's inventory and by requiring the Debtor to maintain segregated accounts for the deposit of proceeds. The Court declines to disregard the clear provisions of the UCC and holds that Yashar's argument is without merit.

Accordingly, and for the reasons stated, it is hereby ordered that the secured claim of Yashar Rug Co., Inc. is disallowed in its entirety. Yashar has an unsecured, nonpriority claim in the amount of $64,243.00.

In the penultimate paragraph of the opinion, Judge Dreher states the conventional solution to Yashar's problem: a *segregated* bank account. A segregated bank account is a bank account that contains only the secured creditor's collateral. If Yashar had taken a security interest in all of Oriental Rug Warehouse's inventory, required that Oriental Rug Warehouse deposit all proceeds of inventory sales to the segregated bank account, prohibited Oriental Rug Warehouse from depositing nonproceeds to that account, required that Oriental Rug Warehouse pay for all inventory purchases from that account, and enforced all of these restrictions, the tracing problem would be solved. Oriental Rug Warehouse's banking records would show every rug to have been purchased with proceeds. Once a debtor is in bankruptcy, the debtor is required by law to maintain such segregated accounts for cash collateral. Bankr. Code. §363(c)(4).

The tracing problem that results from commingling proceeds in a bank account includes not only identification of proceeds remaining in the account, but also proceeds paid out of the account. Suppose, for example, that Yashar had been able to prove that Oriental sold the specific rugs to Yashar and deposited the $5,000 in proceeds from those rugs to a bank account that contained $12,000 of nonproceeds, resulting in a balance of $17,000. Under the lowest intermediate balance test, the funds in the account are proceeds to the extent of $5,000.

Assume further that Oriental purchased Apple, Inc. stock from Ameritrade with a $7,000 check drawn on the account. UCC §9-332(b) provides that "a transferee of funds from a deposit account takes the funds free of a security interest in the deposit account unless the transferee acts in collusion with the debtor in violating the rights of the secured party." Ameritrade is not in collusion and so takes the $7,000 free of Yashar's security interest.

UCC §9-315(a)(2) provides that Yashar's "security interest attaches to any identifiable proceeds of collateral." Are the Apple shares identifiable proceeds of Yashar's interest in the commingled bank account? The answer is yes if proceeds were used to purchase them. *Oriental Rug Warehouse* states that "the intermediate balance rule presumes that a debtor who spends money from a commingled account spends first from his own funds." Because the proceeds remain in the account, the money used to pay for the Apple stock must have been nonproceeds.

On the other hand, §59 of the Restatement (Third) of Restitution and Unjust Enrichment makes clear that in some circumstances a restitution claimant can trace funds out of a commingled account. The rules for doing so are complex and depend on the relative equities between the contestants in a particular case. Their application to the context of secured credit is largely by analogy and so is uncertain. We can find no proposal in case or commentary as to the correct method for tracing collateral out of a commingled account.

B.   Other Value-Tracing Concepts

As we noted in our discussion of the UCC §9-102(a)(64) definition of "proceeds," that term may not encompass all of the forms that the value of a secured creditor's collateral can assume. A secured party who wants to contract as nearly as possible for the value of its collateral, in whatever form it may take, will want to employ some additional value-tracing concepts.

The *product* of collateral is something the collateral produces. The term is most commonly used in the context of agriculture. It has been held that wool is the product of sheep, milk the product of cows (although, as you will see in the next assignment, not everyone agrees), and maple syrup the product of sugar maple trees. These "products" may also be "proceeds" of the collateral named because they "aris[e] out of collateral," UCC §9-102(a)(64), but that is unclear.

Another value the secured creditor may take as collateral is the *profit* from other collateral. "Profit" is another term of art, but with more than one meaning. In a general sense, the word can be used to describe the excess of revenues of a business over the expenses where the business itself is the collateral. In the context of real property, "profit" may be short for *profit à prendre*: "A right or privilege to go on another's land and take away something of value from its soil or from the products of its soil (as by mining, logging, or hunting)." Black's Law Dictionary 1404 (10th ed. 2014). "Profit," used in that sense, relates only to real property.

Two other value-tracing concepts are worthy of mention. *Rents* are money paid for the temporary use of collateral. The *offspring* of collateral is a term most often used with regard to animals. A calf is the offspring of a cow, although it may also be considered the product of a cow.

The concept described by each of these terms is to some degree a value-tracing concept, in that the value of the collateral and the value of the product, profit, rent, or offspring are the same value. That is, as the products, profits, rents, or offspring come into existence, the value of the original collateral declines. The value shifts from the collateral and its potential to the products, profits, rents, or offspring actually produced. Viewing an isolated instance of a cow having a calf, the secured creditor's right to offspring seems to generate an increase in the value of the collateral. But considering reproduction in the entire herd over time, the increase is problematic. Offspring are born, adults are slaughtered (sorry, but there really isn't a nice word for it) and the herd—the collateral—tends to remain the same. Similarly, if the owner of property rents it, the value of the owner's remaining interest in the property will be approximately the value it had before it was rented, less the value of the rent to be paid. The use value of the property during the period of the lease has been added to the expected rents and removed from the owner's reversion. By including the rents or offspring as collateral, the secured creditor is not necessarily claiming more than the value of the property or the cow, but may merely be anticipating transformations of those values.

use value added to rent

Products, profits, rents, and offspring of collateral are all arguably "rights arising out of collateral." Thus they are arguably all proceeds. Assuming they are, adding these terms to a description of collateral in a security agreement adds nothing, at least according to Article 9. Even if a description of collateral does not mention proceeds, their inclusion is implied. See UCC §9-203(f). But, as we shall see in the next assignment, bankruptcy law arguably employs a narrower definition of "proceeds" that leaves room for the concepts of products, profits, rents, and offspring to operate.

C.   Non-Value-Tracing Concepts

Concepts such as "after-acquired property," "replacements," "additions," and "substitutions" in a description of collateral are non-value-tracing in that they can pick up property acquired by the debtor with value that is not derived from the previously-existing collateral. The value in proceeds, product, offspring, rents, or profits arguably comes in whole or in part from previously-existing collateral. The value in after-acquired property, replacements, additions, and substitutions can come entirely from some other source, such as unencumbered property of the debtor, a new loan, or a capital contribution by the debtors' owners.

To illustrate the difference between value-tracing concepts and non-value-tracing concepts, assume that Billie's Toy Shop has $100,000 worth of display equipment and that ZBank has a security interest in its "equipment, including after-acquired equipment." Billie's Toy Shop spends $6,000 to buy additional display cases. To know that ZBank's after-acquired property clause will reach the additional cases, we need only know that the cases are equipment and that Billie's owns them. We do not need to know the source of the $6,000.

Now assume instead that ZBank's security interest was in "equipment, not including after-acquired equipment, but including the proceeds of equipment." If Billie's spends $6,000 to buy the additional display cases, we can know if ZBank's security interest attaches to it only by knowing the source of the $6,000. If Billie's obtained the $6,000 by selling equipment that was already collateral, the $6,000 was proceeds, and the new equipment will be proceeds. If the $6,000 was neither collateral nor the proceeds of collateral, the new equipment will not be collateral either.

In the illustration where the $6,000 did not come from existing collateral, application of the after-acquired property clause increased the total value of ZBank's collateral. ZBank had $100,000 of collateral before the purchase and $106,000 afterward. In the illustration where the $6,000 did come from existing collateral, application of the proceeds doctrine did not change the total value of ZBank's collateral. ZBank had $100,000 of collateral in the debtor's possession before the purchase and $100,000 afterward.

The distinction between after-acquired property and proceeds is a fine one. In practice, the security agreement usually provides that the collateral includes both. In such cases, it may not matter which is being applied and it may be unnecessary to distinguish between the two.

D.   Liability of Buyers of Collateral

If a security interest continues in collateral, the buyer takes "subject to" the security interest. That means the secured party has the right to foreclose against the collateral if the secured debt is not paid. The buyer is not liable for the secured debt unless the buyer "assumes" the debt.

Nor is the buyer bound by provisions of the security agreement. UCC §9-201 provides that "a security agreement is effective . . . against purchasers of the collateral." But Comment 2 to that section claims that

> "security agreement" is used here (and elsewhere in this Article) as it is defined in Section 9-102: "an agreement that creates or provides for a security interest." It follows that subsection (a) does not provide that every term or provision contained in a record that contains a security agreement or that is so labeled is effective.

In other words, "security agreement" should be read to mean "security interest"—except when it shouldn't. (That sounds as bad to us as it does to you, but the law is the law.)

Some buyers—for example, the buyer of a debtor's business—may choose to assume the debtor's debt and become bound by the debtor's security agreement. The debtor who makes such an election is referred to as a "new debtor." UCC §§9-102(a)(56) and 9-203(d). A new debtor is bound by the existing security agreement, including provisions creating security interests in after-acquired property. UCC §9-203(e).

Problem Set 10

10.1.   Firstbank has a perfected security interest in all of the "equipment, inventory, and accounts" of Polly Arthur, who is doing business as Polly's

Plumbing. The contract makes no mention of proceeds, products, offspring, substitutions, additions, or replacements. Are they included? UCC §§9-102(a)(42) and (64), 9-201(a), 9-203(f), 9-204(a).

10.2. Which of the following are collateral of Firstbank under the security agreement described in Problem 10.1 and why? UCC §§9-102(a)(2) and (64), 9-315(a).

a.   The money now in Polly's bank account.

b.   A parrot that Polly took in payment of an overdue account.

c.   A new computer that Polly bought to replace the computer she owned at the time she granted the security interest to Firstbank.

d.   A myna bird that Polly took from Robin Watts in payment for some plumbing work. (Watts didn't have the money to pay for the plumbing work and arranged in advance to trade the bird for the work; Polly did the plumbing while Watts was at her own job; Watts gave Polly the myna bird the following day and Polly kept it as a pet.)

10.3. A few months ago, Equipment Leasing Partners (ELP) financed the Lucky Partners Syndicate's acquisition of a thoroughbred racehorse named Horace. ELP took a security interest in Horace and "all proceeds, products, and profits therefrom." Lucky Partners defaulted on the $7.5 million loan. ELP repossessed Horace and sold him for $2.7 million. Shortly before the repossession, Horace won $500,000 in a race. Lucky Partners has demanded the purse, but the track has not yet paid it. ELP asks you whether they have a valid claim to the purse. What do you tell them? UCC §9-102(a)(64).

10.4. Joey Teigh contracted to buy Billie's Toy Shop, including the leasehold, furniture, fixtures, equipment, goodwill, accounts receivable, and trademarks. Joey hired you to represent her in the closing. In preparing for the closing, you learned that Joey and Billie omitted the inventory from the sale because Firstbank had a security interest in it. You've looked at Firstbank's security agreement and the description of collateral is just "inventory." Is it possible that the security interest encumbers some of the accounts receivable? The other property Joey is buying? (For now, don't worry about whether the security interest could be perfected; confine your inquiry to whether it could attach.)

10.5.   a. ELP consults you about a $35,000 loan to Golan Industries that was made for the express purpose of purchasing an XT-100 copier. Golan signed a security agreement granting ELP a security interest in the copier. (The entire description of collateral reads "XT-100 copier, serial number XEX3088372.") The copier was destroyed in a fire six months ago. Fortunately, the loss was insured. At this point, what is ELP's collateral? UCC §§9-102(a)(12)(A) and (64), 9-203(f).

b.   Unfortunately, ELP was not named as a loss payee on the policy, so the insurance company paid the $35,000 in insurance proceeds to Golan. Golan deposited the check to a little-used bank account that contained $5,000 at the time. At this point, what is ELP's collateral? UCC §9-315(b)(2).

c.   From the account Golan wrote a check for $2,000 to rent another copier for the month it would take to replace the XT-100, leaving $38,000 in the account. At this point, what is ELP's collateral?

d.   Golan then wrote a check from the account for $32,000 to pay the IRS, leaving only $6,000 in the account. The month is up. At this point, what is ELP's collateral? UCC §§9-315(b)(2), 9-332, Comment 3 to UCC §9-315.

10.6.   Your investigation of the Golan account indicates that the $32,000 check that cleared the account was not to the IRS. Golan used the $32,000 to buy another XT-100 to replace the one that had been destroyed. (It seems the price of XT-100s had fallen a bit since the initial purchase.) The new XT-100 was delivered immediately and the debtor is operating it now. If this new information is correct, what is ELP's collateral?

■ END OF DEFAULT PROBLEM SET

10.7   Kruel Motion Picture Studios is in the business of distributing motion pictures in all media and licensing subsidiary rights. Kruel recently purchased the right to distribute a motion picture — a derivative work based on the novel *Blood, Sex, and Secured Credit*. Kruel owns the exclusive right to distribute the film worldwide (the "distribution rights") and the exclusive right to manufacture and sell clothing that incorporates certain trademarks and graphic characters associated with the film (the "character rights"). Kruel granted non-exclusive licenses to several exhibitors to show the film in theaters (the "exhibition rights"). Kruel also granted an exclusive license of the character rights to Target. Both the film exhibitors and Target are obligated under their contracts to pay royalties to Kruel monthly, in amounts that are determined based on the licensees' revenues from tickets and sales. Kruel retains the right to terminate the licenses on default. For the past five years, EuroBank has financed Kruel's operations under a line of credit and has held a security interest in Kruel's "general intangibles."

a.   Does Kruel have a security interest in the licenses owned by Target and the exhibitors? UCC §§1-201(b)(35), 9-109(a)(1).

b.   Does EuroBank have a security interest in the licenses owned by Kruel? In the licenses owned by Target and the exhibitors? §§9-201, 9-315(a)(1), 9-321(a) and (b).

c.   Does EuroBank have a security interest in the royalties owing from the exhibitors and Target to Kruel? UCC §§9-102(a)(2), (42), and (64), 9-203(f).

Assignment 11: Tracing Collateral Value During Bankruptcy

In the absence of bankruptcy, the relationship between the secured party and the debtor is governed almost entirely by contract. If the contract says that the secured creditor has an interest in after-acquired property, then the secured creditor has such an interest. The debtor can use the collateral in whatever manner the contract permits. If the debtor defaults in any of its obligations, the secured party can foreclose.

When a debtor files bankruptcy, the rules change. Even if the debtor is in default, the automatic stay prevents the secured party from foreclosing. In this assignment, we explore other changes in the secured party-debtor relation that result from bankruptcy. Simply stated, these are the bankruptcy-specific rules explored in this assignment:

1. After-acquired property clauses are not effective with respect to collateral the debtor acquires during the bankruptcy case.
2. Secured parties continue to have the right to the proceeds of pre-existing collateral.
3. "Based on the equities of case," the bankruptcy courts have the power to limit secured parties' rights to proceeds. They generally use the power to limit secured parties to value tracing, but they trace value in differing ways.
4. Debtors have the right to use collateral during bankruptcy, but only on the condition that they provide adequate protection to the secured party.
5. If the collateral is cash collateral, such as bank deposits, the debtor must obtain the consent of the secured party or an order of the court before using collateral.

A. After-Acquired Property and the Proceeds Dilemma

Article 9 permits a secured creditor to trace the value of its collateral through concepts such as proceeds or products and also to pick up additional collateral by means of an after-acquired property clause. At state law, it makes no difference whether a creditor obtained its security interest in property acquired after the security agreement as proceeds or by operation of an after-acquired property clause, so long as at least one of the concepts would cover the property in question.

Once the debtor files for bankruptcy, however, the distinction becomes critical. Bankruptcy Code §552(b) permits the secured creditor to trace the value of its collateral. But once the debtor is in bankruptcy, the secured creditor can no longer pick up additional collateral by means of an after-acquired property clause. Bankr. Code §552(a). Bankruptcy Code §552(b) limits value-tracing to five concepts: proceeds, products, offspring, rents, or profits.

The result is that the secured creditor generally can keep the collateral value it has as of the filing of the bankruptcy case, even if that collateral value is transformed, but cannot acquire additional collateral value during bankruptcy. The policy rationale is that once bankruptcy stays creditors from exercising their state remedies, it should safeguard their entitlements. Bankruptcy law prohibits the debtor from favoring one creditor over another in its postpetition dealings. For example, the debtor cannot use property of the estate to pay one prepetition unsecured claim without paying other claims of the same kind pro rata. To permit an after-acquired property clause to operate postpetition would violate this basic principle of bankruptcy.

Consider this example. Wellfoot Electrical Service owes Sunshine Bank $100,000. The loan is secured by a security interest in "all of Wellfoot Electrical's equipment, current and after acquired." At the time of the filing, Wellfoot owns equipment valued at $70,000. While in bankruptcy, Wellfoot trades this equipment for newer equipment that will make Wellfoot's operations more efficient. The bank's security interest attaches to the new equipment as proceeds of the old equipment. UCC §9-315(a); Bankr. Code §552(b). Later, Wellfoot decides to use income from the business to buy a computer system worth $30,000 to handle the billing and paperwork. In the absence of bankruptcy, Article 9 would have permitted the bank's security interest to extend to the newly acquired computer system. Bankruptcy law does not. Bankr. Code §552(a). Because Wellfoot is in bankruptcy, all of its unencumbered assets, including its income, are property of the estate. The unsecured creditors are entitled to those assets (pro rata after payment of priority claims) even though none can reach them while the stay remains in effect.

In effect, Bankruptcy Code §552 permits a secured creditor to trace collateral value from one form to another, but does not permit the secured creditor to convert the unsecured portion of its claim to a secured portion by claiming additional assets. At filing, Sunshine Bank had an allowed secured claim for $70,000 and an unsecured claim for $30,000. Assuming that Wellfoot's trade was for equal dollar value, the bank still had only a $70,000 secured claim afterward.

The same is not true of the computer purchase. If the bank's security interest could attach to the computer, the bank's allowed secured claim would grow to $100,000, and the bank would receive payment in full on the underlying loan. The other unsecured creditors would get nothing in return for the $30,000 spent to enhance the bank's collateral. The bank would receive a windfall at the unsecured creditors' expense.

In our example, Wellfoot traded $70,000 worth of equipment for a different $70,000 of equipment, and bankruptcy law recognized the bank's right to the new equipment as proceeds. What if, to make the trade, Wellfoot had to pay an additional $30,000, from the income of the business and received a single item of equipment worth $100,000 in return? Under UCC §9-102(a)(64), the new equipment would still be proceeds of the old. "Proceeds" are not just the value that can be traced into the new collateral from the old. Under the UCC, "proceeds" includes whatever is received in a transaction in which the debtor disposes of collateral. The courts generally hold the word "proceeds" to have that same meaning as it is used in Bankruptcy Code 552(b). Thus, even though in this second example the bank's after-acquired property clause doesn't operate, the bank's right to "proceeds" of its equipment gives the bank a $30,000 windfall at the unsecured creditors' expense.

With few exceptions, proceeds is an all-or-nothing concept. An item of property is entirely proceeds or not proceeds at all. This creates a dilemma for the bankruptcy system. If, on the facts of our example, the court holds the new equipment not to be proceeds, the secured party has lost its $70,000 of collateral. If the court holds the new equipment to be collateral, the secured party receives a windfall and the unsecured creditors have lost assets ($30,000) that otherwise would have been available for distribution to them.

The problem posed by our example is pervasive in actual business operations, forcing the bankruptcy courts to resolve the dilemma. While we love the following case for its demonstration of that pervasiveness, we warn you that the court's "solution" relies on an incorrect assumption that proceeds are identified based on strict value tracing. As described in Assignment 10, proceeds is an all-or-nothing concept that traces value only loosely.

In re Cafeteria Operators, L.P.

299 B.R. 400 (Bankr. N.D. Tex. 2003)

HARLIN D. HALE, BANKRUPTCY JUDGE.

FACTS

The Debtors operate family-style cafeteria restaurants in several states. The Debtors also own and operate a food preparation, processing and distribution center that processes and delivers various food items, both internally to the Debtors' restaurants and externally to third-party purchasers. On April 10, 2001, the Debtors entered into a $55,000,000 Revolving Credit and Term Loan Agreement ("Credit Agreement") with Fleet National Bank on behalf of itself and as agent for a group of secured lenders (collectively, the "Bank Group"). In connection with the Credit Agreement, Bank Group was granted a security interest in certain personal and real property, including, in relevant part

> [a]ll personal and fixture property of every kind and nature including without limitation all furniture, fixtures, equipment, raw materials, inventory, other goods, accounts, . . . deposit accounts, rights to proceeds of letters of credit and all general intangibles.

On January 3, 2003 (the "Petition Date"), the Debtors commenced reorganization cases under Chapter 11 of the Bankruptcy Code. Immediately thereafter, the Debtors [moved for an order authorizing the use of cash collateral] (the "Cash Collateral Motion").

AUTHORITIES

The starting point in any cash collateral analysis is the language of Bankruptcy Code §363, which states, in relevant part, that a debtor-in-possession may not use, sell or lease cash collateral unless 1) each entity with an interest in the cash collateral consents to or 2) the court, after notice and hearing, authorizes the use of, cash collateral. 11 U.S.C. §363(c)(2). Cash collateral is defined in the Bankruptcy Code as

> cash, negotiable instruments, documents of title, securities, deposit accounts, or other cash equivalents whenever acquired in which the estate and an entity other that the estate have an interest and includes the *proceeds,* products, offspring, rents, or profits of property . . . whether existing *before* or *after* the commencement of a case under this title.

11 U.S.C. §363(a) (emphasis added).

[The court set forth the provisions of Bankruptcy Code §552(a) and (b)(1).] With the passage of the Bankruptcy Code, Congress enacted §552 to limit legislatively the effect of pre-petition liens on the debtor's post-petition property. As noted by one bankruptcy court, "[i]t is beyond question that in enacting §552, Congress sought to preserve the 'fresh start' policy so eloquently stated by the Supreme Court in *Local Loan* by requiring that only security interests in after-acquired property 'arising from, or connected with, preexisting property' be preserved in bankruptcy." Smoker v. Hill & Associates, Inc., 204 B.R. 966, 974 (N.D. Ind. 1997) (citing *Local Loan,* 292 U.S. at 243, 54 S. Ct. 695). The passage of §552 broadened the scope of the *Local Loan* holding to extinguish all liens on after-acquired property, subject to certain exceptions.

Under §552 of the Bankruptcy Code, post-petition property acquired by the debtor's estate, such as revenues generated from operations, is not subject to any liens resulting from pre-petition security agreements unless the pre-petition security agreements create a security interest in pre-petition property and its proceeds, product, offspring, rents or profits and the post-petition property constitutes such proceeds, product, offspring, rents or profits. From a plain reading of §552, revenues generated post-petition solely as a result of the debtor's labor are not subject to a pre-petition lender's security interest.

The parties do not dispute that the Bank Group's security interest extends to virtually all of Debtors' real and personal property—characterized by the Bank Group as a "blanket lien." Instead, the instant dispute is fueled by one primary issue: whether the restaurant revenues are §552 proceeds of property subject to the Bank Group's pre-petition lien.

> [The] acquisition by the estate of additional collateral post-petition does not increase the value of the claim subject to adequate protection. If the value of the original collateral has not diminished, proceeds under §552(b) may be used—pursuant to court order—to pay ordinary business expenses and administrative expenses, consistent with adequate protection.

In re Markos Gurnee P'ship, 252 B.R. 712, 717 (Bankr. N.D. Ill. 1997).

HOTEL REVENUES AS CASH COLLATERAL

In support of its position, the Bank Group relies primarily on a number of real estate cases involving revenues generated by hotels. The issue in these cases typically is whether hotel revenues are "rents" and therefore, the secured lender's cash collateral.

For example, in In re Miami Center Assoc., Ltd., 144 B.R. 937 (Bankr. S.D. Fla. 1992), the court held that §552(b) applies to extend the lender's pre-petition liens to post-petition revenue based, in part, on "the unique nature of hotel financing, [and] the fact that the bulk of hotel revenue is generated from the use of rooms (*as opposed to services*)." (emphasis added).

However, the hotel cases are distinguishable from the restaurant revenue situation in which revenues are derived primarily from services. In fact, one case cited by the Bank Group, In re S.F. Drake Hotel Assoc., 131 B.R. 156, 159 (Bankr. N.D. Cal. 1991), distinguishes hotel revenues from restaurant revenues and notes "[a] hotel operation is unlike a racetrack, restaurant, or retail store, where the primary objective of the customer is to receive a service." The court reasoned that

> [c]ertainly hotels provide services, but so also do apartment and office buildings. Any services that a hotel provides are *incidental* to room occupancy. The hotel guest's primary objective is shelter. That shelter is provided by the land and improvements of the hotel. A hotelier cannot operate a hotel without the real property and improvements, no matter what the extent of the services provided.

The issue with regard to the restaurant industry does not appear to be such a clear cut case.

RESTAURANT REVENUES AS CASH COLLATERAL

In the restaurant context, some authority supports the Debtors' position. In *In re Inman,* 95 B.R. 479, 480-81 (Bankr. W.D. Ky. 1988), the Bankruptcy Court for the Western District of Kentucky noted that

> the restaurant industry, in general, is a service-oriented industry. In comparison with food wholesalers and retailers who sell food products in their natural or packaged state, restaurants expend a great deal of time and energy preparing individual food orders by transforming these natural or packaged foods into menu items. As in any business, the cost of preparing such foods for human consumption is without a doubt passed on to the consumer.

In *Inman,* the secured lender held a security interest in the debtor's inventory. The *Inman* court found that revenues generated by a fast food restaurant did not constitute proceeds from the sale of inventory. The court held that the secured lender did not have a valid, perfected security interest in the resulting cash deposits and concluded that the Debtor's post-petition cash was free of the pre-petition interests of the secured lender.

In a similar vein to the hotel cases, some courts have held that a lender's security interest in real property does not create a post-petition lien on restaurant revenues.

The Bank Group was only able to provide one bankruptcy court opinion that touched on the application of §552 to restaurant revenues. In that case, the court stated, in dicta, that "the initial proceeds of the debtors' restaurant operation were unquestionably 'proceeds' of the bank's pre-petition collateral (such as the food that constituted the restaurant's inventory)" without any discussion of the basis for that general statement. In re Markos Gurnee P'ship, 252 B.R. 712, 720 n. 4 (Bankr. N.D. Ill. 1997).

THE INSTANT CASE

William Snyder, acting CEO and Chief Restructuring Officer of the Debtors, testified credibly that the post-petition cash generated by the Debtors is primarily derived from services provided by the Debtors. The record reflects some of the many services that a restaurant customer purchases, including preparation of the food, some level of food service, the lack of cumbersome dishwashing. Mr. Snyder's testimony indicated that the value of the food component of a meal is less than one-third of the price charged for the final plate of food.

Debtors argue, and the undisputed testimony of Mr. Snyder points out, that the cash generated by the operation of the Debtors' restaurants is derived primarily from the time and energy expended by the Debtors' employees who provide services for which the Debtors' customers pay. Without the labor of their employees, these Debtors would not generate any cash with which to run the businesses.

However, the security interest of the Bank Group is broad and includes the Debtor's pre-petition inventory of food and beverages and other related assets and also extends to Debtors' fixtures and equipment. The only asset converted to cash, though, is the food and beverage inventory. The Debtor's fixtures, *i.e.* the tables, chairs, plates, etc., are not converted to cash. The fixtures remain after the customer has left. The same is true of the equipment, for example the ovens, refrigerators, etc. The revenues generated from the use of fixtures and equipment in the present case does not constitute proceeds under Massachusetts law. Therefore, the cash allegedly generated by Debtors' use of the fixtures and/or equipment in its business does not equate to proceeds of the fixtures and/or equipment. Bank Group, at best, may be entitled to adequate protection from any diminution in value of the fixtures and equipment by virtue of their use. [Editors: Hey, wait a minute. Where does the court get this idea that collateral must be "converted to cash" or diminished in value to yield proceeds? Personal property rents are proceeds under UCC §9-102(a)(64)(A). No property need be converted or diminished.]

This Court agrees with the court in *Inman* that the restaurant industry is a service-oriented industry and that "the cost of preparing food for human consumption is passed on to the consumer." *Inman*, 95 B.R. at 481.

The Court disagrees with the result reached by the *Inman* court, however, that *none* of the revenues generated by a restaurant are proceeds of inventory. In this case, the Bank Group has a security interest in the Debtors' food and beverage inventory. The inventory is being disposed of on a daily basis. Thus, under Massachusetts law, that portion of the revenues acquired as a result of the disposition of the food and beverage inventory constitutes proceeds of such inventory.

Under §363(a), only that portion of the revenues, then, constitutes the Bank Group's cash collateral. [Editors: As a practical solution, this makes sense, but where does the court get this right to split the baby? Under UCC §9-102(a)(64), the diner's payment either is or isn't proceeds. There's no to-the-extent.]

This holding balances the outcome of the hotel revenues cases and the restaurant cases. The hotel cases involve use of real property without real diminishment to the facility, except over a long period of time. Yet, the rents generated thereby are typically cash collateral since they are generated primarily from the use of the real property. The restaurant cases, particularly *Inman,* focus on the fact that the restaurant industry is service-based, yet do not account for the utilization of the secured lender's collateral. In a restaurant, the food and beverages that make up the final product of the restaurant undoubtedly are used up in the process. The reasoned approach, then, is to grant a limited interest in post-petition revenues to secured lenders.

AUTHORITY TO USE CASH COLLATERAL AND
ADEQUATE PROTECTION

The cash collateral generated by Debtors' sale of Bank Group's secured inventory is readily measured—it equals the cost of the inventory used in each sale. The Debtors seek to use Bank Group's cash collateral to continue their day-to-day operation.

Pursuant to §363, the Court authorizes Debtors use of Bank Group's cash collateral, *i.e.* the cash generated as a result of the sale of inventory; however, Bank Group is entitled, pursuant to §363(e), to the following relief as adequate protection. First, Bank Group is hereby granted a replacement lien on the inventory purchased post-petition. If the inventory levels remain the same, the Bank Group's cash collateral is not being utilized by Debtor other than to replenish Bank Group's secured collateral, whether secured by the pre-petition lien or the replacement lien. If the inventory levels decrease, Bank Group is granted a replacement lien in any other assets of Debtor, at the highest available priority as needed to restore and maintain the Bank Group's secured position in inventory as of the Petition Date. With this in mind and upon this condition, Debtor is authorized to utilize cash collateral.

In the *Inman* case, the court ignored the inventory food served by a restaurant and held that nothing was proceeds. In *Cafeteria Operators,* the court recognized that inventory was sold, and held that the price paid was proceeds only to the value of the inventory sold. In Johanson Transportation Service v. Rich Pik'd Rite, Inc., 164 Cal. App. 3d 583 (1985), the court went to the opposite extreme, holding that the proceeds of strawberries delivered by a freight carrier included the full amount paid by the buyer, including the freight charges. What is proceeds may depend on how willing the court is to unbundle the amount paid for the collateral from the amounts paid by the debtor to buy, store, market, and deliver the collateral.

B.   The "Equities of the Case" Solution to the Proceeds Dilemma

In *Cafeteria Operators*, Judge Hale gave a second, sound rationale for splitting the proceeds. The "equities of the case" exception in Bankruptcy Code §552(b) specifically authorizes that result:

> The Bankruptcy Code provides a second, alternative basis to limit the Bank Group's post-petition security interest in Debtors' post-petition revenues and thereby allow the use of post-petition income. [T]he Court finds that the equities of this case warrant a finding that Bank Group's security interest does not flow to all cash generated by Debtors, since all the cash is not proceeds of Bank Group's secured interest in inventory, but instead represents, in large part, the proceeds of Debtors' post-petition toil and effort. Bank Group's pre-petition security interest continues in any cash realized by Debtor as a result of the sale of the inventory, but, based on this record, only to that extent. To grant Bank Group a blanket lien on all of Debtors' cash generated post-petition would represent a windfall to Bank Group, in the face of Debtors' utilization of estate resources, *i.e.* the services of their employees, to increase the value of Bank Group's collateral, and would unfairly deplete the funds available for general unsecured creditors.

Deciding that the proceeds of business operations should be allocated between the debtor's estate and the secured party based on their contributions doesn't entirely resolve the issue. The proceeds of business operations may be worth more or less than the contributions. Recall that in *Cafeteria Operators*, the court held that the Bank Group was entitled to the dollar value of the inventory converted or diminished. That allocated any difference between the total secured creditor contributions and the total proceeds — essentially the profits or losses from operation — to the unsecured creditors.

In the following case, the court faced the question of who was entitled to the proceeds of the sale of encumbered milk by a dairy farm, and chose to split the proceeds on a different basis.

In re Delbridge

61 B.R. 484 (Bankr. E.D. Mich. 1986)

Arthur J. Spector, U.S. Bankruptcy Judge.

Just as the answer to the question of whether the cup is half empty or half full is yes, the question of whether milk is produced by the cow or the farmer is yes. Neither is wrong. The cow can't make milk without being fed, cared for and milked. The farmer alone can't turn feed into milk any more than he can spin straw into gold. What any school child can see is that you need all of the above to produce milk for sale. That is not reason to say that milk is not a product of the cow; it's simply a reason to apply the "equities of the case" language found in §552(b). While I share the concern expressed by those courts which felt that it is unfair to let the creditor with a prepetition lien on milk walk away with the entire cash proceeds of milk produced largely as a result of the farmer's postpetition time, labor, and inputs, §552(b) allows the court leeway to fashion an appropriate equitable remedy, without the need to mangle the English language or cause judicial decision-making to become the object of derisive laughter. Indeed, legislative history is emphatic on this point:

> The provision allows the court to consider the equities in each case. In the course of such consideration the court may evaluate any expenditures by the estate relating to proceeds and any related improvement in position of the secured party. Although this section grants a secured party a security interest in proceeds, products, offspring, rents, or profits, the section is explicitly subject to other sections of title 11. For example, the trustee or debtor in possession may use, sell, or lease proceeds, products, offspring, rents, or profits under section 363.

124 Cong. Rec. H11,097-98 (daily ed. Sept. 28, 1978); S17,414 (daily ed. Oct. 6, 1978).

Although it has been stated, and I agree, that courts should not establish a hard and fast rule or formula when exercising their equitable powers under §552(b) it is often helpful if an easy-to-state and easy-to-apply rule can be formulated. The concepts of equity and mathematics are not necessarily mutually exclusive. [A] rule based on sound economics is more desirable than one founded on nothing more than the judge's own policy predilections. With all due humility, I hereby announce what I hope is such a rule for application in this case and others like it.

"The purpose behind the 'equities of the case' rule of 11 U.S.C. §552(b) is, in a proper case, to enable those who contribute to the production of proceeds during Chapter 11 to share jointly with prepetition creditors secured by proceeds." In re Crouch, 51 B.R. 331, 332 (Bankr. D. Ore. 1985). Since it is established that the farmer's labor, postpetition raw materials and the cow are all integral components of a commercial dairy farming operation, the owners of those commodities, are, in essence, joint venturers in the process of the commercial production and sale of milk. The mathematical equation which follows is intended to yield an equitable division of the products of that joint venture. The formula is as follows:

$$CC = \frac{D}{D + E + L} \times P$$

where: CC = "cash collateral," i.e.: the amount of the milk check which is encumbered by the lender's lien;

D = the average depreciation of the capital, i.e.: the cow;

E = the farmer's average direct expenses such as for feed, supplement, and veterinary services;

L = the average market value of the farmer's or his employees' labor (excluding labor in the production of feed); and

P = the average dollar proceeds of the milk sold.

The rule is easy to state. The lender is entitled to the same percentage of the proceeds of the postpetition milk as its capital contribution to the production of the milk bears to the total of the capital and direct operating expenses incurred in producing the milk. Because the parties are in a direct mathematical relationship, the rule should be easy to apply. Very simply, the larger is the lender's capital contribution to the venture, the larger its share of the proceeds ought to be. Conversely, if the farmer's input in the venture is great, the "equities of the case" compel that his share of the proceeds likewise be great.

C.   The "Net Proceeds" Solution to the Proceeds Dilemma

Delbridge is an example of value-tracing made painfully explicit. Not all courts conduct their value-tracing so precisely. In the following case, the court sets out a different formula for taking account of the debtor's and the secured creditor's respective contributions to postpetition revenues: First, the debtor is reimbursed for expenditures made to generate the postpetition revenue, and then whatever remains is collateral.

In re Gunnison Center Apartments, LP

320 B.R. 391 (Bankr. D. Colo. 2005)

MICHAEL E. ROMERO, BANKRUPTCY JUDGE.

II.   BACKGROUND FACTS

On October 21, 2004, Gunnison Center Apartments, Inc. (the "Debtor"), filed for bankruptcy relief under Chapter 11 of the Bankruptcy Code. The Debtor is a limited partnership comprised of several former mechanic's lienholders, which was formed in order to foreclose on an 87-unit, five-building apartment complex located in Gunnison, Colorado (the "Property") after the developer failed to pay for material and service costs.

   The Property is subject to a Deed of Trust Note, Security Agreement and Deed of Trust (collectively the "Note") currently held by Lenox Mortgage V Limited Partnership ("Lenox"). The Debtor has not made any payments to the holder of the Note since August 26, 2003, and is currently in default.

III.   DISCUSSION

The evidence presented to the Court through witnesses and the admitted exhibits establishes the following:

1. The Deed of Trust and the Security Agreement provide that Lenox is the assignee of rents, issues, profits and income for the Property (the "Rents").
2. On October 6, 2004, prior to the Debtor's bankruptcy filing, Lenox filed an Emergency Motion for Ex Parte Appointment of Receiver for the Property (the "Receiver Motion"), in the State Court. On October 8, 2004, the State Court entered the Ex Parte Order Appointing Receiver (the "Receiver Order").
4. On October 25, 2004, Lenox filed [a demand for segregation and accounting of cash collateral in the bankruptcy court and] stated that it would not consent to the use of Rents.

Section 363(a) of the Bankruptcy Code includes rents or profits from property in its definition of cash collateral. That section provides that the Debtor cannot use cash collateral unless the entity who has an interest in the collateral consents; or the Court, after notice and hearing, authorizes such use. 11 U.S.C. §363(c)(2). In this case, the Debtor argues that by reason of the language contained in the case of In re Morning Star Ranch, 64 B.R. 818 (Bankr. D. Colo. 1986), monies spent for the operation, maintenance, preservation and protection of the Property are not cash collateral and thus, no consent or court authorization is necessary to use those funds. This Court disagrees.

In *Morning Star*, a creditor claiming a secured interest in rents generated in the debtor's hotel operation, sued to prohibit the use of cash collateral. Judge Matheson held:

> When bankruptcy intervenes the property of the debtor becomes subject to the jurisdiction of this Court and the rights of the lender are at least suspended by reason of the automatic stay under 11 U.S.C. §362. The stay deprives the lender of the right to have a receiver appointed. Thus the lender does not become entitled to claim a right to all of the rents collected by the debtor. The lender, instead, is at best entitled to the protection to which he would have been entitled had a receiver been appointed.
>
> It is clear in this case that there would be no proceeds to fight over if the property is not operated. If a receiver were to operate the Debtor's property, he would be required to pay the operating expenses. Indeed, that is precisely what the deed of trust in this case requires. He would also be required to pay for the preservation of the property and that also is what is specified by the deed of trust. Costs of management and preservation would normally include costs for utilities, telephone service, laundry service, maid service, cleaning service, groundskeeping, supplies and the costs of employees to cover such things as reservations, check-in, cashiers, accounting, etc. Further, under normal receiverships, the receiver would be paid a receiver's fee. He might, as well, hire a managing company to manage the property and pay a management fee. He might also engage accountants or attorneys in appropriate circumstances and pay their fees and expenses. All of those costs would come out of the rents received before any monies would be paid over to the lender.

Morning Star, 64 B.R. at 822. Judge Matheson concluded that, although the secured creditor had perfected its interest, the debtor was entitled to use, with supervision, certain of the income generated by the property to pay the same expenses as would a receiver, if one were in place.

As stated by the Court:

> One might argue that there is no "cash collateral" until all of the expenses are accounted for and that only what is left is cash collateral in which the lender has an interest. Conversely the lender can argue that he has an interest in all of the cash, subject only to the payment of reasonable operating and preservation expenses which must be strictly accounted for. Whichever approach is used, the ultimate result is the same.

Id. at 822-23.

———————

Judge Romero's solution, in essence, was to interpret "rents" and "proceeds" as those terms are used in Bankruptcy Code §552(b) to mean "net rents" and "net proceeds." This is not how Article 9 and real estate mavens interpret these terms. To some degree, these differing interpretations result from an ongoing battle between two groups of lawmakers. The Article 9 and real estate mavens struggle to find ways for secured parties to reliably enforce their interests, which often requires putting an end to the debtor's business. The bankruptcy community struggles to find ways to keep those same businesses in operation. The dispute over the meaning of "proceeds" is the result.

D.   Cash Collateral in Bankruptcy

Bankruptcy Code §§363(c)(1) and (b)(1) permit debtors to use their secured creditors' collateral. Thus, if the collateral is a factory, the debtor can continue to operate the factory after filing for bankruptcy. As we have seen, the debtor may also use highly liquid collateral, such as the money in a bank account or the rents that are paid by tenants of an apartment building.

Regardless of the type of collateral, the debtor who uses it must provide adequate protection to the secured creditor against its loss or decline in value. The debtor's use of collateral such as a factory or apartment building ordinarily presents no immediate threat to the interests of the secured creditor. Significant decline in the value of the collateral is likely to occur only over a period of months or years; in the meantime, the secured creditor has access to the bankruptcy court to seek appropriate orders for adequate protection. Bankr. Code §361.

The debtor's use of cash collateral presents a more immediate threat to the secured creditor. The typical use of cash collateral will be to pay expenses incurred by the estate during the bankruptcy case. This may be the wages and salaries of employees who operate the business, the utility bills, or the cost of other supplies. Once the cash collateral is used for such purposes, it may be permanently lost to the secured creditor. The typical solution in such a case is for the debtor to provide adequate protection in the form of a lien on other

property of the estate. Often, that lien is against property which, although not "proceeds" under the definition of UCC §9-102(a)(64), will come into existence only as a result of the cash expenditures. For example, when cash collateral is used to pay employees and for utilities and supplies that are consumed in the manufacturing process, the ultimate result may be to produce factory inventory for sale. The value of the cash collateral becomes the value of the inventory. But the relationship between the two is not tight enough for the inventory to qualify as proceeds of the cash within the definition in UCC §9-102(a)(64). That is because the collateral value is transformed into services and then back into property. The concept of proceeds cannot follow this particular transformation. Nothing can be proceeds of services. Because the new inventory is not proceeds under UCC §9-102(a)(64), the secured creditor is not entitled to it under Bankruptcy Code §552.

An order of the bankruptcy court permitting the use of cash collateral and granting a lien in the resulting inventory as adequate protection can bridge the gap left by UCC §9-102(a)(64). In the example used here, the adequate protection order ensures preservation of the value of the secured creditor's collateral as that value changes form. You should keep in mind, however, that adequate protection orders are not limited by the concept of value-tracing; the court can approve a substitute or replacement lien against property completely unrelated to the collateral that the debtor uses. Recall from Assignment 6 that when Craddock-Terry Shoe Corporation had to provide adequate protection against the declining value of its $700,000 customer list, it did so by granting the creditor a security interest in $700,000 worth of unrelated property.

Because a debtor can dissipate cash collateral almost instantly by using it, the Bankruptcy Code requires notice to the secured creditor and the opportunity for a hearing *before* the debtor can use cash collateral. Bankr. Code §363(c)(2). Nearly all assets of most debtors are fully encumbered by the time they file bankruptcy. Any expenditure of funds by such a debtor is an expenditure of cash collateral. It is a rare business that can go more than a few days without paying anyone for anything. Thus, within a few days of the filing of most bankruptcy reorganization cases, the debtor has to obtain an order from the Bankruptcy Court authorizing the use of cash collateral on an emergency basis. It is not unusual for such "first day" hearings to be held by telephone, at the homes of judges, during court recesses, or at uncivilized hours of the morning.

Problem Set 11

11.1.   On the facts of Problem 10.3, assume that some uncertainty existed as to whether the $500,000 purse was ELP's collateral. Before the matter could be resolved, Lucky Partners filed bankruptcy. Not knowing of the filing, the track paid the purse to Lucky Partners a few days later. The money is now in a trust account, awaiting the court's decision. Is your client ELP's claim to the purse stronger, weaker, or unchanged? Bankr. Code §552.

11.2.   Polly Arthur, from Problem 10.1, filed bankruptcy but continued to run her business. A few days later, she worked for 28 straight hours repairing a dangerous leak at Golan Industries' power plant and billed Golan at $65 an hour for a total of $1,820.

a.   When Polly receives that money, will it be subject to Firstbank's security interest? UCC §9-102(a)(64); Bankr. Code §552.

b.   Would it make any difference if, as part of the work, Polly installed two washers purchased by her more than a month ago from a plumbing supply company for $2 in total.

11.3.   You are still representing ELP against Golan Industries. After the fire that destroyed the copier in Problem 10.5, but before the insurance company paid the claim, Golan filed for bankruptcy under Chapter 11. (The information ELP gave you earlier to the contrary was wrong.) When Golan got the $35,000 in insurance proceeds, it deposited them in its bank account and wrote the $2,000 and $32,000 checks. Those checks have cleared the bank account, leaving only $6,000 in the account. Today ELP got a call from Golan's attorneys notifying it of an emergency cash collateral hearing to be held later this afternoon. What is ELP's collateral in the bankruptcy case? UCC §§9-315(a) and (b); Bankr. Code §§362(d)(1) and (2), 552, 549(a), 363(c)(2) and (e).

11.4.   Your client, Globus Real Estate Investment Trust (Globus) holds a security interest against Hotel Sierra Vista. The description of collateral includes the real property, equipment, inventory, and "all income, rents, royalties, revenues, issues, profits, fees, accounts, deposit accounts, general intangibles, and other proceeds (including without limitation, room sales and revenues from sales of services, food and drink), presently owned or after acquired." Hotel Sierra Vista filed for bankruptcy on October 14 and on that same day the court entered an order that the hotel segregate and account for any cash collateral in the hotel's possession, but also permitting the hotel to "meet its operating expenses from those funds." The value of all collateral for the loan is substantially less than the amount owing to Globus. In accord with the order, the hotel opened a new bank account, deposited all receipts in it, and paid all expenses from it. The hotel's attorney sent you the following list of revenues and expenses for the first 17 days after bankruptcy. Globus wants to know how much money you think should be segregated as cash collateral under Bankruptcy Code §363(c)(4) and why:

	Type	Amount
Revenues	Room charges	$510,000
	Food and drink	121,000
	Total	631,000
Expenses	Room-related	410,000
	Food and drink—labor	70,000
	Food and drink—cost of goods	30,000
	Total	520,000
Operating Profit		111,000

Some of the food and drink is served in the bar and restaurant, some of it is served in the rooms. Assume that neither the value of the hotel nor the value of the food and drink inventories on hand changed during the 17-day period since the filing of bankruptcy.

   a.   If the court follows *Gunnison Center Apartments*, what is your answer?

   b.   If the court applies the "equities of the case" exception in Bankruptcy Code §552(b), what is your answer?

   c.   If the court applies Bankruptcy Code §552(b)(2) literally to the room revenues and declines to make an exception based on the equities of the case, what is your answer?

   11.5.   You also represent Globus in the reorganization of Pine Manor, a 360-unit apartment building that was in foreclosure for more than a year before it filed Chapter 11 yesterday. The apartment building is Pine Manor's only asset, Globus's mortgage is for $9 million, and the apartment building is worth only $7 million. The parties have no reason to believe that value will change during the bankruptcy case. Meredith Johnson, Pine Manor's attorney, filed a motion to use cash collateral along with the petition. The motion seeks use of whatever portion of the rents collected during the Chapter 11 case is necessary to pay the management company that will operate the building during the case and the other postpetition expenses of operation, such as maintenance, repairs, and insurance. The hearing is set for 7 A.M. tomorrow morning. Globus's mortgage extends to "rents and proceeds" of the apartment building and clearly was perfected prior to the filing of the petition. The parties expect $100,000 in rents each month, but no rents are owing or in hand at the moment of filing. Globus wants you to get aggressive with Pine Manor because "it's our property and we are the ones losing money. Pine Manor doesn't even have an equity." Meredith wants you to consent to the cash collateral order. "Every dime we propose to spend is going to benefit your collateral," she says. "There's no point in going to a 7 A.M. hearing when you don't even have an argument." Bankr. Code §§363(a), (c), and (e), 552(b). Working through the following may help you assess the situation.

   a.   What was the amount of Globus's secured claim at the time the petition was filed?

   b.   Was Globus entitled to accrue interest on that amount? To adequate protection payments?

   c.   Will the $100,000 in rent received in the first month after filing be Globus's collateral?

   d.   If the court permits Pine Manor to use that $100,000, to what protection is Globus entitled? How will Pine Manor provide it?

Assignment 12: The Legal Limits on What May Be Collateral

Article 9 places no express limits on what may serve as collateral. Read only Article 9 and you might get the impression that a debtor can encumber anything that has value. Article 9 defines and expressly authorizes the use of broad categories, such as "equipment," UCC §9-102(a)(33), and "general intangibles," UCC §9-102(a)(44), in descriptions of collateral. The use of such categories makes it easy to take all-encompassing security interests. Article 9 makes such broad descriptions of collateral as "all personal property of the debtor" ineffective and this may at first glance seem to be a limit. But as we saw in Assignment 9, it is a limit in form, not in substance. Parties who intend a security agreement in all personal property can easily accomplish that intent by stringing together a list of categories expressly sanctioned by Article 9. For most businesses, "equipment, inventory, accounts, chattel paper, instruments, money, and general intangibles" will cover everything.

Transactions involving certain kinds of collateral, such as real estate and insurance, are excluded from coverage under Article 9. UCC §§9-109(d)(8) and (11). The intention of the drafters in making these exclusions was not to put limits on what can serve as collateral, but merely to yield to otherwise conflicting bodies of secured transactions law.

UCC §9-204(b) places two limits on what may serve as collateral. That section provides that an after-acquired property clause does not attach to consumer goods acquired more than ten days after the lender makes the loan. Assume, for example, that a lender finances a lawnmower and takes a security interest in "lawnmowers, now owned or hereafter acquired." The financed lawnmower breaks and the debtor buys a replacement. The lender's security interest does not reach the replacement mower. UCC §9-204(b) also provides that after-acquired property clauses do not reach commercial tort claims. That provision makes it difficult for a debtor to grant a security interest in a commercial tort claim that does not yet exist at the time the debtor authenticates the security agreement. The apparent purpose of this limit is to prevent debtors from pledging valuable lawsuits before they have any idea what those lawsuits might be.

The key limit that the UCC places on what may serve as collateral is so broad as to be almost invisible. UCC §1-201(b)(35) defines "security interest" as an interest in "personal property or fixtures." State law defines "fixtures" such that only property can be fixtures. The effect is that items must be "property" or they cannot qualify as collateral. Yet, as you will see in this assignment, many things of significant monetary value are not "property." Toward the end of this assignment, we will explore the curious boundary between property and valuable nonproperty and the interesting problems in doctrinal metaphysics that result. But first we examine some limitations arising outside Article 9 that prevent even some items that are property from serving as collateral.

A. Property That Cannot Be Collateral

1. Property of a Personal Nature

During at least the past three decades, there has been a growing consensus that it is inappropriate for creditors to take and enforce *nonpossessory, nonpurchase-money security interests* in property that is highly personal in nature and has little resale value. (A purchase-money security interest is a security interest given to secure either part of the purchase price of the collateral, or money borrowed to pay part of the purchase price of the collateral.) Lenders should not be repossessing and reselling the debtor's false teeth, artificial limbs, or personal clothing. The consensus weakens with distance from the person's body, but still prevails as to furniture, appliances, and household furnishings, so long as they are not of substantial value.

Some might attribute this consensus to human sensibilities and compassion. In testimony before Congress and the Federal Trade Commission (FTC), critics of such repossession and resale focused on the mean-spirited nature of the process. For example, secured creditors threatened to "clean out" their debtors' houses if the debtors did not make payments. Such threats often emphasized those items of collateral used by the children. Repossession was often not so much an effort to collect the debt from the proceeds of the sale of collateral as it was to make good on a threat to deprive the debtor of its use. There was testimony about repossessors who wrenched collateral from the hands of the impoverished debtor, only to take it directly to the city dump.

But, as may already be apparent, the consensus against repossession of personal items has practical underpinnings as well. The chances for conflict in such repossessions is high, making them difficult for the legal system to deal with. A case in which one of us served as a Chapter 7 bankruptcy trustee will illustrate. The debtors were husband and wife, and the husband was "head of the household." Under the law of the state at that time, no property was exempt to a person who was not the head of the household; everything not repurchased by the debtor from the estate had to be surrendered to the trustee for resale. The wife, who was entitled to no exemptions, owned a wedding ring that she could not then afford to repurchase. When the author-trustee requested possession of the ring, she explained its symbolic and emotional importance to her, and ended by looking him dead in the eye and saying, "If you want my ring you are going to have to cut off my finger." Months later, under threat of a contempt citation and in response to the pleas of her own lawyer, she eventually surrendered the ring. Months after that, she was successful in raising the money to buy it back. In the interim, however, a lot of time, effort, and emotions had been spent. (It may be merely coincidence that the author-trustee left the practice of law shortly thereafter to go into teaching.)

In this illustration, the trustee sought to take possession of the ring on behalf of unsecured creditors. In most states, such a problem would not have occurred because the ring would have been exempt from execution under state law and from the estate under bankruptcy law. Centuries ago, exemption law recognized the problems involved in taking possession of personal items from debtors and accommodated to them. But, as you will recall from Assignment 1, these exemptions apply only to the collection efforts of unsecured creditors. The exemption laws themselves do not bar either the grant or foreclosure of security interests in debtors' homes, tools of trade, clothing, household goods, or wedding rings.

In this section, we discuss the existing limitations on the use of low-value personal items as collateral. If an item is exempt, then general unsecured creditors cannot seize it. Exemptions are not, however, effective against secured creditors. If a debtor grants a security interest in exempt property, and, then fails to pay, the creditor can foreclose on the property. Bankruptcy Code §522(f) is a limitation on the secured creditor's right to enforce a security interest in a bankrupt debtor's otherwise exempt property.

Taking nonpurchase-money security interests in personal items became a widespread practice only with the adoption of the UCC in the 1960s. The fledgling consumer finance industry was just developing. Companies in the industry borrowed money from banks at low rates of interest and used it to make small loans to consumer debtors at higher rates. To protect themselves against a high rate of default by consumer debtors, the consumer finance companies took blanket security interests in their borrowers' household goods. When the debtors defaulted, the companies generally threatened to repossess the household goods, and in some cases actually did so. By the mid-1970s, problems with the practice were rampant. Congress sought to deal with them in §522(f) of the Bankruptcy Code it adopted in 1978.

Bankruptcy Code §522(f) permits debtors who file bankruptcy to avoid nonpossessory, nonpurchase-money security interests in property listed in that section, if the security interest prevents the debtor from taking advantage of an exemption otherwise available. Bankruptcy Code §522(f) was aimed squarely at the practices of the consumer finance companies.

Security interests in property in the possession of a secured creditor are excepted from §522(f) avoidance. A bank sometimes takes a security interest in jewelry, coin collections, or the like, and perfects by taking possession of the item and placing it in its vault. Because the bank already has possession of the collateral, repossession is not a problem. Purchase-money security interests in personal items also are excepted from §522(f) avoidance. Department stores can, and some do, take security interests in the property they sell. The department stores are allowed to repossess the property when the purchasers fail to pay for it. The rationale for the purchase-money exception may be that the repossessed items are more likely of value to a seller who is in the business of selling such items. But the rationale is not entirely convincing: If the property repossessed is clothing, mattresses, or electric toothbrushes, even a department store may be taking it to the dump.

Bankruptcy Code §552(f) authorizes avoidance only of a lien that "impairs an exemption to which the debtor would have been entitled" were the lien not in existence. That restricts its protection to the categories of property exempt from the claims of unsecured creditors under state or federal law. But, as we noted above, the protection that Bankruptcy Code §522(f) provides against security interests is considerably narrower than the protection against unsecured creditors that exemption law provides. For a security interest to be avoidable under Bankruptcy Code §522(f), the property must be both exempt *and* of a type listed in Bankruptcy Code §522(f).

Probably the most important difference between the two sets of protections is that the exemption laws typically protect both homes and automobiles, but §522(f) protects neither. In addition, it applies only to liens against the property of debtors who are in bankruptcy. If a debtor is not in bankruptcy, the provision provides no protection. Bankruptcy Code §522(f) does not prohibit the taking of a security interest in the property listed or its enforcement against a debtor absent bankruptcy. In 1985, the FTC published regulations that prohibit both actions. (We have reversed the order of the sections to make them easier to read.)

Federal Trade Commission, Trade Regulation Rules

16 C.F.R. 444 (2015)

§444.2   UNFAIR CREDIT PRACTICES

(a) In connection with the extension of credit to consumers in or affecting commerce, as commerce is defined in the Federal Trade Commission Act, it is an unfair act or practice within the meaning of Section 5 of that Act for a lender or retail installment seller directly or indirectly to take or receive from a consumer an obligation that: . . .

(3) Constitutes or contains an assignment of wages or other earnings unless:

(i) The assignment by its terms is revocable at the will of the debtor, or

(ii) The assignment is a payroll deduction plan or preauthorized payment plan, commencing at the time of the transaction, in which the consumer authorizes a series of wage deductions as a method of making each payment, or

(iii) The assignment applies only to wages or other earnings already earned at the time of the assignment.

(4) Constitutes or contains a nonpossessory security interest in household goods other than a purchase money security interest.

§444.1   DEFINITIONS

(h) *Earnings.* Compensation paid or payable to an individual or for his or her account for personal services rendered or to be rendered by him or her, whether denominated as wages, salary, commission, bonus, or otherwise, including periodic payments pursuant to a pension, retirement, or disability program.

(i) *Household goods.* Clothing, furniture, appliances, one radio and one television, linens, china, crockery, kitchenware, and personal effects (including wedding rings) of the consumer and his or her dependents, provided that the following are not included within the scope of the term "household goods":

(1) Works of art;

(2) Electronic entertainment equipment (except one television and one radio);

(3) Items acquired as antiques; and

(4) Jewelry (except wedding rings).

(j) *Antique.* Any item over one hundred years of age, including such items that have been repaired or renovated without changing their original form or character.

The FTC can enforce these regulations by bringing actions for civil penalties or for cease and desist orders against violators. There is no private remedy under federal law, but most states have enacted "little FTC statutes" that allow private actions against persons engaged in unfair trade practices. Remedies in private actions under these state laws include injunctions, actual damages, small civil penalties in the range of $50 to $300, and modest attorneys fees.

Notice that the list of property in 16 C.F.R. §444.2 is similar to the list in Bankruptcy Code §522(f), but it does not match it precisely. The FTC regulation is in some respects broader and in others narrower than the Bankruptcy Code provision. Both lists are vague and complex. Few consumer lenders can afford to litigate. FTC enforcement is a distant, but real threat. The practical effect has been to discourage generally the use of nonpurchase money Article 9 security interests in consumer finance.

2.   Future Income of Individuals

Perhaps the most valuable thing most debtors "own" is their ability to earn income in the future. A direct attempt to create a security interest in such income is referred to as an *assignment of wages.* Article 9 does not apply to such an attempt. UCC §9-109(d)(3). The reason given for the exclusion is that "[t]hese assignments present important social issues that other law addresses." Comment 11 to UCC §9-109. Non-UCC law in most states restricts the assignment of wages as security or bars it altogether. When states permit some wage assignments, they frequently limit them using one or more of these devices: Assignments of wages cannot be made in consumer transactions, wages can be assigned only after they are earned, or assignments of wages cannot exceed a certain percentage of the debtor's income. You may have noticed that 16 C.F.R. §444.2(a)(3), set forth in the preceding subsection of this assignment, prohibits the taking of security interests in future wages unless the assignment is revocable by the debtor or part of a payroll deduction or preauthorized payment plan.

State laws vary greatly on the extent to which they will permit wage assignments. Hostility to such assignments is usually based on the fear that a creditor's leverage over a debtor is so great in the case of a large wage assignment that the debtor is entirely in the creditor's sway. There is also concern that debtors with encumbered future incomes will have less incentive to work and tend to become public charges. Other state legislatures have seen the matter differently, concluding that debtors should decide what obligations to undertake and what to secure them with.

Under the FTC regulation, debtors can revoke wage assignments at any time. Before the FTC regulation was in effect, the Supreme Court held wage assignments void upon a bankruptcy filing. The Court's broad and powerful language is still quoted today. It reminds us of the emotional underpinnings of wage assignment and the concern that a debtor should emerge from bankruptcy with a fresh start:

> When a person assigns future wages, he, in effect, pledges his future earning power. The power of the individual to earn a living for himself and those dependent upon him is in the nature of a personal liberty quite as much if not more than it is a property right. To preserve its free exercise is of the utmost importance, not only because it is a fundamental private necessity, but because it is a matter of great public concern. From the viewpoint of the wage earner there is little difference between not earning at all and earning wholly for a creditor. Pauperism may be the necessary result of either. The amount of the indebtedness, or the proportion of wages assigned, may here be small, but the principle, once established, will equally apply where both are very great. The new opportunity in life and the clear field for future effort, which it is the purpose of the Bankruptcy Act to afford the emancipated debtor, would be of little value to the wage earner if he were obliged to face the necessity of devoting the whole or a considerable portion of his earnings for an indefinite time in the future to the payment of indebtedness incurred prior to his bankruptcy. Confining our determination to the case in hand, and leaving prospective liens upon other forms of acquisitions to be dealt with as they may arise, we reject the Illinois decisions as to the effect of an assignment of wages earned after bankruptcy as being destructive of the purpose and spirit of the Bankruptcy Act.

Local Loan Co. v. Hunt, 292 U.S. 234 (1934).

3.   Pension Rights

People often save money toward their retirement. When they do so simply by putting cash in a savings account or buying stock, they have an asset that they can use or borrow against. Other people save for retirement either through an employer-sponsored retirement plan or by making payments to a specially designated retirement account such as an IRA. Such retirement plans, if they meet certain requirements, receive favorable tax treatment from the federal government.

As the following case demonstrates, the requirements that make these plans eligible for tax breaks also make the retirement funds ineligible to serve as collateral for a loan. The case involves a profit-sharing plan rather than a pension. But the particular plan was qualified under the Employee Retirement Income Security Act of 1974 (ERISA) so that its relevant legal status was the same as a pension.

In re Green

115 B.R. 1001 (Bankr. W.D. Mo. 1990)

ARTHUR B. FEDERMAN, UNITED STATES BANKRUPTCY JUDGE.

FINDINGS OF FACT

Debtors filed their Chapter 7 bankruptcy petition on July 27, 1989. [Debtor Howard C. Green has been employed as a store manager by Defendant Wal-Mart Stores, Inc. (Wal-Mart) for 16 years.]

Wal-Mart established the Wal-Mart Stores, Inc. Profit Sharing Plan and the Wal-Mart Stores, Inc. Trust (hereinafter referred to as either "Plan," "Trust," or "Wal-Mart Profit Sharing Plan and Trust") on September 1, 1971. The Plan and Trust are apparently qualified under Section 401(a) of the Internal Revenue Code of 1986, as amended (the "Code"), and are subject to the Employee Retirement Income Security Act of 1974 ("ERISA"). As of January 31, 1989, there were 124,780 participants in Wal-Mart Profit Sharing Plan and Trust. Plan assets, which include Wal-Mart common stock, totaled $649,000,000 as of January 31, 1989.

The Wal-Mart Profit Sharing Plan and Trust is intended to be a profit sharing stock bonus plan, investing primarily in Wal-Mart stock to enable Wal-Mart employees to share in the equity ownership of Wal-Mart. The Plan is entirely funded by contributions from Wal-Mart. A separate account is maintained for each participant in the Plan for accounting purposes, but [the assets] are not held as segregated funds.

Mr. Green has participated in the Plan since 1978, and has been one hundred percent (100%) vested in his account balance since June, 1984. [The value of Mr. Green's interest is approximately $100,000.]

Defendant United Savings and Loan Association ("United Savings") is a Missouri state savings and loan association with its principal office located in Lebanon, Missouri. [During 1988, Mr. and Mrs. Green executed and delivered to United Savings for valuable consideration their promissory notes in principal amounts totaling $45,000.00. They also entered into security agreements with United Savings in order to secure the indebtedness represented by the notes with the grant of a security interest in their interests in the Wal-Mart Profit Sharing Plan.] On or about May 9, 1988, [the Debtors] executed, at the request of United Savings, a Wal-Mart Stores, Inc. Profit Sharing Trust Alternative Beneficiary Form for Married Participant, Form B, designating United Savings as beneficiary of [their] interest in the Wal-Mart Profit Sharing Trust.

[The Debtors currently owe United Savings $44,776.50 on the promissory notes.]

The arguments of Wal-Mart and debtors are similar to each other. They submit that the anti-alienation provisions [of ERISA, 29 U.S.C. §1056(d) (1993)] prohibit the assignment and alienation of debtors' interests. Therefore, a valid spendthrift trust has been created, thus preventing the attachment of United Savings' security interest. Wal-Mart [also proposes] various policy arguments in support of their position. For example, they argue that ERISA requires all Plans, as a condition of their non-taxable status, to contain language prohibiting alienation of the interests of participants, that the effect of granting the Trustee's Complaint for Turnover would be to invalidate the anti-alienation provisions, and that the result would be that the entire Wal-Mart Plan and Trust would be stripped of its non-tax status.

CONCLUSIONS OF LAW

3.   SECURITY INTERESTS OF UNITED SAVINGS

It is clear that debtors and United Savings intended to create a security interest in debtors' profit sharing interests to serve as collateral for the debt owing to United Savings. At the time of the execution of the two promissory notes and security agreements, debtors were residents of the state of Missouri. Pursuant to the provisions of the Missouri version of the Uniform Commercial Code, United Savings had a perfected security interest in debtors' beneficial interest in the Wal-Mart Profit Sharing Plan and Trust, even though no financing statement was filed. Accordingly, but for the existence of the anti-alienation provisions, United Savings would have a valid security interest in the debtors' profit sharing plan interest.

The recent case of Guidry v. Sheet Metal Workers National Pension Fund, 493 U.S. 365, 110 S. Ct. 680, 107 L. Ed. 2d 782 (1990), is relevant. In *Guidry,* the Supreme Court protected the ERISA pension interests of a labor union official, who was not in bankruptcy, from the claims of the union which he had defrauded. In doing so, the Court said:

> Section 206(d) (29 U.S.C. §1056(d)(1)) reflects a considered congressional policy choice, a decision to safeguard a stream of income for pensioners even if that decision prevents others from securing relief for the wrongs done them. If exceptions to this policy are to be made, it is for Congress to undertake that task. *Guidry,* 110 S. Ct. at 687-688.

The anti-alienation provisions prohibit the attachment of United Savings' security interest under the precedent established in *Guidry.* The court therefore holds that United Savings' security interest did not attach to the debtors' profit sharing interest due to the existence of the anti-alienation provisions included in the Wal-Mart Profit Sharing Plan.

CONCLUSION AND ORDER

ERISA was intended to allow workers to accumulate monies for retirement by not being taxed on savings until the funds are withdrawn for use. So that such funds would be available at retirement Congress required, as a prerequisite for such preferential tax treatment, that each Plan contain provisions prohibiting the participants from transferring or otherwise alienating their share of Plan assets, and shielding such assets from claims of their creditors until the funds are in fact withdrawn. When withdrawn, the creditors of course could gain access to such funds to satisfy their claims, even though they are the proceeds of an ERISA Plan with the required anti-alienation language.

The plan involved in *Green*, like many pension plans, had thousands of beneficiaries. Other pension plans, such as those set up by a doctor or lawyer sole practitioner to shelter part of his or her income from taxes, may have only one or two. While funds are in the pension plan, the beneficiary may be able, within certain bounds, to determine how the plan funds are invested. In order to qualify for favorable tax treatment, however, the plan must provide that the beneficiary cannot borrow against his or her interest.

Interestingly, the beneficiary ordinarily can withdraw all or part of the funds before retirement. To do so, the beneficiary must pay taxes on the money withdrawn plus a tax penalty equal to 10 percent of the amount withdrawn. Payment of the tax and penalty effectively becomes the price of borrowing against the beneficiary's interest in the plan.

The court in *Green* alludes to the policy Congress was implementing by restricting alienation of qualified retirement plans. The issues are similar to those raised by wage assignments. Some believe it is appropriate to limit the debtor's ability to use the pension as collateral for a loan. If the debtor fails to pay the loan, the debtor may lose the pension to foreclosure and be destitute at retirement. Others believe that use of the pension fund as collateral should be a matter of individual choice. Some debtors might have good reason to borrow, to pay for necessary medical care or to save the debtor's business from failing. The debtor may be unable to borrow at all without use of the pension fund as collateral. Allowing withdrawal of pension funds can be seen as a compromise between these two beliefs.

It is worthwhile to note an exception to the prohibition against the use of pension rights as collateral.

Assignment or Alienation of Plan Benefits

29 U.S.C.A. §1056(d) (2015)

(1) Each pension plan shall provide that benefits provided under the plan may not be assigned or alienated. . . .

(3) (A) Paragraph (1) shall apply to the creation, assignment, or recognition of a right to any benefit payable with respect to a participant pursuant to a domestic relations order, except that paragraph (1) shall not apply if the order is determined to be a qualified domestic relations order. Each pension plan shall provide for the payment of benefits in accordance with the applicable requirements of any qualified domestic relations order. [The section goes on to define a qualified domestic relations order at length.]

———————

Not only do restrictions on alienation depend on the form the transfers take (offering the pension plan as collateral rather than withdrawing money from the plan), but they also depend on the party who is attempting to reach the property in question (beneficiaries of qualified domestic relations orders rather than ordinary creditors). As this provision demonstrates, the policy explanations get more and more tangled as the restrictions on the use of property as collateral become more and more complex.

B.   Future Property as Collateral

Under both the UCC and real property law, a debtor can grant a security interest in property the debtor does not yet own (i.e., in after-acquired property).
When the property comes into existence or into the hands of the debtor, the
security interest attaches. An individual debtor ordinarily cannot effectively
encumber his or her future earnings from personal services, but a business
debtor, whether a corporation or individual, can encumber future earnings of
the business. The business debtor does this by encumbering accounts, including after-acquired accounts, chattel paper, money, and bank accounts—the
income the business will receive over time. When customers later obtain services on credit or for cash, the security interest attaches to the accounts, chattel paper, money, or bank accounts thus created or augmented.

A business that has thus encumbered its future income can escape the
encumbrance by filing bankruptcy. As we saw in the previous assignment,
an after-acquired property clause ceases to be effective once the debtor files.
Bankr. Code §552(a). The creditor is entitled only to the proceeds, products,
offspring, rents, or profits of the collateral existing at the time of the filing.

C.   Valuable Nonproperty as Collateral

Article 9 applies only to transactions "intended to create a security interest in
personal property." If the subject of the transaction is not recognized as "property" for this purpose, the debtor and creditor cannot create a security interest
in it. Policymakers often use this definitional ploy to place limits on what may
be used as collateral. If, as a policy matter, they do not wish to see particular
items of value encumbered, they make their point by classifying the items as
"privileges," "mere expectancies," or some other term that implies they are
not property.

Probably the most important category of nonproperty in the American
economy is *licenses*. The federal government has issued television and radio
broadcast licenses and airport landing rights that alone are probably worth
hundreds of billions of dollars. State and local governments have issued liquor
licenses and taxicab medallions each worth tens or even hundreds of thousands of dollars. Although they are routinely bought and sold, most of these
licenses, rights, and medallions are by law nonproperty. The putative purpose
of this classification is a government decision that the particular license, right,
or medallion should exist only "for the public convenience" or some such purpose. The government theoretically prohibits transfer of the license, right, or
medallion and retains the right to revoke it any time it ceases to be for the public convenience. Laws and regulations classify them as nonproperty in order
to stress their fragile status. Cynics note that classifying these rights as revocable enables politicians to justify giving them away virtually free to their
friends and supporters. The cynics also note that they are rarely revoked, the

restrictions on their transfer are rarely enforced, and that they are routinely bought and sold for huge sums of money.

Some courts take the distinction between property and nonproperty seriously. In determining whether to enforce a security interest in a particular item, they limit their inquiry to whether the item is "property" under the law of the state. For example, in Jackson v. Miller, 93 B.R. 421 (Bankr. W.D. Pa. 1988), the court held a purported security interest in a liquor license to be void and of no effect. The court relied on a provision of state law that stated, "The license shall continue as a personal privilege granted by the board and nothing therein shall constitute the license as property." In the same opinion, the court acknowledged that any security interest taken in a liquor license after the repeal of that statute was valid.

Other courts look beyond classification as property or nonproperty and take a more policy-oriented approach. These courts examine the consequences of permitting or not permitting the taking of security interests in the particular items. They tend to permit the use of licenses as collateral, reasoning that the grant of the security interest in no way restricts the government's right and ability to cancel any license that no longer serves the public convenience. The secured creditor simply takes a security interest in something that might become valueless. The doctrinal explanation is that the license can be property between the licensee and the secured creditor without being property between the government and the licensee. Good-bye consistent theory.

The following case adopts that approach.

In re Tracy Broadcasting Corp.
696 F.3d 1051 (10th Cir. 2012)

HARTZ, CIRCUIT JUDGE.

I. BACKGROUND

Tracy Broadcasting is a Nebraska corporation that operated an FM radio station in Wyoming under a license issued by the Federal Communications Commission (FCC). On May 5, 2008, Tracy Broadcasting executed a promissory note for a $1,596,100 loan from Valley Bank & Trust Company (Valley Bank). The note was secured by an agreement dated December 13, 2007, which granted Valley Bank a security interest in various assets, including Tracy Broadcasting's general intangibles and their proceeds.

On January 23, 2009, Spectrum Scan, LLC obtained a judgment in Nebraska federal court against Tracy Broadcasting in the amount of $1,400,000. Seven months later, Tracy Broadcasting filed a petition under Chapter 11 in Colorado bankruptcy court. It listed assets of $1,223,242.00 and liabilities of $3,045,417.60. The two primary creditors of Tracy Broadcasting were Valley Bank and Spectrum Scan, which was unsecured. The most valuable asset listed was the broadcasting license, with an estimated worth of $950,000. No agreement for sale or transfer of the license was pending at the time.

Under the Bankruptcy Code, property acquired by Tracy Broadcasting after it filed for bankruptcy (such as proceeds of the sale of its FCC license) would not be subject to Valley Bank's lien unless the property was proceeds of property acquired by Tracy Broadcasting before filing and the security agreement "extend[ed] to [the] property . . . acquired before [filing] and to proceeds . . . of such property." 11 U.S.C. §552(b)(1).

II. DISCUSSION

A. Private Interests in Broadcast Licenses

Section 301 of the [Federal Communications Act ("FCA")] "provide[s] for the use of [radio] channels, but not the ownership thereof, by persons for limited periods of time, under licenses granted by Federal authority." Of particular relevance, §310 limits the transfer of rights in a license:

> No . . . license, or any rights thereunder, shall be transferred, assigned, or disposed of in any manner, voluntarily or involuntarily, directly or indirectly, or by transfer of control of any corporation holding such permit or license, to any person except upon application to the Commission and upon finding by the Commission that the public interest, convenience, and necessity will be served thereby.

The FCC has consistently declared that a licensee cannot give a private party a lien on its license that would enable the lienholder to foreclose on the lien and obtain the licensee's rights without FCC approval. "The reason for the policy is that the Commission's statutory mandate requires it to approve the qualifications of every applicant for a license. If a security interest holder were to foreclose on the collateral license, by operation of law, the license could transfer hands without the prior approval of the Commission." On the other hand, for some time the FCC has said that "[a] security interest in the proceeds of the sale of the license does not violate Commission policy." In re Walter O. Cheskey, 9 FCC Rcd. 986, 987 ¶8 (Mobile Servs. Div. 1994):

> [G]iving a security interest in the proceeds of the sale of a license does not raise the same concerns [as granting a lien that would allow the lienholder to obtain the license upon the debtor's default without FCC approval]. When a licensee gives a security interest in the proceeds of the sale of the system, including the license, the licensee's creditor has rights with respect to the money or other assets the licensee receives in exchange for the system and license. The creditor has no rights over the license itself, nor can it take any action under its security interest until there has been a transfer which yields proceeds subject to the security interest. Thus, when the creditor exercises his security interest, the licensee will no longer be holding the license.

Id. at ¶¶8, 9. The FCC has emphasized that permitting such security interests will improve licensees' access to capital.

Courts and commentators have referred to the licensee's present interest in the right to the proceeds of a future sale of the license as a private right or interest, or an economic right. These terms are appropriate because they contrast the right of the licensee to make money on a license (or at least recoup all or part of the licensee's investment in the license) with what the government controls—the use of the electromagnetic-wave spectrum. Under §§301 and 304 of the FCA, a licensee has no ownership rights in a channel of radio transmission or a frequency of the electromagnetic spectrum; the use of the channel (or frequency) is within the regulatory power of the FCC. The FCC's task is to ensure that the spectrum is used in the public interest. But the FCA does not prohibit a licensee from making money from its license—say, when a licensee sells a license (albeit only with FCC approval) and realizes a profit because of the value of listener loyalty to the frequency used by the licensee. In other words, the FCA does not prohibit private interests or rights in value created by the licensee's use of the airwaves.

In our view, it is reasonable to construe §310(d) as permitting the assignment of an interest in a license (such as the right to a portion of the proceeds of the sale of the license) conditional on FCC approval of the sale. Then, once the sale is approved and consummated, the proceeds of the sale can be disbursed in accordance with the assignment. Because the FCC interpretation of §310(d) is a reasonable one, *Chevron* requires our deference to that interpretation.

In sum, we hold that the holder of an FCC license has the right to the proceeds of a sale of that license and may grant a security interest in that right and in the proceeds of that right (that is, the proceeds of a future sale). Arriving at that holding does not, however, end our task in this case. There remains the question whether Nebraska law permits a security interest in the right to the proceeds of the sale of an FCC license, conditional on FCC approval of the sale, to attach to that right before the licensee has entered into a contract for sale of the license.

B. PROPERTY RIGHTS UNDER NEBRASKA LAW

Whether Tracy Broadcasting had sufficient rights in the collateral to support the attachment of a security interest in those rights is a question of Nebraska property law. In our view, Nebraska law recognizes the attachment of an interest in the right to proceeds of a sale of an FCC license when the licensee enters into a security agreement. There can be no dispute that if a licensee's right to the proceeds of a sale of a license is a property interest, it is a general intangible under Nebraska law. *See* [UCC §9-102(42)]. The question raised by the bankruptcy court was whether the licensee's right to those proceeds was sufficiently nonspeculative to constitute a property right that would support attachment of a security interest in that right under [UCC §9-203]. Section 9-203(a) states that "[a] security interest attaches to collateral when it becomes enforceable against the debtor with respect to the collateral," and §9-203(b) states that "a security interest is enforceable against the debtor and third parties with respect to the collateral only if . . . (2) the debtor has rights in the collateral." As we understand the bankruptcy court, it held that the licensee's right to the proceeds of a sale of a license before any agreement to purchase the license has been reached is not a sufficient interest to constitute "rights in the collateral."

In our view, commercial realities require a contrary holding. Recall that the FCC views the right to grant liens on the proceeds of the sale of a license as a means to improve licensees' access to capital. If the security interest could not attach before there was a contract for the sale of the license, the interest would have little value, particularly when the sale results from financial problems of the licensee, the very circumstance for which a creditor desires protection. We can see no policy reason to prevent the attachment of a security interest in the right of the licensee (the right to proceeds of the license's sale) that may well be the licensee's best tool to obtain capital. The right to the proceeds of a potential sale of the license can be worth a great deal. In particular, its value as collateral is that the license can be sold for a tidy sum even if the licensee fails in the business. It is not a right too speculative to be an article of commerce.

Contracts between private parties sometimes create valuable rights that are said not to be property and may not be assignable, but which are in practice routinely transferred. Probably the most common of these are the rights of franchisees. In the typical franchise arrangement, the franchisee pays a substantial amount of money for franchise rights that are valuable but by contract are unassignable. When the franchisee wants to assign the rights, the franchisee first finds an interested buyer for the franchise business. The two enter into a contract for sale of all assets other than the franchise. The contract is contingent on the franchisor's willingness to issue a new franchise to the buyer upon surrender of the franchise currently owned by the seller. If the franchisor is unwilling to issue the new franchise, the sale is off and the unhappy would-be seller continues as franchisee.

Even if the franchisor has no legal obligation to go along with the deal, it ordinarily has two incentives for doing so. The first is that it will be better off with a franchisee that wants to come into the business than with one who wants to get out. The second is that potential buyers of franchises from the franchisor will be willing to pay more for them if they know that the company in fact will approve their sale to an acceptable buyer. Legally, the franchisor has the right to refuse to issue a new franchise to facilitate such a sale, but in practice most franchisors only use that right as a means of controlling the quality of their franchisees. Although the parties agree that the franchise is not property and cannot be assigned, their understanding is that the *value* of the franchise belongs to the franchisee. What is unassignable in law becomes assignable in practice.

The same split of authority that exists with respect to the license cases exists with respect to the franchise cases. If the debtor files bankruptcy, its secured creditor may no longer be able to realize the value of the franchise.

D.   Defeating the Limits on What May Be Collateral

The courts are in agreement that a creditor cannot take a security interest in an FCC license or a franchise that the FCC or the franchisor has deemed not to be property. They are also in agreement that a creditor can take a security interest in the proceeds of sale of such a license or franchise. If the licensor or the franchisor does not approve of the sale, there will be no proceeds and so the security interest in proceeds will be valueless. But if the licensor or the franchisor does approve the sale, the security interest in proceeds will capture the entire sale value of the collateral. It will be every bit as valuable as a security interest in the license or franchise. The secured party has, to a substantial degree, defeated the legal limits on what may be collateral.

The lower court in *Tracy Broadcasting* had interpreted the UCC to reinstate the legal limit. What the seller receives in a sale—the proceeds of a sale in the dictionary sense—are not necessarily "proceeds" as defined in UCC §9-102(a)(64). The lower court in *Tracy Broadcasting* held that the secured creditor had no security interest in any property until sale, and thus the sale proceeds were not "proceeds" within the meaning of UCC §9-102(a)(64). In the absence of bankruptcy the distinction would have no practical effect. The secured party could still claim the proceeds of sale as after-acquired property. But in bankruptcy, the secured party has no security interest at all.

The appellate opinion in *Tracy Broadcasting* protects the secured creditor's interest in the proceeds of sale, even in bankruptcy. It does that by recognizing the secured creditor's prepetition interest in the "proceeds of a future sale"—a right the secured creditor could not enforce—as constituting "property."

Of course, a security interest in the sale and use values of licenses and franchises does not protect the secured creditor from cancellation of the licenses or franchises by the governments or franchisors who created them. But that is a problem the secured creditor would have even if the law permitted the secured creditor to take a direct security interest in the licenses and franchises. An interest in the value of a franchise is not quite as good as an interest in a franchise. The former does not entitle the secured creditor to foreclose, take over the franchise, and run the business itself to maximize the profits. But in or out of bankruptcy, such an interest is an arguable claim to the proceeds of a sale of the license or franchise, which is a lot better than nothing.

E.   Restrictions on the Grant of Security Interests Made Ineffective

UCC §9-408 renders contracts and laws that attempt to restrict the grant of security interests in general intangibles ineffective. The drafters' purpose was to expand the range of collateral available for the protection of secured creditors. Debtors can grant security interests in general intangibles, despite contract provisions and even laws prohibiting such grants. The secured parties cannot enforce their security interests to the detriment of the party protected by the contract provision or law, but the secured parties can sit back and wait for liquidation of the collateral.

As the following case illustrates, however, UCC §9-408 protects only the right to grant security interests in property. If the state law provides that the particular right is not "property," UCC §9-408 doesn't apply.

In re Chris-Don, Inc.

367 F. Supp. 2d 696 (D.N.J. 2005)

MARY L. COOPER, UNITED STATES DISTRICT JUDGE.

The debtor in the underlying bankruptcy filed a voluntary petition for relief under Chapter 11 of the Bankruptcy Code on May 29, 2001. The corporate debtor operated a tavern located in Fanwood, New Jersey. Mr. Straffi was appointed as Chapter 7 trustee after the Chapter 11 proceeding was converted to a Chapter 7 proceeding on motion by the United States Trustee. One of the debtor's assets was a liquor license issued by the Borough of Fanwood ("the license"). The trustee sold the license for a purchase price of $155,000, and held the proceeds pending a determination of the validity of liens attaching to the proceeds.

United's lien stems from a loan of $300,000 it made to the debtor on December 8, 1995 ("the loan"). The debtor granted United a security interest in its business assets, including its general intangibles, as collateral for the loan. United filed a UCC-1 financing statement with the State of New Jersey on December 27, 1995 for the purpose of perfecting this security interest.

The [Alcoholic Beverage Control] Law, originally enacted by the New Jersey legislature in 1933, prevents a licensee from using a liquor license as collateral for a loan. N.J.S.A. §33:1-26 provides:

> Under no circumstances, however, shall a license, or rights thereunder, be deemed property, subject to inheritance, sale, pledge, lien, levy, attachment, execution, seizure for debts, or any other transfer or disposition whatsoever, except for payment of taxes, fees, interest and penalties imposed by any State tax law for which a lien may attach.

The purpose of N.J.S.A. §33:1-26 is "to protect the liquor license from any device which would subject it to the control of persons other than the licensee, be it by pledge, lien, levy, attachment, execution, seizure for debts or the like." Boss Co. v. Bd. of Comm'rs of Atlantic City, 192 A.2d 584 (N.J. 1963).

II.   [UCC §9-408(C)]

The New Jersey legislature enacted revised Article 9 of the UCC in 2001. [UCC §9-408(c)] provides:

> Legal restrictions on assignment generally ineffective. Except as provided in subsection (e), a rule of law, statute, or regulation that prohibits, restricts, or requires the consent of a government, governmental body or official, person obligated on a promissory note, or account debtor to the assignment or transfer of, or creation of a security interest in, a promissory note, health-care-insurance receivable, or general intangible, including a contract, permit, license, or franchise between an account debtor and a debtor, is ineffective to the extent that the rule of law, statute, or regulation:
>
> (1) would impair the creation, attachment, or perfection of a security interest.

This section "allows the creation, attachment, and perfection of a security interest in a general intangible" and thus "enhances the ability of certain debtors to obtain credit." [UCC §9-408 cmt. 2.]

DISCUSSION

II.   N.J.S.A. §§33:1-26 AND [UCC §9-408]

We must determine whether a liquor license is a "general intangible" subject to [UCC §9-408(c)] such that a statute that impairs the creation of a security interest in the license, i.e. N.J.S.A. §33:1-26, would be ineffective under Article 9 of the UCC, as revised in 2001.

A "general intangible," under New Jersey law, is

> any personal property, including things in action, other than accounts, chattel paper, commercial tort claims, deposit accounts, documents, goods, instruments, investment property, letter-of-credit rights, letters of credit, money, and oil, gas, or other minerals before extraction. The term includes payment intangibles and software.

[UCC §9-102(a) (42)]. For a liquor license to be a general intangible, then, it first must be found to be personal property. The revised UCC Article 9, as enacted in New Jersey, does not define "personal property." "Neither this section nor any other provision of this Article determines whether a debtor has a property interest. . . . Other law determines whether a debtor has a property interest ('rights in the collateral') and the nature of that interest." [UCC §9-408 cmt. 3.]

NJDOT argues that N.J.S.A. §33:1-26 is the "other law" that determines whether the debtor has a property interest in the liquor license. We agree. Under N.J.S.A. §33:1-26, the "clear legislative pronouncement that liquor licenses are not property has been consistently supported by case law, all of the cases holding that a license to sell intoxicating liquor is not a property right." Sea Girt Rest. & Tavern Owners Assoc. v. Borough of Sea Girt, 625 F. Supp. 1482, 1486 (D.N.J. 1986).

The Bankruptcy Court, however, found that N.J.S.A. §33:1-26 was repealed specifically when the legislature enacted the Article 9 revisions in 2001. [UCC §9-408(e)] provides:

> Section prevails over specified inconsistent law. Except to the extent otherwise provided in subsection (f), this section prevails over any inconsistent provision of an existing or future statute, rule or regulation of this State, unless the provision is contained in a statute of this State, refers expressly to this section and states that the provision prevails over this section.

Subsection (f) provides that subsection (c) does not apply to certain listed statutes that address workers' compensation claims, state lottery winnings, and structured settlement agreements. The Bankruptcy Court found that the plain language of [UCC §9-408] provides that it overrides N.J.S.A. §33:1-26 because N.J.S.A. §33:1-26 is an inconsistent statute not listed in the exceptions.

We presume, in interpreting a statute, that the legislature was "familiar with its own enactments, with judicial declarations relating to them, and passed or preserved cognate laws with the intention that they be construed to serve a useful and consistent purpose." State v. Greeley, 834 A.2d 1016, 1021 (N.J. 2003). When the legislature enacted [UCC §9-408], the law regarding liquor licenses was clear: (1) N.J.S.A. §33:1-26 provided that liquor licenses were not to be deemed property, except for tax purposes and (2) with narrow exceptions, the "clear legislative pronouncement that liquor licenses are not property [had] been consistently supported by case law," *Sea Girt*, 625 F. Supp. at 1486. The legislature enacted Article 9, which by its own terms applies to personal property as such property is defined by other law, against a backdrop of New Jersey law that provides that a liquor license is not property except in regard to state and federal tax liens and federal due process requirements.

III.   POLICY

The parties have advanced competing public policy arguments in connection with their opposing positions. Appellants argue that policy concerns support reversing the Bankruptcy Court's order. NJABC argues that it and 525 local license issuing authorities oversee approximately 12,500 licenses and they depend on N.J.S.A. §33:1-26 to prevent undisclosed interests from attaching to liquor licenses, e.g., to prevent criminals or other unregulated parties from infiltrating the alcoholic beverage industry. United argues that the Bankruptcy Court's order will not disrupt the state's regulatory scheme for alcohol control; e.g., an otherwise unqualified person will not be able to obtain a security interest in a license. We will not rely on such policy concerns to contradict the clear direction given by the legislature on this issue. The legislature may determine in the future that policy considerations support allowing third parties to hold security interests in liquor licenses. We merely hold that the legislature did not implement such a policy shift when it enacted the 2001 revisions to UCC Article 9 in New Jersey.

Problem Set 12

12.1.   Your client, Commodore National Bank, is contemplating making a loan in the amount of $20 million to superstation KROK-TV. Commodore wants to make sure it has a security interest in each of the items listed below. Can it get such an interest, and, if so, how should the security agreement describe the collateral? UCC §§9-102(a)(2), (33), (42), 9-108(e)(1).

a.   The electronic equipment used in broadcasting.

b.   The station's "peacock" logo, which cost $30,000 to design and test and which is protected by federal and state trademark registrations.

c.   The station's broadcast license, which was issued by the Federal Communications Commission (the lawyer and former member of Congress who prepared the application for the license was paid fees totaling $360,000). UCC §9-408.

d.   The station's reputation for accurate news reporting, which the *Wall Street Journal* recently called "KROK-TV's greatest asset."

e.   The station's cause of action for slander against a former employee who told CNN that KROK had faked news footage of a recent earthquake in Los Angeles.

f.   The $7.3 million in advertising revenues that KROK-TV is expected to earn from its operations in the remainder of the current year (all but a few

hundred dollars of it will be for advertising services rendered before the adver-
tiser pays for them).

12.2.   After Commodore made the loan described in the previous problem,
KROK-TV defaulted, ceased broadcasting, and filed bankruptcy. The case was
converted to Chapter 7 and Marietta Parker was appointed trustee. At the time
of filing, KROK owned nothing not on the list in Problem 12.1. The balance
owing on the loan clearly exceeds the present value of all of the items on that
list. What steps do you take on Commodore's behalf to realize on the loan?
Bankr. Code §§362(a) and (d)(1) and (2), 363(f) and 541(a)(1).

12.3.   After reading the opinion in *Tracy Broadcasting*, Globus (Problem
11.4) wants to know why the post-filing accounts receivable of Hotel Sierra
Vista were not proceeds of the contract right Globus had before the bankruptcy filing to collect the accounts that inevitably would come into existence
after the filing of the petition. Globus points out that hotels have to invest the
capital that produces post-petition accounts before the filing of the petition,
and that if hotel lenders could reach accounts generated post-petition, hotels'
access to capital would be greatly improved. What do you tell Globus?

12.4.   Our client, the Bank of Friend, plans to lend $250,000 to Saul
Finkel to buy an establishment named Harry's Bar. Harry's Bar consists of
furniture, fixtures (including the mounted head of an enormous rhino), and
leasehold, but its most valuable asset is its liquor license. An employee of
the Board of Liquor Control has told you this kind of license is worth about
$160,000. The state law under which this liquor license was issued recites
that "the license shall continue as a personal privilege granted by the board
and nothing herein shall constitute the license as property." The law also
provides a long list of grounds on which the license can be revoked. The
Board's practice, however, has been to revoke licenses only in extreme circumstances or after numerous warnings against continuing violations of the
liquor laws. Because licenses are "personal" and not "property," the Board
maintains that they cannot be sold. But the Board nearly always issues a new
license to a qualified person who buys a bar from an existing licensee. UCC
§9-408.

   a.   What should the Bank of Friend take as security?

   b.   What can the Bank of Friend do to realize the value of this liquor license
if the debtor does not repay the loan?

   c.   Would there be any advantage in requiring that Saul form a corporation
to buy Harry's Bar?

12.5.   Your client, Charles Desmond, is in serious financial difficulty. Takki
Equipment, the creditor who will be the key to Desmond's financial recovery,
is represented by your old law school classmate, Martin Short. Short turned
down all of Desmond's workout proposals until he learned that Desmond had
a vested interest in an ERISA pension plan valued at nearly $300,000. Short
says that if you add a security interest in the pension plan to your earlier offer,
he will recommend it to Takki. Desmond understands that his attempt to
grant a security interest in the pension rights may have serious adverse tax
consequences for him, but he says they won't be nearly as bad as his pending
financial collapse—the only apparent alternative.

a.   If we make the deal Short asked for, what will be the effect?

b.   Are we legally required to tell Short what the effect will be? To tell our client what the effect will be?

c.   Are we permitted to tell Short what the effect will be?

d.   What should you do?

See the Model Rules of Professional Conduct set forth in Problem 8.5, above.

12.6.   a. Zelda Pirosky has come to see you about her financial problems. She owes a considerable amount of money on charge cards, charge accounts, and personal loans. The creditor that is giving her the most trouble is Incredibly Friendly Finance (IFF). Zelda borrowed $2,500 from IFF two years ago. Even though her payments on the account seem to her substantial, interest is running at 36 percent per year (which is the maximum legally permissible rate in your state) and the balance is now over $3,000. The loan application Zelda made asked for a detailed listing of all the property she owned. Zelda listed clothing, furniture, appliances, her four-year-old Toyota automobile, and numerous other items. After IFF approved her application, they asked her to sign a security agreement granting them an interest in the following items: video game set (replacement cost $500), a collection of pictures drawn by her children (no market value), old family photographs dating back to the Civil War (market value unknown), her jewelry (replacement cost about $500), her Toyota automobile (market value $2,000), her portable computer (market value $500), and any "replacements or substitutions." Zelda signed because she wanted the loan. Has IFF done anything illegal? 16 C.F.R. 444.

b.   A few months ago, the video game set broke and Zelda replaced it with a new one, which she bought for $500. ("I know I shouldn't have bought it, but the kids were hassling me more than Bob White," Zelda says. Bob White is the IFF collection officer assigned to Zelda's account.) Does IFF have a security interest in the new video game set? UCC §9-204(b)(1).

c.   During her last conversation with Mr. White, White reminded Zelda of the terms of the security agreement and told her that if she did not get $250 to him by Monday, he very reluctantly would be forced to call the loan and take the collateral. Zelda is frantic. "I can't do without *any* of these things," she says, "but even if I paid Mr. White the $250, he'll just want more." What do you advise? Bankr. Code §522.

Chapter 4.   Default: The Gateway to Remedies

Assignment 13:   Default, Acceleration, and Cure Under State Law

A.   Default

In the first five assignments of this book, we discussed the remedies available to creditors under state law. Creditors have access to those remedies if, and only if, the debtor is "in default." UCC §9-601(a). Article 9 of the UCC does not define default or make any effort to say when a debtor is in it. Defined most simply, *default* is the debtor's failure to pay the debt when due or otherwise perform the agreement between debtor and creditor.

Secured creditors may need to exercise their remedies as soon as a debtor goes into default. Yet, if they exercise their remedies under state law before the debtor goes into default, they act wrongfully and are liable for any damage they inflict. To clear the way for a speedy exercise of remedies, secured creditors generally prefer that the security agreement define precisely what acts or failures constitute default. Secured creditors also prefer that those acts or failures be expansively defined so that in any circumstance in which they may want remedies, remedies will be available to them.

Debtors typically share the secured creditors' preference for precise definition of the terms of default. Debtors, of course, want default defined narrowly and precisely so they can avoid it. The result is that most security agreements contain extensive definitions of default. As to the substance of the definition, the interests of secured creditors and their debtors are in conflict — it is in precisely those situations where secured creditors want to exercise remedies that debtors want contract protection against them. The conflict usually is resolved in favor of the secured creditor: Security agreements nearly always define default expansively. The reason may be that secured creditors are more concerned than debtors about default and more ready to contemplate it, or it may be that such terms merely reflect the relative bargaining power of the parties.

The default provisions that follow are typical of those included in well-drafted security agreements.

Standard Default Provisions

Howard Ruda, Asset Based Financing,
A Transactional Guide 3-285-86 (1997)

11.   EVENTS OF DEFAULT; ACCELERATION

. . . The following are events of default under this agreement . . . :

(a)   Any of Debtor's obligations to Secured Party under any agreement with Secured Party is not paid promptly when due;

* cross default provision - in default if default with any of these agreements - default on car loan then default in business

217

(b)   Debtor breaches any warranty or provision hereof, or of any note or of any other instrument or agreement delivered by Debtor to Secured Party in connection with this or any other transaction;

(c)   Debtor dies, becomes insolvent or ceases to do business as a going concern;

(d)   it is determined that Debtor has given Secured Party materially misleading information regarding its financial condition;

(e)   any of the collateral is lost or destroyed;

(f)   a petition in bankruptcy or for arrangement or reorganization be filed by or against Debtor or Debtor admits its inability to pay its debts as they mature;

(g)   property of Debtor be attached or a receiver be appointed for Debtor;

(h)   Whenever Secured Party in good faith believes the prospect of payment or performance is impaired or in good faith believes the collateral is insecure;

(i)   any guarantor, surety or endorser for Debtor defaults in any obligation or liability to Secured Party or any guaranty obtained in connection with this transaction is terminated or breached.

If debtor shall be in default hereunder, the indebtedness herein described and all other debts then owing by Debtor to Secured Party under this or any other present or future agreement shall, if Secured Party shall so elect, become immediately due and payable. . . .

13.   WAIVER OF DEFAULTS; AGREEMENT INCLUSIVE

Secured Party may in its sole discretion waive a default, or cure, at Debtor's expense, a default. Any such waiver in a particular instance or of a particular default shall not be a waiver of other defaults or the same kind of default at another time. No modification or change in this Security Agreement or any related note, instrument or agreement shall bind Secured Party unless in writing signed by Secured Party. No oral agreement shall be binding.

Under an agreement such as this, virtually any breach of contract by the debtor puts the debtor in default. In fact, the debtor may be in default even if the debtor has performed every obligation under its contract and done everything in its power to placate the secured creditor. In section D of this assignment, we explore the limits of the secured creditor's power under such expansive definitions of default. First, more basic matters beckon.

B.   When Is Payment Due?

Most defaults actually acted upon by secured creditors include defaults in payment. That is, the debtor failed to pay all or part of the loan by the deadline specified in the contract between the parties. To predict the likely legal consequences of failures in payment, it is helpful to understand the commercial contexts in which the particular failures occur. For that reason, we describe some of the more common arrangements for repayment. Keep in mind as you read about them that these arrangements are fixed by contract at the time the loans are made and are therefore subject to almost infinite variation.

1.   Installment Loans

A loan is an *installment loan* if the parties contemplate that the debtor will repay in a series of payments. Ordinarily, these payments will be at regular intervals. They may be due monthly, quarterly, or annually. The payments may vary in amount, but more often all the payments in the series are equal. Probably the most common kinds of installment loans are real estate mortgages and car loans, which usually specify repayment in equal monthly installments over a specified number of years. Installments are the typical form for repayment of a seller or lender who finances the debtor's purchase of a particular item of business equipment, such as an aircraft, a computer, or a drill press, or even an entire business. Even unsecured loans are often made on an installment basis. From the debtor's point of view, repayment in installments is preferable to many of the other repayment contracts discussed here, because it provides the debtor with maximum legal protection against arbitrary action by the lender. The debtor knows that if it makes each payment by the due date and otherwise complies with the loan agreement, it almost certainly will not be in default or subject to creditor remedies. Installment payments also provide a form of enforced budgeting that is absent in single payment loans.

2.   Single Payment Loans

Many secured loans are made payable on a specific date. Often this is because the parties expect that the debtor will have the money to pay on that date. For example, a loan to a chain of gift shops may be payable on January 15 because the debtor will have just completed the Christmas season, its most profitable season of the year. In other instances, loans may be made payable on a specific date that is 60 days, 90 days, or a year later, with no expectation that the debtor will have the money to pay on that date. In such cases, the understanding is usually that if the debtor's financial circumstances remain satisfactory, the bank will renew the note for an additional period, without requiring actual payment. (This is referred to as *rolling the note* or a *rollover.*) The usual understanding is that the bank has no legally binding obligation to roll a note.

This combination of a legally binding document that says one thing and a nonlegally binding understanding that the secured party will do something else is even more apparent in the case of loans payable "on demand." The literal meaning of this term is that the debtor will pay the loan whenever the bank demands the money. (The making of such a demand is referred to as "calling" the loan.) Yet in most situations in which loans are made payable on demand, the parties know full well that if the bank called the loan without warning, the debtor would not be able to pay and would go into default. In a study of 72 debtors, only 22 to 32 percent of them could be characterized as having found new financing after their initial lender terminated them. Ronald J. Mann, Strategy and Force in the Liquidation of Secured Debt, 96 Mich. L. Rev. 159, 215 (1997). One might expect that debtors would be reluctant to agree to repayment terms they know they cannot meet. That appears, however, not to be the case. Statistics issued by the Federal Reserve show that over 30 percent of the dollar amount of all loans by commercial banks is payable on demand. Whether the courts should give literal effect to repayment contracts such as these is considered in section D of this assignment.

3. Lines of Credit

A business's need for capital may vary widely over time. For example, a manufacturer of toys may need substantial amounts of capital to pay suppliers and payroll as it builds inventory in anticipation of the Christmas season. As it receives payment from sales of the Christmas inventory, its need for capital may decline. One way for this toy manufacturer to ensure that it will have sufficient capital for the Christmas season would be to capitalize the business at its peak need and keep the money in a bank account or other liquid investment during the rest of the year. To illustrate, if the debtor assessed its peak capital need at $1 million, the debtor might attempt to raise about $1.1 million through the sale of stock in the company. Debtor would deposit the $1.1 million in a bank account and draw on those funds to meet its peak needs before Christmas. This way of dealing with the problem is rarely practical, because the toy manufacturer would have to pay a high rate of return for the stock investments, while for much of the year the funds would be in a bank account earning a much lower rate of return.

Probably most toy manufacturers prefer to borrow the money when they need it for the Christmas season and pay it back when the season is over. Our toy manufacturer could accomplish this in a crude fashion by borrowing all the money it will need at the beginning of the season under a contract that calls for repayment on a date safely after the end of the season. By that means, the toy manufacturer could make sure it would have enough money to repay the loan when it was due and that it would not go into default. The problem with this approach is essentially the same as with the first. The toy manufacturer would be paying high interest rates to have money during times when it didn't need it and would be reinvesting the same money at much lower rates.

A *line of credit* is a more sophisticated application of the second approach. The bank contracts to lend up to a fixed amount of money (the line "limit") as the debtor needs it. Under most line arrangements, the debtor "borrows" the money simply by writing a check on its bank account. The bank covers all overdrafts up to the limit of the line of credit by drawing against the line, and charges the debtor interest on the money only from the time it pays the money out. As the debtor receives revenues from its operations, it uses the money to pay down on the line of credit obligation, thereby slowing the accrual of interest. A debtor operating under a line of credit may have no cash of its own; all payments may be made from the line and all revenues applied to the line. In some line of credit arrangements, the debtor does not even have a bank account. It pays bills by sending instruction to the bank; the bank makes the payments, charging them to the debtor's loan account. When the debtor receives payments from customers, it forwards the payments to the bank, which logs them in as loan payments.

As we have described the line of credit thus far, the debtor is in the happy position of having to pay its debts only when it has the money to do so. Banks cannot be quite so accommodating. They must know there is some due date, so they can get out of the arrangement if they want. To make that possible, some require that the line of credit fall due at a particular date during the debtor's off season. In the case of our toy manufacturer, that might be in January, when all of its Christmas revenues will be in and its cash needs will be at their lowest. A debtor who can pay the line to zero each year will not mind doing so. Many debtors, however, expect to have an outstanding balance on their line of credit during the entire year. Such a debtor's cash needs are for an indefinite time; yet banks do not make indefinite loans. Here again, the likely solution will be to set a date for repayment with the expectation of a rollover or to make the loan payable on demand with the expectation that the bank will be reasonable about calling it.

C. Acceleration and Cure

1. Acceleration

Assume that Debtor agrees to repay an interest-free loan in ten monthly installments of $10,000 each. Debtor makes the first payment when due and then misses the next two. Creditor sues. But for how much? Absent a contract provision to the contrary, the common law treats the ten installments as ten separate obligations. Debtor is in default only with regard to two payments, and Creditor is entitled to sue only for those two. Creditor will sue for $20,000.

From the creditor's point of view, this must seem entirely unreasonable. The creditor is put to a choice. It can sue now for only two payments and bring additional lawsuits when, as the creditor expects, the debtor misses more payments. Alternatively, it can wait seven more months and then sue for all nine payments at the same time. (In the meantime, the debtor might dissipate its remaining assets or disappear altogether.)

Not surprisingly, most creditors require a provision in an installment loan agreement that opts out of the common law rule. Such provisions are referred to as acceleration clauses. Typically, they state that in the event of default by the debtor in any obligation under the repayment contract, the creditor may, at its option, declare all of the payments immediately due and payable. (Such a provision appears at the end of the Standard Default Provisions in section A of this assignment.) The creditor can then enforce the entire obligation in a single lawsuit.

If the creditor chooses to exercise its option to accelerate, it must do so in the manner specified in the contract. Even if the contract does not require that the creditor give notice of its exercise of the option, some courts require that the creditor do so. For example, the Ninth Circuit has stated that:

> [A] creditor must take affirmative action to put the debtor on notice that it intends to exercise its option to accelerate. . . . Both state and federal courts have made clear the unquestionable principle that, even when the terms of a note do not require notice or demand as a prerequisite to accelerating a note, the holder must take affirmative action to notify the debtor that it intends to accelerate.

In re Crystal Properties, Ltd., 268 F.3d 743 (9th Cir. 2001). Other cases suggest that acceleration does not occur until the debtor receives notice.

The practical effect of acceleration is often to eliminate the debtor's ability to cure its default. Assume, for example, the typical case in which George finances his purchase of a $1 million house by executing an $800,000 mortgage, payable in equal monthly installments, with interest at 8 percent per year. The monthly payments on this mortgage are $5,870.12. George encounters temporary financial difficulties and falls three payments behind, for a total of $17,610.36. The creditor, Federal Savings, sends George a letter stating that George is in default and that if George does not "cure" the default by paying $17,610.36 within ten days, it will exercise its right to accelerate. If George pays the $17,610.36 arrearage before Federal Savings accelerates, the installment payment schedule continues in force and George can continue to pay $5,870.12 each month. If, however, George does not pay the arrearage within the ten-day period and Federal Savings sends George another letter electing to accelerate, the entire mortgage balance of approximately $800,000 becomes due and payable. George can no longer cure the default by paying $17,610.36. Of course, George still has the common law right to redeem the house by paying the entire balance of approximately $800,000. But it is a rare debtor who can't cure by paying the arrearage before acceleration, but can redeem by paying the entire balance after acceleration. So as a practical matter, acceleration usually ends the installment debtor's ability to retain the collateral and permits the creditor to get out of the installment lending arrangement.

2.   The Debtor's Right to Cure

As we noted above, a debtor has the right to cure a default by paying the amount then due. If the debtor cures before the creditor accelerates, the necessary sum may be small. Some debtors, particularly those who get reminders from their creditors, make up the payments in time and get out of jeopardy. The following case illustrates the general rule that once acceleration has occurred, a debtor can cure, or, more accurately, redeem, only by paying the entire amount of the accelerated debt.

Old Republic Insurance Co. v. Lee

507 So. 2d 754 (Fla. Dist. Ct. App. 1987)

UPCHURCH, C.J.

Appellant, Old Republic Insurance Co., appeals an order granting a motion to reinstate a mortgage.

The promissory note that the second mortgage at issue secured provided for monthly payments of $387.85 each. On April 29, 1986, Old Republic declared the note in default because appellees, the Lees, had not made the payments due March and April 19th. The Lees were notified that the mortgage was being declared in default and the unpaid principal balance was being accelerated. On May 16, William Lee sent Old Republic a certified check for the payments due March, April and May 19. Old Republic returned the check and filed suit to foreclose. Lee filed an answer and a motion to reinstate the mortgage on the basis that the Lees had tendered payment and that the property was now for sale and Old Republic would be paid from the proceeds.

The court granted the motion to reinstate finding that there was substantial equity in the real estate subject to the mortgage, that the first mortgage, having a principal balance of approximately $47,000.00 was current, and that the second mortgage of Old Republic was to be paid out of the proceeds of a proposed sale.

We find that the reinstatement of the mortgage and the refusal of the court to order foreclosure was error and reverse. As a general rule of law, a mortgagor, prior to the election of a right to accelerate by the mortgage holder upon the occurrence of a default, may tender the arrears due and thereby prevent the mortgage holder from exercising his option to accelerate. However, once the mortgage holder has exercised his option to accelerate, the right of the mortgagor to tender only the arrears is terminated. . . .

REVERSED and REMANDED for further proceedings consistent with this opinion.

The general rule stated in Old Republic Insurance — which applies to both real and personal property — is that after default, a mortgagor may tender the arrearage. ("Tender" is an immediate offer to perform one's obligations under a contract — in this case, delivery of a check to the mortgagee.) If the mortgagor does that prior to the mortgagee's election to accelerate, the effect is to reinstate the payment schedule. If the mortgagor does not tender prior to the mortgagee's election, the payment schedule is accelerated and the mortgagor has no further right to reinstate. The rule results in a silent race between mortgagor and mortgagee that begins upon default. If the debtor cures first, the debtor wins. If the creditor accelerates first, the creditor wins.

Statutes in some states permit cure and reinstatement of the original loan terms by payment of only the arrearages even after the secured creditor has exercised its contract right to accelerate.

Reinstatement

735 Ill. Comp. Stat. Ann. 5/15-1602 (2015)

In any foreclosure of a mortgage . . . which has become due prior to the maturity date fixed in the mortgage, or in any instrument or obligation secured by the mortgage, through acceleration because of a default under the mortgage, a mortgagor may reinstate the mortgage as provided herein. Reinstatement is effected by curing all defaults then existing, other than payment of such portion of the principal which would not have been due had no acceleration occurred, and by paying all costs and expenses required by the mortgage to be paid in the event of such defaults, provided that such cure and payment are made prior to the expiration of 90 days from the date the mortgagor [is served with summons or by publication in the foreclosure case or submits to the jurisdiction of the court]. . . . Upon such reinstatement of the mortgage, the foreclosure and any other proceedings for the collection or enforcement of the obligation secured by the mortgage shall be dismissed and the mortgage documents shall remain in full force and effect as if no acceleration or default had occurred. . . .

The state legislatures that enact provisions such as these usually limit their application to home mortgages, to consumer borrowers, or to some other circumstances that the legislators believe most require this form of regulation.

▶ Half Assignment Ends

3. Limits on the Enforceability of Acceleration Clauses

A secured creditor can exercise its right to accelerate for even a tiny or fleeting default in payment, as the following case makes clear. But if the secured creditor doesn't promptly assert its rights, it may be met with a claim of waiver or contract modification.

J.R. Hale Contracting Co. v. United New Mexico Bank at Albuquerque

799 P.2d 581 (N.M. 1990)

Ransom, Justice.

The company had been a customer of the bank for about eleven years prior to the circumstances that gave rise to this suit. During this period of time the company entered into numerous revolving credit notes with the bank in gradually increasing amounts. These notes routinely were renewed on or about the due date despite the fact that the company frequently was late a number of days or even weeks in making its payments. The bank seems not to have been troubled by the payments being past due and took no action in each instance other than possibly contacting the company to request that the payments be brought up to date. The company would send a check or the bank simply would deduct the payment from one of the company's accounts at the bank and send a notice of advice regarding the transaction.

The note at issue in this case was executed in November 1982 in the amount of $400,000. This was double the amount of any previous note. The first and only interest payment on the note was due March 1, 1983, and the note itself was due on July 31, 1983. The note provided that:

> If ANY installment of principal and/or interest on this note is not paid when due . . . or if Bank in good faith deems itself insecure or believes that the prospect of receiving payment required by this note is impaired; thereupon, at the option of Bank, this note and any and all other indebtedness of Maker to Bank shall become and be due and payable forthwith without demand, notice of nonpayment, presentment, protest or notice of dishonor, all of which are hereby expressly waived by Maker. . . .

Toward the end of February 1983, J.R. and Bruce Hale, on behalf of the company, approached the bank to borrow additional funds to cover contracting expenses associated with construction at the Double Eagle II Airport in Albuquerque. The existing $400,000 line of credit was fully drawn. Beginning in the first week in March, the Hales met with the bankers several times a week hoping to arrange for additional financing. The company had not made the March 1 interest payment on the existing loan. J.R. and Bruce Hale stated that no one ever contacted them concerning the delinquent payment and the matter never came up during the March meetings. J.R. Hale carried a blank check to these meetings for the purpose of making the interest payment but stated that he forgot to do so. He stated that on one occasion he called the bank officer assigned to his account and asked the officer to remind him at the next meeting and he would make the payment, but the officer had not done so. Apparently, it was necessary for the bank to calculate the interest payment in order to know the specific amount to be paid.

At the same time that the company was seeking to secure additional financing, the bankers had become concerned about the existing $400,000 loan. The financial statements that the company periodically supplied the bank indicated that the company had lost approximately $800,000 during the last six to seven months. While the Hales were under the impression that additional financing was in the works (a loan application to this effect had been prepared and had been taken to the loan committee for discussion), the bank seriously was considering calling in the company's existing obligations. This possibility never was communicated to the Hales as the bank wished them to remain cooperative. After a meeting on March 22 the bank requested and received from the Hales a list of customers for the undisclosed purpose of using it to collect directly the company's accounts.

The bank called a meeting on March 24 and presented the Hales with a letter stating that all amounts due on the $400,000 revolving line of credit were due and payable immediately. The grounds for the acceleration were stated to be that "The promissory note is in default due to your failure to pay the March 1, 1983 interest payment when due, and also due to the Bank's review of your financial situation which causes the Bank to believe that its prospect for receiving payment of the note is impaired." J.R. Hale produced a blank check and offered to pay the delinquent interest charges but the bank would not reconsider. The bank was able to collect the balance of the note with interest, $418,801.86, in about two weeks after exercising its right to set off the company's accounts at the bank and after receiving payments from the company's customers on their outstanding accounts.

WAIVER, MODIFICATION, AND ESTOPPEL DISTINGUISHED

The company's arguments regarding waiver, modification, and estoppel are intertwined and rely upon the same root proposition: that the conduct of the bank negated the express default provision in the note. The distinctions to be made in the application of these concepts, especially in that of waiver and estoppel, have not always been clear in our cases and some discussion on the point is warranted.

Generally, New Mexico cases have defined waiver as the intentional relinquishment or abandonment of a known right. Our decisions recognize that the intent to waive contractual obligations or conditions may be implied from a party's representations that fall short of an express declaration of waiver, or from his conduct. While not express, these types of "implied in fact" waivers still represent a voluntary act whose effect is intended.

In Ed Black's Chevrolet Center, Inc. v. Melichar, 81 N.M. 602, 471 P.2d 172 (1970), we stated that, based upon the honest belief of the other party that a waiver was intended, a waiver might be presumed or implied contrary to the intention of the party waiving certain rights. Following that decision a number of our opinions discussed a waiver "implied" from a course of conduct in terms of estoppel. These cases represent what we would term here as waiver by estoppel. To prove waiver by estoppel the party need only show that he was misled to his prejudice by the conduct of the other party into the honest and reasonable belief that such waiver was intended. The estoppel is justified because the estopped party reasonably could expect that his actions would induce the reliance of the other party. However, unlike the case of a voluntary waiver, either express or implied in fact, the waiver of the contractual obligation or condition and the effect of the conduct upon the opposite party may have been unintentional.

NO ACTUAL WAIVER, EXPRESS OR IMPLIED IN FACT

We believe that the postagreement conduct of the bank does not suggest that the bank actually intended to waive its rights under the contract. When a party accepts a late payment on a contract without comment he waives the default that existed. With repetition his actions may suggest an intention to accept late payments generally. In this case, the overdue interest payment was the first payment due under the contract; the bank had not accepted any earlier late payments on that contract. The payment was overdue, the company did not request an extension, and after twenty-three days the bank declared a default. The parties agree that the matter of the overdue interest payment was not discussed during the series of meetings when the company sought to obtain additional financing. For good reasons, the fact that the bank would declare a default based upon the unpaid interest payment may have come as a surprise to the Hales, the bank's silence may have been misleading in the light of the earlier commercial behavior of the parties, but we do not believe that the bank's conduct during the month of March gives rise to a factual question that it was the bank's actual intention to relinquish any contractual rights. At most, the bank's conduct indicated an intention simply to ignore the delinquency for about three weeks.

NO MODIFICATION

Likewise, we agree with the trial court that the facts of this case do not raise an issue of contract modification. We have concluded in our discussion of the waiver issue that no factual question exists on whether the bank for its part actually intended to waive its right to declare a default based upon the past due interest payment. It follows that there can be no issue of whether the parties intended to substitute a new agreement for their earlier one, or whether the parties mutually agreed to amend the contractual provision concerning default and acceleration, and whether this agreement was supported by consideration.

"WAIVER BY ESTOPPEL" PRESENTED AN ISSUE OF FACT

The company's estoppel argument rests upon an important distinction from actual waiver. Here the previous course of dealings between the parties is relevant to show the meaning that the company reasonably might attribute to the bank's conduct in not mentioning the overdue interest payment. Implicit in [UCC §1-303] is the recognition that, as a practical matter, one party to a contract will use his past commercial dealings with another party as a basis for the interpretation of the other party's conduct. Thus it is to be expected that the company would interpret the bank's behavior during the month of March in light of their earlier dealings and we believe the bank should have been aware of this consideration.

Some of the facts to which we refer can be regarded as silence on the bank's part in the face of an apparent false sense of security of the company. Silence may form the basis for estoppel if a party stands mute when he has a duty to speak. As we have discussed, the circumstances here suggest that the bank reasonably could expect that the company would rely on the bank's failure to request the interest payment. Under these circumstances we believe the bank had a duty to inform the company that the bank would enforce performance under the contract according to the letter of their agreement.

On the question of detrimental reliance we note that the company cannot be said to have been lulled by the postagreement conduct into missing the payment when it was first due on March 1. However, we believe the company reasonably might have been induced into not taking the initiative to correct the delinquency and waiting instead for the bank to request the payment or in some fashion draw the matter to the company's attention. Certainly to have the bank declare a default without warning and then accelerate all payments can be considered the detrimental result of the reliance on the impression that the bank's conduct reasonably might have conveyed.

CONCLUSION

For the reasons stated above, we reverse the district court's grant of a directed verdict in favor of the bank based on the interest default clause and hold that an issue of waiver by estoppel exists to be resolved by the jury.

It is so ordered.

To most people, calling a loan when the debtor is current on the payments probably seems pretty outrageous. But the vast majority of security agreements contain laundry lists of provisions under which debtors can be in default even while current on the payments. The typical agreement permits the creditor to accelerate for any default, however small.

D.   The Enforceability of Payment Terms

As we described in section B of this assignment, debtors and creditors often agree to payment terms that the debtors have no real hope of satisfying. Given the severe consequences of a default, some courts have sought ways of softening those terms. If the facts of a particular case are capable of supporting a defense of waiver or estoppel, these courts may be amenable. (Recall the efforts of the court in J.R. Hale Contracting v. United New Mexico Bank.) But when lending institutions are careful in their administration of the loan, the courts are eventually forced to deal with the ultimate issues: Are harsh payment terms enforceable? Can debtors contract to be at the mercy of their secured creditors?

In a landmark case that helped establish the doctrine of "lender liability," the Sixth Circuit declined to enforce literally the contract between a bank and a borrower engaged in the wholesale and retail grocery business. KMC Co. v. Irving Trust Co., 757 F.2d 752 (6th Cir. 1985). In 1979, Irving and KMC entered into an agreement for a $3.5 million line of credit, secured by an interest in all of KMC's assets. The promissory note was payable on demand. In 1982, KMC sought to draw $800,000 on the line of credit, which would have increased the loan balance to just under the $3.5 million limit. Without prior notice, Irving refused to make the advance. At the time it sought the advance, KMC was attempting to sell its business. Irving's refusal of the advance killed the possibility of a sale and caused the collapse of KMC's business. Irving's defenses were that (1) KMC was already collapsing anyway, and (2) refusing to honor KMC's draw was no different from honoring the draw and immediately making a demand for the entire $3.5 million, which Irving had the right to do under the demand promissory note.

KMC sued Irving for breach of contract, arguing in part that Irving called the loan based on a "personality conflict" between a bank officer and KMC's president. The court instructed the jury that

> there is implied in every contract an obligation of good faith, that this obligation may have imposed on Irving a duty to give notice to KMC before refusing to advance funds under the agreement up to the $3.5 million limit; and that such notice would be required if necessary to the proper execution of the contract, unless Irving's decision to refuse to advance funds without prior notice was made in good faith and in the reasonable exercise of its discretion.

The jury found Irving liable and fixed damages at $7,500,000, the entire value of KMC's business. Irving appealed.

The Sixth Circuit upheld the verdict, saying:

> As part of the procedure established for the operation of the financing agreement, the parties agreed in a supplementary letter that all receipts of KMC would be deposited into a "blocked account" to which Irving would have sole access. Consequently, unless KMC obtained alternative financing, a refusal by Irving to advance funds would leave KMC without operating capital until it had paid down its loan. The record clearly established that a medium-sized company in the wholesale grocery business, such as KMC, could not operate without outside financing. Thus, the literal interpretation of the financing agreement urged upon us by Irving, as supplemented by the "blocked account" mechanism, would leave KMC's continued existence entirely at the whim or mercy of Irving, absent an obligation of good faith performance. Logically, at such time as Irving might wish to curtail financing KMC, as was its right under the agreement, this obligation to act in good faith would require a period of notice to KMC to allow it a reasonable opportunity to seek alternate financing, absent valid business reasons precluding Irving from doing so.
>
> Nor are we persuaded by Irving's reasoning with respect to the effect of the demand provision in the agreement. We agree with the Magistrate that just as Irving's discretion whether or not to advance funds is limited by an obligation of good faith performance, so too would be its power to demand repayment. The demand provision is a kind of acceleration clause, upon which the Uniform Commercial Code and the courts have imposed limitations of reasonableness and fairness. See [UCC §1-309].

In the case that follows, the Seventh Circuit rejected the holding in *KMC*. While the case applies the equitable subordination doctrine from bankruptcy law, the case ultimately turns on the UCC issue of good faith.

Kham & Nate's Shoes No. 2, Inc. v. First Bank of Whiting

908 F.2d 1351 (7th Cir. 1990)

EASTERBROOK, CIRCUIT JUDGE.

Kham & Nate's Shoes No. 2, Inc., ran four retail shoe stores in Chicago. The Bank first extended credit to the Debtor in July 1981. This $50,000 loan was renewed in December 1981 and repaid in part in July 1982. The balance was rolled over until late 1983, when with interest it came to $42,000. In late 1983 Debtor, experiencing serious cash-flow problems, asked for additional capital, which Bank agreed to provide if the loan could be made secure. Debtor and Bank then signed their loan agreement, which opens a $300,000 line of credit. The contract provides for cancellation on five days' notice and adds for good measure that "nothing provided herein shall constitute a waiver of the right of the Bank to terminate financing at any time."

The parties signed the contract on January 23, 1984, and Debtor quickly took about $75,000. On February 29 Bank mailed Debtor a letter stating that it would make no additional advances after March 7. Although the note underlying the line of credit required payment on demand, Bank did not make the demand. It continued honoring draws. Debtor's ultimate indebtedness to Bank was approximately $164,000.

Bankruptcy Judge Coar held an evidentiary hearing and concluded that Bank had behaved inequitably in terminating the line of credit. [The remedy imposed by Judge Coar was to subordinate the bank's security interest to the interests of other creditors, essentially rendering it uncollectible.]

Cases subordinating the claims of creditors that dealt at arm's length with the debtor are few and far between. Benjamin v. Diamond, 563 F.2d 692 (5th Cir. 1977) (*Mobile Steel Co.*), suggests that subordination depends on a combination of inequitable conduct, unfair advantage to the creditor, and injury to other creditors. Debtor submits that conduct may be "unfair" and "inequitable" for this purpose even though the creditor complies with all contractual requirements, but we are not willing to embrace a rule that requires participants in commercial transactions not only to keep their contracts but also do "more"—just how much more resting in the discretion of a bankruptcy judge assessing the situation years later. Contracts specify the duties of the parties to each other, and each may exercise the privileges it obtained. Banks sometimes bind themselves to make loans (commitment letters and letters of credit have this effect) and sometimes reserve the right to terminate further advances. Courts may not convert one form of contract into the other after the fact, without raising the cost of credit or jeopardizing its availability. Unless pacts are enforced according to their terms, the institution of contract, with all the advantages private negotiation and agreement brings, is jeopardized.

"Inequitable conduct" in commercial life means breach plus some advantage-taking, such as the star who agrees to act in a motion picture and then, after $20 million has been spent, sulks in his dressing room until the contract has been renegotiated. Firms that have negotiated contracts are entitled to enforce them to the letter, even to the great discomfort of their trading partners, without being mulcted for lack of "good faith." Although courts often refer to the obligation of good faith that exists in every contractual relation, this is not an invitation to the court to decide whether one party ought to have exercised privileges expressly reserved in the document. "Good faith" is a compact reference to an implied undertaking not to take opportunistic advantage in a way that could not have been contemplated at the time of drafting, and which therefore was not resolved explicitly by the parties. When the contract is silent, principles of good faith—such as the UCC's standard of honesty in fact, UCC §1-201(b)(20), and the reasonable expectations of the trade, UCC §2-103(b) (a principle applicable, however, only to "merchants," which Bank is not)—fill the gap. They do not block use of terms that actually appear in the contract.

We do not doubt the force of the proverb that the letter killeth, while the spirit giveth life. Literal implementation of unadorned language may destroy the essence of the venture. Few people pass out of childhood without learning fables about genies, whose wickedly literal interpretation of their "masters'" wishes always leads to calamity. Yet knowledge that literal enforcement means some mismatch between the parties' expectation and the outcome does not imply a general duty of "kindness" in performance, or of judicial oversight into whether a party had "good cause" to act as it did. Parties to a contract are not each others' fiduciaries; they are not bound to treat customers with the same consideration reserved for their families. Any attempt to add an overlay of "just cause"—as the bankruptcy judge effectively did—to the exercise of contractual privileges would reduce commercial certainty and breed costly litigation. The UCC's requirement of "honesty in fact" stops well short of the requirements the bankruptcy judge thought incident to contractual performance. "In commercial transactions it does not in the end promote justice to seek strained interpretations in aid of those who do not protect themselves." James Baird Co. v. Gimbel Bros., Inc., 64 F.2d 344, 346 (2d Cir. 1933) (L. Hand, J.).

Bank did not break a promise at a time Debtor was especially vulnerable, then use the costs and delay of obtaining legal enforcement of the contract as levers to a better deal. Debtor and Bank signed a contract expressly allowing the Bank to cease making further advances. The $300,000 was the maximum loan, not a guarantee. The Bank exercised its contractual privilege after loaning Debtor $75,000; it made a clean break and did not demand improved terms. It had the right to do this for any reason satisfactory to itself. See also UCC §1-309 (official comment stating that the statutory obligation of good faith in accelerating a term note does not apply to a bank's decision to call demand notes). The principle is identical to that governing a contract for employment at will: the employer may sack its employee for any reason except one forbidden by law, and it need not show "good cause."

Although Bank's decision left Debtor scratching for other sources of credit, Bank did not create Debtor's need for funds, and it was not contractually obliged to satisfy its customer's desires. The Bank was entitled to advance its own interests, and it did not need to put the interests of Debtor and Debtor's other creditors first. To the extent KMC, Inc. v. Irving Trust Co., 757 F.2d 752, 759-763 (6th Cir. 1986), holds that a bank must loan more money or give more advance notice of termination than its contract requires, we respectfully disagree. First Bank of Whiting is not an eleemosynary institution. It need not throw good money after bad, even if other persons would catch the lucre.

Debtor stresses, and the bankruptcy judge found, that Bank would have been secure in making additional advances. Perhaps so, but the contract did not oblige Bank to make all advances for which it could be assured of payment. Ex post assessments of a lender's security are no basis on which to deny it the negotiated place in the queue. Risk must be assessed ex ante by lenders, rather than ex post by judges. If a loan seems secure at the time, lenders will put up the money; their own interests are served by making loans bound to be repaid. What is more, the bankruptcy judge's finding that Bank would have been secure in making additional advances is highly questionable. The judgment of the market vindicates Bank. If more credit would have enabled Debtor to flourish, then other lenders should have been willing to supply it. Yet no one else, not even the SBA, would advance additional money to Debtor.

Although Debtor contends, and the bankruptcy judge found, that Bank's termination of advances frustrated Debtor's efforts to secure credit from other sources, and so propelled it down hill, this is legally irrelevant so long as Bank kept its promises.

At the time these two cases were decided, the UCC defined "good faith" as honesty in fact. In an apparent rejection of *Kham & Nate's Shoes*, the drafters have since changed the definition to "honesty in fact and the observance of reasonable commercial standards of fair dealing." UCC §1-302(b) prohibits disclaimer of the obligation of good faith but allows the parties to "determine the standards by which the performance of those obligations is to be measured," but only "if those standards are not manifestly unreasonable." Thus it is no longer true (if it ever was) that good faith does "not block use of terms that actually appear in the contract." It does block use of terms that fail to observe "reasonable commercial standards of fair dealing" if they are "manifestly unreasonable." Many states, however, have adopted revised Article 1 without the new language, so the rejection of *Kham & Nate's* is far from complete.

In an apparent rejection of *KMC*, Comment 1 to §1-304 provides that

> This section does not support an independent cause of action for failure to perform or enforce in good faith. Rather, this section means that a failure to perform or enforce, in good faith, a specific duty or obligation under the contract, constitutes a breach of that contract or makes unavailable, under the particular circumstances, a remedial right or power. This distinction makes it clear that the doctrine of good faith merely directs a court towards interpreting contracts within the commercial context in which they are created, performed, and enforced, and does not create a separate duty of fairness and reasonableness which can be independently breached.

In other words, the Comment asserts that "good faith" can be used as a shield, but not as a sword. We can see no basis in the UCC text for this limitation. As a result, the dispute over the meaning of good faith remains very much alive.

That meaning determines the scope of the two Article 1 provisions that employ it. UCC §1-304 is the more important of the two. That section provides that "[e]very contract or duty within [the Uniform Commercial Code] imposes an obligation of good faith in its performance and enforcement." Notice that the section applies to "every contract" — which will include every security agreement — and "every duty" — which will include every mandatory provision of the Uniform Commercial Code.

UCC §1-309 — the section applied by the courts in *KMC* and *Kham & Nate's Shoes* — is much narrower. It merely instructs the court how to interpret certain provisions in the event parties choose to include them in the parties' contracts.

E.   Procedures After Default

Once the debtor is in default, the secured creditor usually has a choice of remedies. Those remedies fall into two basic categories: (1) judicial remedies such as foreclosure and replevin, which are administered by the courts, and (2) self-help remedies such as repossession without judicial process, the notification of account debtors, or the refusal to make further advances to the debtor under a line of credit.

The creditor's choice among these remedies is often based on the creditor's assessment of the likelihood that the debtor will resist, the creditor's appraisal of the strength of the debtor's defenses, if any, and the manner in which the sufficiency of those defenses will be determined in each remedial procedure. To illustrate the importance of the differences in procedures, consider the case of

FIGURE 2.   The Spider Ad. This ad ran full page in the *Wall Street Journal* just a few years after the bank was hit with a $105 million verdict for knocking off one of its customers, Port Bougainville of Key Largo, Florida. Should its implication that the bank will not act in an arbitrary manner in calling loans be considered part of the contract of a debtor who signs a demand note? Or should debtors know better than to believe this stuff?

a bank that decides to call a loan secured by all the assets of a restaurant supply company, including equipment, inventory, and accounts receivable. Calling such a loan is almost certain to lead to the closing of the business. Probably the most aggressive approach the bank could take would be to notify the restaurant supply company's account debtors to make their payments directly to the bank. UCC §9-607. The combination of the loss of the account revenues and the reputational damage to the debtor from the giving of notice are likely to destroy the restaurant supply company's business. If the bank has doubts about whether the debtor is really in default, or whether it (the bank) has the right to call the loan, it may be reluctant to employ so harsh a remedy. The bank could wind up on the wrong end of a lender liability action.

Judicial foreclosure would be a more cautious way to proceed. After declaring the debtor in default, the bank would file the foreclosure case. The bank's complaint would set forth the alleged nature of the default and the basis of its right to foreclose. To preserve its defenses — perhaps it wasn't in default, or, if it was, the default resulted from wrongful action by the bank — the restaurant supply company might have to raise them in its answer to the complaint or in a counterclaim. By pressing the foreclosure action to a conclusion, the bank could get a final judicial determination of the respective rights of itself and its debtor before taking irreversible action.

The weakness of foreclosure as a remedy is that it is slow. While the case makes its way through the courts, the debtor may be collecting the accounts, selling the inventory, and allowing the equipment to deteriorate. Replevin offers something of an intermediate course. Recall that in a replevin action the secured creditor can move for an order granting it temporary possession of the collateral. In most jurisdictions, the motion will be heard in the first month of the case. While the debtor is not under compulsion to raise its defenses in response to the motion or lose them, the debtor may choose to do so in an effort to retain possession of the collateral. That may give the secured creditor a basis for assessing the strength of the debtor's defenses.

Problem Set 13

13.1.   Pat Roskoi, a plumbing subcontractor, consults you about a problem she is having with Lincoln State Bank. Pat accidentally missed two $834 payments on her truck loan. Her contract with the bank says that missing two payments is a default and that "upon default, at the secured party's option, the entire balance of the loan shall become due and payable." She noticed her omission before she received any kind of notice from the bank and promptly sent a check for the two overdue payments.

The bank mailed her check back to her with a note stating that the entire loan balance of $33,402 is due and payable. She called the bank, but the person she talked with told her that there was no mistake, and she simply has to pay the entire balance of the loan. Pat says she doesn't have the money and that the loss of the truck would make it impossible for her to continue her business.

    a. Did Pat default?

    b. Did Pat cure? If so, when?

    c. Did the bank accelerate? If so, when? UCC §1-202(f).

    d. Pat asks you whether the bank "can get away with this." What do you tell her? See UCC §9-623, including Comment 2.

    13.2. Your friend, Art Leff, is experiencing what he calls "a temporary cash flow problem." He owes Lincoln State Savings a balance of about $460,000 on his house; his monthly payment is $3,240. He did not make his mortgage payment on the due date last week (October 1) and he is worried about what happens next. Of course, you refused to give any advice without first reading the agreement. The relevant provisions were as follows:

> Default. Upon the occurrence of any of the following events of default . . . (1) the Debtor shall have outstanding an amount exceeding one full payment which has remained unpaid for more than 10 days after the due dates . . . mortgagee shall have all of the rights and remedies for default provided by applicable law and this Agreement, including the right to declare the entire outstanding balance immediately due and payable.

Art wants to delay making his house payments as long as he can and would like you to tell him how long that will be.

    a. Is Art in default?

    b. If Art makes no payments, when will he go into default?

    c. If Art makes no payments, what will be the order of events? When is the last time he can make this and subsequent payments without serious repercussions? What are those repercussions?

    d. What difference would it make if Art's case were governed by the Illinois reinstatement statute?

    13.3. Arthur Oman, a loan officer at Second National Bank, has been given the unpleasant task of "pulling the plug" on one of the bank's customers, Rebel Discount Drugs. Rebel owes $600,000 on a line of credit secured by inventory, equipment, and the debtor's interest under its lease. Rebel's note is payable "on demand." Arthur has come to see you, the bank's lawyer, to discuss the possibility of giving 30 days' notice to Rebel before making the demand. "They won't find another lender in this market," he says, "but I feel like I owe it to Walt Rebel to let him try." In response to your questions, Arthur tells you that Rebel buys its inventory on credit from suppliers, floats them for about 90 to 120 days, and then pays them out of the $4,000 to $8,000 a day that comes in through the cash registers. (Arthur knows this because the agreement between Rebel and the bank requires that Rebel keep its account at the bank and deposit its cash register receipts to the account daily.) Once the bank forecloses, the equipment is probably worth about $80,000 on the resale market and the inventory would probably bring in about $240,000. The lease might bring another $40,000 to $80,000 — assuming the bank can find someone who wants it. Arthur expects that the bank will simply take a $200,000 loss on the balance. The bank has always in the past met its obligations to Rebel and Walt Rebel has never had any complaints about the bank's practices.

    a. Will you approve Arthur's proposal to give notice? If so, how much notice should the bank give?

b.   If you approve Arthur's request to give Walt 30 days' notice, what is the worst that could happen with respect to our collateral during that time?

c.   Will you approve Arthur's request? If so, how should the notice be phrased and delivered?

d.   If you choose to make an immediate demand for payment, how should you proceed?

▶ HALF ASSIGNMENT ENDS

13.4.   On the facts of Problem 13.1, further assume that the bank had already accelerated the loan on its books and mailed notice to Pat before it received Pat's check. The bank cashed her check and promptly sent her a statement showing the entire balance, less the amount of the check, as due and payable. Can the bank continue to claim acceleration now that it has the back payments? UCC §9-601(a).

13.5.   In *Kham & Nate's Shoes*, the bank called the loan 42 days after the bank made it, without any change in the debtor's circumstances. The loan agreement said the bank could do that and Judge Easterbrook held that the good faith requirement does "not block use of terms that actually appear in the contract."

a.   How should a court bound by *Kham & Nate's Shoes* rule if the facts were instead as follows? The loan agreement provided that the bank would extend a $300,000 line of credit to the debtor, secured by all of the debtor's assets. The agreement required the debtor, at the closing, to use $42,000 of the proceeds to pay the debtor's unsecured loan to the bank, leaving the bank fully secured. To assure that the $42,000 payment would not be avoidable as a preference, the loan agreement required that, before closing, the debtor had to file bankruptcy and obtain the bankruptcy court's approval of the loan agreement. The debtor did that. The loan agreement also provided that "the bank may, at any time, for any reason whatsoever or for no reason at all, demand payment and terminate the line of credit." Five minutes after the closing was complete and before the debtor drew any additional funds, the bank called the loan, terminated the line of credit, and refused to advance any more funds. The debtor asserts that the bank is liable for any damages caused by the call because the bank did not call the loan in good faith. UCC §§1-304, 1-309, and the Comments to those sections.

b.   Why might someone would sign such a contract?

13.6.   You represent Angie Littwin and her company, Littwin Mortgage. Two years ago, Littwin lent $600,000 to Lance's Landscaping, Inc. (Lance), repayable in equal monthly payments over seven years. The loan is secured by an interest in all of Lance's equipment; the default provisions of the agreement are those set forth in the standard default provisions in section A of this assignment. Angie has come to see you today because she wants to call Lance's loan. When you asked why, Angie told you it was because Lance had failed for two consecutive years to provide Littwin with proof of liability insurance, as required by the terms of the security agreement. But in response to your questions, Angie admitted that Lance is a strong debtor that has made every payment on time and that the real reason he wants to call the loan is that Littwin itself is in financial difficulty and desperately needs the cash. ("When you need cash," Angie explains, "you don't get it by calling your *bad* loans.") Angie can't get her cash out by selling the loan, because the loan carries such a low rate of interest.

The last due date for proof of insurance was 23 days ago. Angie doesn't know if Lance has the insurance or not. There has never been any discussion of the contract provision requiring it. "Do I or don't I have the right to call this loan?" Angie asks. *Yes*

a.   What is the answer to Angie question? UCC §§1-201(b)(20), 1-304 including Comment 1, 1-309, 9-102(a)(43), and 9-601(a).

b.   What do you think of the argument that by its failure to demand proof of insurance last year, Littwin waived Lance's obligation to furnish proof of insurance this year?

c.   If Littwin calls the loan in bad faith, resulting in the demise of Lance's business, can Lance sue for damages?

d.   Are you willing to continue representing Angie?

e.   If you had to continue, what would you advise?

■ END OF DEFAULT PROBLEM SET

13.7.   Teresa Revez, a personal friend of yours, recently resigned her position in a software development firm in order to start her own golf course supply business. She seeks your advice regarding a number of start-up concerns, including the acquisition of financing. She estimates her capital need (beyond the amount she can invest) at about $300,000 at the peak of the season in May and at about $150,000 at the minimum point in January. To hold her capital needs to that level, she will need to buy her inventory on credit, and perhaps pay the inventory suppliers a little slower than the 60 to 90 days the suppliers want. Teresa has tentatively arranged for a $300,000 line of credit loan from the Bank of Orange, through David Walker, another friend of hers who is a loan officer at the bank.

a.   Teresa was surprised to learn from David that the proposed line of credit would be payable "on demand." Once she is in business, she will have every dime of her money tied up in this business; if the Bank called the loan, she would have no way to meet the call. When she raised this point with David, he told her that line loans are all on demand and it was not something she should worry about. "Bank of Orange has been serving the community for 75 years and has a reputation to protect," he said. "We're not going to do anything unfair or unreasonable." Teresa believes that David is 100 percent sincere, but still wants your opinion as to whether she should enter into this arrangement. What do you advise? Are there any terms that might alleviate Teresa's concerns and still be acceptable to the bank?

b.   Teresa was also bothered by David's statement that she would be signing a note for $300,000, but drawing only half that much money initially. David said that the Bank always has customers sign a note for the line limit, as a matter of convenience. "You don't want to be coming into the bank every time you want a draw," he said. Should Teresa sign a note for $300,000 when she is only drawing $150,000? Would you in such circumstances?

13.8. Assume that the facts are the same as in Problem 13.3, except that Arthur relates these additional facts: Six months ago Walt asked for an increase in his line of credit, and Arthur told him he "thought there would be no problem." The loan committee saw it differently and refused the increase. Walt then wrote an angry letter to the bank, asserting that the bank had "reneged on their commitment" and had also "given false information [about Rebel] on a credit reference." Arthur thinks the "false information" reference is to a conversation Arthur had with a loan officer from First National Bank shortly after the loan committee refused the increase. Rebel applied to First National for a line of credit and First National had, naturally, called Second National. "I didn't tell her anything that wasn't true," Arthur says. Would these facts change your advice?

Assignment 14:   Default, Acceleration, and Cure Under Bankruptcy Law

As we saw in Assignment 13, state law generally enforces the contract between debtor and secured creditor regarding default, acceleration, and the possibility of cure. A contract for repayment of debt in installments usually gives the creditor, upon default, the option to accelerate the due dates of future payments. In some states, statutes intervene, permitting at least some debtors to cure their defaults and thereby reinstate their contracts for payment in installments. Generally speaking, however, once acceleration has occurred, it is irreversible. Without the ability to decelerate, most debtors in most situations cannot recover from their defaults.

To look at acceleration and cure only under state law, however, gives a false impression. To see the relationship between default, acceleration, and cure requires consideration of state and bankruptcy law together. Most of the creditor's rights are found in state law; most of the debtor's rights are found in bankruptcy law. The following case explains how these two sets of laws combine to create a system in which the debtor who has the ability to cure a default and make the installment payments generally will have the opportunity to do so. There is a catch: To get that opportunity, the debtor must file bankruptcy.

In re Moffett
356 F.3d 518 (4th Cir. 2004)

WILKINSON, CIRCUIT JUDGE:

I.

On January 22, 2001, Marlene Moffett purchased a used 1998 Honda Accord from Hendrick Honda in Woodbridge, Virginia. Moffett agreed to pay $20,024.25 with interest in 60 monthly installments, and Hendrick Honda retained a security interest in the vehicle. Under the purchase contract and Virginia state law, Hendrick Honda had the right to repossess the vehicle in the event of default, subject to Moffett's right to redeem it. See [UCC §§9-609, 623]. Hendrick Honda assigned its rights under the purchase agreement to Tidewater Finance Company, which subsequently perfected its security interest. According to the bankruptcy court, the automobile was Moffett's only means of traveling the forty miles from her home to her workplace at the Federal Emergency Management Agency.

Moffett made her payments in timely fashion for approximately one year. Because Moffett failed to make her monthly payments in March and April 2002, however, Tidewater Finance lawfully repossessed the vehicle on the morning of April 25, 2002. Later that day, Moffett filed for voluntary Chapter 13 reorganization. On May 1, 2002, Moffett's attorney notified Tidewater Finance of Moffett's bankruptcy filing and demanded return of the vehicle, according to the Bankruptcy Code's automatic stay and turnover provisions. See 11 U.S.C. §§362(a), 542(a).

II.

Once a debtor files for Chapter 13 bankruptcy, the Bankruptcy Code automatically stays any act by parties to exercise control over, or to enforce a pre-petition or post-petition lien against, property of the bankruptcy estate. 11 U.S.C. §§362(a)(3)-(5) (2003). Any entity that possesses property that the bankruptcy trustee may use, sell, or lease under the Bankruptcy Code is required to turn over or account for the property. Id. §542(a). Before requiring a party to turn over property, however, courts must ensure that the party's interest in the property is adequately protected. Id. §§362(d)(1), 363(e). The central question here is whether Tidewater Finance and the repossessed vehicle are subject to these automatic stay and turnover provisions of the Bankruptcy Code.

A.

We must first determine the nature of Moffett's property interests in the repossessed vehicle, and whether those interests became part of her bankruptcy estate. A debtor's bankruptcy "estate" is automatically created at the time she files for bankruptcy. It broadly includes, among other things, "all legal or equitable interests of the debtor in property as of the commencement of the case." Id. §541(a)(1). The inclusive scope of the bankruptcy estate reflects the desire of Congress to facilitate the financial rehabilitation of debtors. Yet, while federal law defines in broad fashion what property interests are included within the bankruptcy estate, state law determines the nature and existence of a debtor's rights. We therefore must look to Virginia law in determining the nature of Moffett's interests in the vehicle upon repossession.

Because we deal here with a debtor's default on a purchase agreement with a secured creditor, Virginia's Uniform Commercial Code—Secured Transactions ("UCC") controls our analysis. [UCC §9-609] expressly permits a secured creditor to repossess the collateral protecting its security interest after default by the debtor. Upon repossession, Virginia's UCC grants the secured creditor a number of important rights. Here, for example, once Tidewater Finance repossessed Moffett's vehicle, it was permitted to dispose of the vehicle under certain conditions. See [UCC §9-610].

At the same time, however, the UCC grants certain rights to the debtor upon repossession and otherwise imposes duties on a secured creditor in possession of collateral. Most importantly for purposes of this case, [UCC §9-623(c)(2)] granted Moffett the right to redeem the vehicle at any time before Tidewater Finance disposed of it. This right of redemption was further protected by a duty imposed on Tidewater Finance to notify Moffett of any planned disposition, at least ten days prior to disposing of the vehicle. See [UCC §§9-611, 9-612]. Indeed, Tidewater Finance was even required to advise Moffett of her right of redemption. See [UCC §9-614]. Moffett was also entitled to any surplus amount that the secured creditor made in excess of its interest in the collateral. See [UCC §9-615(d)]. Furthermore, the UCC makes clear that Moffett's rights of redemption, notification, and surplus—among other rights—are not extinguished until Tidewater Finance disposes of the repossessed vehicle under [UCC §9-610] or itself accepts the collateral under [UCC §9-620]. See [UCC §9-617]. Since Tidewater Finance has not taken any steps to dispose of the vehicle, Moffett still possessed these rights when she filed for bankruptcy.

These interests, and particularly the statutory right of redemption, are unquestionably "legal or equitable interests" of Moffett's that are included within her bankruptcy estate. See 11 U.S.C. §541(a)(1). As the Supreme Court observed in United States v. Whiting Pools, Inc., 462 U.S. 198 (1983), Congress broadly defined the property of the estate in §541(a)(1) to include all tangible and intangible property interests of the debtor. Indeed, the *Whiting Pools* Court expressly stated that "interests in [repossessed] property that could have been exercised by the debtor—in this case, the rights to notice and the surplus from a tax sale—are already part of the estate by virtue of §541(a)(1)."

Consequently, Moffett's statutory right to redeem the vehicle was properly made part of her bankruptcy estate under 11 U.S.C. §541(a)(1).

B.

We consider next whether Moffett's right to redeem the repossessed vehicle was sufficient to subject Tidewater Finance to the automatic stay and turnover provisions of the Bankruptcy Code. The bankruptcy court found that Moffett's reorganization plan proposes to exercise her right of redemption. Consequently, the court held that Tidewater Finance's security interest was adequately protected and that it must return the vehicle to Moffett.

We agree. [UCC §9-623(b)] permits a debtor to redeem collateral by tendering fulfillment of all obligations secured by the collateral, as well as reasonable expenses from repossessing and holding the collateral. As the bankruptcy court found, Moffett's modified reorganization plan facilitates the exercise of this right of redemption by tendering to Tidewater Finance the full amount due under the contract.

Specifically, the modified plan requires Moffett to make the same monthly installment payments contemplated in the purchase agreement directly to Tidewater Finance, and it provides for the trustee to cure the existing delinquency with payments made over the course of the plan. The estate must pay all applicable interest from the delinquent payments. Moreover, the vehicle is insured. Moffett has now begun to make payments pursuant to the reorganization plan.

It is true that Moffett's reorganization plan does not provide for a lump sum payment of all outstanding debts. However, even if the purchase agreement and [UCC §9-623] require such acceleration of her debts upon default, the Bankruptcy

Code entitles Moffett to restructure the timing of her payments in order to facilitate the exercise of her right of redemption. Section 1322(b)(2) of the Bankruptcy Code permits debtors to modify the rights of holders of secured claims. Section 1322(b)(3) also allows debtors to cure their defaults. Courts have recognized that the Bankruptcy Code permits debtors to restructure the timing of payments to secured creditors by de-accelerating debts, in order to allow debtors to regain collateral necessary to their financial recuperation. Pursuant to these powers, the bankruptcy plan here provided for the payment of all future installments, the curing of all delinquent payments, and the payment of all applicable interest, over the course of the plan. Such a flexible approach to repaying claims is precisely what the Bankruptcy Code allows in order to facilitate a debtor's successful rehabilitation.

Moffett's right to redeem the vehicle is being exercised in the bankruptcy estate, and Tidewater Finance's security interest is thus adequately protected. For these reasons, we find that the bankruptcy court was correct in ordering Tidewater Finance to turn over the vehicle to Moffett.

Bankruptcy protection of the debtor who has suffered an acceleration of installment debt occurs in two stages. In the first stage, which extends from the filing of the bankruptcy case until confirmation, the automatic stay protects the debtor from foreclosure while the debtor attempts to formulate and confirm a plan. In the second stage, confirmation of the debtor's plan reverses the acceleration, the debtor cures its default, and the installment payment contract between the debtor and creditor is reinstated.

A.   Stage One: Protection of the Defaulting Debtor Pending Reorganization

As we saw in Assignment 6, when a debtor files a bankruptcy petition an automatic stay against collection and foreclosure is instantly imposed by operation of law. Unless lifted pursuant to Bankruptcy Code §362(d), the stay of an act against property (e.g., foreclosure) continues until the property is no longer in the bankruptcy estate. The stay of any other act continues until the case is closed or dismissed, or the debtor is granted or denied discharge. Bankr. Code §362(c)(1) and (2). Thus, in a successful corporate Chapter 11 case, the stay may remain in effect until the plan is confirmed. In a successful Chapter 13 case, the stay may remain in effect for the three to five year period of the plan.

A debtor who provides adequate protection to its secured creditor typically will be permitted to use the collateral while the case remains pending. Bankr. Code §§363(b)(2) and 363(c)(2). Thus, if the collateral is a house, the debtor can continue to live in it while seeking to cure and reinstate; if the collateral is a hotel, the debtor can continue to operate it. Keep in mind that the "adequate protection" the debtor is required to provide is only protection against decline in the value of the secured creditor's interest in the collateral. Use of the collateral does not itself trigger an obligation on the part of the debtor to make the installment payments that fall due during the bankruptcy case.

Whether the debtor will be required to make installment payments pending confirmation of a plan depends on the chapter under which the case is pending. Bankruptcy Rule 3015 requires Chapter 13 debtors to file plans within 14 days after the filing of the petition, a limit that the court can extend only for "cause shown." Bankruptcy Code §1326 requires that the debtor "commence making payments not later than 30 days after the filing of the Chapter 13 case." If the plan proposes to reinstate a schedule for installment payments, the Chapter 13 debtor probably will have to resume making the installment payments no later than 30 days after filing the petition.

Chapter 11 is considerably more generous to debtors. Debtors need not begin making payments under the plan until the plan has been confirmed by the court. Empirical studies of Chapter 11 cases indicate that the median time to confirmation is about a year. In the interim, the debtor typically has the best of both worlds: It has the use of the collateral, but need not make the installment payments. (The Chapter 11 debtor may end up having to make some interim payments to the secured creditor if necessary to provide adequate protection. Such payments will be necessary only if the collateral is declining in value and the debtor cannot or does not want to furnish adequate protection in the form of additional collateral. The payments required to provide adequate protection may be more or less than the installment payments.)

B.   Stage Two: Reinstatement and Cure

Reinstatement and cure is a process accomplished through the confirmation of a plan of reorganization in either Chapter 13 or Chapter 11. To understand the legal requirements for accomplishing it, reinstatement and cure must be distinguished from *modification* of the rights of the secured creditor.

1.   Modification Distinguished from Reinstatement and Cure

Modification is sometimes referred to as "rewriting the loan." You saw this technique used in *Till v. SCS* in Assignment 7. Like reinstatement and cure, modification is accomplished through confirmation of a plan that provides for it. The minimum amount the debtor must pay on a modified secured claim is determined in two steps: (1) Determine the amount of the allowed secured claim; and (2) formulate a schedule for payments that will have a value, as of the effective date of the plan, not less than the amount of the allowed secured claim. As shown in *Till v. SCS*, the accepted method for meeting that test is to offer payment of the amount of the allowed secured claim, along with interest at the market rate, from the effective date of the plan, in equal monthly payments over the period of the plan. In cases under Chapter 11, that period can be any period that is "fair and equitable." Bankr. Code §1129(b)(1). If such a plan provision is confirmed over rejection by the secured creditor's negative vote, the confirmation is referred to as a "cramdown." It is not uncommon in cases involving real property for courts to approve payment periods as long as 20 or 30 years.

In cases under Chapter 13, payments under the plan can extend only over the period of the plan. Chapter 13 plans last three to five years. Subject to some exceptions, debtors below their state's median income generally have three-year plans, and above-median income debtors generally have five-year plans. Bankr. Code §1325(b)(4). Chapter 13 plans can modify secured claims paid through the plan with an important exception. Debtors cannot modify the mortgages against their principal residences, Bankr. Code §1322(b)(2), although the courts have ruled this prohibition does not extend to modifications of wholly underwater second mortgages. Debtors are limited to modifying some car loans, mortgages on second homes, and similar kinds of obligations.

By contrast, reinstatement and cure is always a return to the repayment terms agreed to between the debtor and creditor. When a default is "cured" and terms for payment are "reinstated" the debtor takes on two obligations: Any payment that, by the contract between the parties, was due on a date after the reinstatement date remains payable on its original due date; any payment that, by the contract between the parties, is overdue as of the reinstatement date is part of the obligation to cure. As the requirements for cure differ from Chapter 11 to Chapter 13, we discuss them separately.

Modification Compared with Cure and Reinstatement	
Modification (rewrite loan)	*Cure and reinstatement*
Debtor proposes new payment schedule	Debtor returns to original payment schedule
Arrearage is included in payments	Arrearage is paid separately
Interest at a market-based rate set by the court	Interest at the contract rate on the reinstated payments
Debtor pays the unsecured portion to the same extent that debtor pays other unsecured claims	Debtor pays the unsecured portion in full

2.   Reinstatement and Cure Under Chapter 11

The Chapter 11 debtor's right to cure and reinstate is described in Bankruptcy Code §1124(2). That section provides that a class of claims (recall that each class of secured claims ordinarily consists of only a single secured claim) is *unimpaired* if the debtor's proposed treatment of the class under its plan complies with four requirements:

(1) The debtor must cure any default that occurred before or after the commencement of the bankruptcy case. This provision does not state when the cure must be made, but the courts have generally held that cure must be in a lump sum at the effective date of the plan. The amount necessary to cure is determined in accord with the security agreement and applicable nonbankruptcy law. Bankr. Code §1123(d).

(2) The plan must reinstate the maturity of that part of the claim that remains outstanding after cure, as such maturity existed before such default. That is, future payments remain due at the times specified in the original contract.

(3) The debtor must compensate the holder of the secured claim for particular kinds of damages and actual pecuniary losses.

(4) The plan must not otherwise alter the legal, equitable, or contractual rights to which the claim entitles its holder. For example, if the original contract between the parties provided that the debtor would pay the creditor's reasonable attorneys fees for collection in the event of default, that term must continue to be applicable to the debtor's post-reinstatement obligations.

If a class of claims is unimpaired under a Chapter 11 plan, the holder of the claim in the class is conclusively presumed to have accepted the plan and is not entitled to vote on it. Bankr. Code §1126(f). If the plan meets the other requirements for confirmation, it can be imposed on the holder of the unimpaired claim over the holder's objection.

To illustrate the operation of these provisions, assume that Debtor borrowed $100,000 from Firstbank. By the terms of the agreement between them, the loan was repayable with interest at 8 percent per year in equal monthly installments over 25 years. The payment on such a loan is $771.82. The agreement provided that payments were due on the 26th day of each month. Debtor made the first 12 payments when due, missed the next three payments, and then filed under Chapter 11. After filing, Debtor continued to miss payments. Debtor then proposed a plan that specified an effective date ten days after confirmation, obligated Debtor to cure the default and to compensate Firstbank for resulting damages on the effective date of the plan, and thereupon reinstated the contract for repayment. Such a plan would meet the requirements of Bankruptcy Code §1124(2) and the court would impose it on Firstbank over Firstbank's objection. Bankr. Code §1129(a)(8).

Assuming that a year passed between the filing of the Chapter 11 case and confirmation of Debtor's plan on March 4, Debtor's payment obligations under the plan would be as follows. First, on March 14, Debtor would have to make up the 15 missed payments in a single payment of $11,577.30. As damages for its breach, Debtor might have to pay interest on the overdue sums and any attorneys fees and expenses of collection provided for under the contract and incurred by Firstbank as a result of the breach. Bankr. Code §1123(d). On March 26, and the 26th day of each month thereafter, Debtor would be required to make the originally scheduled payment of $771.82.

Why would Debtor have chosen to cure and reinstate this loan rather than modify the repayment schedule through cramdown under Bankruptcy Code §1129(b)(2)(A)(i)? If the loan was secured only by a mortgage against the principal residence of the debtor, modification was prohibited. See Bankr. Code §1123(b)(5). Otherwise, the likely answer is that Debtor wished to preserve some favorable term of the original contract for repayment that Debtor could not preserve in a cramdown. For example, assume that by the time Debtor proposed its plan, the market rate of interest on this kind of loan had increased to 12 percent per year. If Debtor had modified the secured claim through cramdown, Debtor would not have had to make a lump sum cure, but Debtor would have had to pay interest at 12 percent. See *Till v. SCS*, supra. By curing and reinstating the original terms of the loan, Debtor preserved the 8 percent interest rate specified in the original loan contract.

3.   Reinstatement and Cure Under Chapter 13

The Chapter 13 debtor's right to cure and reinstate is described in Bankruptcy Code §1322(b)(5). That section provides that a Chapter 13 plan may "provide for the curing of any default within a reasonable time and maintenance of payments while the case is pending on any . . . secured claim on which the last payment is due after the date on which the final payment under the plan is due." Although this provision is considerably shorter than §1124(2), its effect is to impose much the same four requirements:

(1)   The debtor must cure any default that occurred before or after the commencement of the bankruptcy case. But under Bankruptcy Code §1322(b)(5), the debtor need only cure "within a reasonable time." The courts have given a flexible meaning to this phrase and approved cures over periods of months or years. All seem to agree that the cure need not be in a lump sum at the effective date of the plan. But all seem also to agree that cure cannot extend beyond the period of the plan. Within that range, the courts consider the size of the arrearage and the debtor's ability to pay in determining whether a particular proposal is reasonable.

(2)   Like a Chapter 11 plan, a Chapter 13 plan must reinstate the maturity of the claim as such maturity existed before such default. That is, future payments remain due at the times specified in the original contract.

(3)   Chapter 13 does not expressly require compensation for damages incurred by the creditor as a result of the breach, but directs the courts to look to applicable nonbankruptcy law to determine the amount necessary to cure. Bankr. Code §1322(e). In some states, that law requires payment of interest on the overdue arrearages; in others it does not.

(4)   Like a Chapter 11 plan, a Chapter 13 plan cannot otherwise alter the legal, equitable, or contractual rights to which the holder is entitled.

Debtors who file under Chapter 13 are far more likely to use reinstatement and cure than modification to deal with a long-term secured obligation because Chapter 13 requires full payment of modified claims within the period of the plan; most debtors cannot pay their long-term obligations in such a short time. Bankruptcy Code §1322(b)(2), like Bankruptcy Code §1123(b)(5), prohibits modification of the rights of the holder of a claim secured only by a security interest in real property that is the debtor's principal residence. Under either chapter, reinstatement is the only means available to save the family home once the lender has accelerated the debt.

In Nobelman v. American Savings Bank, 508 U.S. 324 (1993), the Supreme Court gave this mortgagee protection provision an expansive reading. In that case, American Savings held a $71,000 purchase money mortgage against the Nobelmans' condominium, which was worth only $23,500. The Court held that the Nobelmans could not, in their Chapter 13 plan, modify even the unsecured portion of American Savings' claim. To save their $23,500 home, the Court ruled, the Nobelmans had to pay $71,000. Justice Thomas, writing for the Court, based his explanation solely on the language of Bankruptcy Code §1322(b)(2). Justice Stevens, concurring, explained the surprising outcome as implementing a congressional intention "to encourage the flow of capital into the home lending market."

Nobelman prevented the bankruptcy system from relieving the massive residential debt overhang resulting from the 2007 housing market crash. Debtors found themselves with large mortgages on homes that had dropped precipitously in value. Because of *Nobelman*, Chapter 13 debtors could not obtain bankruptcy relief from their mortgages regardless of the values of their homes. There is one exception. The lower courts have interpreted *Nobelman* not to apply to wholly underwater second mortgages.

4. When Is It Too Late to File Bankruptcy to Reinstate and Cure or to Modify?

A debtor can reinstate and cure a default and acceleration even if the deadline for cure under state law has passed before the debtor invokes bankruptcy procedure. Bankruptcy does not just preserve rights existing under state law; it recognizes rights that state law does not. But how far is bankruptcy willing to go in reversing what has already taken place under nonbankruptcy law?

Congress answered this question specifically with respect to reinstatement and cure of a principal residence mortgage in Chapter 13. A debtor can cure and reinstate if the debtor files bankruptcy before the "residence is sold at a foreclosure sale that is conducted in accordance with applicable nonbankruptcy law." Bankr. Code §1322(c)(1). In some states, that will be when the sheriff identifies the winner of the auction held on the courthouse steps. In other states, it will be only when the court has entered an order confirming the foreclosure sale and that order has become final. Although there is no clear authority on the point, we think the rule is probably the same for other kinds of collateral in Chapter 13 cases, and for all kinds of collateral in Chapter 11 cases.

A mortgage or security interest cannot be modified in a bankruptcy case if it no longer exists at the time the case is filed. A mortgage ceases to exist when it has been foreclosed. Depending on the circumstances and the jurisdiction, that may occur as early as entry of the judgment of foreclosure, or as late as confirmation of the sale. Under UCC §9-617(a), "a secured party's disposition of collateral after default . . . discharges the security interest under which the disposition is made; and . . . discharges any subordinate security interest." "Disposition" occurs — and the security interest ceases to exist — when the secured party sells, or contracts to sell, the collateral.

C.   Binding Lenders in the Absence of a Fixed Schedule for Repayment

As we noted in Assignment 13, many lending relationships lack a fixed schedule for repayment. Probably the most common of these is the line of credit that is payable on demand. In that arrangement, borrowing and repayment are expected to occur at the convenience of the debtor — unless the secured creditor decides to call the loan. The debtor's right to cure and reinstate under bankruptcy law is of no avail to debtors in such relationships. Cure and reinstatement only restores to the debtor those contract rights that the debtor enjoyed before default. Debtors whose lines of credit were repayable on demand or at a specific time that has passed have no contract rights that bankruptcy could restore.

Such debtors are protected, if at all, only through their ability to modify the claim or to use the respite of reorganization proceedings to find a willing substitute lender. For modification to yield substantial benefits to the debtor, there must be a substantial loan outstanding at the time of bankruptcy. The automatic stay prevents secured creditors from trying to collect after a bankruptcy filing the money they had advanced to a debtor before the filing. But nothing in bankruptcy law or practice requires a lender to make advances during or after bankruptcy — even if the lenders have contracted to make those advances. See, e.g., Bankr. Code §365(c)(2). If, as is often the case, the line of credit lender simply waits until the debtor pays the line down and then precipitates the bankruptcy by refusing to make further advances, the lender has probably won the game.

Finding a substitute lender may not be out of the question. Many lenders actively seek relationships with borrowers who are in bankruptcy. Some demand a higher price. Some see a benefit to lending to debtors who are stripping away their other debt and have good collateral to offer.

Problem Set 14

14.1.   How does reading Assignment 14 change your response to the situation presented in Problem 13.3? What do you expect Rebel to do if Second National calls the loan without notice? Where is Second National going to come out on this? Bankr. Code §§362(a) and (d)(1) and (2), 363(a), (b)(1), (c), and (e), 1123(a)(5)(E), 1124.

14.2.   Ever since the market for single-family houses collapsed in the town where you practice, you've had a steady stream of debtors looking for ways to save their homes. The circumstances of two of them are described below.

Willard Spivak bought his home three years ago from Rolling Green Developers for $300,000. He financed the home with a 30-year conventional mortgage from Gateway Savings and Loan. The mortgage provides for repayment in equal monthly installments with interest at 8 percent per year. The principal amount of the loan was $240,000. Willard made 29 monthly payments of $1,761.03 each, and then missed the 30th and all subsequent payments. As of yesterday, he is seven months in arrears, a total of $12,327.21.

What is the total amount Willard currently owes on this mortgage? To answer this question, you will need an amortization schedule based on the original terms of the mortgage. Generate one using one of the many "amortization calculators" available online or using a spreadsheet. The total amount owing will be the sum of the missed payments plus the amount that would have been owing if Willard had made those payments. This calculation method implicitly assumes that Willard is not required to pay interest on the overdue payments, no late fees have accrued, and the lender has incurred no attorneys fees for which Willard has liability.

14.3.   On the facts of Problem 14.2, Willard shows you each of the communications he has received from Gateway since he went into default. The first was a "Friendly Reminder;" the second and third were titled "Notice of Delinquency." The fourth was a letter from a law firm detailing the status of the loan and stating that if Willard did not bring the loan current within ten days, the bank would declare a default and accelerate the due dates of all payments. The next letter was from the same law firm, dated 23 days later. It stated that Gateway declared the loan in default, that the entire balance of approximately $246,000 was immediately due and payable, and that if Willard did not pay it within ten days, Gateway would foreclose. The last document Willard shows you is the foreclosure complaint and summons served by the sheriff on Willard yesterday, one month after the last letter. Willard says he is back at work now and has the money to resume payments on the mortgage, but he doesn't know where he can get $12,327.21 to make up the arrearage. When Willard called the bank recently, an officer told him that even if he *does* tender the arrearage now, the bank won't accept it. "You have to pay the whole $246,000," the officer told him. One of the reasons Gateway wants to get rid of this loan is that rates have risen since Gateway made it. Gateway currently charges 11 percent for the same kind of loan. (At that rate, Willard's monthly payment would have been $2,285.58 on the same loan.) The home is probably worth only about the amount of the loan, but Willard wants to keep it.

a. What do you recommend? Bankr. Code §§1322(b)(5), 1322(c) and (d), 1325(b)(4), 1123(a)(5), 1123(b)(5), 1124, 1129(b)(2)(A).

b. If Willard follows your recommendation, what is the minimum Willard must pay to keep the house and when will he have to pay it?

c. Winona Williams bought her home three years ago for $300,000. Thinking that interest rates would go down in a few years, she financed her purchase with an $240,000 purchase-money mortgage from the seller, Marian Case. The terms are remarkably similar to the terms of Willard Spivak's mortgage — the loan is amortized over 30 years with interest at 8 percent per year, for a monthly payment of $1,761.06. The difference is that Winona's mortgage "balloons" at the end of five years — just two years from now. (The term *balloon* means that the entire balance becomes due.) Like Willard, Winona is seven months in arrears, a total of $12,327.42, and Marian Case has accelerated and commenced foreclosure. Winona's home is still worth $300,000 and she'd really like to hold on to it. What do you suggest? Bankr. Code §§1123(a)(5), 1123(b)(5), 1124, 1129(a)(11), 1129(b)(2)(A), 1322(b)(2), 1322(b)(5), 1322(c)(2), 1325(a)(5), 1325(a)(6), 1325(b)(4).

d. Would it help if Winona were to move out of the house, rent it to a tenant, and use that cash flow to rent another house to live in? Bankr. Code §§1123(b)(5), 1129(b)(2)(A)(i).

e. Willard Spivak, felt he couldn't afford your fees, so he didn't take your advice. Instead, he made a deal with Gateway. Under the deal, the amount of his arrearage was fixed at $18,000 ($12,327.42 plus Gateway's attorneys fees) and Gateway gave him six months to pay it. In return, Willard agreed to an increase in the interest rate on the loan from 8 to 11 percent. Now Willard's six months is almost up. He has been making the regular monthly payments of $2,285.58 on the loan at the new interest rate, but hasn't been able to save anything toward the $18,000 payment that is about to come due. Realizing that he is about to default again, Willard is back to see you. Is there anything you can do for him? Bankr. Code §§1123(a)(5), 1123(b)(5), 1322(b).

14.4. a. In *Nobelman*, discussed in section B.3 of this assignment, American Savings held a mortgage in the amount of $71,000 against the debtors' condominium, which had a value of only $23,500. The Supreme Court held that the Nobelmans could not modify the unsecured portion of American Savings' claim. If you represented the Nobelmans at this point, what would you advise with regard to this condominium?

b. If you represented American Savings, what would you advise with regard to this condominium?

c. Is *Nobelman* good policy?

■ End of Default Problem Set

14.5. a. David Walker (from Problem 13.7) has come up with alternatives for Teresa Revez. He now says the bank can lend Teresa the $300,000 she needs on either of two arrangements. The first is to lend her the money at prime plus 2 percent on a demand note. The second is to lend her the money at prime plus 3.25 percent on an arrangement that provides for 30 days' notice prior to call if she is not then in default. Teresa wants your advice on choosing between these options. Considering only these two, what do you recommend? Bankr. Code §§1123(a)(5)(E), 1124, 1129(b)(2)(A)(i).

b. Teresa's expression of concern about having the entire $300,000 outstanding at such a high rate of interest, even when she did not need it, prompted David Walker to sweeten the deal. Now the bank is offering a line of credit for $300,000 on the same terms that they were offering to lend her $300,000 fixed. That is, she can choose between prime plus 2 percent on a demand note or prime plus 3.25 percent on a note with 30 days' notice before cancellation. Having this loan in the form of a line of credit entitles Teresa to pay back to the bank what she doesn't need, and draw it out again when she does need it. Under the options in part (a) of this problem, Teresa would have put the money she didn't need in a bank account at a relatively low rate of interest, so the savings offered by these line of credit options are substantial. Do you see any disadvantages? Which of the two line of credit arrangements seems more attractive?

Chapter 5.   The Prototypical Secured Transaction

Assignment 15:   The Prototypical Secured Transaction

In Part One of this book, we have addressed various aspects of the relationship between a secured creditor and its debtor. In this assignment, we examine a specific example of such a relationship. The example we have chosen is a relationship between a boat dealer and its inventory lender, Otis Finance. The debtors are Bonnie Brezhnev and her corporation, Bonnie's Boat World, Inc. Bonnie's supplier is Shoreline Boats, Inc. Bonnie and these companies are all fictional characters, but the transaction and relationships are, as they say in the movies, "based on a true story."

While the relationships described in this assignment are typical of inventory lending, they are not typical of secured transactions generally. As you have already seen in earlier assignments, secured transactions come in a variety of forms. At one extreme, the secured transaction in which a consumer buys a television may be documented only by a half-page printed form signed when the debtor opens the charge account and a receipt issued for the particular sale. At the other extreme, the documentation for the financing of an office building or industrial plant may be hundreds or even thousands of pages in length. In its complexity, the transaction described in this assignment is perhaps about midway between those extremes.

We will discuss the strategies and motivations of both sides. The legal doctrine governing secured credit is best understood in relation to those strategies and motivations. But given the wide variety of circumstances in which creditors take security, it should come as no surprise that strategies and motivations differ from one kind of secured transaction to another and with the attitudes of different participants to the same kind of secured transaction. Thus, you should be cautious in attempting to generalize our prototype to other kinds of secured lending. To understand why a contract provision exists in the form it does, one must usually see how it operates in a variety of circumstances. At the same time, one must start somewhere, and we have chosen the context of inventory lending.

A.   The Parties

The lender, Otis Finance, is a large financial institution with offices across the United States. Otis offers several kinds of commercial loans. A substantial portion of Otis's business is *floorplanning,* that is, financing the purchase of the inventory that is on a dealer's showroom floor. Floorplan borrowers are typically retailers of relatively high-dollar value items such as mobile homes, recreational vehicles, boats and motors, consumer electronics and appliances, keyboards and other musical instruments, industrial equipment, agricultural equipment, office machines, snowmobiles, and motorcycles.

Bonnie Brezhnev purchased Art's Boat World, Inc. three months ago. She changed the name to Bonnie's Boat World, incorporated Bonnie's Boat World, Inc., and took ownership of the business in the corporate name. The business is located on a commercial highway that passes within a few hundred feet of a lake. The boatyard, located on the narrow strip of land between the highway and the lake, consists of a small indoor showroom, sales offices, three acres of land surrounded by an eight-foot cyclone fence, a boat storage building, and a pier extending into the lake.

B.   Otis Approves Bonnie's Loan

Dissatisfied with the lender who has been financing her inventory, Bonnie makes her first contact with Otis. She visits Otis's local office and meets with Pamela Foohey, an Otis loan officer. They discuss the boat business, Bonnie's plans for the future, the terms on which Otis makes loans, and a number of other subjects. Generally pleased, Bonnie takes the blank form of a loan application with her when she leaves. The application seeks a variety of information about Bonnie and her business, including current balance sheets, income statements, and income tax returns for both herself and the corporation. Because Bonnie has to bring some of the accounting records up to date, it takes Bonnie and her bookkeeper a little over a week to complete the application.

When Pamela receives the application, she immediately orders a credit report from Dun and Bradstreet (D & B). Bonnie's Boat World is a recently formed corporation, and D & B has no information on it at the time they receive Otis's request. To get the information it eventually includes in its report, D & B searches its public record files, interviews Bonnie, and checks with some of the credit references she gives them. Pamela arranges for all of the information she has obtained about Bonnie's to be entered into Otis's proprietary credit scoring system. Based on the results and her own review of the application and credit report, Pamela decides to recommend authorization of the loan.

Pamela presents the loan application to her branch manager a few days later. The branch manager has authority to approve a credit line of this size. Although the branch manager has some concerns about Bonnie's relative inexperience in the retail boat business, the application is otherwise strong and the branch manager approves it. Pamela calls Bonnie that same afternoon to tell her that the loan has been approved and to set a time for closing the transaction.

C. Otis and Bonnie's Document the Loan

Pamela emailed a copy of Otis's standard Agreement for Wholesale Financing (Security Agreement) to Bonnie, and Bonnie discussed it with her own lawyer. Bonnie also emailed to Pamela an authorization for Otis to file a financing statement against Bonnie's, Otis filed the financing statement, and Richard Feynman, an Otis employee, searched the Article 9 filing system to verify the name and address of the bank that financed the boats already in Bonnie's possession. Richard visited Bonnie's Boat World and made a list of all the boats currently in the company's possession. While there, Richard examined the books and records of the business to see how they are kept. Satisfied with what he had seen and been told, Richard advised Pamela that the loan was ready for closing.

A few days later, Bonnie returned to Otis's offices to complete the loan documentation. When Bonnie enters Pamela's office, Pamela has all of the documents on her desk. Bonnie and Pamela go through them one by one, discussing and signing them. Four of these documents, the security agreement, a sample form statement of transaction, the filed financing statement, and the personal guarantee, are relevant to an understanding of the security aspect of the transaction.

1. Security Agreement and Statement of Transaction

Subject to a few omissions indicated, this is the full text of the security agreement Bonnie signs at the closing:

AGREEMENT FOR WHOLESALE FINANCING
(SECURITY AGREEMENT)

This Agreement for Wholesale Financing ("Agreement") is made January 24, 2016 between Otis Finance Corp. ("Otis") and Bonnie's Boat World, Inc., a Missouri Corporation ("Dealer"), having a principal place of business located at 12376 Highway 441, Blue Moon, MO 63131.

Date parties Address

1. Advances Optional. Subject to the terms of this Agreement, Otis, in its sole discretion, may extend credit to Dealer from time to time to purchase inventory from Otis approved vendors. Otis's decision to advance funds on any inventory will not be binding until the funds are actually advanced. Dealer agrees that Otis may, at any time and without notice to Dealer, elect not to finance any inventory sold by particular vendors who are in default of their obligations to Otis, or with respect to which Otis reasonably feels insecure.

Otis decides when to finance inventory

2. Statements of Transaction. Dealer and Otis agree that certain financial terms of any advance made by Otis under this Agreement, whether regarding finance charges, other fees, maturities, curtailments or other financial terms, are not set forth herein because such terms depend, in part, upon the availability from time to time of vendor discounts or other incentives, prevailing economic conditions, Otis's floorplanning volume with Dealer and with Dealer's vendors, and other economic factors which may vary over time. Dealer and Otis further agree that it is therefore in their mutual best interest to set forth in this Agreement only the general terms of Dealer's financing arrangement with Otis. Upon agreeing to finance a particular item of inventory for Dealer, Otis will send Dealer a Statement of Transaction identifying such inventory and the applicable financial terms. Unless Dealer notifies Otis in writing of any objection within fifteen (15) days after a Statement of Transaction is mailed to Dealer:

(a) the amount shown on such Statement of Transaction will be an account stated;

(b) Dealer will have agreed to all rates, charges, and other terms shown on such Statement of Transaction;

(c) Dealer will have agreed that the items of inventory referenced in such Statement of Transaction are being financed by Otis at Dealer's request; and

(d) such Statement of Transaction will be incorporated herein by reference, will be made a part hereof as if originally set forth herein, and will constitute an addendum hereto.

3. Objections to Statements of Transaction. If Dealer objects to the terms of any Statement of Transaction, Dealer agrees to pay Otis for such inventory in accordance with the most recent terms for similar inventory to which Dealer has not objected (or, if there are no prior terms, at the lesser of 16% per annum or at the maximum lawful contract rate of interest permitted under applicable law), but Dealer acknowledges that Otis may then elect to terminate Dealer's financing program pursuant to Section 20, and cease making additional advances to Dealer. Any termination for that reason, however, will not accelerate the maturities of advances previously made, unless Dealer shall otherwise be in default of this Agreement.

4. Description of Collateral. To secure payment of all Dealer's current and future debts to Otis, whether under this Agreement or any current or future guaranty or other agreement, Dealer grants Otis a security interest in all Dealer's inventory, equipment, fixtures, accounts, contract rights, chattel paper, instruments, reserves, documents, and general intangibles, whether now owned or hereafter acquired, all attachments, accessories, accessions, substitutions, and replacements thereto and all proceeds thereof. All such assets are as defined in the Uniform Commercial Code and referred to herein as the "Collateral." All Collateral financed by Otis, and all proceeds thereof, will be held in trust by Dealer for Otis, with such proceeds being payable in accordance with Section 9.

5. Location and Ownership of Collateral. Dealer represents that all Collateral will be kept at Dealer's principal place of business listed above, except as otherwise authorized by Otis in writing. Dealer will give Otis at least 30 days' prior written notice of any change in Dealer's identity, name, form of business organization, ownership, principal place of business, Collateral locations, or other business locations.

6. Dealer's Obligations. Dealer will:

(a) only exhibit and sell Collateral financed by Otis to buyers in the ordinary course of business;

(b) not rent, lease, demonstrate, transfer, or use any Collateral financed by Otis without Otis's prior written consent;

(c) execute all documents Otis requests to perfect Otis's security interest in the Collateral;

(d) deliver to Otis immediately upon each request, and Otis may retain, each Certificate of Title or Statement of Origin issued for Collateral financed by Otis;

(e) immediately provide Otis with copies of Dealer's annual financial statements upon their completion (which in no event shall exceed 120 days after the end of Dealer's fiscal year), and all other information regarding Dealer that Otis requests from time to time. All financial information Dealer delivers to Otis will accurately represent Dealer's financial condition either as of the date of delivery, or, if different, the date specified therein, and Dealer acknowledges Otis's reliance thereon.

(f) pay all taxes and fees assessed against Dealer or the Collateral when due;

(g) immediately notify Otis of any loss, theft, or damage to any Collateral;

(h) keep the Collateral insured for its full insurable value under a property insurance policy with a company acceptable to Otis, naming Otis as a loss-payee and containing standard lender's loss payable and termination provisions; and

(i) provide Otis with written evidence of such insurance coverage and loss-payee and lender's clauses.

7. Reimbursement. If Dealer fails to pay any taxes, fees, or other obligations which may impair Otis's interest in the Collateral, or fails to keep the Collateral insured, Otis may pay such taxes, fees, or obligations and pay the cost to insure the Collateral, and the amounts paid will be: (i) an additional debt owed by Dealer to Otis; and (ii) due and payable immediately in full.

8. Inspection. Dealer grants Otis an irrevocable license to enter Dealer's business locations during normal business hours without notice to Dealer to:

(a) account for and inspect all Collateral;

(b) verify Dealer's compliance with this Agreement; and

(c) examine and copy Dealer's books and records related to the Collateral.

9. Time for Payment. Dealer will immediately pay Otis the principal indebtedness owed Otis on each item of Collateral financed by Otis (as shown on the Statement of Transaction identifying such Collateral) on the earliest occurrence of any of the following events:

(a) when such Collateral is lost, stolen, or damaged;

(b) for Collateral financed under Pay-As-Sold ("PAS") terms (as shown on the Statement of Transaction identifying such Collateral), when such Collateral is sold, transferred, rented, leased, otherwise disposed of, or matured;

(c)   in strict accordance with any curtailment schedule for such Collateral (as shown on the Statement of Transaction identifying such Collateral);

(d)   for Collateral financed under Scheduled Payment Program ("SPP") terms (as shown on the Statement of Transaction identifying such Collateral), in strict accordance with the installment payment schedule; and

(e)   when otherwise required under the terms of any financing program agreed to in writing by the parties.

10. Application of Payments. Regardless of the SPP terms pertaining to any Collateral financed by Otis, if Otis determines that the current outstanding debt owed by Dealer to Otis exceeds the aggregate wholesale invoice price of such Collateral in Dealer's possession, Dealer will immediately upon demand pay Otis the difference between such outstanding debt and the aggregate wholesale invoice price of such Collateral. If Dealer from time to time is required to make immediate payment to Otis of any past due obligation discovered during any Collateral audit, or at any other time, Dealer agrees that acceptance of such payment by Otis shall not be construed to have waived or amended the terms of its financing program. Dealer agrees that the proceeds of any Collateral received by Dealer shall be held by Dealer in trust for Otis's benefit, for application as provided in this Agreement. Dealer will send all payments to Otis's branch office(s) responsible for Dealer's account. Otis may apply:

(a)   payments to reduce finance charges first and then principal, regardless of Dealer's instructions; and

(b)   principal payments to the oldest (earliest) invoice for Collateral financed by Otis, but, in any event, all principal payments will first be applied to such Collateral which is sold, lost, stolen, damaged, rented, leased, or otherwise disposed of or unaccounted for.

11. Finance Charges. Dealer will pay Otis finance charges on the outstanding principal debt Dealer owes Otis for each item of Collateral financed by Otis at the rate(s) shown on the Statement of Transaction identifying such Collateral, unless Dealer objects thereto as provided in Section 3. The finance charges attributable to the rate shown on the Statement of Transaction will:

(a)   be computed based on a 360-day year;

(b)   be calculated by multiplying the Daily Charge (as defined below) by the actual number of days in the applicable billing period; and

(c)   accrue from the invoice date of the Collateral identified on such Statement of Transaction until Otis receives full payment of the principal debt Dealer owes Otis for each item of such Collateral.

The "Daily Charge" is the product of the Daily Rate (as defined below) multiplied by the Average Daily Balance (as defined below). The "Daily Rate" is the quotient of the annual rate shown on the Statement of Transaction divided by 360, or the monthly rate shown on the Statement of Transaction divided by 30. The "Average Daily Balance" is the quotient of

(i)   the sum of the outstanding principal debt owed Otis on each day of a billing period for each item of Collateral identified on a Statement of Transaction, divided by

(ii)   the actual number of days in such billing period.

12. Liquidated Damages, Usury, Account Stated. Dealer will pay Otis $100 for each check returned unpaid for insufficient funds (an "NSF check") (such $100 payment repays Otis's estimated administrative costs; it does not waive the default caused by the NSF check). Dealer acknowledges that Otis intends to strictly conform to the applicable usury laws governing this Agreement and understands that Dealer is not obligated to pay any finance charges billed to Dealer's account exceeding the amount allowed by such usury laws, and any such excess finance charges Dealer pays will be applied to reduce Dealer's principal debt owed to Otis. Otis will send Dealer a monthly billing statement identifying all charges due on Dealer's account with Otis. The charges specified on each billing statement will be:

    (a)   due and payable in full immediately on receipt, and

    (b)   an account stated, unless Otis receives Dealer's written objection thereto within 15 days after it is mailed to Dealer.

13. Late Fees. If Otis does not receive, by the 25th day of any given month, payment of all charges accrued to Dealer's account with Otis during the immediately preceding month, Dealer will (to the extent allowed by law) pay Otis a late fee ("Late Fee") equal to the greater of $5 or 5% of the amount of such finance charges (such Late Fee repays Otis's estimated administrative costs; it does not waive the default caused by the late payment). Otis may adjust the billing statement at any time to conform to applicable law and this Agreement.

14. Default. Dealer will be in default under this Agreement if:

    (a)   Dealer breaches any terms, warranties, or representations contained herein, in any Statement of Transaction to which Dealer has not objected as provided in Section 3, or in any other agreement between Otis and Dealer;

    (b)   any guarantor of Dealer's debts to Otis breaches any terms, warranties, or representations contained in any guaranty or other agreement between the guarantor and Otis;

    (c)   any representation, statement, report, or certificate made or delivered by Dealer or any guarantor to Otis is not accurate when made;

    (d)   Dealer fails to pay any portion of Dealer's debts to Otis when due and payable hereunder or under any other agreement between Otis and Dealer;

    (e)   Dealer abandons any Collateral;

    (f)   Dealer or any guarantor is or becomes in default in the payment of any debt owed to any third party;

    (g)   a money judgment issues against Dealer or any guarantor;

    (h)   an attachment, sale, or seizure issues or is executed against any assets of Dealer or of any guarantor;

    (i)   the undersigned dies while Dealer's business is operated as a sole proprietorship or any general partner dies while Dealer's business is operated as a general or limited partnership;

    (j)   any guarantor dies;

    (k)   Dealer or any guarantor shall cease existence as a corporation, partnership, or trust;

    (l)   Dealer or any guarantor ceases or suspends business;

(m) Dealer or any guarantor makes a general assignment for the benefit of creditors;

(n) Dealer or any guarantor becomes insolvent or voluntarily or involuntarily becomes subject to the Federal Bankruptcy Code, any state insolvency law or any similar law;

(o) any receiver is appointed for any of Dealer's or any guarantor's assets;

(p) any guaranty of Dealer's debts to Otis is terminated;

(q) Dealer loses any franchise, permission, license, or right to sell or deal in any Collateral which Otis finances;

(r) Dealer or any guarantor misrepresents Dealer's or such guarantor's financial condition or organizational structure; or

(s) any of the Collateral becomes subject to any lien, claim, encumbrance, or security interest prior or superior to Otis's.

15. Effect of Default. In the event of a default,

(a) Otis may at any time at Otis's election, without notice or demand to Dealer, do any one or more of the following: declare all or any part of the debt Dealer owes Otis immediately due and payable, together with all costs and expenses of Otis's collection activity, including, without limitation, all reasonable attorneys fees; exercise any or all rights under applicable law (including, without limitation, the right to possess, transfer, and dispose of the Collateral); and/or cease extending any additional credit to Dealer (Otis's right to cease extending credit shall not be construed to limit the discretionary nature of this credit facility).

(b) Dealer will segregate and keep the Collateral in trust for Otis, and in good order and repair, and will not exhibit, sell, rent, lease, further encumber, otherwise dispose of, or use any Collateral.

(c) Upon Otis's oral or written demand, Dealer will immediately deliver the Collateral to Otis, in good order and repair, at a place specified by Otis, together with all related documents; or Otis may, in Otis's sole discretion and without notice or demand to Dealer, take immediate possession of the Collateral together with all related documents.

(d) Otis may, without notice, apply a default finance charge to Dealer's outstanding principal indebtedness equal to the default rate specified in Dealer's financing program with Otis, if any, or if there is none so specified, at the lesser of 3% per annum above the rate in effect immediately prior to the default, or the highest lawful contract rate of interest permitted under applicable law.

All Otis's rights and remedies are cumulative. Otis's failure to exercise any of Otis's rights or remedies hereunder will not waive any of Otis's rights or remedies as to any past, current, or future default.

   16. Sale of Collateral. Dealer agrees that if Otis conducts a private sale of any Collateral by requesting bids from 10 or more dealers or distributors in that type of Collateral, any sale by Otis of such Collateral in bulk or in parcels within 120 days of

(a) Otis's taking possession and control of such Collateral; or

(b) when Otis is otherwise authorized to sell such Collateral;

whichever occurs last, to the bidder submitting the highest cash bid therefor, is a commercially reasonable sale of such Collateral under the Uniform Commercial Code. Dealer agrees that the purchase of any Collateral by a vendor, as provided in any agreement between Otis and the vendor, is a commercially reasonable disposition and private sale of such Collateral under the Uniform Commercial Code, and no request for bids shall be required. Dealer further agrees that 7 or more days' prior written notice will be commercially reasonable notice of any public or private sale (including any sale to a vendor). If Otis disposes of any such Collateral other than as herein contemplated, the commercial reasonableness of such disposition will be determined in accordance with the laws of the state governing this Agreement.

17. Power of Attorney. Dealer grants Otis an irrevocable power of attorney to: execute or endorse on Dealer's behalf any checks, financing statements, instruments, Certificates of Title and Statements of Origin pertaining to the Collateral; supply any omitted information and correct errors in any documents between Otis and Dealer; do anything Dealer is obligated to do hereunder; initiate and settle any insurance claim pertaining to the Collateral; and do anything to preserve and protect the Collateral and Otis's rights and interest therein. Otis may provide to any third party any credit, financial or other information on Dealer that Otis may from time to time possess.

is this standard

18. Time. Time is of the essence. *What does this mean?*

19. Agreement Location. This Agreement is deemed to have been entered into at the Otis branch office executing this Agreement.

20. Termination. Either party may terminate this Agreement at any time by written notice received by the other party. If Otis terminates this Agreement, Dealer agrees that if Dealer:

#15-7

(a)   is not in default hereunder, 30 days' prior notice of termination is reasonable and sufficient (although this provision shall not be construed to mean that shorter periods may not, in particular circumstances, also be reasonable and sufficient); or

(b)   is in default hereunder, no prior notice of termination is required.

Dealer will not be relieved from any obligation to Otis arising out of Otis's advances or commitments made before the effective termination date of this Agreement. Otis will retain all of its rights, interests, and remedies hereunder until Dealer has paid all Dealer's debts to Otis.

21. Assignment. Dealer cannot assign Dealer's interest in this Agreement without Otis's prior written consent, although Otis may assign or participate Otis's interest, in whole or in part, without Dealer's consent. This Agreement will protect and bind Otis's and Dealer's respective heirs, representatives, successors, and assigns.

22. Amendments in Writing. All agreements or commitments to extend or renew credit or refrain from enforcing payment of a debt must be in writing. Any oral or other amendment or waiver claimed to be made to this Agreement that is not evidenced by a written document executed by Otis and Dealer (except for each Statement of Transaction that Dealer does not object to in the manner stated in Section 3) will be null, void, and have no force or effect whatsoever.

23. Severance. If any provision of this Agreement or its application is invalid or unenforceable, the remainder of this Agreement will not be impaired or affected and will remain binding and enforceable.

24. Attorneys Fees and Expenses. Dealer agrees to pay all of Otis's reasonable attorneys fees and expenses incurred by Otis in enforcing Otis's rights hereunder.

25. Binding arbitration. [Editor's note: The two-page arbitration clause was omitted for lack of space in this reproduction. That clause provided that the parties would submit all disputes between them to binding arbitration through the American Arbitration Association.]

26. Jury Waiver. If Section 25 of this Agreement or its application is invalid or unenforceable, any legal proceeding with respect to any Dispute will be tried in a court of competent jurisdiction by a judge without a jury. Dealer and Otis waive any right to a jury trial in any such proceeding.

THIS CONTRACT CONTAINS BINDING ARBITRATION AND JURY WAIVER PROVISIONS.

Otis Finance Corp.   Dealer: Bonnie's Boat World, Inc.

By: *Pamela Foohey*   By: *Bonnie Brezhnev*

Pamela Foohey   Bonnie Brezhnev
Loan officer   President

[Editors' note: We have omitted the Dealer's certification that its Board of Directors adopted a specific resolution authorizing the corporation to enter into this financing arrangement with Otis.]

At the time she signs this agreement, Bonnie has not yet purchased any boats for Otis to finance. Otis disburses no money at this "closing" and there is no Statement of Transaction for Bonnie to approve. Pamela shows Bonnie some information about the pricing of credit by Otis and a sample of a Statement of Transaction prepared on the basis of a hypothetical purchase (see Figure 3). The sequence of events that will occur when Bonnie buys some boats is discussed below.

OTIS FINANCE CORPORATION
Statement of Transaction

Loan #	Manufacturer	Dealer
0216-01	Shoreline Boats	Bonnie's Boat World, Inc.

Model	Serial #	Qty	Unit Price	Amount
Shoreliner Pro	98-P209101X	1	15,566.58	$15,566.58

Finance Terms: Scheduled Payment Plan (SPP)

Loan #	Charge Type	Days/Date	Rate/Amount	Description
0216-01	Finance	31 – 90	Prime -1.00%	per annum of ADB
		91 –	2.4000%	per month of ADB
	Flat	31 –	.2500%	of balance every 1 month
	Late Rate		Prime +5.50%	per annum of ADB of late amount
				Day 1 is date of invoice

"Prime" means the highest prime rate or reference rate of interest publicly announced by JPMorgan Chase Bank, N.A., and such rate in effect on the last business day of any calendar month will be prime for the following calendar month, subject to any minimum prime.

Principal Payments Due
2/4/2016 $15,556.58

Invoice total $15,556.58

Bonnie's Boat World	Otis Finance
12976 Highway 441	P.O. Box 802026
Blue Moon, MO 63131	Cambridge, MO 65254

FIGURE 3.   Statement of Transaction

2. The Financing Statement

Bonnie authorized the filing of the financing statement shown in Figure 4. Otis filed it in Missouri's Uniform Commercial Code filing system. The purpose of the financing statement is to give public notice that Otis claims a security interest in the collateral indicated. We will discuss financing statements at greater length in Part Two of this book.

3. The Personal Guarantee

Although the loans contemplated by the agreement would be made to Bonnie's Boat World, Inc., Otis required that Bonnie personally guarantee repayment. Bonnie signed a one-page document to that effect at the closing.

Lenders such as Otis have at least two reasons for requiring personal guarantees from the owners of their corporate borrowers. First, if the borrower cannot repay the loan, the owners might. The guarantee gives the lender the right to obtain a judgment against the owners and proceed against their assets just as though the owners were the ones who had borrowed the money. In addition,

UCC FINANCING STATEMENT
FOLLOW INSTRUCTIONS

A. NAME & PHONE OF CONTACT AT FILER (optional)

B. E-MAIL CONTACT AT FILER (optional)

C. SEND ACKNOWLEDGMENT TO: (Name and Address)

```
Attn: Sam Spade
Otis Finance
157 Massachusetts Way
Cambridge, MO  65254
```

THE ABOVE SPACE IS FOR FILING OFFICE USE ONLY

1. DEBTOR'S NAME: Provide only one Debtor name (1a or 1b) (use exact, full name; do not omit, modify, or abbreviate any part of the Debtor's name); if any part of the Individual Debtor's name will not fit in line 1b, leave all of item 1 blank, check here ☐ and provide the Individual Debtor information in item 10 of the Financing Statement Addendum (Form UCC1Ad)

1a. ORGANIZATION'S NAME			
Bonnie's Boat World, Inc.			

1b. INDIVIDUAL'S SURNAME	FIRST PERSONAL NAME	ADDITIONAL NAME(S)/INITIAL(S)	SUFFIX

1c. MAILING ADDRESS	CITY	STATE	POSTAL CODE	COUNTRY
12976 Highway 441	**Blue Moon**	**MO**	**63131**	**USA**

2. DEBTOR'S NAME: Provide only one Debtor name (2a or 2b) (use exact, full name; do not omit, modify, or abbreviate any part of the Debtor's name); if any part of the Individual Debtor's name will not fit in line 2b, leave all of item 2 blank, check here ☐ and provide the Individual Debtor information in item 10 of the Financing Statement Addendum (Form UCC1Ad)

2a. ORGANIZATION'S NAME			

2b. INDIVIDUAL'S SURNAME	FIRST PERSONAL NAME	ADDITIONAL NAME(S)/INITIAL(S)	SUFFIX

2c. MAILING ADDRESS	CITY	STATE	POSTAL CODE	COUNTRY

3. SECURED PARTY'S NAME (or NAME of ASSIGNEE of ASSIGNOR SECURED PARTY): Provide only one Secured Party name (3a or 3b)

3a. ORGANIZATION'S NAME			
Otis Finance Corp.			

3b. INDIVIDUAL'S SURNAME	FIRST PERSONAL NAME	ADDITIONAL NAME(S)/INITIAL(S)	SUFFIX

3c. MAILING ADDRESS	CITY	STATE	POSTAL CODE	COUNTRY
157 Massachusetts Way	**Cambridge**	**MO**	**65254**	**USA**

4. COLLATERAL: This financing statement covers the following collateral:

Inventory, equipment, fixtures, accounts, contract rights, chattel paper, instruments, reserves, documents, and general intangibles.

5. Check only if applicable and check only one box: Collateral is ☐ held in a Trust (see UCC1Ad, item 17 and Instructions)   ☐ being administered by a Decedent's Personal Representative

6a. Check only if applicable and check only one box:		6b. Check only if applicable and check only one box:	
☐ Public-Finance Transaction ☐ Manufactured-Home Transaction ☐ A Debtor is a Transmitting Utility		☐ Agricultural Lien ☐ Non-UCC Filing	

7. ALTERNATIVE DESIGNATION (if applicable):   ☐ Lessee/Lessor   ☐ Consignee/Consignor   ☐ Seller/Buyer   ☐ Bailee/Bailor   ☐ Licensee/Licensor

8. OPTIONAL FILER REFERENCE DATA:

FILING OFFICE COPY — UCC FINANCING STATEMENT (Form UCC1) (Rev. 04/20/11)   International Association of Commercial Administrators (IACA)

FIGURE 4.   UCC-1 Financing Statement

personal guarantees can be, and sometimes are, secured by interests in property owned by the guarantors.

The second reason for a lender to take a personal guarantee is to ensure, insofar as possible, that in the event of default, the lender will have the cooperation of the owners. When a corporate debtor becomes insolvent, the owners' interest in the business often becomes worthless. Unless the owners are personally liable for debts of the business, they may not care how much of the debt is repaid. Even if the owners have all of their wealth in the corporation and the corporation is hopelessly insolvent, if the owners are personally liable, they will continue to have an incentive to cooperate with the lender that holds the guarantee. Their incentive is to avoid or minimize the judgments that eventually might be taken against them personally. In the event of competition for the assets of the corporation, the owners are likely to be on the side of the creditor to whom they have given their personal guarantee. Even if the owners can discharge the personal guarantee through bankruptcy, the owners' desire to avoid bankruptcy may also motivate them to repay.

D.   Bonnie's Buys Some Boats

With her floorplan line of credit in place, Bonnie is ready to go shopping. She contacts Shoreline Boat Manufacturing Company and arranges to become a Shoreline authorized dealer. Her choice is in part motivated by the fact that Shoreline is one of the dozen or so boat manufacturers who have signed a Floorplan Agreement with Otis.

1.   The Floorplan Agreement

The Floorplan Agreement provides that if Otis finances purchase of Shoreline boats by dealers such as Bonnie's Boat World and then has to repossess those boats, Shoreline will buy them back at the full invoice price. In the event of default, repossessing the boats will be Otis's problem, but disposing of them will be Shoreline's problem. These are the key terms of the Agreement:

FLOORPLAN AGREEMENT

To: Otis Finance Corp.
157 Massachusetts Way
Cambridge, MO 65254

We, Shoreline Boat Company, sell various products ("Merchandise") to dealers and/or distributors (collectively "Dealer") who may require financial assistance in order to make such purchases from us. To induce you to finance the acquisition of Merchandise by any Dealer and in consideration thereof, we agree that:

1. Warranties. Whenever a Dealer requests the shipment of Merchandise from us and that you finance such Merchandise, we may deliver to you an invoice(s) describing the Merchandise. By delivery of an invoice we warrant the following:

    a.   That we transfer to the Dealer all right, title, and interest in and to the Merchandise so described contingent upon your approval to finance the transaction;

b.   That our title to the Merchandise is free and clear of all liens and encumbrances when transferred to the Dealer;

c.   That the Merchandise is in salable condition, free of any defects;

d.   That the Merchandise is the subject of a bona fide order by the Dealer placed with and accepted by us and that the Dealer has requested the transaction be financed by you; and

e.   That the Merchandise subject to the transaction has been shipped to the Dealer not more than 10 days prior to the invoice date.

If we breach any of the above-described warranties, we will immediately: (i) pay to you an amount equal to the total unpaid balance (being principal and finance charges) owed to you on all Merchandise directly or indirectly related to the breach; and (ii) reimburse you for all costs and expenses (including, but not limited to, attorneys fees) incurred by you as a direct or indirect result of the breach.

   2. Limited Commitment to Finance. You will only be bound to finance Merchandise which you have accepted to finance (which acceptances will be indicated by your issuance of an approval number or a draft or other instrument to us in payment of the invoice less the amount of your charges as agreed upon from time to time) and only if:

a.   the Merchandise is delivered to the Dealer within 30 days following your acceptance;

b.   you have received our invoice for such Merchandise within 10 days from the date of delivery of the Merchandise to the Dealer; and

c.   you have not revoked your acceptance prior to the shipment of the Merchandise to the Dealer.

   3. Obligation to Repurchase. Whenever you deem it necessary in your sole discretion to repossess or if you otherwise come into possession of any Merchandise, in which you have a security interest or other lien, we will purchase such Merchandise from you at the time of your repossession or other acquisition or possession in accordance with the following terms and conditions:

a.   We will purchase such Merchandise, regardless of its condition, at the point where you repossess it or where it otherwise comes into your possession;

b.   The purchase price that we will pay to you for such Merchandise will be due and payable immediately in full, and will be an amount equal to (i) the total unpaid balance (being principal and finance charges) owed to you with respect to such Merchandise or our original invoice price for such Merchandise, whichever is greater, and (ii) all costs and expenses (including, without limitation, reasonable attorneys fees) paid or incurred by you in connection with the repossession of such Merchandise; and

c.   We shall not assert or obtain any interest in or to any Merchandise acquired by us until the purchase price therefor is paid in full.

   4. Waiver. You may extend the time of a Dealer in default to fulfill its obligations to you without notice to us and without altering our obligations hereunder. We waive any rights we may have to require you to proceed against a Dealer or to pursue any other remedy in your power. Our liability to you is direct and unconditional and will not be affected by any change in the terms of payment or performance of any agreement between you and Dealer, or the release, settlement, or compromise of or with any party liable for the payment or performance thereof, the release or non-perfection of any security thereunder, any change in Dealer's financial condition, or the interruption of business relations between you and Dealer.

5. Attorneys Fees and Expenses. We will pay all your expenses (including, without limitation, court costs and reasonable attorneys fees) in the event you are required to enforce your rights against us. Your failure to exercise any rights granted hereunder shall not operate as a waiver of those rights.

6. Termination. Either of us may terminate this Agreement by notice to the other in writing, the termination to be effective 30 days after receipt of the notice by the other party, but no termination of this Agreement will affect any of our liability with respect to any financial transactions entered into by you with any Dealer prior to the effective date of termination, including, without limitation, transactions that will not be completed until after the effective date of termination.

Dated: August 29, 2014
Otis Finance Corp.   Shoreline Boat Company

By: *Tricia McMillan*   By: *Alan R. Shoreline*
Tricia McMillan   Alan R. Shoreline
District Manager   President

The advantage to Otis of this agreement is obvious. If Otis has to repossess Shoreline boats from Bonnie's Boat World, Shoreline has agreed to buy them back for at least their full original invoice price. The advantages to Shoreline are also significant. With the Floorplan Agreement in place, Shoreline can offer qualified dealers nationwide 100 percent financing on the boats they buy from Shoreline, making the boats more attractive to dealers. Shoreline has to be ready to take the boats back if Bonnie's defaults, but if Shoreline had financed the boats itself, Shoreline would have to do that anyway. If Shoreline had financed the boats itself, it would have borne much of the risk of boats being lost, stolen, or destroyed through dealer fraud or otherwise. Under the Floorplan Agreement, Otis bears these risks.

Bonnie's gets three advantages from this agreement. Because the repurchase agreement reduces Otis's risk of loss on resale after repossession, Otis can offer Bonnie's a larger line of credit and finance a larger portion of each purchase than a bank typically could. Additionally, Bonnie's may benefit from time to time from subsidies offered by Shoreline to Otis to provide dealers such as Bonnie's with periods when little or no interest accrues.

2.   The Buy

Bonnie contacts Shoreline and selects the five boats she wants. The total price of the boats is $175,000. In accord with the Floorplan Agreement, Shoreline contacts Otis to obtain approval of the purchase. Otis verifies from its records that both Bonnie's and Shoreline are in compliance with their agreements with Otis and that the purchase will not overdraw Bonnie's line of credit. Satisfied that everything is in order, Otis gives Shoreline an approval number for the purchase. (This is essentially the same thing that happens when you use your VISA card to buy a pair of shoes at the mall.) Shoreline ships the five boats to Bonnie and sends the invoice to Otis. Otis pays the $175,000 to Shoreline, recording it on their books as a loan to Bonnie's.

E.   Bonnie's Sells a Boat

The morning after the Shoreline boats arrive in Bonnie's yard, William and Gladys Homer come to Bonnie's looking for the boat of their dreams. It turns out to be one of the five Bonnie's has just purchased from Shoreline. Bonnie's invoice price from Shoreline is $35,566.58; its invoice price to the Homers is $40,000. Bonnie's will have a gross profit on the sale of $4,433.42.

Arthur Dent, the Bonnie's salesman who helps the Homers pick out the boat, also helps them arrange their financing. Bonnie's has an arrangement with First State Bank under which First State finances 90 percent of the purchase price of a boat for any Bonnie's customer who qualifies. The Homers qualify and First State approves their boat loan on the same day they pick out the boat. The Homers write Bonnie's a check for $4,000, sign a security agreement and authorization to file a financing statement for First State, load the boat on their trailer, and drive off into a sunset filled with monthly payment coupons. On receipt of the security agreement and financing statement, First State deposits $36,000 to Bonnie's bank account.

If Bonnie's financed the purchase of these boats with Otis on a "pay-as-sold" (PAS) basis, part of Bonnie's loan is now due. That is, section 9(b) of the Agreement for Wholesale Financing provides that "Dealer will immediately pay Otis the principal indebtedness owed Otis on each item of Collateral financed by Otis (as shown on the Statement of Transaction identifying such Collateral) . . . when such Collateral is sold." In accord with this provision, Bonnie's sends Otis a check for $35,566.58 that same day. At the beginning of the next month, Otis will bill Bonnie's for the finance charges that accrued during the brief time this $35,566.58 loan was outstanding.

F.   Monitoring the Existence of the Collateral

If Bonnie's had used the $40,000 it received from the Homers to pay other creditors instead of Otis and Otis had then foreclosed, Otis's collateral would have been about that much less than its loan. If Bonnie's repeated this diversion of funds enough times, Otis would soon have no collateral at all. How could Otis discover this developing problem?

The answer is that Otis will send a person to Bonnie's Boat World every 30 to 45 days to verify the continuing existence of the collateral and check its condition. For the first such inspection, Otis assigns its most experienced floor checker, Richard Feynman. Feynman arrives at Bonnie's Boat World unannounced, introduces himself to Bonnie, and goes to work.

Feynman has with him a list of all of the boats Otis has financed for Bonnie's, except those for which Otis has already received payment. For each boat, Feynman's list shows the make, model, and serial number. Feynman begins at one end of the fenced-in property and works his way to the other. For each boat he reads the make, model, and serial number from a metal plate attached to the boat, finds that boat on his list, and checks it off. He also notes the condition of the boat alongside the check mark.

When Feynman is finished, there are still two boats on his list he has not seen. He asks Bonnie about them. One, Bonnie tells him, was sold yesterday and delivered to the customer earlier this morning. Bonnie tells Feynman that she has already mailed the check to Otis for this boat. Feynman does not just take Bonnie's word for that. Instead, he examines Bonnie's check ledger and verifies that Bonnie has written the check. He notes the existence of the purported check on his list; when the check arrives at Otis's offices, he will check the postmark on it. The other boat, Bonnie tells him, is out on the lake on a demonstration. It will be back in an hour or so if Feynman wants to drop by after lunch to check it, Bonnie suggests. Feynman explains to Bonnie that that would be contrary to the established procedure for a floor check: All of the boats must be checked at the same time. Bonnie radios the missing boat and makes arrangements to rendezvous with it. Bonnie and Feynman take a second boat out, meet with the missing boat, and check it off on Feynman's list.

Why couldn't Feynman just stop back after lunch to look at the missing boat? The answer is that the registration plates are not a foolproof method for identifying a boat. Given time to do so, a dishonest debtor could remove the registration plate from a boat Feynman has already checked and substitute a counterfeit plate bearing the make, model, and number of a boat the debtor no longer owns. Feynman checks the boats all at the same time so that he does not have to rely solely on the registration plates; to a large degree, he relies on the number of boats he can see on the premises all at the same time. In addition, the floor check serves as a simulated repossession. Otis wants to know how much collateral it would have recovered had this been a real repossession. If it had been, Bonnie might have been unwilling to tell Otis the location of the missing boat.

Problem Set 15

15.1.   As an attorney for Otis Finance, you have been asked to comment on the floor-checking procedures for a loan of $185 million against 160 million pounds of soybean oil stored in dozens of petroleum tanks in Bayonne, New Jersey. The procedure is as follows: The Otis floor checker shows up in Bayonne unannounced. With an employee of the debtor, Allied Crude Vegetable Oil Refining Corporation, the floor checker climbs the metal staircase that winds around the first tank. From any point along the circular walkway at the top of the tank, the floor checker can see (and taste) the oil. The checker sticks a 40-foot pole into the oil to test its depth. Then the floor checker and the employee move on to the next tank and do the same thing. The quantity of oil in each tank is determined by multiplying the depth of the oil by the surface area. Do you see any problems?

   15.2.   What could the bank lenders in the following story have done to protect themselves against the fraud perpetrated on them?

Miller Indicted on Bank Fraud

Calhoun (Illinois) News-Herald, Nov. 26, 2003, at 1

After federal investigations were completed recently, Calhoun County Ford dealer Stephen Corbett Miller was accused in a federal indictment of defrauding five banks in an effort to retain funding to operate the dealership.

   The grand jury indictment accuses Miller of executing a plan to defraud the Bank of Calhoun County, the Bank of Kampsville, Jersey State Bank, Central State Bank and Citizens Bank from 1993 through February 2003.

   According to the indictment, Miller began working at Calhoun County Ford in 1954, before purchasing the dealership with a business partner in 1977. In 1993 the dealership began having financial problems. This allegedly led Miller to take part in several methods of deception to deceive the financial institutions to continue to lend money for the operation and inventory of the dealership.

   The indictment states that Miller received financing commonly referred to as floorplan financing. In this type of financing, the inventory of the dealership's vehicles is issued to secure loans. The proceeds from the sales are then supposed to be forwarded to the financial institution within 10 days.

   Miller also allegedly double collateralized vehicles. This was supposedly accomplished by using the same vehicles as collateral on two or more floorplan loans without disclosing that the vehicle had already been pledged as collateral.

   Miller is also accused of making false statements to financial institutions when they arrived to conduct floorplan inventory checks. The institutions allegedly were told that the missing vehicles were on test drives or were out on loan to a customer whose vehicle was being serviced.

   Not only did Miller allegedly make false statements to financial institutions, he supposedly practiced the same falsehoods with his customers. Customers who purchased vehicles from the dealership were allegedly told to return their vehicles for warranty or service work, at which time, the license plates were removed and the financial institutions were called to do a floorplan check on the missing vehicles.

   The indictment also states that Miller obtained nominee loans involving the fictitious sales of automobiles, forged and falsified sales contracts for vehicles, in addition to financial contracts for those vehicles.

   Miller also stands accused of obtaining vehicle loans on behalf of other individuals without their knowledge or consent. The proceeds of those loans were then allegedly utilized by Miller to pay the dealership's expenses.

15.3. The law firm you work for is outside counsel to Archer Commercial Finance. For many years, Archer has insisted on personal guarantees from the individuals who own any closely held business they finance. Gordon Jamail, a department head at Archer, has proposed a change in policy. He reels off the names of four potential customers he says have gone to a competitor in the last month alone because by doing so they could avoid Archer's personal guarantee requirement. "The irony," Gordon says, "is that in nine out of ten cases, the judgment we might recover on a personal guarantee would be uncollectible. These people borrow from us because they've already put everything they have in the business." The president of Archer asks for your opinion. What do you tell her?

15.4.   Three years after the events set forth in the reading, Bonnie Brezhnev comes to you for legal advice. For the past two years, the boat business has been lousy. During that time, she has put everything she has into the business, even to the extent of taking out a second mortgage on her home. Still short of working capital, she has been juggling boats, lying to the floor checker, and keeping phony records to back up her lies. On the floor check this morning she was five boats out of trust, a total of about $250,000 on boats she agreed to pay for "as sold." Otis has declared Bonnie's Boat World in default and demanded that she surrender the 35 Shoreline boats remaining in its possession. Over the past couple of weeks, Bonnie has come to the realization that the business cannot survive; what she wants now is to get out of the mess she is in.

a.   Bonnie asks you whether Otis has the right to the boats. Do they? See the Agreement for Wholesale Financing, section 15(c); UCC §§9-601(a), 9-609.

b.   If Bonnie surrenders the boats without a fight, what do you think will happen to her? UCC §9-615(d)(2); 810 Ill. Comp. Stat. 5/9-315.01 set forth in section A.3 of Assignment 10; Agreement for Wholesale Financing, sections 4, 15. Assume these events occur in Illinois and that the prosecutor's policy is to prosecute violations of 9-315.01, but only if the victim presses for prosecution. What happened to Steve Downing when he voluntarily surrendered his automobile in the case bearing his name in Assignment 5?

c.   Does Bonnie have the power to keep these boats? If so, how? For how long?

d.   What advice do you give Bonnie? UCC §1-302; Bankr. Code §523(a)(2)(A), (4) and (6). The Model Rules of Professional Conduct provide in relevant part:

> *Rule 4.4.* In representing a client, a lawyer shall not use means that have no substantial purpose other than to . . . delay or burden a third person.
> *Rule 1.2.* A lawyer shall not counsel a client to engage, or assist a client, in conduct that the lawyer knows is criminal or fraudulent, but a lawyer may discuss the legal consequences of any proposed course of conduct.
> *Rule 1.16.* A lawyer shall not represent a client . . . if the representation will result in violation of the Rules of Professional Conduct or other law.

15.5.   Bonnie consults you prior to signing the agreement with Otis. What is your answer to each of the following questions?

They will bend her a bill

p.263

a. What interest rate will Bonnie pay on her outstanding balance? See Agreement for Wholesale Financing, sections 2, 15(d), and Statement of Transaction.

b. Will Otis have a security interest in Bonnie's lease of the boatyard? In her bank accounts? Agreement for Wholesale Financing, section 4; UCC §§9-109(a) and (d)(11) and (d)(13), 9-604, 9-102(a)(2) and (42), and 9-203(f).

c. Would Bonnie violate her agreement with Otis by permitting an employee to take a boat out for a demonstration ride with a potential customer? If she did, would that give Otis the right to call the loan? Agreement for Wholesale Financing, section 6(b), 14; UCC §§9-201(a), 9-601(a).

d. Given that Shoreline has agreed, as part of the Floorplan Agreement, section 3.b, to buy repossessed boats from Otis at the full amount owing on them, does that mean that Bonnie need not worry about a deficiency judgment on a repossessed boat? UCC §§9-615(d) and (f), 9-602(7) and (8), 9-603(a), and Agreement for Wholesale Financing, section 16. In thinking through this problem, consider three alternative scenarios if Bonnie defaults: (1) Otis repossesses the boats and sells them to Shoreline for the full balance owing on the debt, (2) the boats are destroyed by a hurricane and the insurance company doesn't pay the claim, (3) Otis repossesses the boats in damaged condition, Shoreline is insolvent, and Otis sells the boats to a third party for 40 percent of the balance owing on the debt.

damaged condition 15(d)

■ END OF DEFAULT PROBLEM SET

15.6. As an arbitrator for the American Arbitration Association, you have been assigned a case in which Otis seeks to enforce provisions of the Agreement for Wholesale Financing against a dealer who signed it five years ago and has been borrowing under it since that time. The dealer's attorney argues that the contract is "void for lack of consideration" and "illusory" because nowhere in it does Otis agree to make a loan or necessarily do anything else. What do you think of this argument? See Agreement for Wholesale Financing, section 1.

15.7. It has been a year since Otis entered into this financing arrangement with Bonnie's Boat World. Otis is not happy with the arrangement, in part because Bonnie has been difficult to deal with and in part because the boat business has been bad and Otis would like to get out of it altogether. Bonnie's, however, is not in breach. Can Otis get out of this deal? If so, how does Otis do it? Agreement for Wholesale Financing, section 20. What will be the effect on Bonnie's?

still responsible for all debts

Part Two
The Creditor-Third Party Relationship

Chapter 6.   Perfection

Assignment 16:   The Personal Property Filing Systems

A.   Competition for the Secured Creditor's Collateral

In Part One of this book, we examined the relationship between a secured creditor and its debtor. We focused on how the rights of secured creditors to collect from the debtor differed from those of unsecured creditors. We also examined the procedures by which creditors obtained secured status and the contracts that created those rights.

In Part Two, we shift our focus to the relationship between a secured creditor and others who may claim the same collateral. Our approach remains pragmatic. We ask what the secured creditor must do to prevail over these new adversaries, how effective the secured creditor's rights against them are likely to be, and how expensive these new rights will be to obtain and to enforce.

Debtors sometimes participate in the struggle between their secured creditors and third parties. Other times they have already given up in exhausted resignation and do not care who gets the collateral. The issue now is the rights of a secured creditor against others who also have rights superior to those of the debtor.

Just as debtors come in many different types — consumers and businesses, hard-working but unfortunate people and sleazeballs, wealthy and poor — so do their creditors. An individual debtor in financial trouble is likely to owe money to 20 to 30 creditors, including a home mortgage lender, several credit card issuers, a finance company, the phone company, several local department stores, an auto lender, a cable company, and perhaps some medical providers. A business debtor may owe money to hundreds or even thousands of creditors, including banks, commercial lenders, current employees, retired employees, landlords, suppliers, customers, utility companies, and taxing authorities. Some of these creditors may not have acquired their status voluntarily. The creditor of an individual debtor may be the victim of an automobile accident, a custodial parent with the right to payments for child support, or the IRS. The creditor of a business debtor may be a government agency that has spent money to remove toxic waste from the debtor's property, a competitor injured by the debtor's illegal business practices, or the IRS (it's everywhere!). To complicate matters further, the third party who claims the secured creditor's collateral may not be a creditor at all. It may be someone who bought the collateral from the debtor or someone who claims to remain the owner because the debtor did not pay for the collateral.

A particularly slippery, imaginative, or unfortunate debtor can create a vivid array of contestants for its limited assets. These competitors may see the secured creditor's collateral (or what the secured creditor thought was its collateral) as their only source of recovery or merely as the most convenient or cost-effective one.

The law treats many of the contests over rights to collateral as questions of *priority*. This assignment briefly addresses what it means for one creditor to have priority over another. It also begins a discussion of how creditors obtain priority over one another. The latter discussion extends through the remaining assignments of this chapter.

In Chapter 7 on maintaining perfection we examine what creditors who already have priority must do to keep it. We consider the effect of the passage of time; the filing of bankruptcy; changes in the identity, use, and location of collateral; and changes in the identity and location of the debtor.

In Chapter 8 we examine the concept of priority in more detail. We look at how priority is implemented procedurally, and we use that reality to give further definition to the concept.

In Chapter 9 we explore specific competitions between secured creditors and others over collateral. As we examine these contests one by one, you will see how the rules for resolving them fit together (sometimes well and sometimes badly) to form a single system of lien priority based for the most part on the principle, "first in time is first in right." Along the way, the policies underlying secured credit should become clearer.

B. What Is Priority?

In Part One of this book, we introduced the concept of a *lien*. A lien is a relationship between a debt and property that serves as collateral. If the debtor fails to pay the debt, the secured creditor can foreclose the lien, force a sale of the collateral, and have the proceeds of the sale applied to payment of the debt. We refer to this attribute of a lien as the secured creditor's *remedy*.

In Part Two, we will examine a second and even more important attribute of a lien: *priority*. If there is more than one lien against collateral, each will have a priority. Liens are commonly labeled "first," "second," "third," etc. (You may, for example, have heard of "second mortgages.") A lien with priority higher than another is referred to as the *senior* or *prior lien* and the other is referred to as the *subordinate* or *junior lien*. If the value of collateral is insufficient to pay all of the liens against an item of collateral, the junior liens yield to the senior ones.

To illustrate, assume that David owes Alice $7,000 and Betty $9,000. Each has a security interest (recall that a security interest is a type of lien) in David's BMW, which is worth $12,000. If Alice's lien has priority over Betty's lien and either is foreclosed, Alice will be entitled to $7,000 of the value of the BMW and Betty will be entitled to the remaining $5,000. Once the BMW has been liquidated and the proceeds distributed, Betty will be an unsecured creditor for the $4,000 balance owed to her.

(At this point, we pause to note the complexity of this scheme for resolving competition among creditors. Each creditor's lien is a relationship between an

item of collateral and obligation

obligation and an item of collateral; priority is the relationship between these relationships. Don't be surprised if every implication of this complex scheme does not immediately spring to mind. They will come.)

While we usually think of priority as an attribute of a lien, priority can exist among creditors who do not have liens. For example, it is not uncommon for a large, publicly held company to raise some of its capital by borrowing from banks or insurance companies and some through the issue of unsecured bonds, or *debentures*. One term of the contract between the company and the purchasers of the bonds is that the bond debt is *subordinated* to the bank debt, which means that if the banks and the bondholders ever seek to satisfy their debts from assets of the debtor, the bondholders will take nothing until the banks have been paid in full. Even though the banks and the bondholders have contractually established priority between themselves, both may remain unsecured.

Contracts establishing priority among unsecured creditors are relatively uncommon for the simple reason that debtors frequently encumber all of their assets with liens. Every kind of lien has priority over all unsecured debts. When a debtor is in financial difficulty, even the most senior unsecured status is likely to be, in the metaphor popular among practitioners, "out of the money."

The system of lien priority is so fundamental a social and economic institution that many fail to realize that it is merely one of several ways that a legal system can resolve competition among creditors for the limited assets of a debtor. Some implications of the system chosen become apparent upon consideration of some alternative systems that have been rejected. First, creditor competitions could be resolved by allowing each competitor a pro rata share of the limited assets. Recall from Assignment 7 of this book that this is how competitions are resolved among unsecured creditors in bankruptcy. Second, competitions could be decided on the basis of the status of the competing creditors. Debts deemed more important, such as those owing to employees, taxing agencies, or widows and orphans, might be given higher priority, while less important ones, such as those owing to commercial creditors, might be assigned lower priority. Some of this kind of thinking is embodied in the distributional rules of Bankruptcy Code §§507(a) and 726(a) and in the statutory lien laws discussed in Assignment 37. Third, competitions over the value of a debtor's assets could be resolved by permitting competing creditors to trace and recover the value that each supplied to the debtor. But as the following case illustrates, the current system is comfortable with the idea that creditors share only in the order of their lien priorities, regardless of any competing equities.

Peerless Packing Co. v. Malone & Hyde, Inc.

376 S.E.2d 161 (W. Va. 1988)

NEELY, JUSTICE.

Appellants are twelve companies that supply wholesale products to grocery stores. Appellee is also a wholesaler of grocery products, with operations covering the southeastern states. John Kizer was appellee's co-defendant below. This is an appeal from the trial court's award of a directed verdict for appellee.

Mr. Kizer negotiated an agreement with appellee [to purchase the business of the former ADP store in Beckley]. Under this agreement, Mr. Kizer provided $50,000 for working capital that went into the purchase of inventory. Appellee allowed Mr. Kizer to use its trade name "PIC PAC," subleased the store to Mr. Kizer, sold him the store equipment for $200,000, and provided him with approximately $187,000 in additional inventory. In exchange, Mr. Kizer gave appellee a promissory note for approximately $387,000, plus interest, which was secured by a security interest in the present and after acquired inventory.

Appellee met all requirements of the Uniform Commercial Code (UCC) for perfecting its lien against the store's collateral and appellants do not challenge the technical validity of appellee's lien.

Mr. Kizer opened the store in November 1982. The store sold some goods in addition to those supplied by appellee. Many of these additional goods were supplied by the twelve appellant companies, who delivered the goods several times a week on open account credit extended to the store. None of appellants obtained purchase money security interests in the inventory supplied by them. Purchase money security interests could have given appellants priority over appellee's security interest in the inventory.

By March 1983, it was apparent to appellee that the store was not successful because it was meeting its obligations, in part, by reducing inventory. Also, one of Mr. Kizer's checks for the rent and note payments to appellee was returned for insufficient funds. Agents of appellee approached Mr. Kizer and told him that they were going to take the store back, and either he could voluntarily sign everything over to appellee, or "they would take everything he had." Mr. Kizer then signed a document presented by appellee called a Notice of Default and Transfer of Possession Agreement. This agreement transferred all of Mr. Kizer's rights in the store, equipment and inventory, and the balance of the store's bank account, about $64,000, to appellee. In return, appellee released Mr. Kizer from any liability, including personal liability for any deficiency, on the $387,000 note, the rent on the store and on an additional $54,000 [which was for groceries delivered by appellee and for which Kizer had not yet paid].

Appellee assumed ownership of the store and began operating it with Mr. Kizer as manager. Appellee sent a letter to the appellant vendors stating that appellee had realized on its security interest in the store's assets without assuming any liability to third parties, and would not pay any invoices for deliveries before 31 March 1988, the date appellee took ownership.

Appellants each sued Mr. Kizer for the unpaid accounts, and also sued appellee on a theory of unjust enrichment, with a claim for both compensatory and punitive damages. The cases were consolidated, and each appellant was granted default judgment before trial against Mr. Kizer, who discharged his obligation on the judgments in bankruptcy. At the close of appellants' case against appellee, appellee moved for a directed verdict, which the trial court granted.

I

Appellants also contend that appellee was unjustly enriched by the transfer because appellee, knowing it was going to foreclose on the store, allowed appellants to continue to deliver goods for a week before appellee took over. . . .

Appellee contends that a theory of unjust enrichment is not applicable in a case that is governed by the UCC. Appellee argues that it was entitled to keep the collateral and that it got no more than it was owed by Mr. Kizer. In fact, appellee insists that it "lost" about $130,000 through the transfer.

The trial court agreed with appellee that an unjust enrichment claim is not applicable in a UCC case, and stated in its final order, in part,

> First, the Court concludes as a matter of law that the plaintiffs cannot maintain this action, which is governed by Article 9 of the UCC, on a theory of recovery grounded upon the equitable doctrine of unjust enrichment. Evans Products Co. v. Jorgensen, 421 P.2d 978 (Oregon, 1966). The Court agrees with the rationale of the Oregon Supreme Court at p. 983 that "[T]he purpose and effectiveness of the UCC would be substantially impaired if interests created in compliance with UCC procedure could be defeated by application of the equitable doctrine of unjust enrichment."

We agree with the trial court's order and affirm his ruling with regard to appellants' equitable unjust enrichment claim. As the Oregon Supreme Court pointed out in *Jorgensen*, cited by the trial court in the quote above, although the result of disallowing an equitable unjust enrichment claim in such a case may appear harsh, the unsatisfied creditors, (appellants in the case before us), could have protected themselves either by demanding cash payment for their goods, or by taking a purchase money security interest in the goods they delivered.[4]

In the beginning, there were 13 unsecured creditors. One took a security interest. When the business failed, that one got everything, including goods sold to the debtor by the other 12 creditors and for which those 12 were not paid. That is the power of priority.

C.   How Do Creditors Get Priority?

Central to the system of lien priority is the idea that liens rank in the chronological order in which they were created. There are a few exceptions to this rule, but they are in favor of liens such as property taxes that secure relatively small, predictable obligations. The rationale of the lien priority system depends

---

4. We do not hold that an equitable claim for relief never lies in a case controlled by the UCC As appellants point out, [UCC §1-304)] requires that "[e]very contract or duty within this chapter imposes an obligation of good faith in its performance or enforcement." Some courts have held that equitable claims raised under this section can change priorities explicitly provided in Article 9. However, most of these cases involve situations of virtually fraudulent conduct. The UCC provides justice in the long run in large part through the certainty and predictability of its provisions, which should not be set aside absent truly egregious circumstances verging on actual fraud. In the case before us, even allowing appellants every favorable inference from their evidence, we do not believe they have presented evidence of such circumstances sufficient to disturb the priorities set by the provisions of Article 9.

heavily on the fact that once the priority of a lien is established, any lien created later will be subordinate.

In a very general sense, priority by chronology makes it possible for a creditor to know, at the time it makes a loan, how it will fare in later competitions over the collateral. That is, it knows that it will rank behind liens already in existence and ahead of any liens created later. Because the liens it will rank behind are already in existence, the prospective lender can obtain information about them and, if necessary, contract with the holder regarding their disposition.

Of course, the mere fact that the prior liens exist does not itself ensure that the prospective lender will be able to discover them or to obtain needed information about them. There probably are liens against the inventory and fixtures in the grocery store where you shop, but to a person walking through the store, they are invisible. To ensure that the prospective lender can discover a lien that will have priority over its own, the laws under which liens are created almost invariably condition the priority on the holder taking steps to make existence of the lien public and easily discoverable. The steps that must be taken differ with the type of lien, but nearly all include acts in one of four categories: (1) filing notice in a public records system established for that purpose, (2) taking possession of collateral, (3) taking control of collateral by means of the stake holder's agreement to hold for the secured creditor, or (4) posting notice on the property or where it will be seen by persons dealing with the property. The taking of whatever steps are required is generally referred to as *perfecting* the lien. UCC §9-308(a).

Secured parties usually choose to perfect their liens by public filing. But for particular kinds of property they may choose, or be required, to perfect by some other method. For example, recall from Assignment 1 that an unsecured creditor obtains an execution lien by reducing its claim to judgment, obtaining a writ of execution, and having the sheriff levy on the assets. Under the law of most states, the levy both creates the lien and perfects it by the sheriff's possession.

In the next four assignments we will discuss in more detail the actions that various kinds of creditors must take to perfect their liens in various kinds of collateral. For now, you can think of "perfection" as a step that the holder of a lien must take to give public notice and thereby establish priority. Because priority is based on the time that step was taken, it is important to document the time. To that end, the officers who receive notices for filing immediately record the dates and times of receipt. Similarly, the sheriff who seizes property pursuant to a writ of execution will immediately record the date and time of seizure. When disputes arise, the records of these officers can be used to prove these dates and times. Perfection sometimes can be accomplished in a manner that does not create a date-and-time-stamped public record. In that event, the secured creditor may have to prove the date and time by other evidence.

In the large majority of cases, the dates and times of perfection will determine the priorities of the liens. Notice that in the system thus created, the type of lien is unimportant. Except for the time of their perfection, one lien is the same as another. The assignment of dates and times of perfection makes it possible to quickly and simply determine the priorities among particular Article 9 security interests, mortgages, federal tax liens, execution liens, judgment liens, construction liens, and any others.

As you might guess from the number of pages in the remainder of this book, the model we present here is an oversimplification of the system for perfecting and prioritizing liens. In the real world, the steps for perfecting a lien may be complicated. It may be difficult even to know what they are. The rules that determine priority among liens are made by diverse legislative bodies, and they are not always consistent. Not all priority follows the rule of first in time, first in right. But for now, this simple model will do.

D.   The Theory of the Filing System

A filing system is a means for communicating the existence of a lien from the holder to a person who is considering becoming a creditor of the same debtor. The system's goal is actual communication. Lienholders participate because the law voids their liens if they do not. Prospective creditors participate because the law gives priority to filed liens. The prospective creditors need to know what liens were filed to know who will have priority over them if they lend. A filing system is needed to achieve communication because neither the holder of the existing lien nor the prospective creditor knows the other's identity until the communication occurs.

The filing system allows any lienholder to leave a "to whom it may concern" message for prospective creditors. For an Article 9 security interest, that message is in the form of an *initial financing statement,* also known by its form number, a "UCC-1." Each year, the creditors who take security interests leave millions of these messages in the filing system. And before they take their liens, many filers search the records to see whether prior secured creditors left messages for them.

The filing system gives constructive notice, but it is intended to do more than that. In theory, at least, it is supposed to give actual notice to the later creditor.

For such a system to work, prospective creditors must know that the system exists and that there may be messages waiting in it for them. Of course, banks and most lawyers will have this kind of knowledge. But many consumers and small business people are not aware this system exists. (Neither are some law students who opted not to take this course.)

Unsophisticated lenders often fail to claim their priority by filing; the result is that even later lenders will come ahead of them in priority. Unsophisticated lenders often fail to discover a lien that is on the public record before they obtain their own; the result is that the lien they take will be subordinate to the lien already recorded. Either consequence can be disastrous to a lender who does not expect it. The advantages of a filing system come at a considerable human and economic cost.

The theory of the filing system has suffered considerably in implementation. As we will see in this and the subsequent chapter, filing systems are highly imprecise and difficult and expensive to use. Filing is relatively easy. But searching is relatively difficult and a failed search leads to adverse consequences only if the debtor both previously granted a security interest to a competing creditor and failed to mention that fact on the loan application. As a result, many creditors are lax in searching, and some do not search at all. The following exchange is between Professor Ronald Mann and Joe DeKunder, vice president of NationsBank of Texas, N.A.

Mann: When you do take a pledge of the receivables, even on these really small transactions, do you do a UCC search before you disburse the money?

DeKunder: Yeah, we do a UCC search, yes. Now, I want to qualify that somewhat. We do have situations where we feel that we want to make an exception, and it's a timing factor. Let's say we make a small loan and we do this on blanket receivables, and we want to close that loan tomorrow, let's say—for whatever reason. It's a working capital loan and we want to get it done, and we determine that the search is going to be too lengthy in time, we'll do a post-search. We've already funded the loan, you know. We'll do a search after the fact, just to determine where we are. And frankly, we do that fairly frequently. Now I know that doesn't sound like the prudent thing to do, but what happens in effect is we determine often, just like I mentioned earlier, there are liens that need to be released. We determine sometimes that, obviously, there is nothing there. Sometimes, we are surprised. But at any rate, the post-search is done occasionally. Usually, in those situations we are comfortable with the customer. We are comfortable with the fact that we would make this [loan] unsecured and probably we're just taking this [security interest] as a matter of control.

Mann: But you've done that and gotten burned?

DeKunder: We've done it and gotten burned, yes. . . . Many small business owners, to a degree, don't really understand, sometimes, that someone's even filed . . . a UCC on their collateral. They'll be surprised, they'll say "gosh, I didn't know they did that." Well, you know the obvious question is "you apparently signed the papers." "Well, I didn't know. They never mentioned it. They never said anything about taking a blanket [lien]on my. . . ." Sometimes what happens is that the blanket is already in place by that bank, the customer pays their loan off, they come back and they take another pledge but don't refile the UCC, but it's still in effect.

Mann: It's still there.

DeKunder: It's still there . . . and the borrower didn't know it. He didn't know that they would continue with that. I've had situations where the borrower is quite upset. They will call that other financial institution and say "I didn't know you were gonna. . ."And a lot of times [the other financial institutions will] just go ahead and release it. Some of those things are mechanical in nature; it's like well, they didn't know it, we didn't know it, but it can be resolved if we work it out.

Because only a tiny proportion of debtors grant conflicting security interests that can't be worked out in the manner described by DeKunder, one might suppose that failure to file a financing statement would rarely lead to loan losses. Were that true, secured parties would probably be lax about filing, and searchers would be looking for financing statements that were not there.

To make sure that secured parties take the obligation to file seriously, the drafters of the Bankruptcy Code gave bankruptcy trustees the power to avoid security interests not perfected prior to bankruptcy—even if no one was injured by the secured party's failure to file. The effect is to make the trustees the "police" of the filing system. When bankruptcies are filed, the trustees examine the secured parties' documentation, and sue to avoid the security interests that are not perfected. This ability to avoid unperfected security interests is found in Bankruptcy Code §544(a), which gives trustees the rights of what are generally referred to as "ideal lien creditors" who perfected at bankruptcy. Ideal lien creditors would prevail over unperfected secured parties and so can avoid unperfected security interests.

▶ HALF ASSIGNMENT ENDS

E.   The Multiplicity of Filing Systems

The task of a lender who would search for messages relating to the collateral, lend money, and leave a message of its own is vastly complicated by the fact that there is not just one message center, but many. With a few exceptions, each county in the United States maintains a real estate recording system in which not only real estate mortgages, but also Article 9 fixture filings, are filed. See UCC §9-501(a)(1). Many counties also maintain separate systems for property tax liens, local tax liens, and money judgments. All states except Georgia and Louisiana have state UCC filing systems. See UCC §9-501(a)(2). Georgia and Louisiana have local UCC filing offices in each county or parish, but the county or parish filings can be searched through a statewide index. All states maintain certificate of title systems in which creditors can file notices of security interests in automobiles, and many states have separate certificate of title systems for boats and/or mobile homes. Some states maintain specialized systems for filing against particular kinds of collateral. For example, security interests in Florida liquor licenses are perfected by filing with the state agency that issues the licenses. United States of America v. McGurn, 596 So. 2d 1038 (Fla. 1992). Oklahoma amended its motor vehicle certificate of title statute to exclude vehicles registered by Indian nations and the Cherokee Indian Nation enacted a commercial code authorizing it to record security interests in automobiles. In re Dalton, 58 UCC Rep. 2d 213 (10th Cir. B.A.P. 2005). The federal government maintains yet additional filing systems for patents, trademarks, copyrights, aircraft, and ship mortgages. An international filing system already exists for some aircraft and parts.

Although each of these systems is established by law and charged with keeping particular kinds of messages, the offices that keep the records have almost no communication with one another. If the secured creditor leaves its message in the wrong office, the message almost certainly will be ineffective. If the later lender searches only in the wrong office, it will miss whatever messages were left in the right office.

The statutes that create each of these systems specify, with differing degrees of clarity, the circumstances in which a message should be filed in that system. Usually the type of collateral is determinative. Thus, to decide which system is appropriate for a particular filing, one might have to decide such weighty questions as whether particular collateral is a "ship" or a "boat," a "copyright receivable" or an "account," or a "motor vehicle" or "equipment." The definitions of collateral types are often not intuitive.

Ideally, there would be one and only one correct system in which to file notice of a particular security interest or lien. But with both the state and national governments defining the boundaries of the systems, uncertainties and overlaps are inevitable. The following case both illustrates and discusses the kinds of problems that occur. Because the case arose under a prior version of Article 9, the language quoted by the court does not precisely match the sections indicated in the new section numbers that we have inserted in brackets.

It may seem odd that the debtor who granted the security interest in this case is now claiming "a judicial lien on all assets in the bankruptcy estate." Upon the filing of the bankruptcy case, the debtor became a debtor in possession (DIP). In the latter capacity, the debtor has the rights and duties of a bankruptcy trustee. Bankr. Code §1107(a). Among those rights are the rights of an ideal lien creditor.

In re Peregrine Entertainment, Limited
116 B.R. 194 (C.D. Cal. 1990)

ALEX KOZINSKI, UNITED STATES CIRCUIT JUDGE. Sitting by designation pursuant to 28 U.S.C. §291(b) (1982).

This appeal from a decision of the bankruptcy court raises an issue never before confronted by a federal court in a published opinion: Is a security interest in a copyright perfected by an appropriate filing with the United States Copyright Office or by a UCC-1 financing statement filed with the relevant secretary of state?

I

National Peregrine, Inc. (NPI) is a Chapter 11 debtor in possession whose principal assets are a library of copyrights, distribution rights and licenses to approximately 145 films, and accounts receivable arising from the licensing of these films to various programmers.

In June 1985, Capitol Federal Savings and Loan Association of Denver (Cap Fed) extended to [NPI] a six million dollar line of credit secured by NPI's film library. Both the security agreement and the UCC-1 financing statements filed by Cap Fed describe the collateral as "[a]ll inventory consisting of films and all accounts, contract rights, chattel paper, general intangibles, instruments, equipment, and documents related to such inventory, now owned or hereafter acquired by the Debtor." Although Cap Fed filed its UCC-1 financing statements in California, Colorado and Utah, it did not record its security interest in the United States Copyright Office.

NPI filed a voluntary petition for bankruptcy on January 30, 1989. On April 6, 1989, NPI filed an amended complaint against Cap Fed, contending that the bank's security interest in the copyrights to the films in NPI's library and in the accounts receivable generated by their distribution were unperfected because Cap Fed failed to record its security interest with the Copyright Office. NPI claimed that, as a debtor in possession, it had a judicial lien on all assets in the bankruptcy estate, including the copyrights and receivables. Armed with this lien, it sought to avoid, recover and preserve Cap Fed's supposedly unperfected security interest for the benefit of the estate.

The parties filed cross-motions for partial summary judgment on the question of whether Cap Fed had a valid security interest in the NPI film library. The bankruptcy court held for Cap Fed. NPI appeals.

II

A.   WHERE TO FILE

The Copyright Act provides that "[a]ny transfer of copyright ownership or other document pertaining to a copyright" may be recorded in the United States Copyright Office. 17 U.S.C. §205(a). A "transfer" under the Act includes any "mortgage" or "hypothecation of a copyright," whether "in whole or in part" and "by any means of conveyance or by operation of law." 17 U.S.C. §§101, 201(d)(1). The terms "mortgage" and "hypothecation" include a pledge of property as security or collateral for a debt. In addition, the Copyright Office has defined a "document pertaining to a copyright" as one that "has a direct or indirect relationship to the existence, scope, duration, or identification of a copyright, or to the ownership, division, allocation, licensing, transfer, or exercise of rights under a copyright. That relationship may be past, present, future, or potential."

It is clear from the preceding that an agreement granting a creditor a security interest in a copyright may be recorded in the Copyright Office. Likewise, because a copyright entitles the holder to receive all income derived from the display of the creative work, see 17 U.S.C. §106, an agreement creating a security interest in the receivables generated by a copyright may also be recorded in the Copyright Office. Thus, Cap Fed's security interest could have been recorded in the Copyright Office; the parties seem to agree on this much. The question is, does the UCC provide a parallel method of perfecting a security interest in a copyright? One can answer this question by reference to either federal or state law; both inquiries lead to the same conclusion.

1. Even in the absence of express language, federal regulation will preempt state law if it is so pervasive as to indicate that "Congress left no room for supplementary state regulation," or if "the federal interest is so dominant that the federal system will be assumed to preclude enforcement of state laws on the same subject." Hillsborough County v. Automated Medical Laboratories, Inc., 471 U.S. 707, 713, 85 L. Ed. 2d 714, 105 S. Ct. 2371 (1985). Here, the comprehensive scope

of the federal Copyright Act's recording provisions, along with the unique federal interests they implicate, support the view that federal law preempts state methods of perfecting security interests in copyrights and related accounts receivable.

The federal copyright laws ensure "predictability and certainty of copyright ownership," "promote national uniformity" and "avoid the practical difficulties of determining and enforcing an author's rights under the differing laws and in the separate courts of the various States." Community for Creative Non-Violence v. Reid, 490 U.S. 730. As discussed above, section 205(a) of the Copyright Act establishes a uniform method for recording security interests in copyrights. A secured creditor need only file in the Copyright Office in order to give "all persons constructive notice of the facts stated in the recorded document." 17 U.S.C. §205(c). Likewise, an interested third party need only search the indices maintained by the Copyright Office to determine whether a particular copyright is encumbered.

A recording system works by virtue of the fact that interested parties have a specific place to look in order to discover with certainty whether a particular interest has been transferred or encumbered. To the extent there are competing recordation schemes, this lessens the utility of each; when records are scattered in several filing units, potential creditors must conduct several searches before they can be sure that the property is not encumbered. It is for that reason that parallel recordation schemes for the same types of property are scarce as hen's teeth; the court is aware of no others, and the parties have cited none. No useful purposes would be served — indeed, much confusion would result — if creditors were permitted to perfect security interests by filing with either the Copyright Office or state offices.

The bankruptcy court below nevertheless concluded that security interests in copyrights could be perfected by filing either with the Copyright Office or with the secretary of state under the UCC, making a tongue-in-cheek analogy to the use of a belt and suspenders to hold up a pair of pants. According to the bankruptcy court, because either device is equally useful, one should be free to choose which one to wear. With all due respect, this court finds the analogy inapt. There is no legitimate reason why pants should be held up in only one particular manner: Individuals and public modesty are equally served by either device, or even by a safety pin or a piece of rope; all that really matters is that the job gets done. Registration schemes are different in that the way notice is given is precisely what matters. To the extent interested parties are confused as to which system is being employed, this increases the level of uncertainty and multiplies the risk of error, exposing creditors to the possibility that they might get caught with their pants down.

A recordation scheme best serves its purpose where interested parties can obtain notice of all encumbrances by referring to a single, precisely defined recordation system. The availability of parallel state recordation systems that could put parties on constructive notice as to encumbrances on copyrights would surely interfere with the effectiveness of the federal recordation scheme. Given the virtual absence of dual recordation schemes in our legal system, Congress cannot be presumed to have contemplated such a result. The court therefore concludes that any state recordation system pertaining to interests in copyrights would be preempted by the Copyright Act.

2. State law leads to the same conclusion. [Editors' note: We omit this section of the opinion because the revision of Article 9 made significant changes in language and perhaps in substance. In the omitted section, the court concluded that express provisions of Article 9 yielded to the copyright filing system. The issue under new

Article 9 would be slightly different: Did the filing provisions of the Copyright Act pre-empt the filing provisions of Article 9 with respect to copyrights? UCC §9-109(c)(1).]

As discussed above, section 205(a) of the Copyright Act clearly does establish a national system for recording transfers of copyright interests, and it specifies a place of filing different from that provided in Article Nine. Recording in the Copyright Office gives nationwide, constructive notice to third parties of the recorded encumbrance. Except for the fact that the Copyright Office's indexes are organized on the basis of the title and registration number, rather than by reference to the identity of the debtor, this system is nearly identical to that which Article Nine generally provides on a statewide basis.[10]

The court therefore concludes that the Copyright Act provides for national registration and "specifies a place of filing different from that specified in [Article Nine] for filing of the security interest." [UCC §9-311(a)(1).] Recording in the U.S. Copyright Office, rather than filing a financing statement under Article Nine, is the proper method for perfecting a security interest in a copyright.

Compliance with a national registration scheme is necessary for perfection regardless of whether federal law governs priorities.[13] Cap Fed's security interest in the copyrights of the films in NPI's library and the receivables they have generated therefore is unperfected.

In the second paragraph of Part II.A. of his opinion, Judge Kozinski states that "because a copyright entitles the holder to receive all income derived from the display of the creative work, an agreement creating a security interest in the

---

10. Moreover, the mechanics of recording in the Copyright Office are analogous to filing under the UCC In order to record a security interest in the Copyright Office, a creditor may file either the security agreement itself or a duplicate certified to be a true copy of the original, so long as either is sufficient to place third parties on notice that the copyright is encumbered. Accordingly, the Copyright Act requires that the file document "specifically identif[y] the work to which it pertains so that, after the document is indexed by the Register of Copyrights, it would be revealed by a reasonable search under the title or registration number of the work." 17 U.S.C. §205(c). That having been said, it's worth noting that filing with the Copyright Office can be much less convenient than filing under the UCC This is because UCC filings are indexed by owner, while registration in the Copyright Office is by title or copyright registration number. See 17 U.S.C. §205(c). This means that the recording of a security interest in a film library such as that owned by NPI will involve dozens, sometimes hundreds, of individual filings. Moreover, as the contents of the film library changes, the lienholder will be required to make a separate filing for each work added to or deleted from the library. By contrast, a UCC-1 filing can provide a continuing, floating lien on assets of a particular type owned by the debtor, without the need for periodic updates. See [UCC §9-204]. This technical shortcoming of the copyright filing system does make it a less useful device for perfecting a security interest in copyright libraries. Nevertheless, this problem is not so serious as to make the system unworkable. In any event, this is the system Congress has established and the court is not in a position to order more adequate procedures. If the mechanics of filing turn out to pose a serious burden, it can be taken up by Congress during its oversight of the Copyright Office or, conceivably, the Copyright Office might be able to ameliorate the problem through exercise of its regulatory authority. See 17 U.S.C. §702.

13. When a federal statute provides a system of national registration but fails to provide its own priority scheme, the priority scheme established by Article Nine will generally govern the conflicting rights of creditors. Whether a creditor's interest is perfected, however, depends on whether the creditor recorded its interest in accordance with the federal statute. See UCC §§[9-311(a) and (b)].

receivables generated by a copyright may also be recorded in the Copyright Office." But seven years after *Peregrine*, the Ninth Circuit held that an assignment of royalties was not a "document pertaining to a copyright" and so was not recordable in the Copyright Office. Broadcast Music, Inc. v. Hirsch, 104 F.3d 1163 (9th Cir. 1997).

The recordation requirement recognized in *Peregrine* applied only to copyrights formally registered with the Copyright Office. Most copyrights are not registered. They nevertheless remain valid, enforceable, and valuable. In In re World Auxiliary Power Company, 303 F.3d 1120 (9th Cir. 2002), the court held that security interests in such copyrights could not be recorded in the Copyright Office and that the UCC filing system remained the correct system in which to perfect.

In an omitted portion of the *Peregrine* opinion, Judge Kozinski correctly notes that the federal law governing trademarks (Lanham Act) refers only to recordation of "assignments" and does not mention "hypothecations." Although "assignments" could have been read to include assignments as security, the cases are unanimous in holding that it does not. A federal filing is neither necessary nor sufficient to perfect a security interest in a trademark.

Nevertheless, the Patent and Trademark Office accepts security agreements in trademarks for filing and about 5,000 secured parties file them each year. Fifteen percent of them—about 700 a year—fail to file in the UCC filing system, apparently leaving those filers unperfected. Aneta Ferguson, The Trademark Filing Trap, 49 Idea 197 (2009).

In the following case, the court notes the existence of three other federal filing systems, stating that two (aircraft and railroad) preempt the UCC with respect to filing, but one (patents) does not.

In re Pasteurized Eggs Corporation

296 B.R. 283 (Bankr. D.N.H. 2003)

J. Michael Deasy, Bankruptcy Judge.
[In In re Cybernetic Services, Inc., 252 F.3d 1039, 1043 (9th Cir. 2001),] the Ninth Circuit held that a security interest in a patent was perfected where the assignor had complied with California UCC filing requirements but had not recorded the security interest with the [Patent and Trademark Office]. There, the court concluded that Article 9 of California's UCC governs the method for perfecting a security interest in patents, as Article 9 applies to "general intangibles," which includes intellectual property.

The *Cybernetic* court further concluded that the Patent Act does not preempt the UCC with respect to perfection of security interests, because the Patent Act addresses filings only with respect to transfers in ownership but not with regard to security interests. The *Cybernetic* court underscored this point by noting that the Copyright Act does include such a provision. The court noted that "the Copyright Act governs any 'transfer' of ownership, which is defined by the statute to include any 'hypothecation.'" Black's Law Dictionary defines a "hypothecation" as the "pledging of something as security without delivery of title or possession." By contrast, the Patent Act does not refer to "hypothecation" or security interests. The court concluded that the inclusion of a security interest provision in the Copyright Act "is more evidence that security interests are outside the scope of [the Patent Act]."

In an earlier incarnation of *Cybernetic*, the Ninth Circuit Bankruptcy Appellate Panel pointed to aircraft and railroads as two additional areas in which Congress has established a federal filing system for liens. See Cybernetic Services, Inc. v. Matsco, Inc. (In re Cybernetic Services, Inc.), 239 B.R. 917, 922, nn.13, 14 (9th Cir. B.A.P. 1999). There, the Panel contrasts the Patent Act, which contains no provision regarding perfection of security interests, with statutes that clearly establish a federal filing system and therefore preempt state requirements. Regarding liens on aircraft, "under [49 U.S.C. §44108] the failure to file a security instrument with the FAA administrator precludes constructive notice of the existence of the security instrument and consequently limits the parties against whom it is valid." [Cybernetic Services, 239 B.R. at 923, n.13.] Regarding liens on railroad-related property, 49 U.S.C. §11301 provides that a "mortgage . . . or security interest in vessels, railroad cars, locomotives, or other rolling stock . . . shall be filed with the Board in order to perfect the security interest that is the subject of such instrument." Unlike the language in these statutes, the Patent Act does not contain any language regarding security interests, and therefore does not preempt state law. As such, perfection of a security interest in a patent requires filing a UCC-1 in accordance with state law. Filing a security agreement with the PTO does not perfect the security interest.

The effect of *Cybernetic* is to separate the correct place for filing assignments of patent ownership from the correct place for filing assignments of patents as security. The former is the Patent and Trademark Office, while the latter is the UCC filing system. The same is true for trademarks. But for registered copyrights, the correct place for filing both kinds of assignments is the Copyright Office.

With modern computer technology, maintenance of thousands of isolated filing systems is no longer warranted. See Lynn M. LoPucki, Computerization of the Article 9 Filing System: Thoughts on Building the Electronic Highway, 55 Law & Contemp. Probs. 5 (1992), advocating a system in which each search covers every system. By requiring filing against a corporation in the jurisdiction in which the business is incorporated, new Article 9 has paved the way for joining the record of a UCC filing against a corporation with the other records pertaining to that corporation. But the law has a tradition of staying behind the times, and we suspect that consolidation across filing systems still lies in the distant future.

F. Methods and Costs of Searching

In many filing offices, only employees are permitted access to the records. In those systems, the lender or its lawyer must fill out a form precisely specifying the search requested and send it to the filing officer. In other filing offices a knowledgeable member of the public can walk in and search the records or log in remotely and search them. Nonetheless, in both systems, most lenders and lawyers choose not to deal directly with the filing office. Instead, they hire a "service company" to order or conduct the search for them.

Service companies are private businesses that serve as intermediaries between the lender or lawyer who needs a search and the filing office in which the search is conducted. Unlike many of the filing officers, who are government employees, the service companies will accept search requests by telephone and will expedite them if necessary. If the service company has an office near the records to be searched, a company employee may go to the filing office and either conduct the search or order it "over the counter." If the service company does not have an office near the records, it may nevertheless provide the same service through a local correspondent. The local correspondent typically is an abstract company (known as a *title* or *escrow* company in some parts of the United States), a local UCC search company, or an attorney.

The result is that, in most official searches, the lender pays two fees: that of the filing officer and that of the service company. The filing officer's fee is usually specified by a state statute, and the service company's fee is determined by the service company or its correspondent. A typical fee for searching a single name would be about $50.* To search an additional name or a variation on a name is likely to double the cost of the search. To search in an additional filing office is likely to double it again. About half the typical fee goes to the filing officer, and the other half goes to the service company and its correspondents. If the search identifies relevant filings, the lender will usually wish to purchase copies. A typical search will turn up about ten pages of filings, although the actual number may vary from none to hundreds, depending on the complexity of the debtor's finances and distinctness of its name. Because filing officers typically charge about a dollar a page for making copies, the cost of copies can be considerable. Finally, many searches are conducted at remote locations on short notice, so the lender may also incur charges for overnight deliveries and the like.

Filing is usually a little cheaper than searching, but not much. The service company is likely to charge about $15 per filing and the filing office may charge anywhere from about $10 to $25.

If the client is only an occasional user of the Article 9 filing system, the client will likely want the lawyer to arrange the necessary filings and searches. Involving even a relatively inexpensive lawyer (or an expensive one who delegates the task to a paralegal) can easily triple or quadruple the cost of filing or searching. On the other hand, a lender who deals with a particular filing office regularly may be familiar with the procedures of that office, have an account with the office, and have the ability to search the records or make filings online. (On the websites of some states, it is possible to conduct an unofficial search free.) For such a lender, the cost of filing or searching in that particular office

---

*The authors wish to express their thanks to Ed Hand of UCC Filing and Search Services in Tallahassee, Florida, for the estimates of typical costs in this section.

may be only a fraction of the cost the lender would incur working through a lawyer or a search company.

While the fees incurred by most filers and searchers may seem substantial to a student who is doing law school on $50 a day, they remain small in relation to the amounts of money involved in most commercial lending transactions. For this reason, a lawyer who is uncertain as to the filing office in which a particular search or filing should be made can often solve the problem by searching or filing in more than one system. The possibility has led some observers to advocate filing "everywhere," but that word tends to be used by people other than those paying the bills. We suggest that the issue of where to search and file is one that requires a thorough knowledge of the law and relevant systems, as well as the exercise of judgment in light of the likely cost and the amounts involved.

Problem Set 16

16.1. Bobby Lawful's only valuable possession is a Porsche 911 (lemon yellow, seven-speed transmission) named "Honey." The car is fully paid for and worth about $30,000. Bobby owes about that same amount to Felicia Steinberg, his ex-wife, for child support and alimony arrearages. He also owes a number of other debts, including $36,000 to his business partner, Bernie Keller, for money he borrowed from Bernie over the past few years. Six months ago, Felicia hired you to collect the arrearages for her. You obtained a judgment on the debt, but because Bobby was making the current support payments, the judge declined to hold him in contempt. When Bobby ignored the judgment, Felicia authorized you to have the sheriff seize Honey. In investigating the title to the car, you learned that just over three months ago, Bobby signed a security agreement granting Bernie Keller an interest in Honey to secure the $36,000 debt. Bobby and Bernie went together to the Department of Motor Vehicles and immediately recorded notice of Bernie's lien on the certificate of title.

[handwritten margin note: Bernie Attached + perfected]

    a.   Now where does Felicia stand? Uniform Motor Vehicle Certificate of Title Act §20(b). UCC §§9-102(a)(52), 9-317(a)(2), and 9-311(b).

    b.   Can you go ahead with the execution levy? If you can, should you? UCC §9-401.

16.2. You graduated from law school, passed the bar, and are setting up an office. You want to buy a set of state statutes. You see one advertised in the State Bar Journal for $8,000 by a lawyer who is leaving practice. The price is right and the books are in good condition.

    a.   Is there anything you should do before buying? UCC §9-317(b).

    b.   Would it be any different if you were buying on eBay?

    c.   Would it be any different if you were buying from a used-book dealer? UCC §9-320(a).

16.3. Three Rivers Legal Services referred Stevie Boriskovich to you. Stevie is a Russian immigrant who has been in the United States a little over three years. For most of that time, he worked the graveyard shift at McDonald's, saving the money with which he hoped to start his own business. Five months ago, he found the opportunity he was looking for in a newspaper ad: a street vendor cart with refrigeration for $4,000. Stevie paid the owner, Adam Levitin, $2,000 in cash, signed a promissory note for the balance, quit his job, and went into business for himself selling food and ice cream in the park. About two weeks ago, he received in quick succession (1) a notice that Levitin had filed for bankruptcy and (2) a letter from General Finance Company (GFC), demanding possession of the cart. Along with the GFC letter were copies of three documents. The first was Levitin's promissory note to GFC in the amount of $5,000. The second was a security agreement signed by Levitin more than a year ago granting GFC an interest in the cart to secure the note. The third was a financing statement bearing the date and time stamp of the Secretary of State UCC division. UCC §9-519(a)(2).

In your check of the public records, you found that GFC had done everything necessary to perfect their security interest months before Stevie bought the cart. When you asked Stevie why he had not searched the UCC records before buying the cart, he told you that he did not know such a thing existed.

The partner you work for says that if you take Stevie's case on a pro bono basis, the firm will support you. You like Stevie and would like to help him keep his cart and his dreams. But another lawyer in the firm who does lots of Article 9 work says that Stevie is not protected as a buyer under UCC §9-320(a) because he did not buy in the ordinary course of business, and you accept your colleague's expertise. (You will study this point in greater detail in Assignment 36.) When you asked whether there was any other provision of Article 9 that might provide a defense, she said "No, the whole point of Article 9 is that people are supposed to check the records." You remember a favorite law professor having said that if a sympathetic client has a just case and good facts there's always some legal theory "to hang your hat on," but you also remember that the professor did not teach any commercial subjects. Stevie will be in to talk with you in the morning.

a. What should you tell him? See UCC §§1-103(b), 1-304, 9-201(a), 9-315(a)(1), 9-317(b), 9-402, and the footnote to the *Peerless Packing* case.

b. If you discovered that GFC repossessed three vending carts in the past 12 months, each time from a defrauded buyer, would that help your case?

▶ Half Assignment Ends

16.4.   As the most junior attorney in a firm that represents secured lenders you have been assigned to order UCC filings and searches in anticipation of the various clients' lending against the collateral listed below. (The firm never mentioned this during their summer clerkship program.) In what filing system or systems will you make the filings and conduct the searches?

a.   Keith Pipes, an auto mechanic, has applied to your client, ITT Services, for a consumer loan to be secured by $10,000 worth of tools, which Pipes bought and paid for a couple of years ago to use at the service station he and his wife own and operate. See UCC §§9-109(a), (c) and (d), 9-310, and 9-501(a).

b.   Bernie Wolfson, an inventor, has applied to your client bank for a $400,000 loan to be secured by a patent Bernie obtained several years ago. UCC §§9-311(a)(1), 9-109(c)(1).

c.   Your client is a New York bank that plans to lend $500,000 to famous author Nyl Ikcupol. The loan is to be secured by royalty payments Nyl receives from his New York publisher on the 119 books he has written. See UCC §§9-102(a)(2), 9-109(a) and (c), 9-501(a). Reread the first few paragraphs of section II.A. of *National Peregrine* and the reference to *Broadcast Music* that follows the case.

d.   Your client is a bank planning to make a $600,000 working capital loan to an Indiana dealer in rare automobiles. The collateral will include (1) the dealer's inventory of automobiles, (2) some automobiles that are not for sale, (3) accounts receivable from the sale of automobiles, (4) all of the dealer's rights to its "American Originals" trademark. UCC §§9-311(a)(2) and (d), Comment 4 to UCC §9-311, UCC §§9-501(a), 9-109(a) and (b), 9-102(a)(2), (33), (42), and (48); UMVCTA §§4(a), and 20(a) and (b).

16.5.   A senior partner in your firm specializes in real property work and isn't familiar with the UCC He explains that a bank client is concerned that a debtor might encumber the prospective collateral to a competing creditor at any time, even as the debtor is negotiating with the bank client. The lawyer asks which should be done first, the UCC searches or the filings? UCC §§9-502(d), 9-523(c).

Assignment 17: Article 9 Financing Statements: The Debtor's Name

In Assignment 16, we used the metaphor of leaving messages to explain the function of a filing system. In that assignment we saw that the filer must leave the message in the correct system and the searcher must know to look for it in that system. In this assignment we examine a closely related problem. If the searcher looks in the system where the filing was made, will the searcher be able to find it among the millions of such messages that may be filed there?

A. The Components of a Filing System

Statewide filing systems generally permit the electronic filing of financing statements and other records. Filings are made by filling out a form on the filing office website. To accommodate these paperless filings, the provisions of Article 9 are "media neutral." That is, they are written to be applied to paper filings, electronic filings, or any other sort of filing the future may hold. Thus the term "record" is defined as "information that is inscribed on a tangible medium or which is stored in an electronic or other medium and is retrievable in perceivable form." Accordingly, the filing officer no longer "stamps" the file number on a financing statement; the filing officer "assigns" the file number to a financing statement.

A filing system consists not only of the filed records but also of subsystems for (1) adding new records, (2) searching among the records, and (3) removing obsolete records. The subsystems for adding new records are relatively simple. The clerk who receives a paper filing typically assigns a date and time of filing, makes a copy, and returns the original to the filer with a receipt. Later, someone else in the clerk's office will index the copy and add it to the body of prior filings. Electronic filings are processed automatically.

In many filing systems, subsystems for removing obsolete records do not exist at all: The store of records simply grows each year. The subsystem for removing obsolete records from Article 9 filing systems is discussed in Assignment 22. In this assignment, we focus primarily on the subsystems that search for relevant records in the filing system.

For reasons related more to technology than law, search methods differ widely from one filing system to another. The introduction of new technologies for processing, storing, and searching the records results in important changes in the ways these systems operate. Each new technology spawns a new set of legal problems. For this reason, we think it is useful to understand the system at a broad conceptual level—to understand what the system is designed to do and the basic strategies for accomplishing its goals. This kind of understanding transcends any particular filing system and the technologies in use at the time. Knowing how particular technologies have been implemented in particular systems is important because it is only in the particularity of those implementations that the system generates problems that require the attention of a lawyer. Law functions almost entirely as a facilitator of the technology of its day.

1.   Financing Statements

The Article 9 filing system was designed and implemented before the era of the photocopier. Early filers had to furnish carbon copies of their financing statements to filing officers who had no means of creating additional copies. Searches were conducted by looking through the pieces of paper that were filed. As photocopying came into wide use in the 1960s, some systems began making copies of filed financing statements. But many of the systems went directly from using carbon copies to microfilm as the medium for storing and using financing statements. Microfilm later gave way to microfiche. In both micro-media, the filing officer filmed and stored the financing statements in the order in which they were received.

The statewide UCC systems have switched from micro-media to digital storage of financing statements. The filer may send an image of a financing statement—as it appears in UCC §9-521, but with the blanks filled in—or merely transmit the data necessary to fill the blanks in. In the later event, the filing office creates the financing statement automatically. The financing statements are stored as digital images. Searchers can locate them through the index, view them on the screen, and download them. Still, for both technological and political reasons it remains impossible to search the full text of the financing statements online. Online searches are limited to the index.

[handwritten margin note: Fill in the blanks 9-521 financing statement]

2.   The Index

When a financing statement is filed, the filing office assigns it a unique number, usually referred to as the *file number* or, in some local systems, the *book and page number*. The system uses this number as a means of identifying, indexing, and retrieving the statement.

The typical searcher is a lender who contemplates making a secured loan to the debtor and who wants to discover whether there are prior recorded interests in the debtor's property. This subsequent lender comes to the filing system without a file number. It does not seek a particular financing statement; instead, it wants any and all financing statements that might encumber the prospective collateral. What the typical searcher knows is the name of the prospective debtor and the nature of the proposed collateral. The searcher will be able to find the messages about earlier filed interests only if they are indexed by the description of collateral or the identity of the debtor.

A few kinds of filing systems index by a description of the collateral. The description often includes a number to add distinctness and make searching easier. One example is the *tract index* employed in some real estate recording systems. (Real estate systems are generally referred to as "recording" systems rather than filing systems, but, for convenience, we sometimes use the term *filing systems* to include real estate as well as personal property systems.) Each tract of land in the county is assigned a unique number, and these numbers are written on maps. Searchers find the numbers on the maps and then search the index under the tract number.

The motor vehicle certificate of title system also indexes filings by description of collateral. Each motor vehicle is assigned a Vehicle Identification Number (VIN) at the time of manufacture or importation and a registration number at the time it is licensed for operation on the highways. A searcher can use either number to locate the certificate. All filed liens appear on the face of the certificate.

Both the real estate and motor vehicle filing systems can index by collateral because the collateral has a stable identity. Tracts of land are split or consolidated infrequently, and, even when they are, the land in question remains easy to trace. Similarly, a motor vehicle usually retains its identity throughout its useful life. The system assigns a unique identification number to each tract or vehicle, making it possible to search by number. But for most kinds of collateral governed by the Article 9 filing system — think of tubes of toothpaste on the supermarket shelf or oil in the tanks of a refinery — the assignment of identification numbers is impractical. Nor would it be practical to index directly by the description of collateral. A searcher who intended to lend money against oil in refinery tanks might find thousands of filings under "oil" and have little means for knowing which relate to the oil it plans to take as collateral. The filer who financed the inventory of a supermarket would have to list each type of collateral separately, resulting in thousands of separate notations in the index ("toothpaste," "bread," "milk"). Problems such as these make the indexing of Article 9 financing statements by collateral impractical. Accordingly, Article 9 filing offices typically index financing statements only by the name of the debtor.

UCC §9-519(c) requires that the filing office index financing statements according to the name of the debtor. The index thus prepared typically will include the address of the debtor. The address is often helpful to searchers in distinguishing the debtor who is the subject of their search from other debtors with the same or similar names. Some filing offices include additional information in the index, such as the name and address of the creditor, the date of filing, or even a brief description of the collateral. The file number is also included in the index.

Today, nearly all filing systems use computerized data management systems to generate the debtor name index. Employees of the filing office use keyboards to enter the information to be included in the index from paper financing statements. Electronic filings are indexed automatically.

3. Search Systems

UCC searches run electronically on the index. In some states, the searcher can enter the debtor's name online and the system will immediately return a list of matching entries. In other states, the searcher must submit a search request form and the system fills the request — minutes or days later. Searches return the index entries for exact debtor name matches and whatever near matches the system was specifically programmed to treat as matches. The rules that determine what the program will consider a match are referred to as the program's "search logic." As you will see later in this assignment, the search logic determines not only the results of searches but also the legal sufficiency of the financing statement. Most states have published their search logic as part of the state's administrative code.

The immediate feedback available in some search systems is an important system feature because it enables the user to vary the search until the results are as expected. For example, if the searcher knows there will be financing statements on file against the debtor, but none shows up on the search, the searcher can guess that the searcher misspelled the debtor's name.

The filing office dates and numbers an electronic filing or stamps a paper filing to uniquely identify the record and document the date and time of its filing. The financing statement is effective as of that moment, even though it may take a few days, or even a few weeks, for the filing office to add it to the official index. Thus, at any given time, there will be filed and effective financing statements that the filing officer has not yet added to the index. Because in many filing systems the not-yet-processed documents were once kept in an in-basket on someone's desk, these unindexed and therefore undiscoverable records have come to be known as *the basket.*

Because searches run only in the indexes, they cannot discover financing statements that are still in the basket. For that reason, UCC §9-523(c) authorizes filing offices to respond to search requests with search reports that extend through only the period for which all filings have been indexed. For example, assume that on March 15, the filing office has indexed all filings receive by 5 P.M. on March 1, but has not yet indexed the filings received since that date. Regardless of the period the searcher would like covered by the search, on March 15 the filing office will report the filings "on file on March 1 at 5 P.M." March 1 in this example is the date generally referred to as the "as of date" — the date as of which the search is reported.

Because searches are conducted on the debtor name index, that index is critically important to the functioning of an Article 9 filing system. The vast majority of searchers can find the financing statements they seek only through that index. Moreover, they may be able to find the entries for those financing statements in the debtor name index only if the debtor's name shown on the financing statement is sufficiently similar to the debtor's name as they know it that the computer will return a match, or, if the search is on a hard copy index, the searcher will find the debtor's name and recognize it. Debtors' names as they appear in the index are the searchers' link to the financing statements on file.

B.   Correct Names for Use on Financing Statements

9-506(a)

UCC §9-506(a) provides that "a financing statement substantially complying with the requirements of [part 5 of Article 9] is effective, even if it includes minor errors or omissions, unless the errors or omissions make the financing statement seriously misleading." In the next section, we consider what kinds of errors are considered seriously misleading, but first we address a preliminary question: What is the "correct" name of a debtor that *ideally* would appear on the financing statement? The answer to this question is surprisingly complex.

9-503
9-503(4)
9-503(b)
(c)

The analysis begins with UCC §9-503. That section provides that a financing statement sufficiently provides the name of a registered entity only if it provides the name of the debtor indicated on the public record of the debtor's jurisdiction of origin. As to an individual or partnership, the financing statement must provide the "individual or organizational name of the debtor." UCC §9-503(a)(4). A financing statement is not rendered ineffective by the absence of the debtor's trade name, and use of a trade name alone does not sufficiently provide the name of the debtor. UCC §§9-503(b) and (c). We discuss each of these four types of names separately.

1.   Individual Names

The reference to "individual" names is to the names of human beings, as opposed to the names of artificial legal entities such as corporations, partnerships, or trusts. Unfortunately for all who deal with the filing system, our cultural and social practices are very tolerant of both variations and changes in individual names. An individual's birth certificate and college degree may indicate his name to be "Thomas Lawrence Smith," even though he never uses this form of his name on any other occasion. His friends may know him as "Bucky Smith," while his mother calls him "Tommy," but the line below his signature on documents is always "Thomas L. Smith," and his listing in the phone directory is under "T.L. Smith." If he wants to change any of these to "Tom Smith," most of us will consider that his prerogative and comply.

what is correct Name?

What is the legally correct name of this individual? Article 9 doesn't say. Black letter law tells us that it is the name by which he is generally known, for nonfraudulent purposes, in the community. What community? Black letter law doesn't say, but the implication is that it might be a different community for different legal purposes. His birth certificate is not determinative. In other words, Tom has many names, but no single, unique identifier.

The naming problem is complicated by the fact that an individual can change his or her name. The individual can do so by filing a court action for that purpose. Divorce courts often include desired name changes in their decrees. But an individual can also change his or her name without legal action. All the individual need do is become generally known, for a nonfraudulent purpose, by a different name.

The naming problem is further complicated by a variety of ethnic naming practices that do not fit the traditional American model of first, middle, and last (family) name. Family names come first in Chinese culture, may include the mother's name in Hispanic culture, and are largely unknown in Islamic culture. Immigrants may or may not alter their names to fit the American model. Should a searcher looking for Li Wan search Wan, Li or Li, Wan? And even if the searcher is sure that she understands the correct identification of Li Wan, can the searcher be sure that the filer and the recorder shared that same understanding? To further illustrate the problem, here's an explanation of the Hispanic naming convention:

> Let's take a look at a sample name: Rosa María Muñoz Izquierdo. Rosa María is the woman's name. . . . María is not her middle name — it is part of what we would call her first name. Muñoz is her father's last name. . . . This is what we would call her "last name." Izquierdo is her mother's last name (maiden name) and is used only in conjunction with her father's last name. It is not what we would call her "last name." It is only part of her complete last name. So, we can call her Rosa María Muñoz, Rosa María Muñoz Izquierdo, señora Muñoz or Ms. Muñoz Izquierdo. But we do not call her Ms. Izquierdo! http://www.drlemon.net/Grammar/names. html/.

The implications for the Article 9 filing system are disconcerting. There may be no single version of an individual debtor's name that is "correct," and, even if there is, it may be impossible to know for certain which version it is. To make matters even more complicated, more than one person may have precisely the same name. Together, these characteristics of individual names cause considerable confusion and uncertainty for both filer and searcher in the UCC filing system. With regard to individual names, the indexing system is built on sand.

Reliance on debtor's names as the basis for Article 9 filing and searching has proven to be the Achilles' heel of the Article 9 filing system. High filing and search costs, combined with extensive litigation over name problems led to extensive changes in the 2001 revision to Article 9. These solutions failed, leading to a second set of solutions in the 2010 amendments. The latter provide the states with two alternative individual name provisions to choose between (another dent in the uniformity of the Uniform Commercial Code).

 Neither of these alternatives changes the "correct" or "legal" name of the debtor. For debtors with in-state drivers' licenses, Alternative A makes the correct legal name irrelevant. Instead, filing, and by implication searching, is to be in the name on the debtor's driver's license. For example, if a debtor obtained an in-state driver's license in the name "James McGinty," later obtains a court order changing his name to "Roger McGuinn," but does not change the name on his driver's license, James McGinty is not his correct legal name but is the only name that is sufficient on a financing statement filed against him. A financing statement in his correct legal name, Roger McGuinn, would be insufficient and a creditor who relied on it would be unperfected. Same result for Erica Winston, who married and then called herself Erica Thompson, but who failed to change her driver's license.

Alternative B makes the driver's license name merely a safe harbor. Filings are valid if made in the debtor's correct legal name, in the correct legal first name and surname (apparently regardless of what is indicated to be the middle name), or in the driver's license name. As of this writing, 49 states have adopted the 2010 amendments. The large majority of them have chosen Alternative A.

The 2010 amendments make a subtle change to address ethnic naming conventions. Instead of "last names"—literally the last word in the name—the statute now speaks of "surnames"—the name common to a family. This may ease the problem with Chinese names, but make Hispanic and Arabic names even more problematic. In some states, the driver's license splits the name into first and surname. But in most, the driver's license is just a string of words, leaving it to the Article 9 filer or searcher to make the split at its peril.

2.   Corporate Names

A "registered organization" is an entity "formed or organized solely under the law of a single State or the United States" by the filing of a public organic record with, the issuance of a public organic record by, or the enactment of legislation by the State or United States." UCC §9-102(a)(71). A public organic record is the record "initially filed with or issued by a State or the United States to form or organize an organization . . . or . . . which amends or restates the initial record." UCC §9-102(a)(68). For example, the public organic record for a corporation would ordinarily be the state's copy of the articles of incorporation filed with the state or the corporate charter issued by the state—along with any amendments or restatements. Registered organizations include corporations, limited liability companies, limited partnerships, and a few others. We lump them together for discussion here as "corporations" because the differences among them do not matter for our purposes. What distinguishes registered organizations from other entities is that the state brings them into existence.

That is, corporations can be formed only by obtaining a *charter* or *certificate of incorporation* from the secretary of state of one of the 50 states. The federal government issues charters for a few kinds of corporations, such as national banks. The government's file will show the one and only legal name of the corporation. The corporation can change that name only by filing an amendment with the secretary of state. It follows that a corporation can have only a single correct name at any given time. By examining the documents on file with the Corporations division of the secretary of state, a searcher can discover the precise spelling of a corporate name, including the details of punctuation, hyphenation, and capitalization.

Two other characteristics of corporate names are of significance to the Article 9 filing system. First, in the large majority of states, the name must show that the entity is a corporation. It does that by including one of only a few permissible designators. The most common are "Corporation" or its abbreviation

"Corp.," "Company" or its abbreviation "Co.," "Incorporated" or its abbreviation "Inc.," and "Limited Liability Company" or its abbreviation "L.L.C." If the corporation is formed for a particular purpose, such as to practice a licensed profession, alternative corporate designators may be required. For example, a corporation formed to practice law is a "Professional Association" or "P.A." under Florida law, a "Service Corporation" or "S.C." under Wisconsin law, and a "Professional Corporation" or "P.C." under California law. The primary significance of these rules for the Article 9 filing systems is that they make it possible to identify many names as *not* the names of corporations. For example, in the large majority of states, "McDonald's" cannot be a corporate name, but "McDonald's, Inc." can be. California and Delaware are exceptions; each would, at least in some circumstances, permit the use of "McDonald's" as a corporate name.

The second significant characteristic of the corporate naming system is that no state will permit the formation of two corporations with the same name or confusingly similar names. (A name that differs from another only in its corporate designator is considered confusingly similar. If the state has already incorporated a McDonald's, Inc., it will refuse to incorporate a McDonald's Corporation.) Two corporations can have the same name only if they incorporate in different states. If one adds the state of incorporation to a corporate name, for example, "McDonald's, Inc., a Delaware Corporation," the result is a unique identifier. Together, these characteristics of corporate names make them more reliable and easier to use for filing and searching than individual names. Thanks to Delaware and California's non-standard rules, corporations may also have the same names as individuals. Ruby Tuesday could be someone's elderly auntie or the corporate owner of a place to grab a beer.

3.   Partnership Names

A limited partnership is, for present purposes, a corporation. The name rules discussed in the previous section apply.

General partnerships are formed by contract, express or implied. No state registration is required or permitted. If there is a written partnership agreement, it may assign a name to the partnership. Regardless of the agreement among the partners, however, the legal name of a general partnership is the name by which it is generally known in the community. The name may, but need not, include some indication that the entity is a partnership. If Sally White and Grover Cleveland form a partnership, the name could be "White and Cleveland," "Sally White and Grover Cleveland," "Realty Partners," or even "McDonald's."

In all or nearly all states, a general partnership can become a limited liability partnership (LLP) by filing an election with the state. The filing of that election does not "form or organize" the partnership. UCC §9-102(a)(68). It merely limits the partners' liability. For that reason, most observers conclude that limited liability partnerships are not registered organizations.

4.   Trade Names

A "trade" or "fictitious" name is a name under which a person or entity conducts business that is not its legal name. For example, the purchaser of a McDonald's franchise may incorporate under a name like "McDonald's Restaurants of Atlanta, Incorporated." But if one visits the business premises, one sees only the name "McDonald's" in and about the golden arches. "McDonald's" is a trade name. Many trade names bear no resemblance to the name of the person or entity using them. For example, the Bernard Walker Corporation may do business as "Yellow Cab Company."

Trade names are the subject of several kinds of public record systems. The user of a trade name can register the name with a state or the federal government and thereby lodge a trademark claim to exclusive ownership. Only a small portion of the trade names in use in the United States are so registered; most are simply adopted by a business without additional formality.

Most states have a "fictitious name" statute requiring that *every* person or entity doing business in a name other than its own file notice in a public record system provided for that purpose. Although the statutes typically make failure to file a misdemeanor, there are few prosecutions and no other effective penalties for not filing. Filing does nothing to preserve or to enhance the filer's claim to ownership of the trade name. As a result, most of these fictitious-name filing systems have fallen into disuse. Even large, publicly held companies that own and do business under many trade names often fail to file notices.

As a result, it can often be difficult to determine who or what is doing business under a particular trade name. The drafters of Article 9 deemed trade names too uncertain and too likely not to be known to the secured party or person searching the record to form the basis for a filing system. UCC §§9-503(b) and (c) make clear that trade names are neither necessary nor sufficient to identify a debtor on a financing statement.

5.   The Entity Problem

The difficulty of determining the correct name of a legal entity is easily confused with a much more basic question: Who, or what, can have a name? That is, in the contemplation of the law, who or what will be recognized as a separate entity, capable of being a collateral owner and therefore capable of being the subject of an Article 9 filing? For example, a law school might or might not be an entity as distinguished from the university of which it is a part. A "division" of an incorporated business is not a legal entity unless it is separately incorporated.

The UCC's answer to the entity problem begins with the definition of "debtor" in §9-102(a)(28). A debtor is a "person." "Person" is defined in UCC §1-201(b)(27) to include an individual, corporation, or any other legal or commercial entity. The apparent implication is that an entity might be a debtor under Article 9 and its name might be required on financing statements, even though it is not recognized as a *legal* entity for any other purpose.

Series LLCs are a new form of business organization authorized by statutes in several states. The incorporator files one set of papers to form a series LLC. The LLC can have any number of series and each series can own property, incur liability, and grant security interests. 6 Del. Code § 18-215 (2015) ("[A] series . . . shall have the power and capacity to, in its own name . . . grant liens and security interests."). Property owned by one series is not liable for the debts of another series of the same LLC. The effect is an LLC that functions much like a corporate group.

A series LLC is a registered organization because it is formed by filing a public organic record with the state. One series of a series LLC is not a registered organization because no record of its formation is filed with or maintained by the state. The existence of series are recorded only on the records of the series LLCs. Whether a series LLC is one entity or many remains unclear. As a result, it is also unclear whether the LLC or the particular series that owns the collateral is the "debtor" under UCC §9-102(a)(28).

C. Errors in the Debtors' Names on Financing Statements

In re EDM Corporation

431 B.R. 459, 71 UCC Rep. Serv. 2d 876 (8th Cir. B.A.P. 2010)

Debtor EDM Corporation is a Nebraska corporation which sold and leased emergency vehicles. It was incorporated in 1991, and its official name of record at the Nebraska Secretary of State's office is "EDM Corporation." The Debtor routinely did business as "EDM Equipment," and was commonly known by that name, although it had no registered trade names with the Nebraska Secretary of State. At issue here is the priority of liens in the proceeds of a particular ambulance (the "Ambulance") which had been owned by EDM.

Hastings State Bank, TierOne Bank, and Huntington National Bank each assert a lien against the Ambulance. As stated, the sole issue here is priority.

Over the years, Hastings State Bank made several loans to EDM, in excess of $4.5 million. Hastings filed a financing statement on June 10, 2003, with the Nebraska Secretary of State. Its financing statement identified the debtor as "EDM CORPORATION D/B/A EDM EQUIPMENT." Neither TierOne Bank nor Huntington National Bank disputes that, but for an alleged defect in the way EDM's name appears as the debtor on the financing statement, Hastings would be first in priority because its lien was created, and its financing statement was filed, first.

Nebraska adopted Revised Article 9 of the Uniform Commercial Code, effective July 1, 2001. To put the relevant statutory provisions in context, in practice, a creditor wishing to perfect its lien files with the appropriate governmental authority a financing statement, typically on a standardized form, listing the name of the debtor, the name of the creditor, and a description of the collateral. Once a financing statement is filed, a government employee enters the data from the financing statement into a computerized indexing system. If a potential lender wants to determine for itself whether there are existing liens on the borrower's property, that lender can submit a request to the authority for a lien search (sometimes by conducting its own search on-line). More than 40 states that have adopted Revised Article 9 have also adopted administrative regulations which guide both the governmental authority in entering data from financing statements, as well as the public in conducting searches. Parts of the regulations are often referred to as "search logic." As relevant here, the Nebraska search logic requires that data be entered into the system and indexed based on the exact name listed in the field on the financing statement reserved for the debtor's name. The purpose of this system is to put subsequent creditors on notice of asserted liens and, if everything is done correctly, the search should reveal any financing statements filed.

Hastings asserts that, contrary to the Bankruptcy Court's ruling, a court should not consider §9-506's "seriously misleading" analysis unless the financing statement does not sufficiently provide the debtor's name in accordance with §§9-502 and 9-503. And, Hastings asserts that its financing statement did sufficiently provide EDM's name in accordance with §§9-502 and 9-503 because the words "EDM Corporation" were included in the name provided. We hold both that its financing statement did not provide the name of the debtor, and also that it was seriously misleading.

The Eighth Circuit has emphasized that the purpose of filing a financing statement is to put subsequent creditors on notice that the debtor's property is encumbered. In *ProGrowth v. Wells Fargo Bank*, in interpreting §§9-502(a), 9-504 (relating to the description of the collateral on a financing statement), and 9-506(a), the Eighth Circuit stated:

> The requirements of the UCC concerning filing, notice and perfection all are intended to provide to those dealing with commercial activities knowledge of the status of the commodity with which they are dealing so that they may protect their interests and act in a commercially prudent manner. To that end, the financing statement serves the purpose of putting subsequent creditors on notice that the debtor's property is encumbered. Its function is to warn other subsequent creditors of the prior interest.

In *ProGrowth*, the issue was not about the name of the debtor used in the filing, as is the situation here. Instead, the issue was whether a creditor which was notified of the existence of the lien, due to the UCC filing, had a duty to inquire further as to which specific collateral was covered by it. Because the financing statements in that case put subsequent searchers on notice of a potential lien in the particular assets at issue, the Eighth Circuit held they were sufficient, despite errors in the description of the collateral.

We find it significant that the Eighth Circuit emphasized that the purpose of the filing requirements is to let other creditors know of the existence of the lien. The very first step in that process for creditors is *finding* the UCC statement in the first place, and the way to do that is by searching the records under the debtor's organizational name. In other words, complete accuracy is even more important with the debtor's name than it is with the description of collateral. As one court has stated, with regard to the debtor's name, the legislative language and purpose of the revised UCC "evidenced an intent to shift the responsibility of getting the

"provide the name
cases in which the :
brought by trustees
the sufficiency of tl
challenged, the test
financing statemen
lender under the c
statement. UCC §9-

UCC §9-506(c) t
records of the filin;
office's standard se
the International /
Administrative Rul
does not distinguis
marks and accents,
incorporated, LLC,
nization, (4) ignore
spaces, (6) treats ar
ning with that lette
names, and (8) igno

An official searcl
using the search lo
that a search could
office rules general
always comprehen:
with announced se
what the official se;
the filing office sys
systems are at risk f

The particular se
ing errors the syste
tiniest of errors in
rendering the filing
re Tyringham Hold
name was "Tyring
"Tyringham Holdii
(10th Cir. B.A.P. 20
a space and period
Company." In both
in the debtor's corr
statement under th
search logic, both fi

Under UCC §9-5
official search logic
fective. The drafter
inate the necessity
who knew the cor
with it.

debtor's name right to the party filing the financing statement. This approach would enable a searcher to rely on that name and eliminate the need for multiple searches using variants of the debtor's name, all leading to commercial certainty." And, according to another court, "[p]ost-revision case law is fairly well settled that the burden is squarely on the creditor [filing the financing statement] to correctly identify the name of the debtor."

[Hastings cited since-repealed official comments to §9-503 that implied trade names can be included in addition to the organizational name of the debtor.]

While official comments to the UCC are not binding, they are persuasive in matters of interpretation. However, when considered in conjunction with the rest of the rules and regulations, and keeping in mind the critical importance of accuracy in the debtor's name under Revised Article 9, we do not interpret this comment to endorse the practice of adding superfluous information to a registered organization's *name* in the name field on a financing statement. Rather, it is clear from the language of the statute itself that §9-503 requires that, as to registered organizations, the debtor's name (as listed in the name field on the form) must be "the name of the debtor indicated on the public record of the debtor's jurisdiction of organization." Viewed with §9-503(b)(1), which provides that "[a] financing statement that provides the name of the debtor in accordance with subsection (a) is not rendered ineffective by the *absence of* . . . a trade name or other name of the debtor," and §9-503(c), which provides that "[a] financing statement that provides *only* the debtor's trade name does not sufficiently provide the name of the debtor," we interpret the comment to mean that trade or other names may be added as *other* or *additional* names on a financing statement, but not in place of, or as part of, the debtor's organizational name.

In sum, we interpret §9-503 to mean exactly what it says: if the debtor is a registered organization, then a financing statement "provides the name of the debtor" only if it "provides the name of the debtor indicated on the public record of the debtor's jurisdiction of organization"—nothing more and nothing less. Trade names may be added, but not as part of the organizational name itself. Consequently, because Hastings' UCC statement added superfluous information to EDM's organizational name, it did not sufficiently provide the name of the debtor.

Again, §9-506(a)(iii) provides that, if a search of the records of the filing office under the debtor's correct name, using the filing office's standard search logic, would disclose a financing statement, then the erroneous name provided does not make the financing statement seriously misleading. The undisputed evidence was that a search of the Nebraska Secretary of State's records, using the debtor's correct name, "EDM Corporation," and using the office's standard search logic, did not disclose Hastings' financing statement. Hastings asserts, in effect, that there must be some flaw in Nebraska's search logic and that the Bankruptcy Court allowed the technological deficiencies of the state's search engine to trump a properly filed financing statement. Indeed, at oral argument, Hastings counsel contended that the search logic is contrary to the statute, and so should not serve as the basis for striking down its perfection.

In essence, Hastings asserts that the standard search logic should have found its UCC statement because it should have ignored everything in the field for the debtor's name except the very words "EDM Corporation." The Administrative

Code p
Secretar
the full
of incor
the exa
of "nois
ignored
as a d/b
out clea
ments. \
ness as
using th

We a
insuffici
Accordi

As th
nicate
If the fi
succeec

As th
don't. I
matche
are like
a partic
middle
definiti
searche

If a n
stateme
ing the
existen
cost a le
ting the

Final
does no
filing o
theless
nity for
filing o

Artic
Article
own fir
a lien c
appoin
filer by

Problem Set 17

17.1. In a filing system that uses IACA standard search logic, which of these errors would render a financing statement ineffective? For the individual name problems, assume that the state has adopted Alternative A to UCC §9-503(a).

Correct name	Name as shown on the financing statement under 1a. Organization's Name
a. Heartland Corporation of Iowa	Heartland Corporation
b. Heartland Corporation of Iowa	Heartland of Iowa, Inc.
c. Heartland Corporation	Heartland Corporation, an Iowa corporation
d. HeartLand Corporation	Heartland Corp.
e. The Heartland Corporation	Heartland Corporation
f. K.W.M. Electronics Inc.	K W M Electronics Inc.
g. Heartland Inc.	Hartland Inc.

Driver's license name	Name as shown on the financing statement			
	Individual's surname	First personal name	Additional name	Suffix
h. John Phillip Smith IV	Smith	John		
i. John Phillip Smith	Smith	John	Philip	
j. John Phillip Smith	Smith	J.		
k. Robert Don McErny	Mc Erny	R.	Don	
l. Robert Don McErny	McErny	Robert	Don	Mr.
m. Jose Cruz-Dilan	Cruz-Dilan	Jose		
n. Jose Cruz Dilan	Dilan	Jose	Cruz	
o. Jose Cruz Dilan	Cruz	Jose		
p. Jose Cruz Dilan	Cruz Dilan	Jose		

17.2. Your client, Center Bank and Trust (CBT), plans to lend $2.5 million against equipment, inventory, and accounts receivable owned by Lee Leasing and Bob Lee, the owner of the company.

a. How will you determine what names to search under? If Bob will be a source of information, what questions will you ask him? UCC §§9-503, 9-102(a)(71), and 9-506.

b. If CBT lends to Bob and takes Lee Leasing's property as collateral, which does CBT file against? UCC §§9-102(a)(28), 9-502(a).

c. How will you determine whether the person you are filing against is the owner of the collateral?

17.3. You are a member of your state's Law Revision Commission. The Commission is now preparing the 2010 Amendments to the Uniform Commercial Code for adoption. The Amendments require that the state choose between two versions of UCC §9-503(a). Which Alternative do you prefer, and how would you argue your choice to the other Commission members?

17.4. Isabelle Sterling, the partner you work for, unexpectedly had to travel to Hong Kong. She left you the Tang Aluminum Products file for your client, Global Bank. Global will be lending Tang $1.9 million. The loan is to be secured by an interest in Tang's assets. The closing is set for 16 days from today.

a.   Assuming that the secretary of state is in compliance with UCC §9-523(e), what do you do, and in what order? Can you be ready by the scheduled closing date? UCC §9-523(c).

b.   Assuming that the filing office takes two weeks to process incoming filings to the point that they will show up on a search, that the filing office fixes the "as of" date and time by the state of the records when the search is run, that the filing office takes up to 24 hours to run an "expedited" search, and that the filing office faxes the search to the searcher immediately on completion, what do you do, and in what order? Can you be ready by the scheduled closing date?

■ END OF DEFAULT PROBLEM SET

17.5. In response to your written search request for filings against "John Phillip Smith," the secretary of state sent you a list of 112 financing statements filed against persons with the first name John and the last name Smith. Of those filings, one is against John P. Smith, three are against John Smith, one is against John Philip Smith, Jr., and the remaining 107 are against persons with middle initials other than P or middle names that don't begin with P. Which of the financing statements listed could, as a legal matter, be effective against John Phillip Smith? UCC §9-506(c).

17.6. As the newest associate in the Office of the General Counsel of the Secretary of State, your first assignment is to make a recommendation regarding the search logic for a new computer program that will be used as the exclusive means of searching the UCC filings.

a.   The computer consultants want to know which of the following names should be considered the equivalent of "John Phillip Smith": John Phillip Smyth, John Phillip Smith, Jr., John Philip Smith, Jack Smith.

b.   What is the advantage of returning more names? Fewer names?

17.7.   a.   If the filing office receives an original financing statement on Wednesday, by what day must the filing office index it (and thereby render it searchable)? UCC §§9-519(a) and (h).

b.   If the filing office complies with these sections, the last search report that did not include reference to this financing statement would go out on the following Wednesday. Can you see why? UCC §§9-523(c) and (e).

c.   What happens to a filing office that does not comply with these sections? UCC §§9-524, Comment 8 to UCC §9-523.

17.8.   Find the corporate and UCC filing records of your state online. In nearly every state, both will be maintained by the Secretary of State.

a.   Use the two sets of records to identify a corporation that has one or more UCC filings against it. Print a copy of one of the filings.

b.   Obtain a copy of the Articles of Incorporation and any amendments affecting the debtor's name. (Stop if you would incur fees to proceed further.)

Assignment 18: Article 9 Financing Statements: Other Information

A. Introduction

Financing statements typically are written documents prepared on pre-printed forms or electronic records entered on electronic forms. UCC §9-521 contains standard forms for filing and amending financing statements, but Article 9 does not require their use. The secured party can use its own form or even file a copy of the security agreement as a financing statement.

Filers generally prefer the official form because (1) it prompts them for all required information, (2) the filing fee is typically lower if the form is used, and (3) the filing office can refuse to accept a filing on the official form only for the limited reasons set forth in UCC §9-516(b). Mandatory acceptance is no small advantage because filing officers historically have refused to accept a substantial percentage of all filings they have received.

UCC §9-502(a) requires that three items of information be on an ordinary financing statement for the statement to be effective:

1. The name of the debtor
2. The name of the secured creditor
3. An indication of the collateral covered

UCC §9-520(a) requires the filing officer to refuse to accept a financing statement unless it contains items 1 and 2 and these additional items:

4. The mailing address of the secured creditor. UCC §9-516(b)(4).
5. The mailing address of the debtor. UCC §9-516(b)(5)(A).
6. An indication of whether the debtor is an individual or an organization. UCC §9-516(b)(5)(B).

If a financing statement lacks any of these six pieces of information, other than an indication of the collateral covered, see UCC §9-516(b), the filing officer should refuse to accept it and communicate to the filer both the reason for refusal and the date and time the record would have been filed. UCC §9-520(b). The attempt at filing has accomplished nothing, but, notified of its failure, the filer at least has the opportunity to try again.

This does not mean that the filing officer should refuse filings that contain incorrect information — even if the incorrect information is implausible. Comment 3 to UCC §9-516 provides that "[n]either this section nor Section 9-520 requires or authorizes the filing office to determine, or even consider,

311

the accuracy of information provided in a record." It would seem that if the secured party fills in the key blanks on the financing statement, the filing officer must accept the filing almost irrespective of the content.

B.   Filing Office Errors in Acceptance or Rejection

1.   Wrongly Accepted Filings

If a filing officer mistakenly accepts a filing that contains items 1 through 3 on the above list, but is missing another item or items such that the filing officer was required to reject the filing pursuant to UCC §§9-520(a) and 9-516(b), the filing is nevertheless effective. UCC §9-520(c) and Comment 3 to that section. Why should a filing that the filing officer should have rejected have any effect at all? The answer can be derived from an understanding of how the system functions. First, while the omission might necessitate further inquiry, no one can be misled by the absence of information. The searcher who retrieves a financing statement with blank spaces in it knows it does not have the information that should have been in those blank spaces. The searcher can demand that the debtor provide the information or refuse to lend. Second, if the filing officer had rejected the filing, that would have given the filer the opportunity to correct its error. Because the filing officer accepted it instead, the filer likely will remain unaware of its error until it is too late to correct it. Thus, the effectiveness of the filing saves the filer from its error without inflicting much harm on searchers. Here, as in other decisions they had to make, the drafters were forced to choose between inflicting a burden on filers or on searchers. In this case, they chose to leave it to the searchers to investigate further.

2.   Wrongly Rejected Filings

If the filing officer should accept an initial financing statement, either because it is correct or because the manner in which it is incorrect does not warrant rejection under UCC §9-516, but the filing officer rejects it anyway, then the financing statement will not appear on the public record. Instead, the filing officer will stamp it with the date and time of the attempt to file and return it to the filer. UCC §9-520(b). The failed attempt to file nevertheless perfects the underlying security interest sufficiently to defeat lien creditors. UCC §9-516(d). This is so even though subsequent searchers have no access to the filing and no means of knowing it was made. The explanation for this anomalous result is that the drafters of Article 9 believed (as a matter of faith, not empirical reality) that lien creditors do not search the filing system and therefore cannot be prejudiced by the failure of the financing statement to appear. The non-filing is ineffective against purchasers who are prejudiced by the absence of the record from the filing system. (Recall that, when used in the UCC, "purchasers" includes secured parties, but not lien creditors. UCC §§1-201(b)(29) and (30).) As a result, the drafters reasoned, giving this limited perfected status to security interests for which no filing is on record injures no one.

We will refer to security interests such as these — which are effective against lien creditors, but not sufficient to give constructive notice to purchasers — as "lien-perfected." The mere fact that a filing is lien-perfected is not, however, in itself sufficient to confer priority over secured creditors and other purchasers. UCC §9-338.

C.   Filer Errors in Accepted Filings

If a filer entirely omits from the financing statement a piece of information that is required in UCC §9-516(b), the filing officer can and should reject the filing. UCC §9-520(a). If the required piece of information is merely incorrect, however, that is insufficient reason for rejection. Filing officers are not required to read the filings and are specifically instructed not to evaluate the accuracy of any information contained therein. Properly accepted filings can, and frequently will, contain incorrect information. The effect of errors in the three pieces of information required for effectiveness is different from the effect of errors in the three pieces of information required only to qualify for filing.

1.   Information Necessary Only to Qualify for Filing

The debtor's mailing address, the secured creditor's mailing address, and the indication of whether the debtor is an individual or a corporation are not necessary to the sufficiency of a financing statement. UCC §9-502(a). If the information furnished in response to any or all of these items is merely erroneous (as opposed to omitted entirely), the financing statement qualifies for filing. Such a financing statement, however, will be of limited effectiveness.

Article 9 lumps these limited-effectiveness filings together with wrongly rejected and fully effective filings in the category of "perfected" filings. See, for example, UCC §9-338, referring to limited-effectiveness filings as "perfected." These filings with incorrect UCC §9-516(b)(5) information will be effective against lien creditors, bankruptcy trustees, and others ("lien-perfected"), but not against purchasers who give value and act in reasonable reliance on the incorrect information ("purchaser-perfected"). UCC §9-338.

To illustrate, assume that Firstbank files a financing statement against Debtor Corporation. In filling out the financing statement, Firstbank's employee correctly states the name of the debtor, Firstbank's own name, and the description of collateral, but provides an incorrect mailing address for the debtor. Even if the filing officer notices the error, the filing officer is required to accept the filing. The filing is fully effective against lien creditors, including the trustee in any bankruptcy that Debtor Corporation later files. Only a purchaser who gave value in reasonable reliance on the incorrect information could defeat Firstbank's filing. UCC §9-338.

To understand how a purchaser might give value in reliance on these kinds of information one must consider how searchers use the information. For example, searchers use the debtor's address as a means of determining whether a financing statement relates to their debtor or another debtor with the same name.

To illustrate the problem that may result, assume that First Bank is lending to John P. Smith, who lives in Los Angeles. First Bank conducts a search under that name, which returns 30 filings, all against "John P. Smith" at a San Francisco address. First Bank checks the San Francisco address and discovers that a person named John P. Smith — not First Bank's debtor — lives at that address. First Bank assumes that all 30 filings are against the John P. Smith who lives in San Francisco, and makes the loan. Commercial Finance — one of the 30 filers — in fact lent money to the John P. Smith who lives in Los Angeles. But the clerk who filled out Commercial Finance's financing statement erroneously put the address of the San Francisco John P. Smith on it. Commercial Finance's filing is lien-perfected. Its security interest is subordinated to that of First Bank, however, because First Bank gave value in reasonable reliance upon the incorrect address. UCC §9-338(1).

A financing statement must contain an address for the secured party. UCC §9-516(b)(4). But the failure to include one does not render the financing statement ineffective, UCC §9-502, and an erroneous address cannot be the basis for subordination of the secured party under UCC §9-338. Apparently the only penalty for an erroneous address is that "the secured party is deemed to have received a notification delivered to that address." Comment 5 to UCC §9-516.

2.   Required Information

The debtor's name, the creditor's name, and the indication of collateral are necessary to the effectiveness of the financing statement. If the financing statement substantially complies with the requirement to specify these items, the financing statement will be effective despite "minor errors or omissions unless the errors or omissions make the financing statement seriously misleading." UCC §9-506(a).

In Assignment 17, we considered what errors in the debtor's name will render the financing statement ineffective. Here we consider only errors in the name of the secured party and the indication of collateral. Our theme will be the same as with errors in the debtor's name. Whether an error in a particular item of information is "seriously misleading" depends in part on the function that information serves (or is thought to serve) in the search process. To decide whether errors in financing statement information render the statement seriously misleading, one must first understand why the information is supposed to be there and what impact its omission or distortion can be expected to have on the search process.

a.   Name of the Secured Party.   Searchers may need the name of the secured party for two reasons. First, termination statements, releases of collateral, or subordination agreements are sometimes needed to modify or eliminate prior filings in order to pave the way for the new loan. The name of the secured party on the financing statement tells the searcher who can or must authenticate them. Second, the searcher may need information from the secured party; the secured party's name on the financing statement assures the searcher that it is inquiring of the right person.

This second reason requires some elaboration. The Article 9 filing system is frequently described as a "notice filing" system. See Comment 2 to UCC §9-502. That is, in contrast with the real estate recording system, where recording of the full text of the mortgage may be required, the Article 9 system requires only the recording of a notice of the possible existence of a security agreement. If the searcher wants to know the terms of the security agreement, the searcher is expected to inquire further outside the filing system. The searcher does that by requiring the debtor—typically a person who has applied to the searcher for a loan—to authorize the secured party to furnish information to the searcher. Unless otherwise agreed between the debtor and the secured party, a secured party has the right to respond to a request for credit information (as opposed to bank deposit information) from third parties, but has no obligation to do so. The secured party ordinarily will do so, however, if the debtor so requests, either because of its ongoing business relationship with the debtor or because UCC §9-210 requires the secured party to furnish certain information to the debtor on request. That is, if the secured party refuses to furnish information to the searcher, the debtor will make a formal request for it and the secured party will have to comply. Absent the name of the secured party on the financing statement, the searcher would be dependent on the debtor to tell the searcher of whom it should make these inquiries.

Once one understands that the function of the secured party's name on the financing statement is to identify the holder of the security interest, one should realize that in some cases the secured party's address will be equally necessary. If the secured party's name is John P. Smith, without an address the debtor could steer searchers to any of the hundreds of John P. Smiths in the world. The debtor could easily defraud the searcher by steering the searcher to one who was not the secured party, but would claim to be. But Comment 5 to UCC §9-516 takes the position that the function of the secured party's address is merely to designate a place for sending notices, not to assist in identifying the secured party.

b.   Indication of Collateral.   While a security agreement must contain a description of collateral, a financing statement need only contain an indication of collateral. The difference between the two seems to be only that "all assets" or similar language constitutes an indication, but not a description. UCC §9-504. Courts frequently refer to "descriptions" of collateral in financing statements, and we will do the same. The description of collateral in a financing statement is often identical to that in the security agreement, but that is not always so. For example, a secured creditor may contemplate lending money to the debtor to buy various items of equipment over a period of years. The secured creditor may file a financing statement indicating that the collateral is "equipment," and then, as the debtor buys each item of equipment, the secured creditor may require that the debtor authenticate a security agreement that describes the particular items of equipment. Under these circumstances, the secured creditor will have a perfected security interest in only the equipment described in the security agreements. See UCC §§9-308(a) and 9-203(b)(3)(A). Other equipment owned by the debtor may remain unencumbered.

With the exception already mentioned, the legal standard for adequacy of a financing statement description is the same as that for a security agreement description—that it "reasonably identif[y] the collateral." See UCC §§9-108, 9-504. But given that the description of collateral in a financing statement serves functions different from the description in a security agreement, it should not be surprising if the legal standard is applied differently to the two kinds of descriptions. UCC §9-108 approves of any description that renders the collateral "objectively determinable." To give content to that phrase requires two inquiries. First, what meaning should be assigned to words in the description? When we encountered this issue with regard to descriptions in security agreements in Assignment 9, we concluded that the words should mean whatever the parties intended them to mean provided the intent was expressed objectively. The function of the financing statement, by contrast, is to put searchers on notice of the identity of the collateral. Here, it would make sense to give words their common meaning and to require that they make sense to complete strangers. The second inquiry is how much work can the drafters of the financing statement require of the searcher to link the description to the collateral? In the *Schmidt* case, discussed briefly in Assignment 9, a reference in the description to the ACSC records in another government office required that the searcher (1) know where to look for the ACSC records and (2) go there and look. The court upheld the description. In the *Murphy* case, a reference in the description to whether the item was purchased from the secured creditor required that the searcher (1) somehow obtain access to the records of the store and (2) examine those records. In the *Grabowski* case, the court expressed the traditional view that a filer's description can require a searcher to make inquiry of the secured creditor.

In the case of a financing statement, a creditor may either describe its collateral by "type" or "category" as set forth in §9-108 or may simply indicate its lien on "all assets" of the debtor.

This exceedingly general standard for describing collateral in a financing statement, which is new to the UCC under revised Article 9, is consistent with the "inquiry notice" function of a financing statement under previous law. A financing statement need not specify the property encumbered by a secured party's lien, but need merely notify subsequent creditors that a lien may exist and that further inquiry is necessary "to disclose the complete state of affairs." Uniform Commercial Code Comment 2 [§9-502]. In the present case, Bank of America filed a financing statement indicating it had a lien on the debtors' property consisting of "all inventory, chattel paper, accounts, equipment, and general intangibles." Despite the generality of the Bank's description, it was sufficient to notify subsequent creditors, including South Pointe, that a lien existed on the debtors' property and that further inquiry was necessary to determine the extent of the Bank's lien. For this reason, the Court finds no merit in South Pointe's argument that the description of the Bank's collateral was too general to fulfill the notice function of a financing statement under the UCC.

Grabowski v. Deere & Company (In re Grabowski), 277 B.R. 388 (Bankr. S.D. Ill. 2002).

The court in Teel Construction, Inc. v. Lipper, Inc., 11 UCC Rep. Serv. 2d 667 (Va. Cir. Ct. 1990), took an even more permissive approach to a financing statement description of collateral error than did the court in *Grabowski*. In *Teel*, the financing statement described the collateral as furniture and inventory at a certain address. The address given was nonexistent; the furniture and inventory intended were at another address. The court nevertheless held the financing statement effective, because the particular searcher "knew where Lipper was located and . . . is required to make further inquiry of the secured party in order to determine whether a particular asset is covered by a security agreement."

If our description of *Teel* leaves you wondering just what the function of the description in a financing statement might be, you are not alone. In a classic article, Professor Morris Shanker suggested that descriptions of collateral—in both financing statements and security agreements—should be optional. Shanker, A Proposal for a Simplified All-Embracing Security Interest, 14 UCC L.J. 23, 25-29 (1981). Under Professor Shanker's proposal, if the parties did not include a description, the security interest would reach all property of the debtor rather than none of it, as under current law. Cases like *Grabowski* and *Teel* require the searcher to inquire beyond the description in the financing statement anyway. The searcher can learn what collateral is encumbered from the secured party's statement under UCC §9-210.

The duty to inquire further imposed in cases like *Teel* and *Grabowski* has its limit. In some cases, the description may be so specific as to exclude the possibility that the property in question could be collateral.

[handwritten margin note: 9-210 / secured party / statement]

In re Pickle Logging, Inc.

286 B.R. 181 (Bankr. M.D. Ga. 2002)

John T. Laney, III, United States Bankruptcy Judge.

Pickle Logging, Inc. ("Debtor") is an Americus, Georgia based company doing business in the tree logging industry. In an effort to cure an arrearage to Deere Credit, Inc. ("Movant"), Debtor refinanced eight pieces of equipment. The refinancing was done with Movant.

On April 18, 2002, Debtor filed for Chapter 11 bankruptcy protection. At a hearing held on August 16, 2002 the present issue was raised: whether Movant had a perfected security interest in one specific piece of equipment, a 548G skidder serial number DW548GX568154 ("548G skidder"), which had been mislabeled in both the financing statement and the security agreement as a 648G skidder, serial number DW648GX568154. After hearing testimony from expert witnesses that a 548G skidder is substantially different in appearance, performance, and price from a 648G skidder, the court held that Movant did not have a perfected security interest in the 548G skidder because of the mislabeling. Therefore, Movant was an unsecured creditor as to the 548G skidder. Movant has asked the court to reconsider.

The question is whether Movant's security interest in the 548G skidder is perfected despite the mislabeling on the security agreement and the financing statement.

Pursuant to [UCC §9-203(b)(3)(A)], a security interest in collateral is not enforceable against the debtor or third parties unless the debtor has signed, executed, or otherwise adopted a security agreement that contains a description of the collateral. See also [UCC §9-102(a)(7)]. The description of the collateral in the security agreement and the financing statement, if required, must comport with [UCC §9-108(a)]. See also [UCC §9-504(1)]. The description of collateral is sufficient if it reasonably identifies what is described. See [UCC §9-108(a)]. "The question of the sufficiency of [a] description of [collateral] in a [recorded document] is one of law." Bank of Cumming v. Chapman, 264 S.E.2d 201 (Ga. 1980).

Any number of things could be used to describe collateral and satisfy [UCC §9-108(a)]. A physical description of the collateral, including or excluding a serial number, could be used so long as it "reasonably identifies what is described." The description merely needs to raise a red flag to a third party indicating that more investigation may be necessary to determine whether or not an item is subject to a security agreement. A party does not lose its secured status just because the description includes an inaccurate serial number. However, if the serial number is inaccurate, there must be additional information that provides a "key" to the collateral's identity.

Here, the description in the security agreement and the financing statement are identical. Both documents list a 648G skidder with the serial number DW648GX568154. There is nothing obviously wrong with the model number or the serial number. 648G is a model number for one type skidder sold by Movant. The serial number listed for the disputed skidder is in accordance with other serial numbers issued by Movant.

According to testimony at the August 16, 2002 hearing, Debtor owned more than one of Movant's skidders, including at least two 548G skidders and at least two 648G skidders. There is nothing in either the financing statement or the security agreement that raises a red flag to a third party. A potential purchaser of the 548G skidder in dispute here could easily assume that the skidder is not covered by either the security agreement or the financing statement.

If just the model number was incorrect or if just the serial number was incorrect, the result may be different. It is apparent from the other items listed on the security agreement and the financing statement that the model number is reflected in the serial number. If the model number was not repeated in the serial number, then it would be apparent that something was wrong with one of the two numbers. At a minimum it should raise a red flag to a person of ordinary business prudence that further investigation is necessary. However, with both of the numbers reflecting a 648G skidder, there is nothing to indicate that there was a mistake.

Therefore, the court's order dated September 3, 2002 will not be changed. The 548G skidder is misdescribed in both the security agreement and the financing statement. The rights of Debtor, as a hypothetical lien creditor, are superior to the rights of Movant.

Pickle Logging invalidates a security interest in a situation where both the debtor and the secured party intended one. The invalidation may cause other filers to be more careful in drafting descriptions. It may also enable searchers to ignore a filing that, by its terms, does not include the collateral the searcher plans to take. But the searcher still must consider the possibility that other judges might not decide the case in the same way this one did.

D.   Authorization to File a Financing Statement

The purpose of a financing statement is to advise later lenders of the existence of a prior security interest. If a prior interest exists, the later lender may insist on different terms or decline to lend at all. Consequently, the presence of an incorrect or unauthorized financing statement in the filing system can interfere with the ability of the party named as debtor to borrow money.

To illustrate, assume that a financing statement discovered by State Bank in its search under "Teel, Inc.," showed "Alan Berkowitz" to be the secured party. Teel insisted that Berkowitz was not its secured creditor, but when State Bank contacted Berkowitz, he said he was. Even if State Bank believed Teel, the bank might not be willing to make the loan. The bank may fear that its belief was wrong or that, even if it wasn't, the loan might involve the bank in litigation with Berkowitz. Because of the uncertainty it creates, any filing that *might* encumber particular property makes that property difficult to sell or use as collateral. The title to possibly encumbered property is referred to as "clouded." Most lenders are reluctant to go forward until they can be certain that the title can be "cleared" and the "cloud lifted."

Until 2001, Article 9 provided that a financing statement was sufficient to perfect only if it was signed by the debtor. Even with that requirement in place, the filing of unauthorized financing statements was a significant problem. Prisoners, tax protesters, supporters of the Republic of Texas, and other political protesters realized how easy it was to cloud title to someone's property in the Article 9 filing system — or other filing systems — and filed bogus financing statements to accomplish that. Of course, the victim of a bogus filing could sue, prove the bogus nature of the filing, and have it declared invalid. See, e.g., United States v. Greenstreet, 912 F. Supp. 224 (N.D. Tex. 1996) (holding that the "political" filing of a financing statement by a farmer was ineffective because the alleged debtors had not signed it). But lawsuits are expensive and the victim cannot pass the cost on to a judgment-proof prisoner or protester. Recognizing the ineffectiveness of the signature requirement in protecting public officials and others from bogus liens, some states allow filing offices to reject obviously fraudulent financing statements, and other states provide expedited administrative or judicial procedures to expunge fraudulent financing statements. Sixteen states have criminalized the filing of fraudulent financing statements.

In the 2001 revision, the drafters of Article 9 also decided to abandon the requirement of a signature on a financing statement. The immediate impetus was to facilitate electronic filing of financing statements by high-volume financial institutions. Electronic filings could include debtors' signatures only if those filings included graphics. The UCC filing offices were not up to that technological challenge.

The new system for the prevention of unauthorized filings works as follows. Before filing a financing statement, the secured creditor must obtain authorization from the debtor in an authenticated record. See UCC §9-509(a)(1) ("A person may file [a] financing statement . . . only if the debtor authorizes the filing in an authenticated record."). To make it easy for the secured creditor to obtain such authorization, UCC §9-509(b) provides that "By authenticating a security agreement, a debtor authorizes the filing of [a] financing statement covering the collateral described in the security agreement." Thus, all the creditor need do to obtain the right to file a financing statement against collateral is what it already had to do to become a secured creditor: get the debtor to authenticate a security agreement describing the collateral.

If the person filing a financing statement is not authorized, the financing statement is ineffective. See UCC §9-510(a). That alone, however, will not lift the cloud on title, because the would-be lender still has no way to assure itself that its would-be debtor did not authorize the filing. UCC §9-518 allows the victim of a bogus filing to file an "information statement" that will show up on searches. But the information statement does not lift the cloud on title either. The bogus filing was ineffective without the information statement and remains ineffective after it is filed. UCC §9-518(c). The problem is that the would-be lender has no way to know that the bogus filing is unauthorized and therefore ineffective other than to know and trust its borrower.

With these changes, the Article 9 filing system now stands in stark contrast to the real estate system. Real estate systems typically require not only that the debtor sign the mortgage, but that the signature be both witnessed and *acknowledged*. The witnesses themselves must sign the mortgages. Acknowledgment is before a notary public or other official licensed by the state for that purpose. The notary is supposed to determine the identity of the person making the signature and place the notary's seal on the statement of acknowledgment. If the relatively recent, signature-less system of Article 9 is successful, the real estate system will probably come under pressure to follow the same path.

E.   UCC Insurance

Errors in filing and searching can put millions of dollars at risk. In real estate transactions, the roughly corresponding problems are often dealt with by purchasing title insurance. In recent years, some firms have begun offering a roughly analogous product under the name "UCC insurance." UCC insurance, like title insurance, covers the risk of most kinds of errors in the filing and search processes.

Perhaps the most important difference between the two kinds of insurance stems from the fact that the UCC system does not cover title to collateral. As a result, UCC insurance does not insure against the possibility that the debtor does not own the collateral. It does, however, cover some aspects of attachment, perfection, and priority.

Problem Set 18

18.1.   a.   It's nearly 5:00 on Friday afternoon and you are working on an initial financing statement that *has* to be filed today. You just realized that you don't know your reclusive debtor's mailing address, and there is no way to get it before Monday. Would you be better off leaving that box on the financing statement blank or filling in the address of the vacant lot next door to your office? UCC §§9-520(a) and 9-516(b)(5); Comment 3 to UCC §9-516.

b.   Under pressure, you filled in the address of the vacant lot next door and sent the financing statement to the filing office. The filing office sent the financing statement back to you with a rejection notice stating that the United States Postal Service does not recognize that address. If you don't do anything else, are you perfected? UCC §§9-308(a), 9-310(a) and (b), 9-502(a), 9-516(a), (b)(5), and (d), Comment 3 to UCC §9-516.

c.   Contrary to the facts of *b*, the filing office accepted your financing statement with the incorrect address. Are you perfected? Do you need to take any further action? UCC §§9-520(a) and (c), 9-338.

d.   Rule 8.4 of the Model Rules of Professional Conduct provides that "It is professional misconduct for a lawyer to . . . engage in conduct involving dishonesty, fraud, deceit or misrepresentation." Did you violate that rule?

18.2.   You represent Eric Bradford, a trustee in bankruptcy. One of the duties of a trustee is to examine the financing statements filed by secured creditors for irregularities. Bankruptcy Code §544(a) gives trustees the power to avoid security interests not sufficiently perfected to withstand attack by a lien creditor. That includes any that are unperfected and for which a required financing statement was not filed. See UCC §9-317(a). In cases currently pending, Bradford noted the following irregularities in filed financing statements. Which of the cases should the trustee pursue? Identify any additional information that would help in your evaluation. UCC §§9-502(a), 9-516(b), (d), 9-520(c), and 9-506.

a.   The irregularity is the complete absence of any address for the secured party. The secured party's name is listed as "Roger Fisk." Comment 5 to UCC §9-516; Comment 3 to UCC §9-520.

b.   The irregularity is the indication of collateral in the financing statement as "proceeds from any lawsuit due or pending." At the time the security agreement was signed, the debtor corporation had a $450,000 patent infringement lawsuit pending. After the debtor filed bankruptcy, the court entered judgment for the debtor. UCC §9-108(e) and the last paragraph of Comment 5, UCC §§9-102(a)(13), 9-204(b)(2), Comment 2 to 9-204, and 9-504.

c.   The irregularity is the use of the secured creditor's trade name, Will's Furniture and Appliances, instead of its true name, Wardcorp, Inc. UCC §§9-503(a), (b), and (c), Comment 2 to UCC §9-506.

d.   The irregularity is that the secured creditor's name is listed as "Elizabeth Warren" instead of the correct name, "Lynn M. LoPucki." The paralegal who filled out the financing statement said, "I don't know why I wrote Elizabeth Warren; I really meant to write Lynn M. LoPucki. I guess I got a little confused." UCC §9-506(a); Comment 2 to UCC §9-506.

e.   The irregularity is in the description of the collateral as "Pizza ovens, equipment, and fixtures located at 621 State Street, Madison, Wisconsin." The particular ovens, equipment, and fixtures covered by the security agreement have been at 514 East Washington Avenue, Madison, Wisconsin, at all relevant times. The debtor is Stoney's Pizza Parlour, Inc., a company that has operated stores at both locations at all relevant times. The creditor is Wisconsin State Bank. UCC §§9-504, 9-108.

f.   The irregularity is the complete absence of a description of collateral. The debtor is "Holiday Inn of Westport, Inc." and the creditor is Missouri State Bank. Correct addresses were given for both.

18.3.   After three years of litigation, your client, Ron Smith, has won a judgment against his former employer, the Subterranean Circus, Inc. (SCI), in the amount of $76,000. SCI's lawyer says you might as well forget about collecting—the company has no unencumbered assets. Your UCC search suggests otherwise. There are five financing statements, all showing Glacier Bank as the secured party. Each describes the collateral as "fixtures and equipment located at [a particular address]." The address of the SCI store on Trimble Avenue is not on any of the financing statements and there is no other public record showing any kind of lien against the fixtures and equipment located there. You know from talking with the landlord at the Trimble Avenue location that the fixtures and equipment were installed new and had never been used in any other store. Smith wants to levy on the Trimble Avenue store if the furniture and equipment there are not encumbered, but he is afraid of getting "bogged down in more litigation" if they are.

a.   If Glacier Bank's security agreement includes as collateral the fixtures and equipment located in the Trimble Avenue store, is it possible that Glacier is perfected against them?

b.   What's your next move?

18.4.   You represent Glacier Bank. You get a telephone call from a respectable law firm that represents Ron Smith, a creditor with a $76,000 judgment against SCI, one of Glacier's borrowers. Smith wants to know if Glacier's security interest encumbers the equipment and leasehold at SCI's Trimble Avenue store. In fact, Glacier was supposed to have a security interest in the Trimble assets, but someone did a poor job of drafting.

a.   What do you say to the lawyer?

b.   Would the situation be different if the law firm's client was another bank that had a loan application from SCI? UCC §9-210.

18.5.   Walter's Department Store (from Problem 9.2) has been taking security interests in everything purchased from them on the store's credit card accounts. Last week, Walter's lost two riding lawn mowers that were collateral under their security agreements to neighbors of Walter's bankrupt customers. Unaware of Walter's security interests, the neighbors had purchased the lawn mowers from the debtors prior to bankruptcy. See UCC §9-320(b). When you mentioned to Walter that Walter's would have won the cases had it filed financing statements, Walter asked you to look into doing just that on every Walter's credit card account. Specifically, Walter has the following questions for you.

a.   Does Walter's need permission from each of the thousands of customers involved to file these financing statements? UCC §§9-102(a)(39), 9-509(a), (b), 9-510(a).

b.   What should Walter's use for a description of collateral? UCC §§9-504, 9-108, 9-625(e)(3).

c.   Can you think of any practical problems that are likely to arise?

■ End of Default Problem Set

18.6.   When Kenneth Kettering applied to Second National Bank to borrow money against his restaurant, Fisherman's Pier, the first thing the bank did was to file a financing statement on the form set forth in UCC §9-521. The bank told Kenneth they were filing the statement and Kenneth said that was OK, but nobody thought to get him to sign it because the form has no place for a signature. The bank filed the financing statement on March 1 and conducted a search through that date. The search was clean, and the bank closed on the $320,000 loan on March 15. At the closing, Kenneth signed a security agreement. Two days after the closing, Kenneth disappeared. When the bank searched the title to Fisherman's Pier to prepare for foreclosure, it discovered a financing statement in favor of NationsBank that had been filed March 10. Further inquiry revealed that Kenneth had borrowed $330,000 from NationsBank just before he disappeared. Second National Bank consults you because NationsBank has asked to see the authenticated record authorizing the filing of Second National's financing statement.

a.   Exactly what record would that be? UCC §§9-322(a)(1) and Comment 4, 9-502(d), 9-509(a) and (b), 9-510(a).

b.   Should Second National change its procedures? If so, how?

18.7.   Draft a financing statement to perfect the security interest you took in problem 9.8 and file it with your teacher as filing officer. Standard search logic is in effect unless your teacher otherwise instructs. Do not send filing fees or a formal cover letter. We recommend use of the official form in UCC §9-521. Copies of that form are available in data-enabled pdf format on many UCC filing office websites. Such a form can be completed electronically. Keep a copy of what you file, in case there is a problem with the filing office. UCC §§9-502(a), 9-504, 9-509(a) and (b); 9-516(a) and (b).

Assignment 19: Exceptions to the Article 9 Filing Requirement

For most kinds of security interests, perfection is accomplished by a public record filing. If the filing is not made, the security interest remains unperfected. But there are a number of exceptions to the filing requirement. In this assignment we explore several ways a secured creditor might perfect a security interest without filing.

There are essentially three other ways to perfect. First, a secured party can perfect in some kinds of collateral by taking possession. Second, a secured creditor can perfect in some kinds of collateral by taking control. Third, with respect to other kinds of collateral, a secured creditor may enjoy automatic perfection by operation of law.

Problems involving exceptions to the filing requirement can be analyzed in much the same way as filing problems. Begin by categorizing the collateral. Determine whether perfection will be governed by Article 9, the real estate recording statutes, or other law. Finally, determine what, if anything, that law requires for perfection.

A. Collateral in the Possession of the Secured Party

1. The Possession-Gives-Notice Theory

Both Article 9 and real estate recording statutes recognize *possession* of some kinds of collateral as a substitute for public notice filing. The Article 9 exception appears in UCC §§9-310(b)(6) and 9-313(a). The latter section permits perfection by taking "possession" of the collateral if the collateral is "negotiable documents, goods, instruments, money, or tangible chattel paper."

In functional terms, this exception to the filing requirement is grounded on two assumptions. First, a person who buys or lends against certain kinds of collateral (we will refer to this person as the *searcher*) will look at the collateral before lending against it. Second, looking at collateral in the "possession" of a secured party will alert the searcher to the possible existence of a security interest. We will refer to these two assumptions as the *possession-gives-notice theory*.

Under the possession-gives-notice theory, to require filing with regard to collateral in the "possession" of the secured party would be redundant. Possession would give actual notice to the diligent searcher. In accord with this theory, both Article 9 and real estate recording laws assume that when a secured party is in possession of the collateral, searchers will or should realize that the secured party may have an interest in the property. Based on that assumption, they provide that possession constitutes constructive notice to

324

the searcher and treat the searcher essentially as if the searcher had actual notice of the interest.

To illustrate both the theory and its shortcomings, assume that Thomas Olszynski borrows money from the Seminole Bank & Trust company, using his cast iron lawn dog as collateral. Olszynski drags the lawn dog to the loan closing (on a cart specially made for that purpose). The banker gives Olszynski a check for the loan proceeds and Olszynski turns the lawn dog over to the banker. The banker drags the lawn dog into the bank's vault, unloads it from the cart, and places it among the bags of money. There it will remain until the loan is repaid or the lien foreclosed by sale. Although the Bank does not file a financing statement, the bank will be perfected so long as it retains possession. If Olszynski manages to sell the lawn dog or borrow from some other lender using the lawn dog as collateral while it remains in the bank vault, the law will have no sympathy for that buyer or lender. Had the buyer or lender demanded to see the lawn dog before buying it or lending against it, the buyer or lender would have discovered that it was in the bank vault. Had they known that, the theory goes, they should have been able to figure out that the bank had a security interest in it.

By positing a situation in which the secured party was clearly, unmistakably in possession of the collateral, the lawn-dog-in-the-vault example makes the possession-gives-notice theory appear more reasonable than it is. Even so, the theory stumbles on application of the second assumption: Searchers should be able to guess the meaning of the bank's possession. The facts of a litigated (but unreported) case illustrate the ambiguity. In that case, the debtor solicited investments in a solid gold statue. At all relevant times, the bank held the statue in its vault as collateral for a loan. The debtor told the investors that the bank was holding the statue for safekeeping. Some of the investors viewed the statue. They did not ask whether the bank claimed a security interest in the statue, and the bank did not tell them. Perhaps the particular employee who shepherded them into the room where they viewed the statue did not even know that the bank claimed an interest in it. The investors could see that the bank had immediate control of the statue, but that is hardly the equivalent of a sign that says, "This bank claims a security interest in this gold statue."

Because the investors in the gold statue case were legally unsophisticated, possession did not make them actually aware of the bank's interest. But by operation of law, it constructively gave them notice. The bank prevailed in the case on the theory that the bank was perfected by possession of the statue. The case illustrates an important characteristic of the law governing secured transactions: It favors the more knowledgeable parties who engage in these transactions repeatedly, at the expense of people who stumble occasionally into a system in which "everybody" knows things that they do not.

2.   What Is Possession?

Black's Law Dictionary (10th ed. 2014) gives two definitions for the word "possession": "1. the fact of having or holding property in one's power 2. The right under which one may exercise control over something to the exclusion of all others." These definitions show possession to be not merely an observable fact, but in many situations to depend ultimately on the legal right of the would-be possessor. (When the legal right is devoid of physical control, some courts may refer to the possession as "constructive.")

To illustrate, assume that Oneida Schwin is a law student who lives alone in a rented apartment. At the moment, she is in class. Is she in possession of the television set she owns and that sits on a table in her apartment? We have no doubt that she is. We don't think it matters that Betty the Burglar is immediately outside the door of the apartment or that the door is unlocked. Right now, Betty can more easily exercise power over the television than Oneida, but Oneida remains in possession. Why? Because Oneida has the *right* to control the television, while Betty does not. Oneida has possession not solely from power, but in large part from legal right.

Oneida probably remains in possession of the television even after Betty enters the living room. A searcher who knocks on the door and is greeted by a smiling Betty would almost certainly conclude that Betty is in possession of the television, but the searcher would be wrong. The law looks to legal right, not just physical fact, to determine who is in possession, and once we recognize this we can see that the law's definition of "possession" is at least in part circular. We look to possession to see who has rights and we look to rights to see who has possession.

The legal *right* to control is not determinative of possession. At the moment Betty picks up the television, the observable fact of physical control so overwhelms the legal right to control that we think most courts would say that possession has passed to Betty. Some courts would refer to this as "naked" possession to recognize that few of the attributes of ideal possession had passed to Betty. (The word "naked" also spices up otherwise dull legal opinions.)

A secured party can possess collateral through an agent. See UCC §9-313, Comment 3. Like ownership, agency might be invisible to the searcher. A case one of us litigated will illustrate. The author represented a plaintiff oil company that won the right to possession of a gasoline service station. The order was entered on a Friday afternoon, after the sheriff's office had closed for the weekend. The debtor, another oil company, remained in "possession" and continued to sell the inventory and collect the money. Author and client went to the station and saw that an employee of the debtor oil company was the only person on the premises. The employee had the keys to the building and he sat behind the counter. Was he in possession? The answer is no. The debtor oil company was in possession through him as its agent. Yet, given that the signs on the premises disclosed only the brand of gasoline sold, not the name of the defendant oil company, the true possessor would have been invisible to a searcher who happened by at that moment.

The client introduced himself to the employee, showed him the court's order for possession, and asked if he would like a new job (very much like his current job). Undoubtedly seeing the limited future in the position he then held, the employee said yes. The two agreed on terms, one of which was that the new job started immediately. As author and client walked back to their car, every condition observable to a searcher who looked at the premises was identical to what it had been before. The same employee sat beneath the same sign, collecting money from the same customers in the same way. But assuming the validity of the new employment agreement, the client's oil company was now in possession. Here again, possession shows itself to be a legal construct, not the observable fact some theorists posit it to be.))

possession is legal fact not observable fact

B.   *Possession as a Means of Perfection*

Depending on the type of collateral involved, possession may play any of three roles in the perfection of security interests. Possession is an alternative form of perfection for some types of collateral, an ineffective form for other types of collateral, and, as we discuss later in this section, the sole means of perfecting a security interest in money. UCC §9-312(b)(3). If a debtor offers cash as collateral for a loan, the lender can perfect its security interest only by taking possession.

9-312(b)(3) SI in money

A secured party can perfect in goods, negotiable documents, instruments, tangible chattel paper, and certified securities by filing or taking possession. UCC §§9-312(a), 9-313(a). With respect to instruments, tangible chattel paper, and certified securities, however, a competing secured party that takes possession could, in statutorily defined circumstances, gain priority over an earlier secured party that perfected by filing. UCC §9-330(b), (d). For that reason, secured parties should perfect in those three categories of collateral by possession when practical. (For certified securities "control" is a yet more preferred method.) Filing against any of the five categories of collateral is, however, fully effective against lien creditors and trustees in bankruptcy.

9-312(a) 9-313(a) perfect in goods

9-330(b)(d)

Negotiable documents are outside the scope of this book. "Negotiable documents" is a defined term that includes negotiable warehouse receipts, negotiable bills of lading, and similar documents, but the term does *not* include negotiable promissory notes. See UCC §9-102(a)(30) and the definition of "document of title" in UCC §1-201.

That one can perfect in goods by filing or by possession is good news for the secured creditor who may find one method easier or cheaper than the other in particular circumstances. It is, however, bad news for the searcher who is trying to discover the previous security interest. The effect of such liberalization of the perfection requirement is to impose an additional burden on the searcher. Whenever the collateral subject to a security interest includes goods, the searcher must check both the filing system and the collateral.

For some kinds of collateral, perfection by possession is impossible. Security interests in accounts and general intangibles may be perfected only by filing or automatically; they may not be perfected by possession. UCC §9-313(a). At the most basic level, the rule may be explained by saying that these kinds of property are intangible and therefore incapable of being possessed, but the law can render intangible property tangible simply by recognizing some tangible object as the embodiment of the intangible rights. Thus the secured party who takes possession of a negotiable promissory note is regarded as having perfected in the right to payment it represents. UCC §9-313(a). Similarly, the secured party who takes possession of a negotiable warehouse receipt or bill of lading is regarded as having perfected its interest in the goods in the warehouse or in the hands of the carrier. UCC §9-312(c).

SI in account general intangibles Not by possession 9-313(a)

Notice the circular nature of this explanation: Because the law does not designate a particular document as the embodiment of the promise, the law does not recognize seizure of any document as perfecting the creditor's interest. It might seem that the law could easily resolve the problem by designating a particular document. For example, it might make the certificates issued by the state for liquor licenses or automobile titles the "physical embodiments" of liquor licenses and automobiles. Perfection could then be accomplished by taking possession of the certificates. In neither case would there be a competing document that might be seized by a competing creditor, yet in neither case has the law chosen to take this step.

To understand why the drafters of the law have not taken this step, one need only imagine that they did, for example, by designating the original certificate issued by the state to be the physical embodiment of a liquor license and decreeing that secured creditors can perfect by taking possession of the certificate. The problems that might arise would be numerous. If the state's liquor laws required that the original of the certificate be posted on the debtor's premises, the debtor could not give possession to a secured creditor. The original would have to be distinguishable from copies. For possession of accounts, the law would have to designate some document as the one the secured creditors must possess. The most difficult problem would be informing the millions of people who give or take security interests in accounts precisely how to perfect by possession and how to know if someone else has done so.

To avoid these kinds of problems, the law recognizes physical objects as embodying intangible rights only when business people do. Business practice plays the tune and the law dances, not the other way around.

Ultimately, the impossibility of perfection by possession in accounts and general intangibles results from the lack of any commercial function to be served. Those who want to perfect by taking possession of their debtors' accounts can require their debtors to obtain negotiable promissory notes from the account debtors. The use of negotiable warehouse receipts and bills of lading saves time and effort for those who use them; nobody has yet figured out a way to save significant time and effort by making liquor licenses or copyrights negotiable. If someone did, we suspect there would be pressure to recognize certificates as "embodiments" of these otherwise intangible rights.

By excluding the possibility of perfection by filing, Article 9 protects those who accept money from the possibility that a prior security interest was perfected by filing. The intent is to encourage free negotiability of money, unhampered by the need to conduct searches in the Article 9 filing system. Both "money" and "instrument" are carefully defined in the UCC, and refer only to specialized kinds of property. UCC §§1-201(b)(24) and 9-102(a)(47).

UCC §9-312(a) permits the perfection of security interests in both instruments and chattel paper by filing. Permitting the perfection of security interests by filing in either of these types of collateral might seem to interfere with their negotiability. But UCC §9-330 protects the "purchasers" who take possession of chattel paper or instruments from security interests perfected in them by filing. Because "purchaser" is defined to include those who take a security interest in the chattel paper or instruments as well as those who buy them, the effect is to give priority to some of those who perfect by taking possession over those who perfect by filing. What good is a security interest perfected by filing in these kinds of collateral? It is easy to take and it beats the trustee in bankruptcy — which was probably the whole point of permitting perfection by filing.

Negotiability — essentially the ability to treat the holder of an instrument or money as the owner of it — is of declining commercial importance. Advances in communications and data storage make it progressively easier to identify the source and ownership of funds. Under the old technology, there were many legitimate reasons for transactions in cash, bearer bonds, or notes endorsed in blank. Today there are few, with the result that large cash transactions are suspect and regulated.

B.   Collateral in the Control of the Secured Party

Article 9 recognizes "control" of some kinds of collateral as a substitute for filing. They include deposit accounts, electronic chattel paper, investment property, and letter of credit rights. UCC §9-310(b)(8). Because the methods for taking control differ for each of these four types of collateral and each is in itself a substantial topic, we focus here on deposit accounts and investment property.

9-310(b)(8)

1.   Deposit Accounts

A "deposit account" is the type of property generally referred to as a bank account. See UCC §9-102(a)(29). However, that definition excludes instruments, a term whose definition includes one type of bank account — a bank account represented by a certificate of deposit that can be transferred by indorsement and delivery to the transferee.

UCC §9-104 indicates three ways that a secured party can take "control" of a deposit account. First, the secured party can be the bank in which the account is maintained. Second, the debtor, the secured party, and the bank can authenticate a record instructing the bank to comply with the secured party's instructions with regard to the account. Third, the secured party can become the bank's "customer" by putting the account in the name of the secured party. See UCC §4-104 (defining "customer" as "a person having an account with a bank . . . including a bank that maintains an account at another bank.").

9-104-control of deposit account

The control required to perfect in a deposit account is undermined by UCC §9-104(b), which provides that the secured party's "control" is not abrogated by permitting the debtor to retain "the right to direct the disposition of funds from the deposit account." That is, the secured party is in "control" of the account even though the debtor can write checks on the account and perhaps withdraw the entire amount. The "control" specified in UCC §9-104 is potential control, not actual control.

What kind of notice does control of a bank account give? If the account is in the name of the secured creditor, persons dealing with the debtor can hardly be misled. Anyone attempting to confirm the existence of the debtor's ownership of the account will discover the secured creditor's interest. If the secured party is the bank in which the debtor maintains the account, the drafters of Article 9 assert that "[n]o other form of public notice is necessary; all actual and potential creditors of the debtor are always on notice that the bank with which the debtor's deposit account is maintained may assert a claim against the deposit account." We doubt the drafters were naive enough to think that all or substantially all creditors actually know that a depositary bank can claim the account ahead of them. What they must mean is that they have declared the creditors to be on constructive notice of it.

Parties who wish to encumber a deposit account without putting other creditors on notice could do so by agreement. UCC §9-104(a)(2) does not require that the agreement be filed or made public in any way. UCC §9-342. Those sections simply authorize secret liens.

2. Investment Property

UCC §9-102(a)(49) defines "investment property" as "a security . . . security entitlement, securities account, commodity contract, or commodity account." "Securities" are investment mediums such as stock, bonds, and commodities contracts. To qualify as "securities," the particular medium must be (1) transferable, (2) divisible (that is, there are many shares, bonds, or contracts with the same rights), and (3) a type of medium that is traded in securities markets or securities exchanges. UCC §8-102(a)(15).

The ownership interests in a corporation are usually divided into shares of stock. The ownership interests in a partnership or limited liability company are usually divided into shares or interests. If the terms of those shares or interests so provide, they can be securities governed by Article 8, UCC §8-103(c), and many of the rules set forth below will apply. If they are intended to be traded, the debt obligations of a corporation, partnership, or limited liability company are divided into bonds or notes. Bonds typically are each in the amount of $1,000. If the corporation issues a certificate showing the number of shares or bonds a holder owns, the security is "certificated." UCC §8-102(a) (4). If the corporation merely records the name of the holder and the number of shares or bonds on its own records, the security is "uncertificated." UCC §8-102(a)(18).

A security interest in a security, certificated or uncertificated, may be perfected (1) by filing, UCC §9-312(a), (2) by taking delivery, UCC §§8-106(c)(1), 8-301, 9-313(a), 9-314, or (3) by taking control of the security, UCC §9-106(a). With respect to an uncertificated security, delivery and control occur when the issuer registers the purchaser or the purchaser's non-securities intermediary representative, as the owner. UCC §8-301(b).

The security interest of a secured party having control of investment property has priority over the security interest of a secured party that does not have control. UCC §9-328(1). Control is thus the best method of perfection and so the most important. For a secured party to have control of a certificated security, the certificate must be delivered to the secured party with any necessary indorsement or the certificate must be delivered to the secured party and registered in the secured party's name. Delivery may be by transfer of possession of the certificate to the secured creditor or by the certificate holder's acknowledgment that it holds for the secured creditor. UCC §§8-106(b), 8-301(a). A secured party can take control of an uncertificated security by registering itself as the owner of the security on the records of the corporation. UCC §§8-106(c) and 8-301(b).

A purchaser of securities that registers its ownership with the issuing corporation—with or without obtaining a certificate—is referred to as "directly holding" the security. Most purchasers of securities, however, do not hold them directly. Instead, a brokerage firm—referred to as a "securities intermediary" §8-102(a)(14)—buys the securities on their behalf and acknowledges the investor's ownership in a monthly statement of account. Article 9 refers to such an investor's rights as a "securities entitlement" and a "securities account." Such ownership is referred to as "indirect holding" of the securities.

Although securities entitlements and accounts may appear to their owners to contain uncertificated securities, they seldom do. Most large, public companies have issued certificates for the bulk of their shares to the Depository Trust & Clearing Corporation (DTCC), making the shares "certificated securities." The major stock brokerages have securities accounts with the DTCC. Thus, the stock brokerages hold certificated securities, UCC §8-102(a)(4), but they hold them indirectly. The brokerages, like their customers, own securities entitlements, not securities.

A secured party perfects an interest in a securities entitlement by becoming the entitlement holder or obtaining the securities intermediary's agreement that the latter will comply with the secured party's instructions regarding the entitlement. UCC §8-106(d). For example, if Iman opens a securities account with Merrill Lynch and buys 100 shares of Microsoft stock, Iman owns both a securities account and a securities entitlement to 100 shares of the Microsoft stock owned—probably also as a securities entitlement—by Merrill Lynch. If Iman borrows money from Citibank using the 100 shares as collateral, Citibank might perfect in the shares by becoming Merrill Lynch's customer on the account or by obtaining Merrill Lynch's agreement that Merrill Lynch will follow Citibank's instructions with regard to the account. UCC §8-106(d).

▶ HALF ASSIGNMENT ENDS

C. Automatic Perfection of Purchase-Money Security Interests in Consumer Goods

UCC §9-309(1) creates an exception to the filing requirement for most purchase-money security interests in consumer goods. Security interests that meet the terms of this exception are considered "automatically" perfected. To understand this exception to the filing requirement, one must understand the two concepts from which it is constructed: (1) purchase-money security interest and (2) consumer goods. Each of these concepts is employed elsewhere in the law governing secured transactions, but this is as good a place to study them as any.

1.   Purchase-Money Security Interest (PMSI)

UCC §9-103(b)(1) defines "purchase-money security interest." Unfortunately, the definition is so tangled and complex as to be almost unreadable. Simply put, a security interest is purchase-money to the extent that it secures (1) an obligation to pay the purchase price of the collateral or (2) an obligation to repay a loan, the proceeds of which were intended to be used and were actually used to pay the purchase price of the collateral.

Purchase-money security interests arise in two situations, which correspond to the two parts of the definition in the preceding paragraph. In the simplest situation Pauline Reed buys a piano from Sweigert's Pianos for an agreed price of $20,000. She pays $1,000 down and signs a note promising to pay the remaining $19,000 to Sweigert's. If the note is secured by a security interest in the piano, it is a purchase-money security interest.

In the second situation, Reed makes application to Friendly Finance for a loan that will enable her to buy the piano. She signs a promissory note for $19,000 and a security agreement listing the piano she is about to purchase as collateral. Friendly lends her the $19,000 and she uses that money, together with $1,000 of her savings, to buy the piano from Sweigert's. In the most common form of this transaction, Friendly pays the $19,000 loan proceeds directly to Sweigert's or makes a check out to Reed and Sweigert's jointly to make sure the money is "in fact so used." Notice that from Reed's point of view, this transaction reaches the same end point as the simpler one: Reed pays $1,000 to own the piano subject to a $19,000 security interest. The difference is that in the first transaction, the seller of the piano became the secured creditor; in the second, a third party who provided the financing for the purchase became the secured creditor.

A secured lender can easily lose the purchase-money status of its interest. If, for example, Reed deposits the $19,000 loan proceeds from Friendly to her bank account and then writes a $20,000 check to Sweigert's Pianos, a question may arise as to whether the loan proceeds were in fact used to buy the piano. Assume, for example, that before she deposited the check to her account, the account already contained $21,000 from her income tax refund and her monthly paycheck. Did Reed pay for the piano with the loan proceeds, her tax refund, or her monthly paycheck? That depends on the always somewhat uncertain rules for tracing money through bank accounts. To avoid that uncertainty, and, not incidentally, to prevent Reed from spending the loan proceeds on something other than the collateral, lenders who finance a purchase often pay the loan proceeds directly to the seller for credit against the purchase price.

We will return to the subject of purchase-money security interests in later assignments.

2.   *Consumer Goods*

A purchase-money security interest is automatically perfected only in consumer goods. A PMSI in any other kind of goods must be perfected by the ordinary means required in the UCC for the type of collateral. Thus, the classification as consumer goods determines whether perfection is automatic or whether the secured creditor needs to take some other steps.

UCC §9-102(a)(23) tells us that "consumer goods" are "goods that are used or bought for use primarily for personal, family, or household purposes." It is not the nature of the goods but rather the use to which they are put or the purpose for which they are bought that determines their classification. The same computer might be "consumer goods" if the debtor uses it for family entertainment but "equipment" if the debtor uses it in business.

Courts and commentators all seem to agree that this exception from the filing requirement makes sense only when applied to consumer goods that are of relatively small value. Aside from those who finance the debtor's initial purchase of them, few lend against small-value consumer goods. Those who do rarely search in the filing system, because the amount of money at issue does not justify the expense. Given that filings against small-value consumer goods would be highly unlikely to achieve their purpose of alerting searchers to the existence of the prior lien, lawmakers have been reluctant to put purchase-money lenders to the expense of making them.

Unfortunately for the justification set forth in the preceding paragraph, there is nothing in the definition of "consumer goods" that ensures that they will be of relatively small value. In the following case, the court confronted the problem that arises when the consumer goods are of substantial value and there has been no effective filing.

In re Lockovich
124 B.R. 660 (W.D. Pa. 1991)

Donald J. Lee, United States District Judge.

The facts at issue are not in dispute. On or about August 20, 1986, John J. Lockovich and Clara Lockovich, his wife (Debtors), purchased a 22-foot 1986 Chapparel Villian III boat from the Greene County Yacht Club for $32,500.00. Debtors paid $6,000.00 to Greene County Yacht Club and executed a "Security Agreement/Lien Contract" which set forth the purchase and finance terms. In the Contract, Debtors granted a security interest in the boat to the holder of the Contract. Gallatin paid to the Yacht Club the sum of $26,757.14 on Debtor's behalf, and the Contract was assigned to Gallatin.

The Debtors defaulted under the terms of the Security Agreement to Gallatin by failing to remit payments as required. Before Gallatin could take action, Debtors filed for relief under Chapter 11 of the Bankruptcy Code.

The issue on appeal is whether Gallatin must file a financing statement to perfect its purchase money security interest in the boat. Gallatin's position is that the boat is a consumer good as defined by the [Uniform Commercial Code, Article 9]. Because the boat was a consumer good subject to a purchase money security interest, Gallatin contends it was not required to file a financing statement in order to perfect its security interest. For the reasons below stated, we find that Gallatin has a valid security interest in the boat.

To perfect a security interest in collateral under the Code, [UCC §9-501], a secured party must file a financing statement in the offices of the Secretary of the Commonwealth. Under [UCC §9-309], the Code permits several exceptions to the general rule depending upon the type of collateral. [The court then set out the provisions of UCC §9-309(1).]

There are three significant problems in determining automatic perfection of purchase money interests in consumer goods. First, what is a purchase money security interest? Second, what are "consumer goods"? Third, can massive and expensive items qualify as consumer goods?

It is undisputed in the instant case that the security interest held by Gallatin was a purchase money security interest, [so] therefore the first hurdle has been cleared.

"Goods" are defined as "consumer goods" if they are used or bought for use primary for personal, family or household purposes. The goods are not classified according to design or intrinsic nature, but according to the use to which the owner puts them. Debtors have never maintained that the boat was used for anything other than for their personal use.

The question remaining for this Court is whether a $32,500.00 watercraft can be properly classified as consumer goods under [UCC §9-309(1)]. A Court of Common Pleas in Erie County, Pennsylvania, however, has held that a thirty-three (33) foot motor boat is not a consumer good. Union National Bank of Pittsburgh v. Northwest Marine, Inc., 27 UCC Rep. Serv. 563, 62 Erie Co. L.J. 87 (1979). Though a lower court case is entitled to "some weight," it is not controlling.

It is apparent from the opinion of the Bankruptcy Court, and from the opinion of the court in Northwest Marine, that those courts perceive a void in the Code which does not address the problem of secret liens on valuable motorboats. The court in Northwest Marine stated that this void was "best filled by interstitial lawmaking by the court" until the Legislature acts to bridge the gap. Union National Bank of Pittsburgh v. Northwest Marine, Inc., 62 Erie Co. L.J. at 90.

We disagree. Determining what is a consumer good on an ad hoc basis leaves creditors with little or no guidelines for their conduct. Under the clear mandate of the Code, a consumer good subject to exception from the filing of financing statements is determined by the use or intended use of the good; design, size, weight, shape and cost are irrelevant. Should a millionaire decide to purchase the Queen Mary for his personal or family luxury on the high seas, under [UCC §9-102(a)(23)] of the Code, the great Queen is nothing but a common consumer good. There need be no debate as to cost, size or life expectancy. Creditors must be confident that when they enter into a commercial transaction, they will play by the rules as written in the Code.

Creditors, subsequent creditors and subsequent purchasers under the Code have options available to them that lend appropriate protection. To determine what protections are available to them "by interstitial law-making by the court" is more likely to defeat the intended simplification, clarification, and modernization of the law governing commercial transactions.

There are two legislative solutions to the problem. One is to explicitly require the filing of security interests in motorboats. The other approach, as done in some states, is to limit the value to which the exemption applies. Durable, valuable "consumer goods" upon which a creditor is likely to rely for collateral, encompasses more than motorboats or mobile homes. If motorboats or other expensive items are to be excluded from the dictates of [UCC §9-309(1)], either via specific exemptions or a fixed ceiling price for consumer goods below which no financing statements are required, such determinations are necessarily for the Pennsylvania Legislature.

This Court, therefore, holds that Chapparel Villian III is a consumer good, and pursuant to [UCC §9-309(1)] a financing statement was not required to be filed by Gallatin to perfect the security interest in the boat. Gallatin has a valid security interest in the boat.

On appeal, the Third Circuit affirmed the decision in *Lockovich*, expressly endorsing Judge Lee's comment that "if motorboats or other expensive items are to be excluded from the dictates of §9-309(1), such determinations are necessarily for the Pennsylvania Legislature." Gallatin National Bank v. Lockovich (In re Lockovich), 940 F.2d 916 (3d Cir. 1991).

What if goods are bought with one use in mind, but immediately put to a different use? UCC §9-102(a)(23) is ambiguous on the point. In their landmark treatise on the UCC, Professors White and Summers argued that the intended use at the time of purchase should control. Then they went a step further to argue that creditors should be able to rely on their debtors' written representations regarding intended use. Most courts bought it.

> The case law is clear that where a debtor makes an affirmative representation in loan documents that he or she intends to use goods primarily for personal, family or household purposes, the creditor is protected even if the representation turns out to be erroneous. A debtor who makes representations in a security agreement regarding the intended use of the collateral should be bound by those representations. That is especially true where the debtors fail to inform the creditor that they intend to use the collateral for other than personal, family or household purposes. The classification of the collateral, for purposes of perfection of the security interest, is determined when the security interest attaches. The later use of the collateral for another purpose than as stated in the security agreement is irrelevant in determining whether the security interest is perfected. In re Troupe, 340 B.R. 86 (W.D. Okla. 2006).

These courts miss the fact that future searchers, not the debtor, are the ones who will suffer from the debtor's misrepresentation. Sellers can eliminate the expense of filing by putting boilerplate representations in their sales contracts and debtors can cheerfully sign those representations. Under the White and Summers view, the burden falls on future searchers, who must consider and investigate the possibility that such a secret lien exists.

The alternative view of §9-102(a)(23) is that actual use should control classification of any goods put in use. The intent with which goods were bought should control only if the owner has not yet put them to use. Under this view, if the property is put to a business use, a subsequent searcher need not worry about an automatically perfected PMSI. Cases support each of these views.

Under either view, the lender to a corporation need not worry that the collateral is encumbered by an automatically perfected PMSI in consumer goods. Goods can only be "consumer goods" when the owner is an individual.

D. Security Interests Not Governed by Article 9 or Another Filing Statute

Security interests in a variety of types of collateral are excluded from the coverage of Article 9. They include security interests in wage claims, UCC §9-109(d)(3), insurance policies and claims, UCC §9-109(d)(8), real estate interests, UCC §9-109(d)(11), and non-commercial tort claims, UCC §9-109(d)(12). The reasons for these exclusions vary. Security interests in wage claims, like other assignments of wages, are closely regulated in some states and prohibited in others. Security interests in insurance policies were considered to be special circumstances not appropriate for coverage in a general commercial statute. That view has changed, but the drafters have not amended Article 9. The exclusion of security interests in insurance is problematic because two competing rules govern the priority of security interests in insurance policies. The traditional rule is that the first to notify the insurance company has priority. Some courts, however, hold that the first assignment has priority, regardless of notification. Rose v. AmSouth Bank, 391 F.3d 63 (2d Cir. 2004). In the case of security interests in real estate interests, the purpose of the exclusion is to yield to an elaborate set of recording requirements found in real estate law. The drafters probably excluded non-commercial tort claims because granting security in them is controversial and their inclusion might have made adoption of Article 9 more difficult.

In the following case, the debtor owned a valuable lawsuit and several creditors sought to perfect liens against it. Ultimately all were successful, even the lawyers at Flynn & Stewart who filed an Article 9 financing statement to perfect a security interest that at the time was clearly not governed by Article 9. As you read the case, ask yourself what Flynn & Stewart ought to do next time they have to perfect in a non-commercial tort recovery.

Bluxome Street Associates v. Fireman's Fund Insurance Co.

206 Cal. App. 3d 1149, 254 Cal. Rptr. 198 (Cal. Ct. App. 1988)

Opinion by STRANKMAN, J., with WHITE, P.J., and BARRY-DEAL, J. concurring.

I. PROCEDURAL BACKGROUND AND ISSUES ON APPEAL

In March 1987, a settlement was reached in a legal malpractice action entitled Woods v. Neisar in the Superior Court of the City and County of San Francisco. The settlement provided in part for payment of the sum of $582,500 to Eric H. Woods. This sum was put into a trust account of the law firm of Hassard, Bonnington, Rogers & Huber (Hassard Bonnington), Woods's attorneys in Woods v. Neisar. Hassard Bonnington, appellant Haas & Najarian, appellant Fireman's Fund Insurance Company (Fireman's Fund), and respondent Flynn & Stewart, among others, each claimed a lien on the settlement proceeds.

On May 6, 1987, Woods filed a motion for order establishing lien priorities and allowing distribution of proceeds. Following extensive briefing by all lien claimants and two hearings, the trial court ordered the $582,500 in settlement proceeds to be disbursed as follows: (1) $352,562.14, plus interest, to Hassard Bonnington, pursuant to a retainer agreement which provided for a lien in favor of Hassard Bonnington on any judgment or proceeds recovered in the litigation; (2) $72,500 plus interest to Charles Schilling; (3) the remainder (approximately $150,000) to respondent Flynn & Stewart. [The court concluded that Haas & Najarian and Fireman's Fund held valid liens against the settlement proceeds, but the prior liens consumed the entire settlement, rendering them worthless.]

Appellants Haas & Najarian and Fireman's Fund do not challenge the priority of the liens of Hassard Bonnington or Charles Schilling. Rather, they contend that their liens have priority over the lien of respondent Flynn & Stewart. Flynn & Stewart contends that its lien was created prior in time to those of appellants and that, under the "first in time is first in right" rule, its lien takes priority.

III. VALIDITY OF LIENS

[California] Civil Code section 2881, subdivision 1, provides that liens may be created by contract: "A lien is created: 1. By contract of the parties; or, 2. By operation of law." The liens of Flynn & Stewart and Haas & Najarian were valid contractual liens under this section. The security agreement provides that Woods "grants to Flynn & Stewart, a security interest in any and all of the collateral," defined to include Woods's interest in Woods v. Neisar, to secure payment of a promissory note plus any additional amounts owing arising from the rendition of services by Flynn & Stewart to Woods. Such language describes a lien as defined by Civil Code section 2874.

That Flynn & Stewart is a law firm and the purpose of the lien is to secure payment of attorney fees is immaterial to the creation and enforceability of the lien under Civil Code section 2881, subdivision 1. The lien would be enforceable, barring other factors, even if Flynn & Stewart were not a law firm and the obligation secured were not payment of legal fees.

Fireman's Fund as well as Haas & Najarian next contend that the Flynn & Stewart lien is invalid because the California Uniform Commercial Code (UCC) financing statement filed by Flynn & Stewart incident to the security agreement was void ab initio and did not constitute notice of or perfect the lien.

[handwritten margin note: Null from beginning, as from the first moment when a contract is entered into - if it seriously offends law or public policy]

The security agreement reflects the attorneys' belief that their security interest came within the purview of [Article] 9 of the UCC in that it provides that a UCC financing statement is to be filed with the California Secretary of State to perfect the lien. A financing statement was in fact filed with the Secretary of State.

We agree with appellants that [Article] 9 of the UCC does not apply to the Flynn & Stewart security interest or lien. The security agreement grants to Flynn & Stewart a lien on Woods's interest in a cause of action based upon legal malpractice—a tort cause of action. [UCC §9-109(d)(12)] specifically provides that such lien is not covered by [Article] 9. Because [Article] 9 of the UCC did not apply to Flynn & Stewart's security agreement or lien created thereby, the filing of the UCC financing statement did not operate to provide notice of or "perfect" the lien under [UCC §9-501].

However, although the Flynn & Stewart lien was not perfected under the UCC, and, accordingly, was not entitled to the benefits accorded to a perfected security interest, it nevertheless was valid and enforceable, as discussed ante, under Civil Code section 2881, subdivision 1.

Appellants' next contention is that the Flynn & Stewart lien is unenforceable because there was no notice of the lien. Unlike appellants, who filed written notices of lien in Woods v. Neisar, Flynn & Stewart filed no such notice.

Providing notice of a lien is a statutory prerequisite to the creation or enforceability of certain types of liens. For example, as explained below, the creation of an attachment lien on a litigant's interest in an action is dependent upon the filing of notice of the lien in that action. A judgment lien on real property is created by the recording of an abstract of judgment with the county recorder, and a judgment lien on personal property is created by the filing of notice thereof with the Secretary of State. A mechanic's lien is enforceable only if the claimant first gives notice under Civil Code section 3097, and then records the claim of lien within certain time constrictions.

As to a contractual lien under Civil Code section 2881 on a litigant's interest in a tort claim, however, we find no authority, statute, or case law which requires notice to create such lien.

We conclude that appellants' contentions relating to the validity and enforceability of the Flynn & Stewart contractual lien have no merit.

———————

The court decided that perfection of Flynn & Stewart's lien against Woods' lawsuit was not governed by Article 9 and no other California law established requirements for perfection. From there, the court could have reached any of three conclusions: (1) Flynn & Stewart were perfected because there was no law requiring them to do more than they had done, (2) Flynn & Stewart were unperfected because there was no law specifying any means to perfect, or (3) the court could have established reasonable requirements for perfection, such as placing a notice of the lien in the court file. The court does not explain why it chose the first conclusion over the other two. Other courts might choose differently.

E.   What Became of the Notice Requirement?

In this assignment, we have examined a variety of kinds of security interests that are excepted from the filing requirement. In some cases, the diligent searcher can discover these security interests by viewing or investigating the collateral, examining the court file, or making inquiry with a stakeholder such as a bank, a stock broker, or an insurance company. But in other cases, security interests will be effective against later interests even though the most diligent search would not lead to their discovery. Our most recent addition to this latter category is the automatically perfected purchase-money interest in consumer goods.

In earlier assignments, we noted a number of other situations in which a security interest might be effective, even though it would not be discovered on a diligent search. In later assignments, we will note more.

Prevailing theory holds that the priority granted earlier created interests is justified in part by the fact that those who accepted later interests did so with knowledge of the earlier interests or after choosing not to acquire such knowledge. In many cases, however, the availability of such knowledge is a legal fiction. We offer an alternative justification of these rules: They are principally rules that allocate losses that are thought to be smaller than the cost of loss avoidance.

Problem Set 19

19.1.   As senior associate in the transactional department of your firm, you handle all the perfection questions that come up. This week your colleagues have dropped by with questions about collateral in deals they are doing. Explain the permissible ways to perfect in each of these items of collateral. Be prepared to describe the physical processes.

a.   The cash in the cash registers of a debtor that operates the food and drink concession in a football stadium. The client's concern is the possibility that the debtor will file bankruptcy during a game while the debtor is holding hundreds of thousands of dollars in cash in registers or in armored cars. UCC §§9-312(b)(3), 9-313, Comment 3.

b. A negotiable promissory note. UCC §§9-102(a)(47), 9-312(a), 9-313(a).

c. Money the debtor is keeping in a bank account. UCC §§9-102(a)(29), 9-104, 9-312(b)(1), and 9-314(a) and (b).

d. Shares of stock in General Motors, for which a certificate has been issued. UCC §§8-102(a)(4), 8-106(b), 8-301(a), 9-102(a)(49), 9-106(a), 9-312(a), 9-313(a), 9-314(a), 9-328(1) and (5).

e. The obligations of customers of a used car lot to pay for the cars they purchased. The obligations are evidenced by promissory notes and security interests in the cars purchased. UCC §§9-102(a)(11), 9-312(a), 9-313(a), 9-330(a) and (b).

f. The debtor's bitcoins, which are in the debtor's "wallet" on his own computer. Bitcoins are a "decentralized virtual currency." The currency is issued and verified according to a computer algorithm to persons who furnish computer time to run the algorithm. No one is in control of the system or "owes" a bitcoin. A wallet is a computer program that can communicate with the system to transfer bitcoins. UCC §§1-201(b)(24); 8-102(a)(15); 9-102(a)(2), (29), (42), (49), (61); 9-312, 9-313, 9-314.

19.2. Last year, Ruth and Gene Canard sold their Turkey Burger franchise to Watson Family Restaurants, Inc. They received part of the purchase price in the form of a document titled "Contract for Payment." In the document, Watson promised to pay $500,000 in yearly installments at a stated interest rate. Your client, Casa Grande, is about to lend $300,000 to the Canards, secured by what they have from Watson.

a. How should Casa Grande perfect? UCC §§9-102(a)(2), (42), (47), and (61), 9-310, 9-312(a), 9-313(a), 9-330(d).

b. What if the document gives the Canards a security interest in the franchise and the Canards perfected that security interest properly at the time of the sale? UCC §9-102(a)(11).

19.3. Instead of the "Contract for Payment" that the Canards received in the previous problem, the Canards received only a negotiable promissory note that was an "instrument" within the meaning of UCC §9-102(a)(47). The Canards tell Casa Grande that they cannot give Casa Grande possession of the instrument because Garp Associates is holding it. Garp has a first security interest in the instrument, securing a debt to them in the amount of $60,000. The Canards don't want to pay Garp as part of this transaction because their contract with Garp provides for a substantial prepayment penalty. Casa Grande is willing to make their loan as a second security interest, but they are not willing to risk being unperfected and so possibly unsecured. What do you suggest? UCC §§9-312(a), 9-313, including Comment 3, 9-330(d).

▶ Half Assignment Ends

19.4. Chuck Kettering, former millionaire fallen on hard times, wants to borrow money from our client, Little Silverado Savings and Loan (Silverado). The loan officer is obviously uncomfortable with the loan and seems not to trust Kettering, but Silverado's president, Donald Paul, has been pressuring her to approve it. Paul argues that the appraisals show the collateral to be worth more than twice the amount of the loan, even at foreclosure prices. "If we get a clear UCC search from both the county and the state, and we properly perfect our security interest in the collateral, and insure the collateral, what can go wrong?" The senior partner who advises the bank gave you the following list of proposed collateral and asked you to look into the possibility that there might be liens against the collateral that wouldn't show up on even a diligent search that included a viewing of the collateral. What do you advise? Are there other steps you might take to discover "automatically perfected" security interests? UCC §§9-102(a)(23), 9-309(1), 9-311(b), 9-313(c), (f) and (g).

a.   *A $40,000 mobile home.* It is located in a remote corner of Kettering's estate. State law does not allow for the issuance of a certificate of title for a mobile home.

b.   *A rare book collection.* Valued at $2.5 million, the books are currently on display at the Library of Congress. If the Library were holding possession for someone who claimed a security interest in the books, would it have to tell the searcher? UCC §9-210, 9-625(f) and (g).

c.   *A Mercedes-Benz automobile.* The certificate of title shows no liens.

d.   *A solid gold ingot and 20 unset diamonds.*

e.   *Computer equipment.* The equipment cost about $20,000 at retail and is in Kettering's office, where he uses it principally to review stock quotations.

f.   *A checking account.* The account is at Bank of the West and is in Kettering's name. The bank statements show no interest in favor of Bank of the West or anyone else. UCC §§9-102(a)(23), 9-309(1), 9-311(b), 9-313(c), (f) and (g).

19.5.   a.   When your client Sally loaned her friend Joe $5,000, she took possession of Joe's Rolex watch and gold chain as security. She did not file a financing statement and kept the items in her apartment. Now Joe has filed bankruptcy. Joe's trustee is suspicious of the transaction with Sally because it is completely undocumented. One of his arguments for voiding Sally's security agreement is that Sally was out of town for two weeks on the date Joe filed bankruptcy. During that time, Joe's mother was staying in the apartment where the watch and chain were located. (Joe's mother says she didn't even know the items were there.) Sally wants to know if there is anything to the trustee's argument. Is there? UCC §§9-203(b)(3)(B), 9-310(b)(6).

b.   In a parallel universe, Joe contacted you today to ask that you file a bankruptcy case to stay the foreclosure sale on his home that is scheduled for tomorrow. Sally did loan Joe $5,000 four months ago. But neither Sally nor Joe knew anything about secured transactions. From the time Sally made the loan until now, Joe's watch and chain have been in Joe's safe in his home. No one else saw the watch or chain during that time. After hearing you talk about secured transactions, Joe wants to give Sally possession of the watch and chain now, and then claim in the bankruptcy case that she had possession of them from the time the loan was made. (Admitting that possession was delivered now won't solve Sally's problem because the security interest would be avoided by the trustee as not perfected more than 90 days before the bankruptcy filing.) What's your advice? See Model Rules of Professional Responsibility provisions accompanying Problems 3.3 and 8.4.

■ END OF DEFAULT PROBLEM SET

19.6.   Janet Dakin is in financial trouble. The only bright spot in her financial dealings is that her lawsuit against her former financial adviser, Adam Hershey, goes to trial next week. Adam was on painkillers for most of the three years he managed Janet's investments and the performance of Janet's investment portfolio shows it. In several instances, Adam promised to make particular investments for her but did not. During the three years, $2.5 million turned into $450,000. Adam has offered Janet $800,000 in settlement, but she thinks she can win more. In the meantime, Janet wants to borrow $100,000 from her brother, Will Dakin, using the lawsuit as collateral. Will asks what he should do to perfect. What do you tell him? UCC §§1-201(25), 9-109(d)(12), 9-102(a)(2), (13), (42), (61), 9-309(2).

19.7.   Your client, Sabine Music Manufacturing (Sabine), wants to sell its electronic music tuning equipment to Jersey Music Associates, Inc. (Jersey) for $168,000, payable over seven years with no money down, with the equipment to serve as security for payment of the purchase price. Jersey wants to put the equipment to use immediately, but insists that no financing statement be filed. "Our bank lender will see it on the credit report and go nuts," says Bill Jersey, president of Jersey. Is there any way Sabine can do the deal without taking the risk of Jersey's bankruptcy? Bill Jersey suggests that he can put the music tuning equipment in a separate room, sublease the room to Sabine, and agree that the manufacturing equipment is "at all times in Sabine's possession." Bill, "as Sabine's agent, will control access to the room on behalf of Sabine, permitting Jersey workers to enter the room and use the equipment only as authorized from time to time by Sabine." All this will be in large print, on a sign posted on the door of the room. Sabine wants to do the deal, unless you tell them it won't work. Will it? UCC §9-313(a).

Assignment 20: The Land and Fixtures Recording Systems

The preceding assignments described the personal property filing systems. In its broadest sense, "personal property" refers to anything capable of being owned, that is, all "property," except real property. Real property includes land, certain interests in land such as easements, and permanent structures on land.

The Uniform Commercial Code specifies the filing requirements for security interests in personal property. Real property law—generally state statutes—specifies the filing requirements for mortgages or deeds of trust in real property. The two bodies of law deal with essentially the same issues in different contexts: what documents should be filed in the public records to provide notice to later takers and what should be the effect of failing to file them.

Not only are the bodies of law different, the filings are made in separate systems. Each system has its own offices, systems for filing, indexing, and searching, and language in which to talk about them. For example, the process is referred to as "filing" in the personal property system and "recording" in the real property system. But because these systems are performing essentially the same functions—providing public notice of security interests—in actual operation they are similar.

In some regards, the two systems overlap or conflict. As a result, the holders of some kinds of security interests can perfect them according to real or personal property law and the holders of a few kinds might not be able to perfect them according to either. Some filings that are made pursuant to personal property law must be made in the real property system. Much of the overlap and conflict occur with respect to property that is neither clearly real nor clearly personal—a poorly defined, intermediate category referred to as "fixtures."

A. Real Property Recording Systems

The real property recording systems are generally older than, and physically separate from, the personal property filing systems you studied in Assignment 16. Each state in the United States is divided into counties, and each county maintains a recording system. (In a few areas counties go by other names, or some other governmental unit runs the system.) There are more than 3,000 counties and hence more than 3,000 real estate recording systems. The typical recording system is located in the county seat, either in the courthouse or in a county administration building, and has been in operation for hundreds of years.

Real estate recording systems resemble personal property filing systems in many respects. A person seeking to record a mortgage sends it to the recording office. The clerk charges a fee for recording and immediately stamps the date and time of recording on the face of the mortgage. As in the personal property filing systems, the clerk places the now-recorded mortgage in the basket (literal or metaphoric) for photocopying and indexing. Later, someone in the recording office adds a reference to the mortgage at appropriate places in the indexes, places the mortgage copy in the records in chronological order, and mails the original back to the person who recorded.

Real estate recording systems typically differ from personal property filing systems in other respects. First, the real estate recording system contains not only documents evidencing liens against real estate, but also documents evidencing transfers of ownership—that is, deeds. Recall that bills of sale, the personal property equivalents of deeds, are not filed in the Article 9 filing system. Searchers in the Article 9 filing system may be able to determine who has a security interest in the collateral, but they definitely cannot determine who owns it. The inclusion of deeds in the real estate recording system, combined with more extensive indexing, enables users of the real estate system to determine who owns property as well as who has liens against it. We will explore the implications of this difference in later assignments.

Second, recording in the real estate system costs more than filing in the personal property system. The recording office clerk not only charges the modest filing fee, the clerk also collects a transfer tax based on the value of the property or the amount of the mortgage. For example, when one of the authors sold a Wisconsin condominium for $102,000, the recording fees for the deed and mortgage were $48, while the *transfer fee* was $306. In larger transactions, the fees payable on recording can be considerable. For example, when Rockefeller Center Properties, Inc. recorded $1.25 billion in mortgages against the buildings by that name in New York City, it paid $34.5 million in recording taxes. By contrast, only a handful of states impose transfer fees on grants of security interests in personal property. Article 9 secured parties rarely decline to file a financing statement because of the expense, but real estate secured parties occasionally structure their transactions in ways designed to legally avoid (or illegally evade) the transfer fees. Rockefeller Center Properties left the above-mentioned $1.25 billion in mortgages unrecorded for years. Only when they discovered that their debtor was in financial trouble did they record the mortgage and pay the recording taxes. Not all mortgagees who play these games are so fortunate; some fail to record in time and suffer avoidance of their unperfected mortgages in bankruptcy.

Third, real estate recording systems are not self-purging. When a document is filed, the clerk stamps it with identifying numbers. These are typically the number of the *book* in which it will be bound and the *page* at which it will appear in that book. It will remain permanently on the record. (In many parts of the United States, the recording system still contains records from the seventeenth century.) The advantage of permanent retention is that the thorny issue of continuation does not arise. The disadvantage is that every filing represents a net increase in the number of documents that must be stored and searched.

For our purposes, perhaps the most important difference between the two types of systems is that the debtor's name problem is relatively insignificant in real estate recording systems. The principal reason is that the records reflect the chain of title to the property, up to and including the debtor. The creditor who searched in an incorrect name would not only fail to find prior mortgages against the property, it would fail to find any documents at all. The absence of documents showing title in the debtor would alert the searcher to its error. A second reason is that in most counties, real estate searches can be conducted not only by the names of the parties, but also by *tract*—the description of the property. Some counties maintain tract indexes to facilitate such searching. In many (if not most) counties, private firms known as *abstract* or *title companies* maintain sets of records that duplicate those of the county. That is, they photocopy every document as it is filed in the public records and conduct searches in their own copies. These private systems also enable searches by tract. When the search is conducted by tract, it will reveal a mortgage that bears a correct tract number, even if the record name of the debtor bears no resemblance whatsoever to the correct name of the debtor.

The duplication of real estate public records by private firms has had a profound effect on the recording system in many parts of the United States. As the proportion of searches conducted in private systems has increased, the quality of indexing and the support for searching in the public systems has declined. The indexes in many public systems are replete with errors. Obtaining physical access to the dozens of documents relevant to a particular search may be impossibly time-consuming. In many counties, searching a real estate title in the public records is no longer feasible. Nonetheless, because so few searches are actually conducted in the public records, the effects of public indexing errors are relatively small and the indexes themselves relatively unimportant. For that reason, we do not discuss the problems of indexing and searching the real estate recording systems.

The real estate recording systems have also been spared another problem endemic to personal property recording systems. As you saw in Assignment 16, there is often uncertainty as to which personal property filing system is appropriate for a particular filing. Such uncertainty does not exist with regard to real property recording systems. A document that affects title to real estate in a particular county must be recorded in that county. A document that affects title to real estate in several counties must be recorded in each.

B.   What Is Recorded?

In Assignment 8, we discussed the formalities for the creation of a mortgage against real property. They were, in essence: (1) a mortgage document (2) signed by the debtor and perhaps (3) containing a description of the debt secured and the collateral securing it. We say "perhaps" because there is a split of authority as to whether a mortgage that omits entirely the amount of the debt or expresses it in general terms is valid. And while the description of collateral in a mortgage may be so vague as to render it void, the general rule is that a description does not do so as long as it remains possible to identify the property by a rule of construction or through evidence extrinsic to the mortgage.

In the real estate system, the creditor must record the mortgage document, not merely a notice of its existence. The advantage is that the public record informs searchers not only of the existence of the mortgage but its terms. The disadvantage is that when collateral is added or deleted, or when other important terms change, an additional recording may be necessary.

Real estate law may impose and enforce additional formalities for recording. The most common are the requirements that the mortgage be signed in front of a witness and that it be *acknowledged* before a notary public or some such official, who authenticates the debtor's signature by affixing the official's own signature and seal. Some states, however, omit the witness requirement, the acknowledgment requirement, or both.

Like Article 9, the real estate system has not been very demanding as to the recording of the mortgage holder's identity. Until the 1970s the original lender ordinarily held the mortgage until it was paid off. If the original lender assigned the mortgage, it recorded an assignment showing the new owner. With the growth of mortgage securitization, assignment of mortgages — often several in succession — became the norm. Securitization specialists considered the delays and fees associated with public recordation of those assignments as an unnecessary cost. A group of investors created Mortgage Electronic Registration System (MERS), a private registry that would substitute for the public mortgage filing system. Today, mortgages often name MERS as the mortgagee. As the mortgage is assigned from owner to owner, the assignments are recorded only on the records of MERS. The MERS system has not, however, worked entirely as planned. For example, some states require a foreclosing lender to establish a chain of title showing it is the owner of the mortgage note. U.S. Bank v. Ibanez, 458 Mass. 637, 941 N.E.2d 40 (2011). MERS can make it more difficult for a lender to make this evidentiary showing in court. As a result of this and other uncertainties, some mortgage lenders and investors are backing away from MERS and instead are recording their interests.

C.   Fixtures

Even though buildings are constructed from personal property — bricks, mortar, lumber, nails, and the like — the law considers permanent buildings part of the land on which they are situated. Thus, a mortgage against Blackacre, like a deed to Blackacre, would include any permanent buildings located on it unless they were expressly excluded. Such a mortgage is perfected by filing only in the real estate system; a UCC filing is unnecessary and ineffective. UCC §9-109(d)(11).

Once you realize that "bricks and mortar" can be real property for recording purposes, it should be easy to see that the interface between the real estate and personal property recording systems will necessarily be either uncertain or complex. (In fact, it is both.) That a security interest in a building must be recorded in the real estate system suggests that security interests in everything that is part of the building must be recorded there as well, such as the built-in light fixtures, the light bulbs that screw into them, and maybe even the furniture.

The law defining the scope of a mortgage in real property came into existence long before the UCC was drafted. That law, which was often inconsistent within a state and non-uniform from state to state, determined what property was so related to particular real estate that it would be treated as part of the real estate. Such property was referred to as *fixtures* because the property was usually physically affixed to the real estate.

1.   What Is a "Fixture"?

The drafters of the UCC deferred to real estate law, and they designed around it. They defined "goods" as being "fixtures" when they "have become so related to particular real property that an interest in them arises under real property law." UCC §9-102(a)(41). State law defining what is or is not a fixture is notoriously complex, confusing, and indeterminate. It differs widely from state to state. The big picture is captured by Professor Steve Knippenberg's definition: "You take the world, you shake it, and everything that doesn't fall off is [a fixture]." The three-part test from the *Cliff's Ridge Skiing Corp.* case, below, adds a second level of precision:

> In Michigan, whether personal property becomes a fixture and thereby part of realty is determined by a three-part test: (1) is the property annexed or attached to the realty, (2) is the attached property adapted or applied to the use of the realty, and (3) is it intended that the property will be permanently attached to the realty?

Lest you assume that you can determine whether goods are fixtures by how firmly they are affixed to the real estate:

> Many authorities take the position that any and all machinery essential to the proper functioning of a plant, mill, or similar manufacturing [sic] is a fixture, or is at least so presumed to be, irrespective of the manner in which it is annexed to the realty and *even though it is not attached thereto at all*. This view is sometimes referred to as the "integrated industrial plant" doctrine and represents the modern trend of decisions.

Commonwealth Edison Co. v. The City of Zion, 579 N.E.2d 1082 (Ill. Ct. App. 1991) (emphasis added). Under this doctrine, furniture that is custom-designed for use in a commercial building or free-standing room dividers might be considered fixtures.

In many situations, lawyers will find it impossible to predict whether the courts would consider particular property to be fixtures. In those situations, the best course is to attempt to protect the client regardless of what conclusion the court should later draw. Typically, that will require that searches and filings be made in both the real estate and the personal property filing systems.

2.   How Does a Secured Creditor Perfect in Fixtures?

Nothing in Article 9 prevents the creation or perfection of a security interest in fixtures under the real estate law of the state. UCC §9-334(b). Thus, if some item of property could be encumbered by a real estate mortgage before the adoption of Article 9, it could be encumbered by one afterward as well.

In the case that follows, three creditors claimed perfected security interests in a ski lift. The court decided that the ski lift was a fixture and that all three creditors had perfected their interests in it. The case illustrates the variety of ways a secured creditor can perfect an interest in fixtures.

In re Cliff's Ridge Skiing Corp.

123 B.R. 753 (Bankr. W.D. Mich. 1991)

James D. Gregg, United States Bankruptcy Judge.

On October 28, 1987, Cliff's Ridge Skiing Corporation ("Debtor"), filed for bankruptcy. [The trustee sold a certain chairlift owned by the debtor for $22,500 in cash.]

Three creditors, First National Bank & Trust Company of Marquette ("First National"), Cliff's Ridge Development Co. ("Cliff's Ridge Dev."), and First of America Bank-Marquette, N.A., formerly known as Union National Bank & Trust Company of Marquette ("FOA"), each assert they are legally entitled to the escrowed proceeds and the interest earned therefrom.

FACTS

On July 24, 1980, FOA loaned Cliff's Ridge Dev. the sum of $300,000 pursuant to a note. Repayment of this indebtedness was secured by Cliff's Ridge Dev. executing a mortgage and a security agreement each dated July 24, 1980. The mortgage was properly perfected by recordation with the Marquette County Register of Deeds on August 1, 1980. The mortgage language granted FOA an interest in certain real property owned by Cliff's Ridge Dev. together with "all improvements now or hereafter created on the property . . . and all fixtures now or hereafter attached to the property, all of which, including replacements and additions thereto, shall be deemed to be and remain a part of the property covered by this mortgage." The security interest which granted FOA an interest in all tangible and intangible personal property of Cliff's Ridge Dev. was perfected by the filing of a financing statement with the State of Michigan, Secretary of State, UCC Division, on July 29, 1980. No fixture filing was made with the Marquette County Register of Deeds.

[The Debtor contracted to purchase all of Cliff's Ridge Dev.'s assets and began operating the ski area with the cooperation of one of Cliff's Ridge Dev.'s principals.] The Debtor determined it was advisable to purchase an additional chairlift and the purchase was discussed with a principal of Cliff's Ridge Dev. In April or May, 1982, the Debtor contacted Breckenridge Ski Area to purchase the chairlift on a cash-on-delivery basis. The price paid for the chairlift by the Debtor was $65,000. In addition, the Debtor paid $10,000 for shipping, $7,500 for engineering, and approximately $80,000 for erection of the chairlift.

The chairlift was delivered and installed between August and December, 1982.

On November 22, 1982, Cliff's Ridge Dev. conveyed its ski hill real property to the Debtor pursuant to a warranty deed. The deed given to the Debtor was subject to the prior mortgage granted by Cliff's Ridge Dev. to FOA dated July 24, 1980. Also on November 22, 1982, the Debtor granted Cliff's Ridge Dev. a mortgage respecting the ski hill real property. The mortgage was properly perfected by recordation with the Marquette County Register of Deeds on November 23, 1982. The mortgage does not contain any express language granting Cliff's Ridge Dev. an interest in the Debtor's fixtures, whether then owned or after acquired. Rather, the mortgage only grants an interest in the conveyed real property together "with the hereditaments and appurtenances thereunto belonging or in anywise appertaining."

On December 13, 1982, the Debtor and First National executed a Loan Agreement. The Loan Agreement provides, inter alia, that (1) First National will loan $175,000 to [the Debtor] to be used to purchase the chairlift, (2) First National will receive a perfected security interest in the chairlift. . . . The agreement also includes a representation that the Debtor has, or will obtain, good and marketable title to the chairlift except for liens disclosed to First National. At the time of this Loan Agreement, the parties apparently failed to recognize that Cliff's Ridge Dev. might claim an interest in the chairlift pursuant to its prior mortgage.

At the time the [First National] loan documents were executed, the Debtor had a legal right or interest in the chairlift. The Debtor executed, and First National filed, three financing statements regarding First National's security interest in the chairlift collateral.

First, on December 14, 1982, a financing statement, intended as a fixture filing, was filed where mortgages are recorded with the Marquette County Register of Deeds. [First National] is listed as the secured party. The real property description is attached to the financing statement.

Second, on December 15, 1982, a financing statement, intended as a fixture filing, was filed with the Michigan Secretary of State, Uniform Commercial Code Section. This financing statement was identical to that filed with the Marquette County Register of Deeds.

Third, on December 15, 1982, a financing statement, designated as a "Non-Fixture Statement," was filed with the Michigan Secretary of State, Uniform Commercial Code Section. The chairlift is identified on the financing statement.

DISCUSSION

Is the Chairlift a Fixture?

In Michigan, whether personal property becomes a fixture and thereby part of realty is determined by a three-part test: (1) is the property annexed or attached to the realty, (2) is the attached property adapted or applied to the use of the realty, and (3) is it intended that the property will be permanently attached to the realty? The three-part test remains valid under current Michigan law.

The chairlift was attached to the realty. Concrete pads were poured in the realty prior to the erection of the chairlift. Towers were then bolted to the concrete pads, cables were strung, and about 100 chairs were attached to the cables. The parties have stipulated that "chairlifts are part of ski hills but can be severed from the ski hills and sold." The court finds the chairlift was annexed or attached to the real property.

The parties have stipulated that the chairlift was engineered to be erected on the realty and the chairlift was specially modified to be attached to the realty. The court finds the chairlift was adapted to the ski hill real property for its use and purposes.

Very little testimony exists whether the parties intended to permanently affix the chairlift to the real estate. In the Project Plan, and other documents relating to the Debtor's request to obtain [the First National] financing, it is stated that the loan was intended to finance "construction" and "installation" of the chairlift "improvements" to the realty. Final approval of the requested financing was conditioned upon conveyance of the realty from Cliff's Ridge Dev. to the Debtor. In two financing statements dated December 14 and December 15, 1982, filed by First National, it is stated, "The goods are to become fixtures on 11-24-82." No other evidence regarding intent has been introduced by any party. Under Michigan law, attachments to realty to facilitate its use become part of the realty and, if done by the owner, are presumed to be permanent. Based upon the preponderance of the evidence, the court finds the Debtor intended to permanently affix the chairlift to the Realty.

Under governing Michigan law, all requirements of the three-part test to determine whether personal property has become a fixture have been met. The court concludes that the chairlift in dispute is a fixture.

Creation and Perfection of an Interest in Fixtures

Under Michigan law, there are two methods by which a creditor may create and perfect an interest in fixtures. A creditor may utilize procedures under Michigan real estate law. Alternatively, a creditor may take a security interest in a fixture and perfect that interest under the Uniform Commercial Code as adopted in Michigan ("UCC").

Article 9 of the UCC allows the creation of an interest in fixtures pursuant to state real estate law. Prior to adoption of the UCC, Michigan law was well-settled that once a fixture is annexed or attached to realty, the fixture became part of the realty and title to the fixture is subject to a real estate mortgage.

As stated in Kent Storage Co. v. Grand Rapids Lumber Co., 239 Mich. 161, 164-165, 214 N.W. 111, 112-113 (1927): "It is a salutary rule that whatever is affixed to a building by an owner in complement, to facilitate its use and occupation in general, becomes a part of the realty, though capable of removal without injury to the building." When a fixture becomes complemental to real property, it becomes a permanent accession and becomes part of the realty; the fixture becomes part of the security with regard to any existing mortgage. A mortgage covers fixtures even when they are not expressly mentioned in the mortgage.

Once a mortgage creates an interest in fixtures under Michigan real estate law, the interest must be perfected. Perfection under state real estate law is accomplished by recordation of the mortgage in the county where the real property is located.

The second method by which a security interest in fixtures may be created and perfected is under the UCC without reference to state real estate law. A "security interest" is defined very broadly to mean "an interest in personal property or *fixtures* which secures repayment of an obligation." [UCC §1-201(35)]. (emphasis supplied.) Article 9 of the UCC applies "to any transaction (regardless of its form) which is intended to create a security interest in personal property or *fixtures.*" [UCC §9-109(a)(1)]. (emphasis supplied.)

To perfect a personal property interest in a fixture, and be accorded proper priority, a financing statement must be filed. [UCC §9-310(a)]. To be sufficient . . . a financing statement covering fixtures or goods to become fixtures must: (6) state that it covers this type of collateral; (7) recite it is to be recorded in the real estate records; (8) contain a description of the real estate where the fixtures are located or to be located, which is sufficient to provide constructive notice under state real estate mortgage law; and (9) if the debtor does not have an interest of record in the real estate, the owner of record must be disclosed. [UCC §9-502(b)(4)].

The financing statement which covers fixtures, or goods to become fixtures, must be filed where a mortgage on the real estate would be recorded. [UCC §9-501(a)(1)(B)]. In Michigan, an interest in real estate is properly recorded at the register of deeds in the county in which the real estate is located. When a sufficient financing statement is filed in the proper place, a "fixture filing" occurs. [UCC §9-102(a)(40)]. After a proper fixture filing, a secured party has a perfected interest in the fixtures and may enforce its security interest against other persons according to designated priorities. [UCC §§9-334(c)-(g)].

Do the Creditors Hold a Valid Interest in the Chairlift and the Proceeds?

When a fixture becomes complemental to real property, it becomes a permanent accession and the fixture becomes part of the security with regard to any existing mortgage. The language [regarding after-acquired fixtures] in FOA's prior recorded mortgage is sufficient to create and perfect its interest in the chairlift fixture under state real estate law. FOA retained its interest in the proceeds pursuant to this court's order whereby valid liens would attach to the proceeds of the sale. 11 U.S.C. §§363(e); 361(2); [UCC §9-315(a)(2)].

Cliff's Ridge Dev.'s mortgage grants an interest in the real property together "with the hereditaments and appurtenances thereunto belonging or in anywise appertaining." There is no language in the mortgage relating to "fixtures." An "appurtenance" is an "article adapted to the use of the property to which it is

connected, and which was intended to be a permanent accession to the freehold."
Black's Law Dictionary 94 (5th Ed. West Publishing Co. 1979). An "appurtenance"
is equivalent to a "fixture."

A mortgage covers fixtures even when they are not explicitly mentioned in the
mortgage. If the chairlift became connected to the real property after the grant of
Cliff's Ridge Dev.'s mortgage, Cliff's Ridge Dev. has an interest in the chairlift; the
appurtenance or fixture becomes part of the security with regard to any existing
mortgage. On the other hand, if the chairlift became connected to the real property before the grant of the mortgage, the chairlift would be covered by the subsequent mortgage without a special mention in the mortgage. Therefore, under
state real estate law, Cliff's Ridge Dev. has an interest in the chairlift. Cliff's Ridge
Dev. also has an interest in the proceeds from the chairlift sale in accordance with
the court's prior order.

On December 14, 1982, a financing statement regarding the chairlift was filed
[by First National] where mortgages are recorded with the Marquette County
Register of Deeds. The form of the financing statement meets all the necessary
requirements under the UCC. [UCC §§9-502(a), (b)]. A sufficient financing statement regarding the chairlift fixture was filed in the proper place and a "fixture
filing" occurred. [UCC §§9-102(a)(40), 9-501(a)(1)(B)]. First National therefore
holds a perfected personal property interest in the chairlift under the UCC. It now
also holds an interest in the sale proceeds pursuant to this court's prior order. 11
U.S.C. §§363(e); 361(2); [UCC §9-315(a)(2)].

We omitted the portion of the opinion that tells who won the case, because
it deals with issues of priority among perfected, secured creditors that are
reserved for the final chapter of this book. (Spoiler Alert: For those of you who
can't bear not to know how the case came out, First National got the proceeds
of sale and neither of the others got anything. But the reason for that result
will have to wait.)

As *Cliff's Ridge* illustrates, there is more than one way to obtain and perfect a security interest in fixtures. The court mentions three, a mortgage, an
Article 9 fixture filing and a mortgage as a fixture filing. There is yet a fourth.
By filing an ordinary financing statement in the UCC personal property filing system, a secured creditor can perfect a security interest in goods that are
fixtures. Such a filing does not qualify as a "fixture filing," UCC §9-501(a), but
there is nothing in Article 9 or elsewhere that says one must make a fixture filing to perfect in fixtures. UCC §9-501 does not require filing in the real estate
records to perfect in fixtures; it merely requires filing in the real estate records
to perfect by means of a *fixture filing*. In Assignment 33, we will see that the
perfection obtained in fixtures by a nonfixture filing is of limited effect. For
now, it is important to recognize that a personal property (nonfixture) filing is
a "method permitted by this article" to perfect in property that is fixtures. See
UCC §9-501(a)(2).

Despite its exalted status among commercial law groupies, Article 9 is just
one more state law. Its rules can be, and often are, overridden by other statutes

of the state. As the following case illustrates, if the other statute says that one perfects in a fixture by notation on the certificate of title, one does.

In re Renaud

308 B.R. 347 (8th Cir. B.A.P. 2004)

JERRY W. VENTERS, BANKRUPTCY JUDGE.

[I]n 2001, the Debtors refinanced their purchase of a Spirit mobile home, along with the real property on which it is affixed, by borrowing $33,100.83 from Simmons Bank. The previous lienholder on the mobile home released its lien noted on the certificate of title for the mobile home, and Simmons Bank placed the clean title in the Debtors' loan file. At no time did Simmons Bank note its interest on the certificate of title; rather, Simmons Bank recorded a mortgage on the real property covering "all existing and future improvements, structures, fixtures, and replacements that may now, or at any time in the future, be part of the real estate." The Debtors acknowledged their intent to mortgage both the real property and the mobile home to secure the debt.

With respect to the mobile home, Simmons Bank argues that the bankruptcy court erred inasmuch as it held that the only way to perfect a security interest in a mobile home is to note that interest on the certificate of title. Simmons Bank contends that its mortgage on the real property encompassed the mobile home as soon as the mobile home became permanently affixed to the real property.

The particular issue addressed by Simmons Bank is not new. Courts and legislatures have struggled with the problems of classifying mobile homes that — in their final stages — are every bit as much of the real property as a traditional brick and mortar construction. The particular problem in this case, however, is not necessarily a definition of when an item of personal property becomes annexed to the realty, but rather one of perfecting a security interest in a mobile home and how to maintain that perfection in light of the changing nature of the property from personal to real.

There is no dispute that the Debtors' mobile home is subject to registration under Arkansas certificate of title laws. Ark. Code Ann. §27-14-703 ("Every motor vehicle . . . and every mobile home shall be subject to the provisions of this chapter. . . ."). The fact that a mobile home is without wheels and designed as permanent living quarters does not exempt owners of mobile homes from having to obtain a certificate of title. See §27-14-207(2) (defining a "mobile home" as "every house trailer or other vehicle, with or without wheels, designed for use as living quarters, either permanent or temporary, and, at the time of manufacture, capable of being towed or otherwise transported or drawn upon a highway"). In an apparent attempt to avoid the conundrum of when a mobile home is transmogrified into a fixture or structure affixed to the realty, the Arkansas legislature has established a bright-line rule — the time of manufacture — to determine whether a mobile home is a mobile home or something else. Thus, it would appear that a house trailer or other vehicle designed for use as living quarters and capable of being towed or otherwise transported or drawn on a highway at the time of manufacture will always be a mobile home subject to the certificate of title laws.

Mobile home personal to real property

We can find no exception in Arkansas's certificate of title laws that exempt mobile homes if they are affixed to realty, and counsel for Simmons Bank has pointed to no such exception. We should not provide an extra-statutory exception to Arkansas law when the Arkansas legislature specifically made notation on the certificate of title on a mobile home the exclusive method of perfecting an interest therein. Ark. Code Ann. §27-14-807(a) ("The methods provided in this subchapter of giving constructive notice of a lien or encumbrance upon a registered vehicle shall be exclusive except as to liens dependent upon possession."). If Simmons Bank is unhappy with the conclusion reached by the bankruptcy court, it should petition the Arkansas legislature to change the certificate of title laws pertaining to mobile homes affixed to realty.

About the time *Renaud* was decided, a Michigan court went the opposite way. The difference in outcome resulted from a difference in the wording of the certificate of title statutes. The law is whatever the legislature says it is.

3. Perfecting in the Fixtures of a Transmitting Utility

Article 9 contains special rules for filing against the collateral, including fixtures, of a transmitting utility. The gist of the rules is to permit fixture filings against this type of debtor to be made in the office of the secretary of state rather than in county real estate filing systems. See UCC §9-501(b). The paradigm cases that led to the adoption of this provision were railroads with tracks running through many counties and electric companies with power lines doing the same. Both the tracks and the lines might be fixtures, necessitating filings in all of the involved counties. Absent a special rule, secured creditors would have to include in their fixture financing statements literally thousands of descriptions of parcels of land.

The transmitting utilities provisions of Article 9 may cause more problems than they solve. Read UCC §9-102(a)(81). Under this definition, "transmitting utility" may include businesses such as radio and television stations that do not have lines or tracks running through numerous counties. Moreover, there is nothing in the transmitting utility rule that limits its effect to the special kinds of property that led to its adoption. Presumably, it would apply to the light fixtures in a railroad's headquarters building.

The effect of the rule is to require lenders to consider in every case the possibility that their borrowers qualify as transmitting utilities and, if so, to conduct additional searches in the offices of the secretaries of state. In most cases it will not be prudent for the lenders to dispense with the search of the real property records, because those records may contain mortgages on the railroad rights of way. The transmitting utility provisions are another example of a filing system characteristic we have mentioned several times: Attempts to ease the burdens on filers tend to increase the burdens on searchers and vice versa.

UCC §9-515(f) provides that "if a debtor is a transmitting utility and a filed financing statement so indicates, the financing statement is effective until a termination statement is filed." Continuation statements are thus unnecessary. In one case, a bank filed a financing statement against a railroad but failed to check the "transmitting utility" box. The court held that the financing statement lapsed after five years, rejecting the bank's argument that because "it was clear from the UCC-1 that the debtor was a railroad, it met the 'so indicates' requirement of 9-515(f)." In re California Western Railroad, Inc., 303 B.R. 201, 204 (Bankr. N.D. Cal. 2003).

D.   Personal Property Interests in Real Property

Direct ownership interests in land are real property, but many kinds of indirect ownership are not. For example, if Robin Finkelstein owns Blackacre in fee simple, her interest is real property and a security interest in that interest must be recorded in the real estate system. If she forms a corporation to own Blackacre for her (Robin Finkelstein, Inc.), her interest, the stock of Robin Finkelstein, Inc., is personal property. If she grants a security interest in the stock, Article 9 governs that security interest. Similarly, if Robin and her partner, Alice Li, own Blackacre as joint tenants or as tenants in common, their interest is real property. But if they own it as partners or hold it in trust for themselves, their interest is personal property, even though the partnership or trust owns nothing but real estate. See, e.g., In re Cowsert, 14 B.R. 340 (Bankr. S.D. Fla. 1981) (a beneficial interest under an Illinois land trust is personal property and when given as collateral is classified as a general intangible). A secured creditor perfects its interest in the debtor's interest in the partnership or trust by filing in the Article 9 system.

The creation of a lease of real property is governed by real estate law. Most states require that if the lease is for a period longer than three years, it must be recorded to be effective against purchasers or encumbrancers of the real property. But there is a split of authority as to whether a *lessee's* grant of a security interest in its rights under the lease is governed by Article 9. See UCC §9-109(d)(11); see, e.g., In re Associated Air Services, Inc., 42 B.R. 768 (Bankr. S.D. Fla. 1984) (UCC applies to the use of a real property lease as collateral); In re Hodge Forest Industries, 59 B.R. 801 (Bankr. D. Idaho 1986) (a lease of real property may not be the subject of a security interest because it is excluded from Article 9 by §9-109(a)(11)).

A mortgagee can sell its interest in the mortgage or borrow against it. When the mortgagee does the latter, it usually gives a security interest in the mortgage. (Remember that the mortgagee does not own the land; it merely has a mortgage against the land.) How should such a security interest in a mortgage be perfected? By recording an assignment in the real property records or by filing a financing statement in the Article 9 filing system?

Article 9 deems a security interest in a mortgage to be a security interest in a note — personal property — and thus covered under Article 9. It accomplishes that through two provisions. First, UCC §9-109(b) provides that application of Article 9 to a security interest in a secured obligation (the mortgage note) is not affected by the fact that the note is secured by an interest (the mortgage) to which Article 9 does not apply. Having thus made clear that perfection in the note is under Article 9, the drafters extended coverage to the mortgage by providing in UCC §9-203(g) that attachment of a security interest to a right of payment secured by a security interest in real property (the note) is also attachment of a security interest in the mortgage.

Problem Set 20

20.1. Your client, Secured Lending Partners (SLP), specializes in high-risk secured lending to a class of clientele that, as SLP put it, "the banks won't touch." Billie Ochs, the managing partner of SLP, is negotiating to lend $1.5 million to an untouchable by the name of Pacific Interests. She has the following questions for you. She is a stickler, so be prepared to cite to the governing law.

a.   How should SLP perfect in Pacific Interests' one-third interest in a 160-acre tract of land known as Devil's Valley? Does the form in which title is held matter? UCC §§9-109(a) and (d)(11). For example, what if the land is held in trust? By co-owners as tenants in common? By co-owners as partners?

b.   Billie also wants to make sure SLP is also perfected against the pine trees growing on Devil's Valley. The trees were planted 20 years ago in straight rows for easy harvesting. UCC §§9-102(a)(41) and (44), 9-334(a), (b), and (i), 9-501(a), 9-502(b); Comment 12 to UCC §9-334 and Comment 3 to UCC §9-501.

c.   How should SLP perfect in a parcel of land just west of Devil's Valley? The trees on this second parcel are virgin growth. They include some species that would be of considerable value as timber. (A single walnut tree would be worth $10,000.) UCC §§9-502(c), 9-102(a)(41) and (44).

d.   If SLP perfects by recording a mortgage against the second parcel, does the mortgage have to mention the trees to encumber them?

e.   Pacific Interests holds a mortgage and note from Mark VI Partners to Pacific Interests in the face amount of $200,000. The debt is for the purchase price of certain real property that Pacific Interests sold to Mark VI. The note that evidences the promise to pay is physically incorporated into the purchase money mortgage. Pacific Interests recorded the mortgage and note in the real estate recording system; the original is now in the possession of Pacific Interests. SLP wants a security interest in the note and mortgage. How should SLP perfect it? UCC §§9-102(a)(2) and (47), 9-109(b) and (d)(11), 9-203(g), 9-308(e), 9-310(a), 9-312(a), 9-313(a), 9-330(d).

f.   Pacific Interests owns a corporate subsidiary, Pacific Cellular, Inc. (PCI). Billie tells you that PCI's only asset is a cell phone tower. Because SLP wants to make sure it gets a lien on everything, Billie wants to include a security interest in the tower itself. The steel tower is located on land owned by a local farmer. PCI leases the tower to Verizon under a lease that has five years left to run. The tower is 250 feet tall, is bolted to a concrete foundation, and transmits to adjacent towers by electromagnetic microwaves. UCC §§9-102(a)(11), (41), (44), (49), and (81), 9-314(a), 9-501(b).

g.   How should SLP perfect in a natural gas pipeline that runs through 119 counties in four states? In some counties the pipeline is buried; in others it runs above ground and is bolted to concrete pads. The pipeline is owned and operated by Pipes Holding, Inc. (Pipes), a wholly owned subsidiary of Pacific Interests. In some counties the pipeline runs on land owned by Pipes; in others it runs on easements granted by the landowners to Pipes. UCC §§9-102(a)(41), (44), (81), 9-334(a), 9-502(b).

h.   Pacific Interests also offers something they call "store fixtures" as collateral. These are items owned by Pacific Interests and used in a retail pet store known as Pet World, which is owned and operated by Pacific Interests and is located in a shopping center owned by Oaks Mall, Ltd. The "store fixtures" consist of shelving, counters, cages, cash registers, and similar items. Some are bolted to the building; some are freestanding. The lease between Oaks Mall, Ltd. and Pacific Interests gives Pacific Interests the right to remove the "store fixtures" at the expiration of the lease, provided that Pacific Interests is not then in default. UCC §§9-102(a)(41), 9-501(a), 9-502(b).

20.2.   Representing writer-adventurer Harold Philbrick has never been dull and today is no exception. Six months ago, Harold made a $1 million unsecured loan to Marland, Inc., a company owned by his friend, eccentric multimillionaire industrialist Arnold Edwards. Edwards has disappeared amid rumors of mismanagement and massive debt, leaving his companies in the hands of his estranged stepson, Robert. Harold shows you a napkin, printed with the logo of a bar called "One South" on which the following words have been handwritten:

> Marland, Inc. grants Harold Philbrick a security interest in the Marland manufacturing facility, Marland, Florida, to secure his loan to Marland, Inc.

The napkin bears what Harold says is the signature of Arnold Edwards, though it is difficult to tell because the napkin is torn and has some food stains on it. "I watched Arnold write it," Harold says. "Two other people were at the table when he did it."

The Marland manufacturing facility is a shoe factory located on ten acres of land. The land and building are worth at least $4 million; the machinery and other personal property on the premises, including unshipped inventory, are worth perhaps an additional $1 million. The only encumbrance of record is a real estate mortgage in the original amount of $1.5 million.

Harold wants to know what he should do about his million dollars and his napkin now that Edwards seems to be out of the picture. What do you tell him? UCC §§9-203(b), 9-502(a) and (b), 9-509(a) and (b).

■ End of Default Problem Set

20.3.   Your client, Folds Mobile Homes, sells about 200 mobile homes a year at an average price of about $25,000. When Folds sells a home, it has the buyer execute a promissory note, security agreement, and a standard UCC-1 financing statement. In accord with the advice of its former attorneys, Folds always describes the collateral as "[brand] mobile home, [serial number]" and files the financing statement in the Office of the Secretary of State, UCC

Division, the place specified in UCC §9-501(a)(2). (The state does not permit perfection in a mobile home by notation on a certificate of title.)

Folds repossesses from five to ten mobile homes a year. Until the Bob Barker case, Folds had never had any legal problems with the repossessions. Barker bought a mobile home from Folds about a year ago. He put the home on a lot he owned about four miles outside the city. After Barker disappeared, Folds was served with a summons and complaint in a mortgage foreclosure brought by Pacific Security Finance (PSF). It seems that PSF financed Barker's purchase of the lot and Barker defaulted on his mortgage to them. PSF's complaint alleges that the mobile home is a fixture and hence covered under PSF's mortgage. It also alleges that Fold's security interest in the mobile home is unperfected because it was not filed "in the office where a mortgage on the real estate would be filed or recorded," citing UCC §9-501(a), and "fails to comply with the requirements of" UCC §§9-502(a) and (b).

a.   Allison Folds, the president of Folds, is very upset by the allegation that Folds' interest is unperfected and asks if the allegation is correct. What do you tell Allison?

b.   Does Folds win or lose against PSF? UCC §9-334(e)(1).

c.   Would Folds win or lose if the challenger was a trustee in bankruptcy? UCC §9-334(e)(3).

d.   How should Folds perfect its interest in the mobile homes it sells in the future? UCC §§9-102(a)(41), 9-502(a) and (b).

20.4.   Sam Stoney, owner of Stoney's Pizza Parlour, is refinancing his business with Western Commercial Bank and has asked you to take a look at the documents. A portion of paragraph 20 of the real property mortgage reads as follows:

> In addition, Borrower agrees to execute and deliver to Lender, upon Lender's request, any financing statements, as well as extensions, renewals and amendments thereof, and reproductions of this Instrument in such form as lender may require to perfect a security interest with respect to [the collateral]. Borrower shall pay all costs of filing such financing statements and any extensions, renewals, amendments and releases thereof, and shall pay all reasonable costs and expenses of any record searches for financing statements Lender may reasonably require.

A later provision in the mortgage defines "lender" as including the bank's "successors and assigns."

Sam says that when he read this paragraph in the bank's form mortgage agreement, he was a little irritated. But considering the time and effort he has already put into this refinancing, he doesn't want to pull out and start over unless the clause presents a real and substantial problem. Does it?

Assignment 21: Characterizing Collateral and Transactions

Earlier assignments presented several situations in which the proper method of perfection depends on the type of collateral involved. For example, if the collateral is real property, perfection is by filing in the real estate records of the county where the real property is located. If it is money, perfection is achieved by taking possession. Sometimes the proper method of perfection depends both on the type of collateral and how the court characterizes the transaction. For example, if the collateral is a patent and the transaction is a security interest, perfection is by filing in the Article 9 filing system. But if the transaction is an "assignment"—here meaning a "sale"—perfection is by filing in the U.S. Patent and Trademark Office.

Article 9 makes many other distinctions among types of collateral and transactions. Most of these distinctions are made for the purpose of specifying the appropriate method for perfecting in the collateral. They fall into two categories: distinctions related to place of filing and distinctions related to method of perfection. In this assignment, we examine these distinctions in more detail.

A. Determining the Proper Place of Filing

There are more than four thousand filing systems in the United States. A lender cannot file and search in all of them. Accordingly, Article 9 and related laws attempt to direct each lender to the single proper system.

Some law specifies which filings are properly made in each system. The specification may be based on the intrinsic nature of the collateral, such as when the law directs filing against a copyright in the Copyright Office. It may be based on the use to which the collateral is put, such as when the law requires filing against an automobile that is inventory, but notation on the certificate of title of an automobile that is equipment. Or the specification may be based on type of lien to be perfected, such as where the state provides a separate set of records for perfecting tax liens or judgment liens. Thus, to determine the right systems in which to file, secured parties often must classify collateral and transactions.

B.   Determining the Proper Method of Perfection

Recall that there are essentially five ways that a security interest in personal property can be perfected: (1) by filing, (2) by possession, (3) by control, (4) by giving notice to the stakeholder (on non-UCC collateral such as insurance claims and tort actions), and (5) by doing nothing (automatic perfection). For some kinds of collateral, more than one of these methods will work. Determining which will work in any particular instance depends on the type of collateral involved.

1.   *Instruments Distinguished from General Intangibles*

Omega Environmental Inc. v. Valley Bank, N.A.
219 F.3d 984 (9th Cir. 2000)

PER CURIAM.

We agree with the bankruptcy court and the district court that the Bank perfected its security interest and was entitled to relief from the automatic stay. A security interest in an "instrument" is perfected by possession. See [UCC §9-313(a)]. It is undisputed that at all times relevant to this action the Bank had possession of the [certificate of deposit (CD)]. Therefore, the Bank perfected its security interest in the CD if the CD is an "instrument" as defined in the Uniform Commercial Code (UCC) as adopted by Virginia:

> "Instrument" means a negotiable instrument as defined in [UCC §3-104] or any other writing which evidences a right to the payment of money and is not itself a security agreement or lease and is of a type which is in ordinary course of business transferred by delivery with any necessary indorsement or assignment. . . .

[UCC §9-102(a)(47).] It is undisputed that the CD is neither a "negotiable instrument" nor a security agreement nor a lease. The only question is whether the CD is a writing evidencing a right to the payment of money "which is in ordinary course of business transferred by delivery with any necessary indorsement or assignment."[3]

The bankruptcy court concluded that (1) although the CD is nonnegotiable, it is assignable by its terms and was in fact assigned to the Bank;[4] and (2) the CD "'is of a type which is in ordinary course of business transferred by delivery with any necessary endorsement or assignment,' and as such qualifies as an instrument as defined by [UCC §9-102(a)(47)]." The bankruptcy court rested its decision in

---

3. Although whether the CD is properly characterized as an "instrument" is a question of law reviewed de novo, whether the CD is "of a type which is in ordinary course of business transferred by delivery with any necessary indorsement or assignment" is a question of fact reviewed under the "clearly erroneous" standard.

4. The CD states on its face: "This certificate (and the account it represents) may not be transferred or assigned without [the Bank's] prior written consent and is not negotiable." The CD was assigned to the Bank through a Deposit Account Assignment Agreement.

part upon Panel Publishers, Inc. v. Smith (In re Kelly Group, Inc.), 159 B.R. 472, 480-81 (Bankr. W.D. Va. 1993), which held that promissory notes and certificates of deposit bearing the terms "nonnegotiable and nonassignable" are instruments under [UCC §9-102(a)(47)]. Kelly also rejected the argument that such documents should be characterized as "general intangibles," noting that "the Official Comment set forth in [§9-102] makes clear that [the term 'general intangibles'] was intended to cover types of personal property such as goodwill, copyrights and trademarks that are not usually represented by a particular document."[5]

Kelly's holding that "nonnegotiable, nontransferable" certificates of deposit are "instruments" under [UCC §9-102(a)(47)] has not yet been accepted or rejected by Virginia courts. However, the weight of authority supports the conclusion that a nonnegotiable certificate of deposit, even if bearing words limiting its transferability as in this case, is an "instrument" as defined under UCC Article 9.

Almost every court to face the issue has rejected the argument that the language on the certificate is controlling, i.e., if a certificate of deposit bears the legend "nontransferable" it cannot be "in ordinary course of business transferred" as required by the UCC definition of an instrument. UCC Article 9 provides a uniform method of perfection for security interests in all types of property. Rather than "narrowly looking to the form of the writing, a court should instead look to the realities of the marketplace." Craft Products, Inc. v. Hartford Fire Ins. Co., 670 N.E.2d 959, 961 (Ind. Ct. App. 1996). If there is evidence that the type of writing at issue is ordinarily transferred in the marketplace by delivery with the necessary endorsement, the requirements of Article 9 are met.

The bankruptcy court's finding that the CD in this case is a type of document which is in the ordinary course of business in Virginia treated as transferable by delivery with any necessary endorsement or assignment is not clearly erroneous. The court relied upon a declaration by the president of the Bank, the fact that the CD was actually transferred, and upon the statements in Kelly, to conclude that ordinary commercial practice in Virginia is to treat "nontransferable" certificates of deposit as "instruments." Omega did not claim there was a question of fact as to ordinary commercial practice in Virginia at the time the bankruptcy court entered its order. The majority of the case law concerning the characterization of certificates of deposit also supports the bankruptcy court's conclusion.

AFFIRMED.

---

2.   True Leases Distinguished from Leases Intended as Security

Probably the single most frequently litigated issue under Article 9 is whether a transaction is a security interest or a lease. This issue was discussed briefly in

---

5. "General intangibles" are a catch-all category, defined, in relevant part, as "any personal property (including things in action) other than goods, accounts, chattel paper, documents, [and] instruments. . . ." [UCC §9-102(a)(42).] Security interests in "general intangibles" are perfected by filing a financing statement. [UCC §9-310(a).] The Bank did not file a financing statement in connection with its security interest in the CD.

Assignment 2. For tax and a variety of other reasons unrelated to Article 9 and bankruptcy, parties may decide to structure a particular transaction so it will be characterized as a lease instead of a sale with a security interest — or vice versa. But they do not always succeed in determining how courts will later characterize it.

In the following case, the owner of cattle leased them to a dairy farmer. When the dairy farmer filed bankruptcy, the dairy farmer's bank lender claimed the cattle under an after-acquired property clause in its security agreement. The issue in the case was whether the lease was a "true lease" or a security agreement. It mattered because, if Purdy owned the cows, Citizens bank would have a security interest in them, but if Sunshine owned the cows, Citizens bank would have a security interest only in Purdy's leasehold interest in the cows.

In re Purdy

763 F.3d 513 (6th Cir. 2014)

KAREN NELSON MOORE, CIRCUIT JUDGE.

Between 2009 and 2012, Sunshine Heifers, LLC ("Sunshine") and Lee H. Purdy, a dairy farmer, entered into several "Dairy Cow Leases." Purdy received a total of 435 cows to milk, and, in exchange, he paid a monthly rent to Sunshine. Unfortunately, Purdy's dairy business faltered in 2012, and he petitioned for bankruptcy protection.

I. BACKGROUND

Purdy operated his dairy farm in Barren County, Kentucky. In 2008, he entered into a loan relationship with Citizens First [Bank], using his herd of dairy cattle as collateral. As part of the security agreement, Purdy granted Citizens First a purchase money security interest in "all . . . Equipment, Farm Products, [and] Livestock (including all increase and supplies) . . . currently owned [or] hereafter acquired. . . ." Three days later, Citizens First perfected this purchase money security interest by filing a financing statement with the Kentucky Secretary of State.

In 2009, Purdy decided to increase the size of his dairy-cattle herd. He contacted Jeff Blevins of Sunshine regarding the prospect of leasing additional cattle. Sunshine was amenable to the idea, and on August 7, 2009, Purdy and Sunshine entered into [three contracts involving the 435 cattle in question].

Each of these agreements is titled a "Dairy Cow Lease," and under their terms, Purdy received a total of 435 cattle for fifty months in exchange for a monthly rent. The agreements prohibited Purdy from terminating the leases, and Purdy agreed to "return the Cows, at [his] expense, to such place as Sunshine designate[d]" at the end of the lease term. Additionally, Purdy guaranteed "the net sales proceeds from the sale of the Cows . . . at the end of the Lease term [would] be [a set amount between $290 and $300] per head." Purdy further promised to maintain insurance on the cattle, to replace any cows that were culled from the herd, and to allow Sunshine the right to inspect the herd. When the parties signed these contracts, they also executed security agreements, and Sunshine filed financing statements with the Secretary of State.

In the dairy business, farmers must "cull" a portion of their herd every year, replacing older and less productive cows with younger, healthier ones. [The cattle on the farm at the time of bankruptcy were auctioned. Citizens First and Sunshine are fighting over the auction proceeds.]

Citizens First argued that Purdy owned all of these cattle and, therefore, that they were covered by the bank's perfected purchase money security interest. Sunshine contended that it maintained ownership of the cattle, that Purdy had only a leasehold interest in the cattle, and therefore that the cattle fell outside of Citizen First's security interest.

III. ANALYSIS

The main question in this case is whether the agreements between Purdy and Sunshine are "true leases" or merely "security agreements." A lease involves payment for the temporary possession, use and enjoyment of goods, with the expectation that the goods will be returned to the owner with some expected residual interest of value remaining at the end of the lease term. In contrast, a sale involves an unconditional transfer of absolute title to goods, while a security interest is only an inchoate interest contingent on default and limited to the remaining secured debt. If the agreements are true leases, then Sunshine has a reversionary interest in 435 head of cattle and is entitled to approximately $309,000 [of the $402,354 realized] from the cattle auction. If the agreements represent the sale of the cattle and Sunshine's retention of a security interest, then Citizens First's perfected agricultural security interest trumps Sunshine's interest, and the bank keeps all of the proceeds from the cattle auction.

Under Arizona law, "the facts of each case" dictate whether an agreement is a true lease or a security agreement, [UCC §1-203(a)], and our fact-sensitive analysis proceeds in two steps. First, we employ the Bright-Line Test. According to this test, "[a] transaction in the form of a lease creates a security interest if the consideration that the lessee is to pay the lessor for the right to possession and use of the goods is an obligation for the term of the lease and is not subject to termination by the lessee, and . . . [t]he original term of the lease is equal to or greater than the remaining economic life of the goods." [UCC §1-203(b).] If the lease runs longer than the economic life of the goods, then the lease is a per se security agreement. If the goods retain meaningful value after the lease expires, however, we move to the second step and look at the specific facts of the case to determine whether the economics of the transaction suggest that the arrangement is a lease or a security interest. At all points in this analysis, the party challenging the leases bears the burden of proving that they are something else.

A. Bright-Line Test

No one debates that Purdy lacked the ability to terminate the lease. The question is whether the lease term of fifty months exceeds the economic life of the cattle. The bankruptcy court fixated upon Purdy's testimony that he culled approximately thirty percent of the cattle each year, meaning that the entire herd would turn over in forty months. As a result, the bankruptcy court concluded that the lease term exceeded the economic life of the cattle that Sunshine initially gave Purdy and, therefore, that the lease was a per se security agreement. We disagree and hold that the bankruptcy court erred in its analysis of the cattle's economic life because the court focused upon the economic life of the individual cows originally leased to Purdy, instead of the life of the herd as required by the agreements.

According to the text of the agreements between Purdy and Sunshine, Purdy had a duty to return the same number of cattle to Sunshine that he originally leased, not the same cattle. It made little difference to Sunshine whether it received the exact same cows that it originally leased to Purdy; according to Blevins—Sunshine's owner—"the main thing is to maintain the leasehold, the integrity of the lease numbers." In line with this understanding, the agreements took into account industry practices, such as culling, by requiring Purdy to replace any unproductive cows that he sold. Sunshine protected its interest in the herd by inspecting Purdy's operation, requiring Purdy to carry insurance, and creating a "Residual Guaranty," which stated that the actual cattle returned would be worth at least a set amount. Given these provisions and the testimony of the parties, it is clear to us that the relevant "good" is the herd of cattle, which has an economic life far greater than the lease term, and not the individual cows originally placed on Purdy's farm. Accordingly, we hold that the contracts flunk the Bright-Line Test and are not per se security agreements.

B. Economics-of-the-Transaction Test

The precise contours of the economics-of-the-transaction test are rather unclear, but courts have largely focused upon two particular factors: (1) whether the lease contains a purchase option price that is nominal; and (2) whether the lessee develops equity in the property, such that the only economically reasonable option for the lessee is to purchase the goods. The ultimate question for us, however, is whether Sunshine kept a meaningful reversionary interest in the herd. On the facts presented to us, we hold that Citizens First has also failed to carry its burden of establishing that the actual economics of the transactions indicate that the leases were disguised security agreements.

In this case, neither of the above-mentioned factors suggests that these agreements are something other than true leases because the contracts do not contain an option for Purdy to purchase the cattle at any price, let alone at a nominal one. In fact, the agreements explicitly state that Sunshine retains ownership in the cattle throughout the life of the lease and beyond. Here, even if Purdy wanted to purchase the cattle at $300 per cow, there is nothing in the agreements that obligates Sunshine to sell to him. Sunshine could have retaken possession of its cows and leased them out to Purdy's competitor under the same terms, and there would have been nothing Purdy could have done under the agreement. In our view, this state of play is consistent with a lease.

Finally, whether the parties adhered to the terms of these leases in all facets, in our view, is irrelevant to determining whether the agreements were true leases or disguised security agreements. Neither the bankruptcy court nor the parties have sufficiently explained the legal import of Purdy's culling practices or put forward any evidence that the parties altered the terms of the leases making them anything but what they proclaim to be. Moreover, [UCC §1-203(c)] clearly states that the fact that terms of the lease are unfavorable to the lessee, that the lessee assumes the risk of loss of the goods, or that the lease requires the lessee to maintain insurance on the goods is not alone grounds to find that a contract is a security agreement. As a result, we hold that Citizens First has not carried its burden of proving that the actual economics of the transaction demonstrate that the leases were security agreements.

For those of us who can't tell the difference between a true lease and a security interest and who are skeptical about whether judges can either, UCC §9-505 permits a "precautionary" filing. That filing may characterize the transaction as a lease, but nevertheless will perfect the transaction if some court later holds it to be a security interest.

3. Realty Paper

The term *realty paper* is sometimes used to refer to a promissory note secured by a mortgage or deed of trust. The issue of how to perfect in realty paper was dealt with in Assignment 20. Under UCC §9-308(e), the proper method to perfect in realty paper is to perfect in the right to payment. In most instances, that note will be an "instrument" within the meaning of UCC §9-102(a)(47). When it is, perfection can be accomplished by taking possession of the note, UCC §9-313(a), or by filing, UCC §9-312(a). But there is a twist: only perfection accomplished by possession under the circumstances described in UCC §9-330(d) will achieve priority over a later purchaser, making perfection by such possession preferable.

4. Chattel Paper, Instruments, Accounts, and Payment Intangibles Distinguished

As we saw in earlier assignments, one debt can serve as collateral for another. The debt that serves as collateral can be classified as chattel paper, an instrument, an account, or a payment intangible. These four definitions are, generally speaking, nested. Chattel paper is at the center. If the collateral qualifies as chattel paper, it is chattel paper. UCC §9-102(a)(11). If the collateral qualifies as an instrument, it is an instrument unless it is chattel paper. UCC §9-102(a)(47). If the collateral qualifies as an account, it is an account unless it qualifies as chattel paper or an instrument. UCC §9-102(a)(2). If the collateral qualifies as a payment intangible, it is a payment intangible unless it qualifies as an account, an instrument, or chattel paper. UCC §9-102(a)(61) and (42).

"Chattel paper" means a record that evidences both a monetary obligation and a security interest in goods or a lease of goods. In essence, it is the paper that evidences a secured debt. To illustrate the use of chattel paper as security, assume that Bonnie's Boat World sells a boat to William and Gladys Homer for $20,000, "no money down." At the time of the sale, the Homers sign both a promissory note for $20,000 and a security agreement in favor of Bonnie's. Together, these two documents constitute chattel paper. When Bonnie's sells a boat, it must pay the amount it owes to its inventory lender on the boat. Bonnie's will get the cash from First State Bank by borrowing against or selling its chattel paper (the note and the security agreement from the Homers). First State Bank can perfect its security interest in the chattel paper by taking possession of the paper, UCC §9-313(a), or by filing a financing statement, UCC §9-312(a).

These two methods of perfection are not equivalents. A purchaser of chattel paper who gives new value in the ordinary course of its business and who acts without knowledge of a security interest perfected by filing has priority over the security interest. UCC §9-330(a) and (b). Keep in mind that the definition of "purchaser" is broad enough to encompass both buyers and takers of security interests, including the bank lender in our example. UCC §§1-201(b)(29) and (30). For First State Bank to buy or lend against Bonnie's chattel paper and be assured of first priority, First State Bank need not conduct a UCC search. Even if there are earlier UCC filings against the chattel paper, the bank will have priority over them because the bank has perfected by taking possession.

Why then does Article 9 permit perfection in chattel paper by filing? Permissive filing against chattel paper is part of an ongoing effort by the drafters of Article 9 to scale back the rights of trustees in bankruptcy and lien creditors. Notice that trustees in bankruptcy and lien creditors are not purchasers and thus are not entitled to the benefit of UCC §9-330 priority. By making the permissive UCC filing, those who purchase chattel paper can gain an extra measure of protection. If, for example, they inadvertently leave some of the chattel paper they bought in the debtor's hands and the debtor files bankruptcy or the sheriff arrives, they can rely on their filing to beat out the pesky trustee or lien creditor.

The definition of an instrument has already been discussed. Here we add only that if a writing that otherwise qualifies as an instrument contains a security agreement or lease, it is chattel paper, not an instrument.

An account is a right to payment of a monetary obligation for property sold or services rendered. But if the right to payment is evidenced by chattel paper or an instrument, it does not quality as an account. UCC §9-102(a)(2).

Finally, a payment intangible is "a general intangible under which the account debtor's principal obligation is a monetary obligation." UCC §9-102(a)(61). A general intangible is defined to exclude chattel paper, instruments, and accounts. UCC §9-102(a)(42).

In the case that follows, the parties evoked a careful parsing of these definitions. The "surety" mentioned in the facts is a corporation in the business of guaranteeing payment of debts. If the surety is ever required to pay any of the debts, the surety steps into the shoes of the creditor whose debt it paid.

In re Commercial Money Center, Inc.

350 B.R. 465 (9th Cir. B.A.P. 2006)

MONTALI, BANKRUPTCY JUDGE.

I.   FACTS

Commercial Money Center, Inc. ("Debtor") leased equipment to lessees with sub-prime credit. It packaged groups of leases together and assigned its contractual rights to future lease payments to entities such as NetBank, Inc., FSB ("NetBank"). To enhance the marketability of these payment streams Debtor obtained surety bonds guaranteeing the payments and it assigned its rights under the surety bonds to NetBank. As security for NetBank's receipt of the lease payments and any surety bond payments, Debtor granted NetBank a security interest in the underlying leases and other property. In other words, Debtor assigned NetBank both an interest in the payment streams and an interest in the underlying leases, but it separated the two interests.

A.   TRANSACTION TERMS

In 1999 and 2000 NetBank transferred over $47 million to Debtor in transactions involving 17 pools of leases. Seven lease pools remain at issue. Each transaction involved (1) a Sale and Servicing Agreement ("SSA") among NetBank, Debtor, and a surety company ("Surety"), (2) surety bonds issued by Surety to Debtor, which Debtor assigned to NetBank under the SSA and was supposed to deliver to NetBank, and (3) an indemnity agreement between Surety and Debtor. A typical lease involved 62 payments of which two had been paid at the inception, leaving 60 payments assigned by Debtor to NetBank. Debtor paid Surety a premium equal to approximately two percent of the total of all payments due under each lease.

A sample indemnity agreement between Debtor and Surety, included in the excerpts of record, obligates Debtor and its principals to indemnify Surety and hold it harmless "against all demands, claims, loss, costs, damages, expenses and attorneys' fees whatever, and any and all liability therefore, sustained or incurred by the Surety" under any surety bonds.

IV.   DISCUSSION

Trustee's strongarm powers generally enable him to avoid a pre-petition unperfected transfer by Debtor of an interest in its property. 11 U.S.C. §544. Trustee argues that NetBank's interests were not perfected.

The perfection rules of UCC Article 9 apply not just to security interests for *loans* but also to *sales* of chattel paper and payment intangibles. [UCC §9-109(a)(3)] (with inapplicable exceptions, "this article applies to . . . (c) a *sale* of accounts, chattel paper, payment intangibles, or promissory notes") (emphasis added).

Somewhat confusingly, the UCC uses lending terminology in provisions that are applicable to sales. See [UCC §1-201(b)(35)] ("'Security interest' means an interest in personal property or fixtures which secures payment or performance of an obligation. 'Security interest' includes any interest of a consignor and a *buyer* of accounts, *chattel paper, a payment intangible* or a promissory note in a transaction that is subject to Article 9.") (emphasis added). See also [UCC §9-109], Official Comment 5 ("Use of terminology such as 'security interest,' 'debtor,' and 'collateral' is merely a drafting convention adopted to reach [the] end [of applying 'this Article's perfection and priority rules' to sales transactions], and its use has no relevance to distinguishing sales from other transactions.").

Most perfection is not automatic. One exception is a sale of payment intangibles (referred to as a security interest), which is perfected automatically: "The following *security interests* are perfected when they attach: . . . 3. a *sale* of a payment intangible[.]" [UCC §9-309(3)] (emphasis added).

A. The Payment Streams Are Payment Intangibles, Not Chattel Paper

The UCC distinguishes between the monetary obligation evidenced by chattel paper and the chattel paper itself:

a. In this article:

(11) "Chattel paper" means a *record or records* that *evidence* both a monetary obligation and a security interest in or a lease of specific goods. . . . As used in this paragraph, "monetary obligation" means a monetary obligation secured by the goods or owed under a lease of the goods. . . . [Emphasis added.]

[UCC §9-102(a)(11)].

This language on its face defines chattel paper to mean the "records" that "evidence" certain things, including monetary obligations. Payment streams stripped from the underlying leases are not records that evidence monetary obligations — they are monetary obligations. Therefore, we agree with NetBank that the payment streams are not chattel paper.

If they are not chattel paper, what are they? Most monetary obligations are "accounts" but the definition of account excludes "rights to payment evidenced by chattel paper." Therefore the monetary obligations in this case fall within the payment intangible subset of the catch-all definition of general intangibles. See [UCC §9-102(a)(2)] ("Account" means "a right to payment of a monetary obligation . . . for property that has been or is to be . . . leased . . . [but the term] does not include rights to payment evidenced by chattel paper . . ."); [UCC §9-102(a)(42)] ("General intangible" means any personal property other than accounts, chattel paper, and various other specified types of property, and specifically "includes payment intangibles"); [UCC §9102(a)(61)] ("Payment intangible" means "a general intangible under which the account debtor's principal obligation is a monetary obligation").

Trustee argues that our interpretation of the statute will lead to endless debates over whether particular assignments are actually sales or secured loans. Again, we are not persuaded. Many transactions fall clearly on one side or the other of the sale versus loan dichotomy. When the answer is not clear the UCC contemplates that courts will need to decide the issue. If such decisions are too burdensome on the commercial markets or on litigants then the remedy is with the legislature and not the courts.

Trustee also argues that if UCC Article 9 permits purchases of payment streams to be automatically perfected, as we have held, then this permits secret interests and will wreak havoc on the financing markets. According to Trustee, there is no way for a hypothetical financier to protect itself against the possibility that an entity such as Debtor will transfer interests in the same payment streams more than once. NetBank responds that payment stripping is a bedrock principle of the securitization industry and that Trustee's concerns are misplaced.

NetBank argues persuasively that, if the hypothetical financier is the first to perfect, then generally it will be first in priority. See [UCC §9-322(a)(1)]. For these purposes it does not matter if the transaction was a sale or a secured loan because the UCC covers both, as we have discussed. Nor does it matter if the financier's interest is in the payment streams alone or in the underlying chattel paper leases, because a perfected interest in chattel paper includes the associated payment streams.

A more difficult example is if the financier purchased an interest in the chattel paper leases after Debtor had already sold the payment streams to someone else. The financier might have no way to know of that prior "security interest." The holder of that secret interest might not have filed any financing statements, or taken possession of the leases, or given any other notice because, under our holding, its interest would be automatically perfected under UCC §9-309(3).

[W]e must apply the plain meaning of the statute: the payment streams separated from the underlying leases do not fall within the definition of chattel paper. [UCC §9-102(a)(11)]. Rather, these monetary obligations fall within the payment intangible subset of the catch-all definition of general intangibles. See [UCC §9-102(a)(2)] ("Account") [UCC §9-102(a)(42)] ("General intangible") and [UCC §9-102(a)(61)] ("Payment intangible").

Because the payment streams are payment intangibles, NetBank's interest in them would be automatically perfected upon attachment under [UCC §9-309(3)] if its transactions with Debtor were sales rather than loans. We now turn to that issue.

B. DEBTOR'S TRANSACTIONS WITH NETBANK WERE LOANS, NOT SALES

Despite NetBank's arguments, the transactions bear far more hallmarks of a loan than a sale. Each month Debtor as Sub-Servicer is required to pay NetBank a minimum fixed amount ($258,270.47 in the sample SSA) plus any additional "interest" and "principal" amounts owing to NetBank, regardless of what is or is not paid by the lessees. Debtor's assignment of the Transferred Assets to NetBank is non-recourse but just like many non-recourse loans it is secured by Debtor's property, including the underlying leases and equipment. Debtor as Sub-Servicer bears all costs of collection from lessees, NetBank pays no fees for this expense or any other costs of servicing the leases, and if there is a shortfall at the end of the 60-month Collection Period then Debtor as Sub-Servicer is required to make up the shortfall and pay ongoing "interest" until all "principal" is repaid in full. At that point any residual value in the Transferred Assets is returned to Debtor with no possibility of NetBank receiving more than repayment of the "principal" and "interest" whereas Debtor can retain any subsequent payments and late fees paid by the lessees. In other words, NetBank (1) has none of the potential benefits of ownership and (2) is contractually allocated none of the risk of loss.

These are strong indicia of a loan rather than a sale. The absence of risk "seems to result in a finding of a debtor-creditor relationship in most cases." *Woodson*, 813 F.2d at 271.

We agree with the bankruptcy court that the transactions were loans, not sales. Therefore, NetBank does not satisfy one of the criteria under [UCC §9-309(3)] ("The following security interests are perfected when they attach: . . . (3) a *sale* of a payment intangible[.]") (emphasis added). NetBank's interest was not automatically perfected.

In part IV.A of its decision, the court concludes that the parties stripped the payment streams from the leases, thereby converting the collateral from chattel paper to payment intangibles. Official Comment 5.d. to UCC §9-102 disagrees:

> A right to payment of money is frequently buttressed by ancillary rights . . . such as . . . the lessor's rights with respect to leased goods that arise upon the lessee's default. This Article does not treat these ancillary rights separately from the rights to payment to which they relate. For example, attachment and perfection of an assignment of a right to payment of a monetary obligation, whether it be an account or payment intangible, also carries these ancillary rights. Contrary to the opinion in *In re Commercial Money Center, Inc.* . . . if the lessor's rights under a lease constitute chattel paper, an assignment of the lessor's right to payment under the lease also would be an assignment of chattel paper, even if the assignment excludes other rights.

To reach the result in *Commercial Money Center*, the court had to characterize not only the collateral, but also the transaction. That is, the court characterized the transaction as a security interest in a payment intangible, not the sale of a payment intangible. Ironically, the drafters of Article 9 originally included sales of accounts and chattel paper in its coverage because of the difficulty of distinguishing between sales and security interests. Comment 4 to UCC §9-109 claims that the inclusion of sales of accounts and chattel paper "generally has been successful in avoiding difficult problems of distinguishing between transactions in which a receivable secures an obligation and those in which the receivable has been sold outright." But as the same comment notes, and *Commercial Money Center* illustrates, Article 9 "occasionally distinguishes between outright sales of receivables and sales that secure an obligation."

C.   Multiple Items of Collateral

One can easily get so involved in determining the proper classification of collateral that one does not notice that more than one kind of collateral is involved. In In re Leasing Consultants, Inc., 486 F.2d 367 (2d Cir. 1973), Leasing leased equipment to Plasimetrix Corporation. Citibank took a security interest in "the leases and property leased" and perfected in the manner that was then proper for perfecting a security interest in leases. Only when Leasing later filed bankruptcy did Citibank realize that perfection in the leases wasn't the same thing as perfection in the equipment leased. When Leasing leased the equipment, it retained a reversionary interest — ownership of the equipment itself. That ownership was goods and had to be perfected in the manner appropriate for goods. Citibank hadn't done it, and so lost the case.

The subtlety of Citibank's error becomes apparent when one considers Citibank's conceptualization of the transaction. Citibank believed that the reversion under an equipment lease was part of the lease. By perfecting in the lease, they had perfected in the reversionary interest created by the lease.

The moral of this story is that in many cases there is a step to go through *before* deciding how to classify collateral under the Article 9 scheme. That earlier step is to decide precisely what the collateral is and how that collateral is conceptualized and classified under the scheme of property law. You have already engaged in this process in earlier assignments. For example, in Problem 20.1.a, you had to determine whether the debtor's one-third interest in a parcel of real property was as a tenant-in-common (real estate) or was an interest in a partnership (personal property) in order to determine the proper method of perfection. This assignment has merely made you more conscious of what you were already doing.

Problem Set 21

21.1.   How should the secured party perfect a security interest in each of the following?

a.   *The money owing to the debtor from the purchaser of the debtor's liquor license under an oral agreement?* UCC §§9-102(a)(2), (11), (42), and (61); 9-310(a) and (b), 9-312(a); 9-313(a); 9-314(a).

b.   *A note and mortgage the debtor bought from the mortgagee for 80 percent of its face amount three months ago?* UCC §§9-109(a)(2), (b), (d)(11); 9-203(g); 9-308(e).

c.   *If the secured party in b perfects by filing, against whom should it file?* UCC §§1-201(b)(35); 9-318(b).

d.   *The lessee's interest under a lease of real property.* UCC §§9-102(a)(11) and (42), 9-109(d)(11), and Comment 10 to §9-109.

e.   *Wheat growing in the farmer-debtor's field.* UCC §§9-102(a)(34) and (44), 9-109(d)(11), 9-334(a) and (i), 9-501(a); Comment 4.a. to UCC §9-102 and Comment 12 to UCC §9-334.

f. *The franchise to operate a Burger King restaurant.* (The franchise agreement was signed yesterday. The franchisee has not yet contracted to purchase the land where the restaurant will be located.) The franchise is issued to the debtor and specifically states that it is nontransferable.

g. *An electronic "book entry" certificate of deposit.* The certificate was issued by Citibank in the amount of $2 million to Kennedy Construction Company, but it is not now and never has been evidenced by anything on paper. UCC §§9-102(a)(29), (42) and (47), 9-104, 9-312(a), 9-313(a), 9-314, 9-330(d).

h. *Electronic chattel paper.* UCC §§9-312(a), 9-314(a) and 9-105.

i. The software on a consumer debtor's personal computer, including software written by the debtor. UCC §§9-102(a)(23), (44) and (76), 9-109(c)(1), 9-309(1), 9-310, 9-312(a), 9-313(a).

j. The documentation and manuals for that software.

21.2. You are working as a staff member for the Uniform Law Commission (ULC), and you have been assigned the preparation of a preliminary assessment of a proposal by a ULC member to amend Article 9. The proposal is to have only a single filing system in each state and require that if a debtor is located in the state, all security interests in personal property owned by the debtor be perfected by filing in that filing system. The effect would be to do away with nearly all distinctions among types of collateral except the distinction between "real" and "personal" property collateral. The proposal argues that if all of these distinctions could be eliminated, it would cut the text of Article 9 by one-third and with it the length of the Article 9 course in law schools. With some 15,000 students enrolled in Article 9 courses annually, the savings projected from this source alone might be as much as 315,000 person-hours. (The proposal also suggests that this time in law school be devoted to issues of professional responsibility or sports law.)

ULC does not want your assessment of whether the proposal would pass. They are principally interested in any possible side effects from the change. Are there good reasons for maintaining these separate filing systems and methods of perfection, and making all these distinctions among types of collateral? Restrict your consideration to perfection-related issues. Someone else will report on other uses made of these distinctions.

21.3. Space Corporation owns a satellite that the parties expect will circle the earth for exactly five years and then enter the atmosphere and vaporize.

a. Space Corporation leases the satellite to Communications, Inc. for 60 monthly rental payments of $99,000. Is that a true lease or a security interest? UCC §1-203.

b. Same facts as a., except that the lease provides that Communications can terminate the lease at the end of 59 months.

c. Same facts as a., except that the lease is for 48 months. Communications has an option to rent for an additional 12 months at the same monthly rate. The parties expect Communications to renew because Communications has 60-month leases with several customers.

■ End of Default Problem Set

21.4. Monte Publishing Company has asked your client, Flexible Finance, to finance Monte's acquisition of a custom-built four-color printing press. The press will be manufactured by Thien Tool Company. The cost of the press will be $1.2 million. The parties have agreed that Monte will pay all closing costs and pay Flexible 10 percent interest on the amount of financing outstanding at any given time. Payment will be in equal monthly installments over seven years. Because of sizeable losses Flexible took as a secured creditor in two recent bankruptcy cases, Flexible insists that the transaction be structured as a lease. Flexible would like you to draft the lease and render an opinion that the transaction will be effective as a lease.

Monte and Flexible agree that the expected useful life of the press is probably between five and 15 years, but no one can be sure how long it will in fact be useful and used because the technology is changing rapidly. Monte would like to use the press throughout its useful life; Flexible has no use for the press and does not want possession. If the press has to be resold, the commission on the sale probably would be about 25 percent of the value of the press at the time of sale. As its value approaches zero, brokers will be increasingly unwilling to undertake its sale.

Flexible understands that the lease might not give it exactly what it wants, but it would like you to come as close as possible. What wording do you recommend for the provisions of the lease controlling the lease term and the amount of rent payable? If you recommend that Flexible have a reversionary interest, how should Flexible deal with reversion? UCC §1-201(35).

21.5. Your client, Fidelity Assurance, plans to purchase $26 million of chattel paper presently held by Auto Finance, LLC. What should Fidelity do to assure itself that Auto Finance hasn't stripped the payment obligations from the chattel paper and sold them to someone else?

Chapter 7.   Maintaining Perfection

Assignment 22:   Maintaining Perfection Through Lapse and Bankruptcy

In the preceding chapter, we discussed what secured parties must do to perfect their security interests. In this chapter we discuss what they must do to maintain that perfection over time and how they terminate perfection when it has served its purpose. We begin with the problem of termination.

A.   Removing Filings from the Public Record

From the time it is placed on the public record, a filing or recording serves as constructive notice to the world that a security interest may be outstanding against property of the debtor. The theory is that searchers will discover the existence of a prior holder's interest by examining the public record, and then contact the holder of the prior interest for more information. Ultimately, such searchers must either come to terms with the holder of the prior interest or accept a subordinate position. The prior interest encumbers the property and clouds title to it.

When the debt is paid, both debtor and creditor typically will want to "remove" the filing from the public record. The debtor will want the filing off the record to clear its title to the property. The creditor will want the filing off the record so it won't be bothered by inquiries about property in which it no longer has an interest.

We put "remove" in quotation marks because most filing systems do not permit the literal removal of documents at the request of the parties. All one can do is *add* another document stating that the earlier document is no longer in effect. Nearly all real estate recording systems operate in this manner.

1.   Satisfaction

We begin our discussion of removal of filings with the real property system because removal is easier to master in the real estate context than in the personalty system. When a real estate mortgage is paid, the mortgagee executes a document called a *satisfaction of mortgage* for recording. The satisfaction identifies the mortgage and states that it has been satisfied. Both the mortgage and the satisfaction of mortgage remain permanently in the recording system. It is important to realize that even if the debtor pays the mortgage debt, the mortgage continues to cloud the debtor's title until a satisfaction is recorded. The satisfaction assures persons who deal with the property in the future that the mortgagee cannot make claims against it.

To understand the role that the satisfaction plays in a real estate transaction, consider the following example. Seller owns a beach house that is subject to a mortgage in favor of Western Savings in the amount of $800,000. Seller has contracted to sell the beach house to Buyer, free and clear of the mortgage, for $1 million in cash. Seller, like most of us, does not have $800,000 with which to satisfy the mortgage; she must use the proceeds of sale to pay it. Buyer, like most of us, does not have the $1 million he will use to pay the purchase price. He will borrow the money from Eastern Savings, using the beach house as collateral. Eastern Savings will, of course, insist that the title to the beach house be free and clear of liens other than its own before it will disburse the loan proceeds. But Western Savings will not remove its mortgage from the title until it is paid the $800,000 owing to it. A stalemate looms.

The standard solution to this problem is to set a *closing*—a gathering of all the parties so that they can make a simultaneous exchange of documents and money. At the closing, Eastern will pay the mortgage to Western, using $800,000 of the loan proceeds, and Western will simultaneously deliver a satisfaction of the mortgage to Seller. Seller will deed the property to Buyer. Buyer will sign a new mortgage for the amount of the loan proceeds, and the parties will record all three documents immediately. The satisfaction is Western's assurance to Eastern that Western will make no further claims under the mortgage. Unless Seller can obtain this satisfaction of the old mortgage, Buyer cannot get the new mortgage he needs to pay the purchase price. The transaction will not *close* and the sale will fall through.

Because of the importance of the satisfaction, statutes in most states provide for imposition of a penalty on a secured party who fails to give one to a debtor who has fully paid the mortgage debt. The following statutes are typical:

Arizona Revised Statutes Annotated

(2015)

§33-712   LIABILITY FOR FAILURE TO ACKNOWLEDGE SATISFACTION

A. If any person receiving satisfaction of a mortgage or deed of trust shall, within thirty days, fail to record or cause to be recorded, with the recorder of the county in which the mortgage or deed of trust was recorded, a sufficient release, satisfaction of mortgage or deed of release or acknowledge satisfaction as provided in section 33-707, subsection C, he shall be liable to the mortgagor, trustor or current property owner for actual damages occasioned by the neglect or refusal.

B. If, after the expiration of the time provided in subsection A of this section, the person fails to record or cause to be recorded a sufficient release and continues to do so for more than thirty days after receiving a written request which identifies a certain mortgage or deed of trust by certified mail from the mortgagor, trustor, current property owner or his agent, he shall be liable to the mortgagor, trustor or current property owner for one thousand dollars, in addition to any actual damage occasioned by the neglect or refusal.

Florida Statutes Annotated

(2015)

§701.04   CANCELLATION OF MORTGAGES, LIENS, AND JUDGMENTS

Whenever the amount of money due on any mortgage, lien, or judgment shall be fully paid to the person or party entitled to the payment thereof, the mortgagee, creditor, or assignee, or the attorney of record in the case of a judgment, to whom such payment shall have been made, shall execute in writing an instrument acknowledging satisfaction of said mortgage, lien, or judgment and have the same acknowledged, or proven, and duly entered of record in the book provided by law for such purposes in the proper county. Within 60 days of the date of receipt of the full payment of the mortgage, lien, or judgment, the person required to acknowledge satisfaction of the mortgage, lien, or judgment shall send or cause to be sent the recorded satisfaction to the person who has made the full payment. In the case of a civil action arising out of the provisions of this section, the prevailing party shall be entitled to attorney's fees and costs.

Notice that neither of these statutes requires delivery or recording of a satisfaction of mortgage until long after payment. Consequently, neither requires a mortgagee to deliver a satisfaction of mortgage at the closing at which the mortgagee is to be paid. The law is the same in nearly all states. To address this deficiency, the Restatement (Third) of Property: Mortgages §6.4, asserts that courts can order immediate satisfaction, notwithstanding the existence of a statute to the contrary.

2. Release

Mortgages frequently encumber more than one parcel of real property. If such a mortgage has not been paid in full but the secured creditor is willing to release some of the property from the mortgage lien, the secured creditor accomplishes this by executing a *release* for recording. Most secured creditors release collateral only to the extent that they are required to do so by contract. The debtor typically bargains for the secured creditor's contractual obligation to release collateral before the loan is made.

Provisions requiring the release of collateral on partial payment of the loan are customary in financing the development of real estate subdivisions. For example, assume that High Point Development Company intends to purchase Blackacre, divide it into 100 residential building lots, build a road through it, install utilities, and sell the lots to contractors. Fidelity Savings lends High Point $7 million to buy and improve the property. High Point does so, and begins offering the improved lots for sale. Linda Easterbrook, a professional home builder, is High Point's first customer. Easterbrook agrees to buy one of the lots for $250,000.

Easterbrook will almost certainly demand that she receive the lot free and clear of Fidelity's mortgage. Only then can she use it as collateral for the mortgage she will take out to finance construction of her house. Neither she nor her new lender want the risk that High Point will later default in payment of its mortgage and Fidelity will foreclose against the Easterbrook lot along with the others. But where will that leave Fidelity? The $250,000 that High Point will receive from the sale to Easterbrook will fall far short of the amount necessary to satisfy Fidelity's mortgage.

The usual accommodation between parties like these is that Fidelity will release the Easterbrook lot in return for a partial payment of its mortgage (a *paydown*). Fidelity's mortgage will probably contain a provision requiring it to give the release, contingent on High Point's payment of the *release price*. If the release price for the Easterbrook lot is, for example, $120,000, High Point will use proceeds of the sale to Easterbrook to pay that amount to Fidelity, reducing the balance owing Fidelity to $6,880,000. In return, Fidelity will sign a release of the Easterbrook lot, reducing Fidelity's collateral to 99 lots. Easterbrook will see that the release is recorded.

Notice that Fidelity's collateral-to-loan ratio improves as a result of the sale to Easterbrook. Before the sale, Fidelity has 100 lots as collateral for a $7 million balance outstanding, a ratio of one lot per $70,000 of debt. After the sale, Fidelity has 99 lots as collateral for a $6,880,000 balance outstanding, a ratio of one lot per $69,490 of debt. High Point's $120,000 paydown on each lot sold will pay the debt in full before High Point sells all the lots. With each successive sale, Fidelity will be better assured of payment of the remaining balance.

Absent a release provision in a mortgage, the mortgagee is under no obligation to release collateral on partial payment of the mortgage—even if the debtor offers a paydown that will improve the lender's collateral-to-loan ratio. The mortgagee's only obligation is to execute a satisfaction when the debtor pays the entire balance owing on the mortgage debt. The same rule applies to security interests under Article 9.

3.   Article 9 Termination and Release

If the debtor has paid the secured obligation and the secured party is not required by contract to lend more money, the debtor can demand that the secured party file a *termination statement* within 20 days. UCC §9-513(c)(1). If the secured party fails to do so, the secured party becomes liable for actual damages and, in addition, a civil penalty of $500. UCC §§9-625(b) and (e)(4). Upon the filing of a termination statement, the financing statement to which it relates ceases to be effective. UCC §9-513(d).

Release of collateral from the coverage of a financing statement is accomplished by amending the financing statement. UCC §9-512(a). As under real estate law, the secured party is obligated to file a termination statement upon full payment of the secured debt, but is not obligated to file an amendment deleting collateral on partial payment unless the secured party has contracted to do so.

A termination statement or amendment must identify, by its file number, the initial financing statement to which it relates. In addition, a termination statement must indicate that the identified financing statement is no longer effective. UCC §9-102(a)(80). A termination statement or amendment becomes part of the financing statement to which it relates. See UCC §9-102(a)(39). As a consequence, it appears that minor errors or omissions in the termination statement would be subject to the "seriously misleading" test of UCC §9-506. That is, such errors would not render the financing statement—including the termination statement or amendment—ineffective unless errors make the financing statement seriously misleading.

Anyone can file a termination statement. But a filed record is effective only if it is filed by a person that may file it under §9-509. UCC §9-510(a). That raises the possibility of termination statements that show up on a search but are not effective because the secured parties didn't file them. Searchers are left to figure out which ones they are.

Agency complicates matters even further. Section 9-509(d)(1) provides that a person may file a termination statement if the secured party of record authorized the filing. UCC §9-509(a)(1). When an agent mistakenly files a termination statement, the secured party may argue that it did not authorize the filing of a termination statement or, although it authorized the filing of a termination statement, it did not authorize the filing of *that* termination statement. In the case that follows, the court explains what it means for the secured party of record to authorize a filing:

In re Motors Liquidation Co.

777 F.3d 100 (2d Cir. 2015)

Per Curiam:

BACKGROUND

In October 2001, General Motors entered into a synthetic lease financing transaction (the "Synthetic Lease"), by which it obtained approximately $300 million in financing from a syndicate of lenders including JPMorgan Chase Bank, N.A. ("JPMorgan"). General Motors' obligation to repay the Synthetic Lease was secured by liens on twelve pieces of real estate. JPMorgan served as administrative agent for the Synthetic Lease and was identified on the UCC-1 financing statements as the secured party of record.

Five years later, General Motors entered into a separate term loan facility (the "Term Loan"). The Term Loan was entirely unrelated to the Synthetic Lease and provided General Motors with approximately $1.5 billion in financing from a different syndicate of lenders. To secure the loan, the lenders took security interests in a large number of General Motors' assets, including all of General Motors' equipment and fixtures at forty-two facilities throughout the United States. JPMorgan again served as administrative agent and secured party of record for the Term Loan and caused the filing of twenty-eight UCC-1 financing statements around the country to perfect the lenders' security interests in the collateral. One such financing state-ment, the "Main Term Loan UCC-1," was filed with the Delaware Secretary of State and bore file number "6416808 4." It "covered, among other things, all of the equipment and fixtures at 42 GM facilities, [and] was by far the most important" of the financing statements filed in connection with the Term Loan.

In September 2008, as the Synthetic Lease was nearing maturity, General Motors contacted Mayer Brown LLP, its counsel responsible for the Synthetic Lease, and explained that it planned to repay the amount due. General Motors requested that Mayer Brown prepare the documents necessary for JPMorgan and the lend-ers to be repaid and to release the interests the lenders held in General Motors' property.

A Mayer Brown partner assigned the work to an associate and instructed him to prepare a closing checklist and drafts of the documents required to pay off the Synthetic Lease and to terminate the lenders' security interests in General Motors' property relating to the Synthetic Lease. One of the steps required to unwind the Synthetic Lease was to create a list of security interests held by General Motors' lenders that would need to be terminated. To prepare the list, the Mayer Brown associate asked a paralegal who was unfamiliar with the transaction or the pur-pose of the request to perform a search for UCC-1 financing statements that had been recorded against General Motors in Delaware. The paralegal's search iden-tified three UCC-1s, numbered 2092532 5, 2092526 7, and 6416808 4. Neither the paralegal nor the associate realized that only the first two of the UCC-1s were related to the Synthetic Lease. The third, UCC-1 number 6416808 4, related instead to the Term Loan.

When Mayer Brown prepared a Closing Checklist of the actions required to unwind the Synthetic Lease, it identified the Main Term Loan UCC-1 for termination alongside the security interests that actually did need to be terminated. And when Mayer Brown prepared draft UCC-3 statements to terminate the three security inter-ests identified in the Closing Checklist, it prepared a UCC-3 statement to terminate the Main Term Loan UCC-1 as well as those related to the Synthetic Lease.

No one at General Motors, Mayer Brown, JPMorgan, or its counsel, Simpson Thacher & Bartlett LLP, noticed the error, even though copies of the Closing Checklist and draft UCC-3 termination statements were sent to individuals at each organization for review. On October 30, 2008, General Motors repaid the amount due on the Synthetic Lease. All three UCC-3s were filed with the Delaware Secretary of State, including the UCC-3 that erroneously identified for termination the Main Term Loan UCC-1, which was entirely unrelated to the Synthetic Lease.

A. General Motors' Chapter 11 Bankruptcy Filing

The mistake went unnoticed until General Motors' bankruptcy in 2009. On July 31, 2009, the [Creditors'] Committee commenced the underlying action against JPMorgan in the United States Bankruptcy Court for the Southern District of New York. The Committee sought a determination that, despite the error, the UCC-3 termination statement was effective to terminate the Term Loan security interest and render JPMorgan an unsecured creditor on par with the other General Motors unsecured creditors.

C. The Delaware Supreme Court's Answer

[In an earlier opinion, the Second Circuit certified a question to the Delaware Supreme Court.] In a speedy and thorough reply, the Delaware Supreme Court answered the certified question, explaining that if the secured party of record authorizes the filing of a UCC-3 termination statement, then that filing is effective regardless of whether the secured party subjectively intends or understands the effect of that filing:

> [F]or a termination statement to become effective under §9-509 and thus to have the effect specified in §9-513 of the Delaware UCC, it is enough that the secured party authorizes the filing to be made, which is all that §9-510 requires. The Delaware UCC contains no requirement that a secured party that authorizes a filing subjectively intends or otherwise understands the effect of the plain terms of its own filing.

That conclusion, explained the court, follows both from the unambiguous terms of the UCC and from sound policy considerations:

> JPMorgan's argument that a filing is only effective if the authorizing party understands the filing's substantive terms and intends their effect is contrary to §9-509, which only requires that "the secured party of record authorize [ ] the filing."
>
> Even if the statute were ambiguous, we would be reluctant to embrace JPMorgan's proposition. Before a secured party authorizes the filing of a termination statement, it ought to review the statement carefully and understand which security interests it is releasing and why. If parties could be relieved from the legal consequences of their mistaken filings, they would have little incentive to ensure the accuracy of the information contained in their UCC filings.

DISCUSSION

What remains is to answer the question we reserved for ourselves in our prior certification opinion: Did JPMorgan authorize the filing of the UCC-3 termination statement that mistakenly identified for termination the Main Term Loan UCC-1?

In JPMorgan's view, it never instructed anyone to file the UCC-3 in question, and the termination statement was therefore unauthorized and ineffective. JPMorgan reasons that it authorized General Motors only to terminate security interests related to the Synthetic Lease; that it instructed Simpson Thacher and Mayer Brown only to take actions to accomplish that objective; and that therefore Mayer Brown must have exceeded the scope of its authority when it filed the UCC-3 purporting to terminate the Main Term Loan UCC-1.

JPMorgan's and General Motors' aims throughout the Synthetic Lease transaction were clear: General Motors would repay the Synthetic Lease, and JPMorgan would terminate its related UCC-1 security interests in General Motors' properties. The Synthetic Lease Termination Agreement provided that, upon General Motors' repayment of the amount due under the Synthetic Lease, General Motors would be authorized "to file a termination of any existing Financing Statement relating to the Properties [of the Synthetic Lease]." And, to represent its interests in the transaction, JPMorgan relied on Simpson Thacher, its counsel for matters related to the Synthetic Lease. No one at JPMorgan, Simpson Thacher, General Motors, or Mayer Brown took action intending to affect the Term Loan.

What JPMorgan intended to accomplish, however, is a distinct question from what actions it authorized to be taken on its behalf. Mayer Brown prepared a Closing Checklist, draft UCC-3 termination statements, and an Escrow Agreement, all aimed at unwinding the Synthetic Lease but tainted by one crucial error: The documents included a UCC-3 termination statement that erroneously identified for termination a security interest related not to the Synthetic Lease but to the Term Loan. The critical question in this case is whether JPMorgan "authorize[d] [Mayer Brown] to file" that termination statement.

After Mayer Brown prepared the Closing Checklist and draft UCC-3 termination statements, copies were sent for review to a Managing Director at JPMorgan who supervised the Synthetic Lease payoff and who had signed the Term Loan documents on JPMorgan's behalf. Mayer Brown also sent copies of the Closing Checklist and draft UCC-3 termination statements to JPMorgan's counsel, Simpson Thacher, to ensure that the parties to the transaction agreed as to the documents required to complete the Synthetic Lease payoff transaction. Neither directly nor through its counsel did JPMorgan express any concerns about the draft UCC-3 termination statements or about the Closing Checklist. A Simpson Thacher attorney responded simply as follows: "Nice job on the documents. My only comment, unless I am missing something, is that all references to JPMorgan Chase Bank, as Administrative Agent for the Investors should not include the reference 'for the Investors.'"

After preparing the closing documents and circulating them for review, Mayer Brown drafted an Escrow Agreement that instructed the parties' escrow agent how to proceed with the closing. Among other things, the Escrow Agreement specified that the parties would deliver to the escrow agent the set of three UCC-3 termination statements (individually identified by UCC-1 financing statement file number) that would be filed to terminate the security interests that General Motors' Synthetic Lease lenders held in its properties. The Escrow Agreement provided that once General Motors repaid the amount due on the Synthetic Lease, the escrow agent would forward copies of the UCC-3 termination statements to General Motors' counsel for filing. When Mayer Brown e-mailed a draft of the Escrow Agreement to JPMorgan's counsel for review, the same Simpson Thacher attorney responded that "it was fine" and signed the agreement.

From these facts it is clear that although JPMorgan never intended to terminate the Main Term Loan UCC-1, it authorized the filing of a UCC-3 termination statement that had that effect. "Actual authority . . . is created by a principal's manifestation to an agent that, as reasonably understood by the agent, expresses the principal's assent that the agent take action on the principal's behalf." Restatement (Third) of Agency §3.01 (2006). JPMorgan and Simpson Thacher's repeated manifestations to Mayer Brown show that JPMorgan and its counsel knew that, upon the closing of the Synthetic Lease transaction, Mayer Brown was going to file the termination statement that identified the Main Term Loan UCC-1 for termination and that JPMorgan reviewed and assented to the filing of that statement. Nothing more is needed.

B.   Self-Clearing and Continuation
in the Article 9 Filing System

As we mentioned above, the real estate recording system is committed to keeping your deed to Blackacre for eternity. Documents are added to the system, but none are ever removed from it.

Perhaps cognizant of the record-storage problem confronting the real estate recording systems, the drafters of Article 9 opted for what they call a *self-clearing system*. Financing statements are effective for only five years. (A few states have adopted non-uniform amendments specifying longer periods.) Unless the secured party takes affirmative action by filing a *continuation statement* during the last six months of the five-year period, the financing statement "lapses." UCC §9-515(a) and (c). Only about 30 percent of financing statements are terminated. Another 15 percent are continued. The remaining 55 percent are cleared by lapse. 11 Clark's Secured Transactions Monthly 7 (Jan. 1996). One year after a financing statement lapses, the filing officer can remove it from the records and destroy it. UCC §9-522(a). As a result, an Article 9 filing system may contain only the financing statements filed or continued in the past six years.

Not all Article 9 filing systems are set up to take advantage of this self-clearing feature. Local systems are often integrated with the real estate recording systems in such a way that lapsed financing statements cannot be thrown away. But they lapse just the same.

To understand how the self-clearing feature of the Article 9 filing system works, think of the filed financing statements as each standing vertically on a conveyor belt. At the place where the moving belt begins its horizontal trip, the filing officer places newly filed financing statements on it. The belt carries the filings for six years, at which time they drop off the end into a paper shredder. At four and a half years, the filing statements enter the six-months-long segment of the belt in which they can be continued. If a continuation statement is filed while the financing statement is in this continuation "window," the filing officer pulls the financing statement off the conveyor belt, attaches the continuation statement to it, takes it to the beginning point, and puts it back on the belt, just like a newly filed financing statement.

What about the statements that are not continued? One might think that the conveyor belt should arrive at the paper shredder five years from the point of beginning — that is, as soon as it is out of the continuation window. If the filing officer could process continuation statements immediately on receipt, it probably should. But sometimes the filing officer gets a bit behind in the work. Even though a filing officer receives a continuation statement (and, of course, notes the date and time of filing on it) while the financing statement is in the six-months continuation window, the financing statement may be past the window by the time the filing officer begins looking for it. The conveyor belt extends for a year beyond the continuation window so that the financing statement will not reach the shredder before the busy filing officer can snatch it off the belt.

UCC §9-519(h) requires that the filing officer index records within two days of their receipt by the officer. Why, then, does §9-522 require that the filing officer maintain lapsed records for a year after lapse? Perhaps the reason is that the drafters did not really expect filing officers to comply with UCC §9-519(h). Filing offices traditionally have been one or two weeks behind in indexing new filings and in extreme cases have been more than four months behind. When such delays occur, the filing officers invariably blame their legislatures for not appropriating sufficient funds for the filing offices to carry the workload. No one can prove the filing officer wrong and no penalty is imposed for violating UCC §9-519(h) anyway, making that provision what some refer to euphemistically as "aspirational."

Provided that the secured party files a continuation statement each time its financing statement passes through the continuation window, the financing statement can ride the conveyor belt for decades. Each time it passes the window, the filing officer attaches a new continuation statement and it gets thicker and thicker.

The secured party who wants to maintain the priority of its initial filing must continue that filing rather than simply file a new financing statement. The reason for this requirement may seem obvious, but it is not. Exactly what harm would it cause if a secured party, rather than filing a continuation statement as its earlier financing statement passed through the continuation window, simply filed another financing statement? The second financing statement would be on the belt before the first one reached the shredder. Anyone who searched before taking an interest in the collateral could discover the secured party's interest.

What more does the continuation statement tell them? Only that the priority date of the existing interest is earlier than they might otherwise have supposed. To illustrate, assume that Firstbank filed a financing statement in 2011 and filed a continuation statement in 2015. A search in 2017 would discover the 2011 financing statement with the continuation statement attached. The searcher would know that Firstbank's priority date was in 2011. Had Firstbank filed a second financing statement in 2015 instead of a continuation statement, the 2017 search would discover only the 2015 financing statement; the 2011 financing statement would, by that time, have met the paper shredder. The searcher might have no way of knowing that the 2011 filing was ever made.

So long as new filers entering the system know their own priority, what difference does it make whether the filing system continues to show the initial priority dates of the earlier interests? Perhaps not much. So long as each filer keeps a certified copy of its own filing, the shredding of the filing officer's copy will not prevent the parties from reconstructing the situation. Perhaps the continuation system is designed to guard against the forgery of backdated financing statements after a dispute has arisen. Perhaps a later filer will want to know the order of priority between earlier filers and not trust what they say. Whatever the reasons, UCC §9-515 distinguishes between a continuation statement and a later-filed financing statement, and the courts generally enforce the distinction with a vengeance.

In re Hilyard Drilling Co.

840 F.2d 596 (8th Cir. 1988)

WOLLMAN, CIRCUIT JUDGE.

I

On April 25, 1979, [Hilyard Drilling Co. (Hilyard)] granted [the National Bank of Commerce of El Dorado (NBC)] a security interest in all of its existing and future accounts receivable, and the proceeds thereof. This security interest was perfected by the filing of appropriate financing statements on April 26, 1979.

On April 28, 1983, Paul C. Watson, Jr., [a vice president of Worthen Bank & Trust Co., N.A. (Worthen),] wrote a letter to Hilyard, which stated in relevant part:

> Confirming our telephone conversation, our Loan Committee has approved a renewal of your $550,000 equipment line and your $500,000 short-term working capital line on the following conditions:
>
> 1. That Worthen take a second lien position on accounts receivable. . . .
>
> I do not think that any of these items present a problem to you since we have previously discussed these. I understand that you need to talk with [NBC] regarding the receivables. We acknowledge their first lien and would be happy to do so in writing so that it is clear to everyone that our lien is junior to theirs.

NBC never requested a written acknowledgment. On June 14, 1983, Hilyard granted Worthen a security interest in the same accounts receivable. Neither Worthen's loan documents nor the financing statements it filed on June 14, 1983, stated that Worthen's security interest was subordinate to NBC's security interest.

On July 8, 1983, in connection with the reworking of Hilyard's loans, NBC filed a new financing statement giving notice of its security interest in Hilyard's accounts receivable. NBC did not file a continuation statement within six months preceding April 25, 1984, the expiration date of its 1979 financing statement, as required by [UCC §9-515(d)].

On July 6, 1984, Eugene G. Sayre, Hilyard's attorney, wrote a letter to Steven C. Wade, a commercial loan officer at Worthen, which stated in relevant part:

> The only matter which I want to make absolutely sure is clarified deals with 4.(a) on accounts receivable. Though the Loan Agreement does not reflect it, Hilyard Drilling Company, Inc., has previously made an assignment of its accounts receivable to the National Bank of Commerce of El Dorado, Arkansas. Thus, if the NBC in El Dorado has filed its financing statement and security agreement, Worthen Bank & Trust Company, N.A., would have a "second" position on these assets. As we have discussed, that was the intention of all parties concerned, as reflected in Paul Watson, Jr.'s letter to Ray Hilyard of April 28, 1983.

[Hilyard filed a Chapter 11 bankruptcy petition on January 25, 1985.] The schedule of assets filed in connection with Hilyard's Chapter 11 bankruptcy indicated that the debts to NBC and Worthen exceeded Hilyard's accounts receivable. Worthen filed a motion with the bankruptcy court for the determination of the priority of the security interests in Hilyard's accounts receivable. The bankruptcy court determined that Worthen's security interest was first in priority. On appeal, the district court affirmed the findings of the bankruptcy court.

II

The effectiveness of a financing statement lapses five years from the date of filing, unless a continuation statement is filed prior to its lapse. [UCC §§9-515(a), (c), and (d)]. Thus, unless NBC filed a continuation statement, its April 26, 1979, financing statement lapsed on April 25, 1984, prior to the filing of Hilyard's bankruptcy petition. NBC argues that its July 8, 1983, financing statement should be treated as a continuation statement under [UCC §9-515(c)]. We disagree.

Under [UCC §9-515(d)], a continuation statement must be filed within six months prior to the expiration of the original filing and "must be signed by the secured party, identify the original statement by file number and state that the original statement is still effective." [Editor's note: See UCC §9-102(a)(27).]

NBC admits that its July 8, 1983, financing statement does not satisfy the specific statutory requirements for a continuation statement because it "was not filed within six months of the expiration of the original financing statement, it does not refer to the file number of that financing statement, and it does not state that the original financing statement is still effective." NBC nonetheless argues that its July 8, 1983, financing statement should be treated as a continuation statement because its failure to fulfill the requirements of [UCC §9-102(a)(27)] is "harmless error," comparable to that addressed in [UCC §9-506(a)].

Without determining whether the harmless error concept applies to [UCC §9-102(a)(27)], the bankruptcy court found that NBC's July 8, 1983, financing statement did not substantially comply with the requirements for a continuation statement. This finding is not clearly erroneous.

Financing statements and continuation statements serve distinct and different purposes. A financing statement that does not refer to the original filing cannot suffice as a continuation statement. NBC's failure to file a continuation statement cannot be considered harmless error, because the second financing statement gave no indication that it was filed for the purpose of continuing any other financing statement.

In addition, the fact that Worthen was aware of NBC's once-perfected security interest does not render harmless NBC's failure to file a proper continuation statement. "[S]ince the purpose of statutory filing requirements is, in most instances, to resolve notice disputes consistently and predictably by reference to constructive or statutory notice alone, consideration of a junior creditor's actual notice of a now lapsed prior filing by a competing senior creditor" is precluded. Bostwick-Braun Co. v. Owens, 634 F. Supp. 839 (E.D. Wis. 1986).

III

NBC argues that even if its July 8, 1983, financing statement is not considered a continuation statement, its security interest is first in priority because it was continuously perfected from April 26, 1979, pursuant to [UCC §§9-308(c) and 9-322(a)(1)].

To interpret [UCC §9-308(c)] as providing that a security interest can be continuously perfected by consecutively filed financing statements contradicts the express language of [UCC §9-515(c)]. [UCC §9-308(c)] is applicable to security interests that are originally perfected in one way and then subsequently perfected in some other way, without an intermediate unperfected period. NBC, which initially perfected by filing, subsequently perfected in the same way, by filing, as opposed to "in some other way" as required by the statute. [UCC §9-308(c)] is inapplicable to NBC's security interest in Hilyard's accounts receivable.

Worthen's security interest had first priority pursuant to [UCC §9-322(a)(1)]. NBC's April 26, 1979, financing statement lapsed due to its failure to file a continuation statement, leaving the underlying security interest unperfected. [UCC §9-515(c)]. Following the lapse, the other perfected security interests in Hilyard's accounts receivable advanced in priority. Of the remaining perfected security interests, Worthen's interest had priority because it was first in time of filing or perfection.

The courts have generally been harsh in their treatment of errors in the filing of continuation statements. When creditors file continuation statements after their financing statements have lapsed, the courts uniformly hold the continuation statements ineffective, even if no one was prejudiced by the error. See UCC §9-510(c) (providing that "[a] continuation statement that is not filed within the six-month period prescribed by Section 9-515(d) is ineffective"). Some explain it doctrinally, saying that upon lapse of the financing statement there was no longer a filing to be continued. The result also can be explained through the imagery of the filing system as conveyor belt: By the time the filing officer processes a late-filed continuation statement, the financing statement might already have met its fate in the paper shredder.

It is more difficult to explain why a continuation statement filed too early should be ineffective. That is, nevertheless, the law. See, e.g., UCC §9-510(c), Lorain Music Co. v. Allied Inv. Credit Corp., 535 N.E.2d 345 (Ohio Ct. App. 1987) (continuation statement filed seven months before expiration of five-year period was ineffective; creditor lost his status as first perfected security interest holder when original statement expired).

To explore the problems that early filing might create, assume that Firstbank files its financing statement on April 1, 2011, and then files a premature continuation statement on April 1, 2013. If the continuation statement were held effective, it would continue the filing to March 31, 2021. UCC §9-515(e). Thus, there will be a period of more than six years between the filing of the continuation statement and the lapse of the filing. If we employ the image of the conveyor belt leading to the paper shredder, interrupted only when the filer jogs the filing officer to action by filing another continuation statement, the possibility looms that both financing statement and continuation statement will have gone to the shredder before March 31, 2021, while the filing remains effective.

The actual systems employed to purge lapsed filings no longer resemble the conveyor belt image we invoke. Nothing need go to the shredder unless the filing officer sends it. Considering the low cost of storage of electronic records, we doubt that many filing officers actually destroy their only copy in the few years following lapse.

Upon lapse, the security interest "becomes unperfected" and "is deemed never to have been perfected as against a purchaser of the collateral for value." UCC §9-515(c). The effect is that the security interest—which had priority over the purchaser (probably another security interest)—loses that priority. The implication is that the security interest doesn't lose priority over a similarly situated lien creditor (or the trustee in bankruptcy). Provided that the security interest was perfected at the time the lien creditor levied (or at the filing of the bankruptcy petition), the secured creditor retains priority over the lien creditor or trustee. See Comment 3 to UCC §9-515. The security interest will, however, be subordinate to a lien creditor that levies after lapse and to the trustee in a bankruptcy filed after lapse.

With computerization of the filing systems, the six-month window could be abandoned. If a continuation statement is filed at any time prior to lapse, the filing office should have no difficulty including it in search results. If the filing office does include an early-filed continuation statement, the early filing would not misled searchers.

The effect of technical requirements like the six-month window fall disproportionately on unsophisticated small businesses and individuals who attempt to take security. Law firms, service companies, and commercial lenders have computer systems that remind them to file within the six-month window. (Even so, many fail to file timely and so lose their security.) Small businesses and individuals who take security interests generally do not have such reminder systems. Calls to eliminate the six-month window have, nevertheless, gone unheeded for more than two decades after computerization.

Failure to file a necessary continuation statement timely is both a common error and a common source of legal malpractice claims. Lawyers often assist clients in obtaining and perfecting security interests by filing. The lawyers and clients go their separate ways, and five years later the filings sometime lapse. Such lapses may result in loss to the secured parties if, for example, the debtors file bankruptcy or the debtors use the collateral to secure other loans.

In Barnes v. Turner, 606 S.E. 2d 849 (Ga. 2004), a lawyer assisted Barnes in selling his business and taking a security interest for part of the purchase price. The security interest lapsed five years later, Barnes suffered a loss, and sued the lawyer. In a 5-4 decision with a fiery dissent, the Supreme Court of Georgia held the lawyer liable for malpractice, saying "Safeguarding a security interest is not some unexpected duty imposed upon the unwitting lawyer; it goes to the very heart of why Turner was retained: to sell Barnes's business in exchange for payment." *Barnes v. Turner* effectively imposes on the attorney who perfects a security interest the obligation to arrange—one way or another—for any anticipated continuation.

C.   The Effect of Bankruptcy on Lapse and Continuation

A secured party must file continuation statements at five-year intervals to avoid lapse. No exception is made simply because the debtor has filed bankruptcy. See UCC §9-515(c). The filing of continuation statements during the pendency of the bankruptcy case does not violate the automatic stay. Bankr. Code §§362(b)(3), 546(b)(1)(B).

If a security interest becomes unperfected upon lapse, UCC §9-515(c) provides that "it is deemed never to have been perfected as against a purchaser of the collateral for value." The importance of this provision is in what it does not say. The lapsed financing statement is not deemed unperfected as against a lien creditor or trustee in bankruptcy whose rights arose before lapse. For example, if the debtor files bankruptcy and the secured party's financing statement lapses a week later, the secured party continues to have priority over the trustee. But the secured party would not continue to have priority over a competing secured party whose financing statement did not lapse.

[handwritten margin note: priority over trustee but not a competing secured party]

Although the concept that the filing and searching game goes on even after the filing of a bankruptcy case is easy to grasp intellectually, secured creditors and lawyers never cease to be surprised by the resulting evaporation of their legal rights even while they are in the process of litigating the extent of those rights.

Problem Set 22

22.1.   Your client, the Bank of East Palatka, perfected its $7,280,000 security interest in equipment owned by Horst Manufacturing by filing a financing statement on December 30, 2011. The bank filed a continuation statement on July 7, 2016. Today, March 22, 2020, Jan Swift, a loan officer from the bank, asks you the following questions:

a.   Did the bank file its prior continuation statement at the proper time? UCC §9-515.

b.   Swift wants to put on her calendar the time when she should file the next continuation statement for this filing. When will it be due?

c.   A week after you answered those questions for Jan Swift, Horst Manufacturing filed a case under Chapter 11 of the Bankruptcy Code. Swift expects that the case will probably extend for about two years, but of course that time could vary. Swift would like to know if this changes your advice about the proper time for filing the bank's next continuation statement. What do you tell her? Bankr. Code §§362(b)(3), 546(b)(1); UCC §9-515.

d.   Jan Swift is back to see you. The bankruptcy case turned out to be a lengthy one. The case was still pending when the bank filed its continuation statement on January 6, 2022 — one week after the close of the six-month continuation window. Jan asks you where the bank stands now. UCC §9-515(c), Comments 3 and 4; Bankr. Code §544(a).

22.2.   The discussion with Jan Swift reminded you that you did some UCC closings in your early years of practice but hadn't yet realized the need to calendar your filings for continuation. You pulled the files and found that you filed one of the financing statements five years and two months ago on behalf of Juan Gomez. Gomez had sold his restaurant to The Cantina, Incorporated, and taken back a security interest in all of the restaurant equipment, including after-acquired property. The $600,000 note for the purchase price was amortized over 20 years, with a balloon payment at the end of year six. A quick search in the filing system reveals that you're not the only one who didn't think about continuation; no continuation statement is on file for the financing statement you filed. What do you do now? UCC §§1-106(1), 9-102(a)(39), 9-509(b), 9-510(c), 9-515, 9-516(b)(7); Model Rule of Professional Conduct, Rule 1.4, reproduced in Problem 8.4, above.

22.3. Two weeks ago, the Wriggling Brothers Traveling Circus (founded by the great escape artists) filed under Chapter 11. This was of some concern to you, because your client, Mark Ryerson, holds a $1.2 million first security interest in most of the assets of the circus. Associates Financial Partners (Associates) also holds a security interest in the same property, securing their loan for over $10 million. Both interests were created at the same time, about nine years ago. Ryerson's financing statement was filed first; Associates' later the same day. Both creditors filed continuation statements in a timely fashion.

Associates is represented by Millie Parker. When you spoke to Parker this morning about the bankruptcy case, she tweaked you by casually referring to Ryerson's interest as a "second." When you pointed out that Ryerson filed before Associates, she said that wasn't controlling because Associates had possession of the circus assets on the day the two filings were made. You can't remember anything about possession of the circus assets nine years ago, and neither can Ryerson.

a. According to the documents, the circus assets consisted of tents, bleachers, scaffolding, sound systems, a wide variety of specialized equipment related to performances, elephants, lions, horses, and cages. How, as a practical matter, could Associates have taken possession of those assets nine years ago?

b. Would it matter if Parker were right about possession of the assets nine years ago? UCC §§9-515, 9-308(c), 9-322(a)(1).

c. How would you handle this matter if you had it to do over again from the day Mark Ryerson retained you? UCC §9-339.

22.4. Philip Gandhi, a real estate broker, recently bought 16 lots in Brook Meadow, a residential subdivision, for $3,200,000. He financed the purchase with a $1,600,000 loan from Equity Investment Group (EIG) that is secured by a mortgage against the 16 lots. Gandhi has arranged to sell one of the lots for $300,000. When EIG learned about the sale, they told him that "of course, the entire proceeds of the sale must be applied against the mortgage." Gandhi says he can't do that, because there will be expenses of sale, including the fees of another broker involved in the deal that have to be paid. Gandhi would like you to "get tough with EIG, and free up some of this cash flow." What do you plan to say to EIG?

22.5. a. You represent Firstbank. The bank's security agreement covers 12 fork lifts, a stamping machine, and all "replacements or additions." The bank initially lent $400,000 to the debtor, Beaver Manufacturing, and the loan balance currently stands at $210,174. Beaver authorized, and Firstbank filed, an effective financing statement identifying the collateral as "equipment." Now

Beaver is trying to borrow money against its drill presses. It wants Firstbank to put a release in the filing system for the drill presses and office furniture, neither of which is covered by Firstbank's security agreement. Firstbank does not want to give the release because it hopes to force Beaver to pay the loan off early or agree to a higher rate of interest. Firstbank's security agreement contains no provisions regarding release of collateral. Does Firstbank have to give Beaver the release? UCC §§9-513, 9-512.

b.   If Firstbank doesn't, will Beaver be able to assure another lender that it will have the first filed security agreement against the drill presses? UCC §§9-401(b), 9-502(d), 9-322(a)(1).

c.   Could Beaver solve its problem by demanding from Firstbank a written statement of collateral and showing it to the new lender? UCC §9-210.

22.6.   Joe and Mary Suarez have contracted to sell their house and asked you to handle the closing. The first mortgage, originally given to First Florida Savings and Loan but now serviced by Global Mortgage Service of Newark, New Jersey, is to be paid in full at the closing.

Global has been very difficult to deal with. It was slow to respond to your request for an "estoppel letter" showing the balance owing on the mortgage. When Global did respond, its number, $426,780, was suspiciously high. After a laborious comparison of the mortgage amortization schedule and the Suarezes' payment record, you concluded that the correct balance was $407,110: Global was demanding $19,670 more than what was owed them. When you finally got someone from Global to talk to you on the phone, you discovered that Global had failed to credit the Suarezes for two payments they had actually made (Mrs. Suarez showed you cancelled checks) and had charged the Suarezes' account with "administrative fees" not authorized by the mortgage. The final blow was a $450 fee for recalculating the account and sending you the estoppel letter. Such a fee is neither customary, nor provided for in the mortgage. Despite your protests, the Global representative will not make any change in the estoppel letter.

The mortgage contract provides that in the event of default, the Suarezes will pay the secured creditor's attorneys fees and costs, but does not provide for the secured creditor to pay the Suarezes' attorneys fees under any circumstances. The closing is scheduled for 40 days from today. If you don't have a satisfaction of mortgage from Global, your clients won't be able to convey marketable title to the buyers and the deal may fall through. Mike Schwartz, attorney for the buyer, says his client won't disburse the purchase price unless "there's a satisfaction from Global on the table." The sale price is at about the market, but the Suarezes don't want to lose the sale because it may take a lot of time to find another buyer and they fear that this buyer might sue them. What is your advice? If this property is in Florida, is there any way that the Florida satisfaction of mortgage statute might be of help? Would the Suarezes be better off or worse off if the property was in Arizona?

22.7.   Assume that the sale in the previous problem had been of the Suarezes' business equipment rather than their residence, and therefore governed by Article 9. Would they be in a stronger or a weaker position? UCC §§9-513, 9-509(d).

■ END OF DEFAULT PROBLEM SET

22.8.   Harry Montague, a senior partner in your firm, heard that you took an advanced course in secured transactions in law school and has invited you to lunch. The governor recently appointed Harry to the Uniform Law Commission. (Surely you remember that bunch that shares control of the official text of the UCC and the other uniform and model acts.) The ULC is considering revisions to Article 9. Harry didn't take secured transactions in law school and cheerfully admits that he knows nothing about the subject. Nonetheless, a ULC committee of which Harry is a member is about to vote on a proposed amendment to UCC §9-515 that would permit the filers of financing statements to choose the length of time for which they would be effective. The options would be 5, 10, 15, or 20 years. After that time, the secured parties could still file continuation statements. Harry, whose background is in real estate, doesn't see why there ought to be any time limit on the effectiveness of filings at all. If they need a limit on regular filings, Harry says, how come they don't need one on mortgages that reach fixtures? UCC §9-515(g). Harry asks your opinion. What do you tell him?

22.9.   As a new associate at Simpson Thacher, you have been assigned to clear the title to the assets of General Motors in preparation for closing on a $1.5 billion loan from Simpson Thacher's client, JPMorgan. You discover three termination statements. Two are in connection with financing statements filed more than five years ago and not continued. One is in connection with a financing statement filed within the past five years on behalf of CitiBank. What, if anything, will you do to make sure those terminations statements were authorized? UCC §§9-102(a)(80), 9-509(d), 9-510(a).

Assignment 23: Maintaining Perfection Through Changes of Name, Identity, and Use

Communication in real time is hard enough. As we saw in earlier assignments, a secured creditor who attempts to name its debtor or describe the collateral in which it claims an interest may have difficulty finding the right words. In this assignment, we discuss the additional complexity that arises because communication through the filing system does not occur in real time.

The filer's message may be in the filing system for years before the searcher looks for it. In the interim, the circumstances that shaped the message may have changed. The debtor who comes to the searcher for a loan may have changed its name since the filer put its financing statement on file. If the debtor does not reveal its old name to the searcher, the searcher may search under the new name and not find the financing statement. Collateral described accurately on the financing statement may have changed so drastically in use and appearance that even if the searcher finds the old financing statement, it will be unable to link the collateral it sees to the description on the statement. Remember that one of the changes collateral can undergo is exchange for proceeds. The proceeds may neither look nor be anything at all like the original collateral described in the financing statement. For example, the financing statement may describe the collateral as "beans," but by the time the debtor seeks a loan from the searcher, the debtor may have traded the beans for a circus elephant.

One way to deal with this problem would have been to hold the financing statement ineffective if it would not have been effective as a new financing statement in the changed circumstances. That would have placed responsibility on the filer to monitor the circumstances, discover changes, and make appropriate amendments to the financing statement.

Another way to deal with the problem would have been to hold that an initially effective financing statement remained effective even though circumstances changed. That would have placed responsibility on the searcher to discover the previous circumstances of the debtor and the collateral and then search for statements filed effectively under those circumstances. By thorough investigation, the searcher might have been able to discover what changes had occurred and adjust its search to account for them.

The drafters of Article 9 chose to use a little of each approach, mixing them in a manner sufficiently complex to win them a place in both the law school curriculum and most state bar exams. In this assignment we explore that mix and raise questions about its impact: To what extent are both old filers *and* new searchers required to monitor the collateral, the debtor, or the public record to protect themselves? What is the cost of such monitoring? The cost of failing to monitor?

As you study the balance that has been struck between filer and searcher, you will be tempted to interpret each rule as placing an obligation on filers or searchers to do something. There is no harm in doing so, so long as you realize that in many situations real filers and searchers do not perform their obligations and can't realistically be expected to. These rules don't just tell filers and searchers what to do. In circumstances where potential losses are not worth the effort necessary to avoid them, the rules simply allocate those losses to the filers or searchers.

In this assignment, we focus on the four most important changes in circumstance: (1) changes of the debtor's name, (2) substitution of a "new debtor," (3) changes affecting the description of collateral, and (4) conversion of the collateral into proceeds.

A.   Changes in the Debtor's Name

Individuals, corporations, and other entities can, and sometimes do, change their names. If a debtor changes names between the time a filing is made against the debtor and the time a search for that filing is made, the change may — or may not — cause the communication to fail. To illustrate, assume that Adams Corporation borrows money from Firstbank in 2011 and gives Firstbank a security interest in all of Adams's assets. Firstbank perfects by filing. In 2012, Adams Corporation changes its name to Baker Corporation. Firstbank does not learn of the change of name, so it does not amend its financing statement to reflect it. In 2013, the corporation applies to Secondbank for a loan and offers the same assets as collateral. Secondbank, who does not discover the change of name either, conducts its search only under the name "Baker Corporation." Of course, the search does not discover Firstbank's filing.

That is not to say that Secondbank *could not* have discovered Firstbank's filing through a search. A corporate debtor's change of name is a matter of public record. Even without the debtor's cooperation, Secondbank could have discovered it by (1) insisting that the debtor prove its incorporation under the laws of some state or country, (2) searching the corporate records of that state or country for changes of the debtor's name, and (3) having discovered that the debtor was previously named Adams Corporation, conducting its search in that name as well as in Baker Corporation.

By going to some extra trouble, Firstbank could also have prevented this failure of communication. If Firstbank had been sensitive to changes in its borrower, it might have noticed the change on the debtor's letterhead, checks, or bank accounts. Even if the debtor did nothing to publicize the change, Firstbank could have discovered it by periodically checking the corporate records of the state in which the debtor was incorporated. When it discovered the change, Firstbank could have amended its financing statement to reflect it. By these methods, Firstbank could have minimized the time during which its financing statement was indexed only under an obsolete name, but it could not have entirely eliminated it. For example, even if Firstbank checked the corporate records for borrowers' changes of name every four months, its filings could be indexed under former names for up to four months plus the time it took Firstbank to amend its filing. ✳

Were Adams an individual instead of a corporation, the banks might have found it more difficult to discover her change of name from Juanita Adams to Juanita Baker. Evidence of the change might be in the records of any of thousands of courts or not in any public record at all. Either bank might have discovered the change by checking the debtor's driver's license or other identification, but only if they checked both before and after the change. If the state adopted Alternative A to UCC §9-503, the only change that matters might be the change on the driver's license. The Driver's Privacy Protection Act allows only "a legitimate business" to access the records for this purpose. 18 U.S.C. §2721. Once a creditor discovers an individual debtor's name change, the creditor will want to take the same actions they would with respect to a corporate debtor's name change.

UCC §9-507(c) provides that even though a change in the debtor's name renders a filed financing statement seriously misleading, the financing statement remains effective with regard to (1) collateral owned by the debtor at the time of the name change and (2) collateral acquired by the debtor in the first four months after the change. The seriously misleading financing statement is not, however, effective to perfect a security interest in collateral acquired by the debtor more than four months after the change. ✳

Under this rule, a secured party that financed the purchase of a specific item of collateral (such as a boat) has little reason to concern itself with later changes in the debtor's name. On the other hand, a secured party that is financing the debtor's inventory of boats on a continuing basis does have to concern itself with changes in the debtor's name. The secured party's filing will not be effective against inventory that the debtor acquires more than four months after it changes its name. An inventory financier who fails to notice the debtor's name change for a period of a year might find that its filing is no longer effective against anything of real value.

The name-change rule of UCC §9-507(c) potentially affects every searcher. Even though a search in the current, correct name of the debtor discovers no filings against the collateral, there may be a filing in the debtor's former name that remains effective against the proposed collateral. Depending on the amount of money at stake and the degree to which the searcher trusts the debtor, the searcher may want to investigate the possibility of changes in the debtor's name.

It may have occurred to you in reading the preceding paragraphs that there is one person who could easily keep track of the debtor's name and make sure changes have been promptly memorialized in amendments to the relevant financing statements—the debtor. Although this is true, it is not very helpful. Most security agreements do in fact contain a promise by the debtor to notify the secured party of the debtor's change of name as well as the other kinds of changes that affect the effectiveness of filings. Most debtors, particularly those who have decided to borrow twice against the same collateral, fail to give notice nevertheless. Their failure constitutes a breach of contract, for which they will have civil liability, but that is of little concern to most debtors. If they pay their debts, their lenders won't care whether they gave notice. If they do not pay their debts their lenders can do no more than sue as unsecured creditors. The creditors' damages from nonpayment of the debt and from failure to give notice of the name change are the same damages. The creditor can have only one recovery, so liability for failure to give notice of the name change adds nothing.

The situation would be different if the failure to give notice subjected the debtor to criminal prosecution or even rendered the debt nondischargeable in bankruptcy. It does not. To impose such penalties on a debtor without proof of fraudulent intent would be entirely out of keeping with legal tradition in the United States. We live in a nation founded in large part by people who did not pay their debts in the places from which they came. Our tolerance for debtor misbehavior is relatively high compared with attitudes in other cultures. In spite of this tolerance, or perhaps because of it, the U.S. economy has done relatively well. Neither the criminal nor the bankruptcy authorities are likely to get exercised about even a deliberate failure to comply with a contractual obligation to give notice of a change in circumstances.

For all these reasons, the systems created under the laws governing security in the United States are designed to function without the cooperation of the debtor. Lenders are expected to fend for themselves. B.T. Lazarus v. Christofides, 662 N.E.2d 41 (Ohio App. 1996) illustrates the kind of vigilance required. In that case, the creditor took a security interest in the assets of B.T.L. Inc. The creditor delayed the filing of its financing statement for nearly four months after the signing of the security agreement. In the period between the signing and the filing, B.T.L. Inc. changed its name to Alma Marketing, Inc. The court held the filing ineffective.

You should not conclude from our comments that filers or searchers now stalk their debtors for evidence of changes of name. Changes of name are uncommon. In most instances, either the filer or the searcher will discover them without much effort and take appropriate action. But at the same time, you should realize that the filing system has no fail-safe mechanism for dealing with name changes. Some debtors, particularly those who change their names for the purpose of defrauding their secured lenders, will succeed in borrowing from a second lender who searches, but who does not discover the first lender.

Even though the governing rules are similar, it is important to distinguish changes of name, which are covered by UCC §9-507(c), from the transfer of collateral to a new owner, which is covered by UCC §9-507(a). To illustrate the potential for confusion, assume that while doing business as a sole proprietor, Teresa Williams borrowed money against the equipment of her business and granted a security interest. If Teresa later incorporates the business under the name Williams Electronics, Inc., that is not a change of the debtor's name. That is the formation of a new entity, probably followed by a transfer of the collateral from Teresa to the corporation. The governing law would be UCC §9-507(a). The financing statement filed against Teresa would be effective against the collateral in the hands of Williams Electronics. If Williams Electronics seeks to borrow against the business assets the searcher must be thorough enough to discover the still-effective financing statement filed against Teresa.

B.   New Debtors

"Debtor" is a term ordinarily used to refer to a person who owes payment. Article 9, however, uses the word "debtor" to refer to the person who owns the collateral and the word "obligor" to refer to the person who owes payment. Article 9 defines "new debtor" to refer to "a person that becomes bound as debtor under Section 9-203(d) by a security agreement previously entered into by another person." UCC §9-102(a)(56).

The gist of UCC §9-203(d) is that a new debtor is a person who steps into the shoes of the original debtor by assuming, and agreeing to perform under, the security agreement. The typical new debtor is a person who buys the debtor's business, assumes the debtor's secured loan obligations, and agrees to be bound by the security agreement. But notice that under UCC §9-203(d)(2), a person can be bound as a new debtor by a security agreement without agreeing to it. The person is bound if the person assumes the debts and acquires the assets of the old debtor. Another common type of new debtor is a corporation that acquires the original debtor corporation's assets by merger and by operation of law becomes liable for the original debtor's obligations, including the original debtor's contractual obligations under security agreements.

UCC §9-508(c) treats the transfer of collateral to a new debtor the same as the transfer of collateral to anyone else: A financing statement filed against the original debtor remains effective against the collateral under UCC §9-507(a). If the new debtor's name is different from the debtor's name on the financing statement, UCC §9-508(b) applies the rule contained in UCC §9-507(c): The financing statement remains effective with respect to collateral acquired by the new debtor within four months after the change, but is not effective with respect to collateral acquired by the new debtor later. To make things perfectly clear, UCC §9-508(a) says these rules apply "to the extent that the financing statement would have been effective had the original debtor acquired the rights."

C.   Changes Affecting the Description of Collateral

If the collateral undergoes changes in its appearance, use, or location between the time a filing is made and a search for that filing is commenced, the changes may prevent the searcher from finding the filing or realizing its relevance. To understand these changes, begin by distinguishing two kinds.

Type 1 Changes. The first, which we will call a *type 1* change, is a change in circumstances that did not control the place of filing but that does make the collateral difficult for the searcher to identify as covered by the filing. For example, assume that Firstbank's security agreement correctly describes the collateral as "Coyote Loader, serial number 8203G45," that the debtor holds the loader as inventory at the time Firstbank files its financing statement, and that the financing statement describes the type of collateral as "inventory."

Firstbank is perfected. Later, the debtor begins using the loader as equipment and seeks to borrow against it from Secondbank. Secondbank's search will discover Firstbank's financing statement, but Secondbank may not realize its significance. Secondbank is lending against equipment, and the filing they discover is only against inventory.

UCC §9-507(b) addresses this example. That section provides that even if the change in circumstances has made the financing statement seriously misleading, the financing statement remains effective.

Type 2 Changes. A *type 2* change in circumstances is one that is sufficient to affect the method of perfection that would have been appropriate for the initial filing. For example, assume that Firstbank takes a security interest in the "inventory" of Rabbit's Toyota dealership, which consists of 140 new automobiles. Rabbit begins using one of the automobiles to retrieve parts and to serve as a chase car when delivering serviced automobiles. That automobile thus becomes equipment. As to that automobile, the financing statement is now seriously misleading. UCC §9-507(b) excuses the misdescription, and the financing statement remains effective with respect to that automobile. Firstbank is nevertheless unperfected with respect to that automobile, because notation on the certificate of title is necessary to perfect. UCC §9-311(b). The financing statement retains its effectiveness, but with respect to a non-inventory automobile, that is no effectiveness at all.

In a case dealing with the reverse of that change, Hart, who dealt in automobiles, obtained financing from Blue Ridge Bank for an automobile intended for his own personal use. The bank properly perfected its lien by notation on the certificate of title. Hart later swapped the automobile with another auto dealer. The court held that when Hart put his automobile up for sale it became part of his inventory and the bank's perfection lapsed.

> Even if Blue Ridge Bank had properly perfected its lien during a period of time in which the vehicle was a consumer good, such a lien would not remain perfected "during any period in which [the vehicle] is inventory." See [UCC §§9-311(b) and (d)]. Generally a security interest perfected by compliance with the certificate-of-title statute "remains perfected notwithstanding a change in the use or transfer of possession of the collateral," "except as otherwise provided in subsection (d)," i.e., during any period in which the collateral is inventory. If a security interest in collateral had been properly perfected while the collateral was a consumer good and, then, subsequently, use of the collateral changed to equipment, the security interest would remain perfected. If, however, the use of the collateral changes to inventory, compliance with the certificate of title statute does not remain effective. The first phrase of [UCC §9-311(d)] states that "during any period in which collateral is inventory" the certificate of title statute is inapplicable to perfect a security interest.

Blue Ridge Bank and Trust Co. v. Hart, 152 S.W.3d 420 (Mo. Ct. App. 2005). Thus, in some circumstances, a change in the use a debtor makes of collateral can deprive the secured creditor of perfection.

Real estate law is even less favorable to the secured creditor. The courts have split on the threshold issue of whether a mortgage continues to encumber a fixture once the debtor severs the fixture from the real estate. But most courts agree that a good faith buyer of the fixtures should prevail over the mortgage holder, even though the severance violated the terms of the mortgage.

D.   Exchange of the Collateral

When a debtor exchanges collateral for either property or cash, the effect is to raise many of the same kinds of issues we discussed in the preceding section. Recall from Assignment 10 that on sale, exchange, collection, or other disposition of collateral, a security interest continues in identifiable proceeds. UCC §§9-102(a)(64) and 9-315(a)(2). The holder of the security interest sometimes will want (1) the security interest to be perfected in the proceeds and (2) the perfection to be continuous from the creditor's initial filing. In this section, we examine what the secured creditor must do (if anything) to accomplish those two things.

1.   *Barter Transactions*   315 (d)(1)

Barter is the exchange of one commodity for another in a transaction in which no cash is involved. The rules in UCC §9-315(d)(1) governing perfection in a barter exchange are different from the rules governing perfection in an exchange for cash that is then used to purchase the commodity. In this subsection we discuss only the barter transaction; the rules governing perfection in cash proceeds and proceeds acquired with cash proceeds are discussed in the next two sections.

To understand when secured parties must take action to perfect their interests in proceeds, distinguish three types of barters. We refer to them as *type 0*, *type 1*, and *type 2* so we can retain the numbering from the previous section. In a type 0 barter, the proceeds received by the debtor fall within the description of collateral in the already-filed financing statement. For example, assume that the security agreement described the collateral as "Coyote Loader, serial number 8203G45" and the financing statement, properly filed only in the office of the secretary of state, described the type of collateral as "loader." The debtor trades the Coyote loader for a Caterpillar loader. The security interest attaches to the Caterpillar loader as proceeds even without a statement to that effect in the security agreement. UCC §9-203(f). The security interest is perfected in the Caterpillar loader because the description "loader" is broad enough to encompass it. (Recall that "A financing statement may be filed before a security agreement is made. . . ." UCC §9-502(d).) After this type 0 barter, the secured creditor has a perfected security interest in the new collateral on the basis of the description.

A type 1 barter is an exchange of collateral for noncash proceeds where those proceeds are property not covered by the description in the financing statement but are property in which a security interest could be perfected by filing in the office where the secured creditor's financing statement is already

In February, 1986, Seaway declared bankruptcy under Chapter 11. It sold the Auburn property for approximately $1 million. The funds were placed in a segregated account. Seaway's bankruptcy was subsequently converted to Chapter 7, and Erickson was appointed the bankruptcy trustee.

NBA now claims it has a priority interest in the proceeds of the sale of the Auburn property as "proceeds" from the sale of the AFFS account.

II

A

NBA first argues that it had a perfected security interest in the Auburn property. We disagree.

Under its credit agreement with Seaway, NBA did have a perfected security interest in the AFFS account. Under the terms of the agreement and under the UCC, this interest continued in the "proceeds" of any unauthorized sale of the account. See [UCC §9-315(a)]. NBA need only perfect its interest in the proceeds within [20] days of the sale. [UCC §9-315(c),(d)(3)]. When perfection is impossible due to the actions of the debtor, such an interest may be deemed perfected.

NBA argues that under these principles, its interest in the Auburn property should be deemed perfected. It contends that the sale of the AFFS account was not authorized and that it attempted to perfect its interest in the Auburn property but was prevented by Seaway. We reject NBA's argument.

NBA concedes that by its terms the UCC does not extend to real property. See [UCC §9-109(d)(11)]. NBA cites no case in which a perfected interest in UCC-covered goods has been extended to real property. Good reasons exist not to do so here. To "perfect" an interest in real property under Washington law, a party must record a deed signed by the grantor. An unrecorded interest in property is not binding on a subsequent purchaser in good faith. Such recording statutes are central to real property law.

We agree with the BAP that NBA's perfected security interest in the AFFS account did not extend to the Auburn property.

AFFIRMED.

This case serves to remind secured creditors that while the Uniform Commercial Code gives them great protection by extending their security interests to proceeds, they nonetheless must make sure that those security interests in proceeds are perfected. Here, the secured creditor's problem was that the law governing real estate recording did not contain a provision like UCC §9-509(b)(2) allowing the secured creditor to perfect the security interest in the property into which it could trace its proceeds. The probable reason is that real estate financing is done parcel by parcel. When the debtor sells real estate, the secured party expects to be paid off or to remain secured by the same collateral in the hands of the buyer. It does not expect to leave its loan outstanding and trace the proceeds of its collateral. To put it another way, *Seaway Express* does not result from legislative policy but from legislative neglect. If the designers of the real estate recording system had thought about it, they almost certainly would have adopted a provision like UCC §9-509(b)(2).

2.   *Collateral to Cash Proceeds to Noncash Proceeds*

The debtor may exchange the original collateral for money, then use the money to buy collateral. Provided it can trace its value through both transactions, the creditor's security interest will reach the new property as proceeds of proceeds. UCC §§9-102(a)(12) and (64). In this section we consider the circumstances under which the original filing will give the secured creditor continuous perfection that extends to the new property.

In a type 0 change, the rule remains the same as it did in a barter transaction: The original filing remains effective to cover goods of the same description. To return to our earlier example, the security agreement described the collateral as "Coyote Loader, serial number 8203G45" and the financing statement, properly filed only in the office of the secretary of state, described the type of collateral as "loader." If the debtor sold the Coyote loader for cash, the cash would be proceeds and the security interest would attach to it. So long as the debtor retained the cash and the cash remained identifiable, the secured party would remain perfected in it. If the debtor used that cash to buy a Caterpillar loader, the security interest would attach to the Caterpillar loader as proceeds of the cash and then would remain perfected because the description "loader" is broad enough to encompass it. UCC §9-315(d)(3). In short, the original filing perfected in both loaders because it described both loaders. UCC §9-502(d).

In a type 1 change, however, the exchange results in collateral that is no longer covered by the original description in the filing statement. Consider, again, the earlier example in which the security interest covered inventory and the debtor bartered the inventory for an elephant that would serve as the company's mascot. If the creditor initially perfected its security interest in the inventory, that interest would remain continuously perfected in the elephant without taking further action. Now, assume instead that the debtor sold the inventory for cash and used the cash to buy the elephant. UCC §9-315(d)(3) requires that the secured party file a financing statement to cover the new collateral. Unless the secured party accomplishes that within 20 days of the debtor's receipt of the new collateral, the perfection achieved by the filing is not continuous. If the second filing occurs within 20 days of the debtor's receipt of the new property, the second filing is effective as of the date of the first filing and perfection is continuous thereafter. If the second filing occurs after the end of the 20-day period, it dates only from the time it was made.

Type 2 changes are treated like type 1 changes. Recall that in a type 2 change the new property is of a type that requires filing in a different filing office. Here, also, the secured creditor must make the new filing within 20 days of the debtor's receipt of the collateral. To modify the earlier example, if a debtor sold its

Coyote loader for cash and used the cash to buy an automobile and an aircraft, a type 2 change has occurred. To be continuously perfected in the new property, the secured party must perfect on the certificates of title for the automobile and the aircraft within 20 days of the debtor's receipt of those items. See UCC §9-315(d)(3).

3. Collateral to Cash Proceeds (No New Property)

The debtor may simply sell the original collateral and keep the cash. UCC §9-315(d)(2) grants secured parties continuous, perpetual perfection in identifiable *cash proceeds*. To illustrate the application of that subsection, again assume that Firstbank has a perfected security interest in inventory. The debtor sells some of the inventory for cash and deposits the cash in its bank account at Thirdbank. The bank account is "cash proceeds." UCC §9-102(a)(9). Under the rule of UCC §9-315(d)(2), Firstbank will remain perfected in it even if the money sits in the bank account for months or even years.

If the debtor in this illustration spends the cash proceeds two years later to purchase an elephant, Firstbank will have a security interest in the elephant as "proceeds" and will have twenty days in which to perfect that interest. UCC §9-315(d)(3).

Problem Set 23

23.1. Helen Monette is a compliance officer at Gargantuan Bank and Trust (GBT). Her job is to monitor the collateral securing loans outstanding from the bank. Most of her work is devoted to verifying that collateral is physically in existence, but she occasionally encounters other problems. Currently, Monette is working with Bonnie Brezhnev, owner of Bonnie's Boat World Inc. (BBW). GBT finances BBW's inventory under a financing statement that describes the collateral as "inventory, accounts, and chattel paper." The agreement contains no restrictions on BBW's ability to finance equipment or real estate elsewhere. Assume that the jurisdiction does not maintain a certificate of title system for boats. Today Monette called you with the following list of problems:

a. On a routine inspection of collateral, Monette discovered that, contrary to the provisions of the security agreement prohibiting the use of inventory, Bonnie kept one of the boats at her house and used it personally. Monette warned her not to do it again, but now wonders: Assuming no transfer of ownership to Bonnie personally, did the interlude have any effect on perfection of the bank's security interest? UCC §§9-506(a), 9-507(b).

b. If Bonnie transferred ownership of the boat from her corporation to herself before she took the boat home, what evidence would exist of that fact? If Bonnie did transfer ownership of the boat to herself, is GBT still perfected? UCC §§9-315(a)(1), 9-320(a), 9-507(a).

c. BBW traded one of the boats for a forklift. BBW now uses the forklift to move the boats in and out of storage. Monette says she assumes that the forklift is "ours" because BBW bought it with GBT's collateral, but wonders whether she needs to do anything about perfection. Does she? UCC §§9-315(a) and (d).

d.   Would it make any difference if BBW bought the forklift in subpart c using cash it had received from a customer who bought a new boat? UCC §§9-315(a) and (d).

e.   About a month ago, two of the boats in inventory suffered severe storm damage. The security agreement provided that BBW would insure the boats against storm damage and required that GBT be named as a loss payee on the policy. BBW bought the insurance, but for some reason GBT was not named as a loss payee. Since the storm, BBW changed insurers and GBT is named as a loss payee on the new policy. Monette wonders whether GBT has a perfected security interest in the claim against the former insurer and, if not, what GBT needs to do to get one. UCC §§9-109(d)(8), 9-102(a)(64), 9-315(c) and (d), 9-203(f), 9-109(a).

23.2.   Recently, Monette has been monitoring GBT's inventory loan to South West Appliance Corporation. In a routine check of corporate records, Monette discovered for the first time that six months ago the debtor changed its corporate name to South West General, Inc.

a.   Does Monette need to do anything to make sure GBT remains perfected in all its collateral? UCC §§9-502(a)(1), 9-503(a)(1), 9-512, 9-507(c) and the last sentence of Comment 4 to §§9-507, 9-506, 9-509(d)(1).

b.   What if, instead of inventory, GBT had only a security interest in South West's "construction crane?" Does Monette need to do anything to remain perfected? — *Yes- won't find if under different name*

c.   Assume that the crane was GBT's only collateral. Without GBT's consent, *—Yes* South West sold it for $235,000 in cash, and used the cash to buy a bulldozer. Is GBT perfected in the bulldozer? UCC §§9-315(c) and (d). Does knowing this *proceeds are still* change your answer to *b*? *Yes, SI unauthorized*

23.3.   GBT is about to lend $500,000 to Russell Lair Enterprises (RLE), which operates a small chain of army/navy surplus stores. The loan is to be secured by an interest in substantially all the debtor's assets. The UCC search came back clean, except for a financing statement filed by Suti, a manufacturer of cast iron lawn dogs. The financing statement describes Suti's collateral as "lawn dogs manufactured by Suti." On Helen Monette's physical inspection of the proposed collateral, Monette found only $25,000 worth of Suti lawn dogs. GBT does not care whether the lawn dogs are included in their collateral. Unless you advise otherwise, Monette proposes to go ahead with the loan, without clearing the Suti interest or inquiring further about it. But, first, Monette wants to know: Is there any way the Suti filing could encumber more than the lawn dogs? Is there any way it could be for more than $25,000? UCC §9-315.

23.4.   Your firm represents Arizona National Bank in hundreds of foreclosure cases. The bank has recently had problems with debtors systematically stripping fixtures from their homes during foreclosure and selling them on Craigslist. The client shows you one of the ads, which declares "Stripping House Before Foreclosure." The ad offers "cabinets, countertops, sinks, toilets, stove, refrigerator, and rose bushes from the yard." The bank wants to know what it can do to stop this activity and get some of its property back. UCC

§§9-317(b), 9-507(b). A.R.S. §13-2204 (2015) provides that "[a] person commits defrauding secured creditors if the person knowingly destroys, removes, conceals, encumbers, converts, sells, obtains, transfers, controls or otherwise deals with property subject to a security interest with the intent to hinder or prevent the enforcement of that interest." Defrauding secured creditors is a crime. A.R.S. §13-2201 defines "security interest" as "an interest in personal property or fixtures pursuant to [the Uniform Commercial Code]."

■ END OF DEFAULT PROBLEM SET

23.5.   a.   You represent October National Bank. ONB lent $1 million to Beaver Manufacturing, a local concern that produces and services commercial pumping equipment. The loan documents included a security agreement and financing statement, both of which describe the collateral as "equipment, inventory, accounts, chattel paper, general intangibles, fixtures, money, and bank accounts." You estimate the total value of all collateral at about $750,000. One of Beaver's assets is a bank account at Gargantuan Bank and Trust that contains $85,097. Does ONB have a security interest in the account? UCC §§9-102(a)(29) and (64), 9-109(d)(13), and 9-203(a) and (b); Comment 16 to UCC §9-109.

b.   If ONB has a security interest in the bank account, is it perfected? UCC §§9-104, 9-312(b)(1), 9-314, and 9-315(d)(2).

c.   Does it matter that some of the proceeds have been in the account for as long as 45 days? UCC §§9-315(c) and (d).

d.   Does it matter if Beaver commingled $100 of its own money into the GBT account? UCC §9-315.

23.6.   Although GBT has never had formal procedures for discovering its debtors' name changes, GBT's recent loss of a name-change case has Monette thinking about adopting some procedures. She has three questions:

a.   How often would she have to check the corporate records to make sure she could amend GBT's financing statements in time to avoid loss of collateral? UCC §9-507(c).

b.   To be effective, must a continuation statement include the new name of a debtor that changed its name since the original filing? UCC §§9-102(a)(27), 9-512(a), 9-516(b)(3) and (5), form for Amendments in UCC §9-521.

c.   In the investigation of a loan applicant, how old a change of name could be relevant? UCC §9-515(e).

Assignment 24: Maintaining Perfection Through Relocation of Debtor or Collateral

In previous assignments, we implicitly assumed that every secured transaction occurred within the boundaries of a single state. In this assignment, we relax that assumption and address the problems inherent in using state-based filing systems to keep track of commerce that flows freely from state to state.

A. State-Based Filing in a National Economy

In Assignment 16, we introduced a theory of the filing system. The filing system is a means for a secured creditor who takes a nonpossessory security interest in property of a debtor to communicate the existence of that security interest to others who may later consider extending credit to that debtor. We noted in that assignment that there is not one, but a multitude of filing systems. For a message left in a filing system to reach the later searchers for whom it is intended, the later searchers must be able to determine the correct filing system or systems in which to look. In Assignment 16, we examined how searchers made that determination among state and federal filing systems specialized as to the type of collateral. In this assignment, we examine how searchers make that determination among the statewide filing systems of the 50 states and those of foreign countries.

The rules that specify where to file and search are found in UCC §§9-301 to 9-307. Those rules are framed as conflicts rules that determine the law applicable to "perfection, the effect of perfection or nonperfection, and priority." Because Article 9 has been adopted in all 50 states, the rules governing "perfection, the effect of perfection or nonperfection, and priority" are the same in all 50 states. Generally speaking, it does not matter whether the law of New York or New Mexico applies, because for all practical purposes, those laws are the same. In one important respect, however, they remain different. When the law of New York applies to require the filing of a financing statement in the Office of the Secretary of State, the reference is to an office in Albany, New York. When the law of New Mexico applies, the reference is to an office in Santa Fe, New Mexico. The principal impact of the rules in UCC §§9-301 to 9-307 is to tell filers and searchers the state of the secretary of state's office in which they should file or search.

The rules in UCC §§9-301 to 9-307 govern perfection by possession and perfection by control as well as perfection by filing. In exploring the impact of these sections, however, we deal almost exclusively with perfection by filing.

Perfection by possession and perfection by control are likely to generate few interstate problems. When these kinds of perfection occur at all, they always occur in the right state.

B.   Initial Perfection

1.   At the Location of the Debtor

UCC §9-301(1) states the general rule regarding the correct state in which to file a financing statement. While a debtor is located in a state, the local law of that state governs perfection of a nonpossessory security interest. (If the security interest is possessory, the more specific provision of UCC §9-301(2) would override UCC §9-301(1) and impose the law of the jurisdiction in which the collateral is located.) If the law of the state applies, §9-501(a)(2) will require filing in the statewide filing office of the state for non-real estate-related collateral.

UCC §9-307 contains additional provisions specifying the locations of particular kinds of debtors. An individual debtor is deemed to be located at the individual's "principal residence." The UCC does not define the term. *Black's Law Dictionary* defines a "residence" as "[t]he place where one actually lives, as distinguished from a domicile." The distinction is that residence "just means bodily presence as an inhabitant in a given place," but domicile "requires bodily presence plus an intention to make the place one's home." A person can have only one domicile but may have more than one residence. It is not clear why the UCC drafters used the term "principal residence," or whether they intended the term to have a meaning different from "domicile." Comment 2 to UCC §9-307 says that when doubt arises as to the location of a debtor's principal residence, "prudence may dictate perfecting under the law of each jurisdiction that might be the debtor's 'principal residence.'"

A "registered organization" is "an organization formed or organized solely under the law of one State or the United States by the filing of a public organic record with, the issuance of a public organic record by, or the enactment of legislation by the State or United States." UCC §9-102(a)(71). A "public organic record" is "a record that is available to the public for inspection" and that is "the record initially filed with or issued by a State or the United States to form or organize" the organization or a restatement of that record. UCC §9-102(a)(68). For a corporation, the public organic record would probably be the Articles of Incorporation filed by the incorporator with the state or the corporate charter issued by the state. For a limited liability company, it might be the Articles of Organization.

Virtually every domestic corporation (profit or non-profit), limited partnership, limited liability company, service corporation, or professional association will qualify as a registered organization. Although a few organizations have managed to get charters from more than one government, that is extremely rare. If New York grants a corporate charter to "Acme Enterprises, Inc." and that corporation then applies for and obtains a charter in the same name from another state, the effect is to create a second corporation with the same name, not to obtain a second charter for the same corporation.

UCC §9-307(e) provides that a registered organization that is organized under the law of a state is located in that state. (The provisions of UCC §9-307(b) to the contrary expressly yield to the other provisions of UCC §9-307.) Thus, for example, a Delaware corporation is located in the state of Delaware—even though it may have no offices or employees in that state, do no business in that state, and have all of its extensive operations in Texas. This feature of the new law is deliberate. Because the appropriate state in which to file depends solely on place of incorporation—a matter of public record—the proper place for filing and searching can be determined solely from the public record. Neither filer nor searcher need be concerned with the location of the debtor's collateral or operations.

Early in the Article 9 revision process, the drafters decided to adopt a system in which filing would be in the jurisdiction in which the corporate debtor had its headquarters (referred to as *debtor-based* filing). Filing at the corporate debtor's place of incorporation (*incorporation-based* filing) was initially proposed in the law review article that follows. Empirical data showing that the switch to filing at the debtor's place of incorporation would move only about $3 million a year in filing fees to Delaware from the other 49 states established the political viability of the proposal. But from a systems standpoint, the most important feature of filing at the place of incorporation was placing the UCC filings against a corporate debtor in the same jurisdiction as the corporate records on that debtor. By joining the two sets of files, the secretary of state could make possible a dramatic reduction in filing errors.

Lynn M. LoPucki, Why the Debtor's State of Incorporation Should Be the Proper Place for Article 9 Filing: A Systems Analysis

79 Minn. L. Rev. 577 (1995)

Filers who desire a high level of certainty that their filing was in fact made and properly indexed often conduct a post-filing search to verify that fact. In a collateral-based system, that search will show the filer's financing statement and any effective filings made prior to it in the jurisdiction against the debtor. But that search will tell the filer little about whether the filing is in the right jurisdiction. A debtor-based system has a considerable advantage in this regard. Most filers have sufficient information about their debtors to form some sort of expectation as to how many filings there will be against them. In ordinary circumstances, all of those filings will be made in the same office. If the filer's post-filing search reveals substantially fewer or more filings than expected, the filer can decide whether to investigate further. For example, failure of a post-filing search against a debtor that should have many filings to discover many filings indicates that the filer has filed in the wrong office. I will refer to this system characteristic as the "echo effect."

An incorporation-based system can both provide a strong echo and "trap" some kinds of errors in filings. Because both the corporation records and the statewide

UCC filing records would be under the control of the same Secretary of State, the Secretary could link them electronically. Each time a UCC filing would be made against a corporate debtor, the computer could match the name of the debtor to the names of the corporations formed under the laws of the state. If there were no match, the filing would be erroneous. The system could notify the filer of that fact. If there were a match, the system could display a list of filings against the debtor, the equivalent of the echo effect available in a debtor-based system.[1]

The feedback advantages of an incorporation-based system do not depend on the existence of an automatic computer link between the corporate and statewide UCC filing records. If no such link existed, the filer still could telephone the corporation division of the Secretary of State's office to make the verification.

As increasing numbers of filings are made electronically, error trapping can sharply reduce the number of errors entering the filing system. Although error trapping could not eliminate errors in which the filer mistakes one corporation for another, it could eliminate filings on which the name does not match the name of any corporation formed in the state.

A few states actually implemented point-and-click systems that allowed filers and searchers to select their debtors from lists of the states' corporations. But in 2010, the Article 9 drafters adopted a definition of "public organic record" that declares the correct name for a corporation to be the name on the record the incorporator filed with the state to incorporate and on any record filed or issued by the state to change that name. The effect is to make the corporate name on the state's web site no longer authoritative. Point-and-click systems could have eliminated the name problem in corporate filings, but the "public organic record" definition has made them no longer feasible.

In the United Kingdom, the corporate records are in a single, national system. Extracts of each of the charges (British for "security interests") registered (filed) against a company are included in the company's corporate records. Those records are accessible at the web site for Companies House, the registrar for U.K. companies, but the search is not free.

Some organizations are not incorporated. They include general partnerships and a variety of associations, both for profit and not for profit. UCC §9-307(b)(2) deems such a debtor located at its place of business if it has only one and UCC §9-307(b)(3) deems such a debtor located at its chief executive office if it has more than one place of business. UCC §9-307(a) defines "place of business" to mean "a place where a debtor conducts its affairs." Comment 2 to that section adds "Thus, every organization, even eleemosynary institutions and other organizations that do not conduct 'for profit' business activities, have a 'place of business.'"

[1]. The echo effect is stronger in an incorporation-based system because all effective filings against a debtor will be in the same system. In a debtor-based system, uncertainty about the location of the debtor will cause significant numbers of filers to make more than one filing, leading to the possibility of a false echo.

Determining the location of an organization's "chief executive office" may not be as easy as it sounds. The concept has proven problematic in a number of other contexts, including (1) filing against mobile goods and intangible property under former Article 9, (2) locating corporations for purposes of diversity jurisdiction in the federal courts, and (3) determining proper venue for corporate bankruptcies. In those contexts, courts developed what came to be known as the "nerve center" test: the organization is located in the place from which it is managed — regardless of the location of its operations. That place is referred to as the organization's "nerve center." *Nerve center*

That place might not be much else. To illustrate, assume that San Antonio Hotel Organization (Hotel) owns and operates the San Antonio Hotel in Texas. Jose Sanchez is the chief executive officer. He lives in Tennessee and manages the 100-room San Antonio Hotel from there. Sanchez keeps the books and records on a personal computer in his home. He makes all major decisions for the business, including those regarding the hiring and firing of employees. He is in touch daily with Hector Williams, the on-site manager in Texas. On these facts, a court would be likely to hold that the chief executive office of Hotel is in Tennessee. *chief executive office*

The general rules in UCC §9-307(b) that determine the debtor's location do not apply if the law of the debtor's location does not generally require filing as a condition for obtaining priority. If not, the debtor is deemed located in the District of Columbia. UCC §9-307(c). Because every state in the United States generally requires filing as a condition for obtaining priority, UCC §9-307(c) will apply only when the general rules point to the law of another country.

Dayka & Hackett, LLC v. Del Monte Fresh Produce N.A., Inc.

228 Ariz. 533, 269 P.3d 709 (Ariz. App. 2012)

BRAMMER, JUDGE.

Del Monte Fresh Produce, N.A., Inc. (Del Monte) appeals from the trial court's order granting summary judgment to Dayka & Hackett, LLC (D & H) on its claims of lien priority and conversion regarding the proceeds from the sale of Rolando Castelo de la Rosa and Maria Olivia Aguirre Ramos's (growers) 2008 table grape crop. We affirm.

FACTUAL AND PROCEDURAL BACKGROUND

In January 2007, D & H agreed to finance and sell the growers' 2007 grape crop to be grown in Sonora, Mexico. D & H entered into marketing and security agreements with the growers and, on January 18, 2007, it filed a financing statement pursuant to [UCC §9-307(c)] in Washington, D.C. to perfect its interest. The security agreement granted D & H an interest in the 2007 and any future crops the growers produced, together with any proceeds generated by the sale of the crops. The 2007 grape crop was not profitable and the growers were unable to repay to D & H what they owed. The growers subsequently defaulted on their obligations to D & H, eventually owing $688,587.

Del Monte, unaware of the relationship between the growers and D & H, advanced the growers funds to produce their 2008 crop. After conducting a lien search of the public registry in Sonora, Del Monte entered into a marketing and security agreement with the growers. Under its marketing agreement, Del Monte was obligated to market and sell the crop it was advancing the growers funds to raise, and to pay the growers a portion of the sales proceeds. The growers granted Del Monte a security interest in collateral, which included the 2008 crop and any proceeds from its sale. In May 2008, Del Monte registered its security interest with the public registry in Sonora.

Del Monte marketed the 2008 crop and collected and retained all the sales proceeds. D & H filed a complaint against the growers and Del Monte seeking to enforce its security interest in the growers' 2008 crop and its proceeds. The trial court granted summary judgment in favor of D & H on its conversion claim and awarded it damages of $688,587.71, the amount the growers owed D & H. This appeal followed.

DISCUSSION

D & H recorded its security interest with the Registrar of Deeds in Washington, D.C., on January 18, 2007. Del Monte recorded its security agreement in Mexico's Real Property Registry and Movables Registry on May 7, 2008 in Hermosillo, Sonora, Mexico. To assess which party's filing was effective to perfect its interest and give it priority, we must determine whether United States or Mexican law applies.

The Uniform Commercial Code (UCC) as adopted in Arizona provides that, "while a debtor is located in a jurisdiction, the local law of that jurisdiction governs perfection . . . and the priority of a security interest in collateral." [UCC §9-301(1)]. An individual generally "is located at the individual's principal residence," [UCC §9-307(b)(1)], and it is undisputed that the growers are residents of Sonora, Mexico. However, [UCC §9-307(b)] applies only if:

> [the] debtor's residence . . . is located in a jurisdiction whose law generally requires information concerning the existence of a nonpossessory security interest to be made generally available in a filing, recording or registration system as a condition or result of the security interest's obtaining priority over the rights of a lien creditor with respect to the collateral.

[UCC §9-307(c)]. If the requirements of [UCC §9-307(c)] are not met, the debtor is considered to be "located in the District of Columbia."

Therefore, whether priority is determined by United States or Mexican law depends on whether, during the relevant time period, Mexican law "generally require[d]" such information "to be made generally available in a filing, recording or registration system" in order to obtain priority. Both parties presented expert testimony regarding whether Mexican law during the relevant period satisfied the conditions set forth in [UCC §9-307(c)]. D & H expert Dale Furnish has authored articles and book chapters on Mexican law, has consulted with the Mexican government regarding the amendment of its laws, and has assisted in drafting Arizona's secured transactions laws and the Organization of American States model on secured transactions.

According to Furnish, Mexican law in 2007 and 2008 was a "crazy quilt" of different security devices that did not meet the requirements of [UCC §9-307(c)]. Checking public records in Mexico provided no assurance of the priority of an interest because it was "possible for several common types of credit guaranties to be unrecorded, and still gain priority over even a recorded security interest." According to Furnish, one of the major flaws in the Mexican registration system preventing the growers from being "located" in Mexico is that it did not include a provision stating it applied to any device acting in practical effect as a security interest.

Federal registry

Amendments to Mexico's laws in 2009 recognized and defined a "security interest," created a single federal registry for recording security interests, and generally required that all security interests be recorded in the federal registry. Both Furnish and Bringas Acedo opined that once the 2009 amendments are implemented they will, for the first time, create a system that "'generally requires' recording to establish priority between competing claims or security interests in personal property."

Furnish added that "[e]very authoritative source available agrees that Mexico did not have . . . a law" satisfying [UCC §9-307(c)] in 2007 and 2008. For example, he discussed a 2008 article in evidence authored by Arnold S. Rosenberg and published in the book *Practice Under Article 9 of the UCC* by the UCC Committee of the American Bar Association (ABA). The article classified foreign filing systems into category "A"—jurisdictions clearly satisfying the test in UCC § 9-307(c)—through category "D"—jurisdictions that clearly fail the test. It classified Mexico as a category "D" jurisdiction because "filing is a sufficient but unnecessary step due to the existence of alternative methods of perfecting the secured party's interest without filing."

The expert testimony and secondary authority on the topic establish that Mexico's law in 2007 and 2008 did not meet the requirements of [UCC §9-307(c)] and, therefore, the growers for the purpose of perfecting security interests in their property were located in the District of Columbia pursuant to the statute. Thus, D & H perfected its security interest by filing in the District of Columbia, and its security interest in the 2008 crop and its proceeds had priority over Del Monte's conflicting, unperfected security interest.

---

2.   At the Location of the Collateral

Recall that a fixture filing must be made in "the office designated for the filing or recording of a mortgage on the real property" to which the fixture is attached. UCC §9-501(a)(1). The purpose of this rule is to keep all filings against a parcel of real property or the fixtures attached to it in the same set of records in the county where the land is located. The effect is that all filings and searches regarding a particular parcel of real property can be made in a single filing system—the real property records of the county in which the land is located. (There is one exception: a fixture filing against the fixtures of a transmitting utility is made in the UCC filing system, not the real property filing system. UCC §9-501(b). When the real property lawyers finally realize that this exception exists, they will go nuts.)

For fixture filings to be in the county where the real property is located, they must, of course, be in the state where the real property is located. Thus, the choice of law rule for fixture filings specifies filing at the location of the collateral, not the location of the debtor. UCC §9-301(3). For example, assume that Hotel Sierra Vista, Inc., a California corporation, is the owner of a free-standing walk-in freezer. Regardless of where the freezer is located, non-fixture filings against it must be made in California. If the freezer is affixed to the Hotel property in Reno, Nevada, a fixture filing against the freezer must be made in the county real property records in Reno.

UCC §§9-304 to 9-306 specify the law applicable to the perfection and priority of security interests in deposit accounts, investment property, and letters of credit. Perfection in these kinds of property can be by control of the collateral rather than by filing a financing statement. UCC §9-314. As a consequence, these sections can never determine the proper states in which to file financing statements.

C.   Perfection Maintenance

1.   Through Debtor Relocation

After the secured creditor has perfected its security interest in the collateral by filing in the state in which the debtor is located, the debtor may change its location to another state.

a. Individuals.

An individual debtor would accomplish that by changing his or her *principal residence*. In most cases, such a change will be obvious: The debtor sells his or her house in the original state and a moving van takes the debtor's property to a new house in the destination state. Before the move, the debtor lived and worked in the original state; after the move, the debtor lives and works in the destination state. But many relocations will not be so tidy. Debtors may simultaneously have homes in two states and move back and forth between them. A debtor may own a home in one state but live in a rented home in another. Such a debtor may intend to return to the first state, may intend to remain permanently in the second, or may intend to move to a third. One must at least sometimes be physically present in a state to have one's principal residence there. But if a debtor is sometimes physically present in each of two or more states, the debtor's intentions become determinative. Those intentions may be difficult to discern and may change over time.

When an individual debtor changes his or her state of principal residence, the secured creditor who filed in the original state has four months in which to file in the destination state. UCC §9-316(a)(2). If the secured creditor does not do so, the security interest becomes unperfected, "and is deemed never to have been perfected as against a purchaser of the collateral for value." UCC §9-316(b). The purpose of the quoted language is to distinguish between "purchasers for value," a group that includes secured parties, on the one hand and lien creditors and bankruptcy trustees on the other. A secured party who fails to file in the destination state before the end of the four month period loses to a secured party who perfected before that date, but still prevails over a person who becomes a lien creditor before that date or a trustee in a bankruptcy case filed before that date. The failing secured party loses, of course, to a person who becomes a secured party or a lien creditor after the four month period expires and before the failing secured party otherwise reperfects. The four-month grace period for filing in the destination state applies to security interests that first attach after the debtor's change in location, as well as to security interests that attached — and so were perfected — prior to the debtor's change. UCC §9-316(h).

Security agreements usually require that the debtors declare their jurisdictions of principal residence and notify the secured parties of any changes in them. Experience tells us that debtors will often fail to comply with the latter requirement — particularly debtors who are already in financial difficulty. To protect against loss of perfection, secured creditors will have to discover changes of principal residence and respond. *— purpose of Credit Report*

b. Unregistered Organizations.

The consequences of a change in location of an unregistered organization are the same as for individuals. The secured party has four months to discover the change and file a new financing statement or become unperfected under UCC §9-316.

An unregistered organization can move from one state to another by changing the location of its chief executive office. That might be an uprooting of an entire group of people, office machines, and records, and their transfer to a new address in another state. If it is, it will be easy to spot. But it may be nothing more than a move of the *chief executive officer* from one state to another. Today there are numerous examples of organizations run by chief executive officers who do not work in the same states as their office staffs. The drafters of revised Article 9 rejected location of the chief executive office as the place for filing against registered entities in part because of the ephemeral nature of the chief executive office in modern commerce. It remains the test for unregistered entities only for lack of a better alternative. *Chief executive officer location file for unregistered*

c. Registered Organizations.

No legal procedure exists by which a registered organization can change the state in which it is organized, and thus registered organizations cannot move. Lawyers have, however, developed strategies for accomplishing what amounts to the same thing. To illustrate, suppose those in control of a corporation registered in Michigan merge it into a corporation registered in Florida. After the merger, all of the assets formerly owned by the Michigan corporation will be owned by the surviving Florida corporation.

If, as is often the case, the Florida corporation was incorporated for the specific purpose of the merger and owns no assets except those acquired through the merger, the stockholders of the Michigan corporation can become the sole stockholders of the Florida corporation. After the merger, the Florida corporation will have precisely the same assets and the same stockholders that the Michigan corporation had before the merger. The Florida corporation is a new entity. The Michigan corporation has neither moved nor changed states. The practical effect, however, is the same as if the Michigan corporation had changed its state of incorporation from Michigan to Florida. This strategy is referred to as "reincorporation."

Another strategy for accomplishing such a *reincorporation* is to register a new organization in the destination state and then transfer ownership of the assets of the existing organization to the new one. The assets need not move.

Both strategies—merger and sale of assets—reach precisely the same end. Which is employed will depend on the relative costs of the two transactions. Those costs are principally transfer taxes, attorneys fees, and the costs of giving notice to interested parties.

It is important to realize that reincorporation may be an entirely paper (or paperless) transaction. There may be no change whatsoever in the physical location of the assets or the conduct of the business. The new organization may do business under the same trade name in the same location, and even have the same name on its corporate charter. The only thing that necessarily has changed is the state of organization of the entity that owns the collateral.

Reincorporations, whether by sale or merger, are formally transfers of assets to new entities. The applicable rules are those governing continuation in perfection after transfers of ownership. We turn to these rules in the next section.

2. Through Collateral Transfer

UCC §9-316(a)(3) addresses the situation in which the debtor does not move, but instead transfers the collateral to a debtor located in another state. For filing system operation, such a transfer creates the same problem as a debtor move: A filing against the former debtor remains effective, UCC §9-507(a), yet a search in the state where the current debtor is located will not find it. The solution is the same: Article 9 affords the filer a grace period in which to discover the transfer and perfect by filing in the destination jurisdiction. The grace period, however, is one year instead of four months. If the earlier filer does so, the earlier filer remains continuously perfected and defeats even a competitor who was first to file against the collateral in the destination state.

UCC §9-316(a)(3) also applies when the debtor reincorporates by merger or sale of assets to a corporation in another state. It gives the secured creditor one year in which to discover the merger and perfect in the destination state. The secured creditor's task in discovering the relocation by merger will usually be considerably easier than the secured creditor's task in discovering relocation by sale of assets or a debtor's change of principal residence. The merger will be a matter of public record, generally in both the original and the destination states. Because articles of merger must be filed in the states of incorporation of each of the merging entities, the secured creditor can discover a merger by monitoring the record of its debtor's incorporation in the original state.

If a debtor reincorporates by sale of assets, the transaction may be more difficult for the secured creditor to discover. Consider again the Michigan corporation that seeks to relocate to Florida. The Michigan corporation causes the formation of a new Florida corporation. The Michigan corporation then transfers all of its assets to the Florida corporation in return for all of the stock of the Florida corporation, and distributes the stock to its own shareholders. The Michigan corporation has no assets, but it may continue in existence. Nothing may occur on the corporate records of Michigan that would alert the monitoring secured creditor that the Michigan corporation no longer owns the collateral.

D.   Nation-Based Filing in a World Economy

When Grant Gilmore, the original draftsman of Article 9, proposed in the 1940s that there be "one big filing system," he meant one in each state. More than a half-century later, the drafters of Article 9 implemented his proposal by eliminating county UCC filing systems (but not county real property filing systems). Gilmore's slogan of "one big filing system" has long since been adopted by others who mean by it a single filing system for the entire United States, perhaps operated by the federal government. They were not taken seriously in the drafting of revised Article 9 for precisely the reasons that Gilmore lost his battle at the county level in the 1940s—filing offices are already in place at the state level, and both jobs and political power would be shifted in the move to "one big filing system." The political reality seems to be that this kind of change can occur only when the old system is so hopelessly and obviously out of date that it has become a political embarrassment.

In the meantime, secured transactions have moved from the national level to the international, and the events of the last 70 years have begun to repeat themselves with respect to countries of the world rather than states of the United States. Secured loans from institutions in one country to borrowers in another are becoming routine. Lawyers are attempting to accompany their clients as the clients go international, but lawyers in the destination countries are resisting and struggling to defend their turf. Both lawyers and policymakers have become concerned about the laws of other nations on the subject of secured transactions.

Virtually every country in the world recognizes at least some security devices. This should not be surprising, given that, as we saw in Assignment 2, security devices can be constructed from the devices of ownership, contract, and option. London attorney Philip R. Wood, who has written extensively on differences in world financial laws, identifies a group of

> about 80 English-based states [that allow] a universal monopolistic security over all the assets of the debtor which:
> [1] reaches future assets, including assets coming into existence after the bankruptcy of the debtor;
> [2] imposes few formalities;

[3] imposes no limits on who may take the security;

[4] permits the security to cover all future debt without stating a maximum amount; and

[5] allows the secured creditor privately to appoint a possessory manager to run the business without selling and allows private sales.

Wood classifies the United States and Canada, except for Quebec, as within this group. Wood classifies France as the major trading power most hostile to security; a large group of "Franco-Latin" countries as having "limited security"; and a small but important group led by Germany, Japan, and Russia as having "moderate security." The anti-security groups "allow security over land, but make it more difficult to take security over goods, receivables, investments and contracts." Those jurisdictions do so

by prohibiting non-possessory security and by:

[a] imposing onerous initial formalities and unrealistic taxes;

[b] excluding security for future debt or revolving credits;

[c] insisting on a maximum amount [of debt to be specified in the security agreement];

[d] downgrading the security below priority creditors so that no-one knows what it is worth; and

[e] placing obstacles in the way of enforcement, such as judicial public auction, compulsory grace periods and freezes on enforcement.

Philip R. Wood, Maps of World Financial Law 24-25 (1997).

Requirements for public filing of notice of security interests are less common outside the United States. Where they exist, they are of all four major types: filing at the location of the collateral, filing at the location of the debtor, filing at the place of incorporation, and notation on the certificate of title.

The choice of law rule in UCC §9-301(1) applies among nations as well as among states. Comment 3 to UCC §9-307 gives the following example:

Example 1. Debtor is an English corporation with 7 offices in the United States and its chief executive office in London, England. Debtor creates a security interest in its accounts. Under subsection [9-307](b)(3), Debtor would be located in England. However, subsection (c) provides that subsection (b) applies only if English law conditions perfection on giving public notice. Otherwise, Debtor is located in the District of Columbia. Under Section 9-301(1), perfection, the effect of perfection, and priority are governed by the law of the jurisdiction of the debtor's location — here, England or the District of Columbia (depending on the content of English law).

While the reporters do not give an example going the other way, we submit the following:

Example 2. Debtor is a Delaware corporation with 7 offices in England and its chief executive office in New York. Debtor creates a security interest in its equipment, which is located in England. Under subsection 9-307(e), Debtor would be located in Delaware. Under Section 9-301(1), perfection, the effect of perfection, and priority are governed by the law of the jurisdiction of Debtor's location — here, Delaware.

Finally, it should be noted that revised Article 9 does not purport to reorder the world's filing systems. Although the text places no express limits on its application, Comment 3 to UCC §9-307 notes:

> The foregoing discussion assumes that each transaction bears an appropriate relation to the forum State. In the absence of an appropriate relation, the forum State's entire UCC, including the choice-of-law provisions in Article 9 will not apply.

E.   International Filing Systems

International filing systems are another way to solve the filing coordination problem. The International Registry of Mobile Assets began operating on the Internet in 2006. The registry was established pursuant to the Convention on International Interests in Mobile Equipment and the Protocol to that Convention on matters specific to aircraft equipment (together "the Cape Town Treaty"). Nearly 30 countries have agreed to some or all of the Convention and Protocol. They include the United States, Canada, Mexico, the United Kingdom, France, Germany, Italy, China, and India. But several have done so with reservations that give the Cape Town Treaty limited or no effectiveness in the signatories' home jurisdictions.

Under the Cape Town Treaty, security interests, leases, and, in some countries, other kinds of liens on airframes, aircraft engines, and helicopters can be filed in the International Registry. Airframes and aircraft engines are defined such that the system does not apply to smaller, typically non-commercial aircraft. Aircraft objects are identified by manufacturer's serial number, the name of the manufacturer, and the object's model designation. Protocol VII. Additional protocols are intended in the future to expand the system to cover railway rolling stock and space assets.

Article 29(1) of the Convention states the priority rule: "A registered interest has priority over any other interest subsequently registered and over an unregistered interest." Thus, a secured party or lessor with an interest in an aircraft object to which the Convention applies must register its interest or risk losing its collateral to the holder of a later competing interest.

In accord with the Convention and Protocol, the United States has declared the Federal Aviation Administration to be the "point of entry" for filing in the International Registry. That is, to file in the International Registry, one first files in the FAA's national filing system in Oklahoma City. The FAA authorizes the International Registry filing, and the secured party or lessor then makes that second filing.

This "vertical" linking of the national and international filing systems addresses the principal problem with proliferating filing systems: How those who are required to file and search can know that they must do so, and where. Assuming that the holder of a security interest in an aircraft knows that it must file in the national system and does so, the national system can alert the holder that it is also required to file in the International Registry.

In accord with the Convention and Protocol, the U.S. Declarations except "non-consensual rights or interests" in Convention and Protocol collateral from international registration. The effect of this exception is that mechanics' liens and similar interests continue to have the priority they enjoy under U.S. law, even in competition with internationally registered interests.

Problem Set 24

24.1. Your client, Secured Lending Partners (SLP), has taken the security interests described below. Where should it file a financing statement or other record to perfect in it?

a. A security interest in equipment used in operating a business in New York. Henrik Durst, an individual who lives in New Jersey, owns the equipment and the business. UCC §9-301(1), 9-307.

b. A security interest in fixtures used in the same business and owned by the same person. UCC §9-301(4).

c. A security interest in an automobile used as equipment in the same business and owned by the same person.

d. A security interest in equipment used in operating a business in New York. Sevan Industries LLC, a Nevada limited liability company with its chief executive office in New Jersey, owns the equipment and the business. UCC §9-307.

e. A security interest in a Boeing 747 aircraft owned by AirLeasing, Inc., a Delaware corporation with its headquarters in California. The aircraft is based at an airport in New York and regularly flies outside the United States. UCC §9-311(a).

24.2. You have been assigned to file financing statements on behalf of your client, Firstbank, in connection with a loan in the amount of $500,000 to William Shatner, an inventor and professor of engineering. The collateral is the equipment, accounts, and inventory of Shatner Engineering, a small business located in Tucson, Arizona, that Shatner started before he began teaching. Shatner remains the sole owner of the business. Shatner's ex-wife, Louise Godfrey, runs the business on a day-to-day basis in return for a salary and a share of the profits, but Shatner himself makes all the big decisions. Shatner has a "permanent," tenured job at the University of Missouri in Kansas City. The school is in Missouri, three miles from the Kansas-Missouri state line. Shatner lives in an apartment on the Kansas side of the line, but is hunting for a house nearer the school — probably on the Missouri side of the line. During the summers, Shatner returns to the home he owns just outside of Tucson, Arizona and spends his days working on the business. A friend of yours who knows Shatner well says that Shatner intends to quit teaching in a few years, move to Hawaii, and operate the business from there. UCC §§1-201(b)(25), 9-102(a)(28), 9-301, 9-307, 9-503(a)(4), 9-506(c), and Comment 2 to UCC §9-307.

a. On the foregoing facts, who or what is, or might be, the debtor?

b. In what states should you file?

c. What name or names should be listed on each of the filings?

d.   You just learned that three years ago Shatner formed a Nevada corporation under the name Shatner Engineering Products, Inc. Now where do you file?   *NV too*

e.   As you are going through the papers provided by Shatner when he applied for the loan, you find his most recent tax return where Shatner characterizes his business with Godfrey as a "tenancy in common." In what states should you file? What names should be listed on each of the filings?   *where Shatner, wife location*

f.   You just learned that some of the "equipment" might instead be fixtures. How does your answer change? UCC §9-301(3). – *AR, business location fixture filing*

24.3. a. What, if anything, should Firstbank do to monitor the location of the debtors in Problem 24.2? UCC §§9-316(a) and (b). Keep in mind that if Firstbank is lending at five percentage points above its cost of borrowing, the gross profit on this loan will be $25,000 a year.   *→ ask for updates, public records search*

b.   How would your answer change if the loan were for $25 million? – *federal ucc*

c.   What would be the advantages and disadvantages of a system that required filing against individuals at their place of birth rather than at their principal residences? All states in the United States keep birth records. In some states, they are public records; in others, they are released only at the subject's request. Filing against persons born outside the United States would be in the District of Columbia.   *people move*

24.4. a. Your client, Global Bank, is lending $1.9 million to Tang Aluminum Products to be secured by a first security interest in inventory, equipment, accounts, and general intangibles that Tang recently purchased from Argon, Inc. You have been assigned to do the UCC searches. You already know that the collateral is located in your state and has never been located anywhere else. What inquiries will you make? In what names will you search? In what filing systems will you search? UCC §§9-301(1), 9-307(a)-(e), 9-316(a), 9-507(a), and Comment 3 to UCC §9-507.   *Transfer of collateral 1 yr to file, search Tang your state*

b.   In an alternative universe, you represent XBank, the holder of a security interest perfected against a prior owner of this collateral in another state. Can XBank file a financing statement against Tang Aluminum in this state? UCC §9-509(c).   *yes transfer of sale assets*

24.5. Assume that Afghanistan law gives priority to the first security interest created and that the country has no filing system. Firstbank loans $1 million to Afghan, Inc., an Afghanistan corporation whose headquarters and operations are all in New York. Where is Firstbank required to file a financing statement? UCC §§9-102(a)(71) and (77), 9-301, 9-307(b), (c), and (e), and Comment 3 to UCC §9-307.

■ END OF DEFAULT PROBLEM SET

24.6. You are working for a politically connected firm in Wilmington, Delaware, that does a lot of corporate work, including big bankruptcy cases that come from all over the United States. Carol Lynn Murphy, the youngest partner in the firm, explains that the firm got its start in the 1920s shortly after Delaware replaced New Jersey as the jurisdiction of choice for the incorporation of large public companies. The firm got a big boost in the early 1990s when the Delaware Bankruptcy Court began attracting the bankruptcy reorganization cases of those same large public companies. Today, Delaware is the place of incorporation for over half of all large public companies and the venue for over half of the bankruptcies of large public companies. Because Article 9 provides for filing at the place of incorporation, Murphy envisions a third wave of prosperity for Delaware and the firm.

a.   Murphy asks what you think would happen on the following facts. The other 49 states and the District of Columbia retain Article 9 as promulgated, but Delaware adopts a non-uniform amendment that excuses filing altogether. The Delaware law simply declares all security interests "perfected without filing." Cherokee, Inc., a Delaware corporation whose assets and operations are all located in New York, borrows money from a New York bank and grants the New York bank a security interest. The New York bank does not file a financing statement. A year later, Cherokee, Inc. files under Chapter 11 of the Bankruptcy Code in New York and seeks to avoid the New York bank's security interest as unperfected. UCC §§9-301(1), 9-307.

b.   Would a law that successfully excused some or all UCC filings make Delaware a more or less attractive place for debtors to incorporate? Murphy notes a study by attorney Meredith Jackson, reported in Peter Alces, Abolish the Article 9 Filing System, 79 Minn. L. Rev. 679, 690-691 (1995), indicating that the costs of filing and searching average about $25,000 for loans averaging in the range of $20 million to $70 million.

24.7.   A U.S. government affiliated think tank has been asked to imagine how the world's filing systems will be, or should be, organized 20 or 50 years from now. They would like your opinion on these alternatives: Will there be a single, world-wide filing system? Several worldwide filing systems, each for a different type of collateral? National filing systems with the proper place for filing specified in international treaties? If the latter, will the system be collateral-based or debtor-based?

Assignment 25: Maintaining Perfection in Certificate of Title Systems

Each of the 50 states maintains a certificate of title system for motor vehicles. In each state, a motor vehicle certificate of title act enacted by the legislature governs that system. The most widely adopted certificate of title act is the Uniform Motor Vehicle Certificate of Title and Anti-theft Act (UMVCTA), which has been adopted in 11 states. In most states, a department with the name Department of Motor Vehicles, or something similar, operates the motor vehicle certificate of title system. We will refer to it as "the Department."

For the purpose of inclusion in this system, "motor vehicle" is defined as "a device in, upon, or by which a person or property is or may be transported or drawn upon a highway, except a device moved by human power or used exclusively upon stationary rails or tracks." UMVCTA §1(n). In other words, "motor vehicle" includes cars, trucks, buses, motorcycles, and the like. It does not include bicycles, trains, boats, or aircraft, even though some of these are vehicles that have motors.

For each motor vehicle in a system, the Department maintains a *certificate* that describes the vehicle and shows who owns it. When the system functions properly, there is one and only one certificate of title for any motor vehicle. A copy of a certificate appears later in this assignment. A certificate of title identifies the vehicle by Vehicle Identification Number (VIN), make, and model. It also identifies the owner and the holders of any liens against the vehicle by name and address. On the back of a certificate of title there is usually a form for transferring ownership of the vehicle.

Certificates of title are part of a complex system that serves a variety of purposes, most unrelated to secured credit. Certificates of title are part of the system by which the police identify the owner of a vehicle that is involved in an accident, lost, stolen, or used in the commission of a crime. Certificates of title are also used to transfer ownership of motor vehicles and to keep track of successive annual registrations and taxation of vehicles.

The reason we include an assignment dealing with certificates of title in this course is that for most kinds of property covered by a certificate of title, the face of the certificate is the proper place to record any security interest. (In certificate of title systems, security interests are referred to as *liens* and filing is referred to as *notation of the lien on the certificate of title*.) All states maintain motor vehicle certificate of title systems, nearly all maintain mobile home certificate of title systems, and several maintain motorboat certificate of title systems. Each is physically separate from each other and from the Article 9 filing system.

In the United States, security interests are perfected by notation on the certificate of title in all but a few states. In Canada, security interests in motor

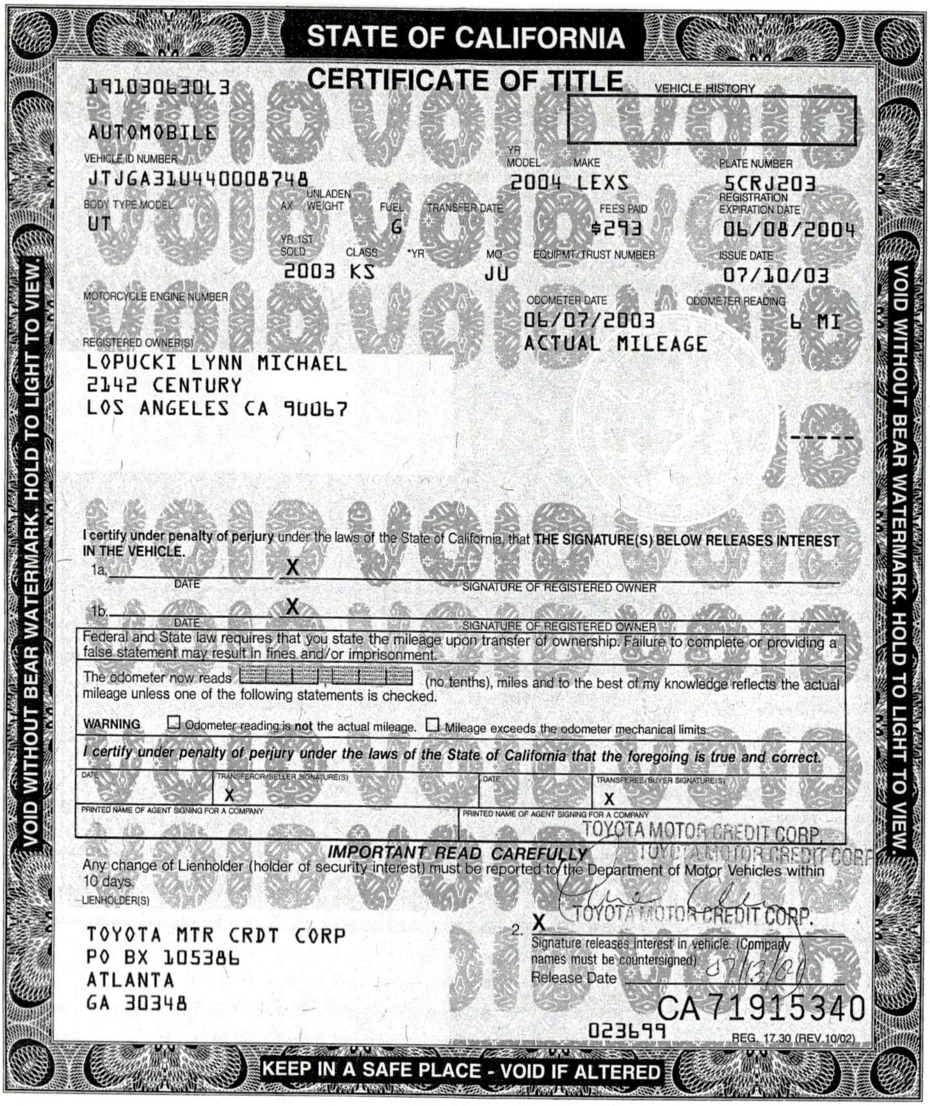

STATE OF CALIFORNIA

CERTIFICATE OF TITLE

VEHICLE HISTORY

1910306306L3

AUTOMOBILE

VEHICLE ID NUMBER: JTJGA31U440008748
YR MODEL: 2004
MAKE: LEXS
PLATE NUMBER: 5CRJ203

BODY TYPE MODEL: UT
AX
UNLADEN WEIGHT
FUEL: G
TRANSFER DATE
FEES PAID: $293
REGISTRATION EXPIRATION DATE: 06/08/2004

YR 1ST SOLD: 2003
CLASS: KS
YR
MO: JU
EQUIPMT/TRUST NUMBER
ISSUE DATE: 07/10/03

MOTORCYCLE ENGINE NUMBER
ODOMETER DATE: 06/07/2003
ODOMETER READING: 6 MI
ACTUAL MILEAGE

REGISTERED OWNER(S)
LOPUCKI LYNN MICHAEL
2142 CENTURY
LOS ANGELES CA 90067

I certify under penalty of perjury under the laws of the State of California, that THE SIGNATURE(S) BELOW RELEASES INTEREST IN THE VEHICLE.

1a. ______ DATE X ______ SIGNATURE OF REGISTERED OWNER

1b. ______ DATE X ______ SIGNATURE OF REGISTERED OWNER

Federal and State law requires that you state the mileage upon transfer of ownership. Failure to complete or providing a false statement may result in fines and/or imprisonment.

The odometer now reads ______ (no tenths), miles and to the best of my knowledge reflects the actual mileage unless one of the following statements is checked.

WARNING ☐ Odometer reading is not the actual mileage. ☐ Mileage exceeds the odometer mechanical limits.

I certify under penalty of perjury under the laws of the State of California that the foregoing is true and correct.

DATE	TRANSFEROR/SELLER SIGNATURE(S)	DATE	TRANSFEREE/BUYER SIGNATURE(S)
	X		X
PRINTED NAME OF AGENT SIGNING FOR A COMPANY		PRINTED NAME OF AGENT SIGNING FOR A COMPANY TOYOTA MOTOR CREDIT CORP.	

IMPORTANT READ CAREFULLY
Any change of Lienholder (holder of security interest) must be reported to the Department of Motor Vehicles within 10 days.

LIENHOLDER(S)
TOYOTA MTR CRDT CORP
PO BX 105386
ATLANTA
GA 30348

2. X TOYOTA MOTOR CREDIT CORP.
Signature releases interest in vehicle. (Company names must be countersigned)
Release Date 07/13/07

CA 71915340
023699
REG. 17.30 (REV.10/02)

KEEP IN A SAFE PLACE - VOID IF ALTERED

VOID WITHOUT BEAR WATERMARK. HOLD TO LIGHT TO VIEW.

FIGURE 5. Sample Certificate of Title

vehicles are filed in the personal property registration systems of the province (the equivalent of the Article 9 filing system in each state in the United States). There are no certificates of title for automobiles. In the late 1980s, New Zealand's Law Commission considered whether New Zealand should adopt a certificate of title system like that of the United States or permit perfection of security interests in motor vehicles by filing financing statements in the personal property filing system, as is done in Canada. The Commission sent a delegation to study and compare the U.S. and Canadian systems firsthand. The following excerpt is from their report:

New Zealand Law Commission, Motor Vehicle Title Systems in the USA and Canada

Preliminary Paper No. 6 (1988)

We give as an example of a Certificate of Title jurisdiction, Illinois. In Illinois, which has had such a system since the 1920s, the motor vehicle title system is a substantial operation with a large computer entry and checking staff. This seemed to be bigger than the registry staff for the whole Personal Property Security Registry in Toronto. The volume of new titles was approximately three million per year and on the day of our visit 27,000 new titles were issued. Many of these were updates of old titles where a transfer of ownership or change in a security interest had occurred. We were informed that the registry had 65 to 70 people working in two shifts and at present was not able to produce a title until about 3-4 weeks after a request was made. During that time the vehicle was driven under a temporary permit. The motor vehicle certificate of title was printed on bank note paper which was difficult to counterfeit and a lamination strip which protects the vehicle information from being altered, allows changes to be detected under retro-reflective light and is of such a form that the removal of the lamination will destroy the information. Before these security features were introduced, several hundred counterfeit or altered titles were discovered each year in Illinois. Since June 1978 when the security features were introduced there has been a continual decrease in counterfeit and altered titles. In addition to Certificates of Title there are separate certificates for junking and salvage.

Vehicle information is processed through the National Crime Information Center and LEADS Hot Check to determine whether a vehicle has been reported stolen. This is not entered on the register itself. Thousands of stolen vehicles have been identified since the implementation of a computerized title system. Illinois has had a title system for motor vehicles since the 1920s.

In the Canadian provinces there are no title systems for motor vehicles. We understand that such a system was considered in Ontario in the 1950s but was rejected as a result of pressure from motor vehicle dealers who were worried about being unable to confer title in a sale effected at the weekend. We did not find this a very convincing reason for the rejection of a title system. The result of not having such a system means that all motor vehicle transactions come under the Ontario Act. In Ontario over 90% of all transactions recorded under the Ontario Act are concerned with motor vehicles or the financing of motor vehicles or dealers. We understand that a similar proportion would apply in the other provinces.

Compared with this a title system takes the pressure off the Article 9 system. In the Article 9 registry in Illinois 600–700 financing statements were filed daily. There were two people working full time entering particulars on the computer and dealing with searches. The system had been computerized in 1972.

There was little doubt to us that the title system seemed to work well in practice and ease the pressure off the Article 9 system, as well as providing prospective purchasers of motor vehicles with notice of security interests without the need to undertake a search. This was due to the degree of specialization involved and in keeping the bulk of motor vehicles transactions off the Article 9 registry. The Canadian provinces have to contend with motor vehicles and a variety of other transactions. There is at the same time also a greater degree of uncertainty regarding the title to motor vehicles in Canadian provinces. While the problems concerned with title are cut down by a Personal Property Security Act they are not eliminated, because, though security interests can be ascertained from the register, the identity of the owner is not itself recorded. However, the ability to obtain searches of motor vehicles by reference either to the debtor or the identification number of the vehicle reduces this shortcoming somewhat.

The optimal system seems to us to be to have a title system for motor vehicles separate from an Article 9 system.

We estimate that new car financing alone results in about 12 million notations on certificates of title annually. That is about four times the number of initial UCC financing statements filed annually.

Why then do certificate of title systems receive so little attention in law school courses in secured transactions? (At one of 40 assignments, a larger portion of this text than most others is devoted to certificates of title.) In part, it is because Article 9, as the product of an earlier generation of legal academics, has a certain cachet in legal academic circles. The motor vehicle certificate of title acts have far less lustrous histories. In part, certificate of title acts receive relatively little attention because the subject is narrow, the transactions routine, and the amounts of money in issue relatively modest. Although there is a small, steady flow of litigation emanating from the certificate of title system, the system has worked more smoothly than Article 9 and produced fewer problems.

Reference to this system as a "certificate of title" system implies that the certificate — the piece of paper issued by the state to the filer — has special importance such as that accorded negotiable instruments or documents. In a few states one can achieve some limited perfection merely by noting the lien on this piece of paper without sending the paper to the state. But with that minor exception, the implication is false. To perfect, the secured creditor must deliver to the Department its application for notation of its lien on the certificate of title.

The certificate for an automobile, motorboat, or mobile home does not control disputes over ownership of a vehicle. It is prima facie evidence of ownership, but if ownership is with a person other than the person shown on the certificate, the certificate is no impediment to proof of that fact. Owner liability statutes adopted in many states make the owner of a motor vehicle liable for the negligence of any person operating it with permission. But the "owner" for this purpose is the true owner, not the person whose name appears on the certificate of title as the owner. Thus, where *A* sells her car to *B*, turns over possession, but does not execute a transfer of the certificate of title so that the certificate remains in *A*'s name, *B* is nevertheless generally treated as the owner.

The certificate has similarly little direct importance in granting and perfecting security interests in motor vehicles. A security interest can be granted by any writing; it need not be noted on the certificate of title to be valid. As will be discussed shortly, strictly speaking, perfection is accomplished not by notation on either the owner's or the Department's copy of the certificate, but by application to the Department for such a notation. When an issued certificate of title differs from the Department's record of that certificate, the Department's record generally controls. The certificate of title system is best regarded as a filing system, closely analogous to the Article 9 filing system.

The certificate of title system has two principal advantages over the Article 9 system. First, the certificate of title system contains title as well as lien information. Searchers in the Article 9 system must determine from off-record sources who is the owner of the collateral they propose to finance. If they finance collateral that is not owned by their debtor, the true owner can reclaim it from them. (This weakness in the Article 9 system is examined in Assignment 35, below.) In a certificate of title system, as in a real estate system, the chain of title is on the public record. A searcher can trace the debtor's title back to its source.

Probably the most important advantage of the motor vehicle certificate of title system is that each item of collateral is identified by two numbers. Every vehicle registered in a state has a license plate number that is unique within the state. Every vehicle also has a vehicle identification number (VIN) assigned at the time of manufacture and unique within the entire United States. Keep in mind that the ultimate purpose of nearly every search of a filing system is ultimately not to determine whether a particular *debtor* has filings against it, but to determine whether particular *collateral* has filings against it. In the Article 9 filing system, searches are conducted by the name of the debtor only because they cannot be conducted by an item of collateral. If an item of collateral has had more than one owner, the searcher must search under the name of each, with the result that multiple searches may be necessary to locate filings against a single item of collateral. The process of discovering former owners is imprecise, which means that Article 9 searching is imprecise as well. Conducting a search by a unique number assigned to the collateral, as can be done in a certificate of title system, eliminates the complexity and uncertainty of using the owner's (debtor's) name. Starting with the VIN, the license number, *or* the name of the current owner, a searcher can immediately locate the certificate. On it will be every current piece of information in the system that relates to the particular vehicle.

Despite the powerful advantages of certificate of title systems, use is not likely to spread to very many kinds of collateral. To operate a certificate of title system, each item of collateral must be assigned a unique number. What made it worth doing this for motor vehicles was not the convenience of a smoothly operating filing system for security interests, but the vulnerability of motor vehicles to theft. Once the numbering system was adopted to control theft, the filing system simply took advantage of it.

The principal weakness of a certificate of title system is in its inability to deal with the addition of parts to, or the removal of parts from, the "whole" — that is, the object, such as the car or the boat, that is the subject of the system. This weakness restricts the use of certificate of title systems to objects, such as cars or boats, that are likely to remain essentially intact throughout their useful lives. The issues that arise when parts are added to or removed from collateral subject to a certificate of title are discussed in section B of this assignment.

A.   Perfection in a Certificate of Title System

Article 9 applies to transactions that create security interests, and to the security interests thus created, in automobiles, boats, mobile homes, and other property subject to certificate of title systems. UCC §9-109(a). However, UCC §§9-311(a)(2) and (3) provide that "the filing of a financing statement otherwise required by this Article is not necessary or effective to perfect a security interest in property subject to [listed certificate of title statutes of this state]" or "a certificate of title statute of another jurisdiction under the law of which indication of a security interest on the certificate is required as a condition of perfection."

The certificate of title act specifies what the secured party must do to perfect. While these acts vary somewhat in their requirements, most are similar to the UMVCTA. UMVCTA §20 provides:

> A security interest is perfected by the delivery to the Department of the existing certificate of title, if any, an application for a certificate of title containing the name and address of the lienholder and the date of his security agreement and the required fee [and registration card]. It is perfected as of the time of its creation if the delivery is completed within ten (10) days thereafter, otherwise, as of the time of the delivery.

Notice that perfection occurs under this provision at the same moment it occurs under UCC §§9-516(a) and 9-308(a), the moment when the filing officer receives the documents and the filing fee. UMVCTA §20 differs in two respects. First, the filing must include the existing certificate of title, if any. For the lien holder who anticipates the problem, unavailability of the certificate is not a serious problem. If the certificate is "lost, stolen, mutilated or destroyed or becomes illegible" the owner or legal representative of the owner is entitled to a replacement. Departments generally will accept both the application for a new title and the application for a lien on that title at the same time. Second, once made, the notation on the certificate of title relates back not just to the filing officer's receipt of the application but to the time of creation of the security interest. This second difference may soon disappear. The Legislative Note at the end of UCC §9-311 advises that states with UMVCTA-type relation-back periods should amend their motor vehicle statutes to eliminate them.

When the Department issues a new certificate of title noting the existence of the lien, it mails the certificate to the secured party rather than to the debtor. UMVCTA §21(d). Until the lien is satisfied, only the secured party (whose name and address are shown on the face of the Department's copy of the certificate) has the right to apply for and obtain a duplicate certificate. UMVCTA §13. Ideally, this would make it impossible for a debtor to obtain release of the lien without the signature of the secured party. In fact, debtors or thieves sometimes manage to obtain "clean" certificates (that is, certificates showing no liens) from the Department where the lien is recorded or from the Department of another state. The erroneous issue of these certificates generates most of the litigation in this area.

Multiple liens against the same collateral pose a special problem in a certificate of title system. Assume that Ozzie Owner granted a security interest in his new Lexus to Firstbank. Later, Ozzie decides to grant a second interest to Larry Lender, who will loan him another $1,000. Larry's application for notation of his lien on the certificate must be accompanied by the existing certificate. But Ozzie, the person to whom he is lending the money, doesn't have the certificate. Firstbank has placed it in their vault for safekeeping. The solution is in UMVCTA §21(c). Larry makes application for notation of his lien on the certificate and gives it to Firstbank. Firstbank is then obligated to send the application and the certificate to the Department for processing. The Department issues a new certificate showing both liens and sends it to Firstbank, the holder of the first lien. UMVCTA §21(d).

The theoretical problems with such a system are numerous. Firstbank might refuse to forward the application because it doubts the authenticity of Larry's lien. Firstbank might have no doubts about authenticity, but might just be slow in sending the certificate. Firstbank might also go to the other extreme, releasing Larry's lien without Larry's authorization. Fortunately for the certificate of title system, such problems seldom arise in practice. Second and subsequent liens against motor vehicles are relatively uncommon. In fact, some states will record no more than two liens on the certificate because that is all that will fit on the form they use.

Searches can be requested by mail or, in most states, online. They can be by license number, VIN, or owner's (debtor's) name. A few states prohibit name searches to prevent unwarranted invasions of privacy.

B. Accessions

Just as personal property can be affixed to real property, creating a fixtures problem, one item of personal property can be affixed to another, creating an *accessions* problem. The accessions problem can occur with regard to property not covered by a certificate of title. For example, when the motor breaks on an industrial machine, the owner may repair the machine by installing a new motor. The new motor is an accession. The accessions problem causes the most difficulty, however, with regard to property covered by certificate of title systems. The certificate issued in a certificate of title system implicitly assumes that the collateral is a whole and is mortgaged as such; the certificate of title is not designed to deal with the possibility of mortgages against particular parts of that whole.

Examples of accessions to certificate of title property include radio equipment installed in an aircraft after it is sold by the manufacturer, the new tires installed on a car when the old ones wear out, or the camper top installed on the back of a pickup truck. In the typical accessions case, one creditor has lent against the accession while another has lent against the item to which it is affixed (the item and the accession are together referred to as the *whole*). The creditor secured by the accession, who may even be a purchase-money financier who perfected before the collateral was affixed, will expect to have priority in the accession over the creditor secured by the whole. In fact, *not* to give the accession-secured creditor priority would enable debtors to routinely defeat security interests just by affixing the collateral to a whole that was financed at some earlier time.

On the other hand, when a creditor secured by a car or truck repossesses its collateral, it does not expect accession-secured parties thereafter to strip the vehicle of its CB radio, let alone the tires, the engine, or the headlights. Yet in a system where accession lenders have priority, that might be a common occurrence. A repossessed car might look exactly like it did the day the secured creditor financed it, but the creditor's security interest might be subordinate to the suppliers of most of the parts. The creditor secured by the whole might well argue that this result too is absurd; a car lender cannot be expected to monitor repairs.

Just as with fixture problems, the courts that resolve accession problems divide affixed property into three categories: (1) that which is not sufficiently related to the whole to be considered part of it and therefore not an accession (e.g., a spare tire); (2) that which is so integrated into the whole that it is part of the whole for financing purposes (e.g., the mixer on the back of a cement truck); and (3) accessions, the property in between that is sufficiently affixed to be reached by a security interest in the whole, but not sufficiently integrated that it can no longer be the subject of separate financing (e.g., automobile tires).

Reexamine the certificate of title shown earlier in this assignment and you will see that it contemplates liens against the car but not against particular parts of the car. If secured parties are shown on the certificate, it is presumed that they have security interests in the entire car. There is no place for recording liens that cover only the radios, custom cabs, or motors. The accession-secured party can perfect its interest in the accession by filing in the Article 9 filing system, but probably only if it does so before the collateral becomes an accession. If perfection in an already-attached accession in the Article 9 system could defeat perfection in the whole in the certificate of title system, the creditor taking a security interest in property covered by a certificate of title statute would have to search in both systems. That may be why UCC §9-311(a)(2) provides that "the filing of a financing statement . . . is not effective to perfect a security interest in property subject to [a certificate of title statute]."

UCC §9-335(d) gives a security interest in the whole perfected by compliance with a certificate of title statute priority over a security interest in an accession to that whole—regardless of the order in which the two security interests were perfected and even though the security interest in the accession attached and became perfected before the accession was affixed and before the security interest in the whole was created. UCC §9-335(e) bars the holder of the subordinate accessions interest from enforcing it, rendering it virtually worthless. To illustrate, assume that Ally Financial finances Dolly's purchase of a new automobile and perfects by notation on the certificate of title. After the warranty on the car expires, it becomes necessary to replace the engine. Joe's Garage sells Dolly a new engine on credit, takes a security interest in it, and perfects before installing the engine in the car. Under UCC §9-335(d), Ally has the first security interest in the car, including the new engine. Joe's Garage has a second security interest in the engine. If Dolly fails to pay Joe's Garage, Joe's Garage cannot foreclose against or repossess the car, because it does not have a security interest in it. Joe's Garage cannot foreclose against or repossess the engine, because it does not have "priority over the claims of every person having an interest in the whole." UCC §9-335(e). On a literal reading of the statute, this would be true even if the car were of sufficient value to satisfy both liens. What *can* Joe's Garage do? It can hope that Ally will eventually force a sale of the property. If Ally does, Joe's Garage can then make a claim against any proceeds of sale in excess of the obligation owing Ally. Alternatively, Joe's Garage can sue as an unsecured creditor. Presumably, the same result would obtain if Joe's Garage sold the engine to Dolly under a contract that prohibited installment in a whole.

UCC §9-335 facilitates the financing of automobiles, aircraft, boats, and other certificate of title property as wholes, and effectively makes it impossible to finance accessions — such as radio equipment or custom cabs — separately. The effect will be to favor those who mass-produce and finance standard units at the expense of those who attempt to customize them. The biggest losers will be those who finance items not intended to be used as accessions, but that are. Under UCC §9-335, any secured creditor whose non-certificate of title collateral is affixed to some other secured creditor's certificate of title collateral effectively loses its interest.

C.   In What State Should a Motor Vehicle Be Titled?

The manufacturer of each motor vehicle assigns it a unique VIN. The manufacturer also issues a *certificate of origin* for the vehicle, which contains both the make and model of the vehicle and the VIN. While the certificate of origin functions in some respects like a certificate of title, a security interest cannot be perfected by notation on the certificate of origin. Instead, while a motor vehicle is inventory in the hands of a manufacturer or dealer, the certificate of title statute is inapplicable. UMVCTA §2(a)(2). Perfection of a security interest in the inventory of a car dealer is accomplished by filing a financing statement, UCC §9-311(d), in the state where the car dealer is incorporated, UCC §§9-301(1), 9-307(e).

Upon sale of the motor vehicle to the first user, the dealer delivers the certificate of origin. That user makes application for the first certificate of title based on the certificate of origin. UMVCTA §4. Once the certificate of title is issued, liens against the motor vehicle can be perfected only by notation on the certificate of title, except while the vehicle is owned by a used car dealer.

In what state should the vehicle be titled? UMVCTA §4(a) answers with the statement that "every owner of a vehicle which is in this state and for which no certificate of title has been issued by [this state] shall make application . . . for a certificate of title of the vehicle." Obviously, this statute cannot be read literally, or it might require two applications when a resident of Texarkana goes out for a cup of coffee. UMVCTA §2(a)(3) may at first glance seem to require titling in a state only if the owner is a resident of the state, but that section protects nonresidents only with regard to vehicles "not required by law to be registered in this state." A combination of case and statutory law requires registration of the vehicles of nonresidents when the nonresidents acquire regular places of abode in the state or use the vehicles in connection with a business in the state for more than a period established by the state. Those periods range from about 30 to 90 days in various states. Merely because a motor vehicle is supposed to be registered in the state does not necessarily mean that it is supposed to be titled there, but it usually does mean that.

The case reporters are full of cases in which owners titled their vehicles in states that are clearly inappropriate. Often, the motivation is to pay registration fees or sales tax in a state that charges a lower rate. These owners may be subject to fines or penalties levied by the state in which they should have titled the car. But the fact that their certificate of title is from the wrong state does not prevent it from being the proper place for a creditor to note the existence of its lien. Perfection can be lost when an owner obtains a second title, but in no case has a security interest in an automobile been held unperfected because the owner obtained the certificate from the wrong state. See UCC §9-303(a).

The point is illustrated in Hoffman v. Associates Commercial Corp., 228 B.R. 70 (1998). That case involved a truck that was garaged in Connecticut and used for transport between Connecticut and New York. Connecticut law required that the owner obtain a Connecticut title. Instead, the owner obtained a Maine title. Maine law authorizes the issuance of titles for vehicles that have no relationship to the state, and charges reduced fees and taxes. Not surprisingly, it has become a truck-title haven. (Titling in Maine is undoubtedly the "contemporary business practice" referred to in Comment 2 to UCC §9-303.) The secured creditor perfected by notation on the Maine title. The debtor filed bankruptcy and the trustee challenged the secured creditor's perfection. The court noted that "[a]n owner's failure to register a vehicle required to be registered in Connecticut is an infraction. An owner's illegal conduct — not registering to avoid paying fees and taxes in Connecticut — does not, however, unperfect a creditor's otherwise validly perfected lien."

D.　Motor Vehicle Registration

Each of the 50 states levies a license tax on automobiles. Except as otherwise provided in reciprocity agreements, within some period after becoming a resident of a state or bringing a car into the state as a nonresident, the owner is required to *register* the car in the state. The owner pays the tax, obtains license plates (tags) from the state, and displays them on the vehicle as proof of payment of the tax and to identify the vehicle.

The registration system in large part duplicates the function of the certificate of title system. A certificate of registration contains much the same information that appears on a certificate of title.

FIGURE 6. Sample Vehicle Registration

There are, however, some important differences between the two systems. First, liens cannot be perfected by notation on a certificate of registration. Second, the certificate of title system exists to keep track of ownership and liens, while the registration system exists to identify vehicles on the street and collect taxes. A vehicle should have only one certificate of title but may be required to have certificates of registration from every state in which the vehicle is operated. (Occasionally, you will see a semi-trailer truck on the highway displaying tiny license plates from as many as 20 states.) Third, not every movement of a motor vehicle that necessitates registration in the destination state also necessitates titling in the destination state. A motor vehicle can sometimes properly be titled in one state and registered in another. See UMVCTA §11.

E. Maintaining Perfection on Interstate Movement of Collateral

1. How It Is Supposed to Work

Marjorie Murphy, a resident of California who lives and works in California, owns a Toyota that is titled in that state. She still owes $10,000 on the car to the Upper Castro State Bank (UCSB). UCSB's lien is noted on the California certificate of title and the title is in the bank's vault. Murphy finds a better job in Georgia and makes the move, taking her car with her.

Georgia's version of the UMVCTA requires that Murphy make application to the Georgia Department of Motor Vehicles for a Georgia title and registration. UMVCTA §4(a). Murphy visits the website of the Georgia Department and prints the forms. UMVCTA §6(c)(1) requires that Murphy's Georgia application be accompanied by her California certificate of title. Because UCSB has possession of the certificate, Murphy calls the bank to ask for its cooperation. Although there is no provision in the UMVCTA requiring UCSB to cooperate, the bank agrees to do so. At the bank's request, Murphy mails it the application and fee, and the bank forwards it with the certificate of title to the Georgia Department. UCSB's cover letter asks the Georgia Department to reflect UCSB's lien on the new certificate and to send the certificate directly to the bank.

Upon receipt of the completed application, the Georgia Department issues a Georgia certificate of title with UCSB's lien noted on it. UMVCTA §9(a)(3). They keep the old California certificate of title on file and mail the new Georgia certificate of title to UCSB. UMVCTA §10. They mail the license plate and certificate of registration directly to Murphy. Using a flat-head screwdriver, Murphy attaches the license plate to the rear of her Toyota (Georgia uses only one license plate), puts the certificate of registration in the glove compartment, and the process is complete.

2. *Some Things That Can Go Wrong*

If the certificate of title systems worked the way they are supposed to, there would be one and only one certificate of title for each motor vehicle. The searcher would need only examine the face of that certificate to determine who had liens and as of what date those liens were perfected.

There are, however, three kinds of problems that commonly occur. The first is when a lien-laden certificate from State *A* is surrendered to the Department in State *B* and the Department inadvertently issues a "clean" certificate. Given that the State *B* Department had the State *A* certificate in its possession in this scenario, issuance of the clean certificate was almost certainly an error, although the error might have been encouraged by fraud. Despite the Department's failure to include the liens on the new certificate, the liens remain perfected against purchasers for up to four months and against lien creditors for as long as State *A* law permits. UCC §§9-316(d) and (e). Having made that error, the Department almost certainly would have made a second by failing to mail the certificate back to the first lien holder who surrendered it. UMVCTA §21(d) requires mailing to the first lien holder *named* in the certificate, and there is no one named on the new certificate. It would be up to each lien holder to notice that the first lien holder had not received the new certificate as it should have and complain.

An even more frequent problem is that a Department issues a new certificate without obtaining surrender of the old one. This might occur when the owner of the vehicle certifies that the original certificate of title has been lost, stolen, or destroyed. UMVCTA §13. It might also occur when the Department excuses surrender under UMVCTA §11. The result is that two certificates are in existence, each arguably covering the vehicle.

UCC §9-303(b) takes the position that when a subsequent certificate of title to property is issued by any state, prior certificates cease to cover the property. The law of the state issuing the most recent (second) certificate for the property governs. UCC §9-303(c). Nevertheless, a security interest perfected by notation on the first certificate remains perfected permanently as against a lien creditor or a trustee in bankruptcy. See UCC §9-316(d). But as against a purchaser for value — such as an Article 9 secured creditor — the security interest remains perfected for only four months after issuance of the second certificate. If the holder of the first lien fails to perfect on the second certificate during that four-month period, the first lien becomes unperfected as against that purchaser, whether the purchaser purchased before or after the end of the four-month period. See UCC §9-316(e). (Remember that secured creditors are "purchasers," under Article 9. See UCC §1-201(b)(29) and (30).) Thus, the trustee in a bankruptcy case commenced after issuance of the second certificate can be defeated by security interests noted on the first certificate before issuance of the second certificate and security interests noted on the second certificate.

Another possible solution to the two-certificates problem is for the state to revoke the improperly issued one, leaving the properly issued certificate to govern. The statutory basis for this solution is UMVCTA §26(a), which authorizes the revocation of a certificate that was "fraudulently procured or erroneously issued." To illustrate, assume that Firstbank perfects by notation on the certificate issued in Illinois. The debtor fraudulently obtains a clean certificate from Alabama and Secondbank perfects by notation on that certificate. Firstbank uses UMVCTA §26(a) to persuade the Alabama Department to revoke the second certificate. Secondbank's security interest remains valid because the revocation does not "in itself, affect the validity of a security interest noted on [the revoked certificate]." But Firstbank's security interest is also arguably valid because after revocation it is on the only remaining certificate. Notice that this is a *strategic* solution to the problem. The lawyer must take action to change the facts before raising the issue and arguing the law.

Some states permit a creditor that loses its lien as a result of filing office negligence to sue the filing officer who committed the error. Recovery is usually from a bond or insurance policy and limited in amount. See, e.g., Va. Code Ann. §46.2-219 (2008) ($100,000 bond).

3. Movement of Goods Between Non-Certificate and Certificate Jurisdictions

Because all 50 states now have certificate of title systems for automobiles and trucks, the movement of automobiles and trucks between certificate and non-certificate jurisdictions has become far less a problem. Such movement remains a problem when automobiles and trucks are, for example, moved between the United States and Canada. In Canada, perfection of security interests in automobiles and trucks is accomplished by filing a financing statement. Because some states have certificate of title systems for boats and mobile homes, while others do not, the movement of boats and mobile homes between certificate and non-certificate states also remains a problem.

Certificate to non-certificate moves. Assume that Steve Harry, a resident of the state of Indiana, owns a boat. The boat is both registered and titled in Indiana. Firstbank has a lien against the boat perfected by notation on the Indiana certificate of title. The bank has possession of the certificate.

Harry changes his principal residence to Idaho, a state that issues certificates of registration for boats but not certificates of title on which a security interest can be perfected by notation. In Idaho, filing in the UCC filing system is necessary to perfect a security interest in a boat. Harry takes his boat with him.

Does Firstbank's security interest remain perfected after the move? The starting point for analysis is to determine whether the boat is still covered by the Indiana certificate of title after it is out of Indiana. First, UCC §9-303(a) assures us that the movement of the goods and Harry's severance of his connections with Indiana are not impediments to continued coverage by the Indiana certificate. UCC §9-303(b) states the two circumstances in which goods cease to be covered by a certificate of title. The first is that the title "ceases to be effective under the law of the issuing jurisdiction" (Indiana). No provision of Article 9 or the UMVCTA suggests that this has happened. The second is that "the goods become covered subsequently by a certificate of title issued by another jurisdiction." We conclude that the boat remains covered by the Indiana certificate. UCC §9-316(d) and (e) do not apply, so Firstbank's security interest remains perfected indefinitely.

Non-certificate to certificate moves. Now assume that Harry's change in principal residence is in the other direction, from Idaho to Indiana, and that prior to the move, Firstbank was perfected in Idaho by the filing of a financing statement. Upon Harry's arrival in Indiana, UCC §9-301(1) makes Indiana law applicable. Under Indiana law, the filing of a financing statement is neither necessary nor effective to perfect in a boat. See UCC §9-311(a)(2). However, Indiana UCC §9-316(a)(2) preserves Firstbank's perfection for four months. To remain continuously perfected, Firstbank must cause an application for an Indiana certificate noting its security interest to be filed within the four-month period.

If Firstbank does not perfect in Indiana within the four-month period, its security interest becomes unperfected and is "deemed never to have been perfected as against a purchaser of the collateral for value." UCC §9-316(b). In this circumstance, Firstbank will be subordinate to a purchaser who buys or takes a security interest before, during, or after the four-month period. Firstbank's interest will not be defeated by a lien creditor who levies within the four-month period. That section is ambiguous on its face with regard to a lien creditor who levies after the four-month period, but a member of the Drafting Committee tells us that the intent was that the secured creditor prevail.

Problem Set 25

25.1. a. Firstbank lends $65,000 to Kahled to purchase a teal blue Jaguar. Firstbank perfects by notation on Kahled's Wisconsin certificate of title and takes possession of the certificate. Kahled moves to Alabama and obtains a clean certificate of title from that state. One month after issuance of the new certificate, Kahled borrows $50,000 from Secondbank. Secondbank takes a security interest and perfects on the Alabama certificate. Six months after issuance of the new certificate, Kahled borrows $45,000 from Thirdbank. Thirdbank takes a security interest and perfects on the Alabama certificate. Seven months after issuance of the new certificate, Kahled files bankruptcy. Is Firstbank perfected?

b.   Change one fact: Firstbank learned of the issuance of the new certificate three months after issuance. Firstbank immediately demanded that Secondbank apply for notation of Firstbank's lien on the Alabama certificate. See UMVCTA §21(c). Secondbank promptly complied, and Firstbank's lien was noted on the Alabama certificate. As between Firstbank and Secondbank, who has priority? UCC §§9-316(d) and (e), 9-337(2).

25.2.   Babs lives in Missouri and owns a Nissan sedan that is titled in Missouri. United Missouri Bank financed her purchase of the car. It applied for the title, had its lien noted on it, and has possession of the certificate. Babs recently moved to New York without notifying the bank of her move.

a.   Four months have passed since her move and she has obtained neither a certificate of title nor a certificate of registration from New York. Is the bank's security interest still perfected? If things continue as they are, how long will the bank's security interest remain perfected? UCC §§9-303, 9-316(d) and (e); UMVCTA §§2(a)(3), 4(a).

b.   Suppose that Babs registers the car in New York and gets New York license plates a week after she arrives. The bank still has the Missouri certificate of title and New York does not issue a certificate of title. Is the bank still perfected? If so, how long will it remain perfected?

c.   Suppose that Babs, rather than the bank, is holding the Missouri certificate of title. A week after her arrival in New York, Babs applies for a New York certificate of title. She surrenders the Missouri title to the New York Department and tells them (falsely) that the bank's lien has been satisfied. Ten days later, New York issues a clean certificate of title for the car. Is the bank's lien still perfected? If so, how long will it remain perfected? UCC §§9-303, 9-316(d) and (e); UMVCTA §§18(c), 26.

d.   Suppose instead that Babs, frustrated at the thought of trying to involve the bank in her title application in New York, gave the New York Department her affidavit stating that she lost her Missouri certificate of title and that it had no liens on it. The clerk issued a clean New York certificate. Is the bank's lien still perfected? If so, how long will it remain perfected? UCC §§9-303, 9-316(d) and (e); UMVCTA §26.

25.3.   Your client, Missouri River Bank, was newly incorporated just a few months ago. The bank plans to finance about a thousand automobiles each year. The bank's plan is to lend only to Missouri residents, require that the cars it finances be initially titled and registered in Missouri, make sure the certificate of title carries a notation of the bank's lien, and retain possession of the certificate. The bank asks you if perfection according to its plan will be adequate to maintain perfection in cars owned by debtors who move out of the state. What is your answer? UCC §§9-303, 9-316(d) and (e).

25.4. Shoreline Boats recently established Shoreline Credit Corporation (SCC) to finance the boats sold by Shoreline dealers at retail in 23 states.

a. SCC would like to know how it should perfect the purchase-money security interests it plans to take in the boats it sells. UCC §§9-310(a) and (b), 9-311(a).

b. How should SCC protect itself against later movement or retitling of the boats? UCC §§9-303, 9-309(1), 9-316(a), (b), (d), and (e), 9-337. (In solving this problem, assume that the statute for titling boats is the same as UMVCTA.) Consider also the possibility that Shoreline's *debtors* may move out of state.

25.5. Missouri River Bank plans to lend $130,000 to Coldwell Construction Company against a bulldozer already owned by Coldwell. Coldwell's offices are in Illinois. Coldwell tells you that the bulldozer is used on various construction sites, all of which are in Missouri. Your client, the bank, asks what it should do to perfect this interest. UCC §§9-301, 9-303, 9-307, 9-311(a); UMVCTA §§1, 2, 4, and 5. What is your answer? If you need additional information, where will you get it?

■ End of Default Problem Set

25.6. Your client was recently injured in an automobile accident. The car that caused the accident was rendered inoperable. Before the police arrived, the driver removed the registration and the license plates from the car and fled the scene on foot. The accident report, which you obtained from the highway patrol, shows only the make and model of the car and the VIN. The police don't seem to be doing much to discover the name of the owner. Can you find it yourself, working only from the public records? Will your method discover the name of the owner if the car is from out of state? From Canada where no certificates of title are issued and the transfer of ownership of a motor vehicle is not recorded on any public record?

Chapter 8.   Priority

Assignment 26:   The Concept of Priority: State Law

This assignment explores in more depth what it means for a secured creditor to have priority. As should already be apparent, the order of priority among creditors can be crucial. Often, it spells the difference between effortless collection of the full amount of the debt and no possibility of collection at all. Reflecting the complexity and importance of priority, we devote the remainder of this book to it.

Because we often speak of priority as a right to be paid first, it may come as a surprise to realize that the "first" used here does not mean first in time. Subordinate lien holders are often paid earlier in time than prior lien holders. The actual meaning of priority is somewhat more difficult to describe. To say that one creditor has *priority* over another is to say that if the value of the collateral is sufficient to pay only one of them, the law requires that value be used to pay the one who has priority. The method by which the law reaches that result can be complicated.

The rules that award priority come into play whenever more than one interest exists in property. They include the rules governing foreclosure sales and the rules governing the rights of competing lien holders to possession of the property after default. We begin first with foreclosure sale procedure.

A.   Priority in Foreclosure

Two basic principles govern the timing of the enforcement of competing liens against the same collateral. First, absent an agreement to the contrary, any lien holder may foreclose while the debtor is in default to that lien holder. The existence of a prior lien does not automatically block the exercise of rights under a subordinate one. Second, no lien holder is compelled to foreclose. Each has the option to extend the debtor's time for payment or simply to forbear from exercising its remedy. A creditor whose priority is sufficient to guarantee that the debt will be paid may see no advantage in foreclosing, even though its debt is in default. Such a creditor may prefer to wait for others to expend the effort and money necessary to resolve the debtor's financial problems. To give effect to these two principles, sale procedures must provide for the possibility that the holders of liens against particular collateral might foreclose in any order, and that some might choose to rely on their security without foreclosing at all.

Notice the specific recognition of these two principles in this statute governing foreclosure:

> Mortgage and other creditors shall be entitled to payment according to the priority of their liens, and not pro rata; and judgments of foreclosure that are conducted in compliance with this part shall operate to extinguish the liens of subsequent mortgages

and liens of the same property, without forcing prior mortgagees or lienors to their right of recovery. The surplus after payment of the mortgage foreclosed, shall be applied pro tanto to the next junior mortgage or lien, and so on to the payment, wholly or in part, of mortgages and liens junior to the one assessed.

Hawaii Rev. Stat. §667-3 (2015).

The holder of virtually any type of lien may foreclose, but the procedure for doing so varies with the type of lien. For example, one state statute may specify the procedure to foreclose a mortgage, another state statute may specify the procedure to enforce a state property tax lien, while a federal statute specifies the procedure for enforcement of a federal tax lien. Even for a particular type of lien, such as a mortgage on real property, the procedure may differ from state to state, or a single state may offer more than one procedure. Notwithstanding the many differences in detail, the general principles common to most foreclosure procedures can serve first as a means of understanding the sale process in the abstract and then as a frame of reference for understanding the specific sale procedures applicable to particular kinds of sales in particular jurisdictions. The principles that follow govern most judicial or foreclosure sales:

1. The sale discharges from the collateral the lien under which the sale is held and all subordinate liens. See UCC §9-617(a). It does not discharge prior liens.

2. The sale transfers the debtor's interest in the collateral to the purchaser, subject to all prior liens. See UCC §9-617(a). A prior lien holder cannot enforce its debt against a foreclosure sale purchaser, because a purchaser does not assume the debt or agree to pay it. But a prior lien holder can enforce its lien against the purchaser. Unless someone pays the prior lien off, the prior lien holder can foreclose on the collateral.

3. Whoever conducts the sale applies the proceeds first to the expenses of sale, then to payment of the lien under which the sale was held, then to payment of subordinate liens in the order of their priority. See UCC §9-615(a). The remaining surplus, if any, is paid to the debtor. See UCC §9-615(d)(1). Neither prior lienholders nor unsecured creditors share in the distribution. Prior lienholders can continue to look to the collateral. Unsecured creditors can obtain judgments against the debtors and levy on the surplus in the debtors' hands.

4. Payment to a lien holder from the proceeds of sale reduces the balance owing. The lien holder is then entitled to a judgment against the debtor for any deficiency, unless a statute provides otherwise. See UCC §9-615(d)(2).

To illustrate the operation of these rules, assume that a debtor's vacation home is subject to a first mortgage lien in the amount of $50,000 and a second mortgage lien in the amount of $30,000. Both mortgages are in default and the holder of the first mortgage forces the sale. The value of the collateral is not yet specified, because it will be determined by bidding at the public auction sale. Sophisticated bidders at the sale would understand that:

1.   The mortgage sale will discharge both liens so that the purchaser will own the vacation home free and clear of them.
2.   The sheriff will use the first proceeds of sale to pay the expenses of sale.
3.   The sheriff will pay the next $50,000 to the first mortgage holder.
4.   The sheriff will pay the next $30,000 to the second mortgage holder.
5.   The sheriff will pay any remaining balance to the debtor (ignoring the claims of unsecured creditors).

For example, if the purchaser bid $100,000 at the sale and the costs of sale were $1,000, the sheriff would pay the costs of sale, pay both mortgage holders in full, and then pay the surplus of $19,000 to the debtor.

If instead the purchaser bid $60,000, the sheriff would pay the costs of sale and the debt owing the first mortgagee in full, and pay the remaining $9,000 to the second mortgage holder. The second mortgage holder could continue to pursue the debtor for the $21,000 deficiency, but the lien of the second mortgage would be discharged from the vacation home and the purchaser would take the home free and clear of both mortgages.

The result is different if the second mortgage holder forces the sale. In that event:

1.   The mortgage sale discharges only the second mortgage lien; the purchaser will take "subject to" the first mortgage.
2.   The sheriff will use the first proceeds of sale to pay the expenses of sale.
3.   The sheriff will not pay anything to the first mortgage holder, but will pay the next $30,000 to the second mortgage holder.
4.   The sheriff will pay any remaining balance to the debtor.

A bidder who understands this difference will, of course, want to adjust for it. One likely adjustment is to stop bidding at $50,000 less than the bidder thinks the house is worth, reserving that amount to pay the first mortgage after the sale is complete. So, for example, if the bidder thought the home was worth $60,000 free and clear, it would bid only up to $10,000 at the sale. The sheriff would apply the $10,000 first to the expenses of sale and then to the second mortgage debt.

What happens if the purchaser at the foreclosure sale does not pay a mortgage to which it takes subject? Although the purchaser is not liable on the debt, the debtor is. But the debtor is not likely to pay a debt to avoid a foreclosure of a lien against property the debtor once owned, but that now belongs to someone else. If no one pays the first mortgage, the first mortgage holder can foreclose and almost certainly will do so. Purchasers usually choose to pay prior mortgages.

Sophisticated bidders at a sale under a second mortgage sometimes arrange with the first mortgagee, before they bid, that if they buy the property they will assume the first mortgage. The deal might call for the bidder to cure any default in the first mortgage and then pay in accord with its original terms, or to pay on new terms negotiated between the parties. The actual terms are not governed by legal rules; they are negotiated in the shadow of what would happen in the absence of agreement. If no deal is struck, the prospective bidder might choose not to bid, or might bid and, if successful, pay the first mortgage.

Not surprisingly, not all bidders at judicial sales understand the rules of priority. Sometimes an unsophisticated bidder bids what he or she considers to be the value of the property, without deducting the amounts to cover the prior liens. To continue with the earlier example, a bidder who values the vacation home at $60,000 might bid the full $60,000, failing to account for the $50,000 mortgage outstanding, rather than bid only $10,000. Such a bid establishes the value of the property as $110,000 (a $60,000 bid for the debtor's interest in the property, subject to a $50,000 mortgage). This bidder is unlikely to learn of the first mortgage in time to correct the mistake. Once the sale is complete, it is unlikely that the purchaser can rescind on the basis of a unilateral mistake; judicial sales are one of the few places in the American economy where the rule of caveat emptor still applies. (See the discussion on the enforceability of judicial sales, even over bidder mistakes, in Assignment 4.)

B.   Credit Bidding Revisited

Multiple liens complicate credit bidding. Recall that "credit bidding" is bidding on credit. If the winning bidder in a foreclosure sale will be entitled to some or all of the sale proceeds, the person conducting the sale is required to extend credit to that bidder for that amount once the bidding is over. Other winners must pay their bids in cash. The person conducting the sale collects from the credit bidder by setting the credit bid off against the amount of the sale proceeds due to the credit bidder. The credit bidder pays the credit bid amount only when the bid is deducted from the sale proceeds.

A secured creditor is entitled to credit bid to the extent—and only to the extent—that the secured creditor would be entitled to the proceeds of sale. If there is only one creditor, the math is easy: FirstMort holds a $100,000 first mortgage and it bids $100,000 at the foreclosure sale. Setting aside sale costs, the transaction is a wash. FirstMort will be the owner of the property, the loan will be satisfied, the mortgage will be extinguished, and FirstMort will pay nothing and receive nothing from the sale—except the house. FirstMort might purchase for less, say $75,000. In that case, the $75,000 purchase price will be credited against the amount owed by the debtor, and the debtor will continue to owe $25,000. That $25,000 is now an unsecured debt. Once again, the mortgage will be extinguished and FirstMort will become the owner, free and clear, of the property. If FirstMort bids more than the outstanding mortgage—say $125,000—it will receive credit for $100,000 and must pay $25,000 in cash. That $25,000 is surplus that will go to the debtor.

If there are multiple creditors, the calculations get a little more complex. To illustrate, again assume that FirstMort holds a $100,000 first mortgage against the collateral. But this time SecondMort holds a $50,000 second lien and Lienor holds a $15,000 third lien against the collateral. If FirstMort forced a sale of this collateral, FirstMort would be entitled to the first $100,000 of proceeds, SecondMort would be entitled to the next $50,000, Lienor would be entitled to the next $15,000, and the debtor would get the rest. At the sale, FirstMort would be entitled to credit bid $100,000, but would have to pay any excess of its bid over $100,000 in cash. SecondMort must bid cash up to $100,000. But SecondMort could bid up to an additional $50,000 on credit. Lienor must bid cash up to $150,000, but could then bid up to an additional $15,000 on credit. If Lienor won the bid at $170,000, Lienor would have to pay $155,000 of its bid in cash.

If SecondMort forced the sale, FirstMort would not be entitled to any of the proceeds of sale, and so could not credit bid. SecondMort could credit bid up to $50,000. Lienor could credit bid up to $15,000, but only on the portion of Lienor's bid in excess of $50,000.

During the auction, no distinction is made between a credit bid and a cash bid. Each bidder simply bids a dollar figure. The distinction is made when the person who conducts the sale requires the high bidder to pay the amount bid. If the high bidder claims a credit to which it is not entitled, the high bidder will be in default on its bid and must either come up with the difference in cash or lose its right to purchase the collateral.

C.   Reconciling Inconsistent Priorities

While the rules governing foreclosure sales and priority in proceeds discussed in the preceding section are typical of many, they are not universal. In some sale procedures the purchaser takes free of all liens against the property and proceeds of sale are distributed first (after payment of the expenses of sale) to the holder of the first lien. Such procedures are relatively rare for two reasons. First, they deprive the holders of senior liens of their option not to foreclose. In such a system, a small subordinate lien could force the liquidation of a large first mortgage. Second, a procedure that foreclosed all liens would bring more parties into each foreclosure proceeding, further complicating the process.

When legislatures create the procedures governing foreclosure and priority in the collateral, their attention is often focused on a particular type of creditor whom they wish to prefer or a dispute between two types of creditors that they wish to resolve. For example, many state legislative staffs have been called on to draft rules that resolve priority disputes between competing execution liens. But if the dispute is between execution liens and security interests, that subject is covered by the Uniform Commercial Code and therefore considered to be within the jurisdiction of the drafters of the Code. The legislature must eventually pass on the rule, but it will be in a different year, in the context of a bill proposing adoption of a set of amendments to the Uniform Commercial Code that cover many other subjects as well. Rules governing the priority of federal tax liens are beyond the power of the state legislature altogether. Congress enacts those rules as part of the Internal Revenue Code. Many other kinds of legislation grant priorities. It should be obvious that in such a system, conflicting rules can be adopted. They often are.

Because all of these liens compete for the value of the same collateral, the conflicts eventually must be resolved. As the courts resolve them, they fuse diverse sets of state and federal statutes into a single system of priority. In the resulting system, all the schemes of foreclosure and distribution have one feature in common: Those creditors whose liens are discharged by the sale share in the proceeds of sale in the order in which their liens have priority. Without this feature, the system of lien priority could not function.

Mortgages usually have priority over judgment liens for the simple reason that when a debtor has judgment liens against his or her property, no one will make a mortgage loan to the debtor. Although the opinion does not explain how the mistake was made, in the following case Bank Leumi Trust made mortgage loans to Joseph Liggett even after his ex-wife Helen Liggett had perfected a judgment lien against his property. The mortgage was subordinate to Helen's lien, but senior to a lien later acquired by Cosden Oil. When Helen forced a sale of the property pursuant to her lien, Cosden Oil argued that even though Bank Leumi Trust's mortgage would be discharged, Bank Leumi Trust could not share in the proceeds of sale. Cosden's argument was supported by the clear language of the statute:

> §5236(g) *Disposition of Proceeds of Sale.* After deduction for and payment of fees, expenses and any taxes levied on the sale, transfer or delivery, the sheriff making a sale of real property pursuant to an execution shall, unless the court otherwise directs,
>   1. distribute the proceeds to the judgment creditors who have delivered executions against the judgment debtor to the sheriff before the sale, which executions have not been returned, in the order in which their judgments have priority, and
>   2. pay over any excess to the judgment debtor.

Had the court not decided that this was a situation in which it should "otherwise direct," Bank Leumi Trust's mortgages would have been discharged, but Bank Leumi Trust would not have been paid from the proceeds of sale. Their mortgages would have been worthless and the proceeds would have gone to Cosden Oil's subordinate lien. This was a possibility that the New York legislature did not address in drafting the statute. The court took the only reasonable course under the circumstances — it ordered otherwise.

One other concept is needed to understand this case. Mortgages and judgment liens ordinarily rank in the order in which they were created. But here, you will see Helen Liggett's later judgment given priority over Bank Leumi's earlier mortgage. The reason for the switch is that, when Helen Liggett filed her lawsuit, she recorded a "notice of pendency" (or "lis pendens" for those who prefer to conduct business in Latin) in the real property records. The notice of pendency reserves a position in the priority queue for whatever judgment is later entered. Bank Leumi should have found this notice when they did their title search. Creditors are entitled to file these notices of pendency only in cases that directly affect the title to real property.

Bank Leumi Trust Co. of New York v. Liggett

496 N.Y.S.2d 14 (N.Y. App. Div. 1985)

MEMORANDUM DECISION.

This case presents an issue of first impression, whether CPLR 5236(g) establishes priority of judgment creditors over mortgages which have been recorded prior to the judgments.

Joseph and Mylene Liggett purchased real property located at 6 Riverview Terrace in Manhattan in September 1974. The following year, the Liggetts transferred the property to Mylene individually. Joseph's first wife Helen Liggett subsequently prevailed in an action for moneys due under their 1970 separation agreement, and obtained a jury verdict of $388,472. In February 1980, Helen commenced a separate action to enforce her judgment in the matrimonial action by setting aside the conveyance of the Riverview Terrace property as fraudulent. She filed a notice of pendency against the property in conjunction with the second lawsuit. The following month a judgment ("the 1980 judgment") was entered in her favor for $508,129, including interest, against Joseph.

Between November 1980 and November 1981, petitioner Bank Leumi Trust Company of New York (Bank Leumi Trust) took successive mortgages on the Riverview Terrace property to secure the amounts of $550,000, $70,000 and $400,000. In February 1982, respondent Cosden Oil & Chemical Company (Cosden Oil) obtained and entered a $144,154 judgment against Joseph.

In September 1983, Helen won partial summary judgment in her action for fraudulent conveyance. By judgment resettled in February 1984, the sheriff was directed to sell the property and to make "distribution out of such proceeds to any judgment creditors in accordance with CPLR 5236(g) in the order of their statutory priority" ("the 1984 judgment").

Bank Leumi appeals only from that portion of Special Term's order which denied its application insofar as it sought a declaration that its mortgages have priority in the distribution of proceeds from the sale over subsequently entered judgments. It concedes the validity of the 1984 judgment and the seniority of Helen Liggett's lien. We disagree with Special Term and reverse for the reasons set forth below.

Special Term misapprehended the issue presented here. This case is unusual since Cosden Oil's judgment is, like petitioner's mortgages, junior in time to the 1980 judgment. Both liens, not just the petitioner's, will be wiped out in the judicial sale. (CPLR 5203(a)(2).) Since there are other judgment creditors in addition to Cosden Oil, junior in time to petitioner, petitioner's mortgages cannot ride through this sale with the purchaser at the sale taking subject to the lien of its mortgages. Cosden Oil has refrained from executing on its judgment in hopes of utilizing the 1980 judgment to gain an advantage over Bank Leumi Trust. Therefore, the real issue is the right to share in the surplus proceeds between petitioner's 1980-1981 mortgages and Cosden Oil's 1982 judgment.

It has long been established that first-in-time priority obtains as between mortgages and judgments. CPLR 5203, not CPLR 5236, contains the substantive provisions concerning the priorities of competing judgment creditors with respect to realty. CPLR 5203 does not purport to determine all priorities among all categories of liens.

It is manifest from the legislative history and the language "unless the court otherwise directs" that CPLR 5236 simply establishes the procedural mechanism for the sale which converts realty into money to pay liens. The purpose of first enacting and later amending CPLR 5239, was, inter alia, to provide a procedural device by which lienors, other than judgment creditors, could stake their claims against the subject property, and have the validity and priority of all liens, including their own, judicially determined prior to a judicial sale. According to Professor Siegel, who recommended the amendment, which resulted from a study made at the request of the Committee to Advise and Consult with the Judicial Conference on the CPLR, the new language, "unless the court otherwise directs":

> recasts the subdivision to permit the court to "otherwise direct" the distribution of the proceeds of the sale when it appears to the court that someone other than those specified in the subdivision has an interest superior to the specified persons. Thus, whenever it appears that, e.g., a lien creditor (whether by way of judgment or mortgage or tax lien or mechanic's lien, etc.) has an interest superior to a judgment creditor (who would ordinarily share in the proceeds under present 5236(e) merely by issuing an execution), the court may apply the proceeds to the superior interest first. Siegel, The Sale of Real Property Pursuant to an Execution Under the CPLR, 10th NY Jud Conf Rep, pp.120, 148 [1965].

All concur.

———————

How did the court know that this was a case in which it should disregard the distributions specified in the statute? The answer has to be that the court knew how the system was supposed to work, and knew it would not work that way if the court didn't order otherwise.

D. The Right to Possession Between Lien Holders

As we previously discussed, one of the basic principles underlying the system of priority is that any lien holder is free to foreclose at any time. But what happens if two lien holders decide to foreclose at the same time? Most courts require that junior lien holders surrender possession to senior lien holders, effectively giving seniors the right of way.

The Grocers Supply Co. v. Intercity Investment Properties, Inc.

795 S.W.2d 225 (Tex. Ct. App. 1990)

CANNON, J.

The facts are undisputed. On February 3, 1989, Grocers Supply perfected a security interest exceeding $600,000 to secure its inventory financing of The Grocery Store, Inc. and Cedric Wise. On March 6, 1989, Intercity Investments obtained a judgment in the county court against The Grocery Store, Inc. and Cedric Wise for approximately $36,000 and on June 22, 1989, the county court issued a turnover order. Grocers Supply was not a party to that suit.

On July 12, 1989, the constable, accompanied by three attorneys for Intercity, levied writs of execution obtained by Intercity on The Grocery Store and took possession of the inventory of groceries, equipment, and other items described in the inventory to the writ of execution. The attorneys for Intercity were aware of the prior recorded security interest of Grocers Supply but did not contact Grocers Supply. Upon learning of the execution on The Grocery Store inventory, appellants filed this action on July 17, 1989, to determine their rights in the property, resulting in the judgment from which this appeal is taken.

In its first cross-point, Intercity contends the trial court erred in awarding possession of the seized property to Grocers Supply. Intercity argues that both Tex. R. Civ. P. 643 and [UCC §9-401] expressly authorize execution against collateral, the sale of which is subject to the existing encumbrance. Appellant argues that when confronted with facts almost identical to those in this case, a Florida court held that [UCC §9-401] does not exempt collateral from execution and that it may be seized and sold by the judgment creditor, subject to the secured party's lien. Altec Lansing v. Friedman Sound, Inc., 204 So. 2d 740 (Fla. Dist. Ct. App. 1967). Intercity also cites First Natl. Bank of Glendale v. Sheriff of Milwaukee County, 34 Wis. 2d 535, 149 N.W.2d 548 (Wis. 1967), wherein the Wisconsin Supreme Court reached the same conclusion. Based upon these two cases, Intercity reasons this is the majority rule. We agree with Grocers Supply that the precedential effect of *Altec Lansing* is highly questionable because of the later case of Brescher v. Assoc. Fin. Serv. Co., 460 So. 2d 464 (Fla. Dist. Ct. App. 1984), in which the court made it clear that the "secured party, upon default by a debtor, may recover possession of a chattel by replevin from a sheriff who has taken possession thereof under execution." Id. at 465.

Texas' version of the Uniform Commercial Code provides that "unless otherwise agreed a secured party has on default the right to take possession of the collateral." [UCC §9-609(a)]. It appears that, with the exception of Wisconsin, other states considering the issue have consistently held that the right of a prior perfected creditor to take possession of its collateral is superior to any right of a mere judgment creditor and that the prior perfected secured creditor may regain possession of the collateral from an officer who has levied on the property at the direction of a judgment creditor. We agree with this interpretation. To hold otherwise would be to take away from the perfected security interest holder the important right of repossession of the collateral.

The security agreement between Grocers Supply and The Grocery Store clearly provided that a judgment against the debtor, or the levy, seizure, or attachment of the collateral constituted a default and upon the occurrence of any of those events, "the entire obligation becomes immediately due and payable at secured party's option without notice to debtor." We hold the right of Grocers Supply, as a prior secured creditor, to take possession of its collateral was superior to the right of Intercity, a mere judgment creditor, and that Grocers Supply could regain possession of the collateral from the constable who had levied on the property.

In its second cross-point, Intercity contends the trial court erred in adjudging against it the transportation and storage costs incurred. Intercity argues that since such costs are not specifically authorized by rule or statute, and since they are not taxable as costs of court, adjudging those costs against Intercity was unauthorized and improper. We disagree. As stated above, the evidence shows that Intercity knew of Grocers Supply's security interest before it seized the collateral, yet they failed to notify appellant before taking action. Intercity's action caused Grocers Supply to incur the additional expense of $24,113.00 in order to recover its collateral. Since someone had to pay this expense, it is appropriate that the one causing the injury be ordered to pay. As pointed out by Grocers Supply, the Oregon Court of Appeals and the Utah Supreme Court have held that a secured creditor with a right of possession of the collateral after default may maintain an action for conversion against one who exercised unauthorized acts of dominion over the property to the exclusion of the creditor's rights. We believe these authorities are sound and support the court's award of the storage and transportation costs.

We modify the judgment and order that The Grocers Supply Co., Inc. have judgment against Intercity Investment Properties, Inc. for $24,113.00, such sum being the amount which The Grocers Supply Co., Inc. paid to discharge the warehouseman's lien on the property seized under the writs of execution.

As modified, we affirm the judgment of the trial court.

Comment 5 to UCC §9-609 recognizes the rule of *Grocers Supply:*

More than one secured party may be entitled to take possession of collateral under this section. Conflicting rights to possession among secured parties are resolved by the priority rules of this Article. Thus, a senior secured party is entitled to possession as against a junior claimant. Non-UCC law governs whether a junior secured party in possession of collateral is liable to the senior in conversion. Normally, a junior who refuses to relinquish possession of collateral upon the demand of a secured party having a superior possessory right to the collateral would be liable in conversion.

Where does this leave the junior creditor? If it cannot seize property of the debtor and force a sale merely because the holder of a senior lien whose debt is in default objects, what can it do to collect its debt? If the answer is that it cannot collect until the senior lets it, a junior lien is next to useless. The point has not gone unnoticed.

Frierson v. United Farm Agency, Inc.
868 F.2d 302 (8th Cir. 1988)

[Merchants held a first security interest in collateral owned by United Farm Agency, Inc. (UFA). When Frierson levied on the collateral, Merchants demanded that Frierson return the collateral to UFA.] With respect to Merchants' and UFA's arguments under Article 9 of the Uniform Commercial Code, see [UCC §9-101], et seq., we agree with the district court. As the district court stated:

Most secured loans provide for numerous events which constitute default, many of which are technical in nature and are inserted in the loan documents to enable the lender to declare the note in default when even a relatively minor problem arises with the loan or the debtor. Thus, at any given time many secured loans are technically in default, but are never treated as such by secured creditors. In addition, a secured party will occasionally, as Merchants has done in this case, ignore a default which is more than just a technical default. If a secured creditor with a security interest over all the debtor's property is permitted to rely on a default, whether technical or not, to prevent another creditor from executing on the debtor's property, while treating the loan as not in default when dealing with the debtor and others, severe inequities would result. Such an approach would be against both the spirit and the letter of the Uniform Commercial Code.

672 F. Supp. at 1276.

Merchants cannot refuse to exercise its rights under the security agreement, thereby maintaining UFA as a going concern, while it impairs the status of other creditors by preventing them from exercising valid liens. Allowing Merchants to do so would fly in the face of all Article 9, which is premised on the debtor's ability to exercise rights in the property. See [UCC §9-401]. Regardless of whether the funds in question are viewed as collateral or as proceeds, Article 9 requires that Frierson take the remaining funds subject to Merchants' security interest if the bank refuses to exercise its remedies under the code. [UCC §9-315(a)]. Merchants' security interest in the funds will continue, and Merchants can trace and recapture when it chooses to declare the loan in default and accelerate the debt.

UCC §9-401 does not say that an unsecured creditor who has obtained a judgment against the debtor can levy on collateral encumbered by another creditor's security interest. It merely says that the issue "is governed by applicable law other than this article." The most obvious feature of that other law will be statutes authorizing judgment creditors to levy on the debtor's property. Those statutes make no exception for encumbered property.

We think there are at least two ways to reconcile *Grocers Supply* with UCC §9-401. The first is the reasoning in *Frierson*: The right of the senior to possession is not the right to possession for the purpose of leaving the debtor in business and frustrating collection by junior lien holders. The senior lien holder must foreclose or stand aside so junior lien holders can foreclose. The second begins with the observation that *Grocers Supply* requires the junior lien holder to surrender possession to the senior, but it does not bar the junior from continuing with the sale. Under some sale procedures at least, property can be sold even though it is not physically present.

E.   UCC Notice of Sale

Lien holders other than the one forcing a sale need to know that the sale is occurring. Senior lien holders whose debts are in default may wish to demand possession and conduct their own sales. Junior lien holders may wish to protect their interests by bidding at the senior lien holders' sales.

Providing notice is not easy. Liens may be perfected in a variety of ways that make them difficult or impossible to discover. If the foreclosing creditor cannot discover them, the foreclosing creditor cannot give them notice. There is, however, strong pressure to terminate all subordinate liens in a sale. If Article 9 sales did not discharge those liens, such sales would be very risky places to shop and prices might suffer.

UCC §9-611 responds to the dilemma by requiring foreclosing secured parties to give notice of sale, but only to lien holders who are easy to find — those who have properly indexed financing statements on file or who have perfected by compliance with a federal statute or state certificate of title statute.

To take advantage of this UCC §9-611 safe harbor, the foreclosing secured party requests a search of the UCC filing system 20 to 30 days before the "notification date." The notification date is the date on which the foreclosing secured party will send notice of sale. If the search results arrive before the notification date, the foreclosing secured party sends notice to the lien holders named in the search result and also sends notice to any lien holder who furnished the foreclosing secured party with an authenticated notice of its claim. Provided that those required notices are sent, all subordinate liens are discharged. That is, if UCC §9-611(c) does not require notice to the holder of a properly perfected valid lien, the lien is discharged without notice.

F. Rule Variation Across Systems

Liens come in numerous varieties. This book has focused on Article 9 security interests, but has also explored real property mortgages, deeds of trust, judgment liens, tax liens, and several kinds of judicial and statutory liens. The systems by which each of these types of lien is created, perfected, and enforced are largely separate from one another, but sometimes share elements. For example, judgment liens are recorded in the real property records and in some states, also in the Article 9 filing system. The holders of Article 9 security interests rarely sue for judicial foreclosure, but when they do, the procedures for sale will likely be the same as those for real property foreclosures.

Because all of these systems are creating, perfecting, and enforcing liens, all must address the same issues — such as providing notice to later lenders, determining the priority of liens against the same collateral, and distributing the proceeds of sale. On some of these issues, the system's creators are constrained by lien system imperatives that apply across lien types. For example, every kind of lien must be stackable; that is, it must be possible for the courts to rank its priority against every other lien in the same collateral. Another example is that the holders of liens discharged by a sale must be eligible to share in the sale proceeds and the holders of liens that survive the sale must not. Thus, even though UCC §9-615(a) controls the distribution of proceeds from an Article 9 sale, state statutes, such as N.Y. C.P.L.R. §5236(g), control the distribution of the proceeds from an execution sale, and state mortgage foreclosure statutes control the distribution of proceeds from a foreclosure sale, all must follow the same rule. Proceeds go first to the costs of sale, then to the lien under which the sale was held, and then to subordinate liens. No other distribution would work.

On other issues, the systems are free to diverge, and sometimes do. The holder of a prior perfected security interest that is in default is entitled to take possession from a sheriff who holds the property for sale under a writ of execution — thus probably preventing the sale. But the holder of a prior perfected execution lien clearly cannot prevent the sale. The sheriff sells the property pursuant to both writs. Similarly, the holder of a prior perfected mortgage has no right to prevent the holders of junior mortgages from foreclosing. The junior holder can race to foreclose until the senior holder discharges the junior holder's lien though its own foreclosure.

Article 9 expressly addresses nearly every issue in detail. But for many lien systems, the law consists of a few sentences and perhaps a few cases. Sometimes the most recent cases are decades old and were decided in business contexts that have changed dramatically — casting doubt on their continued vitality. In such systems, the best way to resolve the unaddressed issues is by analogy to a similar, better-documented system. A lawyer who cannot find law for the system in issue should assume that system will be held to work like the better-documented ones.

Problem Set 26

26.1.   Your client, Katherine Kinski, has investigated an upcoming fore-closure sale for the purpose of bidding at it. The sale is being conducted by the sheriff under a final judgment of foreclosure in favor of John Gottleib on a mortgage securing a debt in the amount of $10,000. The judgment specifi-cally forecloses a subordinate mortgage in the amount of $29,000, but makes no mention of a senior mortgage in the amount of $17,000. Kinski has exam-ined the property and concluded that she is willing to pay up to $25,000 to own the property free and clear of all liens. The sheriff's expenses in conduct-ing the sale are $200. How much should Kinski bid at the sale? Compare UCC §9-617(a).

26.2.   A 2004 Rolls Royce automobile worth $75,000 was seized by the sheriff under a writ of execution on an $8,000 judgment. The car is subject to a first security interest in the amount of $60,000 and a second in the amount of $30,000. Both secured creditors are aware of the sale; neither has objected or demanded possession of the collateral. The expenses of conducting the sale are estimated at $200. If all bidders understand the sale procedure, what do you expect will be the highest bid at the sale? Compare UCC §9-617(a).

26.3.   You represent Diamond Head National Bank, which holds a first security interest against some mobile equipment owned by Henry Walker, securing a debt in the amount of $270,000. Walker is current on his pay-ments. Diamond Head considers the loan very safe because, even at a sher-iff's auction sale, the bank is confident the equipment would bring at least

$400,000. From friends at the Club, you have heard that Walker is in financial difficulty and the holder of some kind of second lien is forcing a sale of the equipment.

a.   If this information is correct, is there any reason for Diamond Head to be concerned? UCC §§9-611(c)(3), 9-617(b), 9-625(b).

b.   Can Diamond Head protect its position by purchasing the equipment at the sale? UCC §9-615(a).

c.   Can Diamond Head prevent the sale? UCC §§9-609(a), 9-401.

d.   Assuming that the creditor forcing this sale was an Article 9 secured party, was Diamond Head entitled to receive notice of this sale? UCC §9-611 and Comment 4 to that section.

26.4.   You had never intended to get so intimately involved in debtor-creditor relations, but a friend needs to borrow $100,000 from you. She is willing to give you a second mortgage against the house she recently bought for $1.2 million. The house is subject to an $800,000 first mortgage and appears to be easily worth more than $900,000.

a.   If your friend defaults on the $100,000 loan and you have to look to the house for repayment, what will you do?

b.   Will taking that action ensure recovery of your $100,000?

c.   What will happen if your friend makes the payments on your mortgage, but defaults in payments under the first mortgage?

d.   Can you protect yourself against default under the first mortgage by a provision in your loan or mortgage agreement?

26.5.   After the decision in *Grocers Supply*, Bob Gorman, president of Intercity Investments, directed the sheriff to surrender possession of The Grocery Store inventory to Grocers Supply and paid Grocers Supply $24,000 in satisfaction of the judgment. Gorman discharged the attorneys who represented Intercity in the execution and came to you for advice on how to collect Intercity's $36,000 judgment against The Grocery Store and Cedric Wise. It appears that after its victory in court, Grocers Supply instructed the sheriff to return the inventory to The Grocery Store, the sheriff has done so, and The Grocery Store is back in business. Wiser from his earlier experience, Gorman contacted Grocers Supply and told them that he intended to execute on the inventory again to enforce his judgment. Grocers Supply objected, saying that they preferred that the inventory remain in place, and threatened that if Gorman executed "it will just be a repeat of the earlier case." Gorman thinks the inventory is worth more than enough to pay both liens, and Grocers Supply is only objecting in order to protect The Grocery Store. "If they can do this," Gorman says, "any debtor with a cooperative secured creditor can beat its judgment creditors." What do you tell Gorman?

26.6.   Your firm has just picked up a new client, Fidelity Mortgage. Fidelity is an Alaska lender that frequently lends against real property, taking a first mortgage in the property. You review Fidelity's current standard loan documents and you notice they say nothing about property taxes, which may range anywhere from 1 to 3 percent of the value of the property each year. Alaska Stat. §29.45.300 has a provision of the type common in most U.S. jurisdictions: "Property taxes, together with penalty and interest, are a lien upon the property assessed, and the lien is prior and paramount to all other liens or encumbrances against the property." If they are not paid within two years, the state forecloses the property tax lien and the property is sold to the highest bidder at auction. The proceeds of sale are applied first to the tax and then to subordinate liens.

a.   If one of Fidelity's debtors fails to pay property taxes and the state forecloses, what is the effect on Fidelity's mortgage?

b.   If such a foreclosure is already under way against one of Fidelity's mortgagors, what can Fidelity do to protect itself?

c.   What suggestions do you have for reforming Fidelity's standard form contract?

■ End of Default Problem Set

26.7.   You represent Commercial Finance, a commercial lender. It holds a second mortgage in the amount of $2.3 million against an industrial plant. (That amount includes principal, interest, attorneys fees, and the estimated costs of conducting the mortgage foreclosure sale.) The plant is the only asset of the debtor, Industrial Manufacturers, Inc. (Industrial). The principals of Industrial have personally guaranteed payment of the mortgage debt, but it is unclear whether any deficiency against them will be collectible. The foreclosure of Commercial's mortgage is complete and the sale is set for next week. The first mortgage in the amount of $4.1 million in favor of City State Bank is in default, but the bank has not yet begun to foreclose. Commercial has asked you to prepare the bidding strategy for the upcoming sale. It believes that if the property were marketed and sold privately, it would bring between $4.2 million and $5.6 million, with the most likely resale price being about $5 million. Commercial estimates its out-of-pocket costs of buying, holding, and reselling the plant at $200,000, and an additional $300,000 of interest and attorneys fees will accrue on the first mortgage during the time it would take to resell the plant. How much should Commercial bid at the sale? Organize your answer by assuming a resale of the property for exactly $5 million, then explain how the numbers change if the property actually brings more or less.

Assignment 27: The Concept of Priority: Bankruptcy Law

As we discussed in Assignments 6 and 7, security interests and liens survive the filing of a bankruptcy case. Through confirmation of a plan in a case under Chapter 11, 12, or 13, bankruptcy can reduce the amount of the lien to an amount equal to the value of the collateral as determined by the court, adjust the interest rate based on some market rate, and extend the time for repayment. In addition, during bankruptcy, some kinds of liens can be *avoided* entirely because they are unperfected (Assignment 30) or are preferences (Assignment 31). Except to the extent these things occur, security interests and liens survive and retain their relative priorities in bankruptcy.

At the most fundamental level, "priority" means that when the value of collateral is sufficient to pay only one of two lien creditors, the law will seek to ensure that the value is applied to payment of the one who has priority. In this sense, the meaning of "priority" does not change when the debtor goes into bankruptcy.

In other respects, the meaning of "priority" does change. Recall the two basic principles of priority with which we began Assignment 26. First, absent an agreement to the contrary, any lien holder may foreclose at any time after default. As we discussed in Assignment 6, the automatic stay contradicts that principle: The secured creditor cannot foreclose until the stay is terminated. Bankr. Code §362(a). Secured creditors can seek relief from the stay, but there is no assurance it will be granted. Bankr. Code §362(d)(1) and (2). The second basic principle was that no lien holder could be compelled to foreclose. Although the debt might be in default, it remained the right of the secured creditor to choose the time to foreclose its own lien and to force a sale. As will be discussed in this assignment, the rules of bankruptcy procedure contradict that principle as well: The trustee or debtor in possession can sell the secured creditor's collateral "free and clear of liens," effectively foreclosing the secured creditor's lien on the trustee's or debtor's own timetable. Thus, while the debtor is in bankruptcy, the secured creditor continues to enjoy its priority, but the meaning of "priority" has been altered.

This transfer of control over the timing of foreclosure from the secured creditor to the trustee or debtor in possession signals an important difference in the focus of the state remedies and bankruptcy systems. In accord with the terms of the security agreement explicitly agreed to between the debtor and the secured creditor and implicitly agreed to by others who chose to become creditors knowing of the secured creditor's lien (or, when the others are unsecured creditors, knowing that the debtor could later grant a lien that would defeat them), the state remedies system puts the most senior secured creditor's interests first. The bankruptcy system gives less credence to these supposed agreements and focuses instead on maximizing the value of the bankruptcy estate for the benefit of all concerned. To accomplish that goal, it may compel secured creditors to leave their collateral in place so that the business of the estate can continue or so that the debtor can go on earning a living. This is not done for the benefit of the fully secured creditors. Most fully secured creditors could recover as much through foreclosure as they could through bankruptcy. Instead, the bankruptcy system holds fully secured creditors in place primarily for the benefit of the marginally secured or unsecured creditors and the debtor. This change in focus too can be thought of as a change in the meaning of "priority" as a case moves from the state remedies system to the bankruptcy system and perhaps back again if the bankruptcy case is dismissed.

In the remainder of this assignment, we take a closer look at three ways in which the priority rights of secured creditors are diminished in bankruptcy. The first is through the trustee or debtor in possession's ability to sell collateral free and clear of liens; the second is the trustee or debtor in possession's ability to grant liens senior to existing liens; and the third is the shift in focus from the protection of more senior creditors to the protection of more junior ones.

A.   Bankruptcy Sale Procedure

As we touched on briefly in Assignment 7, during a bankruptcy case the trustee or debtor in possession can sell collateral. These sales may be judicial sales, held pursuant to an order of the court and confirmed afterward by the court, or they may be nonjudicial sales held pursuant to the powers vested in the debtors in possession (DIPs) or trustees by statute. See Bankr. Code §§363(b)(1) and (c)(1).

As in foreclosure sales under state law, in bankruptcy sales the collateral may be sold subject to the liens of secured creditors. Once such a sale is complete, the collateral ceases to be "property of the [bankruptcy] estate," the automatic stay expires, and, if the debt is in default, the secured creditor will be free to foreclose. Bankr. Code §362(c)(1) and (2). Again, as in a state law foreclosure action, purchasers in such a sale acquire only the debtor's equity in the property. Ordinarily they will deduct from their offers the additional amounts they expect to pay later to secured creditors to clear the title to the property. If the liens against collateral exceed its value, no one may be willing to buy it subject to the liens. The collateral is then considered "burdensome" to the estate and the debtor or trustee can abandon it. Bankr. Code §554.

Abandonment, like sale, removes the property from the estate, revests the property from the DIP (acting on behalf of the estate) to the debtor (acting on its own behalf). Bankr. Code §362(c)(1) and (2). Provisions of the automatic stay that prohibit acts against property of the estate no longer apply. But provisions of the automatic stay that prohibit acts against the debtor or against property of the debtor continue to apply. The secured creditor who wishes to foreclose after an abandonment may still need to obtain a stay lift before doing so.

Unlike state law, bankruptcy law provides an alternative procedure under which a trustee or DIP can sell collateral "free and clear" of the liens of secured creditors. Bankr. Code §363(f). A sale free and clear of liens works much the same way as a foreclosure sale by the first lien holder in the absence of bankruptcy. The buyer takes unencumbered title to the property and presumably pays its full value as the purchase price. The liens are transferred to the proceeds of sale, with the ultimate effect that the proceeds are applied to the liens in the order of their priority.

In the absence of bankruptcy, a secured creditor can choose the time at which it will foreclose. Although another secured creditor with a prior lien can foreclose against it, neither the debtor nor secured creditors with subordinate liens can involuntarily dislodge the secured creditor from its position against the collateral by anything less than full payment. The ability to sell free and clear of liens in bankruptcy deprives the secured creditor of this control over the timing of foreclosure. If the trustee or DIP can prove grounds for selling the collateral free and clear of liens, the trustee or DIP—*not* the secured creditor—chooses when to sell. The difference is critical to a lien holder who will recover nothing from an immediate sale free and clear of liens, but who might recover from a later sale if the property appreciated in value or was sold in a better market.

In the case that follows, a defaulting debtor won the right to sell a secured creditor's collateral over the secured creditor's vehement objection. According to a two-year-old appraisal, the collateral had been worth enough to cover nearly the entire amount of the creditor's $600,000 lien, but the court's decision authorizes its sale for an amount barely sufficient to pay the prior liens. The objecting creditor's $600,000 lien will be wiped out with only nominal payment.

In re Oneida Lake Development, Inc.

114 B.R. 352 (Bankr. N.D.N.Y. 1990)

STEPHEN D. GERLING, UNITED STATES BANKRUPTCY JUDGE.

This contested matter comes before the Court on the motion of Oneida Lake Development, Inc., d/b/a Wood Pointe Marine ("Debtor") for an order pursuant to §363 of the Bankruptcy Code (11 U.S.C.A. §101-1330) (West 1989) ("Code"), permitting it to sell all of its real estate, together with all physical assets to Raymond H. Bloss ("Bloss") for the sum of $750,000.00 in accordance with the terms of a written purchase offer which is subject to the approval of this Court.

At [a] hearing objections to the sale were interposed by Thomas K. Crowley ("Crowley") and Wood Pointe Venturers ("WPV"), both judgment creditors, while Merchants Bank & Trust Company of Syracuse ("Merchants"), conditionally objected to the sale seeking only to have its junior mortgage paid in full upon closing.

FACTS

Debtor filed a voluntary petition pursuant to Chapter 11 of the Code on September 11, 1989. On November 11, 1989 Debtor entered into a contract for the sale of its real property designated as the Wood Pointe Marina at Oneida Lake, New York for the sum of $750,000.00. The contract also included all inventory and equipment, excepting boats subject to any floor plan agreement.

It does not appear that the contract was expressly contingent upon the approval of this Court, although it does contain a reference to "Bankruptcy proceedings." (See Offer to Purchase attached to Debtor's Motion Papers.)

As of the date of filing, it appears that the Debtor's real property was encumbered by three mortgages, three judgments and delinquent real estate taxes totaling in excess of 1.3 million dollars.

While there apparently is no dispute with regard to the validity of the three mortgages and the delinquent real property taxes, the Debtor has commenced an adversary proceeding to set aside two of the three judgments as preferences, and those proceedings are presently pending.

The third judgment in the sum of $600,000 is held by WPV and while the Debtor's moving papers suggest that it too will be either compromised or become the subject of a similar adversary proceeding, no such proceeding has as yet been commenced.

It is apparent that if all three judgments are set aside, a sale price of not less than $750,000.00 will be substantially in excess of the remaining liens. The Bloss offer, however, provides for the purchaser to assume the first and second mortgages and for the Debtor to take back a third mortgage securing $140,000.00, so that the Debtor will only receive $250,000.00 in cash at the time of closing.

Debtor has provided the Court with an appraisal of the real property prepared in 1987 reflecting the fair market value at 1.25 million dollars, however, a revision of that appraisal as of November 30, 1989 reflects a significant decrease in that value.

ARGUMENTS

At the hearing held before the Court on December 19, 1989, both Crowley and WPV objected to the sale. However, in his Memorandum of Law filed January 2, 1990, Crowley purports to withdraw its objection based upon (1) improper notice, and (2) Code §363(f) and now urges the Court to approve the sale "upon the terms set forth both in the Debtor's motion and at the hearing."

WPV also faxed a Memorandum of Law to the Court on January 2, 1990 in support of their objection to the sale. WPV contends that a sale pursuant to Code §363(b) requires notice and a hearing, and that the hearing must be an evidentiary hearing. WPV contends further that such a hearing is also necessary to determine the issues raised by Code §363(f).

WPV also postures that Debtor cannot comply with Code §363(f) since there is no bona fide dispute as to its judgment (§363(f)(4)), that the sale will not produce a full money satisfaction of its judgment (§363(f)(5)), and that the remaining subsections of Code §363(f) are concededly inapplicable.

Crowley's Memorandum of Law argues that WPV's judgment is in bona fide dispute and that, in fact, Debtor's counsel has indicated its intent to commence an adversary proceeding challenging WPV's judgment as a preference, thus complying with the requirements of Code §363(f)(4). Crowley also contends that Debtor's sale may be approved pursuant to Code §363(f)(3) since a proper interpretation of that subsection requires the Court to value the secured creditor's lien at the actual value of the collateral subject to the lien, and not at the face amount of the lien, thus adequately protecting the lien which is all that a secured creditor is entitled to under the applicable provisions of the Code dealing with secured claims.

DISCUSSION

Turning to a consideration of Code §363(f), there appears to be no dispute that that section authorizes a debtor to sell its property free and clear of liens and encumbrances, so long as it can satisfy any one of the five subsections. It is equally clear that subsections (f)(1), (2) and (5) cannot be complied with by the Debtor. At issue then is whether the Debtor has established compliance with either subsection (3) or (4).

Subsection (f)(3) authorizes a sale by debtor free and clear of liens and encumbrances only where the sale price "is greater than the aggregate value of all liens on such property."

Both the Debtor and Crowley argue in their respective Memoranda of Law that the term "value" as utilized in Code §363(f)(3) must be defined by reference to Code §506(a)(1) which defines secured status as extending only to "the value of such creditor's interest in the estate's interest in such property," thus negating the contention that value is determined by looking solely to the face amount of the lien in analyzing Code §363(f)(3).

Crowley cites the well-reasoned opinion of Bankruptcy Judge Howard Buschman, III, in In re Beker Industries Corp., 63 B.R. 474 (Bankr. S.D.N.Y. 1986), which supports the concept that the value and not the amount of the liens is what the Court must look to in applying Code §363(f)(3).

Bankruptcy Judge Buschman suggests that the Code's statutory scheme authorizes a debtor to deal with its secured assets by insuring simply that the secured creditor receives only the value of its secured claim in debtor's property, even though that may be significantly less than the face amount of the claim by referencing Code §1129(b)(2)(A)(i) and §1129(b)(2)(A)(ii).

While Judge Buschman acknowledges that there is significant authority to the effect that *value* as used in Code §363(f)(3) is synonymous with *amount*, this Court believes that the *Beker* analysis comports with Congressional intent in utilizing the term "value" versus the term "amount" in the statute. *Beker* does point out, however, that the Court must conclude that the proposed sale price is the best price obtainable under the circumstances and further that it must find special circumstances justifying the sale for less than the amount of liens over the objection of a secured creditor.

Applying the rationale of *Beker* to the instant case, the Court concludes that, even without conducting an evidentiary hearing, which would only serve to significantly delay a sale of the marina property, the current appraisal submitted by Debtor in light of the bidding that occurred on December 19, 1989, is the best possible price that could be obtained for the property. That further both the status of the non-consenting creditor WPV as a non-consensual judgment lienor whose judgment is at least arguably subject to attack under Code §547 and the apparent rapid depreciation of the property provide special circumstances which suggest that the Debtor has met the requirements of Code §363(f)(3).

Turning to an analysis of Code §363(f)(4), both Debtor and Crowley contend that that subsection has been satisfied, since at a minimum, the lien of WPV, the objector, is in bona fide dispute, and should that lien be avoided, the [$750,000 offer] would easily exceed the sum of all of the other existing liens and leave significant equity for the Chapter 11 Debtor.

WPV postures that in order to satisfy the requirement of "bona fide dispute" the lien must be the subject of an adversary proceeding and there must be a high probability that the adversary proceeding will result in the avoidance of the lien. WPV points out that the validity of the judgment lien is not presently the subject of any adversary proceeding.

Bankruptcy Judge A. Thomas Small's decision in In re Millerburg, 61 B.R. at 125 (Bankr. E.D.N.C. 1986) is cited by both Crowley and WPV in support of their respective positions. However, the Court believes that WPV reads more into Judge Small's decision than its plain language will support.

WPV construes *Millerburg* as requiring that the facts must suggest that the debtor has a high probability of success in the adversary proceeding which seeks to avoid the lien in order for a bona fide dispute to exist within the meaning of Code §363(f)(4).

Bankruptcy Judge Small simply observed, however, that the facts in that particular case suggested that the debtor would have a high probability of success in avoiding the creditor's lien as a preference under Code §547, however, the debtor had not even commenced an adversary proceeding. The Court commented that "the potential preference action against GMAC would certainly qualify as a bona fide dispute for purposes of §363(f)(4)." Id. page 128.

This Court reads *Millerburg* as supporting the position of Crowley and the Debtor, and it concludes that Code §363(f)(4) has been satisfied even though the Debtor has not as yet commenced the adversary proceeding versus WPV.

———————

Under nonbankruptcy law, it probably would have been impossible for the debtor to sell WPV's collateral over its objection and free of its lien. Absent foreclosure by a senior lien, WPV could have sat tight, accrued interest, and waited for a better market or a better buyer. But the debtor's bankruptcy filing changed all that. If the value of the collateral rises back to $1.25 million, it will be the buyer, Bloss, not the lien creditor, WPV, who reaps the benefit.

One circumstance in which the bankruptcy power to sell free and clear of liens can achieve greater economic efficiency than the nonbankruptcy foreclosure sale procedure is where the amounts and priorities of competing liens against the collateral are in doubt and the collateral is depreciating in value. By selling free and clear of liens and transferring the liens, whatever their priority and amount, to the proceeds of sale, the debtor or trustee can prevent further losses.

Consider, for example, the case of two creditors who hold mortgages against a shopping center that is under construction. The debtor is in financial difficulty and has defaulted in payments under both mortgages. Work on the property has ceased and the building now sits idle. Assume that the two mortgage holders are unsure which mortgage is entitled to priority.

In the absence of bankruptcy, one of the creditors would file a foreclosure action, alleging that the other was subordinate. The court would determine the priority of the mortgages before entering final judgment of foreclosure. Only then could the sale be held. The litigation might go on for years, while interest accrued and the property remained vacant.

In a bankruptcy case, the debtor or trustee could effect a sale free and clear of the two mortgages. Bankr. Code §363(f)(4). The buyer could resume construction immediately while the proceeds of sale earned interest in a bank account under the control of the bankruptcy court. The court could then determine the priority of the two mortgages at its leisure.

Just as in a nonbankruptcy foreclosure sale, secured creditors in a bankruptcy sale free and clear of liens are protected by their right to "bid in" the amounts of their liens. Bankr. Code §363(k). But in this regard, the major strength of the sale free and clear of liens is also its great weakness. The secured creditor who is unsure of the amount and priority of its lien may face a difficult problem in determining how much to bid.

B.   The Power to Grant Senior Liens

As we discussed in the preceding section, a trustee or DIP can elect to sell encumbered collateral. Alternatively, the trustee or DIP can keep the property and offer it as collateral for post-petition loans. In the latter case, the trustee or DIP may be able to alter the priority of preexisting liens in ways not possible at state law.

Under state law, liens generally rank in priority in the order in which they are created and perfected. As we saw in earlier assignments, the usual procedure for lending against collateral is to inspect the collateral and search the public records to determine what liens currently encumber it. Thus, the lender can know before making the loan what priority its security interest initially will have. Moreover, because liens *rank in priority in the order in which they are created*, the lender can also know that its initial priority will not change. That is, if there are no liens against the collateral at the time a creditor lends and perfects its security interest, the lender's security interest will become a first lien. Once it becomes first, it will remain first; competing liens will be subordinate because they were created at a later time. The value of the lender's security interest may still fluctuate with the value of the collateral, but the lender can rest assured that whatever that value may be, the lender has the first claim to it.

Even under state law, there may be exceptions to the rule that the first lien created and perfected has first priority. But the exceptions are rare and generally of a manageable nature. The example we have used before is that, under the statutes of most states, property taxes assessed against collateral constitute a lien prior to all others, including first mortgages. To maintain their first position, first mortgage lenders generally seek to compel their debtors to pay the property taxes as they accrue. If their debtors do not pay the property taxes, the secured creditors pay them and foreclose. This approach is feasible because property taxes accrue at predictable times and in predictable amounts that are generally small in relation to the amount of the first mortgage. Property taxes are not the only exception. In a few states, the lien of a person who repairs collateral, such as a mechanic, will have priority over preexisting security interests. Here, too, the creditor's strategy is likely to be to pay such liens as they accrue in order to maintain a first position.

Once a debtor is in bankruptcy, this seemingly fundamental tenet of security—that the lien first created and perfected has first priority—no longer holds. In limited circumstances, the trustee or DIP can borrow additional money from a *post-petition lender*, secured by a lien prior to existing liens. Bankr. Code §364(d). Before doing so, the trustee or DIP must notify the holder of the first lien of its intention. If the holder objects (which it almost certainly will), the court must hold a hearing to determine that the Code prerequisites to such borrowing have been satisfied. The prerequisites are that (1) the estate is unable to borrow the money without granting a prior lien and (2) there is adequate protection of the interest of the secured creditor whose lien is being displaced.

The Bankruptcy Code permits the granting of prior liens on the theory that additional, postpetition financing is often essential to the successful operations of the business. If it is not forthcoming, the business may fail and its future income may be lost. If the senior lender is adequately protected from loss, it presumably will suffer no loss from its demotion in priority. By permitting the debtor to do what is necessary to keep the business running, the debtor may be able to protect the junior creditors (and, not incidentally, itself) against loss without harming anyone.

Why, then, are secured creditors usually so unhappy about this supposedly win-win strategy? First, the secured creditor typically gains nothing from the transaction. It was already secured, and probably would have come out just fine in a foreclosure. Second, the adequate protection dispensed by the bankruptcy courts is no guarantee against loss. To illustrate, assume that the DIP seeks to borrow from Newlender and grant Newlender a first mortgage against property already encumbered by Oldlender's mortgage. On the DIP's motion, the bankruptcy court decides that the value of the collateral is well in excess of both mortgages and that the excess (the "cushion of equity") will provide Oldlender with adequate protection. Further assume that the court's decision proves to be wrong, either because the property was never worth as much as the judge thought or because it later declined in value. The DIP then sells the property, free and clear of liens, for less than enough to pay both mortgages. The DIP pays Newlender in full and applies whatever is left to Oldlender's mortgage debt. What happens to the unpaid balance of Oldlender's mortgage debt? If you guessed that the judge pays it out of the judge's salary, you were wrong. In fact, it becomes an unsecured claim. Although it has priority over virtually all other kinds of unsecured claims, Bankr. Code §507(b), it might not be paid because the estate has insufficient assets. Although this scenario occurs with some frequency, neither of the authors has ever known a judge or a debtor even to apologize.

Granting senior liens to postpetition lenders is not a common occurrence, but the effect of permitting it is nevertheless profound. In essence, it transforms priority from the right of the secured creditor to be paid first to the mere right to adequate protection against nonpayment. Oldlender in the above illustration can be likened to a mountain hiker who, having arrived first on a dangerous ledge, positions herself as far from the edge as possible. As other hikers arrive behind her, they ask that she move a little closer to the edge to make room for them against the mountainside. When she protests, they tell her she'll still be safe, because the distance between her and the edge will still be adequate. Probably her best retort is that if it's so safe out there, why don't *they* stand there and let *her* stay against the mountainside? To understand the somewhat disingenuous position of the Bankruptcy Code on this point, consider that the trustee must prove two things to make Oldlender stand closer to the edge: (1) it's safe out there and (2) the debtor couldn't find anyone else who would stand out there.

At the inception of the following case, John Hancock Insurance Company held a $4 million first mortgage on the debtor's building, which was worth only $2.2 million. By a feat of legal alchemy, the debtor used Bankruptcy Code §364(d) to borrow even more money against the building—and put the new lender ahead of John Hancock.

In re 495 Central Park Avenue Corporation

136 B.R. 626 (Bankr. S.D.N.Y. 1992)

HOWARD SCHWARTZBERG, UNITED STATES BANKRUPTCY JUDGE.

DECISION ON APPLICATION FOR AN ORDER AUTHORIZING SENIOR SECURED CREDIT UNDER SECTION 364(D)

495 Central Avenue Corp. ("495 Central Avenue"), the debtor in this Chapter 11 case, has moved pursuant to 11 U.S.C. §364(d) for an order authorizing it to borrow funds from either Leon Silverman ("Silverman") and Tom Borek ("Borek"), shareholders of the debtor, or from third-party lenders supported by the personal guaranties of Silverman and Borek and permitting the lender to obtain a security interest senior to all existing security interests. John Hancock Mutual Life Insurance Company ("Hancock"), a secured creditor which holds a first mortgage on the debtor's property, opposes the debtor's motion. Hancock contends that the debtor has failed to meet the requirements of 11 U.S.C. §364(d) asserting that the debtor has not demonstrated that it has been unable to obtain credit by any other means and that the debtor has failed to show that Hancock's position is adequately protected.

FINDINGS OF FACT

1. The debtor, 495 Central Avenue, filed with this court on September 5, 1991, a voluntary petition for reorganizational relief under Chapter 11 of the Bankruptcy

Code. The debtor thereafter continued in possession and control of its assets as a debtor in possession in accordance with 11 U.S.C. §§1107 and 1108.

2. The debtor's primary asset is real property and a building located at 495 Central Avenue, Scarsdale, New York. The debtor leases space in the building to various commercial tenants.

3. The debtor acquired the premises at 495 Central Avenue from Viewpoint Realty Corporation ("Viewpoint") in April, 1991. The debtor took the property subject to an existing mortgage held by Hancock. In addition, the debtor paid Viewpoint $202,500.00 in cash and executed a purchase money mortgage in the amount of $200,000.00 payable to Viewpoint over five years in six-month installments. The purchase money mortgage is subordinate to Hancock's secured position.

4. Hancock holds a mortgage on the property in the principal amount of $3,950,000.00. In October, 1988, Viewpoint executed a promissory note and a mortgage to Hancock secured by the premises. Hancock duly recorded the mortgage. Under the terms of the security agreement, principal and interest are payable in monthly installments over a period of five years and the entire amount of unpaid principal is due on November 1, 1993. In the event of default, Hancock has the right to accelerate the entire debt. The agreement also requires real estate taxes to be placed in an escrow account on a monthly basis.

5. Under the security agreement, $35,418.34 is the monthly amount presently payable to Hancock on the mortgage and $12,954.64 must be escrowed for real estate tax liability each month. Because the debtor purchased the property at 495 Central Avenue subject to Hancock's mortgage, the debtor must make required payments to avoid foreclosure. While the debtor only purchased the property subject to Hancock's mortgage, the debtor did not assume the promissory note that Viewpoint had executed in favor of Hancock. Therefore, Viewpoint remains obligated on the mortgage note held by Hancock. Thus, Viewpoint, the former owner of the property, will be liable for any mortgage deficiency in the event of a foreclosure.

6. The debtor violated the terms and provisions of the mortgage held by Hancock by failing to make the required monthly mortgage payments on July 1, 1991. Following the default, Hancock accelerated the entire debt which totaled $3,937,993.25 and, in August, 1991, commenced a foreclosure action in New York State Supreme Court, Westchester County. That action was stayed upon the debtor's filing of the bankruptcy petition pursuant to 11 U.S.C. §362(a).

7. The debtor has moved in this court for an order permitting it to obtain credit under 11 U.S.C. §364(d), either from its shareholders, Silverman and Borek, or from a third-party lender, which would prime the secured positions of Hancock and Viewpoint. The debtor asks the court to grant its motion on the grounds that it has met the requirements imposed by 11 U.S.C. §364(d). First, the debtor contends that it has shown through its appraiser that Hancock's secured position is adequately protected. The debtor also argues it has established, through the testimony of Silverman as well as an independent expert witness, that alternate financing could not be obtained. Hancock opposes the debtor's motion arguing that the debtor has failed to demonstrate that the requirements of 11 U.S.C. §364(d) have been met. Hancock further argues that the motion should be denied because subordination of its position would violate 11 U.S.C. §1129(b), which provides that

secured claims are entitled to priority over junior claims. Viewpoint, the second mortgagee, does not oppose the debtor's motion.

8. Silverman, the president of the debtor, explained that the debtor needed to borrow money to enable it to make structural changes in the building at 495 Central Avenue to attract new tenants. [The court discussed Silverman's negotiations with prospective tenants and the kinds of renovations the prospective tenants wanted.]

14. The debtor needs money to renovate the building in order to enter into a lease agreement with Leather Center. Silverman testified that he has diligently sought to borrow funds on behalf of the debtor from various financial institutions. He stated that every bank has refused to lend the debtor money despite his and Borek's offers to guarantee the debt personally.

15. Henry Farrand ("Farrand"), a Commercial Loan Officer at Hudson Valley National Bank, is a commercial loan specialist and was certified as an expert in this case in commercial lending practices under Federal Rule of Evidence 702. Farrand testified that, in his opinion, all legitimate financial institutions would refuse to lend the debtor money because such a loan would be junior to Hancock's secured position. He explained that banks ordinarily demand a first position on commercial real estate loans and that a junior lien or an administrative priority simply will not suffice.

16. Roger Miller ("Miller"), the debtor's real estate appraiser, valued the building at 495 Central Avenue at $2,250,000.00. Miller utilized the income approach in making his valuation, basing his appraisal on the net income that the property is presently capable of producing. According to Miller, the income approach is the method typically used by appraisers to value income producing property such as the debtor's building.

17. Miller testified that additional rental revenue would enhance the building's market value. In his opinion, if the debtor invested $625,000.00 in renovating the property in question, its value would immediately increase to $3,500,000.00 because, after the infusion of capital, the building would be capable of producing higher rental income. Miller explained that this figure is based upon the current discounted value of the cash flow which he predicted the building would generate during the next seven years. According to his cash flow projections, Miller estimated that the building would be worth $4,000,000.00 in three years and $5,000,000.00 in five years.

18. Steven Levine ("Levine"), Hancock's appraiser, employing the income approach to valuation, concluded that the debtor's building is presently worth $2,200,000.00. Levine testified that the market value of the property would rise if its ability to produce rental income increased. He testified that after the proposed renovations, the building would be worth approximately $2,800,000.00.

19. Both experts agree if improvements of the property are made with the proposed borrowed funds, the property will increase in value. They differ, however, as to the extent of the increase in value. It is no surprise that Hancock's expert appears to be extremely conservative in calculating the expected increase in value, whereas the debtor's expert is overly optimistic in his view. The court finds that the proposed improvements will probably cause the property to increase in value to approximately $3,000,000.00. This amounts to an increase of $800,000.00 over the $2,200,000.00 appraised value expressed by Hancock's appraiser.

20. In light of the fact that the projected property improvements to be made with the requested credit will exceed the $650,000.00 loan, it follows that Hancock's secured interest will be adequately protected after the approval of the proposed $650,000.00 senior loan.

DISCUSSION

The procedure by which a debtor may obtain credit is set forth in 11 U.S.C. §364. 11 U.S.C. §364(d)(1) enables a debtor to obtain financing secured by a lien senior to all other interests. A debtor in possession has the rights, powers, and duties of a trustee pursuant to 11 U.S.C. §1107(a). Therefore, 495 Central Avenue, as a debtor in possession, may utilize 11 U.S.C. §364(d) to obtain credit. The debtor has the burden of proving that the requirements of 11 U.S.C. §364(d) have been met. In this case, the debtor has presented substantial evidence that both prongs of 11 U.S.C. §364(d) have been satisfied.

INABILITY TO OBTAIN ALTERNATE FINANCING

The first prong of 11 U.S.C. §364(d) requires the debtor to show that alternate financing is unavailable. Because superpriority financing displaces liens on which creditors have relied in extending credit, the debtor must demonstrate to the court that it cannot obtain financing by other means. The Bankruptcy Code permits a debtor to borrow money in various ways less onerous to secured creditors. 11 U.S.C. §364. A debtor, pursuant to 11 U.S.C. §364(b), may incur unsecured debt as an administrative expense with priority status under 11 U.S.C. §507(a)(2). If the debtor cannot obtain credit as an administrative expense, it may acquire a loan that is either unsecured but senior to all administrative expense claims, secured by a lien on property that is not secured, or secured by a junior lien on property already secured. 11 U.S.C. §364(c). If the debtor cannot obtain financing by any of these means, the debtor may invoke 11 U.S.C. §364(d) and obtain credit secured by a lien on property senior or equal to a prior lien.

In this case, it is clear that apart from 11 U.S.C. §364(d), the debtor cannot obtain credit. Section 364(d)(1) does not require the debtor to seek alternate financing from every possible lender. However, the debtor must make an effort to obtain credit without priming a senior lien. Silverman, on behalf of the debtor, has repeatedly tried to procure financing from various banks and lending institutions. Nevertheless, he testified that he was unable to receive financing in exchange for an unsecured position. No one was willing to lend the debtor money as an administrative expense or as an expense senior to all administrative claims.

Silverman also could not obtain credit secured by a lien junior to Hancock's secured position despite his diligent efforts. He stated that the banks were simply not interested in lending to the debtor. Farrand, a specialist in commercial lending practices, substantiated Silverman's testimony and explained that most banks lend money only in return for a senior secured position. The debtor cannot obtain financing secured by a lien on unencumbered property pursuant to 11 U.S.C. §363(c)(2) because there is no property in the estate which is not already subject to a lien. The debtor's property is encumbered by Hancock's lien which exceeds its appraised value.

ADEQUATE PROTECTION

The second prong of 11 U.S.C. §364(d) requires the debtor to show that the interests of the holder of an existing lien on the property are adequately protected. The Bankruptcy Code does not expressly define adequate protection. However, 11 U.S.C. §361 sets forth examples of this concept. Although 11 U.S.C. §361 presents some specific illustrations of adequate protection, the statute is not exclusive. Rather, it suggests a broad and flexible definition providing in pertinent part as follows:

> When adequate protection is required under section . . . 364 of this title of an interest of an entity in property, such adequate protection may be provided by . . .
>
> (3) granting such other relief, other than entitling such entity to compensation allowable under section 503(b)(1) of this title as an administrative expense, as will result in the realization by such entity of the indubitable equivalent of such entity's interest in such property.

11 U.S.C. §361.

The statute confers upon "the parties and the courts flexibility by allowing such other relief as will result in the realization by the protected entity of the value of its interest in the property involved." House Report No. 95-595, 95th Cong., 1st Sess. (1978). The goal of adequate protection is to safeguard the secured creditor from diminution in the value of its interest during the chapter 11 reorganization.

In the instant case, to determine whether Hancock is adequately protected, the court must consider whether the value of the debtor's property will increase as a result of the renovations funded by the proposed financing. Although appraisers for both sides disagree as to what the value of the building would be following the infusion of approximately $600,000.00, there is no question that the property would be improved by the proposed renovations and that an increase in value will result. In effect, a substitution occurs in that the money spent for improvements will be transferred into value. This value will serve as adequate protection for Hancock's secured claim.

CONCLUSIONS OF LAW

2. The debtor's motion to obtain senior priority financing under 11 U.S.C. §364(d) is granted because the statutory requirements have been satisfied. The debtor has shown that it could not incur debt by less onerous means. The debtor has also established that Hancock's secured position is adequately protected because the infusion of capital into the building will increase the value of the property.

3. The debtor may borrow money from Silverman and Borek, shareholders of the debtor, as a senior priority loan under 11 U.S.C. §364(d) because the statute does not prohibit such a loan.

SETTLE ORDER ON NOTICE

Some readers may have trouble with the court's finding that spending $650,000 on improvements to this $2,200,000 building will increase its value to $3,000,000. If the building plus the $650,000 are worth $3,000,000, why isn't the building worth $2,350,000 as it is? The answer is that the court believes the $650,000 will be a profitable investment. It is the building, plus the $650,000, plus the profit resulting from the debtor's time and effort that will be worth $3,000,000.

Notice also that the court in *495 Central Park Avenue Corp.* adopts some of the colorful language of the bankruptcy lawyers. The court speaks of the proposed post-petition mortgage that will "prime" the first mortgage — meaning that it will have priority over it. It also talks of a "super priority," a phrase used to refer to the priority the court can grant to a new lender under Bankruptcy Code §364(d). (The same terminology is more commonly used to refer to the priority under Bankruptcy Code §507(b) of an adequately protected creditor whose protection proved inadequate.)

C.   Protection of Subordinate Creditors

As noted earlier in this assignment, nonbankruptcy law emphasizes the protection of senior lien holders. Once the debtor is in default, a senior lien holder controls the timing of its own foreclosure, even though that foreclosure may have severe adverse effects on the positions of other lien holders and unsecured creditors. The power of the senior creditor to foreclose will be felt by all subordinate creditors, even as the subordinate creditors cannot force the senior to take any action.

Bankruptcy policy shifts the emphasis, positing essentially that the collection efforts of senior lien holders should be stayed if (1) the senior lien holders are adequately protected against loss (that is, the bankruptcy court does not think they are being asked to stand too close to the edge) and (2) the stay is likely to facilitate the collection efforts of subordinate creditors.

Bankruptcy policy can be thought of as analogous to the concept of triage in medicine. When resources are scarce, the injured are divided into three groups: (1) those who cannot benefit greatly from care because their injuries are relatively minor (they are told to wait), (2) those who cannot benefit greatly from care because their injuries are so severe they will die anyway, and (3) those who can benefit most from care because their injuries constitute a serious but probably not fatal threat. The scarce resources are expended on the third group. Bankruptcy policy can be viewed as dividing creditors into three analogous groups. In the first are adequately protected secured creditors who are likely to recover the full amounts of their claims regardless of what happens in the bankruptcy case (the automatic stay compels them to wait). In the second group are the holders of debts and liens so subordinate that they are unlikely ever to be paid, regardless of what happens in the bankruptcy case. Bankruptcy lawyers and judges talk about them as no longer having a real interest in the case. As with triage in medicine, bankruptcy policy focuses its attention and resources on the plight of the third group of creditors: those whose priority is sufficiently high that they may be able to be paid through an efficient and effective liquidation or reorganization, but not so high that they will be paid in any event.

To those versed solely in nonbankruptcy law, this emphasis on the rights of creditors of intermediate priority may seem contrary to the concept of priority itself. But it is important to keep in mind that the large majority of lenders consider the effects of both state law and bankruptcy law in determining what loans they will make and the terms upon which they will make them. As we noted at the outset, the concept of priority is defined not by state law, but by state law and bankruptcy law together.

Problem Set 27

27.1. Katherine Kinski (from Problem 26.1) is back in your office. The fore-closure sale she investigated was never held. About an hour before the sale was to take place, the debtor filed under Chapter 7 of the Bankruptcy Code and the sheriff concluded that continuation of the sale was barred by the automatic stay. Kinski contacted the Chapter 7 trustee, who told her that in two weeks he would sell the property at auction sale free and clear of liens. How much should Kinski bid at the auction? Bankr. Code §§363(b)(1), (f), (k), and (m).

27.2. You represent the Sicilian State Bank (SSB), which holds an $800,000 second security interest in railroad cars. In the current depressed market, the cars are worth only about $1 million. The first security interest in the amount of $1.1 million is held by Citibank. SSB made the loan two years ago when the market for railroad cars was at its peak and the collateral was worth $3 million. SSB thinks that within a year or two the market will come back and the cars will again have that value.

The debtor who owns the cars has filed for a Chapter 11 bankruptcy and proposes to sell the cars, free and clear of liens, for their current market value. If the cars are sold for $1 million, who will get what? Is there anything SSB can do to prevent the sale? Bankr. Code §§363(b), (f), and (k).

27.3. Toi San Development is the owner of an office complex currently under construction. Liens against the property total $5 million. The first is in favor of American Bank, the construction lender, in the amount of $4 million. The remainder are mechanic's liens filed by suppliers and subcontractors who have not been paid. If the complex is sold in its present state of completion, it will bring only about $2 million. The cost of completing it will be about $1.5 million. Even then, it will be worth only about $4 million, still less than the amount of the liens.

Although Toi San Development is not in bankruptcy, it is out of cash and in financial trouble. The office complex is its only significant asset. Wendy Toi San, the owner of Toi San Development, has asked for your help in borrowing the money necessary to finish the project. American is preparing papers for foreclosure and says there is no way the bank is putting another dime into this project. What are your ideas for getting financing to complete the construction? What legal obstacles will you face? Bankr. Code §§364, 506(a)(1).

27.4. Despite your attorney's advice to the contrary, you made the $100,000 loan to the friend described in Problem 26.4 and took a second mortgage against the house. Just as your attorney predicted, your friend defaulted on both mortgages and the first mortgage holder has filed for judicial foreclosure of its $800,000 mortgage loan. The house still appears to be worth as much as $1.2 million, but housing sales are slow and there are no buyers on the horizon. Even if there were, your friend is not yet ready to sell. You are not in bad shape financially, but as a first-year associate in a medium-size firm, there is no way you can raise $800,000 to pay off the first mortgage. What do you think will happen if the foreclosure sale is held? Where do you stand if your friend files for bankruptcy? Bankr. Code §§362(a) and (d)(1) and (2), 363(b) and (f), 506(a)(1).

27.5. With your new knowledge of bankruptcy priority, reconsider Problem 22.4.

Chapter 9.   Competitions for Collateral

Assignment 28:   Lien Creditors Against Secured Creditors: The Basics

In Assignment 16, we introduced a crude model of priority among liens. That model ranked liens chronologically in the order in which they were perfected. In Assignment 26, we refined the model by noting that the rules governing priority among the various kinds of liens are contained in diverse bodies of law. To list just a few, Congress determines the priority of tax liens, a complex superstructure of organizations controls the priority rules contained in the UCC, and state legislatures control priority among judicial liens. The courts are left to deal with the resulting inconsistencies. In this chapter, we examine these rules as they were written, one competition at a time.

Along the way, we will consider the effects of two circumstances that have spawned their own special rules of priority: future advances and purchase-money status. As to future advances, the principal issue is whether the priority date of a later advance should be the date of that advance or the date of the earlier transaction in which the future advance was contemplated. As to purchase-money status, the principal issue is what steps a later purchase-money lender must take to have priority over earlier competing liens. We will see that the rules governing future advances and purchase-money lending, like the rules governing priority generally, differ from one competition to another.

In this assignment, we discuss three competitions, all involving lien creditors. They are (1) lien creditor against lien creditor, (2) lien creditor against Article 9 secured party, and (3) lien creditor against real estate secured party.

A.   How Creditors Become "Lien Creditors"

The prototypical lien creditor is an unsecured creditor who won a judgment against the debtor, obtained a writ of execution, and then obtained a lien by levying on specific property of the debtor. UCC §9-102(a)(52) defines "lien creditor" somewhat more broadly as including any "creditor who has acquired a lien on the property involved by attachment, levy or the like."

As used in this definition, attachment is not the process described in UCC §9-203. It is a legal remedy in which the plaintiff in litigation obtains a writ and delivers it to a sheriff, marshal, or other law enforcement officer, who then levies on property of the debtor. In a few jurisdictions, "attachment" is virtually a synonym for "execution." But in most, the distinction between attachment and execution is that an attachment occurs before judgment is entered, while execution occurs afterward. As you might expect, property seized pursuant to

attachment is not immediately sold; it is held by the sheriff pending the outcome of the litigation.

Two other procedures by which an unsecured creditor may obtain lien
creditor status are worthy of mention. *Garnishment* is the process by which a
judgment creditor in most states reaches debts owing from a third party to
the debtor or property of the debtor that is in the hands of a third party. The
garnishing creditor becomes a lien creditor at the moment the writ of garnishment is served on the third party. In many jurisdictions, an unsecured creditor
can garnish before obtaining a judgment in certain kinds of cases, subject to
numerous statutory and constitutional restrictions. However, garnishment of
wages prior to judgment has been held unconstitutional. A few states prohibit
garnishment of wages even after judgment.

The second procedure worth mentioning is the recordation of a judgment
for money damages. In nearly all states, recordation of a money judgment in
the real property recording system creates and perfects a lien against all real
property owned by the debtor within the county. The judgment lien thus created will also reach any such property that the debtor later acquires while the
judgment lien remains perfected.

Also, in a growing minority of states, including both California and Florida, a
judgment creditor can record its judgment — or a notice of it — in the Uniform
Commercial Code filing system or a separate statewide system, and thereby create and perfect a lien against some kinds of personal property of the debtor. This
ability to perfect a judgment lien by filing is an alternative to perfection by levy.

Judgment Liens on Real and Personal Property

Cal. Civ. Proc. Code (2015)

§697.310

(a) Except as otherwise provided by statute, a judgment lien on real property
is created under this section by recording an abstract of a money judgment with
the county recorder.

§697.510

(a) A judgment lien on personal property described in Section 697.530 is created by filing a notice of judgment lien in the office of the Secretary of State pursuant to this article.

§697.530

(a) A judgment lien on personal property is a lien on all interests in the following personal property that are subject to enforcement [of a money judgment] at
the time when the lien is created if the personal property is, at that time, any of
the following:

(1)   Accounts receivable, and the judgment debtor is located in this state.

(2) Tangible chattel paper, as defined in [UCC §9-102(a)(79)], and the judgment debtor is located in this state.
(3) Equipment, located within this state.
(4) Farm products, located within this state.
(5) Inventory, located within this state.
(6) Negotiable documents of title, located within this state.

The filing officer indexes the notice of judgment lien thus filed in the same system with financing statements. A search of the Article 9 filing system will disclose the existence of the judgment.

Last, but certainly not least, a trustee in bankruptcy, including a debtor in possession under Chapter 11, has the rights of a hypothetical ideal lien creditor that obtained a lien on all property of the debtor at the instant the bankruptcy case was filed. The lien creditor is "ideal" from the trustee's point of view in that it has no debilitating history or knowledge. For example, even if none of the debtor's creditors could prevail over an unrecorded mortgage because they all knew about it, the debtor's trustee, as an ideal lien creditor, could still prevail over it. See Bankr. Code §544(a). The trustee's rights as an ideal lien creditor are the subject of a later assignment in this book. We alert you to their existence now, because they lend added significance to the subject of this assignment. It is essential to know the rights of a lien creditor in order to calculate the rights of a trustee in bankruptcy.

B. Priority Among Lien Creditors

The rules governing priority among competing lien creditors are generally found in state statutes. They set up a first-come, first-served system. That is, the first creditor to take the legally designated crucial step has the first lien, the second to take that step has the second lien, and so forth. The laws generally award a lien priority as of one of four dates; we list them roughly in their frequency of use with respect to personal property.

1. *Date of levy.* The reference here is to the date on which the sheriff or other officer took possession of particular property. Some states honor only actual physical possession by the sheriff; others consider various kinds of constructive or symbolic possession adequate. In the former jurisdictions, the sheriff actually hauls moveable property back to a warehouse maintained for the purpose of holding property subject to a lien. In the latter, it may be adequate for the sheriff to post a notice on or about the property stating that the property is in the sheriff's possession.
2. *Date of delivery of the writ.* A writ of execution, attachment, or garnishment typically is issued by the clerk of the court on the request of a

creditor who is entitled to it. The creditor then delivers the writ to the sheriff. In a minority of states, including Illinois, writs of execution rank in the order in which they are delivered to the sheriff with instructions for levy on the property in issue. The lien comes into existence only on levy and may then be said to "relate back" to the date of delivery to the sheriff. This means that if two executions are delivered to the sheriff but only one is levied, then only the one levied is a lien. If and when the other execution is levied, it will have priority as of the date the other execution was delivered to the sheriff.

3. *Date of service of a writ of garnishment.* Service is the delivery of the writ by the sheriff to the garnishee. The garnishee is typically a bank or an employer.

4. *Date of recordation of judgment.* The date will be the date the judgment is delivered to the filing or recording officer. (In the large majority of states, this recordation is in the real property records and creates liens only in real estate.)

In a competition between writs of execution, the majority rule gives priority to the first to levy on the particular property. For example, in California, "A levy on property under a writ of execution creates an execution lien on the property from the time of levy. . . ." Cal. Civ. Proc. Code §697.710 (2011). Recall that a *levy* occurs when the sheriff takes possession of property pursuant to a writ of execution or attachment.

C. Priority Between Lien Creditors and Secured Creditors

Priority between a lien creditor and a nonpurchase-money Article 9 secured creditor depends on whether the lien creditor "becomes a lien creditor" before the secured creditor does either of two things: (1) perfects its security interest or (2) files a financing statement and complies with UCC §9-203(b)(3).

Article 9 defines "perfection" in a highly technical manner. UCC §9-308(a). A security interest is perfected only after it has attached and the "applicable steps required for perfection" have been taken. If, for example, the step taken to perfect is to file a financing statement, perfection will occur at the time of attachment or of filing, whichever is later. The important thing to notice here is that filing and perfection are not the same thing; they may or may not occur simultaneously.

The lien creditor's priority date in this context is the date on which the lien creditor "becomes a lien creditor." UCC §9-317(a)(2). In states that follow the majority rule regarding priority among execution creditors, an execution creditor becomes a lien creditor at the time of the levy. In states that follow the minority rule, an argument can be made that the execution creditor becomes a lien creditor upon delivery of the writ to the sheriff. But in most of those states, there exists either a statute or dicta to the effect that even though priority dates from delivery of the writ, the lien comes into existence only upon levy.

In the case that follows, a bumbling prosecutor competes with a bumbling defense attorney for priority in the spoils of crime. As you read the case, you may want to make a list of their failed efforts at the simple task of obtaining and perfecting a lien. The case also serves as a reminder that secured transactions are pervasive in every area of law. Security is a principal means by which the legal system determines rights in property. Not even criminal lawyers can escape the need to know something about it.

People v. Green

22 Cal. Rptr. 3d 736 (Cal. App. 2004)

RICHLI, J., with RAMIREZ, P.J., and WARD, J., concurring.

Penal Code section 186.11 (section 186.11) is sometimes known as the "Freeze and Seize Law." It defines an "aggravated white collar crime enhancement." When such an enhancement applies, it allows the trial court, before trial, to enjoin the defendant from disposing of assets; it then allows the trial court, after trial, to levy on those assets to pay restitution to victims.

FACTUAL AND PROCEDURAL BACKGROUND

On July 6, 2000, sheriff's deputies executing a search warrant seized items from Douglas Green. These items included those at issue in this appeal: two cars, a motorhome, a boat and boat trailer, a jet ski and jet ski trailer, three all-terrain vehicles, a computer, various computer peripherals, a digital camera, a copier, a fax machine, four two-way radios, and $10,900 in cash. We will refer to these collectively as "the property."

On August 15, 2000, a complaint was filed charging Green with grand theft, burglary, and forgery. Green retained attorney Lawrence Buckley to defend him. When Buckley asked for a $25,000 retainer, Green told him "he did not have access to that much money because the Sheriff had taken all of his money and personal property." They therefore agreed that Buckley would have an attorney's lien against the seized property for $25,000.

Buckley filed a motion on Green's behalf for the return of any seized items that were not contraband or evidence. The People filed [an] opposition to the motion which stated, "Pursuant to Penal [C]ode section 186.11[, subdivision](e)(1), the Court is requested to preserve those items of value siezed [sic] pursuant to the search warrant." On August 3, 2001 at least with respect to the property involved in this appeal, the trial court denied Green's motion for the return of seized items.

On August 29, 2001, in exchange for legal services in this case and in certain civil cases, Green gave Buckley a promissory note for $80,000. He also signed a written security agreement, purporting to give Buckley a security interest in the property and its proceeds, to secure the note and any other present or future debts. Buckley filed a "Notice of Lien," asserting a lien on the property for $80,000 in attorney fees and costs.

On September 12, 2001, Buckley filed a UCC-1 financing statement listing the property and its proceeds. However, he was unable to perfect his security interest in the cash because the sheriff had possession of it. See [UCC §§9-312(b)(3), 9-313(a), (c), (f)]. Likewise, he was unable to perfect his security interest in the vehicles because the sheriff had possession of the title documents. See [UCC §9-311(a)(2)]; Veh. Code, §§6300-6303, 9919-9922.

On October 11, 2001, following a jury trial, Green was found guilty as charged; all enhancements were found true. On October 25, 2001, Green entered into a plea bargain, pursuant to which the jury verdict was vacated: Green pleaded no contest to two counts of forgery, one count of conspiracy, and one count of grand theft; he admitted the white collar enhancement with respect to the conspiracy count; and he was sentenced to seven years in prison. The trial court ordered Green to pay restitution to the victims as follows: $95,661.41 to MBNA America (MBNA), $93,330 to Washington Mutual, and $59,800 to Wells Fargo. As part of the plea bargain, Green agreed that the property could be sold and the proceeds could be used for restitution. [The sheriff sold the property.] The net proceeds of the auction were $33,426.95.

The People then filed a motion for a hearing concerning the disposition of the proceeds. The trial court found insufficient evidence that the property had been purchased with stolen funds: "[L]ogically, you would assume that given the business that Mr. Green did or the legitimate business he didn't do, most of his income must have come from these illegitimate businesses. But nobody has been in a position to go and trace all of these sources of money from which he secured the Seedoos [sic], the boats, the cars, and all that. And absent being able to do that, nobody is able to conclusively prove that all of these items came from the money that was stolen from the victims in these cases."

COMPLIANCE WITH PENAL CODE SECTION 186.11

The People plainly did not file a proper petition. The only kind of petition section 186.11 permits is a petition for "a temporary restraining order, preliminary injunction, the appointment of a receiver, or any other protective relief necessary to preserve the property or assets." §186.11(e)(2). Because the property had already been seized pursuant to the search warrant, the People felt there was no need to petition for protective relief.

The only property, however, that may be levied on pursuant to section 186.11 is property that is subject to a preliminary injunction. No petition, no preliminary injunction; no preliminary injunction, no levy.

THE VALIDITY OF BUCKLEY'S SECURITY INTEREST

This brings us to the People's contention that Buckley's security interest was not perfected. We discuss this contention solely as to the vehicles and the cash; as to all of the other property, it was perfected, by Buckley's UCC-1.

A restitution order is enforceable as a money judgment. Pen. Code, §§1202.4(i), 1214(b). Generally speaking, a judgment creditor can obtain an execution lien by levying on personal property of the judgment debtor. Code Civ. Proc., §697.710. Alternatively, with respect to a few specific kinds of personal property, a judgment creditor can obtain a judgment lien by filing a notice of lien with the Secretary of State. Code Civ. Proc., §§697.510, subd. (a), 697.530, subd. (a). Either type of lien has priority over an unperfected security interest. [UCC §9-317(a)(2).]

Under the Uniform Commercial Code, upon default, a secured party has the right to immediate possession of the collateral, including proceeds. [UCC §§9-607(a) (2), 9-609(a)(1), (b)(1), (b)(2).] A perfected security interest has priority over an unperfected security interest. [UCC §9-322(a)(2).] An unperfected security interest, however, is not null and void. Among other things, it has priority over an unsecured creditor's claim. [UCC §9-201(a).]

As far as we can tell from the record, none of the victims had levied on the property or filed a notice of judgment lien. Accordingly, when the trial court held a hearing to determine the disposition of the proceeds, the victims were still just unsecured creditors. They had no right to any particular property. Buckley, by contrast, had the immediate right to possession of the proceeds of the property, up to the amount he was owed; whatever that was, it exceeded the proceeds.

It follows that the trial court should have awarded all of the proceeds to Buckley.

People v. Green demonstrates the importance of procedure to the priority scheme. The People seized Green's assets and demanded that the court retain them for restitution purposes before Green granted a security interest to Buckley. But seizures and demands are not enough to create lien rights in unsecured creditors: The unsecured creditors must levy.

Both lawyers had numerous opportunities to win priority in *People v. Green*. Buckley won only because he bungled less. Who would have won if both lawyers had play the secured transaction game expertly? In a footnote to *People v. Green*, the court suggests Buckley:

> Section 186.11 gives the People no way to prevent the dissipation of assets before a complaint or indictment has been filed. Here, for example, by July 6, 2000, when the search warrant was executed, Green knew the police were on to him. On August 15, 2000, he retained Buckley and made his first attempt to apply the property to Buckley's legal fees. Yet it was not until February 26, 2001, when the People filed an amended complaint with aggravated white collar crime enhancements, that they were in a position to obtain injunctive relief.

In other words, if criminals give their lawyers Article 9 security interests before they are indicted and the lawyers file financing statements, the lawyers will come ahead of the victims. The scheme won't work if the collateral is shown to be the proceeds of crime, but that, as *People v. Green* illustrates, is a difficult showing to make.

People v. Green is unusual in that a lien creditor and a secured creditor took the steps to ensure their priority in a piece of collateral at about the same time. Most competitions for priority between lien creditors and secured creditors involve no race to the courthouse or the filing office and no close measurement of which party completed the necessary tasks first. Instead, most UCC §9-317(a)(2) cases will involve either a trustee in bankruptcy or a creditor who took the steps necessary to become a lien creditor against the property. (Recall that every bankruptcy filing immediately gives the trustee the rights of an ideal lien creditor that levied at the moment of the filing of the petition.) After becoming a lien creditor, that person asserts that an apparently prior secured creditor failed to properly perfect its interest. The claim is often based on a defect in the secured creditor's filing. The issue is not when the secured creditor perfected, but whether the secured creditor perfected at all.

▶ Half Assignment Ends

D.   Priority Between Lien Creditors and Mortgage Creditors

Priority between lien creditors and mortgage creditors is governed by real estate law. Real estate law generally gives priority to the first lien created, and then reverses the result only if the failure to perfect offends the state's recording statute. In most states, a judgment lien creditor against real property is not entitled to the benefit of the recording statute. The result is that a mortgage granted before the judgment creditor became a lien creditor by recording its judgment has priority over the judgment lien, even though the judgment lien was the first lien perfected.

E.   Purchase-Money Priority

As we mentioned previously, the fundamental principle underlying the system of priority among liens is that liens rank in the order in which they become public. Because the liens that will have priority are already public, one who contemplates taking a lien can evaluate the priority it will have before accepting it.

When a second-in-time interest takes precedence over an earlier interest, the cognoscenti describe the second secured creditor as "priming" the first. One of the most frequent events of priming occurs with *purchase-money security interests* (PMSIs), which may be granted and perfected long after the competing liens they prime. PMSIs are an exception to the fundamental principle of first in time is first in right, but the exception is not nearly so broad as it at first appears. In the context of competition between security interests and lien creditors the exception is brief and unlikely to cause difficulty for the holders of earlier interests. Under the rule stated in UCC §9-317(e), a PMSI can prime a lien creditor's interest only if the PMSI attaches to the collateral before the creditor obtains its lien against that collateral. If the PMSI attaches first, the holder of the PMSI has a 20-day grace period in which it can perfect and thereby defeat a lien that came into existence between the dates of attachment and perfection of the PMSI. That 20-day grace period runs from the debtor's receipt of delivery of the collateral. This means that if a debtor buys property on secured credit and the lien creditor levies on the property before the secured creditor perfects its interest, the lien creditor will prevail unless the secured creditor perfects its interest within 20 days of the time the debtor received delivery of the property. One effect is that a purchase-money secured creditor that went public later can defeat a lien creditor who went public up to 20 days earlier.

The reason for allowing a 20-day grace period is to facilitate sales of personal property on secured credit. The grace period makes it possible for the seller to give immediate delivery to the buyer, without first filing its financing statement. Absent the grace period, purchase-money secured sellers might feel the need to file before delivery. The result might be to delay sale transactions.

The benefits of the grace period do not come without cost to the system. Relation back of the PMSI might surprise and disappoint the lien creditor who levied on the debtor's new property after running a UCC search and finding it apparently free and clear. But the injury is likely to be relatively minor. Through its unsuccessful levy on the property, the lien creditor may have suffered additional expense and delay, but no lien creditor is likely to advance additional funds to the debtor on the basis of the deceptively clear title. Lien creditors who are concerned about the possibility of secret purchase-money liens might choose to delay their levies for 20 days after the debtor acquires new property to see if a PMSI shows up on the public record. But we don't think that happens often. Lien creditors are usually in a hurry to establish their priority. Probably most will levy and wait to see if a purchase-money secured party turns up later.

Problem Set 28

28.1. Melinda Hu is in financial difficulty. Her friend, Phyllis Goldman, decides to lend her $20,000, which is to be secured by scaffolding and construction equipment owned by Melinda and located in Melinda's construction yard. On March 7, Melinda signs a security agreement and promissory note, but Phyllis does not disburse the money. Phyllis files a financing statement that same day and orders a search. On March 10, the sheriff levies on the equipment pursuant to a writ of execution in favor of Star Plastering. On March 11 Phyllis receives from the filing officer the report of her expedited search showing Phyllis's interest to be the first filed against the equipment.

   a.   As matters now stand, is Phyllis perfected? UCC §§9-308(a), 9-203(b).

   b.   If Phyllis makes the $20,000 loan despite the levy, will she have priority over Star in the equipment? UCC §9-317(a).

28.2.   The local credit bureau reported today the entry of a judgment in the amount of $125,000 in favor of Sheng Electronics, an unsecured creditor of Conda Copper. Conda Copper also owes a $50,000 unsecured obligation to one of your clients, RFT Enterprises. Billy Williams, the owner of RFT, is concerned that by the entry of this judgment, Sheng will obtain priority in Conda's assets. "I have been patient with Conda, and they haven't," says Williams. "Why should my account be subordinated to theirs?" Can you think of a way that Williams could get priority over Sheng? UCC §§9-317(a) and 9-201(a).

28.3.   Your client, National Business Credit (National), specializes in asset-based lending to small businesses that are in financial distress. All of National's loans are nonpurchase-money loans secured by tangible personal property. All are made in a state with clear precedent that a creditor "becomes a lien creditor" only when the sheriff takes actual physical possession of the property levied on. Because many of its debtors are high-risk, National wants to make sure its procedures are perfect. Ned Williams, head of the loan department, explains the theory under which National operates: "First, we get our own financing statement on file. Then we search to make sure no one filed ahead of us and we check the collateral to make sure it's in the possession of the debtor. Typically, we disburse within two weeks of the time we file and within a few days after we receive the search report." Ned wonders if, aside from an error in the search or physical verification, "there's any way an execution creditor could come ahead of us." What do you tell him? UCC §§9-317(a)(2), 9-308(a). If there is a problem, what should he do about it?

▶ HALF ASSIGNMENT ENDS

28.4.   a.   On June 1, Debtor grants a real estate mortgage to *M*, who does not record. On June 2, *C* levies on the real estate. As between *M* and *C*, who has priority?

b.   Assume the facts are the same as in *a*, except that the collateral is personal property and Article 9 governs. As between *M* and *C*, who has priority? UCC §9-317(a).

28.5.   Bonnie Brezhnev, the owner of Bonnie's Boat World (BBW), calls to ask your advice. Earlier in the day, BBW sold a $70,000 Bayliner Boat to Edith Jones. BBW ran an "instant" credit check, which missed the fact that Edith's former husband, Orville, held an unrecorded judgment against her in the amount of $80,000 for unpaid alimony and child support. Edith paid $7,000 of the purchase price of the boat by check and signed a promissory note for the balance. Along with the note, she signed a security agreement in favor of BBW. Edith immediately took possession of the boat and the documents landed in the in-basket of BBW's bookkeeper for processing.

As a result of some good detective work, Orville and a sheriff's deputy were waiting a block away when Edith rolled out of BBW's yard with the boat in tow. Orville and the sheriff followed her to the marina. As soon as she stopped, the sheriff levied on the boat and took possession of it. Assume that the jurisdiction has no statute authorizing certificates of title for boats of this type.

a.   Is BBW perfected? If not, what must it do to perfect?

b.   Bonnie wants to know if you can get the boat back from the sheriff, and if so, how long that is going to take. What is your advice?

See The Grocers Supply Co. v. Intercity Investment Properties, Inc., in Assignment 26. See also UCC §§9-102(a)(23), 9-308(a), 9-309(1), 9-317(a) and (e), 9-609.

28.6.   a.   Bonnie Brezhnev calls back with some bad news and some good news. The bad news is that she checked the documents after her earlier conversation with you. The space for the signature on the security agreement is blank. The good news is that Edith is at this very moment sitting in Bonnie's office, willing to sign the security agreement if you say it is okay. "I'd rather you got the boat than that #\@$%&*," Edith tells Bonnie. What do you tell Bonnie? UCC §9-317(e).

b.   If Edith had her own lawyer, what advice would that lawyer give her? Is that a problem for you? Rule 4.3 of the Model Rules of Professional Conduct provides:

> In dealing on behalf of a client with a person who is not represented by counsel, a lawyer shall not state or imply that the lawyer is disinterested. When the lawyer knows or reasonably should know that the unrepresented person misunderstands the lawyer's role in the matter, the lawyer shall make reasonable efforts to correct the misunderstanding. The lawyer shall not give legal advice to an unrepresented person, other than the advice to secure counsel, if the lawyer knows or reasonably should know that the interests of such a person are or have a reasonable possibility of being in conflict with the interests of the client.

■ END OF DEFAULT PROBLEM SET

28.7.   You are a member of the UCC Drafting Committee. The committee is considering a proposal to incorporate provisions permitting judgment creditors to obtain liens by filing their judgments in the statewide UCC filing systems. The provisions are similar to California Civil Procedure Code §§697.310 and 697.530 set forth in section A. Do you think such provisions are in the public interest? Why or why not?

28.8.   Assume that the state in which National (Problem 28.3) operates adopts statutes identical to California Code of Civil Procedure §§697.510 and 697.530 (set forth in section A), but its law otherwise remains the same. Should National change its loan procedures? UCC §9-317(a)(2).

28.9.   Assume that the state in which National (Problem 28.3) operates adopts the rule in effect in some states that a judgment creditor's lien dates from the delivery of the writ of execution to the sheriff, but its law otherwise remains the same. Should National change its loan procedures? UCC §9-317(a)(2).

Assignment 29: Lien Creditors Against Secured Creditors: Future Advances

A. Priority of Future Advances: Personal Property

As we discussed in earlier assignments, secured creditors often continue to disburse money to their debtors after the initial loan transaction. For example, the secured party with an interest in the debtor's inventory and accounts receivable may advance additional funds each time the debtor acquires additional inventory or accounts. Similarly, the lender who finances construction of a building may make advances (referred to as *draws*) as the building reaches particular stages of completion.

Of course, most of the secured parties who make these advances would be unwilling to do so if the secured party's interest might be subordinate to a lien creditor who levied on the collateral before the secured party made the advance. Such a secured party theoretically could protect itself against that possibility by repeating its search for lien creditors before making each new advance and refusing to make the advance if one has intervened. That would, however, be expensive. Instead, UCC §9-323(b) gives future advances priority over the lien, provided the creditor making the advance does not have knowledge of the lien. The rule enables a secured creditor to conduct one search at the time it begins its lending relationship with the debtor and make future advances without fear of unknown lien creditors.

But the exception for future advances made without knowledge of the lien is not the only exception in UCC §9-323(b) in favor of secured parties who make future advances. The section provides two other exceptions. First, every secured advance made within 45 days after the lien's creation is entitled to priority over the lien, even if the secured creditor making the advance knows of the lien's existence. Second, every advance made "pursuant to commitment entered into without knowledge of the lien" is similarly protected. UCC §9-323(b)(2). Knowledge at the time of the advance, even if the advance is more than 45 days after the lien's creation, does not prevent the lender making the advance from having priority, provided the advance is made pursuant to a commitment made when the creditor did not have knowledge of the lien.

The reason for giving priority to advances made by the secured party with actual knowledge of the lien during the 45 days after its creation is technical. Comment 4 to UCC §9-323 makes a half-hearted attempt to explain. Only by giving unconditional priority over lien creditors to secured creditors' future advances made during the 45-day period could the drafters qualify those future advances for the maximum priority over IRS tax liens available under the Tax Lien Act, 26 U.S.C. §§6321 et seq. Keep in mind, however, that the provision enables secured creditors to prevail over lien creditors in these circumstances; it is not restricted to contests involving the IRS.

The exception in favor of advances made "pursuant to a commitment entered into without knowledge of the lien" is considerably more difficult to justify. The secured creditor who makes advances pursuant to commitment can do so knowing of the lien and secure in the knowledge that its security interest will prevail over the lien. To illustrate the justifications for the exception and give you the opportunity to evaluate the arguments, we present our discussion in the form of a debate between a bank and a lien creditor.

Bank: The same reasons that warrant a priority for advances we make without knowledge of the lien also warrant a priority for advances we *commit* to make without knowledge of the lien. The appropriate time to consider our state of knowledge is when we commit; at the time of the advance, we have no choice.

Lien Creditor: That is simply not true. Suffering a judgment lien is nearly always a default under the bank's security agreement, so once you know of a lien, you are not obligated to make further advances. Yet UCC §9-102(a)(69) defines "pursuant to commitment" such that these optional advances are pursuant to commitment. In nearly every instance where you make an advance "pursuant to commitment" with knowledge of the lien, you had the right to refuse to make it.

Bank: But for us to refuse to make advances pursuant to commitment because you became a lien creditor in the interim, we would have to know you did. Without the "pursuant to commitment" exception, we would have to search before making each advance.

Lien Creditor: Not so. You could lend without searching even if the "pursuant to commitment" exception did not exist. The "without knowledge" exception in UCC §9-323(b) would still protect you against liens you did not know about. The "pursuant to commitment" exception only comes into play when you know of the lien and make advances anyway.

Bank: But if we had to lend without knowledge to have priority, you could easily destroy our protection under the exception, merely by notifying us of your levy. We'd have to stop making future advances and the debtor's business would be history.

Lien Creditor: What's wrong with that?

Bank: Many of these businesses can be saved if we continue to make advances.

Lien Creditor: You're not the right ones to make that decision. You have priority in the debtor's assets for the amounts you already advanced. In most cases, you are going to get paid whether or not the debtor's business survives. It is more likely our money than yours that is at risk in the decision on whether to continue the business. We are the ones with the right incentives to decide whether the business should continue or not—but the law gives you the power to decide.

Bank: Who has the right incentives will vary from case to case. But we are the ones with the big money at stake. A lone tort creditor or supplier shouldn't be able to sabotage a multimillion dollar lending relationship.

Lien Creditor: If you can make discretionary advances against any property we lien and take it from us, how are we *ever* supposed to get paid?

Bank: Who said you were supposed to get paid?

B.   Priority of Nonadvances: Personal Property

Most security agreements provide that in the event of default, the debtor will pay the secured creditor's reasonable costs of collection, including attorneys fees. In complex transactions, the debtor often agrees to pay many other kinds of expenses that may be incurred by the secured creditor before or after default. The secured creditor does not advance these amounts to the debtor. Do these *nonadvances* qualify for priority over lien creditors under UCC §9-323(b)? In the following case, the court addresses that question.

Uni Imports, Inc. v. Exchange National Bank of Chicago

978 F.2d 984 (7th Cir. 1991)

CRABB, DISTRICT JUDGE.

FACTS

On August 12, 1987, Exchange National Bank and Aparacor, Inc. executed a document entitled "Security Agreement," which granted Exchange a security interest in Aparacor's assets at Exchange. On October 9, 1987, the two executed a note due April 30, 1988, which incorporated the security agreement and established a revolving line of credit of up to $7.2 million for Aparacor and related entities. After the note expired, Exchange continued to make advances of funds without an additional written agreement.

On November 18, 1988, UNI obtained a $66,000 judgment against Aparacor in the United States District Court for the Central District of California. UNI registered the judgment in the United States District Court for the Northern District of Illinois. On January 12, 1989, UNI tried to enforce the judgment against Aparacor's assets at Exchange by delivering a writ of execution to the United States Marshals Service. The marshals service served the writ on Exchange the following day, but Exchange refused to turn over any of Aparacor's assets, contending that it had priority status.

Exchange continued to advance money to Aparacor. By February 26, 1989 (45 days after Exchange had been served with the writ), the principal balance of Aparacor's loan had grown to approximately $2.8 million from a balance of approximately $780,000 as of January 12, 1989. Between February 26, 1989 and March 2, 1989, Exchange advanced an additional $274,000 to Aparacor. Between March 2 and May 31, 1989, Exchange made additional payments of over $2 million as follows:

Advances to Assignee	$ 636,595
Payment of Sales Commissions	419,080
Payment of Real Estate Taxes	728,753
Payment of Interest under modification Note to Mar. 2	27,056
Payment of Mechanics' Lien	2,200
Payment of Legal Fees	30,708
Letter of Credit Draws	277,716
Miscellaneous	19,326
TOTAL	$2,141,438

After March 2, 1989, Exchange credited to Aparacor's outstanding balance the following: credit collections from accounts receivable, $2,584,638.21; proceeds from the sale of real estate and equipment, $1,414,287.30; and proceeds from the application of a certificate of deposit, $51,203.00, for a total of $4,050,128.51.

On September 27, 1990, UNI petitioned the district court for turnover of Aparacor's assets in the possession of Exchange. The court granted the petition and this appeal followed. UNI's $66,000 judgment has not been satisfied. Aparacor still owes $938,553.78 to Exchange.

OPINION

When a person in need of money borrows a lump sum secured by specific collateral, such as real estate, the question of priorities between the lender and any subsequent person who obtains a judgment against the borrower is relatively straightforward: the judgment creditor's interest is subordinate to the lender's, so long as the lender has obtained and perfected a security interest in the borrower's realty before the lien attaches. This straightforward situation becomes complicated when the borrower wants a line of credit rather than a lump sum loan and when the collateral is a constantly changing one in the form of inventory or accounts receivables. Scholars and practitioners have debated whether the lender's security interest in the collateral attaches from the outset, that is, from the first advance under the line of credit (the "unitary" theory), or whether each advance gives rise to a new security interest, each of which arises no earlier than the time the creditor extends value (the "multiple" theory).

[UCC §9-323(b)] rests on the assumption that the multiple theory is operative for future advances, that is, each advance gives rise to a new security interest, which arises when the creditor extends value. See Dick Warner Cargo Handling Corp. v. Aetna Business Credit, 746 F.2d at 133:

> Sections [9-323(b) and (d)] generally accepted Coogan's conclusion that security interests relating to advances created subsequent to the intervention of a third party as lien creditor or purchaser should be subordinated to the interest of the third party.

Section [9-323(b)] applies to situations in which there is a "perfected" security interest in existence when the judgment lien attaches. (Perfection occurs when a debtor signs a security agreement containing a description of the collateral, value has been given and the debtor has rights in the collateral. [UCC §9-203(b)(2)].) Under [§9-323(b)], future advances are protected (1) in all cases for 45 days following attachment of the lien; (2) beyond 45 days if the secured party makes the advance without knowledge of the lien; and (3) beyond 45 days if the secured party is committed to make advances, provided the commitment was entered into without knowledge of the lien.

Left unanswered by the drafters of [§9-323(b)] was the question of the treatment of the other parts of a secured obligation such as interest and collection expenses. Were these different parts of the obligation subsumed by the term "advances" (and treated identically) or did they give rise to their own security interests and, if so, did those security interests arise when value was given or at the outset when the obligation was entered into? In the only case to address this issue, Dick Warner Cargo Handling Corp. v. Aetna Business Credit, 746 F.2d 126 (2d Cir. 1984), the Court of Appeals for the Second Circuit concluded that the separate parts of the obligation were not intended to be treated as advances. Although the court did not say so explicitly, in effect it treated such obligations as giving rise to their own security interests, at least some of which arose with the execution of the financing agreement.

In *Dick Warner*, [the secured party, Aetna Business Credit and its borrower, Best Banana, entered into a security agreement that obligated Best Banana to indemnify Aetna for various expenses that Aetna might have to incur in connection with the loan and to reimburse Aetna for its expenses in enforcing or protecting its security interest or its other rights in the transaction. Best Banana defaulted under the agreement, Dick Warner obtained an execution lien against the collateral, and then Aetna incurred expenses that Best Banana was obligated under the security agreement to reimburse].

The Second Circuit held that Aetna's interest in the [collateral] had priority over Dick Warner's lien, based on Best Banana's undertaking in the original financing agreement to reimburse Aetna for attorneys' fees and other expenses it might incur in defending against suits such as Dick Warner's. According to the court, the drafters of [§9-323(b)] did not intend to include such expenditures by the lender in the term "advances" because the lender's obligation to advance funds to the borrower differs from the lender's obligation for expenses in connection with the loan, such as attorneys' fees. Expenditures in the latter category

> do not constitute "advances" as that term is commonly used; in the ordinary meaning of language, "advances" are sums put at the disposal of the borrower—not expenditures made by the lender for his own benefit.

Id. at 130. The Second Circuit suggested use of the term "nonadvances" for the debtor's obligation to pay interest and indemnify the lender for various expenses it has incurred. The court held that a lender that perfects its security interest with respect to such obligations is entitled to protection against a subsequent lien creditor. In other words, the lender is entitled to priority reimbursement insofar as a prior-perfected security interest

> secures a nonadvance obligation relating to a transaction prior to the levy, like that of the debtor to pay interest or even to reimburse the creditor for attorneys' fees incurred reasonably and in good faith with respect to loans made prior to the imposition of the lien or otherwise protected by it.

Id. at 134. The court took the view that the drafters of [§9-323(b)] never intended to include nonadvance obligations under this section. Thus, although for the purpose of the section, advances were treated as multiple (giving rise to a new security interest with each new advance), the treatment of future "nonadvance" obligations was not affected by the new [§9-323(b)]. Such obligations retained their unitary character, relating back to the original agreement. They continued to have priority over a later judicial lien if they had been undertaken before the lien attached, even if they did not mature until after attachment. The court acknowledged that a straightforward reading of [§9-323(b)] would not support such an interpretation, but concluded that it was what the drafters must have meant and that any other result "would be so plainly unreasonable and inconsistent with commercial practice that such an interpretation must be avoided." *Dick Warner*, 746 F.2d at 134.

The result reached in *Dick Warner* is not wholly convincing. As a general rule, security interests under Article 9 do not arise until value is extended. The court does not explain satisfactorily why it should be different for "nonadvances." Although protecting nonadvances benefits revolving credit lenders and thus, presumably improves debtors' chances of obtaining such loans, it does so at the cost of squeezing out lien creditors. One can reasonably ask whether it is fair or commercially useful to strike the balance in favor of the financier. After all, the lender in these situations has a close and continuing relationship with the debtor, enabling him to supervise and control all of the debtor's transactions, whereas the judgment lien creditor may well be an involuntary creditor of the debtor. See Grant Gilmore, The Good Faith Purchase Idea and the Uniform Commercial Code: Confessions of a Repentant Draftsman, 15 Ga. L. Rev. 605, 627 (1981) ("The financing assignee, who serves a useful function in providing working-capital loans is not an ignorant stranger. He does not need to be insulated, as a matter of law, from the risks of the transactions in which [his borrowers] engage. Because he can investigate, supervise, and control, he should be encouraged to do so and penalized if he has not done so.") The drafters of the 1972 amendment noted this unfairness with respect to future advances:

> It seems unfair to make it possible for a debtor and secured party with knowledge of the judgment lien to squeeze out a judgment creditor who has successfully levied on a valuable equity subject to a security interest, by permitting later enlargement of the security interest, by an additional advance, unless that advance was committed in advance without such knowledge. [Footnote omitted.]

UCC §9-312 (1972) Reasons for 1972 Change. Ironically, the possibility of squeeze-out posed by future advances is less than for nonadvance value. Future advances have the positive value of enlarging the estate; reimbursing the secured creditor for nonadvance value only depletes the estate. In *Dick Warner*, for example, Best Banana was obligated to pay Aetna a $7500 minimum monthly charge. Aetna had no incentive and no apparent obligation to stop the running of the charge, other than the declining [value of the collateral].

Nonetheless, the *Dick Warner* result is endorsed by the Permanent Editorial Board for the Uniform Commercial Code. In light of [the Board's] commentary and the holding of the Second Circuit, we conclude that the Illinois courts would hold [nonadvances not to be advances for purposes of §9-323(b)]. This conclusion is not the end of the inquiry in this case, however. It remains to be determined just which non-advance payments and expenditures have priority under UNI's lien. Neither *Dick Warner* nor the Permanent Editorial Board's commentary can be read as giving priority to every expense claimed by a secured creditor, whenever incurred and for whatever purpose. [The court went on to distinguish nonadvances relating to advances made before the levy (which have the priority of the first advance) from nonadvances relating to advances made after the levy (which have only the priority of the future advance).]

Uni Imports gives the secured creditor's nonadvances—typically interest, attorneys fees, and expenses of collection accruing on the debt owing to the secured creditor—the priority of the advances to which they relate, unrestrained by UCC §9-323(b). The result is that after a levy, the prior secured debt continues to grow in amount, each day reducing a little of what the levying creditor will ultimately collect. The 45-day limit does not apply. Grant Gilmore's complaint was that the rule encourages secured creditors carelessly to leave their secured debts outstanding even after default—provided only that the collateral is worth more than the debt owing to the secured creditor. When secured creditors do that they themselves incur no risk, but their non-advance accruals eventually eliminate any equity from which junior creditors might recover.

▶ Half Assignment Ends

C.   Priority of Future Advances and Nonadvances: Real Property

The law governing real estate transactions is even more tolerant of future advances made after a lien creditor perfects an interest in the collateral. In the following case, the Supreme Court of Mississippi holds that advances made on a home equity loan have priority over an earlier recorded judgment. A home equity loan is essentially a line of credit secured by a second mortgage in the debtor's home. Within the dollar limit of the line, the debtor-homeowner is permitted to take draws and make payments as the debtor-homeowner chooses. As the case demonstrates, the home equity lender is given priority over intervening interests such as recorded judgment liens, which enables the home equity lender to make future advances without searching for such interests. As the court points out, that rule is even more generous to home equity lenders than the UCC rule is to secured creditors.

Shutze v. Credithrift of America, Inc.

607 So. 2d 55 (Miss. 1992)

ROBERTSON, J.

II

In the early 1980s, Hobart W. Gentry, Jr., and Georgia C. Gentry owned Lot 53 of Rosewood Heights Subdivision to the City of Hattiesburg, Mississippi, commonly known by street number as the residence at 1105 North 34th Avenue. At all times relevant hereto, this property has been subject to the lien of a deed of trust, the beneficiary of which was Deposit Guaranty Mortgage Company and its predecessors in interest. The Deposit Guaranty lien was a conventional, residential first mortgage.

The first of today's combatants is Credithrift of America, Inc. On April 8, 1981, the Gentrys negotiated a second mortgage, home equity loan with Credithrift, borrowing the sum of $23,679.36. The Gentrys executed and delivered a second deed of trust conveying a security interest in the 34th Avenue property to Ben Hendrix, trustee for the benefit of Credithrift, and this deed of trust was duly recorded in the land records of Forrest County, Mississippi. Of considerable consequence, this deed of trust contains a future advance clause, in legal colloquia sometimes a "dragnet clause," which reads as follows:

> In addition to the indebtedness specifically mentioned above and any and all extensions or renewals of the same or any part thereof, this conveyance shall also cover such future and additional advances as may be made to the Grantor, or either of them, by the beneficiary.

The clause went on to provide that the conveyance in trust secured

> any and all debts, obligations, or liabilities, direct or contingent, of the grantor herein, or either of them, to the beneficiary, whether now existing or hereafter arising at any time before actual cancellation of this instrument on the public records of mortgages and deeds of trust, whether the same be evidenced by note, open account, overdraft, endorsement, guaranty or otherwise.

Nothing in any of the papers obligated Credithrift to make any future advances.

Enter Thomas E. Shutze, our other combatant. Shutze resides in Lamar County, Mississippi, and apparently had business dealings with the Gentrys, the nature of which is not disclosed in the record, nor is it important, except that on September 20, 1984, the County Court of Forrest County entered a judgment in favor of Shutze and against Hobart W. Gentry, Jr., in the original principal sum of $4,541.78. This judgment was duly enrolled in Forrest County on October 23, 1984, and its lien thereupon acquired the powers our law provides.

Re-enter Credithrift—eleven months later. By this time, the Gentrys had reduced their indebtedness to Credithrift to $11,215.13. On August 23, 1985, the Gentrys again refinanced—"renewed"—their loan with Credithrift and executed a new note in the principal sum of $14,150.26, repayable in installments at interest. The future advance—"the new money"—the Gentrys received was $2,784.13. Credithrift again regarded the renewal and advance as within the dragnet clause of the 1981 deed of trust which it in no way canceled or released, although it did take the precaution of a new deed of trust.

Over the next several years, the Gentrys struggled financially. It appears they made their payments to Credithrift through the Spring of 1988. At some point thereafter, they abandoned all and left for the West Coast and are believed in Reseda, California. Their creditors immediately resorted to the 34th Avenue residence to satisfy their respective debts.

No one questions that Deposit Guaranty Mortgage Company held a good, valid and perfected first lien and security interest by virtue of its 1978 deed of trust. Second mortgage holder Credithrift and judgment lien creditor Shutze, however, litigated below regarding their respective rights, and particularly the priority thereof with regard to Credithrift's future advance of $2,784.13 made after Shutze perfected his judgment lien.

IV

A

Shutze concedes the 1981 deed of trust established Credithrift's priority the moment it was recorded, regarding of like priority the 1983 renewal and refinancing and any other indebtedness within the dragnet's reach, up until October of 1984. Shutze's point is that on October 23, 1984, he enrolled his judgment to the tune of some $4,541.78 plus interest and that, from and after that date, he held by law a lien on all of Gentry's property in the county. He argues further that his judgment lien is entitled to priority as of the date of enrollment, and in this he is correct. Credithrift does not dispute this. Indeed, our question is not which lien came first. All admit that the lien of Credithrift's April 8, 1981, deed of trust has priority over Shutze's October 23, 1984, judgment lien.

The more difficult question concerns the 1985 future advance of $2,784.13. Witczinski v. Everman, 541 Miss. 841, 846 (1876), though decided a good while back, speaks perceptively to the point.

> A mortgage to secure future advances, which on its face gives information as to the extent and purpose of the contract, so that a purchaser or junior creditor may, by an inspection of the record, and by ordinary diligence and common prudence, ascertain

the extent of the encumbrance, will prevail over the supervening claim of such purchaser or creditor as to all advances made by the mortgagee within the terms of such mortgage, whether made *before or after* the claim of such purchaser or creditor arose. [Emphasis supplied.]

The *Witczinski* future advance clause was far less elaborate than Credithrift's but was nevertheless held "enough to show a contract that is to stand as a security for such indebtedness as may arise from future dealings between the parties," by reason of which the Court held it "sufficient to put a purchaser or encumbrancer on inquiry." *Witczinski*, 51 Miss. at 846.

[F]or priority purposes, the lien securing the future advance takes its date from the recording of the original deed of trust and by operation of law reaches forward to secure the advance made after intervening rights became perfected. The reason we permit this is the same we found in *Witczinski* almost 120 years ago. Third parties dealing with the debtor Thomas E. Shutze in today's case are given notice by the public record that the recorded lien secures any future advances. Those third parties are charged at their peril to inquire of the debtor and prior secured creditors. The device of a subordination agreement or notice to terminate may be available but, failing some legally effective contract or notice rearranging rank, third parties cannot be heard to complain when the original secured creditor's future advances are accorded the priority its publicly recorded instrument imports.

Nothing said here turns on the fact that in 1985, at the time of its last advance to the Gentrys, Credithrift had no actual knowledge of Shutze's judgment nor the lien thereof. We quite agree with the point Shutze stresses on appeal, that the Circuit Court erred when it held Credithrift prevailed by reason of its lack of actual knowledge. Shutze's enrolled judgment became notice to the world from and after October 23, 1984, and the fact that Credithrift did not know of it in no way affects Shutze's rights. Where Shutze fails is in his inability to see that Credithrift's lien was perfected three-and-a-half years prior to his judgment lien and, by reason of the dragnet clause, Credithrift's lien reaches forward and secures the 1985 renewal and advance. Credithrift's dragnet clause had been a matter of public record since 1981, and under *Witczinski* and progeny would-be creditors such as Shutze were charged with knowledge thereof and with a duty of diligent inquiry regarding further details, before doing business with Gentry whether on open account or otherwise.

All of this makes perfectly good sense in today's world. Our citizens and their secured creditors need the flexibility dragnet clauses provide. The demands of our agricultural credit economy are as great as in the days of *Witczinski*. Draws on construction loans and disbursements under lines of credit are other common examples of future advances businessmen need and secured lenders make. Second mortgage home equity loans are a more recent area of need. Many Mississippians need to borrow substantial sums with which to educate their offspring and to borrow by the semester as tuition payments become due. They and their lenders need the security of the knowledge that their priority position will remain fixed to the date of the original deed of trust or security agreement, so that they can save "time, travel, loan closing costs, costs of extra legal services, recording fees, et cetera," as in Newton County Bank v. Jones, 299 So. 2d at 218. There is no reason our law should demand new title searches incident to each advance. Any other view could imperil the student's education in mid-stream. The same may be said for opportunities our citizens pursue in many other areas of social and economic life. The public records system each county maintains affords third parties full opportunity for knowledge which, if pursued with diligence, protects such third parties from being blind-sided. And because they will know we mean what we say, creditors do not have to record a new deed of trust every time a future advance is made which, if nothing else, avoids cluttering up the land records.

B

There is another dimension. The Uniform Commercial Code as originally enacted in Mississippi treated the priority of liens securing future advances the same as our cases noted above. Effective July 1, 1986, we amended our law to limit the lien's priority (though not its enforceability) to future advances made within forty-five days of perfection of an intervening lien or without actual knowledge of the new lien. [UCC §9-323(b)]. This enactment does not directly reach real estate secured transactions. [UCC §§9-109(a) and 9-109(d)(11)]. It does, however, pronounce the public policy in an area on its face indistinguishable in principle from real estate secured transactions. Dragnet clauses legally identical to Credithrift's abound in personal property security agreements across this state. We perceive no good reason why this legal language should have one meaning and effect where the security is personalty and an altogether different meaning and effect where the security is realty. We sharpen the point when we see dragnet clauses in mixed security agreements, where the collateral is a combination of real and personal property and a single dragnet clause says all collateral stands to secure all future advances.

If we imported [UCC §9-323(b)] into our law of real estate secured transactions, we would cut back the reach of the dragnet clause. We need not take that step today, for Credithrift prevails even under the UCC. The Chancery Court found as a fact that, at the time of its 1985 refinancing and advance, Credithrift "had no actual notice of [Shutze's] judgment." The point for the moment is, given the findings of fact, Credithrift prevails even under amended [UCC §9-323(b)] if we enforced it by analogy.

———————

Obtaining a judicial lien against personal property is generally a more intrusive process than obtaining one against real property. The usual means of obtaining a judicial lien against personal property is for the sheriff to take possession of the property by levy. Both the debtor and the lien creditor are likely to know that the lien has been created and there is a good chance the secured creditor will find out as well. The usual means of obtaining a judicial lien against real estate is for the creditor to record its judgment in the real estate records. Unless the lien creditor thereafter conducts a search, it will not know whether its lien attached to any property of the debtor. While the debtor typically will know that the judgment was entered, it is unlikely to discover that the judgment was recorded until it tries to sell or borrow against the property. We do not see, however, why this difference in intrusiveness justifies real property law affording greater protection to prior mortgagees than the personal property system provides to prior secured creditors.

Even with regard to real property, not all jurisdictions follow the *Shutze* view. The *Shutze* court gave Credithrift's future advance priority over the earlier judgment, even though Credithrift was not obligated to make it. Surely that court would reach the same result with regard to a future advance the mortgagee was obligated to make. Other jurisdictions refuse priority to such *optional* advances made by the mortgagee with knowledge of a subsequent lien, but give priority to *obligatory* advances. This distinction between "optional" and "obligatory" advances is similar to the UCC distinction between advances made "pursuant to commitment" and those that are not.

Problem Set 29

29.1. A year ago, Carol Dearing lent $1,000 to her friend, Bob Muzzetti. Bob gave her a security interest in his 32-foot Bayliner boat (worth about $32,000), and saw that her financing statement was duly filed. Business Credit Associates (BCA) recently recovered a judgment against Muzzetti in the amount of $45,000. Yesterday, March 1, they levied on the boat. It now sits in the sheriff's compound, behind an eight-foot cyclone fence that is topped with concertina wire.

Now Bob is back to ask another favor of Carol. What Bob wants is an additional advance of $31,000. Bob's lawyer, John Sung, says that the advance will protect the boat from judicial sale. "Even if they go through with the sale, they won't get anything," he says. Carol, who has been your client for years, asks whether this will work. Consider these issues:

a. If Carol doesn't make the requested advance, what is likely to happen and how do BCA, Bob, and Carol come out?

b. If Carol makes this advance, will the advance be secured? UCC §§9-203(b)(3)(A), 9-204(c).

c. If Carol makes this advance and the sale is later held, how do BCA, Bob, and Carol come out? UCC §§9-201(a), 9-323(b).

29.2. Assume that instead of representing Carol Dearing, you represent BCA in its attempt to collect the $45,000 judgment. You assess the value of the boat at $32,000. The sheriff's sale is set for March 29, just a few days from now. In preparation for bidding at the sale, you conducted a UCC search and discovered Carol Dearing's financing statement. Because you believe that a deficiency judgment against Muzzetti may be collectible, you don't want to bid higher than the value of Muzzetti's equity in the boat. But to know how much that is you need to know the amount secured by Dearing's interest.

When you called Dearing, she said she would have to consult her attorney before giving you that information. Although she said she would call you back, you have not heard from her.

a. How do you plan to get the information? UCC §9-210.

b. If you can't get the information, what will be your bidding strategy at the sale? UCC §§9-323(b) and (d).

c. Can a court help you with this problem? UCC §9-625(a).

▶ Half Assignment Ends

29.3. Mortgagor borrows $50,000 from Mortgagee, and executes a note and mortgage that state that future advances up to an additional $25,000 may be made by Mortgagee in the future. However, Mortgagee has no obligation to make such advances. The mortgage also states that it secures interest at 10 percent per annum and Mortgagee's attorneys fees in any collection action. Thereafter *J* obtains a judgment for $100,000 against Mortgagor and properly records it so as to impose a lien on Mortgagor's real estate. Mortgagee has actual knowledge of this lien. Then Mortgagee lends and Mortgagor accepts an additional $25,000 advance. Mortgagor defaults on the loan, owing the full balance and $10,000 in interest. After default, Mortgagee incurs $5,000 of attorneys fees that are recoverable against Mortgagor under the terms of the mortgage. As between Mortgagee and *J*, who has priority in the real property?

29.4. Debtor borrows $50,000 from Secured Party and executes a note and security agreement that state that future advances up to an additional $25,000 may be made by Secured Party in the future. However, Secured Party has no obligation to make such advances. The security agreement also states that it secures interest at 10 percent per annum and Secured Party's attorneys fees in any collection action. Secured party perfects. Thereafter, *J* obtains a judgment for $100,000 against Debtor and becomes a lien creditor by levying on the collateral. Secured Party has actual knowledge of the lien. Sixty days after the levy, Secured Party lends and Debtor accepts an additional $25,000 advance. Debtor defaults on the loan, owing the full balance and $10,000 in interest. Secured Party incurs $5,000 of attorneys fees that are recoverable against Debtor under the terms of the security agreement. As between Secured Party and *J*, who has priority in the personal property? UCC §9-323(b).

29.5. You represent Sheng Electronics (from Problem 28.2). In preparing to levy, you ran a UCC search on Conda Copper, the judgment debtor. Your search turned up three financing statements filed a little over three months ago. Each names a different secured party and describes the collateral as "all of the assets of Conda Copper." From your discovery earlier in the case, you know that at the time of those filings Conda Copper was in such bad financial condition that you doubt anyone would have been stupid enough to lend them money unsecured.

a. What do you think is going on?

b. What should you do? UCC §§9-317(a) and 9-323(b). Uniform Voidable Transactions Act §§3(a), 4(a) and (5)(a).

Assignment 30: Trustees in Bankruptcy Against Secured Creditors: The Strong Arm Clause

Back in Assignment 7 we discussed the fact that security interests generally retain their priority when the debtor goes into bankruptcy. That is not true, however, as to *unperfected* security interests. Under Bankruptcy Code §544(a), sometimes referred to as the *strong arm clause*, a bankruptcy trustee or debtor in possession has the power to avoid most kinds of security interests that remain unperfected as of the time of filing of the bankruptcy case. If the trustee or debtor in possession avoids a security interest, the once-secured creditor loses the benefit of it and is thereafter treated as an unsecured creditor. Because perfection of a security interest is so likely to be challenged in bankruptcy, bankruptcy is often referred to as the acid test of the perfection of a security interest.

A. The Purpose of Bankruptcy Code §544(a)

Courts often attribute Bankruptcy Code §544(a) to a policy against *secret liens*. They see §544 as reinforcing the requirements of Article 9 that creditors give public notice of their security interests whenever feasible. The creditors can do that by filing notice of the security interest in an appropriate public record or by taking possession of tangible collateral. Generally speaking, if secured creditors have perfected their liens in the manner required by law prior to bankruptcy, the policy is considered satisfied. If secured creditors have not, their security interests are considered secret liens and the trustees or debtors in possession can sometimes avoid them.

Courts and commentators frequently speak of bankruptcy trustees as "policing" compliance with Article 9 perfection requirements. Trustees do so by inspecting security documents, checking the secured creditors' compliance with filing requirements, and bringing actions in bankruptcy court to avoid the security interests they discover are unperfected. Although we know of no empirical data on the point, most commentators assume that the large majority of legal attacks on the perfection of security interests are brought by bankruptcy trustees. Attacks by other secured creditors or buyers are far less common.

If the trustee is successful in avoiding a security interest, the interest is "preserved for the benefit of the estate." Bankr. Code §551. The trustee, in effect, steps into the shoes of the unperfected secured creditor and enforces the security interest for the benefit of the estate and, indirectly, the unsecured creditors.

B.   The Text of Bankruptcy Code §544(a)

If, instead of writing what they did, the drafters of Bankruptcy Code §544(a) had written that "the trustee can avoid unperfected security interests and liens," they would have accomplished essentially the same thing. Law students and lawyers alike would have been spared a great deal of suffering and anguish. Relating the complex language of Bankruptcy Code §544(a) to its simple effect is one of the most difficult tasks facing students of secured credit.

Probably the reason that the drafters did not simply authorize the avoidance of "unperfected security interests and liens" is that Bankruptcy Code §544(a) was intended to apply to a wide variety of statutory and judicial liens authorized under the laws of each of the 50 states. Not all of the statutes under which those liens arise use the word "perfection." And, as you have already seen, liens may be sufficiently "perfected" to prevail against one kind of competitor at a time when they are not sufficiently perfected to prevail against another. Simply authorizing the avoidance of unperfected security interests and liens would have left the courts with the job of interpreting hundreds of statutes to determine the moment of perfection in numerous scenarios against varieties of competitors. Instead, the drafters tried to speak with greater precision by establishing a standard for lien avoidance that the courts could apply without regard to the type of competing lien involved or the statutory language authorizing that competing lien.

The technique the drafters came up with was to invent three hypothetical persons who might compete with those holding less than perfect liens in debtors' property. They gave the trustee the right to step into the shoes of the one who would have the greatest rights against the particular competitor and defeat any liens that hypothetical person could defeat. Federal law determines the characteristics of the three hypothetical persons. Aside from the characteristics specified, the trustee has the freedom to imagine the characteristics of the most powerful creditor possible, the *ideal lien creditor*, and to assume the rights of a lien creditor with those characteristics. Courts with more literary flair than we can muster refer to such a creditor as "the ideal creditor, irreproachable and without notice, armed cap-a-pie with every right and power which is conferred by the law of the state upon its most favored creditor who has acquired a lien by legal or equitable proceedings." E.g., Havee v. Belk, 775 F.2d 1209 (4th Cir. 1985). Federal law leaves it to state law, however, to determine what rights these ideal lien creditors have against others. Because the outcomes of contests between the trustee as "ideal lien creditor" and competing creditors depend upon state law, those outcomes differ from state to state. The result is that the impact of §544(a) differs from state to state, and the bankruptcy courts must interpret hundreds of statutes to resolve disputes between hypothetical unsecured creditors and real secured creditors.

Bankruptcy Code §544(a) gives the trustee the power to avoid "any transfer" that could be avoided by one of the three hypothetical persons. The Bankruptcy Code §101 definition of "transfer" is broad enough to encompass the voluntary grant of a security interest or the involuntary suffering of a judicial or statutory lien. It also includes other kinds of transfers, but in this book we restrict our consideration to the trustee's ability to avoid grants of security interests and liens.

1.   The Judicial Lien Creditor of §544(a)(1)

Under Bankruptcy Code §544(a)(1), the trustee can step into the shoes of a hypothetical "creditor that extends credit to the debtor at the time of the commencement of the case, and that obtains, at such time and with respect to such credit, a judicial lien on all property on which a creditor on a simple contract could have obtained such a judicial lien." For a real creditor to have these characteristics is impossible. Even if a real creditor extended credit at the time of the commencement of the bankruptcy case, that creditor could not obtain a judicial lien at the same moment.

Why did the drafters choose this contortionist as their hypothetical lien creditor? They wanted to test perfection as of the filing of the bankruptcy case. Giving the hypothetical lien creditor its lien only as of the commencement of the bankruptcy case prevents the trustee from challenging a security interest for being unperfected at some earlier time. Allowing the hypothetical lien creditor to be other than a simple contract creditor would have created the same problem, because other kinds of creditors are sometimes accorded rights that relate back to some earlier time. The following South Carolina statute, for example, gives tort victims a lien that dates not from the date the tort victim becomes a lien creditor, but from the date of the accident.

Lien on Motor Vehicle for Damages

S.C. Code Ann. §29-15-20 (2015)

When a motor vehicle is operated in violation of the provisions of law or negligently, carelessly, recklessly, willfully or wantonly and any person receives personal injury or property is damaged thereby or a cause of action for wrongful death arises therefrom, damages recoverable therefor shall be and constitute a lien next in priority to the lien for State and county taxes upon such motor vehicle . . . and the person sustaining such damages . . . may attach such motor vehicle in the manner provided by law for attachments in this State. But this lien shall not exist if the motor vehicle was stolen by the breaking of a building under a secure lock or when the vehicle is securely locked.

If a bankruptcy trustee were permitted to imagine a creditor like the tort creditor in the statute and step into that creditor's shoes, the trustee could defeat virtually any competitor. The limitation that the hypothetical lien creditor must extend credit only at the time of the commencement of the case is also explained by examples such as this South Carolina tort creditor.

In cases where the interest under attack is a lien or security interest, the only characteristics of the hypothetical lien creditor that seem to make any difference are (1) that the hypothetical lien creditor obtains its rights through the exercise of judicial remedies such as execution, attachment, garnishment, levy, and the like, and (2) that the hypothetical lien creditor obtains its rights at the moment of the filing of the case. To describe the effect of §544(a)(1) another way, it is as though the trustee were a judgment creditor who exercised every remedy available to unsecured creditors under state law against all of the debtor's property at the moment of the filing of the bankruptcy case. The trustee will win any competition that such a judgment creditor would win under state law. What competitions would such a judgment creditor win under state law? When the competing claim is a security interest, the applicable state law will be UCC §§9-317(a)(2) and 9-323(b). Under it, ideal lien creditors defeat unperfected security interests for which no effective financing statement and security agreements exist, but lose to other security interests.

As an ideal lien creditor, the trustee is unburdened by knowledge that a party who actually dealt with the debtor might have. As the following case illustrates, treating the trustee as an ideal lien creditor means the trustee will win against a secured party with a defect in its documentation.

In re Duckworth

776 F.3d 453 (7th Cir. 2014)

HAMILTON, CIRCUIT JUDGE.

I. FACTUAL AND PROCEDURAL BACKGROUND

The parties filed cross-motions for summary judgment based on the following undisputed facts. On December 15, 2008, David L. Duckworth borrowed $1,100,000 from the State Bank of Toulon. The transaction was executed through a promissory note that was dated and signed on December 15 and an Agricultural Security Agreement dated two days earlier, December 13, 2008. The security agreement said that Duckworth granted the State Bank of Toulon a security interest in crops and farm equipment. The promissory note referred to the security agreement. The security agreement identified the debt to be secured, but the identification had a critical mistake. The security agreement said that it secured a note "in the principal amount of $_____ dated *December 13, 2008*." But there was no promissory note dated December 13. Both the December 15 promissory note and the security agreement were prepared by the bank's loan officer. In 2010, Duckworth filed a petition for bankruptcy protection under Chapter 7 of the bankruptcy code.

II. ANALYSIS

Illinois adopts the familiar principle that an unambiguous contract is interpreted by the court as a matter of law without use of parol evidence. The relevant provisions of the security agreement are unambiguous as applied to these facts. [T]he security agreement refers clearly to a December 13 promissory note that the parties agree never existed. The promissory note that the Bank seeks to secure was signed and dated on December 15.

To cure the mistaken date in the security agreement and connect it to the December 15 promissory note, the bank relies primarily on parol evidence, from outside the four corners of the document. The bank relies on the December 15 promissory note itself and testimony regarding the bank's and the borrower's intentions.

The testimony of both the bank officer who prepared the documents and borrower Duckworth makes clear that the bank made a mistake in preparing the security agreement. We are confident that the bank would have been able to obtain reformation—even of an unambiguous agreement—against the original borrower if he had tried to avoid the security agreement based on the mistaken date.

A bankruptcy trustee is in a different position, however. A bankruptcy trustee is tasked with maximizing the recovery of unsecured creditors. To assist in this task, trustees may exercise the so-called strong-arm power: the trustee is deemed to be in the privileged position of a hypothetical subsequent creditor and can avoid any interests that a hypothetical subsequent creditor could avoid "without regard to any knowledge of the trustee or of any creditor." See 11 U.S.C. §544(a). The strong-arm power is a "blunt information-generating tool" that encourages lenders to give public notice of their security interests by harshly penalizing those who fail to do so. Jonathan C. Lipson, *Secrets and Liens: The End of Notice in Commercial Finance Law,* 21 Emory Bankr. Dev. J. 421, 450-51 (2005).

The bank argues that constructive notice may still be imputed to a trustee using the strong-arm power. The concept of constructive notice comes from state real property law and defines the property rights of good faith purchasers. A good faith purchaser cannot avoid the claims of creditors who have complied with state recording laws that provide public notice of the ownership of and liens on property. For that reason, constructive notice constrains a trustee who seeks to use the specific strong-arm power of a good faith purchaser of property.

But the trustee here does not need to assume the role of a good faith purchaser to avoid the lender's interest. The trustee can use other strong-arm provisions and stand in the shoes of other subsequent creditors, to which the limitations of constructive notice do not apply. The trustee may avoid the bank's security interest by acting as a hypothetical judicial lien creditor. 11 U.S.C. §544(a)(1). Such a trustee, unconstrained by constructive notice, may "void a security interest because of defects that need not have misled, or even have been capable of misleading, anyone." *In re Vic Supply Co.,* 227 F.3d at 931.

We therefore must treat the trustee as if he were a hypothetical later lien creditor and ask if the bank has a valid security interest that could be asserted against such a creditor. We conclude that the bank's asserted security interest is not valid against such a later creditor. Such a creditor would be entitled to rely on the text of a security agreement, despite extrinsic evidence that could be used between the original parties to correct the mistaken identification of the debt to be secured.

In *Martin Grinding,* we held that parol evidence about the original parties' intentions could not be used to correct a mistake in a security agreement by adding,

agreement as meaning what it says, even if the original parties have made a mistake in expressing their intentions. The judgments of the district courts are REVERSED and the cases are REMANDED for proceedings consistent with this opinion.

The decision in *In re Duckworth* illustrates how unforgiving the secured credit system can be of errors in security interest documentation. The parties to the initial transaction agreed that the "December 15" obligation was the intended secured obligation. No "December 13" obligation existed. As an ideal lien creditor, the trustee was not charged with notice of the mistake and could avoid the bank's interest. This decision is in the context of the trustee's avoiding power. We wonder if the court would have applied the same strict standard in favor of a second secured creditor that made its loan without knowledge of the first secured creditor's error.

2.   The Creditor with an Execution Returned Unsatisfied

Under Bankruptcy Code §544(a)(2), the trustee can choose to step into the shoes of a hypothetical "creditor that extends credit to the debtor at the time of the commencement of the case, and obtains, at such time and with respect to such credit, an execution against the debtor that is returned unsatisfied at such time." The original purpose of this provision was to remedy a shortcoming in §544(a)(1). Under §544(a)(1) the trustee could not avoid some fraudulent transfers that occurred prior to bankruptcy. Only a creditor with an execution returned unsatisfied was eligible for the remedies that would reach the fraudulently transferred property in the hands of the third party. Because the subject of fraudulent transfers is beyond the scope of this book, so too are the details of §544(a)(2). But this provision is a reminder of the expansive sweep of the Bankruptcy Code.

3.   The Bona Fide Purchaser of Real Property

If the property in dispute is real property other than fixtures, the trustee can step into the shoes of a hypothetical bona fide purchaser who bought and paid for the property (that is, "perfected such transfer") at the time of the commencement of the bankruptcy case. The bona fide purchaser must, however, be one "against whom applicable law permits such transfer (the lien under attack) to be perfected." To put it another way, the trustee gets the rights of a bona fide purchaser only in circumstances where the competing transfer was capable of perfection. While the language used in Bankruptcy Code §544(a)(3) is as foggy as any in the Code, courts are fairly consistent in interpreting it. They allow the trustee to prevail only where (1) the competing creditor was supposed to do something to perfect its lien (that is, "applicable law . . . permits . . . perfect[ion]" against a later bona fide purchaser) and (2) the competing creditor failed to do it. If the competing creditor was supposed to perfect and did, the competing creditor prevails over the trustee because the competing creditor would prevail over a bona fide purchaser who bought the collateral after the competing creditor perfected.

Bankruptcy Code §544(a)(3) does not give the trustee the rights of a hypothetical bona fide purchaser in a fight over fixtures. With regard to fixtures, the trustee has only the lesser rights of a hypothetical judicial lien creditor.

In a case involving real estate, the trustee can use his or her rights as a hypothetical lien creditor or as a hypothetical bona fide purchaser. But, as the following case illustrates, the rights of a bona fide purchaser of real property are generally greater than those of a lien creditor.

Midlantic National Bank v. Bridge

18 F.3d 195 (3d Cir. 1994)

BECKER, CIRCUIT JUDGE.

I

The underlying facts are not in dispute. On March 31, 1987, the debtor, Frank Bridge, obtained a $260,000 mortgage loan from Midlantic National Bank (Midlantic) to finance the construction of improvements on his property at 94 South Main Street in Ocean Grove, Monmouth County, New Jersey. The mortgage was recorded on April 3, 1987, in the Monmouth County Clerk's Office. In 1988, Bridge and Midlantic agreed to refinance the loan and, on October 18, 1988, Bridge secured another mortgage on the Ocean Grove property for $260,000. Bridge used the proceeds from the note underlying this mortgage to discharge the debt from the original mortgage.

Throughout these transactions with Midlantic, Bridge was represented by counsel who also acted as the settlement agent for the October 18, 1988 transaction, and, as such, was required by Midlantic to record the new mortgage. Bridge's counsel subsequently certified that the mortgage had been sent for filing and was now the primary lien on the Ocean Grove property. Unbeknownst to Midlantic and Bridge, however, the October 18, 1988 mortgage was not recorded, although on July 13, 1990, the original mortgage was marked satisfied.

On August 15, 1990, Bridge filed a voluntary petition under Chapter 7 of the Bankruptcy Code in the Bankruptcy Court for the District of New Jersey. As of this time, the new mortgage was unrecorded and remained so until September 12, 1990, when Midlantic ultimately recorded it.

In December of 1991, Midlantic initiated an adversary proceeding in the bankruptcy court. Although it conceded that in view of the failure to record the mortgage, the New Jersey recording statute appeared to favor the trustee, see N.J.S.A. 46:22-1 (1989), Midlantic argued that it retained an equitable lien on the Ocean Grove property, which was superior to all other interests in the property because the doctrine of equitable subrogation operated to place it in the position of its discharged first mortgage.

III

A

On October 18, 1988, Bridge executed a written agreement that pledged the Ocean Grove property as security for the funds advanced to him by Midlantic in the refinancing transaction. While the resulting mortgage was unrecorded, it resulted in an equitable lien on the Ocean Grove property.

Accordingly, we now must examine whether the doctrine of equitable subrogation enables Midlantic's unrecorded equitable lien to trump the strong arm powers of the trustee.

B

Generally, when a creditor advances funds to a debtor to pay an existing debt and takes a new mortgage to secure the loan there is no subrogation because the new security manifests the creditor's intent to rely upon it, rather than upon the old security, which was discharged. Sometimes, however, a creditor's new security may prove to be defective due to fraud or some kind of mistake. In such cases, the doctrine of equitable subrogation can operate to subrogate the new creditor to the position of the lender whose lien was discharged and permits the new creditor to assert its right to priority against subsequent claimants.

New Jersey courts have implemented the doctrine in situations in which "a state of facts fraudulently concealed from the lender, or of which he was ignorant, impaired the lien of the new mortgage." [Home Owners' Loan Corp. v. Collins, 184 A. 621, 623 (N.J. Eq. 1936).] In such instances, New Jersey courts have permitted an equitable lienholder to defeat the intervening interests of lien creditors and levying execution creditors. Since the rights of transferees of real property are at issue in this case, however, we concern ourselves with the trustee's status as a hypothetical bona fide purchaser under §544(a)(3) and the interrelationship of the rights of such a bona fide purchaser and an equitable lienholder under New Jersey law.

Midlantic asserts that, according to the doctrine of equitable subrogation, the interest of an equitable lienholder is superior to the trustee's interest as a bona fide purchaser. Thus, Midlantic argues, it should be subrogated to the position of its first discharged mortgage on the Ocean Grove property and escape the trustee's strong arm powers under §544(a)(3).

Even in title disputes when parties have not sought equitable subrogation, the New Jersey courts have espoused [the holding in Gaskill v. Wales, 36 N.J. Eq. 527 (E&A 1883)] that a bona fide purchaser of real property for value without actual or constructive notice, takes title to the property free from unrecorded equitable liens.

C

. . . As a hypothetical bona fide purchaser, the trustee is deemed to have paid value for the Ocean Grove property and is deemed to have perfected (i.e., recorded) his interest as legal title holder in the subject property as of the date of the bankruptcy petition's filing. The trustee has the status of a hypothetical bona fide purchaser who is deemed to have searched the title of the Ocean Grove property as of the petition's filing. [The court then rejected precedent dealing with personal property as inapposite.]

The trustee here took title on August 15, 1990, at the time the bankruptcy petition was filed. The first mortgage was marked satisfied on July 13, 1990; but the second mortgage was not recorded until September 12, 1990, hence when the trustee took title, there was no recorded mortgage. The short of it is that, since a bona fide purchaser acquiring title under such circumstances would have taken clear of the mortgages, the trustee must also take clear of the mortgages. We therefore conclude that, under New Jersey law, the rights of the trustee, as a hypothetical bona fide purchaser of real property for value without notice, prevail over the rights of Midlantic, as the holder of an unrecorded equitable lien, and prevent the operation of equitable subrogation in this case.

The order of the district court will be affirmed.

Proposals have recently been made to extend the rights of the trustee in bankruptcy to those of a bona fide purchaser in all cases — whether the collateral is real estate or personalty. In most cases, the shift would not change the result. The trustee will beat the holder of an unperfected, unfiled security interest under either rule. But *Midlantic* demonstrates that the change would make a difference in at least some cases.

C. The Implementation of Bankruptcy Code §544(a)

Bankruptcy Code §544(a) makes certain transfers avoidable, but it does not *require* the trustee to avoid them. When a transfer is avoidable, the trustee has the discretion to avoid it or not, as may be in the interests of the estate. In Chapter 7 cases, the discretion is almost invariably exercised in favor of avoidance. In Chapter 11 cases, the debtor in possession usually wields the trustee's discretion with regard to avoidable transfers. Bankr. Code §1107(a). The debtor in possession often has reason not to avoid transfers that it could avoid. To understand the reasons for this difference, it is helpful to understand the different contexts in which trustees and debtors in possession operate.

1. Exercise of Bankruptcy Code §544(a) Discretion by Chapter 7 Trustees

As we mentioned in Assignment 6, Chapter 7 trustees are professional persons, usually lawyers, appointed by the U.S. trustee to administer the bankruptcy estates of strangers. They are paid for their work from the estate. Their claims for compensation are subordinate to the rights of secured creditors, equal in priority to other expenses of administration, and senior to virtually every other kind of claim. They are required to perform extensive duties in every case, Bankruptcy Code §704, but they are paid reasonable compensation only in cases where there are sufficient funds in the estate to pay them.

More than 99 percent of Chapter 7 cases are filed by the debtor. Most debtors have no nonexempt assets to begin with. Most others liquidate their own estates before filing, by paying creditors, granting security interests, or converting assets into property that will be exempt from the estate. In about 93 percent of all Chapter 7 cases, no assets are available for distribution to unsecured creditors. In those cases, the trustee receives $60 from the filing fee paid by the debtor. The trustee's attorneys fees go unpaid. See Bankr. Code §330(b).

If the trustee manages to avoid one or more security interests or liens against property of the debtor, that property becomes property of the estate. Bankr. Code §§541(a)(3) and (4). The proceeds of its sale are available to pay the expenses of administration, including the fees of the trustee for administering the estate. If the trustee cannot avoid some security interest or lien and the case is otherwise a no-asset case, the trustee gets only the $60.

The $60 trustee fee remains the same as it was in 1994, although inflation has eroded 50 percent of its value. In cases where the debtor has *in forma pauperis* status and therefore does not pay a filing fee, trustees do not even receive the $60. Also, the number of bankruptcy cases has been declining to their lowest per capita rate in 25 years, meaning fewer cases for each Chapter 7 trustee. To make a reasonable living and to pay staff and overhead, Chapter 7 trustees are increasingly reliant on the cases where they can find assets to administer. Lawyers use the phrase "eat what you kill" to describe one of the ways revenues can be divided among the lawyers in a firm; the system for compensating Chapter 7 trustees elevates the concept to an entirely new level.

In addition to the risk they take as trustees, trustees who are lawyers usually retain themselves to do the estate's legal work, including filing actions for avoidance. The avoiding actions represent additional legal work for the attorney-trustees, which they are delighted to have if they will be paid for it. In a large percentage of cases, it works out that the fees of the trustee and the attorney for the trustee will be paid only if they are successful in avoiding someone's security interest or lien. Working in this incentive system makes trustees particularly vociferous advocates. Their zeal often prompts the more genteel breed of lawyer who defends banks and finance companies in avoidance actions to refer to trustees as "junkyard dogs." The result of this compensation system is that in Chapter 7 cases, policing of the perfection requirements of Article 9 and other lien statutes is stringent. Trustees attack and avoid security interests on grounds that may appear to be technicalities to the uninitiated—a missing notary signature, a wrong date in the security agreement, a mistakenly filed termination statement, or a slight misspelling of the debtor's name in a financing statement.

If a secured creditor files a proof of claim in a bankruptcy case, the secured creditor must attach evidence of its security interest. The trustee is supposed to examine that evidence carefully and perhaps even conduct a search of the public records to verify that the financing statement was filed. If the secured creditor does not file a proof of claim, the trustee may nevertheless demand that the secured creditor informally furnish proof of the validity and perfection of the security interest. Either way, once the trustee has the documentation, the trustee may examine it for errors, such as a misspelled name or an incorrect place of filing that might render the lien unperfected and therefore vulnerable to avoidance. The trustee can bring an action under Bankruptcy Code §544(a) whether or not the secured creditor has filed a proof of claim in the Chapter 7 case. Under Bankruptcy Code §546(a), the trustee has up to two years from the time of his or her appointment in which to bring the action.

2.   Exercise of §544(a) Discretion by Chapter 11 Debtors in Possession

Trustees are rarely appointed in Chapter 11 cases. Ordinarily, the debtor serves as debtor in possession (DIP) and in that capacity exercises its discretion to bring or not bring avoiding actions. If a DIP is successful in avoiding a secured creditor's lien, the effect is to change that creditor's status from secured to unsecured. That, in turn, will generally reduce the formerly secured creditor's leverage in the negotiation of a plan. But even an unsecured creditor is entitled to absolute priority over shareholders. If, as is usually the case, the persons in control of the debtor are shareholders, they may have little to gain by avoiding the security interest. The secured creditor will have lost its priority over the other creditors, but the total amount of debt will remain the same and the shareholders will remain subordinate to all of it. Moreover, DIPs and their owner-managers often have reasons *not* to avoid transfers made by the debtor in the period prior to the bankruptcy filing. For example, the transfer of a security interest may be to the owner-managers themselves, to their friends or relatives, or to persons with whom they have ongoing business relationships. If, for example, the DIP voids the defectively perfected lien of a key supplier, the supplier may refuse to make sales in the future. That may increase the DIP's costs or disrupt its operations if the supplier is the only available source.

The DIP is a fiduciary and is bound to act in the interests of the estate. If the DIP abuses its discretion by failing to bring an avoiding action that clearly should be brought, some bankruptcy courts permit the unsecured creditor's committee to sue in place of the DIP. In extreme cases, failure to bring the avoiding action may be grounds for the appointment of a trustee.

About 70 percent of Chapter 11 cases eventually are converted to Chapter 7. When that occurs, a Chapter 7 trustee is appointed. As you might expect, the appointment of the Chapter 7 trustee often results in an abrupt change of policy toward the avoidance of unperfected security interests. So long as the conversion and appointment occur within two years of the commencement of the Chapter 11 case, a newly appointed Chapter 7 trustee will have sufficient opportunity to examine the secured creditors' documentation and file avoiding actions against secured parties who were not perfected at the time the Chapter 11 case was filed. Bankr. Code §546(a).

D.   Recognition of Grace Periods

Many of the state statutes that require public filing to perfect a lien also provide the creditor with a grace period within which to make the filing. If the creditor files within the grace period, it will have priority over anyone who becomes a lien creditor in the interim. An example is UCC §9-317(e), which gives the holder of a purchase-money security interest 20 days from the debtor's receipt of possession of the collateral in which to file. If the holder files within that time, it has priority over a lien creditor who becomes such between the time the security interest attaches and the time of filing. Another example of such a grace period is found in UCC §9-324(e), which governs the rights of the holder of a purchase-money security interest in collateral other than inventory against the holder of a competing security interest. A third example is a mechanic's lien law, which typically requires recording of a claim of lien within 90 days of the lien holder's completion of work. If the holder records in a timely fashion, the lien relates back to some earlier date, usually the date construction commenced on the job or the date the lien holder commenced construction on the job.

What happens when the debtor goes into bankruptcy during such a grace period and before the secured creditor has perfected? For example, assume that Sandra Smith buys a new car from Big Motors, grants Big Motors a security interest, signs the application for a certificate of title showing the lien to Big Motors, and takes the car home. Two days later, while the application is still sitting in a basket in Big Motors' offices and Big Motors therefore remains unperfected, Smith files bankruptcy. In these circumstances, Big Motors can still perfect by delivery of its application to the Department of Motor Vehicles within the ten-day grace period of UMVCTA §20(b). If it does so, Big Motors' rights will be superior to those of the trustee in bankruptcy.

This result flows from the combination of three provisions of the Bankruptcy Code: Bankruptcy Code §362(a)(4) automatically stays "any act to . . . perfect . . . any lien against property of the estate"; Bankruptcy Code §362(b)(3) creates an exception from the stay to permit perfection "to the extent that the trustee's rights and powers are subject to . . . perfection under section 546(b)"; Bankruptcy Code §546(b) makes "the rights and powers of a trustee . . . subject to any generally applicable law that permits perfection of an interest in property to be effective against an entity that acquires rights in such property before the date of perfection." UMVCTA §20(b) and UCC §9-317(e) both meet this test because they permit perfection of a security interest to be effective against a person who became a lien creditor before the date of perfection of the security interest.

Problem Set 30

30.1.   You are employed as attorney for the trustee in the Chapter 7 bankruptcy of Gargantuan Industries, Inc. Gargantuan filed under Chapter 11 of the Bankruptcy Code on April 15, and the case was converted to Chapter 7 on October 15. The trustee, a political appointee who is new to this kind of work, asks you which of the following she can avoid under Bankruptcy Code §544(a).

a.   Wyandotte State Bank financed Gargantuan's acquisition of new machinery about eight months prior to the bankruptcy filing. At the closing, one of the attorneys handed the signed financing statement to a paralegal and instructed her to "file it." The paralegal did—she put it in the "Wyandotte State Bank loan to Gargantuan Industries, Inc." file in the attorney's office. The bank's attorney discovered the error after Gargantuan filed its Chapter 11 case. The attorney filed the financing statement on April 22. Bankr. Code §§544(a), 301, 348(a), 362(a)(4) and (b)(3), 546(b); UCC §9-317(a)(2).

b.   Same facts as above, but the bank discovered its error and properly filed its financing statement on April 14, one day before Gargantuan filed under Chapter 11.

c.   Torgeson, a creditor secured by an interest in some front-loaders, listed the debtor as "Gargantuan Industries" on the financing statement, but omitted all of the information required by UCC §9-516(b)(5). As a result, the filing still shows up on a search under the correct name of the debtor, but it is impossible to tell that the filing is against Gargantuan Industries, Inc., rather than a business using Gargantuan Industries as a trade name. UCC §§9-338, 9-506(a), 9-520, and Comment 3 to §9-520.

d.   Glasco, Inc., a creditor secured by an interest in other equipment of Garguantuan, filed a financing statement five years prior to July 15. Glasco has not filed a continuation statement. UCC §§9-317(a)(2), 9-515(c), Comment 3 to UCC §9-515; and Bankr. Code §362(b)(3).

e.   Florida National Bank made a "secured" loan to Gargantuan about two years before the filing of the Chapter 11 case. Gargantuan signed a promissory note, a security agreement, and a financing statement, but the description of the collateral in the security agreement was left entirely blank. The trustee learned of that fact from a young attorney named Grace Washington who had been an associate with the firm that represented the bank. A partner in the firm instructed Grace to fill in the blank and "maintain client confidentiality." Instead, Grace resigned her position with the law firm that represented the bank and eventually told the trustee what had happened. ("I cannot tell a lie," she said later in her deposition.) On April 24, after Grace had resigned but before she spoke with the trustee, Benny Arnold, another young associate with the same firm, filled in the description of collateral with words identical to those on the filed financing statement. On the following day, both the bank and Gargantuan acknowledged in writing that the completion correctly expressed their original intention. UCC §§9-203(b), 9-308, 9-317(a)(2), and 9-323(b); Bankr. Code §§362(a)(4), 544(a). What happens to Grace and Benny? See Model Rules of Professional Conduct set forth in Problem 8.5, above.

f.   On April 6, nine days before it filed under Chapter 11, Gargantuan bought a new Lexus automobile for use by its executives. Gargantuan signed a security agreement in favor of Union Bank, which financed the purchase, but as of the time of filing of the petition, Union Bank's application for a certificate of title showing its lien was still sitting on someone's desk at the bank. As soon as Union Bank learned of the Chapter 11 filing on April 25, an employee of the bank hand-delivered the application to the Department of Motor Vehicles. Bankr. Code §§544(a), 362(a)(4) and (b)(3), 546(b); UCC §§9-317, 9-311(a) and (b); UMVCTA §20(b); Comment 8 to UCC §9-317. Did Union Bank's delivery of the application violate the automatic stay?

g.   On April 8, one week before Gargantuan filed its petition, the Yarn Shop, Inc. delivered its writ of execution to the sheriff along with instructions to levy on an automobile owned by Gargantuan. Two days after the filing of the Chapter 11 case, the sheriff, who was unaware of the filing, levied on the automobile and took possession of it. Bankr. Code §§362(b)(3), 544(a), 546(b); UCC §9-317; Assignment 28, Section B.

30.2.   A senior partner in your firm has asked you to review and comment on the firm's procedures for closing on sales of businesses. She describes one of the problems as follows:

> At the time of closing, we often receive all of the transfer documents and purchase price in trust for the parties. Once we have all of the documents and all of the money, we are authorized to record and disburse. The person entitled to the money usually wants it at the earliest possible moment. If that person is our client, we want to give it to them as soon as we can do so without unreasonable risk on our part. We never disburse until we have sent all financing statements and certificate of title applications to the appropriate offices, but in some cases we disburse before those documents are received by those offices. We don't always represent the lenders, but we always undertake to perfect their interests. Is our practice of early disbursement safe? In particular, what happens if we have already disbursed the proceeds of sale and the purchaser files bankruptcy before the documents are received and recorded by the filing offices?

What is your answer? Bankr. Code §§362(a)(4) and (b)(3), 544(a), and 546(b); UCC §§9-311 and 9-317; UMVCTA §20(b).

30.3.   You represent Optimistic Industries in its case under Chapter 11. The company's massive size is fueled by even more massive debts. The company has assets worth about $10 million. All of those assets are collateral for a secured debt of about $8 million which is owed to Optimistic's line-of-credit lender, Oriental State Bank. Optimistic also has unsecured debt of approximately $20 million. Oriental has indicated its opposition to any plan of reorganization and is attempting to withdraw from its relationship with the company. Other lenders are willing to come in, but none will extend $8 million in credit against a mere $10 million in assets.

Earlier today, you got your first break in the case. You discovered that the financing statement Oriental filed three years ago misspelled Optimistic's name in a manner that causes it not to show up in a search.

a.   What is the legal effect of this defect? Bankr. Code §544(a); UCC §§9-317(a)(2) and 9-506.

b.   To how much money is Oriental State Bank entitled under the Chapter 11 plan? Bankr. Code §1129(b)(2)(A).

c.   To how much money are the unsecured creditors entitled under the Chapter 11 plan? Bankr. Code §1129(b)(2)(B).

d.   To how much money are the shareholders entitled under the Chapter 11 plan? Bankr. Code §1129(b)(2)(C).

e. Assume Optimistic proposes the following plan of reorganization: Oriental State Bank's claim will be reduced to $5 million and will remain secured. The unsecured creditors will receive a second security interest for $2 million and will be entitled to an additional $2 million, for a total of $4 million. The shareholders will retain ownership of Optimistic, which is estimated to have a value of $1 million. Should Oriental accept this plan?

f. Should the unsecured creditors accept this plan?

■ END OF DEFAULT PROBLEM SET

30.4. The court in *Midlantic v. Bridge* rested its ruling on the greater protection given to a bona fide purchaser of real estate for value than to a judicial lien creditor. Thus, the case probably comes out differently if the property had been personal property rather than real property. Should the rule in Bankruptcy Code §544(a) be the same for real property and personal property? If so, what should the uniform rule be?

could spend that last evening granting security interests in all their assets to their favorite creditors, thereby depriving the remaining creditors of any recovery at all. Preference law permits the avoidance of such security interests.

B.   What Security Interests Can Be Avoided as Preferential?

1.   Generally

Bankruptcy Code §547(b) states which "transfers" can be avoided as preferences. To be avoidable, a transfer must satisfy each element of that subsection. Even if it does, it may nevertheless be excepted from avoidance by Bankruptcy Code §547(c). The elements of Bankruptcy Code §547(b) are the following:

a. §547(b). Transfer. Only a "transfer of an interest of the debtor in property" can be avoided as a preference under §547(b). Bankruptcy Code §101 sets forth a broad definition of "transfer." It includes "each mode, direct or indirect, absolute or conditional, voluntary or involuntary, of disposing of or parting with property or with an interest in property. . . ." The transfers that trustees most commonly seek to avoid are payments. But the creation and perfection of a security interest is clearly a transfer within the meaning of this section. In this assignment, we focus on the avoidance of security interests and leave the avoidance of other transfers, including payments, for the course on bankruptcy.

b. §547(b)(1), to or for the benefit of a creditor, and §547(b)(2), for or on account of an antecedent debt. The transfer must have been to a party who, at the time of receipt, was already a creditor. Bankr. Code §§547(b)(1) and (2). The principal effect of this limitation is to shelter from avoidance interests securing loans that were secured from the time they were made. To illustrate, Firstbank agrees to lend $100,000 to Debtor on a secured basis. Debtor executes a security agreement and financing statement. Firstbank files the financing statement and then makes the $100,000 advance. Debtor files bankruptcy the next day. The transfer of this security interest is not avoidable as a preference. It was not made "for or on account of an *antecedent* debt" because no debt was owing from Debtor to Firstbank until the transfer of the security interest was complete. Now suppose that Debtor's trustee in bankruptcy could prove that at the closing of this $100,000 loan, Firstbank's representative gave Debtor the check before Debtor signed the security agreement and financing statement and transferred the security interest to Firstbank. The existence of the debt preceded the existence of the security interest, making the transfer of the security interest arguably "for or on account of the [the $100,000] debt." Prior to 1979, trustees sometimes made arguments such as this. To silence these arguments, Congress enacted the exception in Bankruptcy Code §547(c)(1) that prohibits avoidance of a transfer that was intended to be a contemporaneous exchange for new value and that was in fact a substantially contemporaneous exchange.

c. §547(b)(3). Insolvency. If the debtor is solvent at the time of the transfer, the transfer is not avoidable as a preference. See Bankr. Code §547(b)(3). The rationale is that when a debtor is solvent, it has assets sufficient to satisfy all of its creditors. Paying or securing one creditor does not harm others because the debtor still has sufficient assets to pay or secure the others. If they choose to remain unsecured creditors, they choose to assume the risk that the debtor might no longer have sufficient assets when they finally try to collect—even if the insufficiency develops a few days or a few weeks later. This perfectly reasonable-sounding rationale does not look quite so good when you see the insolvency requirement in operation. Creditors whose debtors are hopelessly insolvent at bankruptcy claim those debtors were solvent a month or two earlier when the debtors granted the creditors' security interests. The debtors may actually have been insolvent, or the creditor may just be relying on the difficulty the debtors or their trustees will have in proving it. The facts underlying a debtor's solvency or insolvency are complex and often uniquely within the knowledge and control of the debtor. To protect the estate, Bankruptcy Code §547(f) arms the trustee trying to set aside the transaction with a presumption that the debtor was insolvent for 90 days before the filing. To retain an otherwise preferential security interest on the ground that the debtor gave it while solvent, the secured creditor must prove solvency.

d. §547(b)(4). The Preference Period. To be avoidable, the transfer must have occurred within the preference period. Bankr. Code §547(b)(4). Once again, the preference period is 90 days for transfers to most creditors and one year for transfers to insider creditors.

e. §547(b)(5). The Improvement Test. To be avoidable, the transfer must have improved the creditor's position. That means the transfer must have enabled the creditor who received it to recover more than the creditor would have if the debtor had been liquidated under Chapter 7 without making the transfer. The purpose of preference law is to achieve a pro rata distribution; if the transfer did not result in the creditor's getting more than its pro rata share, there is no reason to avoid it. Nearly any transfer of a security interest that meets the other requirements for avoidance will meet this one. Secured claims are paid in full up to the value of the collateral in bankruptcy and unsecured claims are rarely paid in full. The secured creditor who gets a security interest without paying new value for it almost certainly comes out ahead. If the debtor could be liquidated in the hypothetical Chapter 7 for enough to pay all creditors in full, the prebankruptcy transfer of a security interest to one creditor does not improve that creditor's position in the sense discussed here. But such a transfer would be from a solvent debtor and would be unavoidable as a preference for that reason alone.

2. When Does the "Transfer" of a Security Interest Occur?

The highly technical nature of preference law is nowhere more evident than on the issue of when the transfer of a security interest occurs. The precise time of the transfer is important for two reasons. First, the transfer can be avoided only if it occurs within the preference period. Second, both state law and example, the security interest would be within the safe harbor of §547(c)(5) and the trustee could not avoid any of it.

Because it is measuring aggregate changes in the value of the collateral and the amount of the debt rather than individual transactions, §547(c)(5) employs what is referred to as a *two-point test* of whether the receivables and inventory lender has improved its position. In re Ebbler, Furniture and Appliances, Inc., 804 F.2d 87 (7th Cir. 1986), gives a particularly succinct explanation of the two-point test:

> The first step in applying section 547(c)(5) is to determine the amount of the loan outstanding 90 days prior to filing and the "value" of the collateral on that day. The difference between these figures is then computed. Next, the same determinations are made as of the date of filing the petition. A comparison is made, and, if there is a reduction during the 90-day period of the amount by which the initially existing debt exceeded the security, then a preference for section 547(c)(5) purposes exists. The effect of 547(c)(5) is to make the security interest voidable [only] to the extent of the preference. Of course, if the creditor is fully secured 90 days before the filing of the petition, then that creditor will never be subject to a preference attack.

Id. at 89-90.

In this subsection, we have used the example of accounts and inventory financing. But the Bankruptcy Code definitions that determine the scope of the §547(c)(5) exception for "inventory and a receivable" are much broader than their UCC counterparts. Bankruptcy Code §547(a) defines "inventory" to include farm products and "receivable" to include instruments, chattel paper, and payment intangibles.

C. Strategic Implications of Preference Avoidance

When applied to debtors who are forced into bankruptcy with little warning, preference law probably has the effect its drafters intended. Creditors who were promoted from unsecured to secured status on the eve of bankruptcy are demoted to their former status. Debtors are discouraged from making such transfers because they won't stick.

Many debtors, however, are able to choose when they will file bankruptcy. These debtors can make the preferential transfers they wish, wait until the preference period expires, and then file. The reported cases are full of debtors who exercised this strategy. The transfers remain unavoidable because they were not within the preference period.

Savvy unsecured creditors usually can overcome this strategy. Because the transfer of a security interest is made only when it is perfected, the event that starts the preference period running is usually a public one. Unsecured creditors often monitor the public records for grants of security. When one appears, they demand an explanation of the debtor. If the debtor cannot or will not justify the transfer to their satisfaction, the unsecured creditors petition for involuntary bankruptcy before the preference period expires. The petition prevents the preference period from expiring and renders the transfer avoidable if the other elements of §547(b) are present.

Ironically, the unsecured creditor that monitors, discovers the preferential transfer, files the involuntary petition, and thereby enables the trustee to avoid the transfer, receives only its pro rata share of the recovery after the expenses of the litigation (possibly including payment of the unsecured creditor's attorneys fees incurred in bringing the petition) have been paid. The watchdog gets no special reward.

As a result, the most sophisticated watchdogs don't bark. They approach the debtor privately, point out their ability to file an involuntary petition and thereby upset the transfer, and cut a deal. They may themselves get preferential treatment directly from the debtor (in which case another red flag might go on the public record) or the creditor that is already preferred may agree to share its bounty with them. In either event, preference law fails to accomplish its purpose. All it does is to shift wealth from the less sophisticated to the more sophisticated players.

Even if the debtor is in bankruptcy, the mere fact that a transfer is avoidable as a preference does not ensure that it will be avoided. Bankruptcy Code §547(b) says that the trustee *may* avoid the transfer, not that the trustee *must*. In a Chapter 7 case, the trustee will be a disinterested member of the panel of trustees, a lawyer or member of another profession, who makes his or her living from administering the estates of strangers. For these trustees, preference avoidance is a major source of income and expense money. Most of these trustees are like hungry pit bulls. They are likely to avoid whatever prepetition transfers they can.

In a Chapter 11 case, the debtor in possession administers the estate and, at least initially, exercises the discretion to avoid or not avoid avoidable preferences. The debtor in possession is unlikely to avoid a preference, often for the same reason the debtor made the preference in the first place. The transferee may be a friend, a business associate, or a supplier whose cooperation is necessary to the continued operation of the business. Even if the transferee is a person with no other leverage against the debtor, the debtor may strike an agreement, express or implied, by which the transfer remains undisturbed and the transferee votes in favor of the debtor's plan.

When debtors in possession have abused their discretion by refusing to avoid preferences, unsecured creditors' committees have sometimes sought to exercise the discretion themselves. They have petitioned the bankruptcy court to allow them to bring the preference avoidance action that the debtor will not. Particularly in egregious circumstances, the bankruptcy courts have tended to allow creditors' committees to bring these preference avoidance actions in the name of the estate.

Problem Set 31

31.1.   As the newest associate at a glamorous, big-city bankruptcy firm, you have been assigned the Wooden Industries bankruptcy. Wooden filed under

Assignment 32: Secured Creditors Against Secured Creditors: The Basics

In this assignment we examine the rules governing priority among Article 9 security interests. These rules appear in UCC §9-322. As we discuss them, keep in mind that they do not apply to competitions between Article 9 security interests and other kinds of liens (except agricultural liens). If the competitor is a lien creditor, UCC §9-317(a) applies. If the competitor is a real estate mortgagee, UCC §9-334 applies. If the competitor is a federal tax lien, the Federal Tax Lien Act applies. These are just a few examples. Because the rules governing priority among different kinds of liens are spread among so many bodies of law, priority is a subject that must be learned one competition at a time.

A. Nonpurchase-Money Security Interests

1. *The Basic Rule: First to File or Perfect*

The basic rule governing priority among security interests is in UCC §9-322(a)(1). Between the holders of two security interests in the same collateral, the first to file or perfect has priority. In other words, the priority date of a security interest is the earlier of the dates on which the secured party filed with respect to the interest or perfected it. As between two security interests, the one with the earlier priority date has priority. The holder who gains priority by first filing or perfecting retains it so long as the holder remains continuously filed or perfected. UCC §9-322(a)(1).

To illustrate the basic rule, assume that on December 1, Bank1 files a financing statement against collateral the debtor already owns, but neither lends money nor enters into a security agreement with the debtor. So far, Bank1 is not even a creditor, let alone a perfected secured creditor. On December 5, Bank2 files a financing statement against the same collateral and perfects by entering into a security agreement with the debtor and lending money. On December 10, Bank1 perfects by entering into a security agreement with the debtor and lending money. Bank1 has priority, because Bank1 filed *or* perfected (it filed on December 1) before Bank2 filed or perfected (it filed and perfected on December 5).

The explanation for this complex rule is itself complex, and not entirely satisfactory. The drafters sought by this rule to "[protect] the filing system." The concept is explained in Comment 4 to UCC §9-322. Given the rule, a secured party can file a financing statement before either lending or agreeing to lend,

UCC §9-502(d), search the filing system at its leisure (or perhaps, more to the point, at the leisure of the filing officer) to make sure its financing statement is the first on file, and then lend without worrying that a competing secured party might have perfected since the filing.

The trouble with this explanation is that it justifies a "first to file" rule rather than the "first to file or perfect" rule of UCC §9-322(a)(1). The reference to "perfection" was probably added to deal with the situation in which one of the competitors perfected without filing — that is, automatically or by taking possession. In all probability, the drafters acted without malice in adopting the "first to file or perfect" language — they just wanted to cover all cases with a single pronouncement.

To illustrate the operation of the rule, assume that US Bank and Trust (USBT) contemplates lending against assets already owned by, and in the possession of, Davis Industries. USBT files a financing statement on September 1. USBT waits for the Secretary of State to process all filings through September 1, which the Secretary of State manages to do by September 15. Knowing that its priority date against competing security interests will be the date of its September 1 filing, USBT also knows that any filing with priority over its own is now in the index and discoverable. USBT orders its search for filings against Davis Industries. The search report it receives on September 22 shows its filing to be the only one on record against Davis as of the effective date of the search, September 1.

Because the rule is first to file or *perfect*, USBT must also view the collateral to make sure it is not in the possession of the holder of a competing security interest. The ideal time to conduct this inspection would be at the moment USBT files on September 1. That inspection would ensure absolutely that no competing secured party had priority over USBT by virtue of filing or perfection by possession.

If USBT conducts the visual inspection on September 7, there is the possibility that the competing creditor was perfected by possession until September 6 and relinquished possession on that day only after filing a financing statement. The competing creditor would be continuously perfected, UCC §9-308(c), but its financing statement would not show up on USBT's search because the search would only cover the period through September 1. Neither secured creditors nor their lawyers are likely to lose much sleep over such a possibility — unless a *very* large amount of money is at issue.

Notice that UCC §9-322(a) assigns priority without reference to either creditor's state of mind. The drafters intend that the first to file or perfect have priority even if the first knows that the debtor intended that another creditor have priority and even if the first believed itself to be subordinate at the time it filed or perfected. White and Summers explain:

> One justification for the rule is certainty. Under [§]9-322, no disappointed secured creditor can assert trumped up (or true) facts from which a compassionate court might find sufficient knowledge to subordinate the winner of the race. If the competitor filed first or perfected first, as the case may be, that is the end of it; that party wins even if aware of the other party's prior but unperfected claim.

James J. White & Robert S. Summers, Uniform Commercial Code §24-3 (6th ed. 2010).

UCC §9-325 sets forth an important exception to the rule of first to file or perfect. That section subordinates security interests perfected against a transferee to those perfected against the transferor. To illustrate, assume that Firstbank takes a security interest against all equipment of DebtorTee, including after-acquired property, and perfects by filing a financing statement on March 1. On April 1, Secondbank takes a security interest in all of the assets of DebtorTor and perfects by filing a financing statement. On May 1, DebtorTor sells an item of equipment — an automated chicken scratcher — to DebtorTee. Because Secondbank did not authorize the sale free and clear of its security interest, the interest continues to encumber the chicken scratcher in the hands of DebtorTee. Firstbank's security interest attaches to the chicken scratcher pursuant to the after-acquired property clause. Firstbank is perfected in the chicken scratcher because its financing statement is sufficiently broad to cover it.

Which of the two banks has priority? Simply applying the rule of UCC §9-322(a)(1), it would seem that Firstbank has priority: It filed against the chicken scratcher before Secondbank did. But UCC §9-325 gives priority to Secondbank, because Secondbank perfected in the chicken scratcher before DebtorTor sold it to DebtorTee.

Even without UCC §9-325, someone who understood how the Article 9 system of priority functioned would have realized the necessity for the §9-325 exception. Security interests rank in order of perfection so that lenders can discover the security interests to which they will be subordinate. If a lender to DebtorTor could be subordinate to a security interest filed earlier against DebtorTee, that lender's search could not discover prior competing interests. The lender could not search for filings against DebtorTee because even DebtorTor may not yet have identified DebtorTee as a potential transferee.

2. Priority of Future Advances

In competitions between Article 9 secured creditors, the rule regarding future advances is essentially the rule you saw applied between a mortgage holder and a lien creditor in Shutze v. Credithrift of America in Assignment 29. Provided only that the secured creditor's financing statement "covers the collateral," all advances made by the secured creditor to the debtor have priority as of the filing of the financing statement. This rule is implicit in UCC §9-322(a)(1).

To illustrate, reconsider the scenario in which Bank1 files a financing statement against collateral owned by the debtor, Bank2 files and perfects in the same collateral, and Bank1 then perfects by taking a security interest in the collateral and making an advance against it. We concluded that Bank1's interest had priority over Bank2's interest because Bank1 was the first to file or perfect. If Bank1 later makes additional advances against the collateral, those advances will have the same priority as the first. They will have priority over Bank2's security interest.

The justification for this priority under Article 9 is the same given for the priority of future advances in real estate law. Bank1's filing put Bank2 on notice of the possible existence of a security interest that might secure future advances, so Bank2 should not be heard to complain if such advances are made. An important function of an Article 9 financing statement is to put searchers on notice of present and future interests that may prime the one they intend to take. So long as searchers understand the rule regarding priority of future advances, the financing statement will in fact convey notice to searchers. The understanding is that one who takes a second security interest agrees to take subject to the amount outstanding under the first filing and any future advances the holder of the first may later make.

This justification is less persuasive under Article 9 than under real estate law. Under real estate law, the future-advance clause must appear in the mortgage and the mortgage must be recorded. To gain actual notice of the possibility of future advances, one need only know how to search and how to read. Under Article 9, only the financing statement need be on the public record. Rarely will it mention the existence of the future-advance clause in the security agreement. In fact, the security agreement containing the future-advance clause need not yet be in existence. To realize the possibility of future advances under Article 9, one must know a little law as well as how to search and read.

An important function of the future-advance rule under Article 9 is to relieve the lender who will make future advances from the necessity to file and search in conjunction with each advance. The same is true in the real estate system. In both systems, once the lender achieves priority with regard to its security interest, it can make future advances secure in the knowledge that they will have that priority.

Who would take a second security interest in a system in which the first can increase without limit? The takers fall essentially into three categories: (1) lenders who do not understand the future-advance rule, (2) creditors who hope to benefit from their second interest but do not advance funds in reliance on it, and (3) lenders who protect themselves against future advances by contract with the holder of the first interest. UCC §9-339.

Subsection (a) of UCC §9-322 refers to the priority of a "security interest." Ironically, the security interest whose priority date is fixed by filing may not yet be in existence at the time. The filing has the effect of reserving priority for whatever security interest the debtor later grants in favor of the filer — limited, of course, by the description of collateral in the financing statement.

Can a single financing statement secure more than one such interest? To illustrate the problem, assume that the debtor gives the bank a security interest in the debtor's inventory of auto parts. The parties file a financing statement describing the type of collateral as "inventory" and the bank advances funds under the first promissory note and security agreement. Later, the debtor gives the bank a security interest in the debtor's inventory of automobiles and the bank advances funds under a second promissory note and security agreement. The parties do not file a second financing statement. On these facts, both advances have priority as of the filing of the financing statement. See UCC §§9-322(a) and 9-502(d). A single financing statement is adequate to perfect any number of security interests, to the limits of the description of collateral in the financing statement.

3.   Priority in After-Acquired Property

Recall from Assignment 9 that Article 9 permits the grant of a security interest in property the debtor does not yet own. The security agreement can describe the collateral to be acquired specifically ("John Deere tractor bearing serial number 5843F877Y99") or in general terms ("any inventory or equipment the debtor acquires in the future"). Debtors who grant security interests in after-acquired property often do not even contemplate acquiring any property of the kind described. If the debtor later acquires property that fits the description in the security agreement, the security interest attaches. UCC §9-203(b).

If the description of collateral is broad enough to cover the after-acquired property, the filing covers it. As against other Article 9 secured creditors of the debtor, the after-acquired lender's priority dates from the time of its filing. UCC §9-322(a)(1). To put it another way, a security interest has the same priority with respect to after-acquired property that it has with respect to the original collateral.

To illustrate, assume that Bank1 files a financing statement on April 1 against the equipment of Davis Industries and Bank2 files such a financing statement on April 5. On April 11, Davis Industries signs a security agreement granting a security interest in equipment, including after-acquired equipment, to Bank2. Bank2 makes an advance. On April 15, Davis Industries signs such a security agreement in favor of Bank1 and Bank1 makes an advance. On April 20, Davis Industries acquires its first and only item of equipment, a Giant Mashing Machine. On these facts, Bank1 has priority over Bank2 in the Giant Mashing Machine. Under UCC §9-322(a)(1), Bank1's priority dates from the filing of its financing statement.

The most common commercial use of after-acquired property clauses is in inventory-secured financing. The typical debtor is continually selling inventory and replacing it with new inventory. If an inventory-secured lender's interest did not reach property acquired after the initial loan transaction, in a few days or a few weeks little collateral would remain. The debtor and creditor could solve this problem without the use of an after-acquired property clause: They could simply enter into a new security agreement every time a new shipment of inventory arrived. That would be cumbersome. Instead, nearly all inventory loan agreements provide that after-acquired inventory will serve as collateral for all amounts outstanding under the loan. The lender perfects its interest in both currently owned and after-acquired inventory by the filing of a single financing statement.

Many regard the validation of after-acquired property clauses as the most important innovation in Article 9. They argue that modern-day inventory lending could not exist without the use of after-acquired property clauses and that without such lending, the overall level of economic activity would be considerably lower. To understand the factual assertions on which their argument is based, consider the example of Sally Raj, who is planning to open a stereo store in a small shopping center. Sally estimates the cost of the inventory the store will need to open at $100,000. She has $100,000 that she has raised through savings and unsecured borrowing from friends, but she will have to use nearly all of that money to rent and furnish store space, hire employees, and get the business under way. How will she buy the inventory she needs? Most suppliers of inventory for stereo stores are themselves short of working capital. They will sell their products on credit, even unsecured credit, but they are unwilling to "carry" a debtor for more than 30 to 60 days after the sale. They want to be paid quickly so they can reinvest the money in their own business. If all of Sally's suppliers would sell on 30 to 60 days' credit, if they would sell her enough to adequately stock the store, and if Sally could sell all of that inventory for cash quickly enough to pay her suppliers when due, Sally would not need inventory financing. But that is a lot of "ifs."

Most people in Sally's situation find it necessary to seek an inventory loan from a bank or finance company. We discussed inventory lending at some length in Assignment 15. The lender will take a security interest in the debtor's inventory (which may be nothing at the time the loan is closed), including after-acquired inventory. A common arrangement would be for the bank to lend 60 percent of the cost of the inventory. The bank chooses this particular level of financing because it is the level at which the bank feels "secure" — that is, the bank estimates that in the event of default on the loan, they could take possession of the inventory, sell it, and net about 60 percent of its cost.

Each time a new shipment of inventory arrives, Sally sends proof of its arrival to the bank and the bank deposits 60 percent of the invoice amount to Sally's bank account. Each day the business is open, Sally deposits all of the proceeds from sale of inventory to the same bank account, and the bank takes an amount equal to what they lent against the items of collateral that have been sold. From time to time, an employee of the bank might stop by the stereo store to make sure there is as much inventory there as the bank thinks there is. So long as Sally's revenues are sufficient to pay her debts as they fall due, the bank is always fully secured, Sally has sufficient inventory, and the suppliers get paid on time. If her revenues are insufficient, the bank can make itself whole by selling the inventory and Sally and the suppliers will have to take the hit. That is the meaning of priority. The secured party with priority comes first, and everyone else gets only whatever is left.

[handwritten margin note: — Meaning of priority]

▶ HALF ASSIGNMENT ENDS

B. Purchase-Money Security Interests

1. *Purchase-Money Security Interests Generally*

Under UCC §9-324(a), a purchase-money security interest in collateral other than inventory has priority over a conflicting security interest in the same collateral if the purchase-money security interest is perfected not later than

owned by the debtor. Within days, or even hours, of the arrival of a new shipment of inventory, the inventory-secured lender will make advances against it. The inventory-secured lender will do so on proof that the debtor is in possession of the inventory, without investigating whether the debtor has paid for it. (In fact, the understanding is usually that the debtor will *not* have paid for the inventory at the time it borrows against the inventory.) The inventory-secured lender may or may not require the debtor to use the loan proceeds to pay for the inventory, but the understanding is that the debtor will grant no PMSIs in it.

If these understandings applied to all inventory financing, a flat prohibition on PMSIs in inventory would have been appropriate. But some inventory lenders are willing to allow their debtors to take advantage of some purchase-money secured financing. Even these more tolerant lenders must, of course, have some way of knowing that others are financing some of the debtor's inventory. Inventory-secured lenders do not want to lend in reliance on collateral that is fully encumbered by a prior interest.

To protect against such double borrowing, it is not enough that the inventory lender learn of the purchase-money secured financing. The inventory lender must learn of the financing before disbursing against the collateral. If a purchase-money secured lender against inventory could, like its noninventory counterpart, obtain priority by filing a financing statement 20 days after delivery, the debtor would have (and spend) its double financing long before the inventory lender learned of the conflict.

These special needs of inventory financiers are reflected in the special rules in UCC §9-324(b). These rules permit purchase-money priority in inventory only on these conditions:

1. The purchase-money financier must perfect no later than the time the debtor receives possession of the collateral, and
2. The purchase-money financier must give advance notice to the inventory lender that it expects to acquire a purchase-money security interest in inventory. To give this notice, the purchase-money lender first searches the filing system for the names and addresses of all secured parties with a filing against inventory of the type it plans to sell. The lender then sends the notice to each of the inventory lenders. Like a financing statement, the notice expires at the end of five years. The purchase-money supplier can avoid expiration by repeating the notice at intervals of less than five years.

As Comment 4 to UCC §9-324 explains,

> The notification requirement protects the non-purchase-money inventory secured party in such a situation: if the inventory secured party has received notification, it presumably will not make an advance; if it has not received notification . . . any advance the inventory secured party may make ordinarily will have priority under Section 9-322.

Most important, the protection comes without any necessity for the inventory lender to search the filing system before making each advance.

If the security agreement prohibits liens against inventory other than the lien of the inventory lender, a notification pursuant to UCC §9-324(b) is a notification to the inventory lender that the debtor is about to go into default. To avoid that, debtors typically refuse to grant purchase-money security interests to their suppliers. The suppliers typically have little choice but to sell on unsecured credit and hope that the debtor pays.

4.   Purchase-Money Priority in Proceeds

Assume that a seller manages to acquire purchase-money priority in property of the debtor. What happens when the debtor exchanges the collateral for proceeds? Of course, the seller must take whatever action is required under UCC §9-315(d) to continue its perfection in the proceeds. But will it have purchase-money priority over a competing security interest perfected by an earlier filing against the debtor naming those proceeds as original collateral?

Generally speaking, the answer is yes. Purchase-money priority under UCC §9-324(a) extends to the "collateral or its proceeds." To illustrate the operation of this rule, assume that Bank1 has perfected a security interest in the equipment of Davis Industries and Bank2 has perfected a security interest in the accounts of Davis Industries. Seller sells a piece of equipment to Davis Industries, retaining a PMSI. Seller perfects within the 20-day grace period of UCC §9-324(a), thereby obtaining priority over Bank1. Davis later sells the piece of equipment to Buyer, resulting in an account owing from Buyer to Davis that is proceeds of the equipment. Seller has a security interest in the account as proceeds of the sale of its collateral. UCC §9-315(a)(2). In addition, Seller's purchase-money priority flows through to the account, giving Seller priority over Bank2's earlier filing against "accounts." UCC §9-324(a).

The rule that purchase-money status flows through into proceeds is subject to an important exception. The exception, found in UCC §9-324(b), is that purchase-money status in inventory flows only into chattel paper, instruments, and cash proceeds. The limitation prevents purchase-money status from flowing into other kinds of proceeds, most notably accounts. Even the flow-throughs of purchase money status into chattel paper, instruments, and cash deposits are themselves limited by the provisions of UCC §§9-327 and 9-330(a) and (d). Those provisions protect purchasers of the chattel paper or instruments and secured parties with control of the deposit account into which the cash proceeds are deposited.

9-324(b) exception [handwritten margin note]

The reason for the exception was to facilitate account financing. To understand the perceived necessity for the exception, assume that Davis Industries had no financing statements on file against it when it approached Bank1 for a loan against its accounts receivable. Absent the exception, the unencumbered accounts would not have been adequate collateral for a loan in any amount. Bank1's fear would be that after it perfected its security interest and advanced funds against the accounts, SomeOther Bank would make a purchase-money loan against inventory. As Davis Industries converted the inventory to accounts through sales, SomeOther Bank's purchase-money priority would flow through into the accounts, priming Bank1's lien. By limiting SomeOther

PMSI

Bank's purchase-money status in the proceeds of inventory to just the chattel paper, instruments, and cash proceeds, the exception arguably makes it possible for Bank1 to lend against Davis's accounts.

A later purchase-money inventory lender can protect itself against the possibility that such an account lender exists. The inventory lender would know of the account lender from the outset, because the account lender would have filed a financing statement before the inventory lender entered the picture. (If the inventory lender filed first, it could have filed against both the inventory and the accounts, and would have had priority over the later account lender on that basis.) The inventory lender can refuse to lend unless the debtor arranges to pay the inventory lender upon sale of the inventory. The obvious source of that payment is the advance made by the account lender each time a new account comes into existence. The arrangement can provide for the account lender to pay an appropriate portion of each advance directly to the inventory lender.

C.   Priority in Commingled Collateral

Collateral is *commingled* when it is mixed with other property. Commingling may occur when the debtor deposits cash collateral to a bank account that also contains funds that are not proceeds. It may occur when a debtor mixes corn purchased from one supplier with corn purchased from another, or it may occur when a debtor manufactures a car using steel purchased from one supplier and aluminum purchased from another.

The commingling of funds in a bank account was discussed in Assignments 10 and 11. Here we discuss the commingling of goods. Distinguish two situations. The first is where the identity of the collateral is lost by commingling as the collateral becomes part of a product or mass. The effect is that the security interest "continues in the product or mass." UCC §9-336(c). For example, assume that Firstbank holds a security interest in a shipment of potassium nitrate that the debtor combines with other chemicals to manufacture fertilizer. Under UCC §9-336(c), Firstbank's security interest continues in the resulting shipment of fertilizer even though the potassium nitrate constitutes only a small part of the fertilizer.

If more than one security interest attaches to a product or mass as a result of commingling, the interests rank equally and share in the proportion that the cost of each debtor's contribution bears to the total cost of the product or mass. For example, assume that Farmer Green sells wheat to Processing Co. for $20,000 and Farmer Brown sells wheat to Processing Co. for $80,000. Processing Co. commingles the two shipments. Further assume that Farmer Green's wheat is subject to a security interest in favor of PCA in the amount of $20,000 and Farmer Brown's wheat is subject to a security interest in favor of WestBank in the amount of $20,000. PCA and WestBank have equal priority in the commingled wheat and are entitled to the proceeds of its sale. They will share in proportion to the two farmers' contributions, not in proportion to the obligations owing them. PCA will be entitled to 20 percent of any proceeds from the sale of the commingled wheat; WestBank will be entitled to 80 percent. If, due to a decline in wheat prices, Processing Co. sells the commingled wheat for $10,000, PCA will be entitled to $2,000 and WestBank will be entitled to $8,000.

The second situation is where the identity is not lost, as where a replacement part is installed in a machine. (The identity of the replacement part is not lost because we can still see the part and perhaps take it back out of the machine.) Such a replacement part is an *accession*. If the secured party has taken a security interest in only the replacement part, UCC §9-335 will apply. The secured party's interest will continue to be perfected, and will have priority over later-perfected interests in the whole. But the accession-secured party's remedies may be severely impaired by UCC §9-335(e). Under that section, any secured party with priority over the accession-secured party is entitled to prevent removal of the accession from the whole. For example, assume that Firstbank has a security interest in Debtor's generator that is perfected by filing. Debtor installs the generator in Debtor's machine. Firstbank continues to be perfected in the generator. If Secondbank perfects in the machine after installation of the generator, Firstbank's interest has priority over Secondbank's. UCC §§9-335(c), 9-322(a). What if Secondbank perfected its interest in the machine before Firstbank perfected in the generator? Again, UCC §9-335(c) refers us to other provisions of Part 3 of Article 9. Firstbank will have priority in the generator if its security interest is purchase-money, see UCC §9-324(a); otherwise Secondbank will have priority, see UCC §9-322(a)(1).

Problem Set 32

32.1.   In late July, Dawgs & More (Dawgs) applied to Bank One for a loan against its lawn dog manufacturing equipment. Without committing to make the loan, on August 1 Bank One filed a financing statement against Dawgs showing the equipment as collateral. Also in late July, Dawgs applied for a similar loan from Bank Two. On August 5, Bank Two approved the loan and filed a financing statement against Dawgs showing the equipment as collateral. Bank Two and Dawgs signed a security agreement on August 5 and Bank Two advanced funds to Debtor. On August 7, C-Dogs, a supplier and judgment creditor of Dawgs, became a lien creditor by levying on the equipment. On August 10, Bank One received the report of their UCC search showing their financing statement to be in first position. They approved the loan to Dawgs. Bank One and Dawgs signed a security agreement, and Bank One advanced funds against the equipment. As soon as the check from Bank One cleared, the owner of Dawgs wired the Bank One loan proceeds to Freeport in the Bahamas, where they paused only long enough to join the proceeds from the Bank Two loan, and then continued on to places unknown. Who has priority in the equipment? UCC §§9-203(b), 9-308(a), 9-317(a), 9-322(a)(1).

32.2.   On March 21, Centurian National Bank lent $1 million to AirCo. Centurian took a security interest in "flight simulation equipment, now owned or hereafter acquired" and perfected by filing a financing statement naming

AirCo as debtor. On July 21, First National Bank lent $1.5 million to FlightCo, took a security interest in "flight simulation equipment, now owned or hereafter acquired" and perfected by filing a financing statement naming FlightCo as debtor. On November 4, FlightCo sold an MD-80 simulator to AirCo and deposited the $750,000 in proceeds to FlightCo's bank account at Centurian.

a.   As between Centurian and First National, who has priority in the MD-80 simulator? UCC §§9-322(a)(1), 9-325, and 9-507(a).

b.   FlightCo also owes $2.5 million to Centurian. The boilerplate agreement that FlightCo signed when it opened the Centurian account stated that "customer grants a security interest to Centurian in this deposit account to secure any amounts now, or in the future owing to Centurian." Centurian hasn't done anything about perfecting that interest. As between Centurian and First National, who has priority in the $750,000? UCC §§9-104, 9-203(b)(3)(D), 9-315(a)(2), (c), and (d)(2), 9-327, and Comment 4 to §9-327.

32.3.   A year ago, George Sol Estes borrowed $75,000 from Octopus National Bank (ONB) to purchase a computer for his dry cleaning business. The security agreement he signed at that time provided that the collateral would consist of the computer and any "substitutions, replacements or accessions." The security agreement contained no provision regarding future advances, because none was contemplated at the time. ONB filed a financing statement indicating that the collateral was "equipment."

ONB has just approved a $400,000 line of credit for George, to be secured by the dry cleaning equipment in his shop. Molly Parker, the loan officer at ONB, tells you that she knows she must prepare a new promissory note and security agreement, but wonders if she must also prepare and file a new financing statement. UCC §§9-108(b)(3), 9-322(a)(1), 9-502(d).

32.4.   a.   A year ago, Carol Dearing lent $1,000 to her friend, Bob Muzzetti. Bob gave her a security interest in his 32-foot Bayliner boat and saw that her financing statement was properly filed in accord with the law of the state. About a month later, Business Credit Associates (BCA) lent Muzzetti $45,000, taking a security interest in several items of collateral, including the boat. BCA also filed an effective financing statement. Muzzetti fell behind in his payments to BCA and yesterday, March 1, BCA repossessed the boat. The boat now sits in the repo agent's compound, behind an eight-foot cyclone fence that is topped with concertina wire.

Now Bob is back to ask another favor of Carol. What Bob wants is an additional advance of $31,000 "to protect the boat from sale by BCA and prevent BCA from collecting." Carol, who has been your client for years, asks whether this will work. What do you tell her? UCC §§9-322(a)(1), 9-609(a).

b.   Assume that Carol had filed a financing statement against Bob before BCA repossessed, but Bob had not authenticated a security agreement and Carol had not lent any money. Would the scheme work under these circumstances? Comment 4 to UCC §9-322.

32.5.   On the heels of its bad experience with Bob Muzzetti, your client, BCA, has sensed the need for a change in the way it does business. While its high-risk lending remains profitable overall, BCA does not want to continue being victimized by the likes of Bob Muzzetti and Carol Dearing. Restricting its loans to first security interests is not a practical solution because nearly all of

BCA's borrowers have given security interests in their collateral and the creditors who have taken them want to retain their current priority until they are paid. Is there anything else you can suggest? UCC §9-339.

▶ HALF ASSIGNMENT ENDS

32.6.   Sara Wisnewski has been manufacturing high-quality speakers for audio systems since 1979. Her speakers are among the best available and her prices are reasonable. For the past few years, orders have been running in excess of her manufacturing capacity and she has been unable to fill all the orders she receives from dealers.

At the same time, she has been losing a considerable amount of money on bad debts. In your initial conference, she told you about a case in which she sold $150,000 worth of speakers to a dealer, who promptly filed bankruptcy. The dealer still had most of her speakers in stock when it closed its doors, but the bankruptcy court gave them to the inventory lender. Sara literally ended up having to buy her own speakers back from the bank to fill other orders. Her attorney in the bankruptcy case explained to her that "the bank got the speakers because they had the first security interest."

a.   Sara thinks she should have the first security interest and she'd like you to tell her what she needs to do to get it. What do you tell her? UCC §§9-102(a)(48), 9-324(a) and (b).

b.   What problems do you foresee? What can Sara do about them?

■ END OF DEFAULT PROBLEM SET

32.7.   John A.E. "Potsie" Pottow is under a lot of pressure in his job at Centurian National Bank. Pottow's freewheeling lending policies have generated a number of "nonproducing assets." (To put it as politely as possible.) "One more," Potsie says, "and I may no longer be viable in my current position."

Potsie tells you this in the context of a discussion of the Paul Grumman loan. Until yesterday, Grumman's deteriorating financial condition looked like it would be the bale of straw that broke the camel's back. Centurian's loan to Grumman is in the amount of $1 million and is unsecured. The financial statements Grumman has given Centurian from time to time have always shown Centurian's principal competitor, First National Bank, as the holder of a $5 million security interest in all of Grumman's assets (principally equipment, inventory, and accounts). In the event of liquidation, Potsie is sure the assets will yield less than $5 million. Two weeks ago, desperate for ideas, Potsie ran a UCC search under Grumman's name.

Yesterday, a miracle happened. Potsie received the Secretary of State's search report in the mail. The certificate, which Potsie has laid gently on the desk in front of you, shows no filings against Paul Grumman. Potsie says he is sure that the assets are in Grumman's possession and that "Paul Grumman" is the correct name of the debtor — sure enough to bet his career on it.

To seize his opportunity, Potsie has tentatively cut a deal with Grumman. Centurian is to advance an additional $400,000 to Grumman. In return, Grumman will grant a security interest in favor of Centurian that will secure both the $1 million advance already outstanding and the new $400,000 loan. "The way I figure," Potsie says, "that will leave us with a $1.4 million first on almost $5 million in collateral."

The bankruptcy expert in your firm tells you that the old $1 million advance will remain vulnerable as a preference for 90 days, but the new $400,000 advance will not. From her point of view, Centurian has something to gain and nothing to lose by making the new loan — *provided that Centurian will have priority over First National*. Potsie would like you to give your opinion that Centurian will have priority. If Potsie loses his job, you worry that the firm may not be able to hang onto Centurian's business, perhaps putting your job in jeopardy as well.

a.   Is there any way that First National could have an effective financing statement that doesn't show up on an official search in the state in which Grumman's business is located? UCC §§9-316(a) and (b), 9-338, 9-502(d), 9-506(c), 9-507(a), 9-515(c), 9-516(d), 9-517.

b.   How can you find out if such a financing statement exists, without shooting yourself in the foot? UCC §9-322(a)(1) and Comment 4 to that section. For example, what if you search under "Gruman" (an incorrect spelling) and find First National's filing?

c.   What should you do?

d.   Is there an ethical issue here?

32.8.   Potsie Pottow, who is still hanging on at Centurian National Bank, has made an appointment with you to discuss a letter he received from Mark Kauffman, attorney for Weil's Feed and Seed (WFS). For years, WFS has been the only feed supplier to Potsie's borrower, the now-defunct Murray Cattle Company. Now WFS has surprised the bank by claiming a security interest "of equal priority with the bank" in Murray's cattle and its inventory of manure, and a prior security interest in the feed on hand. WFS has a financing statement on file against Murray, but WFS filed it two years after Centurion's and it covers only "feed." Potsie says he is sure that WFS never served a §9-324 notification on the bank.

Kauffman's letter contains copies of WFS's security agreement and financing statement. His argument is that when the cattle ate the feed, WFS's collateral became part of the "mass" (the cow) and, some time later, part of the collateral became the "product" (the manure). Kauffman cites UCC §9-336. Potsie wants to know if he should take the Kauffman letter seriously or whether "it's just bull****." What do you tell him? UCC §§9-102(a)(34) and (48), 9-324.

32.9.   Your new client, the Equitable Lending Group (ELG), specializes in high-risk, high-profit lending. It lends to debtors in possession under Chapter 11 and buys nonperforming loans from other institutions and restructures them. ELG is now interested in a new lending concept and would like your opinion on it. Potsie Pottow, who recently moved to ELG from his position at Centurion and brought ELG to you, explains a typical case.

Silicon Microchip (SM) is a manufacturer of computer components. Its business is fundamentally sound, but the company is overburdened with debt. First National Bank has a perfected security interest in its inventory and accounts, worth about $6 million, securing First National's loan in the amount of $8.2 million. The SM-First National relationship is currently in a holding pattern while the parties attempt to renegotiate. While they are doing that, ELG wants to finance SM's acquisition of new inventory and have purchase-money priority over First National in both the inventory and the accounts that arise when that inventory is sold. Potsie says he can handle the problem of monitoring the collateral, but wants you to tell him whether ELG can get the priority it seeks without agreement from First National. Potsie says the folks at First National will be "mad as hell" when they see what ELG is doing, but "they're so conservative they'll still be having meetings about it six months from now. In the meantime, we'll be making six points over prime. As long as we've got first priority, it's zero risk." Can ELG get priority? UCC §§9-324, 9-401(b).

Assignment 33:   Priority in Land and Fixtures

In this assignment, we explore the law governing priority among the holders of liens on real property. In section A, we begin with the paradigm case of competition among mortgages. In section B, we consider the priority of mortgages in the special circumstance of a building that is under construction. There we introduce a new kind of competitor, a form of statutory lien known as a *construction* or *mechanic's lien*. In section C, we return to Article 9 of the Uniform Commercial Code to consider competitions among mortgages and Article 9 fixtures filings. In the final section, we consider some special circumstances in which ordinary, nonfixture filings can give secured creditors priority in goods that are fixtures under real estate law.

A.   Mortgage Against Mortgage

As you read about the rules governing priority among real estate mortgages, keep in mind that they are merely *default* rules that apply in the absence of an agreement among the parties. In most cases, a mortgagee contracts with the debtor for its priority. That is, the mortgage signed by debtor and mortgagee provides that it is a first, second, or fifth mortgage. So long as the debtor has such an agreement with all of the mortgagees and the agreements are consistent, the agreements determine priority among the mortgages. Only when there is some kind of slip-up or ambiguity in the contracting do the rules discussed in this section determine priority.

The rules governing priority among real estate mortgages are similar to those governing priority among security interests. As under Article 9, unperfected security interests in real property are binding on the debtor who grants them. The real estate rules give somewhat wider effect to these unperfected mortgages and deeds of trust, but the ultimate result is that real estate mortgages, like security interests in personal property, typically rank in the order in which they are perfected. Like an Article 9 security interest, a mortgage can secure future advances. It can reach after-acquired property, but it will be subordinate to a purchase-money mortgage in the same property provided that the purchase-money mortgage is recorded timely.

1.   Recording Statutes: The Rules of Priority

Most of the rules of priority among interests in real estate are embedded in the statutes that govern recording and specify its effect. One that is not is the rule governing priority among unrecorded mortgages. Recall that under UCC §9-322(a)(3), unperfected security interests rank in the order in which they attach.

Example 1. Debtor grants an Article 9 security interest to *A*; then Debtor grants an Article 9 security interest to *B*. Neither *A* nor *B* perfects. *A*'s security interest has priority over *B*'s.

Under Article 9, this rule had almost no practical importance, because the holder of the later-created interest nearly always could alter the priority by filing. The rule governing priority among unperfected mortgages is the same as the rule illustrated in Example 1.

In the mortgage context, however, the rule has a much wider effect, because the priority thus gained is not so easily upset by the recording of one of the mortgages. The protection available to one who records a mortgage under some real estate recording statutes is narrower than the protection available to one who records an Article 9 financing statement.

While the protection available to Article 9 filers is essentially the same throughout the United States, the protection available to real estate recorders varies significantly from state to state. To understand the differences among recording regimes, begin by distinguishing three archetypes: *race, notice,* and *race-notice* regimes. (Actual recording statutes are highly varied and seldom match any of these archetypes, but understanding the archetypes will help you know what to look for when you study an actual recording statute.) Under a pure race statute, the first mortgage recorded has priority, regardless of the mortgagee's state of mind.

Example 2. Debtor grants a mortgage to *A*; then debtor grants a mortgage to *B*. At the time *B* acquires its mortgage, *B* knows of the mortgage to *A*. *B* records, then *A* records. *B* has priority.

UCC §9-322(a) is often characterized as a "race" statute because under Article 9, "a filing secured creditor prevails even over those unrecorded security interests of which he was aware." Langley v. Federal Deposit Ins. Corp., 484 U.S. 86 (1987). Here is an example of a real estate recording statute that is generally characterized as a race statute:

Race Statute

North Carolina General Statutes §47-20(a) (2015)

No deed of trust or mortgage of real or personal property, or of a leasehold interest or other chattel real, or conditional sales contract of personal property in which the title is retained by the vendor, shall be valid to pass any property as against lien creditors or purchasers for a valuable consideration from the grantor, mortgagor or conditional sales vendee, but from the time of registration thereof. . . .

Under a pure "notice" statute, the order in which competing mortgages are recorded does not matter at all. The statute provides, in essence, that if a second mortgagee acquires an interest in the property without notice of the first, the second prevails. The holder of the first mortgage can prevent that from happening by recording its mortgage immediately upon receiving it; recording will constitute constructive notice to later takers. Thus, the statute gives an incentive to record promptly. But the outcome of the case will never depend on which mortgagee recorded first.

Example 3. Debtor grants a mortgage to *A*; then debtor grants a mortgage to *B*. At the time *B* acquires its mortgage, *B* knows of the mortgage to *A*. *B* records. *A* has priority.

The following statute is generally considered a "notice" statute:

Notice Statute

Massachusetts General Laws Ch. 183, §4 (2015)

A conveyance of an estate in fee simple . . . shall not be valid as against any person, except the grantor, . . . his heirs and devisees and persons having actual notice of it, unless it . . . is recorded in the registry of deeds for the county or district in which the land to which it relates lies.

While the statute is not clear on the point, the intention apparently is that *A*'s recording is effective only against *B*s who receive mortgages after the recording. Those later *B*s have constructive notice of *A*'s mortgage. Provided that *B* took prior to *A*'s recording, *B* would prevail over *A*, without regard to whether *B* even recorded at all.

The most common kind of real estate recording statute is a blend of the race and the notice statutes. Its catchy name is *notice-race statute* (or, for those of us who grew up in another part of the country, *race-notice*). A notice-race statute provides, in essence, that if the recipient of the second conveyance takes the conveyance without notice *and* records before the holder of the first conveyance does so, the second conveyance has priority.

Example 4. Debtor grants a mortgage to *A*; then debtor grants a mortgage to *B*. At the time *B* acquires its mortgage, *B* does not know of the mortgage to *A*. *B* records. Then *A* records. *B* has priority.

Notice-Race Statute

New York Real Property Laws §291 (2015)

A conveyance of real property . . . may be recorded in the office of the clerk of the county where such real property is situated. . . . Every such conveyance not so recorded is void as against any person who subsequently purchases or acquires by exchange or contracts to purchase or acquire by exchange, the same real property or any portion thereof . . . in good faith and for a valuable consideration, from the same vendor or assignor, his distributees or devisees, and whose conveyance, contract or assignment is first duly recorded. . . .

B can lose in two different ways under a notice-race statute. If *B* knows of the mortgage to *A* at the time *B* acquires its mortgage, or if *B* loses the race to the courthouse, *B* will not have priority under the statute. *A* will prevail under the general common law rule that the first conveyance has priority over the second. The "notice" portion of notice-race rules is based on knowledge at the time of the conveyance. Subsequent notice is irrelevant. Thus, if *B* takes its mortgage without notice of *A*'s prior mortgage, learns of it, and then hurries to record before *A* does, *B* will prevail.

A notice-race statute gives both *A* and *B* incentives to record promptly upon receiving their mortgages. By recording, *A* can prevent later transferees from gaining priority; a later-created mortgage can defeat an earlier one only by winning the race to the courthouse. If *B* takes without notice of the prior mortgage to *A, B* too has an incentive to record promptly. If *B* records before *A, B* will have satisfied both requirements and will have priority over *A*. If *A* records first, *A* wins because *A* was, by definition, without knowledge of the transfer to *B* at the time of the transfer to *A* (it hadn't happened yet), and *A* recorded first.

2.   Who Is a Good Faith Purchaser for Value?

Most recording statutes protect only good faith purchasers for value. Few recording statutes specify who is a good faith purchaser for value, but there is much law on the subject. "Value" or "valuable consideration" generally must be more than just a nominal consideration. (Compare UCC §1-204, which takes a contrary view.) A $20,000 mortgage given in return for a peppercorn would not be entitled to the protection of the recording statute. On the other hand, a mortgagee should not be denied the protection of the recording statute merely because it made a good deal in an arm's length exchange. That the $20,000 mortgage was exchanged for goods worth only $15,000 does not mean that it was not given for value.

Often, a mortgage is given to secure a preexisting debt. In those situations, the question may arise whether the mortgage is given for value.

Example 5. On February 1, *O* borrows $25,000 from *A* on an unsecured basis. On July 1, *O* grants *A* a mortgage against Blackacre. Whether *A* acquires its mortgage "for value" depends on what, if anything, *A* gave in exchange for the July mortgage. The majority view distinguishes mortgages granted with the hope of winning forbearance from the grantee from mortgages explicitly exchanged for a legally binding extension of the due date for payment. Only the latter constitutes "value."

As is discussed in section B, below, those who acquire liens against the collateral by legal proceedings are not "purchasers." To be a purchaser, one must take in a voluntary transaction.

3. Purchase-Money Mortgages

Most states recognize some kind of priority for purchase-money mortgages. The California statute set forth below, like UCC §9-317(e), gives a purchase-money mortgage priority over some liens created and perfected before the purchase-money mortgage comes into existence. In contrast, Pennsylvania's statute appears to leave the purchase-money mortgage subordinate to liens perfected before the purchase-money mortgage is delivered.

Purchase-Money Mortgages

California Civil Code §2898(a) (2015)

A mortgage or deed of trust given for the price of real property, at the time of its conveyance, has priority over all other liens created against the purchaser, subject to the operation of the recording laws.

Purchase-Money Mortgages

42 Pennsylvania Consolidated Statutes §8141 (2015)

Liens against real property shall have priority over each other on the following basis:

(1) Purchase money mortgages, from the time they are delivered to the mortgagee, if they are recorded within ten days after their date; otherwise, from the time they are left for record. A mortgage is a "purchase money mortgage" to the extent that it is:

(i) taken by the seller of the mortgaged property to secure the payment of all or part of the purchase price; or

(ii) taken by a mortgagee other than the seller to secure the repayment of money actually advanced by such person to or on behalf of the mortgagor at the time the mortgagor acquires title to the property and used by the mortgagor at that time to pay all or part of the purchase price, except that a mortgage other than to the seller of the property shall not be a purchase money mortgage within the meaning of this section unless expressly stated so to be.

(2) Other mortgages and defeasible deeds in the nature of mortgages, from the time they are left for record. . . .

We elaborate on a point we made earlier: Archetypes are useful in learning how the system works, but real property law is highly variable from state to state on nonfunctional detail and, occasionally, even on more basic matters.

B.   Judgment Liens Against Mortgages

An unsecured creditor can obtain a lien against the debtor's real property by suing the debtor, obtaining a judgment against the debtor, and recording the judgment in the real estate recording system of the county where the real property is located. The judgment will constitute a lien against real property owned by the debtor at the time of recording and real property the debtor later acquires. (This right to later property should seem familiar; it is the equivalent of an after-acquired property clause in an Article 9 security agreement.)

The rules governing priority between a judgment lien and a mortgage are similar to those governing priority between mortgages. The recording of the judgment both creates and perfects the judgment lien. Unless the recording statute changes the result, priority between a judgment lien and a mortgage depends on which was first created. In some states, the holder of a judgment lien is entitled to the benefit of the recording statutes. Notice, for example, that the North Carolina Statute in section A of this assignment provides that an unrecorded mortgage is not valid to pass title as against a "lien creditor." The holder of a judgment lien is such a lien creditor. Thus, if the judgment lien is recorded in North Carolina before the competing mortgage, the judgment lien has priority even if the mortgage was created first.

In most states, however, the recording statutes do not protect judgment lien or other lien creditors. The New York recording statute set forth earlier in this assignment is an illustration: It protects only "purchasers." (A mortgagee under real property law, like a secured party under the UCC, is a "purchaser." See UCC §§1-201(b)(29) and (30) defining "purchaser" as including only those who take in voluntary transactions.) Thus, in New York, an unrecorded mortgage has priority over a recorded judgment, provided that the mortgage was created before the judgment was recorded.

To complicate matters further, the courts are not bound to give the word "purchasers" its UCC meaning when that word appears outside the UCC A few states protect lien creditors as "purchasers" under recording statutes.

C.   Mechanics' Liens Against Construction Mortgages

Perhaps the mortgagee's most common competitor for priority is the inaptly named *mechanic's lien*. Contrary to the ordinary meaning of the terms, persons who supply labor or material used in the construction of buildings or other improvements on land receive "mechanics' liens" to secure their payment, while the mechanic who fixes your car gets an *artisan's lien*. A few states use the plain language *construction lien*, but that term doesn't seem to be catching on, so we yield to long-standing custom in our usage here. Mechanics' liens are "statutory" liens — that is, they arise by operation of law pursuant to the statute creating them. All 50 states have such statutes. The purpose of these liens is to protect those who supply labor or material incorporated into the construction of a building. The protection comes in the form of a lien against the real property into which the labor or material was incorporated.

To understand the competition between mechanics' liens and mortgages, one must start with an understanding of the context in which mechanics' liens arise.

1. A Prototypical Construction Financing Transaction

Sick of apartment living, Ozzie Owner has decided to build the house of his dreams. After an extensive search, he finds the perfect lot in a subdivision owned by Valerie Vendor. Ozzie enters into a contract to buy the lot from Valerie for $200,000. The contract is contingent upon Ozzie obtaining acquisition and construction financing acceptable to him. With the help of architect-homebuilder Conrad Contractor, Ozzie comes up with a design for the house. Conrad and Ozzie then enter into a contract whereby Conrad agrees to build the house on Ozzie's lot and Ozzie agrees to pay $800,000 for it. This contract too is contingent upon Ozzie obtaining acquisition and construction financing acceptable to him. Ozzie's last stop is at the Beaufort Bank, where he applies for and is offered acquisition and construction financing in the necessary amount of $1 million. The loan closing and the commencement of construction are scheduled for April 1.

The construction loan agreement between Ozzie and the bank provides for disbursement in five *draws* of $200,000 each. The bank will pay the first $200,000 draw when Ozzie obtains clear title to the lot on which the house is to be built. The next three draws will be payable at particular stages of construction. The second draw will be paid when the concrete slab has been poured. The third will be paid when the roof is on. The fourth will be paid when the house is "weathered in" — that is, when windows and walls are in place so that wind and rain are excluded. The fifth and last $200,000 draw is payable only after construction is complete in accord with the plans. This arrangement is designed to suit the interests of both Ozzie and the bank. Ozzie needs money to buy the land and to pay Conrad, subcontractors, suppliers, and laborers while the house is under construction. But the bank does not want to lend Ozzie money before he has a use for it (cash tends to disappear) or in amounts that exceed the value of the collateral. The further construction has progressed, the more the partially completed house will be worth. Hence the five-draw disbursement. The bank will lend for each stage of construction only when that stage is complete.

It is easy enough to see how Ozzie will earn the first draw. He need only arrange for a closing at which Valerie will deed the lot to him and be paid with the first draw check from the bank. But if Ozzie has no cash of his own, how will he advance construction to the pouring of the slab when he will be entitled to the next draw? Typically, the answer is that Conrad Contractor does the construction on credit, looking to the draw for payment. Conrad Contractor does not put his own money in the project either. Instead, he chooses subcontractors who will do the work on credit. One of them is Randy Rock, the concrete subcontractor who will pour the slab. Randy, who lives in the country and has seven dogs who sleep under the porch, is no financier either; he is counting on Sandy's Sand and Gravel for supplies and on John Williams to drive the truck and do the pouring and leveling. Randy will pay them when he gets the draw. Ultimately, it is John (the laborer) and Sandy (the materialman) who are going to finance this construction.

But how do John and Sandy — and everyone else in the chain — know that when the bank pays the draw, the money will filter down to them? For example, what if the bank pays the second draw check to Ozzie, Ozzie pays Conrad, and Conrad uses the money to pay his alimony payment and a couple of subcontractors that worked on a house he built a few months ago? (A sizeable number of contractors use their draw checks in precisely these ways.) Theoretically, the bank could contract to pay everybody directly, but that rarely is practical. Hundreds of people may work on or supply materials to even a small construction job; the bank has no way of knowing their identity, let alone their arrangements for compensation. Neither does Ozzie, or even Conrad. Each subcontractor contracts to do its work; it is up to the subcontractor to decide how to get it done and who participates. Last-minute changes in the construction team are common; even the plumbing subcontractor may not know the name of the person who is out on the site hooking up the pipe.

Mechanic's lien laws address this problem in two ways. First, they require that each person in the construction chain hold the draw money they receive *in trust* and use the trust funds only to make *proper payments*. Proper payments are payments that go only to subcontractors, laborers, and materialmen who work under the payor, until all of those people have been paid in full. Only the balance remaining is the payor's and available for payment of the payor's alimony. The statutes typically provide that the making of improper payments from construction draw money is embezzlement and subject the persons making them to criminal penalties. This aspect of mechanic's lien law protection does not rely on the concept of security and for that reason is outside the scope of this book.

The second manner in which the mechanic's lien law seeks to ensure payment to everyone who supplies labor or materials to a construction site is by entitling all such persons to mechanics' liens. To claim its lien, a contractor, subcontractor, materialman, or supplier must record a *claim of lien* in the real estate recording system by a deadline that typically is 90 or 120 days after the claimant completes its work on the building. (Yes, there are often tales of would-be lien holders going back to the site to put in a light bulb and thereby arguably reviving an expired deadline.)

To illustrate, when Rock finishes pouring the slab, he will expect payment from Conrad within a few weeks. If the payment is not forthcoming, Rock will prepare a claim of lien against Ozzie's property and file it in the real estate recording system. Rock will then have a mechanic's lien against the land and the partially completed house on it.

When the draws from a construction loan are sufficient and applied to proper payments, everyone who works on the job will be paid on time. No one will have reason to file a claim of lien. When claims of lien do appear on the public record, they signal that something has gone wrong. Once a construction project is in financial difficulty, subcontractors, suppliers, and laborers may refuse to extend further credit, thereby bringing construction to a halt. Resumption of construction may be difficult to achieve because those asked to supply labor and materials on credit fear not being paid. The rescheduling of their work may put the work in conflict with other jobs they are doing. During the inevitable delays, the physical condition of a partially completed building may deteriorate from exposure to the elements. All these factors tend to cause the value of the partially completed building to decline. The rule of thumb is that when liens are filed, the work stops, and everybody is in trouble.

The capacity of a claim of lien to doom a construction project is both its strength and its weakness. Owners and contractors may pay the lienor who threatens to record a claim of lien because they fear the consequences. But in the strange world of debtor and creditor, the weakness of defaulting owners and contractors may also be their strength. Such owners and contractors often argue to their unpaid lienors that by filing claims of lien, they would be cutting their own throats. Filing of the lien will stop construction and prevent the owners and contractors from reaching the only possible source of payment: the next draw.

What if the recording of a claim of lien does not result in payment? The answer is that the lienor must bring an action for judicial foreclosure. In most states, the statute of limitations for an action on a mechanic's lien is one year and runs from the filing of the claim of lien. If the action is not filed by the end of the year, the lien expires and the debt becomes unsecured. If lienor and owner wish to extend payments over a longer period of time, they will usually wish to substitute a mortgage for the mechanic's lien.

2.   Who Is Entitled to a Mechanic's Lien?

While mechanics' liens are usually associated with the construction of buildings, the statutes of many states provide for liens in favor of virtually anyone who participates in the making of any improvement to real property. The New York Lien Law is illustrative. (We have reversed the order of the two sections for easier reading.)

New York Lien Law

(2015)

§3.   MECHANIC'S LIEN ON REAL PROPERTY

A contractor, subcontractor, laborer, materialman, landscape gardener, [or] nurseryman . . . who performs labor or furnishes materials for the improvement of real property with the consent or at the request of the owner thereof, or of his agent, contractor or subcontractor . . . shall have a lien for the . . . value, or the agreed price, of such labor . . . or materials upon the real property improved or to be improved and upon such improvement, from the time of filing a notice of such lien as prescribed in this chapter. . . .

§2.   DEFINITIONS . . .

2. Real property. The term "real property," when used in this chapter, includes real estate, lands, tenements and hereditaments, corporeal and incorporeal, [and] fixtures. . . .

3. Owner. The term "owner," when used in this chapter, includes the owner in fee of real property, or of a lesser estate therein, a lessee for a term of years, a vendee in possession under a contract for the purchase of such real property, and all persons having any right, title or interest in such real property, which may be sold under an execution in pursuance of the provisions of statutes relating to the enforcement of liens of judgment. . . .

4. Improvement. The term "improvement," when used in this chapter, includes the demolition, erection, alteration or repair of any structure upon, connected with, or beneath the surface of, any real property and any work done upon such property or materials furnished for its permanent improvement, . . . and shall also include the drawing by any architect or engineer or surveyor, of any plans or specifications or survey, which are prepared for or used in connection with such improvement and shall also include the value of materials actually manufactured for but not delivered to the real property. . . .

9. Contractor. The term "contractor," when used in this chapter, means a person who enters into a contract with the owner of real property for the improvement thereof. . . .

10. Subcontractor. The term "subcontractor" when used in this chapter, means a person who enters into a contract with a contractor and/or with a subcontractor for the improvement of such real property . . . or with a person who has contracted with or through such contractor for the performance of his contract or any part thereof.

11. Laborer. The term "laborer," when used in this chapter, means any person who performs labor or services upon such improvement.

12. Materialman. The term "materialman" when used in this chapter, means any person who furnishes material or the use of machinery, tools, or equipment . . . either to an owner, contractor or subcontractor, for, or in the prosecution of such improvement. . . .

20. Persons. The term "persons" when used in this chapter, includes an individual, partnership, association, trust or corporation.

---

3.   *Priority of Mechanics' Liens*

Statutes that fix the priority of mechanics' liens usually distinguish the obvious construction of buildings from the not-so-obvious casual alteration or repair of a building. A lien for an alteration or repair, such as the installation of a new furnace in an existing building, takes priority as of the recording of the claim of lien. By contrast, liens that arise out of the construction of a building typically all take priority as of the same date. In most states, that date is the date of the commencement of construction.

In re Skyline Properties, Inc.

134 B.R. 830 (Bankr. W.D. Pa. 1992)

A mechanics' lien for services which constitute alterations and repairs takes effect and has priority as of the date the mechanics' lien claim is filed. In the case of erection and construction, the lien of a claim takes effect and has priority "as of the date of the visible commencement upon the ground of the work of erecting or constructing the improvement." 49 Pa. Cons. Stat. Ann. §1508(a) (Purdon 1965).

The within matter involves the following relevant dates: Visible commencement of construction: April 20, 1987; Bank's mortgage: June 5, 1987; Mealy Claim filed: September 23, 1987.

Thus, if Mealy's work is erection and construction, Mealy's Claim has priority over the Bank; if the work is an alteration or repair, the Bank's mortgage takes priority.

Section 1201(10) of the Mechanics' Lien Law defines "erection and construction" as follows:

> "Erection and construction" means the erection and construction of a new improvement or of a substantial addition to an existing improvement or any adaptation of an existing improvement rendering the same fit for a new or distinct use and effecting a material change in the interior or exterior thereof.

49 Pa. Cons. Stat. Ann. §1202 (Purdon 1965).

The Bank asserts that no buildings were erected nor constructed in conjunction with Mealy's work and Mealy's lien is for alterations and repairs. Thus, the Bank asserts that Mealy's lien takes priority as of the date of filing of the Claim and not the date of visible commencement of the work.

The concern in determining whether the work is "erection and construction" or "alterations or repairs" is whether a substantial change to the existing structure has occurred such that any third party, such as the Bank, would be on notice that potential liens could exist. A change in the appearance or use of a building is sufficient to give such notice.

If there is a construction lender in the picture, the project is probably "erection or construction." The liens will date from the commencement of construction. The construction lender will want its mortgage to have priority over any mechanics' liens eventually filed. The simplest, most direct way of accomplishing that is to record the construction mortgage before the commencement of construction. Draws paid after creation and recording of the mortgage will be *future advances* that will in nearly all circumstances have priority over liens arising out of the construction. But how can the construction lender be sure at the time it records its mortgage that construction has not yet begun? The usual method is for someone from the bank to examine the property to make sure there are no visible signs of recent construction and to prepare dated photographs so the bank will later be able to prove that in court.

Is the lack of any visible sign of construction on the site a sufficient basis for concluding that construction has not yet begun? The court faced that issue in the case that follows.

Ketchum, Konkel, Barrett, Nickel & Austin v. Heritage Mountain Development Co.

784 P.2d 1217 (Utah Ct. App. 1989)

JUDITH M. BILLINGS, JUDGE:

Appellants filed actions to foreclose their mechanics' liens recorded against property being developed as a ski resort in Utah County. The construction lender, Guaranty Savings and Loan Association ("Guaranty"), moved for partial summary judgment claiming its trust deed had priority over all mechanics' liens on the property.

In October 1972, Heritage Mountain Development Co. ("Heritage"), began the planning and development of a ski resort. The master plan for the ski resort contemplated the common development of three contiguous parcels of property in Utah County: 110 acres owned in fee simple; 41 acres leased from the State of Utah ("Leased Property"); and 4500 acres of federal land under a special use permit ("Permit Property").

Beginning in April of 1983, an engineering firm surveyed and staked the boundaries of the property. In June 1983, Heritage obtained a predevelopment loan from Guaranty. To secure the loan, Heritage executed a trust deed on the property. Guaranty recorded the trust deed on September 15, 1983. At the time of this loan, Guaranty knew that appellants had performed extensive design work on the project. Between June and September of 1983, appellants and others resumed design work on the project.

The long-term financing for the ski development fell through and no additional on-site construction took place. Heritage abandoned the project by the summer of 1984 and left appellants and other contractors unpaid.

I.   EFFECT OF OFF-SITE ARCHITECTURAL WORK ON MECHANICS' LIENS PRIORITY

Appellants claim that, under Utah Code Ann. §§38-1-5 and -10 (1988), their pre-trust deed, off-site design work on the project gives their mechanics' liens priority over Guaranty's trust deed. We disagree.

Under Utah law, architects' services are lienable. Utah Code Ann. §38-1-3 (1981) expressly provides for liens for architectural services:

> [L]icensed architects and engineers and artisans who have furnished designs, plats, plans, maps, specifications, drawings, estimates of cost, surveys or superintendence, or who have rendered other like professional service, or bestowed labor, shall have a lien upon the property upon or concerning which they have rendered service, performed labor, or furnished or rented materials. . . .

Guaranty does not challenge the validity of the appellants' liens, but claims its trust deed has priority over all valid mechanics' liens under the statutory scheme. Priority of mechanics' liens, including architectural liens, is governed by Utah Code Ann. §38-1-5 (1988), which provides:

> The liens herein provided for shall relate back to, and take effect as of, the time of the commencement to do work or furnish materials on the ground for the structure or improvement, and shall have priority over any lien, mortgage or other encumbrance which may have attached subsequently to the time when the building, improvement or structure was commenced, work begun, or first material furnished on the ground. . . .

Lien statutes are construed broadly in order to achieve their protective purpose. Further, the phrase "commencement to do work" is construed in favor of the lien claimant.

The precise statutory construction issue presented is the meaning of the language "commencement to do work or furnish materials on the ground for the structure or improvement" in section 38-1-5. The district court construed this section to require the commencement of visible, on-site improvements without regard to whether a subsequent lender had actual notice of prior off-site lienable work such as appellants.

This issue has never been squarely dealt with by Utah courts. However, Utah case law discussing priority under section 38-1-5 has emphasized visible work performed on the property or the presence of materials, giving notice that work has commenced on the property. In Calder Bros. Co. v. Anderson, 652 P.2d 922 (Utah 1982), the court rejected the lien claimant's claim of priority because "[a]t no point up to and including the time [the lender's] mortgage was recorded, was it evident from the inspection of the premises that an improvement had been commenced." The court stated that "visible evidence of work performed provides notice to any interested party that work has commenced."

The majority of other jurisdictions which have considered the issue of whether off-site services of architects and engineers constitute the commencement of work for purposes of the priority of mechanics' liens have answered in the negative. Although each statutory scheme is unique, the decisions are in harmony that physical notice of work on the property must be present before mechanics' liens have priority over other third parties, especially lenders.

If this court were to allow architects' work to establish the "commencement" of the project, not just architects' liens but all other liens would relate back to the date of the architectural work. Under Utah Code Ann. §38-1-10 (1988), all mechanics' liens are on equal footing for purposes of priority. Accordingly, a trust deed recorded after attachment of a mechanics' lien is inferior in priority to that lien and all other mechanics' liens filed on the property.

We believe the predictability sought by the mechanics' lien statutory scheme would be undermined if actual notice of architectural work by a third party claiming priority qualified this off-site design work as "commencement to do work" for priority purposes under section 38-1-5. First, it would multiply litigation over the issue of whether the third party had actual notice. Second, all mechanics' liens for work performed on the project, not just the work of the architect, would suddenly take priority over a secured lender with the consequent adverse impact on construction financing. Finally, and most importantly, had the legislature intended priority under section 38-1-5 to be affected by actual notice, it could have so stated but did not.

We are persuaded that the policy of giving third parties notice of possible mechanics' liens requires visible, on-site construction to qualify for "commencement of work" under section 38-1-5. Thus, the off-site work of architects does not constitute commencement of work under section 38-1-5.

IV.   PRE-TRUST DEED, ON-SITE IMPROVEMENTS

Appellants finally contend that their liens can relate back to surveying, staking, and soil core sampling work performed on the Leased Property prior to the recording of the trust deed. Once again, appellants contend that because the work is "lienable," it automatically constitutes "commencement of work" under section 38-1-5. However, the "mere fact that work was a proper subject of a lien cannot establish priority where it does not give notice of commencement." Clark v. General Elec. Co., 243 Ark. 399, 420 S.W.2d 830, 834 (1967).

This court has previously considered the issue of whether surveying work is sufficient to establish relation back under section 38-1-5. In Tripp v. Vaughn, 747 P.2d 1051 (Utah Ct. App. 1987), the court concluded that the staking, which was the only visible manifestation of the surveyor's work, was not "sufficiently noticeable or related to actual construction to impart notice to a prudent lender."

Utah's position is consistent with the majority of jurisdictions which have ruled that preparing the soil, leveling the ground, placing survey stakes, and taking soil samples do not constitute "visible" on-site improvements required to establish priority under mechanics' liens statutes.

Based on the authority discussed, we conclude there was no pre-trust deed work sufficient to qualify for commencement of work because surveying, staking, and soil testing do not constitute a visible on-site improvement as required by Utah law for relation back under sections 38-1-5 and -10.

In some states, the owner can file a notice of commencement of construction and mechanics' liens will have priority as of that filing.

D.   The Priority of Article 9 Fixture Filings

In Assignment 20, we discussed the fact that an Article 9 security interest can exist in goods that are fixtures under real estate law. Article 9 authorizes the perfection of such an interest by a "fixture filing" in the real estate recording system. UCC §§9-102(a)(40), 9-501(a)(1)(B), and 9-502(b). The priority achieved by fixture filings is governed by the rules stated in UCC §9-334.

1.   Priority in Fixtures Incorporated During Construction

The distinction between a fixture filing made during construction and a mechanic's lien that arises during the same period is important. The following examples may help to make that distinction:

Example 1.   Debtor, Inc. is building a 200-unit apartment building on its property. During construction, Debtor, Inc. buys 200 water heaters from the H_2OT Co. If H_2OT Co. delivers the water heaters to the construction site, H_2OT Co. has a mechanic's lien against the land and building that it can perfect by recording a claim of lien. H_2OT Co. will have this lien even though the parties did not sign a security agreement.

Example 2.   Now assume that, on the same facts, Debtor, Inc. and H_2OT Co. executed an agreement granting H_2OT Co. an Article 9 security interest in the water heaters. Because the hot water heaters will become fixtures, H_2OT Co. should perfect this interest by a fixture filing in the real estate records. H_2OT Co. might also wish to file its claim of lien at the same time, but Debtor, Inc. might find the latter filing distressing.

Notice that the mechanic's lien in Example 1 encumbers the entire apartment building property, while the fixture filing in Example 2 encumbers only the fixtures described in it, the water heaters. If H_2OT Co. forecloses the security interest in the water heaters, only the water heaters will be sold. Because the construction mortgage has priority over H_2OT Co.'s security interest, the holder of the construction mortgage can prevent H_2OT Co. from removing the water heaters. UCC §9-604(c).

These two liens may also differ in their priority against the construction mortgage. The mechanic's lien will have priority as of the commencement of construction, which may be months before Debtor, Inc. purchased the water heaters. But it will have priority over the construction mortgage only if construction commenced before Firstbank recorded the mortgage — an unlikely possibility. The Article 9 security interest will have priority as of the time the fixture filing is made. Accordingly, the fixture filing will have priority over the construction mortgage only if H_2OT Co. made the fixture filing before Firstbank recorded the mortgage. See UCC §9-334(h). In practice, the construction lender will virtually always record first, thereby giving it priority over both the mechanic's lien and the Article 9 security interest.

Notice that H_2OT Co.'s security interest is subordinate to Firstbank's construction mortgage even if H_2OT Co.'s security interest is a purchase-money security interest and Firstbank's construction mortgage is not a purchase-money mortgage. See UCC §§9-334(h) and 9-334(d). If H_2OT Co. sells hot water heaters to Debtor, Inc. after recording of the construction mortgage, H_2OT Co. can obtain priority over Firstbank only if Firstbank agrees to subordinate. UCC §9-339.

2. *Priority in Fixtures Incorporated Without Construction*

Again, the basic rule is that Article 9 fixture filings and mortgages rank in the order in which they are recorded in the real estate recording system. UCC §§9-334(c) and 9-334(e)(1). In the typical case, the mortgage will have been recorded during the construction of the building or some other time long before the fixture is purchased and incorporated into the building. Generally, the nonpurchase-money fixture financier will be subordinate to whatever mortgages exist at the time of fixture filing. If this result is unacceptable to the fixture financier, the fixture financier may wish to seek the mortgagee's consent to the security interest. UCC §9-334(f)(1).

There are two important exceptions to the basic rule. First, the fixture filing will have priority over the mortgages if the debtor has the right under the mortgages to remove the fixtures. Second, the fixture filing will have priority over the mortgages if the security interest is a purchase-money security interest in goods affixed after the mortgage is in place and the fixture filing is made not later than 20 days after the goods become fixtures. UCC §9-334(d). To illustrate, assume that after Firstbank's mortgage is recorded against Debtor, Inc. and construction of the apartment building is completed, Debtor, Inc. finds it necessary to replace all the hot water heaters in the building. If H_2OT Co. sells the water heaters to Debtor, Inc., retains a purchase-money security interest in them, and makes a fixture filing before they are installed or within 20 days after they are installed, H_2OT Co.'s security interest will have priority over Firstbank's mortgage in the hot water heaters.

As is true of security interests and liens generally, the priority of a fixture filing is important not just for its effect on the distribution of proceeds from a sale of collateral. The priority of a fixture filing also determines the secured party's right to possession after default. The fixture-secured party has the right to remove the fixture from the real property if the security interest in the fixture has priority over the owners and encumbrancers of the real estate. UCC §9-604(c). Otherwise, the secured party can only wait in the hope that someone else will liquidate the collateral.

E. Priority in Real Property Based on Personal Property Filing

A "fixture filing" is a financing statement filed in the real property recording system that meets the requirements of UCC §9-502(b). A secured creditor can perfect in fixtures (1) by making a fixture filing, (2) by recording a mortgage against the real property to which the fixtures are attached, or (3) by filing an ordinary financing statement in the Article 9 filing office. In this section, we refer to the third method as a "personal property filing against fixtures" to distinguish it from a fixture filing.

The general rule is that personal property filings against fixtures are subordinate to real property owners and encumbrancers. UCC §9-334(c).

("Encumbrancer" is essentially the Article 9 term for a mortgage holder. UCC §9-102(a)(32).) The priority for real property owners and mortgagees is apparently intended to enable them to assure themselves of priority without having to search outside the real property recording system.

Personal property filings against fixtures are cheaper and easier to make than fixture filings. To see why, consider the options available to the credit-seller of a type of property that might be affixed to real estate. To make a fixture filing, the seller must identify the real property and its owner, obtain the property's legal description, include the owner's name and legal description in the filing, and pay real property recording fees and taxes. At the time of the sale, even the buyer may not yet have determined the real property to which it will affix the collateral.

By contrast, the seller can make a personal property filing immediately on sale, using nothing but the description of the property sold. Article 9 filing fees are smaller and only a few states tax their filing. If the loan size is insufficient to justify the expense and trouble of both a fixture filing and a personal property filing against fixtures, even a sophisticated secured party may choose to make only the latter.

A personal property filing against fixtures has priority over three kinds of competitors. The first is lien creditors, including the trustee in bankruptcy. See UCC §9-334(e)(3) and Comment 9. The Article 9 drafters justified their grant of priority to a personal property filing against fixtures on the assertion that "generally, a judgment creditor is not a reliance creditor who would have searched the records." We doubt the accuracy of this assertion. Unsecured creditors commonly monitor the public records through various reporting services, and many judgment creditors search before they levy. More to the point, the fact that many creditors do not search does not warrant the enforcement of personal property filings against those who perfected liens in real property after searching the real property records.

The second kind of competitor a personal property filing against fixtures can trump is an owner or encumbrancer with respect to certain kinds of "readily removable" fixtures. Recall that, in general, the UCC leaves the defining of "fixtures"—and therefore the determination of which filing system must be used—to the real estate law of the state. UCC §9-102(a)(41). Real estate lawmakers have in some jurisdictions defined "fixtures" so broadly as to include property that can be easily removed.

The Article 9 drafters struck back in UCC §9-334(e)(2). That section does not challenge real estate law's characterization of such property as fixtures or prevent encumbrance of the property through recordings in the real estate system. It does, however, permit personal property filings to defeat those mortgages and fixture filings with respect to readily removable factory or office machines, equipment that is not primarily used in operation of the real property, or replacement domestic appliances. To illustrate, by making personal property filings, sellers of replacement kitchen appliances can get priority over the mortgages against the homes in which the kitchen appliances are later installed.

Read literally, the priority granted to personal property filings in UCC §9-334(e)(2) may be broad. Property intended to be affixed to real estate is generally designed to be readily installable, which usually means it will be readily removable. For example, a ski lift that is bolted to concrete foundations can probably be unbolted just as easily. The three categories of collateral listed in §9-334(e)(2) thus arguably except the large bulk of what real property law characterizes as "fixtures."

A third kind of competitor a personal property filing against fixtures may be able to defeat is a later fixture filing. UCC §9-322 awards priority among competing filers without distinguishing between fixture filings and personal property filings against fixtures. The first to file or perfect wins. We see no policy reason for the failure to distinguish between these types of filings, and much mischief may flow from that failure. The most prominent bit of mischief is that every Article 9 fixture filer needs two searches: one in the real estate records in which the fixture filer will file and one in the UCC filing system in which a personal property filer would file against the collateral. Double the searching may mean double the costs.

Problem Set 33

33.1.   Fifteen years ago, Wanda Fish recovered a judgment against her ex-husband, Marshall, for $350,000 in lump-sum alimony. Marshall resolved never to pay it, and moved to California. Five years ago, Wanda tracked him down, established her judgment in California, and recorded it in the county where Marshall lived. Because Marshall had no assets at the time, she did not pursue the matter further. Later, Marshall prospered. On March 1 of this year, Marshall paid $1,000,000 in cash to buy a house: $200,000 of that was from his savings, the other $800,000 was a loan from Security Finance. The mortgage to Security Finance was a purchase-money mortgage and that fact was recited in it. As a result of the sudden death of an office employee, Security Finance did not record their mortgage until March 10. As between Wanda and Security Finance, who will have priority in Marshall's home? The California statute regarding priority of a purchase-money mortgage is set forth in this assignment. Assume that the California recording statute is the same as New York Real Property Laws §291, also set forth in this assignment.

33.2.   Add these facts to those of the preceding problem: Marshall discovered Security Finance's delay in recording, and he borrowed $500,000 from Pacific State Bank on March 8. (Marshall moves quickly.) Pacific State recorded on the same day. Marshall used part of the loan proceeds to purchase airfare to the Bahamas and has not been seen since.

   a.   As between Security Finance and Pacific State, who has priority in Marshall's house?

   b.   As between Wanda and Pacific State, who has priority in Marshall's house? See Cal. Civ. Proc. Code §697.310(a) in Assignment 28.

   c.   If all three end up in court together, who will win?

33.3.   a.   George Onasis, the trustee in bankruptcy for William Miller, has retained you to advise on avoidance matters. Eighteen months before filing bankruptcy, Miller bought a mobile home on credit from Folds Mobile Home Sales (Folds). Folds took a security interest in the mobile home, and filed a nonfixture financing statement in the office of the Secretary of State. The state in which this took place does not issue certificates of title for mobile homes. Under its laws, the mobile home was a fixture even before Folds filed its financing statement. Onasis asks your opinion as to whether the estate has priority over Folds. Bankr. Code §544(a), UCC §§9-102(a)(40), (41), and (52); 9-317(a); 9-334(e)(3) and (4); 9-501(a); Comment 4 to UCC §9-501.

b.   Another creditor has surfaced in Miller's bankruptcy. After Miller affixed the mobile home to the real property, Commercial Finance extended credit to Miller, took a security interest in the mobile home, and made a fixture filing in the real estate records in the county where the real property is located. As between Folds and Commercial Finance, who has priority? UCC §§9-102(a)(32), 9-322(a), 9-334(a) and (c).

33.4.   a.   Two months ago your client, Sound City, Inc., sold a sound system to Jake's Bar and Restaurant during Jake's remodeling. The installer spent three days on the site, running wiring from the stage to the control booth and from there to speakers throughout the premises. Most of the wiring is above the drop ceiling, but some was fished through the conduits used in the electrical wiring of the building. Speakers are bolted to walls and ceiling beams; some of the control panels are built in. Jake was supposed to pay for the sound system as soon as it was installed. Instead, he complained about the quality of the sound and had the installer back every few days. Now the installer says that Jake's complaints are bogus and "he's just stalling for time." Sound City has neither promissory note nor security agreement. What do you recommend?

b.   You discovered that the reason Jake was stalling for time was that he was in the process of refinancing the bar and restaurant. Before you could do anything, the new lender, Mercantile Bank, recorded their mortgage. Assuming that the bank acted in good faith and without knowledge that Sound City had installed the sound system, where does this leave you?

33.5.   Sound City has contracted for another installation. The job is similar to the one they did for Jake's Bar and Restaurant, except this time the customer is Dub's Lounge. No remodeling will be done, and the customer will pay in installments over a period of 18 months after installation. Bill Sauls, the owner of Sound City, says he wants at least the right to "rip everything back out if they don't pay for it." In response to your questions, he says he doesn't know whether Dub's owns the place where the installation will be done or whether they rent it. Nor does he know whether there are mortgages outstanding against the property.

a.   Assume Sound City installs a sound system on Dub's authority and Dub's doesn't pay for it. Will Sound City be entitled to a mechanic's lien? If it is, will that be an adequate remedy?

b.   Assume Sound City decides to make a fixture filing. Whose authorization does Sound City need? UCC §§9-102(a)(28), 9-203(b), 9-502(b)(4), 9-509, 9-604(c), and 9-334(f). For example, if it turns out that Dub's has the premises under a long-term lease from the fee owner, Realty Partners Ltd., do you have to have a contract with Realty Partners, or can Sound City do the deal on Dub's signature alone? UCC §§9-334, 9-502(b)(4).

c.   Does your answer to question b change if Sound City is installing a sound system in a new building that is under construction? UCC §§9-334(d), (e), and (h). In the construction scenario, would Dub's consent in writing to removal of the sound system in the event of default be of help? UCC §9-334(f).

33.6.   In 2001, Northcorp lent $500,000 to Cliff's Ridge Skiing and took a security interest in all ski-lifts located on the resort property. Northcorp perfected by filing a financing statement in the UCC filing system. In 2002, Finance America lent $1 million to Cliff's Ridge Skiing and took a security interest in the same collateral. Finance America perfected by making a fixture filing in county real property records. In 2003, Refi America lent $24 million to Cliff's Ridge Skiing, took a security interest in the real property, and perfected by recording a mortgage in the real property records. In 2008, Cliff's Ridge Skiing closed its business and filed under Chapter 7 of the Bankruptcy Code. With the consent of these three creditors, the trustee sold the resort property for $22 million and sold the lifts separately for $400,000. Assuming that the lifts are fixtures, who is entitled to what proceeds? UCC §§9-102(a)(40), 9-334(c) and (e)(1), 9-322(a)(1), and 9-501(a)(2); Comment 4 to UCC §9-501.

■ End of Default Problem Set

33.7.   Three years ago, your client, Barney Wells, loaned $75,000 to his brother Wilbur to help Wilbur buy a small apartment building in New York. Wilbur executed a mortgage against the property to Barney at the time, but Barney did not record it because he thought recording might offend Wilbur. Since then, Wilbur's financial condition and Barney's relationship with him have grown progressively worse. Concerned about rumors of profligacy and financial ruin, Barney finally recorded his mortgage two weeks ago and purchased a title and encumbrance search. The search shows four encumbrances against the property:

1. A mortgage in favor of Walter Weyrauch in the amount of $45,000 recorded four years ago (the mortgage is actually on a different piece of property owned by Wilbur; it shows up on your search because the mortgage contains an after-acquired property clause).
2. A judgment for $38,000 in favor of Talbot Financial Services, Inc., recorded two years ago.
3. A mortgage in favor of Allie Toklas, recorded one year ago in the amount of $60,000.
4. The mortgage to Barney Wells.

Each of the four documents is regular on its face. Barney says Toklas is a close friend of Wilbur; he does not recognize the other two names. Barney estimates that the property is worth about the amount of his mortgage. Barney acknowledges that he "screwed up" by not bringing this matter to you at the time of the loan, but he wants to know if there is anything you can do for him now. Is there? Can you imagine any facts consistent with what Barney has told you that would make his mortgage valuable? Or is he, as Wilbur told him yesterday, "dead in the water"? New York Real Property Laws §291. Assume that New York defines "purchase-money mortgage" in accord with 42 Pennsylvania Consolidated Statutes §8141 and gives it priority in accord with California Civil Code §2898 (all three sections are reproduced in this assignment).

Assignment 34: Multiple Items of Collateral, Marshaling, Cross-Collateralization, and Purchase Money Priority

Multiple items of property can serve as collateral for a single debt. In addition, a single item of collateral can secure multiple debts to the same secured party. The latter relationship is referred to as *cross collateralization*. Both these phenomena can occur in the same transaction. That is, multiple items of collateral can serve as security for multiple debts. The language of the security agreement generally specifies what property serves as collateral for what debts and the law generally gives effect to that specification.

Section A of this assignment describes these two relationships in more detail. Section B describes the baseline rights of the secured party in these relationships. Section C explains how the doctrine of marshaling of assets limits those baseline rights. Section D examines the effect of cross-collateralization on purchase money status.

A. Multiple Items of Collateral and Cross-Collateralization Provisions in Security Agreements

To set the stage for the analysis that follows we begin with a story. Assume that South Bank lends $50,000 to Michael Williams, secured by Red Mars, Williams's racehorse. The horse is worth $70,000. As you saw in the early assignments of this book, in the event of default South Bank could foreclose by selling the horse and pay itself from the proceeds. If Red Mars were lame at the time of foreclosure and sold for only $1,000, South Bank would get the $1,000 and be entitled to a judgment against Williams for the $49,000 deficiency. UCC §9-615(d)(2). The deficiency judgment would be unsecured.

Now assume that prior to his default, South Bank lent Williams an additional $50,000 to acquire Green Mars, another horse also worth $70,000. South Bank could have treated this second loan as entirely separate from the first. That is, it could have prepared a second note and security agreement, securing the second $50,000 loan by a security interest in Green Mars. Each horse then would have been collateral for only the corresponding loan. Williams would have been personally liable for any deficiency on either loan.

Continuing with this scenario, if Williams had defaulted on both loans and South Bank foreclosed, the separateness of the two loans might have put South

Bank at a disadvantage. For example, if Red Mars had sold for $1,000 and Green Mars had sold for $70,000, the result would have been a $49,000 deficiency judgment against Williams on the first loan and a $20,000 surplus in favor of Williams on the second. South Bank would have had the right to enforce its $49,000 deficiency judgment against Williams's interest in the surplus, but in doing so, South Bank could have employed only the remedies available to an unsecured creditor. South Bank would have been subject to any exemptions Williams might have had under state law and been subordinate to any junior liens then existing against Green Mars. If Williams got his hands on the $20,000 surplus before South Bank could enforce against it, Williams might have spent the money or used it to pay other creditors.

A secured creditor may have no way of knowing at the time of the loan which particular items of collateral will be most valuable at the time of foreclosure. In our first illustration, Green Mars was the valuable one. But it might have been Red Mars that sold for $70,000 and Green Mars that sold for only $1,000. The risk of collateralizing each loan separately is that South Bank could have a deficiency on one loan at the same time that it had a surplus on the other. Indeed, if Red Mars had turned out to be worth enough to satisfy both loans, with separate collateralization, South Bank might still be facing a $49,000 deficiency on its loan against Green Mars. Williams's other creditors might be able to beat South Bank to the $50,000 surplus from the sale of Red Mars.

Cross-collateralization is the usual method for solving this problem. When South Bank makes the second loan to Williams, it requires him to sign a security agreement stating that both horses are collateral for the entire balance of each loan. The effect is that, in the event of default on either loan, South Bank would be entitled to foreclose against either horse or both horses, and apply the proceeds to the two loans in any manner South Bank chose. If Red Mars were lame at the time of the sale and were to bring only $1,000, but Green Mars were to sell for $70,000, South Bank would get both the $1,000 and the $70,000 in its capacity as a secured creditor. As a secured creditor, South Bank would not be subject to any exemptions to which Williams might be entitled. Security interests created and perfected after that of South Bank would be subordinate. South Bank could lose money only if the total value of the two horses were less than the total amount owing on the two loans.

In the above example, South Bank did not anticipate making a second loan to Williams against a second horse. If it had, South Bank could easily have provided for both security interests in a single set of documents. You are already familiar with the necessary contract provisions. The security agreement would secure all obligations owing from Williams to South Bank, including future advances (a future-advance clause). It would provide for a security interest in Red Mars "and all racehorses hereafter acquired by the debtor" or some such language (an after-acquired property clause). Perhaps the only document Williams would sign at the time of the second loan would be a promissory note for the additional $50,000. The effect is that South Bank's loans would be cross-collateralized and secured by multiple items of collateral. Every item of collateral would secure every dollar of debt.

B.   The Secured Creditor's Right to Choose Its Remedy

A secured creditor generally has the right to choose when it will foreclose. We now add the rule that a creditor secured by more than one item of collateral generally has the right to choose when it will foreclose against each. To illustrate, consider again the situation where South Bank has lent $100,000 and secured the loan with a security interest in both horses. Upon default, South Bank would have the right to foreclose against Green Mars, see how much it could recover at the sale, and then decide when and whether to foreclose against Red Mars. If Green Mars sold for enough to pay the entire debt, South Bank might be saved the time and trouble of trying to squeeze money out of a lame horse. If South Bank collected only $70,000 from the sale of Green Mars, it need not immediately proceed against Red Mars. It could wait and see what Williams did about paying the remaining balance.

Under this general rule, a creditor secured by multiple items of collateral might have numerous strategic options. A secured creditor that wanted to force its debtor into bankruptcy reorganization with minimum effort (perhaps to get court supervision of the debtor's payouts) might file an action for replevin of just a single item of collateral — but one without which the debtor could not continue in business. The creditor's intent would not be to take possession of the item and sell it, but to leave the debtor no practical option other than to "voluntarily" file for bankruptcy reorganization.

The general rule we have just discussed may seem too generous to the secured creditor. But the opposite rule — a secured creditor must foreclose against all of its collateral or none — would be completely unworkable. A secured creditor's collateral might be scattered through dozens of jurisdictions, necessitating the simultaneous filing of actions in all of them. The creditor might have to bring several forms of action and join numerous owners. Some of the collateral might be of such little value that the creditor would prefer to abandon it, but making that determination might require extensive investigation. In most circumstances, these problems do not arise because the applicable rule permits the creditor to foreclose against part of the collateral without waiving or abandoning its rights against the rest.

1.   *Debtor-Enforceable Limits on the Secured Creditor's Right to Choose Its Remedy*

Limits in favor of a debtor on a secured creditor's right to choose the sequence in which it will proceed against its various items of collateral are rare. Yet some exist. A secured party might bring so many separate foreclosure actions against a debtor that the court would bar further actions as a nuisance. A few states (most notably California) have "single action" rules. The California version states that "[t]here can be only one action to enforce payment on a debt secured by a mortgage on real property." A creditor in one of these states who forecloses against one parcel of real estate omitting another may find that it has lost the omitted parcel as collateral. These single action rules do not apply to personal property. UCC §9-604(a)(1) specifically authorizes secured creditors to sever the foreclosure against personal property collateral from their foreclosure of the same security interest against real estate collateral, and foreclosure against one piece of personalty does not, in ordinary circumstances, bar later foreclosure against another.

2.   *Release of Collateral*

A corollary of the secured creditor's right to choose what collateral it will proceed against is that all collateral remains encumbered until the debt is paid in full. To illustrate, assume that South Bank has made a $100,000 loan to Williams secured by the $140,000 value of the two horses. Williams finds a buyer who will pay $70,000 in cash for Green Mars. He wants to make the sale. The buyer, of course, insists on receiving clear title. If this sale were in the ordinary course of Williams's business, that would be no problem. Under UCC §9-320(a), a buyer in the ordinary course of business would take free of the security interest of South Bank. But Williams is not in the business of selling horses, so the buyer will not take free of the security interest. See UCC §9-317(b), 9-323(d).

How can Williams clear South Bank's security interest from the title? One way would be for Williams to pay his debt to South Bank and insist that South Bank file a termination statement under UCC §9-513(c). Provided that South Bank has no obligation to make further advances to him, the bank will be obliged to comply. But to trigger his right to a termination statement under UCC §9-513(c), Williams must pay the entire $100,000 debt. That he cannot afford to do, because he is receiving only $70,000 for Green Mars and he doesn't have the other $30,000 he needs.

Hat in hand, Williams goes to South Bank to ask that the bank *release*—that is, voluntarily surrender, its right to Green Mars as collateral. Williams explains his predicament to the loan officer. He proposes that the loan officer attend the closing on his sale of the horse. In return for a release of Green Mars from South Bank's security interest, Williams offers to apply $50,000 of the proceeds of sale to South Bank's loan—that is, the buyers will pay $50,000 to South Bank and $20,000 to Williams. South Bank will then have a $50,000 loan outstanding secured by Red Mars, which is alone worth $70,000. South Bank will still be oversecured and, Williams argues, have no significant risk of loss. After a brief review of the file, the loan officer advises Williams that his proposal is not acceptable to South Bank and that it will be necessary for Williams to pay the full balance of the loan at closing. Williams thinks about that for a few minutes and decides to increase his offer.

"How about if I just pay you the full $70,000 I am getting for Green Mars?" Williams asks. "The $30,000 balance on your loan will then be secured by a horse worth $70,000."

"I'm sorry," says the loan officer, "but in cases like this it is the bank's policy to insist upon full payment at closing."

At this point, Williams is more than just a little annoyed. "You have no *reason* to insist on full payment at closing. You're getting every penny from the sale. You'll be better off as a result of this sale. Now you have collateral worth 140 percent of the loan; after the sale I've arranged, you'll have collateral worth 233 percent of the loan."

"I'm sorry," the loan officer says, repeating himself, "but in cases like this it is the bank's policy to insist upon full payment at closing."

Now Williams is really agitated. "You're *preventing* me from repaying this loan," he says. "I can't sell both horses at the same time and expect to get full value for them. I've arranged a sale that is entirely for your benefit, and you are making it impossible for me to do it. What you're doing is illegal."

At the sound of the word "illegal," the loan officer perks up. He begins speaking slowly and deliberately. "This bank is not *preventing* you from doing anything. You signed the security agreement and we are just insisting on our rights under it. You *say* that at $70,000 you are getting full value for Green Mars, but we have no way of knowing that. You *say* that Red Mars is worth $70,000 and so we'll be oversecured, but for all we know, the horse could be lame. It's not our job to figure out all this stuff every time you want to sell some of the collateral. We don't know anything about horses; we're a *bank*." Now the loan officer is just as agitated as Williams. "If it's such a great deal to have Red Mars as collateral for a $30,000 loan, why don't you borrow the $30,000 from somebody else and pay us off?"

"How am I going to get some other bank to make the loan when you've already made it and are trying to weasel out of it? You might as well have called my loan!" Williams was on his feet, storming out of the loan officer's office.

"We just want our rights under the contract," the loan officer yells at the retreating debtor. "The contract you *signed*."

The loan officer in this story was not being entirely honest with Williams. His real reason for insisting on the bank's rights under the contract was that state bank examiners were pressing the bank to reduce the size of its outstanding loan portfolio. Insisting on their rights under their contracts is one of the few legal ways a bank can do that. But then Williams was not being entirely honest with the loan officer. He stormed out in such a hurry because he had to meet with the veterinarian who had just taken her second look at the problem with Red Mars's leg.

In other circumstances, the bank might have been willing to negotiate for the release of Green Mars. South Bank might have had the horses appraised and, if they did, certainly would have required that Williams pay for the appraisals. They might also have taken this opportunity to cure any perceived defects in the loan documents by having Williams sign new ones, or to request that Williams give additional collateral. South Bank might have required a paydown of the loan in an amount more or less than the full $70,000 Williams was getting for the sale of Green Mars.

Sophisticated debtors often negotiate release clauses as part of the initial loan agreement. For example, assume that Williams anticipated this problem with South Bank. Before acquiring the second horse, he might have negotiated for the right to a release of either horse upon payment of a specified portion of the loan. South Bank would probably have required a paydown of more than half the loan to obtain a release of one of the two horses. Alternatively, South Bank might have required that Williams give advance notice of the release request and pay for South Bank to appraise the horses immediately prior to release. That would have enabled them to use a percentage paydown formula that ensured they would be more secure after the release than before.

Debtors do not need release clauses for collateral that is inventory. UCC §9-320(a) sets as the default rule that a sale of inventory automatically releases the property sold from any security interest created by the seller. The rule can be varied by agreement, and some inventory loan agreements do require that the debtor obtain the consent of the secured party to the sale of each item of inventory. (This method typically is used for "big ticket" items such as aircraft or industrial machinery, where a single transaction is big enough to warrant this kind of attention.) The most common response, however, is to leave the default rule in effect and provide in the security agreement for payoff of particular portions of the loan upon sale of particular portions of the collateral. To illustrate, if the collateral for the loan is two horses of equal value, the agreement might provide that immediately upon sale of either horse the debtor must repay 65 percent of the loan.

C. Marshaling Assets

An oversecured creditor's election to proceed against one item of collateral rather than another can determine the fate of other unpaid creditors. Consider again our previous example in which Red Mars and Green Mars are each worth $70,000, and South Bank has a first security interest in both horses for $100,000. Add to the facts that Williams has given Becky Sansei a second security interest in Green Mars, securing her loan to Williams in the amount of $40,000. Later, Williams defaults on his payments to South Bank and the bank forecloses. If the bank repossesses Green Mars and sells it, the sale will discharge Sansei's security interest. UCC §9-617(a)(3). The bank will be entitled to all of the sale proceeds. UCC §9-615(a). Sansei will then have nothing but an unsecured claim. Sansei will be left to compete as an unsecured creditor for Williams's equity in Red Mars or his other nonexempt assets.

Notice that if, instead of repossessing Green Mars first, South Bank had repossessed Red Mars first and sold it for $70,000, Sansei would have been assured a full recovery. Application of the $70,000 in proceeds of the Red Mars sale to South Bank's loan would have reduced the balance to $30,000. If South Bank later sold Green Mars for $70,000, South Bank would have been entitled to only the first $30,000, leaving just enough to pay the $40,000 balance owing to Sansei under her second security interest. The point of this example is that South Bank's decision to pursue Red Mars or Green Mars first determines whether Sansei can recover from her collateral at all.

1.   Marshaling as a Limit on the Secured Creditor's Choice

Marshaling assets is an equitable doctrine developed to limit the senior secured creditor's choice of which collateral to pursue. When the doctrine applies, it requires that a creditor such as South Bank look for its recovery to the asset not encumbered by junior liens, so that the holders of the junior liens, such as Becky Sansei, can recover from the only collateral available to them. As the following case illustrates, when this doctrine operates to the benefit of junior lienors, it is usually to the detriment of the debtor's unsecured creditors.

In re Robert E. Derecktor of Rhode Island, Inc.

150 B.R. 296 (Bankr. D.R.I. 1993)

ARTHUR N. VOTOLATO, UNITED STATES BANKRUPTCY JUDGE.

Robert E. Derecktor of Rhode Island, Inc., which for approximately 13 years had conducted a ship building and repair facility in Portsmouth, Rhode Island, filed a Chapter 11 petition on January 3, 1992. Since the filing the debtor has operated in varying but limited fashion, and is presently in the final stages of total liquidation, with no future operations contemplated.

Before us is the Rhode Island Port Authority's Motion wherein it asks this Court to order marshaling as to Federal Deposit Insurance Corporation's (FDIC) interest in the Debtor's assets. Several unsecured creditors oppose the relief sought by the Port Authority on the ground that to allow marshaling would diminish or wipe out any dividend they might otherwise receive.

FACTS

The relevant facts, as they appear below, are not in dispute: On April 13, 1979, the Port Authority loaned Derecktor $6,500,000 for the acquisition of facilities and equipment to be used in its ship building and repair business. As collateral for the loan the Port Authority retained a security interest in all of Derecktor's then owned and after acquired fixtures, furniture, furnishings, equipment, machinery, inventory, and other tangible personal property. As of February 15, 1992, the Debtor owed $4,975,000 to the Port Authority on the original obligation.

On October 23, 1987, to purchase a 20,000-ton floating dry dock (Dry Dock III), Derecktor borrowed $6.5 million from, and executed a purchase money security mortgage to Bank of New England-Old Colony. As additional collateral, Derecktor granted the bank a security interest in all of its presently owned and after acquired machinery, docks, equipment, inventory, personal property, and general intangibles. As of February 6, 1992, approximately $5.8 million was due on this loan.

On December 21, 1988, Bank of New England loaned Derecktor $2,500,000 more, and received a security interest in Debtor's accounts, contracts, contract rights, inventory, and equipment. This security interest also covered the balance due on the original $6.5 million loan. As of February 6, 1992, approximately

$1.2 million remained due on the December 1988 loan. When Bank of New England was deemed insolvent, FDIC became its successor-in-interest, entitling it to payment under Derecktor's obligations to Bank of New England.

As is evident, both FDIC and the Port Authority have a security interest in some of the same collateral, namely the equipment, inventory, machinery, and Dry Dock III. FDIC has the senior secured position on Dry Dock III, and it has the only security interest in the Debtor's intangibles, accounts, contracts, and contract rights. The Debtor's major assets include: (1) Dry Dock III; (2) an assignable tug boat contract (the Assignment); (3) a claim against Insurance Company of North America (INA Settlement); and (4) equipment, machinery, and inventory. The parties have agreed to liquidate the assets in the most efficient manner, and to defer the resolution of the marshaling issue pending the disposition of the assets.

Dry Dock III, the first asset liquidated, was sold in July, 1992 for $6.6 million. The Tug Assignment and the INA Settlement were both approved on September 25, 1992, producing approximately $2.1 million from the Assignment, and $650,000 from the INA Settlement. The equipment, machinery, and inventory were sold in January, 1993, and proceeds were approximately $1.0 million.

In the normal course, i.e. without marshaling, because Dry Dock III was the first asset liquidated, FDIC would apply the entire $6.6 million against its $7.0 million secured claim. The balance of its claim would then be satisfied from the proceeds of the Tug Assignment, and thereafter the funds remaining from the Assignment and INA Settlement would be used to pay junior secured creditors, and finally unsecured creditors. Again, without marshaling, the Port Authority's security interest would extend only (after the Dry Dock III proceeds go to FDIC) to the equipment, machinery, and inventory and therefore, it would recover, at best, $1.0 million of its $5.0 million claim. Through marshaling however, the Port Authority can realize the benefit of its second secured position on Dry Dock III, with FDIC looking first to the INA Settlement and the Assignment for payment, and thereafter to Dry Dock III, leaving a surplus for junior lienors.

DISCUSSION

The present dispute concerns the propriety of applying the doctrine of marshaling to the facts before us. Marshaling is an equitable doctrine which "rests upon the principle that a creditor having two funds to satisfy his debt may not, by his application of them to his demand, defeat another creditor, who may resort to only one of the funds." Sowell v. Federal Reserve Bank, 268 U.S. 449, 457, 69 L. Ed. 1041, 45 S. Ct. 528 (1925). The purpose of the doctrine is to "prevent the arbitrary action of a senior lienor from destroying the rights of a junior lienor or a creditor having less security." Meyer v. United States, 375 U.S. 233, 237, 11 L. Ed. 2d 293, 84 S. Ct. 318 (1963). Equity requires the senior creditor to look first to property which cannot be reached by the junior creditor, but only if the senior creditor or third parties are not prejudiced.

To apply the marshaling doctrine, three elements must be present: (1) the existence of two creditors of the Debtor; (2) the existence of two funds owned by the Debtor; and (3) the ability of one creditor to satisfy its claim from either or both of the funds, while the other creditor can only look to one of the funds.

The instant controversy falls squarely within these requirements: (1) FDIC and the Port Authority are two creditors of the Debtor; (2) there are (more than) two funds of the Debtor available for these creditors, i.e. sale proceeds from Dry Dock III, the Assignment, the INA Settlement, and the equipment, machinery, and inventory; and (3) FDIC can satisfy its claim from all of the Debtor's funds, while the Port Authority can only look to Dry Dock III and the equipment, machinery, and inventory for payment.

The unsecured creditors object to the application of the doctrine on the ground of prejudice, in that marshaling will give the Port Authority more security than it originally bargained for. The FDIC's claim is roughly $7.0 million, which would be almost entirely satisfied from the proceeds of the Dry Dock III sale. If FDIC were paid these proceeds, the Port Authority's recovery on its $5.0 million claim would be limited to approximately $1.0 million from the sale of the equipment and machinery, and the balance of its claim would be rendered unsecured. However, if FDIC is required to look first to the proceeds from the Assignment and the INA Settlement before looking to Dry Dock III, the Port Authority will receive an additional $2.0 million on its secured claim. While it is clear that marshaling in this manner will deplete the funds otherwise available to unsecured creditors, we do not find such a result to constitute legal prejudice, in the marshaling context.

The history and intended purpose of the doctrine, as well as a review of the more recent cases addressing the issue, support this conclusion. Historically, marshaling has been applied for the benefit of the junior secured creditor by preserving its collateral through a court established order of distribution of secured assets. This is accomplished by requiring the senior secured creditor to look first to its single interest collateral, i.e. property that the junior secured creditor cannot reach, before looking to the shared collateral to satisfy its claim, and this of course invariably results in a diminution of the funds available for unsecured creditors. If we were to accept the unsecured creditors' argument regarding prejudice, the doctrine of marshaling would rarely, if ever, be utilized in bankruptcy because its application almost always results in diminished assets for the unsecured creditors.

The Port Authority bargained for security on its loan, whereas the unsecured creditors did not, and this allows the junior secured creditor to realize the benefit of its bargain. The caveat against causing harm or prejudice to others applies only to parties having equity equal to the party seeking to invoke marshaling. As the Supreme Court in *Meyer* stated,

> [Marshaling] deals with the rights of all who have an interest in the property involved and is applied only when it can be equitably fashioned as to all of the parties. Thus, state courts have refused to apply it where the rights of third parties having equal equity would be prejudiced.

Here, the parties do not stand on equal footing—the Port Authority's rights as a secured creditor are legally superior to those of the unsecured creditors, and accordingly the "prejudice" argument does not apply in this instance.

Accordingly, based upon all of the foregoing, the Port Authority's Motion requesting FDIC to marshal its interest in Debtor's assets, is GRANTED.

The doctrine of marshaling assets is subject to several limitations on its applicability. Notice, for example, Judge Votolato's comment in passing that the doctrine of marshaling assets can be applied "only if the senior creditor [is] not prejudiced." In Matter of Woolf Printing Corp., 87 B.R. 692 (Bankr. M.D. Fla. 1988), the senior creditor, Mac Papers, had a security interest in the proceeds of a life insurance policy and also in the debtor's personal property, including furniture, fixtures, equipment, inventory, and accounts receivable. The junior creditor, NCNB, had a security interest only in the proceeds of the life insurance policy. The insured was dead, and the proceeds of the life insurance were in the hands of the court. The court refused to require Mac Papers to recover from the personal property, thereby denying NCNB any recovery from its lien at all. The court explained its decision in terms of "equity":

> NCNB argues Mac Papers should satisfy its debt by first looking to the Debtor's personal property. In order to accomplish this satisfaction, Mac Papers would have to have relief from the automatic stay, then sell the property to satisfy the debt with the sale proceeds. There is no evidence to show the time frame within which the property could be sold. On the other hand, if Mac Papers were not compelled to marshal, it would be able to look to the insurance proceeds first. This is ready cash which would be immediately available. Upon a review of the characteristics of the two funds it is clear that compelling Mac Papers to look to the Debtor's personal property prior to the insurance proceeds would cause undue delay in satisfying the debt. Since marshaling would injuriously affect the secured interests of Mac Papers, this Court declines to compel the requested equitable relief.

While the *Woolf Printing* court's idea of equity (NCNB should not recover at all rather than put Mac Papers through the delay of personal property foreclosure) is probably not widely shared, the case stands as a good reminder that marshaling assets is available only when the court thinks it ought to be.

Another limitation on the doctrine of marshaling assets is that it generally cannot be used to compel the senior creditor to foreclose against homestead property. If the senior creditor has both homestead and nonhomestead property to which it can look for recovery, a creditor with a junior lien on only the nonhomestead property cannot force the senior creditor to foreclose against the homestead. If the homestead is exempt to a dollar limit, the homestead is subject to marshaling up to that limit.

The courts are split as the situation in which the first lienor has the right to seek payment from either or both of two funds and each fund is subject to a subordinate lien. Consider for example, the situation in which Sansei holds a $40,000 second security interest in Green Mars and Rodriguez holds a $50,000 second security interest in Red Mars. On these facts, some courts hold that it is no more "equitable" to require the holder of the first security interest, South Bank, to look to Red Mars for its recovery in a suit brought by Sansei than it is to require South Bank to look to Green Mars for its recovery in a suit brought by Rodriguez. Neither Sansei nor Rodriguez can use marshaling assets to force the bank's choice of a remedy. Another possible outcome is that each of the junior liens is compelled to bear the burden of the first lien in proportion to the value of the fund to which that junior lienholder has a claim. If each horse is worth

$70,000 and South Bank is entitled to $100,000, Sansei and Rodriguez are each entitled to $20,000. Yet other courts would permit the earlier-perfected of the two second liens to force marshaling against the later perfected. Thus, if Sansei perfected before Rodriguez, Sansei would be entitled to $40,000 and Rodriguez would be entitled to nothing.

2. Equitable Assignment as an Alternative to Marshaling

As you read the description of *Woolf Printing* you may have wondered what would have happened if NCNB had offered to eliminate the prejudice to Mac Papers by paying the expenses Mac Papers would incur in foreclosing and making cash immediately available to Mac Papers in the form of an interest-free loan secured by Mac Paper's interest in the debtor's personal property. Mac Papers would have suffered no prejudice and NCNB would have been able to recover. The same result could be reached another way: Let Mac Papers recover from the insurance policy, but give NCNB Mac Papers's rights against the personal property. Faced with situations like *Woolf Printing*, where the prejudice to the senior creditor from marshaling assets was merely procedural, some courts have done precisely that. That is, they deny marshaling and let the senior creditor recover from the most convenient source. But as a condition of doing so, they require the senior creditor to assign its security interest in the unforeclosed collateral to the junior creditor. The effect is like marshaling, but the risks and procedural burdens have been transferred to the junior creditor.

The case of *Janke v. Chace* illustrates this *equitable assignment* remedy. Jack Chace owned 280 acres of land, subject to a mortgage in favor of Farm Credit Bank of Omaha. At the time of the dispute, this mortgage had been paid down to $19,000. Chace sold two of the 280 acres to his son, James Chace. The mortgage continued to encumber the two acres. James was married to Diana Janke. The couple borrowed $116,000 from Diana Janke's parents (the Jankes) to build a house on the two acres and gave the Jankes a mortgage on the house and two acres. James and Diana defaulted in payments on this mortgage and the Jankes foreclosed. At that time, the house and two acres were worth less than the $116,000 owing against them. After the foreclosure judgment was entered, the Jankes requested that the court "marshal the assets" by requiring Farm Credit to look to the remaining 278 acres for payment of its $19,000 and letting the Jankes have all the proceeds from the house and two acres. Farm Credit resisted.

The court concluded that the doctrine of marshaling assets was inapplicable because the requirement of a "common debtor" was not met. (Jack Chace was debtor to Farm Credit; James Chace and Diana Janke were debtors to the Jankes. Nobody owed both loans.) For that reason, the court denied marshaling and allowed Farm Credit to recover its $19,000 from the proceeds of the sale of the house and two acres. The court concluded, nevertheless, that "equitable principles" required a remedy for the Jankes. It ordered that the $19,000 be treated not as a payment of the mortgage to Farm Credit but as a purchase of it. That is, upon receiving the $19,000 from the foreclosure of the house and two acres, Farm Credit had to assign to the Jankes all of its right, title, and interest in the $19,000 note and mortgage. Farm Credit would have its $19,000 from the house and two acres, but the Jankes could then recoup their loss by recovering $19,000 from the 278 acres owned by Jack Chace.

3. Can Unsecured Creditors Marshal?

In *Derecktor*, Judge Votolato permitted marshaling assets *against* unsecured creditors. That is, he forced the senior creditor to look for recovery to the only assets from which the unsecured creditors could hope to recover. There are cases that hold to the contrary when the debtor has filed bankruptcy. Doctrinally, the argument for this minority view goes as follows. Bankruptcy Code §544(a) gives the trustee or debtor in possession the rights of an ideal lien creditor. Thus, any attempt to marshal against a bankruptcy estate is an attempt to marshal against a junior lienor. As we noted above, the doctrine of marshaling assets cannot be used by one junior lienor to the detriment of another.

Acceptance of this argument protects the bankruptcy trustee and, through the bankruptcy trustee, the unsecured creditors, from the attempts of other lienors to marshal against them. But it provides only a limited ability for the bankruptcy trustee to marshal against others. Marshaling doesn't produce additional assets; it merely shifts assets from one application to another. Marshaling is always *for* someone's interest and *against* someone else's. A bankruptcy trustee cannot marshal against other lien holders for reasons already stated; it cannot marshal against unsecured creditors because it already represents all of the unsecured creditors; it cannot marshal against the debtor because the debtor has no interests separate from the estate (all of the debtor's interests in property have already become property of the estate pursuant to Bankruptcy Code §541(a)(1)). The only circumstance in which a bankruptcy trustee can marshal at all is where some of the collateral is owned by a person other than the debtor. Only a minority of courts permit marshaling in that circumstance.

4. Marshaling Against Property Owned by Third Parties

It is not unusual for a creditor to take a security interest in property that does not belong to its debtor. To illustrate, assume that Mark Aman has decided to open a clothing store in the local shopping mall. He forms a corporation, Aman Corporation, that will own the business. The corporation then applies to Power Bank for a loan to be secured by its fixtures, equipment, and inventory. Power Bank agrees to make the loan to the corporation, but only on the condition that Mark further secure the loan with a mortgage against a beach house he owns personally. Mark does so.

Assume that Janus, an unsecured creditor of the corporation, obtains a judgment, levies on the fixtures, equipment, and inventory, and seeks marshaling to compel Power Bank to look to the beach house for its recovery. Assuming further that Mark's beach house has no liens against it that are junior to Power Bank's, the bank's recovery from it will not injure other lienors. Provided that Mark Aman is solvent, marshaling will injure no one but him.

Nevertheless, the courts split on cases like this where a lienor seeks to compel marshaling against the assets of a third party. The objection is expressed in the *common debtor* requirement. Most courts read that requirement to have two parts. The marshaling must be between two or more creditors of the same debtor *and the funds or assets must be in the hands of that common debtor*. Here the marshaling is between two creditors of the corporation, but the assets subject to marshaling (the beach house and the assets of Aman Corporation) are owned by different debtors. Janus's attempt to marshal against Power Bank fails the second part of the common debtor requirement. As one court put it: "it is well settled that a creditor who has a claim against two debtors, one a principal and the other a surety, cannot be compelled by another creditor of the principal debtor to exhaust his remedy against the surety before proceeding against the principal." Gaines v. Hill, 147 Ky. 445, 144 S.W. 92, 94 (1912) (citations omitted). The rationale for this rule has been explained as follows:

> A surety is not a "fund" or "security" in the sense in which those terms are used in connection with the principle of marshaling so as to permit or require a senior creditor to look first to the surety for satisfaction of its claim. Where a fund is held by a surety or guarantor, marshaling is barred because the debtor does not hold the funds which are in the hands of the surety or guarantor and, therefore, are not assets subject to marshaling. Thus, in the absence of some special equity, the principle of marshaling assets is not applicable to a case where one of the funds is the property of a surety of the common debtor. As a result, a creditor cannot be compelled to satisfy its debt from the sureties of a debtor before resorting to a fund or collateral security on which the creditor has a lien.

UPS Capital Business Credit v. C.R. Cable Construction, Inc., 181 S.W.3d 44, 48 (Ky. App. 2005).

Other courts impose only the first part of the common debtor test. There need be only a debtor who owes money to both creditors—here Aman Corporation—and the common debtor requirement is met regardless of who owns the encumbered property. In those courts, Janus could marshal against Power Bank.

Now assume that instead of Janus becoming a lien creditor, the corporation had gone into bankruptcy; a trustee had been appointed to represent the interests of the unsecured creditors of the corporation; and the trustee, asserting his status as a lien creditor, tried to use marshaling to force Power Bank to look to the beach house. Given that the trustee has the rights of a lien creditor, it should not surprise you that the analysis is the same as when Janus attempted to marshal. The trustee loses in the majority of courts, and wins only in those that employ a one-part common debtor test. As we discussed in the preceding section, if the trustee cannot use marshaling to force a secured creditor to look to property owned by a third party, there remains no situation in which a trustee can use marshaling.

▶ HALF ASSIGNMENT ENDS

D.   The Effect of Cross-Collateralization on Purchase-Money Status

Purchase-money status is an important attribute of a security interest, in part because it enables a security interest that is second in time to prevail over liens and security interests perfected earlier. The knowledge that its interest will be first in priority even if it is not first in time enables the purchase-money lender to extend credit without conducting a search of the filing system.

Historically, a security interest has been considered purchase money only to the extent that the collateral secures an obligation that is the purchase price of the collateral. This rule survives the drafting of new Article 9 with regard to collateral other than inventory. UCC §§9-103(a) and (b)(1). But to determine the extent to which collateral secures only its purchase price can be difficult both as a matter of fact and of theory. Two types of problems contribute to the difficulty.

First, the secured creditor may not keep a separate account for the purchase-money obligation. For example, Becky Sansei sells Green Mars to Williams for $40,000 and takes a security interest for the purchase price. At the closing on this sale, the parties cancel Williams's earlier-executed promissory note to Sansei in the amount of $300,000 and Williams signs a new one in the amount of $340,000. At this point, $40,000 of the $340,000 obligation is the purchase price of Green Mars. Even if the entire $340,000 is secured by the security interest in Green Mars, that does not prevent $40,000 of the security interest from being purchase money. UCC §9-103(f)(1). This is the so-called dual status rule: A security interest may be part purchase money and part nonpurchase money. Nor would the purchase-money status of the $40,000 be lost merely because the entire $340,000 were secured by other collateral in addition to Green Mars.

The purchase-money status of the security interest in Green Mars becomes less clear when $3,000 of interest accrues on the note and then Williams pays $10,000. The new balance is $333,000, but how much of that is the purchase price of Green Mars?

UCC §9-103(g) addresses the problem by placing the burden of establishing what part of the balance is the purchase price of Green Mars on the secured creditor. Sansei must provide the court with evidence showing what payments or accrual were made. UCC §9-103(e) tells Sansei how to apply the payments she receives. If the parties have agreed to a method, she must follow it. If they have not, Williams can direct the application of the payments as he makes them. If he fails to do so, Sansei must apply the payments to obligations that are unsecured before applying them to payments that are secured. Among secured obligations, she must apply them first to the oldest.

The second type of problem in determining the extent to which security interests are purchase money is the problem of aggregating collateral. To understand the problem, assume that Sansei sells both Green Mars and Red Mars to Williams and takes $80,000 of the purchase price in the form of a promissory note secured by Green Mars and Red Mars. That is, the price of each horse is cross-collateralized by a security interest in the other horse. Is this a single purchase-money security interest in which the two horses are the purchase-money collateral and the $80,000 is the purchase-money obligation? Or are there two purchase-money security interests, each to the extent of $40,000 and each encumbering only one horse?

To illustrate why it matters, assume that after the loan is made, Sansei releases Red Mars for a payment of $10,000 because the horse is lame. Is the remaining $70,000 obligation an obligation "incurred as . . . the price of the collateral"? Though UCC §9-103 does not address the point, some authorities take the position that "the collateral" is whatever is sold in the transaction in which the purchase-money obligation arose. That is, a security interest can be purchase-money even though cross-collateralized, provided that the entire purchase-money obligation arises on a single occasion. Under that rule, Sansei could have a $70,000 purchase-money obligation in a horse that never alone had a price nearly so high.

UCC §9-103(b)(2) sets forth an even more liberal rule for purchase-money security interests in inventory. If the two horses would be inventory in the hands of Williams and the creditor is secured by both, the entire $80,000 can be a purchase-money security interest in each of the horses, even though they were not purchased at the same time. As the following illustration from Comment 4 to UCC §9-103 shows, an inventory lender can have a purchase-money security interest in an item of inventory that secures an obligation that is not even arguably the purchase price of that item.

> Seller (S) sells an item of inventory (Item-1) to Debtor (D), retaining a security interest in Item-1 to secure Item-1's price and all other obligations, existing and future, of D to S. S then sells another item of inventory to D (Item-2), again retaining a security interest in Item-2 to secure Item-2's price as well as all other obligations of D to S. D then pays to S Item-1's purchase price. D then sells Item-2 to a buyer in ordinary course of business, who takes Item-2 free of S's security interest.

The Comment explains:

> Under subsection (b)(2), S's security interest in Item-1 securing Item-2's unpaid price would be a purchase-money security interest. This is so because S has a purchase-money security interest in Item-1, Item-1 secures the price of (a "purchase-money obligation incurred with respect to") Item-2 ("other inventory"), and Item-2 itself was subject to a purchase-money security interest.

Although this rule plays fast and loose with the English language, it is directed against a serious practical problem. Absent the rule, an inventory lender that advanced money against successive deliveries of collateral as they arrived would have not a single purchase-money security interest in the debtor's inventory but a series of purchase-money security interests each in the collateral delivered on a particular occasion. Such a secured party could meet its obligation of establishing the extent of its purchase-money security interest in particular items of collateral, UCC §9-103(g), only by keeping track of which items of inventory were sold. That might be a simple matter with regard to automobiles or other such collateral where the parties are already keeping track on a serial number basis, but it would impose an additional and perhaps excessive record-keeping burden with regard to groceries in the hands of a restaurant supply house or a grocery store.

Problem Set 34

34.1. Your client, Paula Jones, holds a second mortgage on a house owned by Rupert Waldoch. Waldoch apparently has defaulted in payments under the first mortgage and the mortgage holder, Watson Federal Savings, has filed a complaint for foreclosure. The complaint recites that the amount outstanding on the first mortgage is $440,000; your investigation indicates the house to be worth not more than about $400,000.

a.   If no additional relevant facts come to light, what do you expect to recover?

b.   What additional facts might yet entitle Paula to recover by virtue of her second mortgage?

34.2. When David Paul filed for bankruptcy, he owned only two non-exempt assets, a 22-unit apartment building and a yacht. The first mortgage on the apartment building was in the amount of $4,500,000 and was held by University City Bank. The first security interest in the yacht was in the amount of $4,000,000 and was held by Capital Equities. The $4,000,000 note to Capital Equities was also secured by a second mortgage against the apartment building. Paul's lawyer, William Hurst, held a second security interest in the yacht securing payment of $250,000 for legal work done by Hurst more than a year before the bankruptcy filing. By consent of all parties, the Chapter 7 trustee sold the two assets free and clear of liens and the liens were transferred to the proceeds of sale.

a.   The apartment building sold for $6,600,000; the yacht for $2,500,000. The three lien holders and the trustee all claim the proceeds of sale. Who is entitled to them?

b.   If the yacht had sold for only $2,000,000, who would have been entitled to the money?

34.3. About six months ago, you obtained a judgment in the amount of $10,000 on behalf of your client, Miller's Feed and Seed, against Estelle LeNotre. At that time you recorded the judgment in the real property records of the county. Under the majority rule and local law, by recording, the judgment became a lien against real property owned by the debtor in the county. Your investigation since that time reveals the following additional facts. LeNotre owes a balance of $440,000 to Production Credit Association (PCA). The loan is secured by a first security interest in her farm machinery and by a second mortgage against her farm. The first mortgage on the farm is held by National City Bank and is in the amount of $350,000. LeNotre owes $540,000 to the Small Business Administration (SBA). That loan is secured by a first mortgage against her home and a second against her farm machinery. Your best estimates of value are that the farm machinery is worth $550,000, the farm is worth $600,000, and the home is worth $630,000. The home appears to be an exempt homestead under the debtor-creditor laws of the state. If your estimates of value are correct and LeNotre owns no other property, is your judgment collectible? What problems do you foresee and how do you plan to deal with them?

▶ HALF ASSIGNMENT ENDS

34.4. On October 1, Becky Sansei sells a Sansei submersible robot to Michael Williams for $700,000. Williams pays $200,000 in cash and signs a promissory note for the remaining $500,000. Williams also signs a security agreement granting Sansei a security interest in "all Sansei equipment now owned or hereafter acquired" to secure "all obligations owing from Williams to Sansei." The security agreement makes no mention of purchase-money status and provides no rules for applying payments. The robot will be equipment in the hands of Williams.

a. Is Sansei's security interest purchase money? If so, to what extent? UCC §§9-103(a) and (b).

b. On November 1, Sansei sells a Sansei miniature submarine to Michael Williams for $600,000. Williams pays $200,000 in cash and signs a promissory note for the remaining $400,000. The submarine will be equipment in the hands of Williams. In what amount is the submarine encumbered?

c. Is Sansei's security interest in the submarine purchase money? If so, to what extent?

d. Assume that no interest is accruing on either obligation. On November 2, Williams pays Sansei $10,000. Sansei deposits Williams's check and credits $10,000 against the $900,000 shown owing on Sansei's books. Now what is the extent of Sansei's purchase-money security interest in the submarine? UCC §9-103(e); Comment 7b to UCC §9-103.

e. Would your answers to question c be different if the collateral were inventory in the hands of Williams? UCC §§9-103(a) and (b); Comment 4 to UCC §9-103.

34.5. On May 31, Bonnie's Boat World, Inc. purchases two Coyote Loaders for $90,000. Coyote takes a security interest for $50,000 of the purchase price. Bonnie's borrows another $40,000 from Firstbank against the loaders, without mentioning Coyote's lien. Firstbank takes a security interest in the loaders, disburses the loan proceeds directly to Coyote, and perfects by filing a financing statement on June 1. Coyote perfects by filing a financing statement on June 2, and delivers the loaders to Bonnie's on June 3. Bonnie's bought and uses the loaders as equipment.

a. Who has priority in the loaders? UCC §§9-324(a) and (g).

b. What should the losing party have done to avoid this unexpected setback?

34.6. Otis Finance plans to finance an inventory of boats that Bart's Boat World will purchase from Shoreline Boats. In accord with their usual practice, Otis filed a financing statement covering "inventory" and conducted a search for other filings against Bart's. The search discovered a financing statement filed by Firstbank covering "inventory." Bart tells Otis that Firstbank is financing only Bart's inventory of Bayliner boats. Otis wonders whether they need a subordination agreement with Firstbank or whether they can simply give notice as required by UCC §§9-324(b) and (c) and begin lending. They ask you to consider the following possible scenario: Firstbank lends Bart's $100 to help make the down payment on a Shoreline boat and Bart's uses the money for that purpose. The description of collateral in Firstbank's security agreement is sufficiently broad to cover a Shoreline boat.

a. On these facts, would Firstbank have a purchase-money security interest in the Shoreline boat? UCC §§9-103(a) and (b).

b. If so, for how much money? UCC §9-103(b)(2).

c. Between Firstbank and Otis, who would have priority in the Shoreline boat? UCC §§9-324(b), (c), and (g).

d. Would your answer to question c be different if Otis filed and began lending first, Firstbank gave notice to Otis under UCC §§9-324(b) and (c), and then Firstbank lent Bart's $100 to help make the down payment on a Shoreline boat and Bart's used the money for that purpose?

■ END OF DEFAULT PROBLEM SET

34.7. Willard Kurtz, a friend of yours from college, asks that you take a look at a contract for him before he signs. For several years, Willard has been looking for a five-acre tract of wooded land on a river at a reasonable price — not an easy bill to fill — and he has finally found it. The document he shows you is titled "Contract for Deed." The contract provides for a sale price of $300,000, payable with interest at 9 percent in equal monthly installments of $3,800.30 over a period of ten years. Upon payment of the full purchase price, the owner, Rancho Mirage Development, Inc., will transfer the property by deed, free and clear of all encumbrances. The contract gives Willard the right to prepay the outstanding balance at any time and to receive his deed at the time of payment. The title search you ordered on the property shows a mortgage in the original face amount of $9.4 million. The mortgage is signed by Rancho Mirage Development, Inc. and is in favor of Robert L. Henderson, the former owner of the property. It encumbers about 60 five-acre parcels, in addition to the tract Willard is buying. Based on your knowledge of real estate in the area, you estimate that all 60 tracts together are probably worth more than $20 million.

a. What are your concerns as you advise Willard whether to buy under this contract?

b. Would it change your mind if Rancho Mirage had already sold over half the tracts in this development and was receiving monthly payments from purchasers that were well in excess of the payment Rancho Mirage must make each month to Henderson?

34.8. In a parallel universe, you represent Rancho Mirage in the scenario described in the previous problem. Willard Kurtz has just refused to close and Mr. Mirage is worried about whether he can sell *any* of his tracts. What do you recommend?

Assignment 35: Sellers Against Secured Creditors

After-acquired property may seem to spring from nowhere, but it does not. In most instances, someone sells it to the debtor. If the debtor buys from the true owner of the property, does so honestly, and pays the purchase price, the transaction is unlikely to present legal issues of significance. The secured creditor who obtains its interest from the buyer can have a security interest only in what the buyer purchased. The disputes arise in two kinds of cases. The first is where the debtor buys from someone who has less than full ownership of the collateral. The second is where the debtor induces the sale through questionable conduct, such as fraud, misrepresentation, or payment by worthless check, and then fails to pay for the collateral. In either kind of case, the secured creditor may have rights to the collateral even greater than its debtor-transferor.

We begin this assignment by examining the limits on what a debtor who does not have full ownership of the collateral can transfer to its secured lender. Then we turn to the rights of the true owner of what the debtor purports to encumber to recover the property from the debtor's secured lender. In that regard, we consider various protections available to sellers, including purchase-money security interests, rights of reclamation, and actions against secured creditors for unjust enrichment.

A. Limits of the After-Acquired Property Clause

UCC §9-203(b)(2) does not require that the debtor be the owner of collateral in order to grant a valid security interest in it. The debtor need only have "rights in the collateral." The usual rule is that a debtor's grant of a security interest in collateral in which the debtor holds only a limited interest conveys only a security interest in the limited interest. For example, assume that Debtor leased a computer from LeaseCo under a one-year lease. Debtor grants Bank a security interest in the computer. Bank probably will be held to acquire only a security interest in Debtor's leasehold. It is not true, however, that the transferee of a security interest can never obtain greater rights than those of its debtor-transferor. To understand why and in what circumstances the secured creditor can obtain greater rights, it is first necessary to understand the basic rules governing title to personal property.

1. Rules Governing Title to Personal Property

In 1990, a thief stole a car belonging to a Philadelphia man. Some months later, the man found the car again by an odd coincidence. A taxicab pulled up in front of the man while he was standing beside a city street. Despite the markings of the cab company, the man recognized the cab as the car he had lost. (His clue was a piece of tape he had placed on the car before it was stolen.) He called the police. They tracked the cab down and verified that it was indeed the car previously stolen from the man. The cab company, however, was not the thief; it had purchased the car for value, in good faith, from a used car dealer. As between the man and the cab company, who gets the car?

The answer is that, because the car was stolen, the man (the "true owner") prevails over the cab company (the "good faith purchaser for value"). The rule of law that yields this result is generally referred to as the *void title rule*. An outright thief obtains no title (a "void" title) to the property he or she steals. Thus the purchaser from the thief (in this case the used car dealer) obtains no title, and thus can convey no title to the taxicab company. This reasoning is grounded, of course, in the even more basic assumption that one who does not have title cannot convey title. That assumption is often expressed in Latin, *nemo dat qui non habet* (or just "*nemo dat*" to be *very* cool).

It is easy to take a rule like *nemo dat* too seriously. A title is merely a legal construct. It exists only because the law says it does. There are no physical limitations on what a title can do. A title can spring into existence from nowhere if a court of sufficient authority solemnly so declares. It can disappear just as suddenly. The rule of *nemo dat* does not cause the result in the taxicab case or necessitate the void title rule. What the rule of *nemo dat* does is to provide a convenient metaphor for keeping track of and explaining the outcomes in the variety of cases that can arise. In short, if a thief steals the property from the true owner, the true owner can recover the property regardless of who the competing party is or how that party acquired its interest. The rule can apply even against the shopper who buys a piano from a retail store in a shopping mall.

A key policy behind the rule is to discourage theft. Theft is most profitable when the stolen goods can be reintroduced into the stream of commerce and ultimately sold to good faith purchasers for their full value. The rule of *nemo dat* makes that difficult. A good faith purchaser who is not careful about the source of the goods it buys always runs the risk that a true owner will appear and reclaim them. If Edith buys her piano from a reputable store and it turns out to be stolen, she will lose the piano, but she will have a cause of action against the store. The store in turn will have an action against its seller. Assuming that all sellers in the chain are financially responsible, the loss will fall on the person who dealt with the thief.

The equities change if the true owner also dealt with the thief; appropriately, the result changes as well. To illustrate, if the true owner of the Philadelphia taxicab lost his car not to a thief who snatched it off the street at night but to a car dealer who agreed to repair it for the true owner but sold it instead, the true owner could not have recovered it from the taxicab company. See UCC §§2-403(2) and (3). Notice that this result violates the rule of *nemo dat*. A car dealer to whom a car is entrusted for repair does not have title to the car, but under UCC §2-403(2) can pass good title to a buyer in the ordinary course of business. In this illustration, the owner who selected the garage had a better opportunity to avoid the loss. As between the owner and the subsequent buyer, the owner must bear the loss.

The taxicab company would also win over a true owner who lost the car in a *transaction of purchase*, even if the true owner was defrauded in the transaction. This would be the case, for example, if a con artist bought the car from the true owner with a check drawn on a nonexistent bank account. The true owner would be able to void the transaction as against the con artist for fraud, but if the taxicab company bought the car from the con artist in good faith for value before the true owner caught up with it, the taxicab company would prevail. UCC §2-403(1). That provision deals with the *nemo dat* argument by saying that the con artist obtains a voidable title through his or her fraud, and that the holder of a voidable title has the power to transfer a good title to a good faith purchaser for value.

2. Rules Governing Security Interests in Personal Property

One of the great favorites of American law is the good faith purchaser for value. The drafters of the UCC applied considerable skill and cunning to cast secured creditors in that role. They defined "purchaser" as a person who takes by purchase, and defined "purchase" as including taking by "mortgage, pledge . . . or any other voluntary transaction creating an interest in property." UCC §1-201(b)(29) and (30). When a creditor acquires a security interest in collateral, the creditor "purchases" the collateral and receives whatever protection purchasers have elsewhere in law. The creditor can "purchase" through the operation of an after-acquired property clause, even though the creditor makes no additional advance and does not rely on its newly acquired rights.

The drafters also played fast and loose in defining "value" such that "any consideration sufficient to support a simple contract" would qualify. UCC §1-204. Thus, a secured creditor can be a purchaser for value even when it acquires its interest for nominal value — or for no value under an after-acquired property clause. Adding all this together, a secured creditor can be a good faith purchaser of collateral for value even though the secured creditor does not purchase the collateral in the ordinary sense of the word "purchase," has bad intentions, and pays nothing for it.

Among the rights that a secured creditor obtains through these remarkable feats of definition are the rights of a good faith purchaser under UCC §2-403. The secured creditor can prevail over the true owner of goods even if the title of its transferor, the debtor, was avoidable because the debtor procured it through fraud.

There have been some famous cases that have played this rule out to its extreme. Perhaps the most lively is In re Samuels, 526 F.2d 1238 (5th Cir. 1976). In that case, CIT had financed the inventory of Samuels's slaughterhouse. Samuels bought cattle from Stowers over an 11-day period and paid for the purchases by check. On the twelfth day, Samuels filed bankruptcy. The checks bounced, and Stowers wanted his cattle back. CIT claimed the cattle under the after-acquired property clause in its security agreement. CIT ultimately prevailed in a hotly contested case that twice made its way to the Fifth Circuit Court of Appeals. The court reasoned that CIT was a good faith purchaser for value. Even though Samuels never acquired good title to the cattle, he had the power under UCC §2-403(1) to transfer good title to CIT simply by bringing the cattle within the scope of CIT's after-acquired property clause.

Correctly perceiving how outrageous it is for Article 9 secured creditors to steal sellers' property in this manner, but mistakenly thinking that the problem was unique to livestock, Congress granted the sellers of livestock in such "cash sales" priority over inventory lenders, but not without first taking a shot at the UCC drafters:

> It is hereby found that a burden on and obstruction to commerce in livestock is caused by financing arrangements under which packers . . . give lenders security interests in . . . livestock purchased by packers in cash sales . . . when payment is not made for the livestock and that such arrangements are contrary to the public interest. 7 U.S.C. §196.

The drafters have not responded to this comment on the reasonableness of UCC §2-403.

3. *The Filing System as an Exception to* Nemo Dat

The concept of a filing system is inconsistent with the rule of *nemo dat.* Assume that *O* is the true owner of Blackacre. *O* executes and delivers a deed to *A.* Despite *A*'s failure to record, *A* is now the true owner. *O*, who no longer has title, executes and delivers a deed to *B* for value. If *B* records without knowledge that *A* is the true owner, *B* becomes the true owner. The title "springs" from *A* to *B*, enabling *O* to transfer what *O* did not have.

B. Suppliers Against Inventory-Secured Lenders

Sally Raj relied on a bank loan against inventory to start her stereo store on a shoestring. Sally bought $100,000 worth of inventory, but the bank lent only $60,000 against it. Where did Sally get the other $40,000? The answer is that she got it from her suppliers in the form of a *float.* In the week before Sally opened her store, she bought her $100,000 of inventory on unsecured credit from the suppliers. The invoices for that inventory came due 30 to 60 days later. By then, Sally had not only the $60,000 from her inventory financier, but also another $40,000 from sales of inventory. She then paid for the original $100,000 of inventory, purchased more on credit to replace what she sold, and borrowed 60 percent of the cost of the replacements. As these bills came in, she repeated the cycle. Provided that Sally could turn over at least $40,000 of inventory every 30 to 60 days, she would always have at least that much in unsecured credit from her suppliers. In essence, Sally is borrowing twice against the same property.

After a few months of operation, Sally discovers that her cash flow is insufficient to pay her bills as they become due. She might deal with the situation by using some of her sales revenues to pay creditors other than the bank instead of depositing it all to her bank account, as her contract requires. If she does, she is in breach. The bank might not discover her breach; it might think the low amount she deposited represents the entire proceeds of her sales. (If so, the bank would think the remaining inventory that serves as its collateral is larger than it actually is.) If the bank does discover Sally's breach, it probably will call the loan, and Sally will be in a full-fledged financial crisis.

Sally will probably elect to deal with the situation by disappointing some of her suppliers instead of the bank. If she waits an average of 90 days rather than 45 to pay her invoices, she will have an additional $40,000 of float. Her "slow pay" should be a warning sign to the suppliers that Sally may be in financial trouble. If the suppliers are making substantial profits on their sales to Sally, they might be willing to accept the additional risk. If they are not, they will stop selling inventory to Sally, and perhaps even sue her for the outstanding balance. But they will do so as unsecured creditors. Their remedy will be slow and probably ineffective.

If Sally's business closes, the bank will have the right to take possession of the inventory and sell it. UCC §9-609(a). As a secured creditor, it will have priority over the suppliers in the inventory. The result is somewhat ironic. The supplier who sold Sally 25 compact disc changers just two weeks ago (and has not been paid for them) stands by helplessly while the bank sells the changers and pockets the proceeds. Proponents of the broad scope of the Article 9 "floating lien" against after-acquired property argue that there is no unfairness here. The bank that made the inventory loan put suppliers on notice of its security interest when it filed its financing statement. Even if the supplier did not check the records or learn of the bank's interest through a credit report, the supplier should have anticipated — and probably did — that its buyer would grant a security interest to an inventory financier. If the supplier wanted the ability to reclaim its products in the event Sally did not pay for them, the supplier should have insisted that Sally grant the supplier a security interest. Such a security interest would have been a purchase-money security interest with priority over the bank. UCC §9-324(b). By failing to take such an interest, the supplier agreed to take the risk of unsecured status and perhaps even extracted compensation for that risk in the form of higher interest on the account or a higher price for the product it sold.

Opponents of the broad scope of the Article 9 floating lien on after-acquired property argue that while the carefully calculating supplier of the proponent's argument may be common, it is far from universal. In many applications, the concept of after-acquired property is deceptive. If suppliers often don't understand the system and therefore don't charge adequately for the risks they assume, it is no answer to say that they *ought to*. Even if they do understand, they may be unable to extract competing security interests because other financiers with more leverage, such as banks and commercial lenders, insist on having the only interest in the inventory.

C. Sellers' Weapons Against the After-Acquired Property Clause

Many sellers are shocked to discover how helpless they are when the debtor fails to pay the purchase price and the secured creditor claims the property sold as its collateral. They naturally search for legal devices that will enable them to repossess what they sold if the debtor does not pay for it.

1. Purchase-Money Security Interests

Theoretically, sellers have the option to timely comply with the purchase-money requirements of Article 9 and thereby obtain priority in the property they sell. But recall that many lenders bar their debtors from granting purchase-money security interests. To grant such an interest is a breach of the security agreement that will entitle the inventory lender to call the loan. As a result, many sellers are unable to retain security interests in what they sell.

2. Retention of Title

A seller's first reaction to the treatment of sellers under Article 9 may be to decide not to sell on credit. The seller has that option, and it is an effective protection. Some sellers, however, will fall into the trap of *contracting* to sell, with title to pass to the buyer only when the buyer pays for the goods. For example, S, the owner of goods, might give possession of goods to B pursuant to an agreement that says (1) S continues to own the goods, (2) B will purchase the goods for $30,000, to be paid in installments, and (3) B will become the owner upon payment of the last installment. As you have already seen in earlier assignments, such a contract is treated as an immediate sale, with the seller retaining a security interest. UCC §2-401(1) provides that "Any retention or reservation by the seller of the title (property) in goods shipped or delivered to the buyer is limited in effect to a reservation of a security interest." If the seller did not anticipate this treatment, the seller probably will not have filed a financing statement or given the notice necessary to retain an effective purchase-money security interest. In that event, the seller's security interest will be subordinate to that of the inventory secured lender.

▶ Half Assignment Ends

3. Consignment

Consignment is an arrangement in which the owner of goods (the *consignor*) entrusts the goods to an agent or bailee (the *consignee*) for sale. When the consignee arranges a sale of the goods, title passes directly from the consignor to the buyer. The consignee remits a portion of the sale proceeds to the consignor and keeps the rest as a fee for selling the goods. By the consignment contract, unsold goods remain the property of the consignor and the consignee ultimately returns them to the consignor.

Consignment is used in a variety of situations. The owner of a piece of jewelry may deliver it to a jewelry store "on consignment." The deal is that the jewelry store will try to sell it. If the store does, the store will remit the sale proceeds to the consignor, less the store's commission. If the store does not sell the piece, the store will return it to the consignor. This type of consignment is also common between artists and art galleries.

Consignment is also a common arrangement between clothing manufacturers and retail clothing stores. The consignee is an independently owned and operated store, just like any other retail store. The store's customers — and more importantly, the store's creditors — may be completely unaware that the store does not own the goods it is selling.

Economically, this consignment relationship may be no different from the seller-buyer relationship of other manufacturers with competing stores. The consignee store receives a fee for selling the goods; the buyer store keeps the gross profit from selling the goods — simply the difference between the wholesale and retail prices of the goods. The consignee store pays nothing for the goods unless they are sold; the buyer store probably buys on liberal credit terms that accomplish the same thing. The consignor continues to own unsold goods; the seller probably agrees to accept return of unsold goods. The defining difference between consignment and seller-buyer relationships is in who owns the goods pending sale. But the owner may be difficult to identify, because when the transactions go as planned, ownership doesn't matter.

The UCC recognizes essentially three types of consignments. The first is the group excluded from Article 9 coverage, UCC §9-109(a)(4), by excepting them from the Article 9 definition of "consignment," UCC §9-102(a)(20). The excluded group includes (A) consignments in which the consignees do business under the name of the consignor (largely franchisees), (B) small consignments, defined as those in which no single delivery of goods exceeded $1,000 in value, and (C) consignments by consumers, such as the jewelry owner in the example above. Some of these consignments are regulated by laws other than Article 9.

The second type recognized by Article 9 is the consignment referred to in UCC §9-102(a)(20)(D) — the consignment that is merely a disguised security interest. Recall that a security interest is an interest in property contingent on the nonpayment of a debt. An arrangement in which the "consignee" was not entitled to return the goods, for example, would be a disguised security interest because the seller would have no interest in the goods in the absence of default. These consignments are treated in all respects as security interests under Article 9.

The third type of consignment is the group defined as "consignments" in UCC §9-102(a)(20). The interest of the consignor in these transactions is included in the definition of "security interest." Other provisions of Article 9 specify that other aspects of the consignment be treated the same as they would have been in a buyer-seller arrangement. UCC §9-319(a), for example, allows creditors of the consignee to acquire judicial liens and security interests in the goods. Thus, generally speaking, both the second and third types of consignments are treated as security interests for purposes of perfection and priority.

4. The Seller's Right of Reclamation

If a buyer receives goods while insolvent, the seller has the right to reclaim them. To "reclaim" goods is to take them back from the buyer. The right is, however, subject to the rights of the buyer's secured creditors that attached to the goods in the hands of the buyer. A narrow version of the right to reclaim appears in UCC §2-702(2). The seller's demand under that section may be made against any insolvent buyer and must be made within ten days of the buyer's receipt of the goods, but apparently the demand need not be in writing. A broader version appears in Bankruptcy Code §546(c). The seller's demand under that section is only effective if the debtor is in bankruptcy, must be made within 45 days of the debtor's receipt of the goods (and not later than 20 days after the commencement of the bankruptcy case), and must be in writing.

In most cases, the buyer will have granted a security interest in its inventory. Those security interests will attach to purchased goods immediately upon their identification to the contract for sale. The right to reclaim will generally be ineffective, because it is subject to those security interests. The secured creditors will have the right to possession of the goods and that right will probably translate into a right to insist that the debtor be permitted to retain possession. Eventually the debtor will sell the goods, the right of reclamation will expire, and the secured creditor or the buyer/debtor will get the proceeds of sale.

In the following case, tobacco companies that sold inventory to the debtor on credit just a few days earlier tried to reclaim what they sold. Not only had the inventory lender not supplied a penny of the purchase price of that inventory, but the inventory lender had literally lain in wait for the new inventory to arrive. Nevertheless, the court held that the inventory lender was a "good faith" purchaser entitled to priority over the tobacco companies' right to reclaim.

In re M. Paolella & Sons, Inc.

161 B.R. 107 (E.D. Pa. 1993)

RAYMOND J. BRODERICK, UNITED STATES DISTRICT JUDGE.

Since this Court has determined that the findings made by the Bankruptcy Court are not "clearly erroneous," we summarize the relevant facts as found by the Bankruptcy Judge as follows:

The debtor, M. Paolella & Sons, Inc., was the largest wholesale distributor of tobacco products in the Delaware Valley. On January 26, 1982, the debtor and MNC Commercial Corp. (MNC) entered into a financing agreement that provided a line of credit secured by virtually all of the debtor's assets, i.e., receivables, inventory, and equipment. These security interests were perfected by filings pursuant to the Uniform Commercial Code ("UCC"). Initially of two-year duration, the agreement was renewed and was in effect up to January 26, 1986. The financing agreement was asset-based in that it provided the debtor with a line of credit determined by a formula whereby the debtor could borrow against 85% of eligible accounts receivable and 60% of eligible inventory.

In October 1982, the debtor requested and MNC permitted an increase in credit to enable the debtor to participate in a special buying program offered by the tobacco companies. Thereafter, the debtor's loan was always out of formula. That is, after October 1982, the amount advanced by MNC always exceeded the sum of 85% of eligible receivables plus 60% of eligible inventory. Although MNC attempted repeatedly to bring the loan within formula, MNC agreed on several occasions to increase the amount of the overadvance to enable the debtor to participate in the tobacco companies' special buying programs; the debtor participated in these programs regularly.

As a consequence of the loan being out of formula, MNC, pursuant to the financing agreement, exercised considerable control of the debtor's business operations. Each business day the debtor would submit a report disclosing daily information as to receivables and weekly data as to the inventory. In addition, the debtor submitted weekly reports denoting invoices received. The financing agreement also gave MNC reasonable access to the debtor's premises during regular business hours and at other reasonable times, in order to conduct audits of its collateral. Pursuant to the agreement, MNC conducted frequent audits of the debtor's operations. MNC used all of this information to calculate the value of its collateral, the daily loan balance, and the additional loan sums then available to the debtor.

By the early part of 1984, MNC became concerned about the debtor's ability to repay its loan. At this time, MNC classified the loan in the "watch" category and further reduced the classification to "substandard" by October 1985.

In May 1985, the debtor and MNC discussed plans to liquidate debtor's assets and repay all of the debtor's creditors. Robert Stewart [MNC's president] was aware of the liquidation plan, which was expected to be complete within three to five months with a "target date" of January 1, 1986. A condition of the plan was the debtor's reduction of the overadvance by $50,000 per week.

In September 1985, the debtor started to sell its assets. [From the proceeds of sales of debtor's subsidiaries, debtor paid MNC $3,217,300 and provided MNC with $560,000 in promissory notes as additional collateral.]

In the latter part of 1985, MNC decided to inventory the debtor's goods and sent Mr. Baldwin, MNC executive vice-president, to physically count all tobacco products. Mr. Baldwin conducted three audits in the early-morning hours of January 8, 15, and 21, 1986. The inventories were conducted while the debtor was closed for business, and there was no one in the warehouse except the audit team and the debtor's representative.

In expectation of an orderly liquidation, Michael Paolella began informing certain tobacco companies that he would not be renewing personal loan guarantees. He did not inform these companies, however, of his liquidation plans.

American Tobacco had previously obtained a letter of credit in the amount of $120,000 from the debtor secured by Maryland National Bank. The letter allowed American Tobacco to draw upon the letter if payment from the debtor was more than thirty days overdue. The letter required that American Tobacco be given notice if the letter was to be canceled or not renewed. On January 3, 1986, twenty-two days before the deadline for notification, Maryland National Bank sent notice to American Tobacco that the letter of credit would not be renewed [with respect to invoices issued after January 10, 1986].

American Tobacco was aware that the letter of credit would not be renewed by January 9, 1986, when its employee, Frank Gallagher, contacted Michael Paolella regarding the notice of non-renewal. Gallagher wanted to ascertain whether the decision not to renew had been made by the debtor or by the bank. Gallagher was not entirely satisfied with Paolella's explanation that the non-renewal was the debtor's decision. Accordingly, he called Maryland National Bank and was referred to Cromwell at MNC. Gallagher called Cromwell on Wednesday, January 15, 1986, and Cromwell confirmed that the decision not to renew the letter of credit was the debtor's. It appears, however, that the decision not to renew the letter of credit was MNC's.

In the interim, American Tobacco, despite Gallagher's dissatisfaction with Michael Paolella's explanation regarding the letter of credit, continued to sell tobacco inventory to the debtor after January 10, 1986 and during the period when the letter of credit had expired.

[Through special buying programs announced by the tobacco plaintiffs in December 1985, the debtor purchased $1.9 million more inventory than usual in January 1986.]

On Tuesday, January 28, 1986, MNC decided not to advance the funds to honor the debtor's checks presented the previous day; Paolella was informed of this decision on Wednesday, January 29, 1986. Paolella told Cromwell that MNC should take over and operate the debtor. On Thursday, January 30, 1986, MNC notified the debtor that the loan was in default and requested immediate repayment of the entire balance and possession of all collateral securing the loan. In addition, Rick Sell, MNC's audit manager, took possession of the debtor's assets and secured the warehouse.

Also on January 30, 1986, credit collection managers from several tobacco companies came to the debtor's business in Philadelphia after their companies learned that the debtor's checks had been dishonored by Maryland National Bank. On Friday, January 31, 1986, despite entreaties by Paolella that the debtor be given until Monday, February 3, 1986 to liquidate its assets, the tobacco company plaintiffs filed an involuntary bankruptcy petition against the debtor.

[A trustee appointed by the Bankruptcy Court liquidated the debtor's assets, selling the inventory for $4.5 million, 75 percent of debtor's cost.] As a result of the trustee's liquidation of the estate, MNC received a distribution totaling $6,606,678.37.

The five tobacco company plaintiffs filed proofs of claim as follows: American Cigar—$23,923.40; American Tobacco—$283,671.51; Lorillard—$759,636.04; Philip Morris—$1,712,608.13; and Reynolds—$1,181,585.70.

VI.   RECLAMATION UNDER THE UNIFORM COMMERCIAL CODE §2-702

[T]he five tobacco companies delivered reclamation notices to the debtor pursuant to [UCC §2-702(2)], which states in pertinent part that "where seller discovers that the buyer has received goods on credit while insolvent he may reclaim the goods upon demand made within ten days after the receipt." However, [UCC §2-702(3)] makes the seller's reclamation "subject to the rights of a buyer in ordinary course or other good faith purchaser under [UCC §2-403]."

In this case, the parties agree that the debtor received the goods while insolvent and that the tobacco companies made demand to reclaim within ten days after receipt of the goods. Thus, the only issue remaining is whether MNC is a "good faith purchaser" for purposes of [UCC §2-702(3)].

[The court quoted Creeger Brick v. Mid-State Bank, 385 Pa. Super. 30, 560 A.2d 151 (Pa. Super. Ct. 1989):]

> It seems reasonably clear from the decided cases that a lending institution does not violate a separate duty of good faith by adhering to its agreement with the borrower or by enforcing its legal and contractual rights as a creditor. The duty of good faith imposed upon contracting parties does not compel a lender to surrender rights which it has been given by statute or by the terms of its contract.

Similarly, Judge Easterbrook reasoned in *Kham & Nate's Shoes*:

> Firms that have negotiated contracts are entitled to enforce them to the letter, even to the great discomfort of their trading partners, without being mulcted for lack of "good faith." Although courts often refer to the obligation of good faith that exists in every contractual relation, this is not an invitation to the court to decide whether one party ought to have exercised privileges expressly reserved in the document. "Good faith" is a compact reference to an implied undertaking not to take opportunistic advantage in a way that could not have been contemplated at the time of drafting, and which therefore was not resolved explicitly by the parties. When the contract is silent, principles of good faith—such as the UCC's §1-201(b)(20) (formerly §1-201(19)) fill the gap. They do not block use of terms that actually appear in the contract.

Kham & Nate's Shoes, 908 F.2d at 1357 (citations omitted). Thus, it is plain that under Pennsylvania law, a creditor that enforces a financing agreement in a manner consistent with the clear terms of the agreement and the expectations of the parties acts in "good faith."

In this case, the contract that must be examined to determine whether MNC acted in "good faith" is the financing agreement between MNC and the debtor. The Bankruptcy Judge found that MNC's overall plan, i.e., to gather information without alerting the other creditors of its future plan to cease funding the debtor when the warehouse was full, constituted inequitable conduct that deprived MNC of its status as a "good faith purchaser" under [UCC §2-702(2)]. Notably, the Bankruptcy Judge did not find that any of these actions were outside the scope of the financing agreement. It is clear from the Bankruptcy Judge's exhaustive ninety-three page opinion that MNC did not overstep its rights under the financing agreement. [The court reversed the Bankruptcy Judge and denied reclamation.]

It is a rare debtor whose inventory is not encumbered. The interpretation of UCC §2-702(3) that recognizes the inventory secured lender as a good faith purchaser to whom the seller's right of reclamation is subject practically eviscerates the right of reclamation granted in UCC §2-702(2). Inventory can no longer be reclaimed the moment the inventory security interest attaches.

The right to reclaim in Bankruptcy Code §546(c) lacks even the good faith requirement. Under that section, the secured creditor need only have "prior rights" to prevail over the reclaiming seller. Those prior rights are found in the provisions of Article 9 that give effect to after-acquired property clauses against unsecured sellers.

Lawyers refer to what the five tobacco companies in *Paolella* did as "feeding the lien." Feeding the lien benefits the secured creditor directly by increasing the amount of its collateral. It benefits the debtor by adding to the debtor's inventory. The losers are the suppliers who ship the inventory.

5.   *Express or Implied Agreement with the Secured Creditor*

The most direct means for a seller to protect itself against the buyer's inventory secured lender is by agreement with the secured lender. Inventory secured lenders often sincerely intend that the money they advance to the debtor be used to pay those who supply the inventory. If approached by the seller and debtor together with a request to do so, many inventory secured lenders will disburse loan proceeds directly to the seller to pay for the debtor's purchases. Some inventory secured lenders insist on doing so. An agreement by the inventory secured lender to pay for the goods is enforceable by action against the lender.

Ordinarily, however, the debtor does not want the secured lender to pay suppliers directly. Recall that when Sally Raj decided to open her stereo store, she could only do so if she could get a $40,000 float from her suppliers. Direct payment would eliminate the float. Suppliers are reluctant to insist on direct payment from the inventory secured lender if such payment is not customary in the industry. Such a request may imply to the inventory secured lender that the debtor is in financial difficulty. Rather than join in such a request, the debtor may take its business to a competing supplier.

Inventory-secured lenders have another motive for not wanting to make direct payment. As you saw in *Paolella*, when a collapsing debtor manages to buy additional inventory on credit, the purchase can directly benefit the lender. To illustrate, assume that the liquidation value of the inventory of Sally's Stereo Store is $55,000 and the amount owing on the inventory loan is $60,000. If Sally can buy an additional $5,000 worth of inventory on unsecured credit, the new inventory will "feed the [bank's] lien" — that is, it will increase the amount of the collateral without increasing the amount of the debt. If the bank waits for the new inventory to arrive and then calls the loan without disbursing against it, the bank has shifted $5,000 of value from the supplier to themselves. To the extent that the bank agrees in advance to pay suppliers directly, it has eliminated the possibility that purchases such as these will feed its lien. The bank will be able to obtain additional collateral only by paying for it.

6. Equitable Subordination

A seller who is subordinate to a secured creditor under Article 9 also might look to the doctrine of equitable subordination. The following excerpt is from the same opinion presented earlier in this assignment on reclamation. In it, the court makes clear its opinion that there is nothing inequitable about feeding a lien.

In re M. Paolella & Sons, Inc.
161 B.R. 107 (E.D. Pa. 1993)

It is a long-standing principle that bankruptcy courts, sitting as courts of equity, have the authority to subordinate claims on equitable grounds. Nevertheless, equitable subordination is an extraordinary departure from the "usual principles of equality of distribution and preference for secured creditors." *In re Osborne*, 42 B.R. at 992.

Section 510(c) of the Bankruptcy Code codified pre-existing case law allowing bankruptcy courts to adjust the status of claims on equitable grounds. Because of Congress' clear intent that §510 codify then-existing principles of equitable subordination, most courts applying the doctrine have adopted the three-prong test articulated by the United States Court of Appeals for the Fifth Circuit on the eve of the Bankruptcy Code's enactment:

(i) The claimant must have engaged in some type of inequitable conduct.
(ii) The misconduct must have resulted in injury to the creditors of the bankrupt or conferred an unfair advantage on the claimant.
(iii) Equitable subordination of the claim must not be inconsistent with the provisions of the Bankruptcy Act.

In re Mobile Steel Co., 563 F.2d 692, 700 (5th Cir. 1977).

Although there is general acceptance of the Mobile Steel three-part test, courts have struggled to define the precise conduct that constitutes grounds for equitable subordination. Generally, there are three categories of conduct that satisfy the first prong of the three-part test: (1) fraud, illegality, or breach of fiduciary duties; (2) undercapitalization; and (3) claimant's use of the debtor as a mere instrumentality or alter ego.

Further, in applying equitable subordination principles, the courts differentiate between insider and non-insider claimants.

In this case, the Bankruptcy Judge found that MNC did not participate in the debtor's management, determine its operating decisions, or have any presence on its board. It was Michael Paolella who controlled the debtor, who decided that the debtor would participate in tobacco company purchase programs, and who decided that the debtor would expand and then later liquidate. We agree with the Bankruptcy Court's finding that MNC is neither an insider nor a fiduciary of the debtor.

Although courts have struggled to articulate the misconduct that must be established to subordinate non-insider claims, it is clear that the non-insider's misconduct must be "gross or egregious."

V.   THE BANKRUPTCY COURT'S CONCLUSIONS OF LAW REGARDING EQUITABLE SUBORDINATION

For purposes of the doctrine of equitable subordination, it is not inequitable for a non-insider creditor to monitor a debtor closely, pursuant to a valid financing agreement, for the purpose of choosing the most advantageous time to foreclose on a loan that has been out of formula for several years. Not only is it not inequitable conduct, but MNC would have been derelict in its duty to its own stockholders and depositors, if it had failed to obtain additional information so as to exercise its contractual right not to lend at a propitious time relative to tobacco company creditors. This principle has even more force in cases such as this one, where the Bankruptcy Judge found that all creditors were aware of the debtor's precarious financial position. Accordingly, there was no reliance by any creditor that MNC would continue funding; nor was there an explicit or implicit promise by MNC to continue funding. Indeed, the Bankruptcy Judge found that the tobacco plaintiffs knew that the debtor was overleveraged and knew that there was a risk that MNC might declare the loan in default or refuse to advance additional loan funds or make available to the debtor the proceeds of its receivables. Yet, knowing for some time of the substantial risk of nonpayment of their outstanding invoices, these tobacco companies continued making unsecured loans to the debtor. Within this context, MNC's conduct hardly can be considered inequitable under the doctrine of equitable subordination.

The *Paolella* court's characterization of the creditor as a non-insider is key to the outcome. As the court notes, there is a "dearth of cases subordinating the claims of non-insiders." If the secured creditor is an insider — and especially if the secured creditor owes fiduciary duties — a court is more likely to order equitable subordination.

Another case illustrates the point. Pursuant to a divorce settlement, a court had ordered James Mesa to pay Renee Feresi's mortgage within five years. The court also ordered that obligation secured by a security interest in a limited liability company (LLC) that Feresi and Mesa had co-founded. Feresi took no steps to perfect the security interest. Without Feresi's knowledge, Mesa later borrowed money from Hartley, the third member and president of the LLC, and gave Hartley a security interest in the same collateral. Hartley knew of Feresi's security interest but perfected without alerting her. The court held that Hartley's interest should be equitably subordinated to Feresi's.

Feresi v. The Livery, LLC

182 Cal. Rptr. 3d 169 (Cal. Ct. App. 2014)

Feresi had no reason to protect the priority of her own security interest in the same property because she was unaware that her partner held a conflicting interest. Hartley took advantage of Feresi's ignorance by concealing this from her, and betrayed her trust and confidence by perfecting his security interest ahead of hers. In doing so, Hartley breached the fiduciary duties of loyalty and good faith he owed to Feresi. The primacy of Hartley's security interest in Mesa's share of the LLC must succumb to the infection of his duplicity and silence. The trial court properly refused to enforce the security interest held by Hartley's pension plan.

EQUITABLE SUBORDINATION

Hartley contends the UCC sets a "hard line" that requires courts to disregard the equities and accept "harsh results" to ensure that commercial transactions are simple, clear and uniform. Hartley observes that the statutory priority given to the holder of a perfected security interest must be upheld even if the holder is unjustly enriched at the expense of an unsecured creditor.

We conclude that if a fiduciary engages in inequitable conduct with respect to a person to whom a fiduciary duty is owed, then its claim, lien or security interest may be wholly or partially subordinated. The doctrine of equitable subordination has deep common law roots and is based upon the inherent power of a court of equity to do justice as circumstances dictate. While the doctrine is most frequently asserted in bankruptcy court because it has statutory support in section 510 of the Bankruptcy Code, it has also been employed, though sparingly, in other contexts.

Equity and thus equitable subordination should be invoked with caution by the courts. But where, as here, a petitioner has shown: (1) the fiduciary engaged in inequitable conduct; (2) the misconduct resulted in injury to the petitioner or conferred an unfair advantage on the fiduciary; and, (3) invocation of the remedy of equitable subordination will not be inconsistent with the Commercial Code, then the remedy has a place.

The UCC itself acknowledges that its provisions are to be supplemented by "principles of law and equity." [UCC §1-103(b)]. The UCC filing system provides a mechanism for creditors to establish the priority of security interests they secure from debtors and allows them to determine if others already have a claim on collateral. It sets the priority of valid security interests in the same collateral through a registration system. The statutory scheme is not intended to provide a vehicle for creditors to take advantage of persons with whom they have a fiduciary relationship. The application of equitable principles in this case strengthens the statutory scheme. Not rewarding the product of sharp practices in the creation of a security interest lends stability and security in commercial transactions among fiduciaries.

---

7.   Unjust Enrichment

Recall that the unsecured creditors who fed the secured creditors' lien in *Peerless Packing Co., Inc. v. Malone & Hyde, Inc.* in Assignment 16 sued for unjust enrichment. The court denied recovery, stating that an unjust enrichment claim is not applicable in a UCC case because "the purpose and effectiveness of the UCC would be substantially impaired if interests created in compliance with UCC procedure could be defeated by application of the equitable doctrine of unjust enrichment."

Since *Peerless*, the courts have become more receptive to unjust enrichment claims, but only slightly. For example, the Supreme Court of Colorado said:

> The central issue in this case is whether a creditor that holds a perfected security interest in collateral can be held liable to an unsecured creditor based on a theory of unjust enrichment for benefits that enhance the value of the collateral. We conclude that this question cannot be answered categorically. Such a dispute involves tension between the priority system established in Article 9 of the Uniform Commercial Code (UCC or the Code) and equitable principles of unjust enrichment. Although the policies underlying the UCC support a uniform, reliable system of priorities among creditors, we are unwilling to hold that alteration of that hierarchy of priorities is never necessary to implement the equitable principles on which the doctrine of unjust enrichment is based. There is obvious tension between the doctrine of unjust enrichment and the priority system established by Article 9. When an unsecured creditor confers a benefit upon a secured creditor by adding to or enhancing the creditor's collateral and a claim for unjust enrichment against the secured creditor is recognized, the secured creditor in effect loses its priority status despite its compliance with the procedures set forth in Article 9. We have recognized in other settings, however, that the scope of the remedy under the doctrine of unjust enrichment "is broad, cutting across both contract and tort law, with its application guided by the underlying principle of avoiding the unjust enrichment of one party at the expense of another." [Cablevision of Breckenridge v. Tannhauser Condominium Assn., 649 P.2d 1093, 1096-1097 (Colo. 1982)].
>
> The UCC priority system thus reflects the legislative judgment that the value of a predictable system of priorities ordinarily outweighs the disadvantage of the system's occasional inequities. At the same time, however, the Code recognizes that equitable principles may require alteration of the priority system in particular circumstances.
>
> In a situation where a secured creditor initiates or encourages transactions between the debtor and suppliers of goods or services, and benefits from the goods or services supplied to produce such debts, equitable principles require that the secured creditor compensate even an unsecured creditor to avoid being unjustly enriched. The equitable claim is at its strongest when the goods or services are necessary to preserve the security, as in *Producers Cotton Oil.* A secured creditor can protect itself from unjust enrichment claims by remaining uninvolved or by informing the proper parties of its intent not to pay for debts incurred in maintaining, enhancing, or making additions to secured collateral.

Ninth District Production Credit Association v. Ed Duggan, Inc., 821 P.2d 788
(Colo. 1991).

Problem Set 35

35.1. a.   The Faith Diamond was stolen from the Faith Family Museum.
The thief sold it to Borges, a professional fence. Borges sold it to Madame
Downs, an English baroness who claims not to have known Borges's true profession at the time. Her story is made somewhat more credible by the fact that
she paid the reasonable value of the diamond, not the reduced price that a
stolen diamond would be expected to bring. If a representative of the Faith
Family Museum claims the diamond from Madame Downs, who wins?

   b.   Add some more facts. The representative didn't find the diamond that
quickly. Instead, Madame Downs took the diamond to Fairchild and Sons,
a retail jewelry store, and selected a setting for a diamond ring. The proprietor suggested that Madame Downs stop back in a week to pick up her ring.
During the week, Fairchild and Sons sold the diamond to Curtis Whittington,

"BECAUSE OF FINANCIAL DIFFICULTIES, WE
SOLD YOUR LUGGAGE TO ANOTHER AIRLINE."

Reprinted with special permission of North American Syndicate.

a customer who visited Fairchild's store in the Flamingo Mall. Whittington grossly overpaid for the diamond and had no suspicion of its tortured history. Fairchild and Sons filed for bankruptcy. When Whittington made a gift of the ring to the Guru Maraji during his U.S. tour, the story hit the newspapers. The Museum, Madame Downs, the trustee in bankruptcy for Fairchild and Sons, Curtis Whittington, and the Guru all claim the diamond. Now who prevails?

c.   What if Madame Downs had purchased the diamond from the museum and taken it to Fairchild, but Fairchild had sold it to Whittington instead of setting it in a ring as Downs and Fairchild had agreed? UCC §2-403(2) and (3).

35.2.   When the customer pictured in the cartoon sues the airline to whom his luggage was sold, who wins? The airlines sell more than 68,000 pieces of unclaimed luggage each year to a store in Scottsboro, Alabama, which then sells the luggage and the items from the luggage to the public. The airline in the cartoon probably has one or more employees whose duties include selling the luggage. UCC §§1-201(b)(9), 2-104(1), and 2-403.

35.3.   Your client is Willis Trillian, a novelist of considerable repute. Willis has asked you to take a look at the contract he is about to sign with Big Brown Publishing for publication of his latest book. The contract provides that:

1)   The Author hereby grants and assigns to the Publisher . . . the sole and exclusive right to publish, cause to be published, sell, and license others to sell, in book form or in any other form, in the United States of America and elsewhere, in the English language and in any other language, the work tentatively entitled "Blood, Sex, and Secured Credit."

2)   The Publisher agrees to pay to the author, his representatives, or assigns a royalty of 15 percent of the amount charged by the Publisher for copies of said Work, less returns.

Big Brown was recently acquired by Paramount Communications. The rumors are that Big Brown was heavily leveraged in the transaction, but you cannot confirm those rumors because Big Brown is privately held and does not disclose financial information. Willis wonders what he risks losing if Big Brown files bankruptcy and what changes in the contract would be necessary to protect him fully.

a.   If Big Brown filed bankruptcy two weeks after the book was published and before Willis received any royalties, what rights would Willis have?

b.   When we expressed concern about the contract terms Big Brown proposed, Big Brown offered this modification: "The publisher shall register the copyright in said work in the name of the Author and the Author shall remain the owner absolute of such copyright." Willis asks, "If worse came to worst, at least I'd still have the copyright, right? I could look for a new publisher?" What do you tell him? UCC §9-109(a)(1).

c. What modification to the contract between Trillian and Big Brown could assure that Trillian will own the publishing rights if Big Brown does not pay the royalties?

▶ HALF ASSIGNMENT ENDS

35.4. You represent Foster Musical Manufacturing, a small company that manufactures musical instruments and sells them directly to retail stores. In the past two years, it has suffered a number of losses when customers have gone out of business or filed for bankruptcy. Each time, an inventory secured lender has taken possession of some of Foster's products and sold them. Frances Foster, the owner of Foster Musical Manufacturing, wants to do something about it. "Don't tell me to raise our prices to cover these losses," Frances tells you. "We can't. Our good customers will just go elsewhere; they don't want to pay for our bad customers."

a. Would selling on consignment do any good? UCC §§1-201(b)(35), 9-103(d), 9-109(a), 9-319(a), 9-324(b).

b. Could Frances use her right of reclamation to protect herself? UCC §2-702(3); Bankruptcy Code §546(c).

c. Can you think of anything else that might help?

35.5. Potsie Pottow (your old friend and client from Assignment 32) is back. After a short stint in the unemployment lines, Potsie is now a loan officer for SwissBank, Ltd. SwissBank ("Not really a bank," Potsie tells you, "but they've got a lot of money and they make a lot of loans") has some nasty exposure on a chain of gift shops called Gifter. Gifter is "headed for the tank," Potsie says. A balance outstanding of $950,000 is on a demand note, secured by inventory worth not more than $400,000. Accounts receivable are also covered, but they are minimal because most customers use charge cards and the debits are processed very quickly. Potsie's manager has authorized him to call the loan, but Potsie has what he thinks is a better idea. In four months, the Christmas season will begin. By then, Gifter will have drawn down the remaining $50,000 on its $1 million line of credit. Then, in a period of about two months, their inventory will increase to $700,000. "We wait for the additional inventory to arrive and then we call the loan," Potsie tells you. "Unless the folks at Gifter are real idiots, they file Chapter 11, we get adequate protection on a secured claim of $700,000, and we finish the Christmas season hand in hand. We lose $300,000 instead of $550,000." What do you tell Potsie? UCC §§2-702, 9-322(a)(1), 9-324(b); Bankr. Code §§506(a)(1) and 510(c).

Assignment 36: Buyers Against Secured Creditors

A. Introduction

In the preceding assignment we discussed property that came in the debtor's door and fell under the spell of the secured creditor's earlier security interest. In this assignment we look at property that goes out the debtor's door and may or may not fall out of that spell.

Secured creditors have a variety of expectations about possible sale of their collateral by the debtor. The bank that lends against the inventory of a retail store typically expects the debtor to sell the collateral and apply the proceeds to payment of the debt or the purchase of new inventory that will serve as collateral. The insurance company that provides financing for an apartment building may expect the debtor to sell the building without paying off the loan, but, if so, the insurance company expects that its mortgage will continue to encumber the building in the hands of its new owner. The finance company that makes a car loan may expect the debtor to repay the loan in full as a condition of selling the car. All these scenarios share two characteristics. First, the secured creditor recognizes that the debtor has the right to sell the collateral. Security does not interfere with the free alienability of property. See UCC §9-401. Second, the secured creditor expects to be protected as to the *value* of its interest. The protection may be in the form of a lien on the proceeds the debtor receives from the buyer, a continuing lien on the collateral in the hands of the buyer, payment of the loan, or some combination of these protections.

Buyers have a variety of expectations as to what, if anything, they must do to make sure they get good title to what they buy. The consumer who buys a refrigerator from a store in the mall does not expect to search the public records, but does expect to be protected against preexisting security interests. This expectation of protection without search is not limited to consumers: After all, Wal-Mart doesn't search the UCC records when it buys refrigerators from a manufacturer or wholesaler either. But buyers of real estate have a very different set of expectations. Even the young couple buying their first home are likely to be aware of the expectation that there must be a search of the real estate records and, if there is not, they may find that the property they buy is saddled with mortgages that others were supposed to pay. The buyer of a negotiable instrument does not expect to search public records, but probably knows that it must take possession of the instrument at the time it buys or risk taking subject to a security interest in favor of the person who does have possession.

It is possible to view these expectations as the product of law. When doing that, we might say, for example, that the buyer of real estate realizes it must search because the law subjects its title to mortgages of record, including those of which the buyer is not aware. But it may be more useful to view the law as the product of these expectations. When doing that, we might say that the law subjects the buyer's title to mortgages of record because the custom of searching is so strong that the buyer *should* know of those mortgages.

B.   Buyers of Personal Property

The general rule governing sales of encumbered personal property is that buyers take subject to pre-existing security interests. The rule is reflected in UCC §§9-201 and 9-315(a). The former section provides that "a security agreement is effective . . . against [subsequent] purchasers." The latter provides that even in the absence of a provision to that effect, "a security interest continues in collateral notwithstanding sale." The personal property rule is, however, riddled with exceptions.

1.   *The Buyer-in-the-Ordinary-Course Exception: UCC §9-320(a)*

Every purchaser of real estate is expected to search the public records before paying the purchase price and is deemed to have notice of what it would have found. The same is not true for buyers of most kinds of goods. To charge the buyer of milk from a grocery store with constructive notice of what the buyer would have found on a search of the public records under the name of the grocery store would be absurd. One might think that the distinction in what the law expects of a real estate shopper and a grocery shopper results from the difference in the amounts of money involved. Perhaps the amounts typically involved in the two kinds of transactions contributed to the decision to make the real-personal distinction. But we think the distinction is principally an accident of history perpetuated by custom. Some real estate purchases involve only a few hundred dollars, but the system expects a search; some purchases of goods involve millions of dollars, but the system does not. In addition, a search is expected for some kinds of goods, including automobiles, aircraft, and mobile homes.

Whatever the reason, those who buy goods sold by a seller in the ordinary course of the seller's business need not search. The limitation of this indulgence to buyers of goods is found in the definition of "buyer in the ordinary course of business" in UCC §1-201(b)(9). Only buyers of goods can be buyers in the ordinary course of business.

The ordinary course of whose business? Under UCC §9-320(a), a buyer in the ordinary course of business can take free of a security interest created by its seller. "Buyer in the ordinary course of business" is defined in UCC §1-201(b)(9). "Buying" is "in the ordinary course" only if it is "from a person in the business of selling goods of that kind." Thus, the buy must be in the ordinary course of the *seller's* business, not the *buyer's* business. To illustrate, assume that Linda Westerbrook buys and sells used traffic lights. State Street Bank holds a perfected security interest in her inventory. When she sells a traffic light to Peter Kollander (who knows nothing about how Linda finances her business) and installs it in his living room, the sale is in the ordinary course of Linda's business, UCC §9-320(a) applies, and Peter takes free of State Street's security interest. When Linda buys a used traffic light from Disney World, UCC §9-320(a) does not apply. (For those not from around here, Disney World is an amusement park.) This buy is in the ordinary course of Linda's business. Although Disney World may sell a traffic light from time to time, selling traffic lights is not in the ordinary course of Disney World's business. Linda would not take free of a security interest granted by Disney World to its bank.

In the foregoing example, it was a consumer buyer who took free of a security interest granted by his seller. UCC §9-320(a) is not limited to consumer buyers. If Linda sold one of her traffic lights to Neiman Marcus (a fancy department store chain), for display or for resale, Neiman Marcus would be a buyer in the ordinary course of Linda's business, and Neiman Marcus would take free of the State Street Bank security interest.

The buyer's knowledge. UCC §9-320(a) protects a buyer in the ordinary course of business "even though the buyer knows of [the security interest's] existence." UCC §1-201(b)(9) limits "buyer in the ordinary course of business" in a manner that may at first seem to contradict UCC §9-320(a). One cannot be a buyer in the ordinary course if one knows "that the sale to him is in violation of the . . . security interest of a third party." Comment 3 to UCC §9-320 explains: "Reading the definition together with the rule of law results in the buyer's taking free if the buyer merely knows that a security interest covers the goods but taking subject if the buyer knows, in addition, that the sale violates a term in an agreement with the secured party." In other words, merely knowing that Neiman Marcus has granted a security interest in its inventory should not prevent shopper Edith Parker from taking free of the security interest under UCC §9-320(a). Many, if not most, businesses that sell goods from inventory have granted security interests in their inventories. Those security agreements almost invariably authorize the debtors to sell the collateral free and clear of the security interests. UCC §9-320(a) entitles Edith to assume that is true of every merchant's inventory security agreement until she learns otherwise with respect to a particular merchant.

As we noted above, some inventory security agreements impose conditions on the sale of collateral. For example, a bank that finances the inventory of a yacht dealer may want to be involved in and scrutinize every sale. The security agreement employed in such a relationship may prohibit sales of yachts from inventory except with the express written consent of the bank for sale to the particular buyer. A customer who knows that this dealer has inventory financing will not be bound by this sale condition if it does not know of the condition, but will be bound if it does. If the customer knowingly buys in violation of the condition, the customer takes subject to the bank's security interest.

"Created by the buyer's seller." Assume that First National Bank holds a security interest in all personal property owned by Disney World, including its single

traffic light, to secure a loan in the amount of $90 million. Disney World sells the traffic light to Linda in a sale that is not in the ordinary course of Disney World business. As previously noted, Linda takes subject to First National's security interest. Not realizing that the traffic light is encumbered, Linda sells it to Neiman Marcus. Does Neiman Marcus take free of First National's security interest under UCC §9-320(a)? The answer is no. Although Neiman Marcus is a buyer in the ordinary course of business, under UCC §9-320(a), it takes free only of "a security interest created by [its] seller," Linda Westerbrook. It does not take free of security interests created by her predecessors in title.

The effects of this limitation of UCC §9-320(a) become even more surprising when Neiman Marcus decides to sell vintage traffic lights as a Christmas special from its store in the Galleria Mall. When Christmas shopper Edith Parker buys one as a gift for her husband George, both may be in for a surprise. The traffic light inside their gift-wrapped package may have a $90 million perfected security interest firmly attached to it. George, as the owner of the traffic light, is a debtor under UCC §9-102(a)(28). First National is entitled under UCC §9-509(c) to file a financing statement against him. Should Disney World default on its debt to First National, the bank would be entitled to hunt George down and repossess the traffic light. (One of us heard a lender's representative refer to this as "going knocking on doors.")

The farm products exception. UCC §9-320(a) omits from its protection those who buy farm products from a person engaged in farming operations. But the federal Food Security Act provides them parallel protection. That law provides:

> Except as provided in subsection (e) and notwithstanding any other provision of Federal, State, or local law, a buyer who in the ordinary course of business buys a farm product from a seller engaged in farming operations shall take free of a security interest created by the seller, even though the security interest is perfected; and the buyer knows of the existence of such interest.

7 U.S.C. §1631(d) (2005). The exceptions in subsection (e) of §1631 provide farm lenders with various ways of notifying prospective buyers of their security interests. The security interests of lenders who do give notice continue in the collateral notwithstanding sale. The result is that farm lenders can preserve their security interests somewhat more easily than nonfarm lenders. The details of the Food Security Act system are, however, outside the scope of this book. For our purposes it is sufficient to see that the farm products exception of UCC §9-320(a) may not be much of an exception at all.

When does a buyer become a buyer? At the moment a bankruptcy petition is filed or the moment that a secured creditor takes possession of its collateral, there typically will be some people who have contracted to buy some of the collateral but who have not yet completed their transactions. If such a person is a "buyer" within the meaning of UCC §9-320(a), the person will take free of the inventory lender's security agreement and be able to keep what was bought. If the buyer has paid part of the purchase price, the buyer will get credit for that part, and owe the balance.

If the person is not yet a "buyer," then the person is merely the seller's unsecured creditor. As a creditor, the person is legally entitled to return of the down payment or damages for loss of the benefit of his or her bargain. Payment in full is, however, unlikely. Like other unsecured creditors of bankrupt debtors, the buyer-wanabee-now-creditor is likely to end up with only a few cents on the dollar. Because the law treats buyers so much better than unsecured creditors, the moment when a person becomes a "buyer" within the meaning of UCC §9-320(a) can be of tremendous importance. As the following case illustrates, there are many permutations of this problem and much remaining uncertainty.

Daniel v. Bank of Hayward

425 N.W.2d 416 (Wis. 1988)

SHIRLEY S. ABRAHAMSON, J.

This case presents the following issue: When does a retail purchaser who makes a down payment on a motor vehicle but does not take title to the vehicle become a "buyer in ordinary course of business" under [UCC §1-201(b)(9)] and [UCC §9-320(a)] to prevail over the security interest of the motor vehicle dealer's floor plan financier?

In Chrysler Corp. v. Adamatic, 59 Wis. 2d 219, 208 N.W.2d 97 (1972), this court concluded that a purchaser becomes a buyer in ordinary course of business when he or she takes title to the goods. We conclude that the purchasers in this case became buyers in ordinary course of business when the vehicle was identified to the contract. To the extent that our decision in the Chrysler case is inconsistent with our decision in this case, we overrule the Chrysler case.

The facts in the record are undisputed. Joseph and Marijane Daniel, the purchasers, entered into a motor vehicle purchase contract in May 1983 with Don Hofstadter, Inc., a motor vehicle dealership in the City of Hayward. The purchasers agreed to purchase a 1984 Chevrolet van which had not yet been manufactured and to trade in the older motor home. According to the contract, the cash price of the vehicle was $12,077.55; the trade-in allowance was $8,675.55; and the amount the purchasers owed on delivery was $3,402.00. The contract described the motor vehicle and its various accessories but did not set forth the vehicle identification number because the vehicle had not been manufactured when the contract was signed.

The purchasers signed over title to their existing motor home and delivered the home to the dealership. The dealership sold the motor home on or about June 6, 1983. The record does not reflect how much the dealership received on the sale of the motor home, and it is not clear whether the Bank received any of the proceeds.

The dealership did its financing, including floor plan financing on new vehicles, with defendant Bank of Hayward (Bank). The floor plan financing operated as follows: There was a master note in the original sum of $150,000 dated April 19, 1982. When the dealership would order a new vehicle from General Motors, the Bank would receive a copy of that order. Prior to GM's delivery of the new vehicle to the dealership, GM would send the Bank a sight draft which included the vehicle identification number. The Bank would then prepare an individual floor plan note in the amount of the draft and the dealership would sign it. When the individual note was signed by the dealership, the Bank would pay GM. GM would then send the Manufacturer's Statement of Origin (MSO) to the Bank which retained the MSO. Because the MSO is necessary to obtain title to the motor vehicle, the Bank effectively controlled delivery of title to the retail purchaser and ensured itself of being paid. This procedure was unusual. Ordinarily, GM would send the MSO directly to the dealership. The Bank used the unusual procedure in this case because it was concerned about the financial status of the dealership.

On September 30, 1983, the Bank received a sight draft from General Motors for the van the purchasers had ordered. The dealership executed a floor plan note in the amount of $9,905.22 to pay General Motors for a 1984 Chevrolet van, I.D. No. 1GCGG35M6E7105325. The parties agree that the van bearing this identification number is the vehicle the purchasers ordered. The Floor Plan Note conveyed a security interest in the van to the Bank on September 30, 1983.

Sometime on Friday, October 21, 1983, the Chevrolet van was delivered to the dealership. On Saturday, October 22, 1983, the Bank discovered that its debtor, the dealership, was removing used vehicles from the lots. Because these used vehicles were collateral for the Bank's loans, the Bank called all loans and secured the lot so that no vehicles could be removed. The purchasers' Chevrolet van was among the new vehicles on the lot when the Bank took possession of the dealership's premises.

On October 24, 1983, the purchasers went to the dealership to complete the purchase of the van.

The Bank was willing to release the van only if the purchasers paid in full the Bank's interest in the van pursuant to the Floor Plan Note, namely, $9,905.22. According to their contract with the dealership, the purchasers did not owe the dealership $9,905.22. By virtue of the trade-in, the purchasers owed the dealership only $3,402.00. Because the purchasers needed the van to go to Florida, they [paid] $9,905.22 and they then took title to and possession of the van. They brought this action against the Bank to recover damages "to the extent of the over-payment together with consequential damages including interest on the monies that plaintiff had to borrow to meet the extorted demands of the bank, actual attorney's fees incurred and a great inconvenience all to their damage in the sum of $15,000."

As we stated previously, the sole question in this case is: When do purchasers who make a down payment under a contract for sale and have not taken title to the vehicle achieve the status of buyer in ordinary course of business? If the purchasers in this case became buyers in ordinary course of business prior to the Bank's seizing the van, their interest in the van takes priority over the Bank's perfected security interest.

We examine first the relevant provisions of the Wisconsin Uniform Commercial Code. [UCC Article 9] establishes a priority system for determining the rights of parties who claim competing interests in secured property. As a general rule, the holder of a perfected security interest has an interest in the secured property which is superior to the interests of the debtor, unsecured creditors of the debtor and subsequent purchasers of the secured property. [UCC §9-201] thus protects the secured creditor. The Code provides, however, exceptions to the rule that the secured creditor has priority over purchasers of the collateral. A principal exception to the rule is found in [UCC §9-320(a)], captioned "protection of buyers of goods," which permits a buyer in ordinary course of business as defined in [UCC §1-201(b)(9)] to take free of a security interest created by the seller. The Code thus recognizes a potential conflict between the buyer in ordinary course of business and the seller's secured creditor and attempts to seek a fair accommodation between the two. [UCC §9-320(9)] severs the inventory lender's security interest in favor of the buyer in ordinary course of business. In order to prevail over the Bank's perfected security interest, the purchasers in this case must qualify as buyers in ordinary course of business, as that term is defined in [UCC §1-201(b)(9)].

The exception for a buyer in ordinary course of business accommodates the interests of all parties. Buyers desire to be free of the lender's interest after they have committed themselves to paying for the goods. A buyer cannot easily determine how the seller finances its inventory, nor can the buyer afford to negotiate subordination agreements with the seller's lenders for each purchase made. Secured creditors at some point expect to surrender their security interest in the goods and look to the proceeds of a sale for repayment of the loan. The secured creditor thus depends on the goods being sold. The secured lender expects a constant flow of inventory in and out of the seller's possession; it is usually in the business of lending funds and is in a better position to take precautions against the loss of its security.

Although the Code protects the buyer in ordinary course of business, the Code provides no explicit guidance to the question presented in this case, namely when does a purchaser under a contract for sale achieve the status of buyer in ordinary course of business. There are at least five possible dates on which a purchaser may be viewed as having achieved the status of buyer in ordinary course of business: (1) the date of initial contract; (2) the date the goods are identified; (3) the date title passes to the purchaser; (4) the date the purchaser gets delivery; and (5) the date the purchaser accepts the goods.

Relying on Chrysler Corp. v. Adamatic, 59 Wis. 2d 219, 208 N.W.2d 97 (1973), the Bank maintains that the purchasers can not become buyers in ordinary course of business who take free of the seller's secured creditor until the purchasers take title or delivery of the van. Because the purchasers in this case did not take title or delivery, the Bank contends that the purchasers do not take free of its interest as the dealership's secured creditor.

We have reconsidered our analysis in *Chrysler* and are persuaded by the reasoning of the commentators and courts which have, since our decision in Chrysler Corp. v. Adamatic, addressed the issue presented in this case. The commentators and courts have, for the most part, opted for an earlier date than the date that title passed as the time when a purchaser achieves the status of a buyer in ordinary course of business.

We conclude that we erred in relying on the date of transfer of title as the date on which a purchaser becomes a buyer in ordinary course of business. Reliance on the concept of title is contrary to the thrust of the Uniform Commercial Code and the commentary. The drafters of the Uniform Commercial Code tried to avoid giving technical rules of title a central role in furthering the policies of the Uniform Commercial Code. See [UCC §§2-401, 9-202]. Although title questions may be of significance in determining some issues under the Code, we conclude that reliance on title to interpret [UCC §9-320(a)] is an unduly narrow and technical interpretation.

Courts have overwhelmingly rejected a definition of buyer in ordinary course that focuses on whether title has passed. These courts reason that the inventory financier is better able to guard against the risks inherent in this type of financing than is the average retail buyer because the financier is more knowledgeable and has the resources to guard against the risks. These courts conclude that placing the burden on the buyer would inhibit retail sales.

Furthermore, focusing on the words "in ordinary course," these courts reason that a court must consider the substance of the transaction; a court must look to the customary manner in which sales are made in the seller's business and to the expectations of the buyer under the contract. The language "in ordinary course" indicates deference to commercial practice and is consistent with the purposes and policies underlying the Code "[t]o permit the continued expansion of commercial practices through custom, usage and agreement of the parties." [UCC §1-103(a)(2)]. If it is customary in the seller's business to sell goods in a particular manner (e.g., seller and purchaser enter into a contract for sale and purchaser makes a down payment), then the court may find that the purchaser who makes a down payment without taking title is a "buyer in ordinary course of business."

The purchasers in this case ask the court to reject the title or delivery date in this case and adopt an "identification" date as the date on which they became buyers in ordinary course of business. The purchasers rely on [UCC §2-501(1)], which provides that a buyer obtains a special property interest on identification. [UCC §2-501(1)] provides:

> The buyer obtains a special property and an insurable interest in goods by identi-fication of existing goods to which the contract refers even though the goods so identified are nonconforming and he has an option to return or reject them. Such identification can be made at any time and in any manner explicitly agreed to by the parties. In the absence of explicit agreement identification occurs:
>
> (a) When the contract is made if it is for the sale of goods already existing and identified;
>
> (b) If the contract is for the sale of future goods...when goods are shipped, marked or otherwise designated by the seller as goods to which the contract refers. . . .

The purchasers argue that adoption of the identification date strikes a fair bal-ance between the interests of the buyer in ordinary course and the secured party. The purchasers argue that once the goods have been identified they have an insur-able interest in the goods and can maintain an action against a third party who has injured them through his or her dealings with the goods. The purchasers reason that their interest at identification justifies considering them buyers in ordinary course at that time.

The purchasers conclude that they became buyers in ordinary course of business when the van became identified to the contract, that is, when it was produced or when GM sent the Bank the sight draft including the vehicle identification num-ber. We need not decide in this case which is the appropriate date of identification.

Whichever date, the purchaser would prevail over the Bank. Because the purchasers do not ask this court to adopt the date of contract as the triggering date for transforming the purchasers to buyers in ordinary course, we need not decide this issue.

We merely hold today that the purchasers became buyers in ordinary course of business when the goods became identified to the contract. We rest our decision on the circumstances surrounding the transaction in this case and the manner in which sales are made in this industry.

This case presents the situation that [UCC §9-320(a)] was designed to address. The purchasers were ordinary retail consumers purchasing a vehicle from a dealership, an entity in the business of selling vehicles. The purchasers made a down payment and signed a contract. The Bank as financier of the inventory authorized the sale of the inventory. It was only through the sale of the inventory that the Bank would receive cash from the dealership to repay the loan. The Bank knew of the purchasers. The Bank knew of the purchase order and paid the manufacturer for the vehicle in question on September 30, 1983.

In its amicus brief the Wisconsin Bankers Association states that protecting the purchasers in this case will make a security interest in inventory an unworkable concept. The position we adopt today is the position most courts have adopted, concluding that the floor plan financier can guard against the risks. The Bank was in a better position than the purchasers to guard against the risk of loss. Most retail purchasers probably have never heard of the Uniform Commercial Code and would not know how to go about protecting their interest. The Bank, on the other hand, is in the business of lending money and has access to information about how to protect itself, as best it can, against risk of loss. Accordingly, under the facts of this case, we hold that the purchasers were buyers in ordinary course of business upon identification of the merchandise to the contract. The purchasers assert that the van had been identified to the contract before the Bank took over the dealership's premises and that their interest prevails over the Bank's. Because it is unclear whether the Bank disputes the date of identification, this issue may have to be resolved in remand.

The judgment of the circuit court is reversed and the cause remanded.

Sales of goods remaining in the possession of the seller. After *Daniel*, the drafters revised UCC §1-201(b)(9) to add that "[o]nly a buyer that takes possession of the goods or has a right to recover the goods from the seller under Article 2 may be a buyer in ordinary course of business." That addition changed the *calculus* for determining buyer in ordinary course status, but it did not change the *result* in consumer-buyer cases such as *Daniel*. Comment 9 to UCC §1-201 identifies UCC §§2-502 and 2-716 as the relevant provisions of Article 2 governing the right to recover goods. UCC §2-502 gives consumer buyers the right to recover from their sellers goods that have been identified to the sale contract. That means consumer buyers will be buyers in ordinary course from the time the goods are identified to the contract for sale.

Most business buyers—even if they have paid the full purchase price—do not have an Article 2 right to recover. Until those buyers take possession, they cannot be buyers in the ordinary course and their rights remain subject to those of the seller's inventory lender. When business buyers leave possession with sellers, the possession requirement often defeats business buyers' reasonable expectations. Some courts have pushed back against the possession requirement by holding that business buyers who leave what they bought in the possession of the seller nevertheless have "constructive possession" of it. They are thus buyers in ordinary course and take free of the inventory lender's security interest.

For example, in In re Western Iowa Limestone, Inc., 538 F.3d 858 (8th Cir. 2008), dealers purchased 18,400 tons of agricultural lime. The dealers "inspected the ag lime and accepted it at [the seller's] place of business." But, by agreement of the parties, the lime remained, along with all of the lime owned by the seller, "in a single fungible pile until resold to [the dealers'] customers and removed from the premises." In the seller's bankruptcy, the court held that the requirement of UCC §1-201(9) that the buyer take possession to be a buyer in ordinary course of business was met with respect to lime still in the fungible pile because the dealers were in "constructive possession" of it.

Sales of goods with certificates in the possession of the secured party. The *Daniel* case describes the bank's effort to control the dealership by controlling the Manufacturer's Statement of Origin (the MSO). The dealer needs the MSO to obtain the initial certificate of title. Once a certificate of title has been issued, the owner is required to surrender it as a prerequisite to issuance of a certificate of title to the owner's transferee. Thus it might seem that secured creditors could prevent sale of their automobile collateral by retaining possession of the certificates of title. Such efforts, however, have generally been unsuccessful.

In First National Bank of El Campo v. Buss, 143 S.W.3d 915 (Tex. App. 2004), for example, several buyers bought used automobiles from Greg's Auto Sales. Each paid for a vehicle and took possession of it. The buyers completed title applications and left the applications with the dealer. Unbeknownst to the buyers, the titles were in the hands of First National Bank, Greg's inventory lender. The bank refused to surrender the titles without payment. The Texas certificate of title act "declared that the non-transfer of certificates of title renders the sale void." The Texas Court of Appeals held that the buyers were buyers in the ordinary course of business under Article 9 and that the provisions of Article 9 were in conflict with and superseded the provisions of the certificate of title act. The buyers got the cars.

Sales of goods in the possession of the secured party. Daniel v. Bank of Hayward illustrates that a buyer in the ordinary course of business can defeat the inventory lender's security interest without taking possession of the goods. In that case, the seller-debtor, Don Hofstadter, Inc., had possession. What if, instead, the Bank of Hayward had possession of the vehicle at the time the Daniels purchased it? Could the Daniels still have bought the vehicle in the ordinary course of business and taken free of the bank's now doubly perfected security interest? If so, it would seem to be virtually impossible for a secured creditor to prevent its debtor from selling collateral free of the creditor's security interest. Even collateral resting in the bank's vault would not be safe. On the other hand, the

Wisconsin Supreme Court determined that the Daniels were buyers in the ordinary course of business even though they had never seen the van they bought. For all the Daniels knew, their van might have been in the bank's vault.

Tanbro Fabrics Corp. v. Deering Milliken, Inc., 350 N.E.2d 590 (N.Y. 1976), illustrates both the problem and the solution. The secured creditor, Deering, had possession of 267,000 yards of a certain fabric as security for an account owing from Mill Fabrics, the debtor, to Deering. Mill Fabrics sold the fabric to Tanbro. Tanbro was familiar with the industry practice of leaving goods in the possession of the seller's seller as security and hence did not find it unusual to be buying fabric the seller did not possess. Tanbro paid the purchase price to Mill Fabrics. Mill Fabrics promptly went belly-up without paying Deering. Deering refused to give the fabric to Tanbro and Tanbro sued. The court held that Tanbro was a buyer in the ordinary course of Mill Fabrics' business and that Tanbro therefore took free of Deering's security interest.

Some of the drafters of former Article 9 were apoplectic over *Tanbro Fabrics*. Although they never managed to overturn that decision, the drafters of revised Article 9 have. UCC §9-320(e) provides somewhat mysteriously that "Subsections (a) and (b) do not affect a security interest in goods in possession of the secured party under Section 9-313." Comment 8 explains that UCC §9-320(e) "rejects the holding of Tanbro Fabrics Corp. v. Deering Milliken... and, together with Section 9-317(b), prevents a buyer of collateral from taking free of a security interest if the collateral is in the possession of the secured party." This disturbing reversal of *Tanbro Fabrics* becomes even more disturbing when one takes into account that a secured party can possess collateral through an agent or as the consequence of the person in actual possession authenticating a record stating that it holds possession for the secured party's benefit. Comment 3 to UCC §9-313. Possession through either method may be invisible to the buyer.

2.   The Failure-to-Perfect Exception, UCC §§9-323(d) and (e), 9-317(b) and (d)

Buyers who do not qualify for the ordinary course of business exception have no exemption from the search requirement. They are expected to search the UCC records and are charged with constructive notice of the filings they would have found. Accordingly, unless the secured party authorized the debtor to sell free of a perfected security interest, a buyer of goods not in the ordinary course, or the buyer of other tangible UCC collateral irrespective of whether it is in the ordinary course, takes subject to it. UCC §9-315(a)(1). But such a buyer not in the ordinary course can take free of an unperfected security interest if the buyer gives value and receives delivery without knowledge of the security interest. UCC §9-317(b). The rules are the same for intangible collateral, with the exception that delivery is not required because intangibles cannot be delivered. UCC §9-317(d).

To illustrate, assume that Thomas Redding plans to open a frozen yogurt store. He needs a walk-in cooler to refrigerate the yogurt mix. He spots one for $6,000 on eBay. The owner, Peter's Pizzas, used the cooler to store food and drinks in connection with its pizza business, but the business closed a few weeks ago. Because Peter's Pizzas is not in the business of selling coolers, the sale of this cooler to Redding will not be a sale in the ordinary course. Redding will take subject to any perfected security interest in the cooler, including even some future advances Peter's Pizzas might receive from its lender after Redding's purchase. UCC §§9-323(d) and (e). For that reason, Redding is well advised to search the public record before paying the purchase price.

If, instead, Redding bought his cooler from Paul's Restaurant Supply, a company that sells, among other things, used coolers, he would not have been expected to search the public record. He would have taken free of any security interest given by Paul's Restaurant Supply. UCC §9-320(a).

▶ HALF ASSIGNMENT ENDS

3. The Authorized Disposition Exception: UCC §9-315(a)(1)

All types of UCC collateral are subject to the *authorized disposition* exception in UCC §9-315(a)(1). A security interest does not continue in the collateral if "the secured party authorized the disposition free of the security interest."

This exception is broader than may at first appear. First, the exception does not depend for its operation on equities in favor of the buyer. It can apply in favor of a buyer who did or did not search the public record. It can apply in favor of a buyer who knows or does not know of the security interest or the secured creditor's authorization to sell.

Second, the authorization to sell need not be express. In numerous cases, the courts have held that a secured creditor who knew that the debtor was making sales of collateral in violation of provisions of the security agreement, and did not object, thereby waived the provisions and "authorized" the sale so that the buyer took free of the security interest. For example, in Gretna State Bank v. Cornbelt Livestock Co., 463 N.W.2d 795 (Neb. 1990), the bank held a security interest in the debtor's cows and hogs, which were farm products under UCC §9-102(a)(34). The security agreement expressly prohibited sale of the collateral without the prior written consent of the bank. The debtor sold some of the cattle without written consent, and the bank sued the buyer. The court held that the bank's security interest did not continue in the cattle after their sale because the sale was "authorized" within the meaning of UCC §9-315(a)(1). The court relied on the fact that the debtor previously had sold cattle and hogs without the bank's written consent on numerous occasions, the bank knew about many of those sales, and the bank had not objected to them or rebuked the debtor for having made them. The court concluded that the bank had thereby waived the security agreement provision requiring its consent to sales and authorized such later sales as the debtor might make.

For the authorized disposition exception to apply, the authorization must be to dispose of the collateral free of the security interest. This element of the authorization also can be express or implied.

But Article 9 leaves unresolved a split of authority as to conditional authorizations. To illustrate, assume that Gretna State Bank holds a security interest in cattle owned by Cornbelt Livestock Co. Gretna authorizes Cornbelt to sell 30 head of cattle free of Gretna's security interest, but only on the condition that Cornbelt immediately pay the proceeds of sale to Gretna as a payment on the loan. Cornbelt sells the cattle to Butler, receives the proceeds from Butler, but does not pay them to Gretna. In an action by Gretna to enforce its security interest in the cattle now owned by Butler, the courts split. Some treat the disposition as authorized; others do not. The courts are more likely to treat the disposition as authorized if Butler does not know of the condition, but that factor is not determinative.

In the case that follows, the secured creditor expressly authorized the sale, but only on the condition that the loan be paid in full. The court holds the condition binding on the purchaser, even though the secured creditor agreed to withhold knowledge of the condition from the purchaser.

RFC Capital Corporation v. EarthLink, Inc.

55 UCC Rep. Serv. 2d 617 (Ohio App. 2004)

KLATT, J., BOWMAN and PETREE, JJ., concur.

[RFC loaned $12 million to Internet Commerce & Communications, Inc. ("ICC"), a publicly traded company that provided Internet access, among other services, to its customers.] To secure the loan, ICC granted RFC a security interest in, among other assets:

> All of [ICC's] customer base, which shall include but not be limited to all of [ICC's] past, present and future customer contracts, agreements, lists, documents, computer tapes, letters of agency or other arrangements, any customer list relating thereto and any information regarding prospective customers and contracts, agreements, goodwill and other intangible assets associated with any of the foregoing.

[In late 2000, ICC was in financial trouble and agreed to sell the customer base to EarthLink for a "bounty" of $190 per customer.] ICC represented that it had 97,000 customers who could transfer to EarthLink. Thus, if all 97,000 customers transferred to EarthLink and paid for two months of service, EarthLink would pay ICC a total of $18,430,000.

[Cliff Bryant, EarthLink's director of acquisitions] asked if RFC knew of the proposed sale of the customer base, and Mr. Hanson [ICC's employee] assured him that RFC knew of the sale and had agreed to release the collateral. [A]t the time ICC and EarthLink executed the EarthLink Agreement, RFC was considering the release of its security interest, but it had not agreed to do so.

After RFC's financial review of ICC, RFC drafted the "Second Amendment to the Loan and Security Agreement" ("Second Amendment") to address the sale of the customer base. RFC and ICC executed the Second Amendment on April 2, 2001. Section 11 of the Second Amendment provided that:

> The Lender hereby consents to the sale of the Purchased Accounts by [ICC]. Upon the performance by [ICC] and [its wholly owned subsidiary] of all their obligations under

the Loan Agreement and this Amendment, the Lender agrees to release its security interest in the Purchased Accounts.

Neither ICC nor RFC informed EarthLink of the Second Amendment. In fact, Mr. Hanson forbade RFC from contacting EarthLink. Despite RFC's knowledge that EarthLink expected the customer base to be delivered free and clear of any security interest, RFC followed Mr. Hanson's instructions.

Ultimately, only 25,144 former ICC customers paid EarthLink for either dial-up or web hosting service for two consecutive months. Because EarthLink had paid for 40,000 customers, but only received 25,144 customers, EarthLink determined that it did not owe ICC any further payments.

On May 24, 2002, RFC filed suit against EarthLink, alleging conversion, tortious interference with a contractual relationship, unjust enrichment, impairment of RFC's security interest, and a right to an accounting. RFC claimed that, as a secured party, it was entitled to a recovery from EarthLink because EarthLink took and damaged its collateral without obtaining a release.

The case was submitted to the jury, which found EarthLink liable and awarded RFC $6 million. On June 23, 2003, the trial court entered judgment for RFC in the amount of $6 million plus post-judgment interest. EarthLink then filed this appeal.

EarthLink contends that RFC expressly authorized the release of its security interest when it consented to the sale of the customer base in the Second Amendment. We disagree.

In [UCC §9-315] the UCC drafters [made] it explicit that a security interest continues in collateral "unless the secured party authorizes the disposition *free of the security interest.*" Construing the two sentences of Section 11 together, we conclude that RFC authorized the sale of the customer base, but made that collateral subject to its security interest until ICC performed its contractual obligations. Because RFC retained its security interest, despite its consent to the sale, the customer base remained encumbered as long as ICC's contractual obligations went unperformed.

EarthLink [also] contends that the condition RFC imposed upon the release of its security interest (i.e., ICC's performance of its contractual obligations) was ineffective against EarthLink because satisfaction of the condition was outside of EarthLink's control. Consequently, EarthLink reasons that, even though ICC did not perform its contractual obligations, RFC's security interest was released.

As EarthLink points out, there is a split in authority regarding whether a conditional consent cuts off a secured party's interest in the collateral. The line of authority EarthLink relies upon holds that, "a condition imposed on an authorization to sell is ineffective, unless performance of the condition is within the buyer's control." Production Credit Assn. of Baraboo v. Pillsbury Co., 392 N.W.2d 445, 448 (Wis. 1986). These courts reason that a condition requiring performance only the seller can provide is not a "real" condition because it "makes the buyer an insurer of acts beyond its control." First Natl. Bank & Trust Co. of Oklahoma City v. Iowa Beef Processors, Inc., 626 F.2d 764, 769 (10th Cir. 1980). Under this view, the third party purchaser who agreed to no condition has superior rights over the secured party who permitted the collateral to be placed on the market.

Not surprisingly, RFC directs us to the contrary line of authority, which holds that regardless of the nature of the condition, "no authorization exists where the debtor fails to satisfy the conditions of the creditor's conditional consent." Northern Commercial Co. v. Cobb, 778 P.2d 205, 208 (Alaska 1989). These courts reason that the UCC does not prevent a secured party from attaching a condition or limitation to its consent. Further, these courts maintain that a buyer can protect itself by searching UCC filings to ascertain whether a security interest exists and then contacting the secured party to determine whether there are any conditions attached to the consent.

After reviewing the authority on each side of this issue, we are persuaded that any and all conditions a secured party places upon its consent must be satisfied for the consent to be effective. We do not agree with the reasoning of *First Natl. Bank & Trust Co. of Oklahoma City, supra,* and its progeny that a conditional consent should be construed as a full authorization of a release because the condition is out of the buyer's control. Rather, we hold that it is the buyer, who has the power to ascertain any potential conditions prior to sale and the status of those conditions, that must bear the consequences of purchasing another's collateral.

By giving the secured party the power to authorize the release of the security interest, the UCC places the secured party in a superior position over a third party purchaser. Thus, the onus is on the third party purchaser to determine if a security interest exists and ensure that the secured party fully authorizes the release of that security interest. If the third party purchaser does not conduct a search of UCC filings or does not obtain a release, it must bear the risk and/or burden of buying potentially encumbered collateral.

This burden, however, is relatively light. When purchasing goods that are subject to a security interest, the buyer must simply communicate with the secured party disclosed in the UCC filing to determine what conditions, if any, the secured party has placed upon its consent to a release. If a secured party discloses that it will only consent if the seller satisfies a condition (whether it be a condition precedent or subsequent to the release), the buyer can then investigate the likelihood of the condition occurring, value the collateral in the context of the potentially ongoing security interest and generally assess the risk of going forward with the transaction. If the buyer determines that the risk presented by the conditional consent is too high, it can decide not to consummate the deal. While the condition may only be in the seller's power to satisfy, the decision to purchase the collateral is totally within the buyer's power.

In the case at bar, RFC agreed to release its security interest in the customer base "upon the performance by [ICC] . . . of all [its] obligations under the Loan Agreement and [the Second] Amendment." This provision reflected RFC's consistently-held position that it would only release its security interest if ICC either paid off or paid down the loan. ICC, however, did not satisfy either of these conditions. Therefore, RFC never authorized the release of its security interest in the customer base.

EarthLink's ignorance of the condition contained in the Second Amendment until after it transferred ICC's customers to its system and its inability to satisfy the condition itself are not significant factors in our analysis. By not obtaining a full release of RFC's publicly-disclosed security interest, EarthLink assumed the risk that the customer base would remain encumbered by that security interest.

_____

The court seems to be saying that EarthLink should have searched the UCC records, discovered RFC Capital's security interest, and insisted on a release of that interest before paying the purchase price. The problem with that interpretation of the "unless" clause in UCC §9-315(a)(1) is that a released security interest no longer exists. Thus, if the buyer insisted on a release it would not need the "unless" clause, and if the buyer didn't insist on a release the "unless" clause would not be applicable. The "unless" clause would never apply.

4. The Consumer-to-Consumer-Sale Exception: UCC §9-320(b)

When a sale of goods is outside the ordinary course of business, even consumer buyers are expected to play the search-and-file game. Assume, for example, that Steve Waldoch offers to sell his riding lawnmower to Thomas Redding for $600. If Sears holds a security interest in the lawn mower that is perfected by filing and Sears has not authorized the sale, Redding will take subject to it. Redding is not protected by UCC §9-320(a) because Waldoch does not deal in lawnmowers. See UCC §1-201(b)(9). Redding is not protected by UCC §9-320(b) because of the exception in that section in favor of secured parties who have filed a financing statement. Ordinary people would consider it absurd that Redding be expected to search the public record before buying a lawnmower in a garage sale. But you should realize by now that the drafters of Article 9 were not ordinary people.

We refer to the exception in UCC §9-320(b) as the consumer-to-consumer-sale exception because the exception applies only if the goods are consumer goods in the hands of the seller before the sale and consumer goods in the hands of the buyer after the sale. The requirement that the goods be held for personal, family, or household purposes of the seller prior to the sale is contained in the main part of section (b); the requirement that they be held for personal, family, or household purposes of the buyer after the sale is contained in subsection (b)(3). The buyer in a consumer-to-consumer sale is protected from an automatically perfected purchase-money security interest (PMSI) in consumer goods. Thus, if Sears had not filed a financing statement in the illustration given in the previous paragraph, but instead relied on its PMSI protection from UCC §9-309(1), the consumer-to-consumer-sale exception of UCC §9-320(b) would apply to permit Redding to take free of Sears' perfected security interest.

Even if consumers knew they would lose to PMSIs perfected by filing, searching in small consumer goods transactions would not be cost effective. Rarely do consumers do it. Making the effectiveness of a security interest depend on making a filing that no one will search for or discover makes no sense to us. The drafters probably came up with this rule because they believed that secured creditors would file only on expensive consumer goods, and that consumers would regularly search before purchasing those goods. If that was the drafter's thinking, they should have written "cheap" into the definition of consumer goods. Their failure to do is inexcusable. It has been cured by the legislatures of a few states by placing a dollar limit on the definition of consumer goods.

C.   Buyers of Real Property

The general rule resolves the competition between buyer and mortgagee on the basis of first in time. That is, if the mortgage was created before the debtor sold the property to the buyer, the buyer takes subject to the mortgage. If the sale takes place first, it will be free of a later mortgage granted by the debtor-seller. A recording statute may reverse either of these results. One who buys in good faith, for value, without notice of an unrecorded mortgage may take free of it under the recording statute. Similarly, one who takes a mortgage in good faith, for value, without notice of an unrecorded deed may have priority over the rights of the buyer pursuant to the recording statute. If a mortgage is recorded before the debtor sells the property, its priority over the rights of the purchaser is pretty much absolute. All purchasers of real property are expected to search the public record, are deemed to have notice (*constructive notice*) of duly recorded mortgages, and take subject to them. No exceptions are recognized for sales in the ordinary course of business or even sales to consumers.

To illustrate, assume that Bob Mason sees a four-color glossy magazine ad for five-acre tracts of land in the Rocky Mountains. He emails the Mountain Development offices in Denver and they send a salesman to Bob's home in New York. In good faith, Bob pays the salesman $20,000 in return for a deed that recites the conveyance of lot 237 "free and clear of all liens and encumbrances." Unknown to Bob, American Finance holds a first mortgage against Mountain's entire inventory of lots, including lot 237, to secure a $1.2 million loan that American made to Mountain Development. American recorded its mortgage in Colorado before Bob purchased the lot. Bob purchased in the ordinary course of American's business, but he nevertheless takes lot 237 subject to the $1.2 million mortgage. Although Bob did not search the public records and therefore did not know of the mortgage before paying his money, the law regards that as his fault, not his virtue. Consumer Bob, like every other purchaser of real property, is expected to search, and he takes with constructive notice of all duly recorded mortgages.

If the mortgage exists but remains unrecorded at the time Bob buys lot 237, the recording statute of the state will govern the validity of the mortgage against Bob. Recording statutes, which we discussed in Assignment 33, apply to conveyances by deed to purchasers, as well as conveyances to lenders by mortgage.

The applicable statute may be a pure *race statute*, such as the North Carolina statute reproduced in Assignment 33. It may be a *notice-race statute*, such as the New York statute also reproduced in Assignment 33. In either case, Bob will prevail so long as he records his deed before American records its mortgage. If the statute is a pure *notice statute*, such as the Massachusetts statute also reproduced in Assignment 33, Bob will prevail even if American records after Bob buys but before Bob records. (Remember, Bob is a buyer against an unperfected security interest.) Thus, in general, a bona fide purchaser of real estate for value will take free of a prior unrecorded mortgage if that purchaser records before the mortgage holder records.

Had Bob contacted a lawyer, the lawyer would have recommended a search of the public records before Bob paid for the land. The search would have discovered the mortgage. It then would have been up to the debtor, Mountain Development, to obtain a release of lot 237 from American's mortgage. Bob would simply have refused to pay the purchase price until the record title to lot 237 was clear.

The importance of searching title has become so much a part of real estate purchases and sales that in every state some group — usually lawyers or title companies — routinely handles sales, checking all the paperwork to make certain that liens have been properly cleared from the property before the purchase money is released to the seller. Title searches also partly explain why it takes so much longer and is so much more expensive to buy a home than to buy a car or a boat, even when the latter sales are financed and the goods are valuable.

Problem Set 36

36.1.   Alecia Card bought a used 1992 "Lindy Delux Housecar" (the Lindy) from the used car lot of Sunrise R.V. She paid for the recreational vehicle with a $23,000 cashier's check and drove it home. The salesman at Sunrise assured her that she would receive title to the Lindy directly from the Division of Motor Vehicles within two weeks. When the title did not arrive as promised, Alecia complained to Sunrise.

Eventually she learned the history of the Lindy. A man named Bruce Markell purchased it from All Seasons R.V. over a year ago. Markell granted All Seasons a security interest in the Lindy to secure a part of the purchase price. In the security agreement, Markell agreed "not to transfer any interest in the vehicle." A few weeks ago, Markell violated the security agreement by trading the Lindy to Sunrise R.V. (Sunrise) for another recreational vehicle. UCC §9-401(b). At the time he sold the Lindy to Sunrise, Markell still owed All Seasons $17,000 of the purchase price. Sunrise bought the Lindy subject to that lien and agreed to pay it. Instead, Sunrise deposited Alecia's $23,000 to its operating account and spent the money on rent and other expenses. Alecia also learned that Markell did not notify All Seasons that he was selling to Sunrise and did not obtain All Seasons' permission to sell.

a.   Alecia wants to sue to remove All Seasons' lien from the title to the Lindy. How good is her case? UCC §§9-315(a), 9-320(a).

b.   If Alecia had insisted on seeing the certificate of title for the Lindy before she paid her $23,000, what would she have learned? See UCC §9-311(d) and Comment 4 to that section; form for motor vehicle certificate of title in Assignment 25.

36.2.   Alecia Card is back to see you for the fourth time since you represented her in the *All Seasons* case. Although she is a bright, energetic, friendly person, she has been asking questions that seem . . . well, a little too basic. Even before today, you had been suspecting that Alecia might be showing signs of paranoia. In your meeting this morning, Alecia explained that she has been shopping for a piano, has found a reconditioned one she likes for $10,000 at the American Piano Company in the Galleria Mall, and would like you to "represent her at the closing." Covering your surprise, you told her that most people who buy things in the mall just represent themselves. "Yes," she replied matter-of-factly, "but they haven't been through what you and I have." You told her you'd think about it and give her a call this afternoon.

a.   Is there anything to her fears? UCC §9-320(a).

b.   Can the problem be dealt with by a thorough search of the public records? UCC §9-507(a), including Comment 3.

c.   Should you recommend a psychiatrist or try to deal with this yourself? If you try to deal with it yourself, what will you say to Alecia and what will you do to get ready for the "closing"?

d.   Is this a problem that is unique to used goods, or could it occur with respect to new goods as well?

e.   The Truth in Lending Act, 15 U.S.C. §1666i, provides in relevant part that:

> [A] card issuer [bank] . . . shall be subject to all claims . . . arising out of any transaction in which the credit card is used as a method of payment . . . . The amount of claims . . . *asserted by the cardholder may not exceed the amount of credit outstanding with respect to such transaction* at the time the cardholder first notifies the card issuer . . . of such claim.

If Alecia uses a credit card to buy the piano, does that solve the problem?

36.3.   Charles Hayward, president of the Bank of Hayward, was really angry about the bank's loss in the *Daniel* case. Fresh from a meeting of bankers in which they all grumbled about "the end of inventory financing," he would like your advice on damage control. The bank finances several motor vehicle dealerships. Before the *Daniel* case, the bank sent inspectors out at unpredictable times to physically inspect the inventory. Each inspector carried a list of vehicle ID numbers for the vehicles against which the bank had lent money. As the inspector found each vehicle on the lot, the inspector checked it off on the list. If a dealer could not satisfactorily account for all of the vehicles on the list, the bank would consider calling the loan.

a.   "After *Daniel*," Charles says, "the presence of a vehicle on the lot means nothing. The dealer could already have sold it and been paid for it. The lot could be full of vehicles, but every one of them sold to a prepaying buyer." Do you agree?

b.   "Under *Chrysler*," Charles says, "we controlled delivery of the title to the retail purchaser by holding the MSO. Now the buyer doesn't need title; they can just sue us for it." Is he right?

c.   The *Daniel* court said that "The bank . . . is in the business of lending money and has access to information about how to protect itself, as best it can, against risk of loss." Charles wants to know how the bank can protect itself. What do you suggest?

36.4.   Charles Hayward is back. He would like your opinion of "a great new scheme" he just heard about at a meeting of bankers. The bills of lading for new vehicles will provide that from the moment of identification of a new vehicle to a dealer's contract for sale until the vehicle actually arrives on the dealer's lot, the manufacturer and the carriers will hold possession of the vehicle as agents for the bank that finances the dealer's inventory. That way, Hayward says, buyers like the Daniels won't be entitled to vehicles on which they have made down payments unless those vehicles actually arrive on the dealers' lots before repossession.

a.   Is Hayward right? UCC §§9-313(a) and (c), 9-315(a) and (c), 9-317(b), 9-320(a) and (e); Comment 3 to UCC §9-313.

b.   Is there any way the bank can use UCC §9-320(e) to prevail even as to vehicles actually delivered to the dealer's lot?

c.   What advice would you give to people like the Daniels who want a car custom-made for them, but are faced with the inevitable demand from the dealer for a substantial down payment?

▶ HALF ASSIGNMENT ENDS

36.5.   Davis Department Store sold a combination TV-stereo-VCR-popcorn popper to Beavis on credit for $1,925. Beavis paid no money down, but signed a promissory note and security agreement. Davis filed a financing statement in the statewide UCC records. The security agreement provided that Beavis "agrees not to sell the collateral" and that any purported sale "shall be void and of no effect." Six months later, Beavis lost his job at the meat processing plant and moved to Tennessee. Before leaving, he held a garage sale at which he sold the entertainment unit to his friend Butthead for $960. Butthead didn't know about the security agreement with Davis Department Store and (wouldn't you know it?) made the mistake of paying by check. Davis identified Butthead as the buyer from Beavis's checking account records.

a.   Is Davis entitled to repossess the entertainment unit from Butthead? UCC §§1-201(b)(9), 9-315(a), 9-320, 9-401.

b.   If so, does Davis have to refund Butthead's $960?

c.   Did Butthead convert Davis's collateral?

36.6.   Your client, University City Bank (UCB), has a security interest in the inventory of Sound City, Inc. Sound City sells sound systems at retail to consumers and businesses. The security agreement between UCB and Sound City authorized sales only in the ordinary course of business, prohibited sales on credit, and required that "Debtor deposit all proceeds of sales of collateral to Debtor's account #937284 at University City Bank." UCB perfected the security interest by filing a financing statement. On October 20, Sound City, Inc. filed under Chapter 7 of the Bankruptcy Code. The trustee abandoned the inventory, the debtor surrendered it to UCB, and UCB sold it and applied the proceeds to the inventory loan. A deficiency of $36,000 remains owing to UCB on the Sound City loan. Through discovery, you learned of the following transactions that took place before the filing of the bankruptcy petition:

a. Sound City sold a sound system to Rhonda Fried for $12,000. Rhonda paid $2,000 in cash and signed a negotiable promissory note for the remaining $10,000. There is no evidence that she knew of the restrictive provisions of the security agreement. Sound City deposited Rhonda's check to an account with a bank other than UCB and used the money to pay a utility bill. About a month later, Sound City sold the Rhonda note for $9,200. UCB has been unable to determine what Sound City did with the proceeds. Rhonda has missed several payments on the promissory note. Is UCB entitled to repossess the sound system from Rhonda? UCC §§9-315(a), 9-320, 9-323(d) and (e), 1-201(b)(9).

b. George Paulos is a lawyer who has been representing Sound City for several years. As of July 17, Sound City owed George $16,458 for legal services rendered in two employment discrimination suits. George agreed to accept a $14,000 sound system as partial payment and Sound City installed it in his home. Is UCB entitled to repossess the sound system from George? UCC §§1-201(b)(9), 9-315, 9-320, 9-323(d) and (e).

c. As of July 17, could George have solved his problem by structuring his transaction differently? UCC §9-404(a)(2).

■ END OF DEFAULT PROBLEM SET

36.7. Robert and Edward Sherrock are partners in Sherrock Brothers, a Toyota dealership. Ed tried to call you early this afternoon, but you were in a meeting and he was unable to get through. Your secretary took a lengthy message and now relates it to you. Ed called from Dover Motors, the Toyota dealership in a nearby city. He bought two cars from Dover and made arrangements to pay for them by transfer of funds later this afternoon. Dover agreed to keep the cars for a few days until Sherrock Brothers could send a couple of drivers to move them. After he left Dover's lot, Ed had second thoughts. He had heard some rumors that Dover was in financial difficulty, so he called you to find out if it's okay to leave the cars there until he gets back from Chicago in two days. Actually, you were on your way out of town as well. Does this have to be dealt with now? UCC §§9-320, 1-201(b)(20), 2-102, 2-403(2) and (3). Consider two possibilities:

a. Dover sells the two cars to buyers in the ordinary course of business and then files bankruptcy.

b. Dover files bankruptcy and Dover's inventory lender claims the cars.

36.8. Sara Wisnewski (from Problem 32.6) is back again. She has been thinking about what you told her, and has an idea. Deutsche Credit Corporation will finance the inventory of her corporation, Wiz Musical Manufacturing Corporation (Manufacturing), under a security agreement that provides for release of collateral only when Deutsche is paid. Sara proposes to set up a separate corporation, Wiz Musical Marketing Corporation (Marketing). Manufacturing will sell the inventory to Marketing subject to Deutsche's security interest. Marketing will sell the inventory to retail stores. UCC §9-320(a). The retail store will not take free of Deutsche's lien because it was created by Manufacturing, not "the buyer's seller" (Marketing). The retail stores won't know the instruments are subject to Deutsche's security interest, but that won't make any difference to them provided they pay what they owe. If they don't, justice will prevail. Deutsche will repossess the instruments and Sara will buy them back from Deutsche. Best of all, Sara does not have to rely on purchase-money status to beat the retail store's inventory lender, so she does not have to comply with UCC §9-324(b). Will this work? UCC §§1-302, 9-315(a), 9-322(a), 9-325, 9-507(a), 9-602.

Assignment 37: Statutory Lien Creditors Against Secured Creditors

When the term *statutory lien* is used in its narrow sense, as it is in the Bankruptcy Code, it means a lien that arises by operation of a statute. But the term is also used in a broader sense to include any lien that arises by operation of law, which includes liens that arise under common law or equity.

A statutory lien, used in this broader sense, is one of the three major categories of liens. The other two, which we have been working with throughout the course are *consensual liens* and *judicial liens*. Consensual liens arise by contract between debtor and creditor. This category includes security interests, mortgages, and deeds of trust. Judicial liens arise as the result of some act taken during litigation. This category includes execution, attachment, and garnishment liens, as well as judgment liens that arise against real property upon the recording of a money judgment in the real property recording system. Statutory liens differ from consensual liens in that the debtor need not give consent for the lien to arise; they differ from judicial liens in that the creditor need not engage in litigation to acquire the lien.

Although most kinds of statutory liens arise without any action on the part of the lien holder, some kinds of statutory lien holders must take steps to perfect. For example, a mechanic's lien holder typically has to record a Claim of Lien in the real property recording system within 90 days of the last date on which the lien holder furnished labor or materials, or it loses its lien. The laws of many states require that the holder of a lien for improvements or repairs to personal property retain possession of the property for the lien to remain in effect, a requirement that is analogous to perfection by possession.

A. The Variety of Statutory Liens in Personal Property

Most states recognize dozens of different types of statutory liens; among the 50 states there are well over a thousand statutes granting liens to particular kinds of creditors. Federal law also creates dozens of types of statutory liens. The federal tax lien is the one of greatest economic importance. In this section, we reproduce examples of these statutes, which, taken together, illustrate the nature and variety of this kind of legislation.

1. Artisans' Liens

Black's Law Dictionary defines "artisan" as a person skilled in some kind of trade, craft, or art requiring manual dexterity, such as a carpenter, plumber, tailor, or mechanic. At common law, artisans had liens against personal property they improved or repaired. Persons successfully claiming artisans' liens have included jewelers, laundry operators, garage mechanics, and accountants. To retain its lien at common law, the artisan had to retain possession of the property; if the artisan surrendered possession of the property, the lien was lost.

Most state legislatures have codified the artisan's lien. Some have done so in general terms that essentially track the common law. Others have created separate lien rights for particular kinds of artisans. California is an example of a state that has done both. Its general artisan's lien law provides:

Personal Property Lien for Services, Manufacture, or Repair

Cal. Civ. Code §3051 (2015)

Every person who, while lawfully in possession of an article of personal property, renders any service to the owner thereof, by labor or skill, employed for the protection, improvement, safekeeping, or carriage thereof, has a special lien thereon, dependent on possession, for the compensation, if any, which is due to him from the owner for such service; a person who makes, alters, or repairs any article of personal property, at the request of the owner, or legal possessor of the property, has a lien on the same for his reasonable charges for the balance due for such work done and materials furnished, and may retain possession of the same until the charges are paid. . . .

This California statute expressly excepts motor vehicles, vessels, mobile homes, and commercial coaches from coverage because California, like many states, has a more specific statute that covers them.

2. Garage Keepers' Liens

Persons who repair motor vehicles are in most states entitled to common law artisans' liens, but a substantial minority of states have enacted a statute specifically entitling garage keepers and mechanics to liens. (Although the liens awarded by these statutes are commonly referred to as *mechanics' liens*, in most states "mechanics' liens" are liens in favor of persons who supply labor or materials for building construction. The liens of garage mechanics in those states may be referred to as *artisans' liens* or the statute may give them another name.) The following is the garage keeper's lien law in Maine:

Garage Keeper's Lien

10 Me. Rev. Stat. Ann. (2015)

§3801 VEHICLES, AIRCRAFT AND PARACHUTES

Whoever performs labor by himself or his employees in manufacturing or repairing the ironwork or woodwork of wagons, carts, sleighs and other vehicles, aircraft or component parts thereof, and parachutes, or so performing labor furnishes materials therefor or provides storage therefor by direction or consent of the owner thereof, shall have a lien on such vehicle, aircraft or component parts thereof, and parachutes for his reasonable charges for said labor, and for materials used in performing said labor, and for said storage, which takes precedence of all other claims and encumbrances on said vehicles, aircraft or component parts thereof, and parachutes not made to secure a similar lien, and may be enforced by attachment at any time within 90 days after such labor is performed or such materials or storage furnished and not afterwards, provided a claim for such lien is duly filed as required in section 3802. Said lien shall be dissolved if said property has actually changed ownership prior to such filing.

§3802 FILING IN OFFICE OF SECRETARY OF STATE; INACCURACY DOES NOT INVALIDATE LIEN

1. FILING. A lien described in section 3801 is dissolved unless the claimant files the following documents in the office of the Secretary of State within 90 days after providing the labor, storage or materials:
A. A financing statement in the form approved by the Secretary of State; and
B. A notarized statement that includes an accurate description of the property manufactured or repaired; the name of the owner, if known; and the amount due the claimant for the labor, materials or storage, with any amount paid on account. . . .

———————

The Maine statute is unusual in requiring that the garage keeper file notice of its lien with the Secretary of State. In most states, the garage keeper perfects its lien by retaining possession of the vehicle and loses the lien if it surrenders possession of the vehicle.

3. Attorneys' Charging and Retaining Liens

Under the law of every state, attorneys are granted statutory liens to secure the payment of at least some kinds of fees. These liens are of two general types. A "charging lien" is a lien that attaches to the client's recovery in an action against a third person. A "retaining lien" is a lien that attaches to documents and records that the client has delivered to the lawyer for use in connection with the representation. The following statute is narrower than some in that it grants only a charging lien. It is broader than some in that the charging lien attaches upon the case being "placed in [the attorney's] hands"; some attach only upon the attorney filing a lawsuit on behalf of the client.

Attorney's Lien for Fees; Enforcement
Ill. Comp. Stat., ch. 770, act 5 (2015)

Sec. 1. Attorneys at law shall have a lien upon all claims, demands and causes of action, including all claims for unliquidated damages, which may be placed in their hands by their clients for suit or collection, or upon which suit or action has been instituted, for the amount of any fee which may have been agreed upon by and between such attorneys and their clients, or, in the absence of such agreement, for a reasonable fee, for the services of such suits, claims, demands or causes of action, plus costs and expenses. . . . To enforce such lien, such attorneys shall serve notice in writing, which service may be made by registered or certified mail, upon the party against whom their clients may have such suits, claims or causes of action, claiming such lien and stating therein the interest they have in such suits, claims, demands or causes of action. Such lien shall attach to any verdict, judgment or order entered and to any money or property which may be recovered, on account of such suits, claims, demands or causes of action, from and after the time of service of the notice. On petition filed by such attorneys or their clients any court of competent jurisdiction shall, on not less than five days' notice to the adverse party, adjudicate the rights of the parties and enforce the lien.

Illinois nevertheless recognizes a common law right to a retaining lien. "A retaining lien allows an attorney to retain papers and property of a client until the attorney fees are paid or the client posts a security for payment." Shelvy v. Wal-Mart Stores, East, L.P. v. U.S. Xpress Enterprises, Inc., 2013 WL 6081514 (N.D. Ill.).

4.   Landlord's Lien

Although landlords' liens have in recent decades fallen into disfavor, the large majority of states recognizes a landlord's lien in at least some landlord-tenant contexts. The most common context is between a landlord and a tenant-farmer who is growing crops on the property. Many states recognize the lien in commercial contexts such as shopping center leases and some even recognize it in the residential context. In most states, the landlord's lien is against personal property of the tenant that remains on the leased premises, but in a few, it is against all personal property of the debtor. While no statute is typical, the following provides an example:

Landlord's Lien

Or. Rev. Stat. Ann. (2015)

§87.146.   PRIORITIES OF LIENS

(1) Liens created by ORS . . . 87.162 have priority over all other liens, security interests and encumbrances on the chattel subject to the lien, except that taxes and duly perfected security interests existing before chattels sought to be subjected to a lien created by ORS 87.162 are brought upon the leased premises have priority over that lien.

§87.162.   LANDLORD'S LIEN

(1) [A] landlord has a lien on all chattels, except wearing apparel as defined in ORS 18.345(1), owned by a tenant or occupant legally responsible for rent, brought upon the leased premises, to secure the payment of rent and such advances as are made on behalf of the tenant. The landlord may retain the chattels until the amount of rent and advances is paid.

5.   Agricultural Liens

Stockman Bank of Montana v. Mon-Kota, Inc.

180 P.3d 1125 (Mont. 2008)

JUSTICE JIM RICE delivered the Opinion of the Court.

This case involves claims by a number of competing creditors asserting priority in certain sugar beet revenues. Stockman Bank served as the primary lender for Hardy Farm, Inc. (Hardy Farm), a North Dakota farming corporation, for the 2002 growing season, lending Hardy Farm [approximately $5.4 million]. Pursuant to the relevant security agreements between Stockman Bank and Hardy Farm, Stockman Bank took a security interest in certain of Hardy Farm's personal property, including its crops and crop revenues (the subject of this action) to secure repayment of said loans. Stockman Bank perfected a security interest in the personal property by filing the appropriate financing statements in North Dakota and Montana.

AGSCO is a North Dakota corporation that sells agricultural chemicals to growers in North Dakota and Montana. Capital Harvest is a corporate affiliate of AGSCO. AGSCO sells agricultural chemicals through its own retail stores, and Capital Harvest finances the purchase of those chemicals. During the 2002 growing season, AGSCO sold Hardy Farm roughly $500,000 in agricultural chemicals and services using a line of credit approved by Capital Harvest. On October 29, 2002, Capital Harvest filed an agricultural lien with the office of the Montana Secretary of State for the agricultural chemicals furnished, pursuant to § 71-3-901 et seq., MCA.

Generally defined, an agricultural lien is a non-consensual charge or encumbrance upon property created by operation of law when a person supplies goods or services to another engaged in the business of producing farm products. These liens commonly cover suppliers of seed, fertilizer, and pesticides, as do Montana's statutory liens, and allow them to be filed without the farmer's consent. At issue here is one of several agricultural lien statutes, § 71-3-901 et seq., MCA, which addresses fertilizer and pesticide liens. Section 71-3-901, MCA, describes who is eligible to have a fertilizer and pesticide lien:

> A person, firm, corporation, or partnership that under contract, express or implied, performs labor or services or furnishes material in crop dusting or spraying grains or crops, whether by aerial or ground application, for the purpose of fertilization or weed, disease, or insect control for promoting the growth of the grains or crops has a lien upon all grains or crops dusted or sprayed for and on account of the labor or service performed and material furnished, upon complying with the provisions of this part.

The time and manner of filing on the lien is also set forth in statute:

> A person, firm, corporation, or partnership that is entitled to a lien under this part shall, within 90 days after the last labor or service was performed or material furnished in crop dusting or spraying grains or crops, file in the office of the secretary of state a statement of agricultural lien as provided in 71-3-125.

Section 71-3-902(1), MCA.

Revised Article 9, like its predecessor, provides a comprehensive scheme for the regulation of security interests in personal property and fixtures, but unlike the original Article 9, also brings within its scope non-possessory agricultural liens—an area of law in which Montana already had a significant body of statutes. Thus, this Court must determine how the two bodies of law interact.

Critical to an accurate reading of the agricultural lien provisions within Revised Article 9 is an understanding that *agricultural liens are not security interests.* A security interest is defined as "an interest in personal property or fixtures that secures payment or performance of an obligation," [UCC §1-201(b)(37)] while an agricultural lien is "an interest, *other than a security interest,* in farm products. . . ." [UCC §9-102(a)(5)]. Thus, the UCC defines these interests in mutually exclusive terms. Consequently, when the UCC drafters desired to apply a particular provision to both agricultural liens and to security interests, the drafters expressly referred to both. Thus, merely because collateral consists of farm products does not automatically turn an agricultural lien into a security interest. This conceptual separation between "security interest" and "agricultural lien" means that agricultural liens are only partially incorporated into Revised Article 9.

The attachment rules in Revised Article 9, set forth in [UCC §§9-203 et seq.] are made applicable to interests arising from a "security agreement," defined as "an agreement that creates or provides for a security interest." [UCC §9-102(a)(73)]. Thus, the mutually exclusive definitions immediately come into play. Because, as discussed above, agricultural liens are not "security interests," the Revised Article 9 attachment rules are not applicable to agricultural liens. "[I]nstead, agricultural liens attach according to the particular rules in the statute that creates them." *See* Julian B. McDonnell, *Farm Financing Under Revised Article 9,* in *1D Secured Transactions*

Under the Uniform Commercial Code 26-1, 26-14 (2003). Stockman Bank does not contend that Capital Harvest's agricultural lien did not attach under Montana law.

While attachment makes an agricultural lien effective as between the supplier and the debtor, perfection is the mechanism by which a supplier establishes his or her priority in relation to other creditors of the debtor in the same collateral. Section 71-3-902(1), MCA, set forth above, clearly delineates the procedure to be followed to perfect an agricultural lien: filing a statement of agricultural lien in the office of the Secretary of State within ninety days after furnishing the last labor or service. Stockman Bank does not contend that Capital Harvest's lien statement was insufficient to perfect its lien for purposes of Title 71.

Agricultural liens are granted a "superpriority status" by the Montana agricultural lien statutes, which provide: "The lien for labor or services performed or material furnished as specified in this part *shall be prior to and have precedence over any mortgage, encumbrance, or other lien* upon said grain or crops. . . ." Section 71-3-904, MCA. Under the statute, this superpriority status is not dependent upon being the first to file. However, Stockman Bank's argument is that Capital Harvest's lien, though perfected for purposes of the agricultural lien statute, was not perfected for purposes of the UCC, and thus did not obtain priority over the Bank's earlier perfected secured interest.

Consistent with the priority given to liens under our agricultural lien statutes, Revised Article 9 recognizes that an agricultural lien may be granted priority by local law over a competing Article 9 security interest. "A perfected agricultural lien on collateral has priority over a conflicting security interest in or agricultural lien on the same collateral if the statute creating the agricultural lien so provides." [UCC §9-322(g)]. However, the critical point here, which gives rise to Stockman Bank's argument, is that this UCC provision recognizes the priority only of a *"perfected* agricultural lien." Further, the UCC defines what it means by the term "perfected agricultural lien:" "An agricultural lien is perfected if it has become effective *and all of the applicable requirements for perfection in [UCC §9-310] have been satisfied.*" [UCC §9-308(b)]. Thus, even though Montana's fertilizer and pesticide lien statute purports to grant an agricultural lien absolute priority over "any" other security interest if perfected under Title 71, Revised Article 9 requires that an agricultural lien must also satisfy the requirements of [UCC §9-310], in order to be perfected and obtain priority over security interests established under the UCC.

We do not believe these provisions are irreconcilable. It is clear from the above discussion that Revised Article 9 acknowledges existing agricultural lien statutes and expressly incorporates them into its priority scheme. We thus believe the Legislature did not intend for the agricultural lien statutes to be superseded by the later passage of Revised Article 9, but, rather, for these two statutes to work in coordination. Revised Article 9 likewise recognizes and respects the "superpriority" granted to agricultural liens by local law, but simply requires that those liens also be perfected in satisfaction of [UCC §9-310].

In summary, although agricultural lienors must satisfy the perfection requirements of [UCC §9-310], in addition to the perfection requirements of the lien statutes, by doing so they will be insulated from Revised Article 9's "first in time" rule and retain the "superpriority" status of their liens. Here, Capital Harvest's perfection efforts were required to have complied with the prerequisites of [UCC §9-310], in addition to satisfying Title 71's requirements, in order to obtain priority over Stockman Bank's previously perfected secured interest.

We now turn to Capital Harvest's argument that its filing of an agricultural lien statement with the Montana Secretary of State, pursuant to § 71-3-125, MCA, also satisfied Revised Article 9's requirements for filing a UCC financing statement to perfect an agricultural lien.

[UCC §9–502] provides: "[A] financing statement is sufficient only if it: (a) provides the name of the debtor; (b) provides the name of the secured party or a representative of the secured party; and (c) indicates the collateral covered by the financing statement." In comparison, a Title 71 agricultural lien statement not only includes the information required on a UCC financing statement—the name of the debtor, the name of the secured party or a representative of the secured party, and the collateral covered by the financing statement—but also requires that the statement be signed by the lienor, describe the service or product furnished, state the county in which the farm products are located, and state other details with regard to the particular type of agricultural lien being filed. *See* § 71-3-125, MCA. Moreover, the information provided by the Title 71 agricultural lien statement is filed in the same centralized computer system as a UCC financing statement. Indeed, § 71-3-125, MCA, which governs the filing of agricultural lien statements, was amended in 1999 by Senate Bill 153—the same bill that enacted Revised Article 9—to provide that the Montana Secretary of State shall "record the agricultural lien statement on the centralized computer system as set forth in [UCC provision] 30-9A-502." Section 71-3-125(4)(a), MCA.

As we have noted, perfection is the process a creditor uses to establish its priority in relation to other creditors of the debtor in the same collateral by giving notice of its interest. Moreover, "[t]he main reasons for including agricultural liens within the scope of Revised Article 9 were to require these interests to be publicly known through an Article 9 filing and to curb 'secret liens.'" Eric J. Pullen, Revised Article 9 of the Uniform Commercial Code and Agricultural Liens in Texas, 40 Tex. J. Bus. L. 1, 15 (2004). This interest was pursued in Montana by requiring that agricultural liens be filed in the same depository as documents perfecting other secured interests. Capital Harvest filed a Title 71 lien statement, containing all of the information required in a UCC financing statement and more, which was placed in the same centralized computer system as a UCC financing statement would have been placed. The notice purpose was thus fulfilled by Capital Harvest's filing, and no further purpose would have been served had Capital Harvest also filed a duplicative UCC financing statement.

As a condition of perfection, Article 9 requires the holders of agricultural liens to file financing statements. UCC §§9-308(b), 9-310(a). Agricultural lien holders who fail to file remain unperfected and subordinate to perfected secured creditors, lien creditors, trustees in bankruptcy, and buyers. UCC §9-322(a). The system works only if the sellers of feed and seed, crop dusters, and farmers who rent a little land to a neighbor are aware of the need to file and do so.

The case of Dean v. Hall, 50 UCC Rep. Serv. 2d 618 (E.D. Va. 2003), illustrates the difficulty facing unsophisticated creditors. Dean leased two parcels of land to the Halls. When the Halls failed to pay $12,000 of rent, a landlord's lien against the crops the Halls were growing on the land arose automatically in favor of Dean. A Virginia statute dating back to the 1880s stated that lien was "valid against creditors," which would have included Colonial Farm Credit, the Halls' crop lender.

But the court held that Dean's lien was an "agricultural lien" within the meaning of UCC §9-102(a)(5). Because Article 9 requires filing to perfect an agricultural lien, the court also held that Dean was unperfected. That left Colonial Farm Credit with priority in the crops.

The agricultural lien holder who does file a financing statement will enjoy priority as of the filing. UCC §9-322(a). For most, that will still mean subordination to the security interests of banks and other farm lenders, because the latter will have filed financing statements in earlier growing seasons and continued them. If the statute that creates the agricultural lien expressly gives it priority over other security interests, UCC §9-322(a) yields to that statute. UCC §9-322(g).

To qualify for this superpriority treatment, UCC §9-322(g) requires that the agricultural lien be perfected. To perfect, the lienor must file a financing statement. UCC §9-310(a). The lienor does not, however, need to file its financing statement before its competitor to gain priority over the competitor. It could file even during litigation over priority. But if the debtor files bankruptcy, the automatic stay will cut off the lienor's right to perfect, giving the lienor's competitor priority.

The interplay between secured lenders and agricultural lien creditors illustrates a dynamic tension in the law. As secured lenders win changes through the UCC drafting process that enable them to lock up more of their debtors' assets with perfected security interests, less of the assets remain to satisfy the claims of the unsecured creditors who supply goods and services to farms. Groups representing these sorts of unsecured creditors tend not to have seats at the UCC drafting table but have influence in state legislatures and Congress. What secured creditors take through the UCC process, these groups may be able to take back through the legislative process for other laws.

For example, the federal Perishable Agricultural Commodities Act (PACA) imposes a "statutory trust" that gives sellers and suppliers of perishable agricultural commodities — including farmers — priority in payment even over secured creditors of the buyers. Although PACA does not create a lien, the trust it creates functions in much the same way. As the following case illustrates, the trust even gives the sellers and suppliers priority over interests that secured parties perfected against buyers of the perishables before they bought the perishables.

Nickey Gregory Co., LLC v. AgriCap, LLC

597 F.3d 591 (4th Cir. 2010)

NIEMEYER, CIRCUIT JUDGE:

I

The Perishable Agriculture Commodities Act, which was enacted in 1930 to suppress unfair and fraudulent business practices in the marketing of perishable commodities, was amended in 1984 to provide unique credit protection to sellers of perishable agricultural commodities. Because sellers of perishable commodities had a need to move their inventories quickly, they were often required to become unsecured creditors of their purchasers, whose credit they were often unable to verify. As these sellers of perishable commodities increasingly suffered the risk of the uncollectability of amounts owed by the purchasers, especially because the purchasers gave superior security interests to their lenders, Congress enacted the 1984 amendments to protect the commodities sellers by giving them a priority position over even secured creditors.

The 1984 amendments create, upon the sale of perishable agricultural commodities, a trust for the benefit of the unpaid sellers of the commodities on (1) the commodities, (2) the inventory or products derived from them, and (3) the proceeds of the inventory or products. As amended, PACA requires that purchasers of perishable agricultural commodities maintain the trust by retaining the commodities or their proceeds until the commodities sellers are paid, and it makes it unlawful to "fail to maintain the trust as required."

The trust created by PACA is a "nonsegregated 'floating' trust" on perishable agricultural commodities and their derivatives until all sellers of such commodities are paid. Because the governing regulations specifically contemplate the comingling of trust assets without defeating the trust, the trustee of such a trust is permitted to convert trust assets into other property, provided that the trustee honors its obligation to "maintain trust assets in a manner that such assets are freely available to satisfy outstanding obligations to sellers of perishable agricultural commodities."

PACA trusts thus give sellers of perishable agricultural commodities a right of recovery that is superior to the right of all other creditors, including secured creditors. Indeed, in the event of bankruptcy, trust assets do not even become a part of the bankruptcy estate.

General trust principles govern PACA trusts unless the principle conflicts with PACA. Thus, when trust assets are held by a third party, resulting in the failure of the trustee to pay unpaid sellers of perishable agricultural commodities, the third party may be required to disgorge the trust assets unless the third party can establish that it has some defense, such as having taken the assets as a bona fide purchaser without notice of the breach of trust.

II

Robison Farms, LLC, a South Carolina limited liability company that operated in Greenville, South Carolina, was, during the relevant periods, engaged in the business of distributing produce to restaurants and school systems in North Carolina and South Carolina. It purchased the produce from wholesalers who sold the produce to Robison Farms on credit under the protection of PACA's trust arrangement. Two of its suppliers, Nickey Gregory Company, LLC, and Poppell's Produce, Inc., who are the plaintiffs in this action, sold their produce to Robison Farms on a continuing basis, extending short term credit to Robison Farms "subject to the statutory trust authorized by [PACA]," as indicated on their invoices.

In early March 2005, when Robison Farms was experiencing financial difficulties, it applied to AgriCap, L.L.C., for financing to provide it with working capital "to restructure [its] payables." AgriCap approved a line of credit that was geared to the amount of Robison Farms' accounts receivable. As Robison Farms assigned accounts receivable to AgriCap, AgriCap advanced Robison Farms 80% of the face amount of the receivables, up to a limit of $500,000 outstanding at any given time. As AgriCap collected on the receivables, it retained the 80% amount and remitted the remaining 20% to Robison Farms, less its fees and interest for the period during which its advances on the accounts receivable were outstanding.

Notwithstanding this financing arrangement, Robison Farms continued to experience financial difficulties. Even though the produce suppliers continued to deliver produce throughout the spring and early summer, Robison Farms stopped paying them on May 11, 2006, and on July 17, 2006, it closed its doors for business. Less than a month later, Robison Farms filed a Chapter 7 bankruptcy petition to liquidate all of its assets. After receiving a portion of the amounts owed them from the bankruptcy estate, Nickey Gregory and Poppell's Produce are still owed $66,411.25 and $40,284.61, respectively, for a total of $106,695.86.

Nickey Gregory and Poppell's Produce commenced this action against AgriCap, contending that the accounts receivable that AgriCap received from Robison Farms after May 11, 2006, were, under PACA, trust assets held by AgriCap for the benefit of unpaid commodities sellers such as them.

III

When Congress made this policy choice to make the unsecured credit extended by commodities sellers superior to the position of lenders holding a security interest in those commodities and proceeds, it recognized the difficulty that lenders might have in administering their secured loans. Indeed, it received testimony to that effect from the American Bankers Association. In the end, however, Congress determined that those concerns were outweighed by other considerations:

> The Committee believes that the statutory trust requirements will not be a burden to the lending institutions. They will be known to and considered by prospective lenders in extending credit. The assurance the trust provision gives that raw products will be paid for promptly and that there is a monitoring system provided for under the Act will protect the interests of the borrower, the money lender, and the fruit and vegetable industry. Prompt payment should generate trade confidence and new business which yields increased cash and receivables, the prime security factors to the money lender.

H.R. Rep. No. 98-543, at 4 (1984).

Thus, when Robison Farms purchased perishable agricultural commodities from the sellers in this case, the commodities and the proceeds from them became assets of the PACA trust, to be maintained to pay the sellers' loans *before* payment of any other loan, whether secured or not. As relevant to this case, in May 2006, when the invoices of the commodities sellers went unpaid, the accounts receivable generated from the resale of the commodities to the school systems and restaurants, being proceeds of the commodities, were PACA trust assets that had to be maintained for payment *first* to the unpaid commodities sellers.

If Robison Farms had transferred these trust assets to AgriCap by means *of a sale* in exchange for cash, the transaction would have been nothing more than a permissible conversion of trust assets from one form to another—*i.e.,* from accounts receivable into cash. Following this form of transaction, the accounts receivable would no longer have remained trust assets, and the commodities sellers would not have had any claim for payment from them. Thus, AgriCap would have been entitled to collect on the accounts receivable and to retain the proceeds without interference by Nickey Gregory and Poppell's Produce.

But if, in contrast, Robison Farms had transferred the accounts receivable to AgriCap *as collateral for a secured loan,* the receivables and their proceeds would have remained trust assets, even though held by AgriCap. As AgriCap has asserted, such a transfer again is permitted by PACA. But PACA provides that any security interest so created would be subject to the interest of unpaid commodities sellers.

It is therefore highly relevant to the disposition of this case to determine whether Robison Farms' accounts receivable were indeed *sold* for value to AgriCap under a factoring agreement or whether they were simply subjected to a security interest *to collateralize a loan* that AgriCap made to Robison Farms. If the accounts receivable were only subjected to a security interest, then the security interest was subordinate to the prior statutory trust created for the benefit of the commodities sellers.

Ultimately, the court concluded that "Robison Farms' accounts receivable were held by AgriCap as collateral for a loan and therefore were subject to a PACA trust." PACA gave the commodities sellers priority over AgriCap's security interest, so AgriCap should have paid money collected on the accounts to the sellers until they were paid in full before paying anything to itself. Because AgriCap misdirected the money, it was liable to the sellers for damages. If AgriCap had bought the accounts instead of lending against them, AgriCap would have been entitled to *all* money collected on the accounts.

A trustee who knowingly misapplies trust funds is liable to the extent of the loss to the beneficiary. Thus PACA may impose personal liability on the particular owner or officer who directs the misapplication of trust funds.

▶ HALF ASSIGNMENT ENDS

B.   Statutory Liens in Bankruptcy

The bankruptcy system generally recognizes and gives effect to liens and priorities that creditors perfected under nonbankruptcy law prior to the filing of the bankruptcy case. In general, bankruptcy law gives effect to statutory liens as well.

There are, however, three types of statutory liens that the trustee in bankruptcy can avoid. See Bankr. Code §545. The first is a lien that becomes effective not when the debt arises but only after the debtor is in financial difficulty. See Bankr. Code §545(1). Given that provision, legislatures have no reason to create such liens. By their terms, such liens are ineffective before the debtor is in bankruptcy; by §545(1), they are ineffective afterward. Not surprisingly, legislatures seldom bother enacting such statutes—which probably suits Congress just fine.

Under §545(2), the trustee can avoid a statutory lien that, at the time of the filing of the bankruptcy case, was not sufficiently perfected to be effective in the absence of bankruptcy against a hypothetical bona fide purchaser. To illustrate, some statutory lien laws require that the lien holder make a public filing or give notice to a stakeholder to perfect the lien. If failure to perfect would make the lien ineffective against a bona fide purchaser—or if even a properly perfected lien of the type would be ineffective against a bona fide purchaser—the trustee can avoid the statutory lien. Bankruptcy takes a statutory lien seriously only if state law takes it seriously.

Under §§545(3) and (4), the trustee can avoid statutory liens for rent and liens of distress for rent. "Distress for rent" was a self-help remedy available to landlords at common law. Without notice to the debtor or the opportunity for a hearing, the unpaid landlord could have the help of the sheriff in seizing property of the tenant. The remedy was declared unconstitutional in its most common form, but still survives in some others. Because the procedure for obtaining a distress lien includes filing a lawsuit, distress liens are arguably judicial liens. The drafters of Bankruptcy Code §545 probably mentioned them separately to make sure that a distress lien could not survive avoidance of the underlying lien for rent.

Prior to enactment of the Bankruptcy Code in 1978, not only were landlords' liens fully effective in bankruptcy cases, but the Bankruptcy Act gave priority to unsecured claims for rent. The legislative history gives no clue as to why, with hundreds of kinds of statutory liens to choose from, Congress chose to nail the landlords. At that time, the procedure of distress for rent was intimately tied to the landlord's lien for rent. The most common forms of distress had been declared unconstitutional, perhaps throwing landlord's liens into general disrepute. In any case, the event stands as testimony to the arbitrary (or perhaps it would be more accurate to say political) nature of statutory liens and creditor priorities in general.

When the trustee avoids a statutory lien in bankruptcy, the lien is "preserved for the benefit of the estate." Bankr. Code §551. That is, the trustee has the rights of the holder of the avoided lien, including the right to the lien's priority. To illustrate, assume that the debtor owns property worth $10,000 that is subject to a first statutory lien in the amount of $7,000 and a subordinate security interest in the amount of $20,000. If the trustee avoids the statutory lien, the trustee will then be entitled to the first $7,000 of value in the property and the holder of the security interest will be entitled to the remaining $3,000. The secured creditor in second position neither benefits nor loses from the trustee's avoidance of the first lien.

C. The Priority of Statutory Liens

A statutory lien has the priority specified in the law that creates it. The statutory provisions addressing priority are often complex, giving priority in some circumstances and withholding it in others. Overall, statutory liens probably have priority over security interests more often than not.

There are three types of rules governing priority between statutory liens and security interests. One type gives priority to the lien or to the security interest based on which is first in time. A second type gives priority to the statutory lien regardless of the order in which the two arose. The third gives priority to the security interest regardless of the order in which the two arose. If the statute gives priority on the basis of first in time, it will probably, but not necessarily, specify what the holder of the lien or security interest must do first in order to prevail. Security interests are usually dated as of filing or perfection. Statutory liens may be dated as of the time the lien holder gives value, contracts to give value, files a claim of lien, or takes some other action.

To illustrate the various approaches to priority in the context of garage keepers' liens, assume that Ally Financial advances $10,000 to Mildred Washington to buy a new car and secures the loan with a purchase-money security interest. Ally perfects the lien by having it noted on the certificate of title by the Department of Motor Vehicles. After the one-year warranty on the car expires, the car develops mechanical problems and Mildred takes the car to Central Auto Repair for repair. The repairs, all of which are authorized by Mildred, cost $3,000. Mildred is unable to pay for them. Under the most commonly applied rule, Central Auto Repair's lien has priority over Ally's security interest. Under the other two rules, Ally's lien has priority.

Most security interests in automobiles are purchase-money security interests taken at the time the debtor acquires the automobile. In the context of garage keepers' liens, a rule based on which lien is first in time nearly always gives priority to the security interest. As a consequence, we sometimes think of the rules as coming in only two categories: those that give priority to the garage keeper and those that give priority to the secured creditor. There are more statutes of the former type than of the latter.

The context in which landlords' liens arise is different. The debtor that operates a store in a shopping center may sign a lease that, with renewal options, runs for 30 years or more. In most jurisdictions, the landlord's lien is held to arise upon the signing of the lease and to attach to personal property when it is first brought upon the premises. Under the rule of first in time, such a landlord's lien is likely to be subordinate to the security interest of the bank that finances the debtor's initial purchase of fixtures, equipment, and inventory. But during the term of such a long lease, the debtor may refinance the equipment and inventory several times. The landlord's lien will prevail over these later lenders. In the context of landlords' liens, the rule of first in time, first in right will sometimes give priority to the landlord and other times to the secured party.

Most states follow the rule of first in time, first in right with regard to landlord's liens, but some states give priority to the landlord regardless of when the competing liens arise, and some states give priority to the secured party regardless of when the competing liens arise.

Since 1979, the rules determining priority between landlord and secured party have declined sharply in importance. In that year, a new Bankruptcy Code took effect. It included §§545(3) and (4), which authorized avoidance of landlord's liens in bankruptcy. Considering the high likelihood that a failing debtor will pass through bankruptcy on its way out of existence, a lien that can be avoided in bankruptcy does not provide very much security. Since 1979, commercial lessors have increasingly included in their leases provisions granting themselves Article 9 security interests in their debtor's property then on the premises or later brought onto it. The effect of such provisions is to create a consensual "landlord's lien," that trustees in bankruptcy have no power to avoid.

UCC §9-333 addresses the issue of priority between security interests and liens arising by operation of law. That section grants no lien and determines the relative priority of a statutory lien only if the statute or rule of law creating the lien does not. UCC §9-333 provides as the default rule of priority that a lien by operation of law has priority over even an earlier perfected Article 9 security interest. The liens to which this default rule applies are narrowly defined. The lien must be (1) in favor of a person who furnishes services or materials in the ordinary course of his or her business, (2) for the purchase price of the services and materials, (3) on goods in the possession of the lien holder. The lien holder must have furnished the services or materials "with respect to [the] goods" against which the lien holder claims. Essentially, the liens described are possessory artisans' liens. Landlords' liens are not affected by UCC §9-333; they are excluded from the coverage of Article 9. See UCC §9-109(d)(1).

In situations to which UCC §9-333 applies, it reverses a presumption in case law that statutory liens are subordinate to mortgages and security interests unless the statute creating the lien clearly specifies to the contrary.

In the following case, the court construes a California lien statute to determine whether it gives the lienors priority over previously recorded security interests. The facts of the case illustrate the potential importance of such liens in the context of a failing business. Those in control of such a business may help themselves, their friends, and (in this case) their attorneys to whatever assets remain by granting security interests. Absent a statutory lien, "outsiders" such as employees, tort creditors, and occasional suppliers will be out of luck.

Myzer v. Emark Corporation

45 Cal. App. 4th 884, 53 Cal. Rptr. 2d 60 (Cal. App. 1996)

HUFFMAN, J.

[In 1992, Emark Corporation was in financial difficulty. The corporation granted security interests to secure debts allegedly owing to the corporation's counsel (Rieck & Crotty) in the amount of $170,000 and to the corporation's director (Keig) and chief financial officer (Rummel) in the amounts of $772,993 and $129,210 respectively.]

the secured creditors. Secured creditors can and do take steps to protect themselves. Among the means that secured creditors can use are the following:

1. *Covenants.* Most secured lenders require, as a condition of the loan, that the debtor agree not to do anything that would give rise to a statutory lien. Such covenants are relatively ineffective. They do not bind statutory lien holders who are not party to them. The covenant will be in the security agreement, and most garage keepers, for example, will not see that document before they perform a repair. While the debtor will be liable for breach of the covenant, a debtor who incurs a statutory lien and fails to discharge it by payment is almost certainly insolvent. Any judgment the creditor recovers against such a debtor for breach of this covenant is likely to be uncollectible. Besides, the damages are likely to be measured by the unpaid balance of the loan that was not satisfied from the collateral. Thus, the action for breach of the covenant adds nothing but an alternative, unneeded basis for the entry of an unsecured judgment for the amount of the debt.

2. *Payment.* Most statutory liens that have priority over earlier perfected security interests are relatively small and predictable in amount. Real property taxes are a good example. Every state levies an annual tax on real property. The tax varies in amount from about 1 percent to about 3 percent of the total value of the property. Mortgages against real property are typically in an original amount between about 50 percent and 100 percent of the total value of the property. The tax is thus small in relation to the mortgage. Mortgages typically provide that the debtor will make timely payment of the property tax. Default in payment of the tax is a default under the mortgage, giving the mortgagee the right to foreclose. Because the tax debt is relatively small, the mortgagee can prevent the taxing authority from foreclosing by paying the taxes. Most mortgages give the mortgagee the right to do that and add the amount so paid to the amount due under the mortgage. While the mortgagee might lose an amount equal to a year's taxes because of the debtor's failure to pay them, it cannot lose its collateral to foreclosure. Many mortgages require that the debtor pay the taxes to the mortgagee in advance, so that the mortgagee can pay them to the taxing authority.

3. *Waiver.* Some statutory lien laws permit the lien holder to waive its rights. If the debtor has sufficient leverage with the lien holder to extract such a waiver, the secured creditor may, as a condition of its loan, require that the debtor obtain the waiver. For example, in some states it is customary for those who supply labor or materials in the construction of a building to waive their liens in advance. The debtor simply refuses to hire any subcontractor or supplier that will not waive its statutory lien. The debtor does this because construction lenders will not lend to debtors who do not obtain waivers. In these jurisdictions, mechanic's lien holders and construction lenders are permitted to and do contract out of the statutory rule giving liens, and perhaps priority, to the mechanic's lien holders.

4. *Monitoring.* Statutory liens that prime prior perfected mortgages and security interests can arise in substantial amounts in favor of creditors who have no reason to give waivers. For example, statutes in about 14 states give the state's environmental cleanup lien priority over earlier perfected security interests

and mortgages. One such statute is that of the environmentally active (pun intended) state of New Jersey:

Cleanup and Removal of Hazardous Substances

N.J. Rev. Stat. §58:10-23.11f (2015)

a. (1) Whenever any hazardous substance is discharged, the department may, in its discretion, act to clean up and remove or arrange for the cleanup and removal of such discharge. . . .

f. Any expenditures of cleanup and removal costs and related costs made by the State pursuant to this act shall constitute, in each instance, a debt of the discharger to the fund. The debt shall constitute a lien on all property owned by the discharger when a notice of lien, incorporating a description of the property of the discharger subject to the cleanup and removal and an identification of the amount of cleanup, removal and related costs expended by the State, is duly filed with the clerk of the Superior Court. . . .

The notice of lien filed pursuant to this subsection which affects the property of a discharger subject to the cleanup and removal of a discharge shall create a lien with priority over all other claims or liens which are or have been filed against the property, except if the property comprises six dwelling units or less and is used exclusively for residential purposes, this notice of lien shall not affect any valid lien, right or interest in the property filed in accordance with established procedure prior to the filing of this notice of lien. The notice of lien filed pursuant to this subsection which affects any property of a discharger, other than the property subject to the cleanup and removal, shall have priority from the day of the filing of the notice of the lien over all other claims and liens filed against the property, but shall not affect any valid lien, right, or interest in the property filed in accordance with established procedure prior to the filing of a notice of lien pursuant to this subsection.

This statute gives environmental cleanup liens against commercial property priority over earlier-recorded mortgages. An environmental cleanup lien can easily exceed the entire market value of the property, rendering the prior perfected security interests worthless. Faced with a statute such as this, the secured lender's best response may be to monitor its debtor's activities to make sure that the need for a cleanup does not arise. Such monitoring begins at the time the loan is made. Through its own employees or a subcontractor, the secured lender will inspect the property for environmental contamination that might later require cleanup. If such contamination is present, the secured creditor can refuse to lend until the debtor has cleaned the property and paid the bills. Because even a later contamination can give rise to a prior lien, the secured creditor must continue to monitor the debtor's activities after the loan is made.

Statutory lien laws that force secured lenders to monitor the activities of their debtors are highly controversial. They have the potential to provide a social benefit by preventing environmental contamination, pension under-funding, nonpayment of taxes, and numerous other social ills. But in accomplishing that, they require lenders to involve themselves in activities outside their traditional role and may make lending more costly.

Problem Set 37

37.1. Debtor owns an original painting by Vincent Van Gogh, which is subject to a duly perfected security interest in favor of Firstbank. The painting was damaged in an attempted burglary and Debtor takes it to Elisa Morse, a specialist, for repair. Morse repairs the painting. When Debtor proves unable to pay for the repair, Morse retains possession. Pressed by this and other financial problems, Debtor files bankruptcy. As between Morse, Firstbank, and the Chapter 7 trustee, who has priority? Bankr. Code §§101 (definition of "statutory lien"), 545, 547(c)(6); UCC §§9-333, 9-109(d)(2). Assume that only the UCC and California Civil Code §3051, set forth in section A of this assignment, apply.

37.2. Norman Farms sold 400 bushels of California tomatoes to American Produce, a licensed dealer in perishable agricultural commodities. Norman failed to take a security interest in what it sold, but it did include in its invoice the statement that "The perishable agricultural commodities listed on this invoice are sold subject to the statutory trust authorized by section 5(c) of the Perishable Agricultural Commodities Act." American paid by check. American sold half the tomatoes to Star Markets, a regional grocer in Massachusetts and the other half to Haunt's Cannery in Mississippi. Both Star and Haunt's paid American by electronic cash transfer. Star sold their Norman tomatoes to retail customers over the next five days. Haunt's canned their half of the Norman tomatoes and sold them to Publix, a regional grocer in Florida. Publix has not yet paid the purchase price to Haunt's, but has received delivery of the cans in its Jacksonville warehouse. Two years ago, Haunt's assigned all of its "accounts" to FirstBank, and FirstBank perfected by filing a financing statement. American's check to Norman Farms bounced, and it now appears that American is deeply insolvent. Norman asks you whether there are sources other than American Produce from which Norman Farms might recover. Are there?

37.3. Gill Seed is a Montana supplier of seed to Montana farmers for planting a variety of crops. Peter Gill, the owner of Gill Seed, is in your office. Peter explains that his business makes a substantial portion of its sales on credit. Most customers make the payments when due. But given the risks that come with farming, some don't. Gill has recently suffered significant losses from nonpayment and bankruptcies. In most cases, the farmers had borrowed from banks to fund their operations, and the banks had mortgages and security interests covering the farmers' land, crops, and equipment. Peter would like to know what he can do, if anything, to protect himself. Peter says he knows that other businesses like his take security interests, but he is uncomfortable with that. His concern is that he would alienate his paying customers by asking them to sign documents and seeming not to trust them. (He is less concerned about offending those who do not pay.) What advice do you give? The relevant Montana statutes are reproduced in the *Stockman Bank* case in section A of this assignment.

37.4.   Jean Widdington bought a car for $8,000. Ally lent Widdington $7,000 of the purchase price and secured the loan with a purchase-money security interest. Ally had its lien noted on the certificate of title. When the engine overheated, Widdington took it to Central Auto Repair. Although Widdington's contract with Ally required that she notify Ally and obtain their permission before contracting for any repair costing more than $2,500, she did neither. The repair cost $3,500. Central Auto Repair asserted a lien under the following Wisconsin statute, gave proper notice under Wisconsin Statute §779.48, and eventually sold the car at auction for $5,500.

Mechanic's Liens

Wis. Stat. Ann. (2015)

§779.41

(1) Every mechanic and every keeper of a garage or shop, and every employer of a mechanic who transports, makes, alters, repairs or does any work on personal property at the request of the owner or legal possessor of the personal property, has a lien on the personal property for the just and reasonable charges therefor, including any parts, accessories, materials or supplies furnished in connection therewith and may retain possession of the personal property until the charges are paid. The lien provided by this section is subject to the lien of any security interest in the property which is perfected as provided by law prior to the commencement of the work for which a lien is claimed unless the work was done with the express consent of the holder of the security interest, but only for charges in excess of $1,500.

§779.48 ENFORCEMENT . . .

(2) Every person given a lien by §779.41 . . . may in case the claim remains unpaid for two months after the debt is incurred . . . enforce such lien by sale of the property substantially in conformity with [UCC §§9-601 through 9-628] and the lien claimant shall have the rights and duties of a secured party thereunder. . . .

------

   a.   Does Central have a lien?
   b.   If so, with what priority in relation to Ally? UCC §9-333.

c. Is the buyer's title free and clear of Ally's security interest? UCC §9-617.

d. Who is entitled to the $5,500? UCC §9-615.

e. What would the result be under Maine law? See 10 Me. Rev. Stat. Ann. §§3801-3802, set forth in section A of this assignment.

37.5. One of your first clients after you set up in solo practice was John Gage, who owns a local restaurant. Gage gave you a will his former lawyer prepared for him seven years ago and instructions for preparing a new will. Drafting the new will required sophisticated tax research and Gage agreed to pay for it. After you had invested about 15 hours in the project, Gage instructed you to stop work because he had decided not to change wills. A week ago, you sent Gage a bill for $1,800 (reduced from your regular billing rate because the job had been canceled). Gage has not paid the bill, but he is now in your office seeking return of the original will. When you asked about payment of your bill, Gage said that you should "send me another copy." You have the distinct feeling that if you give Gage the original will, he will never pay you. What do you do now? See 770 Ill. Comp. Stat. 5/1, set forth in section A of this assignment and the case reference that follows it. Assume that Illinois law applies.

Rule 1.16 of the Model Rules of Professional Conduct provides:

> Upon termination of representation, a lawyer shall take steps to (d) the extent reasonably practicable to protect a client's interests, such as giving reasonable notice to the client, allowing time for employment of other counsel, surrendering papers and property to which the client is entitled and refunding any advance payment of fee or expense that has not been earned or incurred. The lawyer may retain papers relating to the client to the extent permitted by other law.

▶ HALF ASSIGNMENT ENDS

37.6. a. You represent Oaks Mall, Ltd., a shopping center whose business is located in Oregon. Buffy Oaks, the CEO of Oaks Mall, consults you regarding Powder Puff, Inc. For 12 years, Powder Puff's sole place of business has been a store in the Oaks Mall. Powder Puff is now six months in arrears in the payment of rent for a total of $42,000, and has just closed the store. Does Oaks have a lien against any of the following assets: equipment (estimated value $25,000), inventory (estimated value $25,000), and fixtures remaining in the store (estimated value $25,000), equipment that Powder Puff recently removed from the store (estimated value $5,000), and accounts receivable that are not proceeds of the collateral (estimated value $10,000)? See Oregon Statutes §§87.146, 87.162 in section A of this assignment. UCC §§9-333, 9-109(d)(1) and (2).

b. Five years ago, Powder Puff obtained a loan from Secondbank. Secondbank perfected a security interest in all of Powder Puff's "fixtures, equipment, and inventory." The amount currently owing on that debt is $80,000. All of the fixtures and equipment were in the store before Secondbank made its loan. Powder Puff acquired the inventory presently on hand with funds supplied by Secondbank. Secondbank complied with the requirements of UCC §9-324(b) for obtaining purchase-money status in the inventory. Between Secondbank and Oaks Mall, who has priority? UCC §§9-203(a) and (b).

c.   In addition to the creditors mentioned above, Powder Puff has $100,000 in unsecured debt owing to 25 creditors. If Powder Puff's assets are liquidated outside bankruptcy, how much will each creditor get? If Powder Puff liquidates the assets in Chapter 11, how much will each creditor get? Bankr. Code §§545, 547(c)(6), 551.

d.   Powder Puff makes a restructuring proposal that calls for sale of Powder Puff's assets and the collection of its accounts receivable. From the proceeds, Powder Puff will pay $21,000 to Oaks, $45,000 to Secondbank, and the remaining $24,000 will be divided pro rata among the unsecured creditors, including the unpaid portion of Secondbank's debt. Powder Puff says that unless Oaks and Secondbank agree to its proposal, Powder Puff will file under Chapter 11 and liquidate under the protection of the Bankruptcy Court. Buffy asks how she should respond to this offer. What do you tell her?

37.7.   Governor Margaret Delgado was elected in large part on the basis of her promise to "put the environment first." As a legal aide to the governor, you have been assigned to evaluate a proposed change in the priority of the state's lien for environmental cleanup. Under current law, the state has a lien for its expenditures made to clean up contaminated property. The lien is subordinate to earlier perfected mortgages. The state frequently cleans up a property only to find that its lien is worthless. Earlier mortgages absorb the entire value of the property. The governor would specifically like to know how well environmental cleanup lien priority is working in states that give cleanup liens priority over mortgages. What questions would you ask to find out, and of whom would you ask them?

Assignment 38: Competitions Involving Federal Tax Liens: The Basics

The U.S. government is one of the principal competitors for debtors' assets. It competes on the basis of hundreds of kinds of obligations, including taxes, criminal fines, small business loans, student loans, accidental overpayments of Social Security benefits, and many others. In this assignment, we examine the government's rights with regard to the most frequent of these obligations, the debt for unpaid taxes. The government's receipts from taxes now exceed $3 trillion per year. At any given time, delinquent taxes total some $130 billion owed by about 12.4 million taxpayers.

Debtors owe many kinds of taxes to the U.S. government. Probably the largest amounts owing at any given time are for income taxes. Although they account for many tax delinquencies, income taxes are not the principal source of tax losses for the U.S. government. The threat of criminal prosecution and large civil penalties is generally sufficient to cause debtors who have money to pay their income taxes. Tax losses are usually incurred on taxes owing from debtors with business losses; they often do not have the money to pay. A debtor with business losses will tend not to owe income tax. Income tax delinquencies sometimes result in federal tax liens, but only a small percentage of federal tax liens arise from income taxes.

By far the most common source of federal tax liens is payroll taxes, in the form of federal withholding taxes and Social Security contributions owed by employers to the U.S. government. Provisions of the Internal Revenue Code (IRC) require that every employer "deduct" from every employee's pay the estimated income tax the employee will owe to the government at the end of the year and pay that money directly to the Internal Revenue Service (IRS). (We put "deduct" in quotes because the word implies that the employer takes money from a fund when in fact the employer may never have had the money it "deducts.") The Federal Insurance Contributions Act (FICA) divides the Social Security tax levy, imposing half on employers and half on employees. FICA requires that the employer "deduct" the employee's half of the tax from the employee's pay and pay both halves directly to the IRS. If the payroll is small, the employer is required to forward the money for these taxes to the IRS quarterly; if larger, the employer is required to forward the money more frequently.

For many businesses, payroll taxes are a substantial portion of cash flow. Considering that most payroll taxes are deducted from the pay of employees, it might seem that employers should have little trouble paying them. But the "deduction" is a legal fiction; the employer may never have had the "deducted" funds in the first place. To illustrate, assume that Rhonda is an employer who has agreed to pay her only employee, Ernie, $1,000 a week.

Based on current tax rates and Ernie's personal circumstances, Rhonda is required to withhold $250 a week for Ernie's income taxes and an additional $80 for Social Security. At the end of the week, she pays Ernie $670. Rhonda's half of the Social Security is an additional $80, for a total of $410 that Rhonda is supposed to pay the IRS. Because Rhonda's payroll is small, she need only pay the IRS four times a year. For now, she keeps the $410. At the end of the 13-week quarter, she will make a single payment to the IRS in the amount of $5,330.

If Rhonda is in financial difficulty and unable to pay all of her bills as they become due, things may not work so smoothly. As Rhonda decides which bills to pay and which to leave for later, those bills the nonpayment of which will immediately bring her business to a close are likely to be highest on her list. That probably will include Ernie's $670 paycheck each week, because if Ernie doesn't get paid, he will quit. It probably will include the utility company if it is about to turn off the lights, and it will include payments to suppliers whose products are needed and who will deliver them only for cash. What about the payroll taxes owing to the IRS? Their nonpayment represents no threat to Rhonda's business — at least until they become due. When they do, Rhonda may not have the money, having spent it on later payroll, utility bills, and suppliers. Or Rhonda may never have had the money in the first place. What happens if she doesn't pay the taxes? Immediately, not much. In all likelihood, it will take the IRS weeks to discover that Rhonda did not make the payment. Penalties will accrue in the interim. Tax law designates the money collected for these taxes as held in a "trust fund" even in the absence of any separate account for these receipts, and it imposes penalties for nonpayment from the day these "trust funds" are due. Rhonda may be well aware that her knowing and intentional failure to pay these "trust funds" to the IRS is a crime and that the resulting liability will be nondischargeable in bankruptcy. But frightening as trust fund liability may be in the long run, in the short run it pales beside the problems of a person whose business is failing. People like Rhonda pay what they must to keep their businesses and their hopes alive. While the IRS sleeps on its rights, people like Rhonda lie awake at night worrying about their mounting liabilities to that sleeping giant.

Eventually, the sleeping giant will awaken. When it does, it will not charge Rhonda with the crime she committed by embezzling the "trust funds" she used to pay the light bill; too many employers have done the same thing to attempt to prosecute them all. Instead, the IRS will assess the amount of payroll tax due and then, within a matter of weeks or months, file a Notice of Tax Lien against Rhonda. When it files the Notice, the U.S. government enters the competition that has been the subject of the second half of this book. The IRS files about 500,000 Notices of Tax Lien each year.

Provided that Rhonda was the decision maker for her business, Rhonda's liability for unremitted trust funds would have been the same even if she had incorporated. The Internal Revenue Code imposes liability for trust fund taxes not just on the corporation whose taxes were not paid, but also on the individuals "responsible" for the nonpayment.

A.   The Creation and Perfection of Federal Tax Liens

1.   Creation

I.R.C. §§6321 and 6322 govern the creation of a federal tax lien. When the IRS determines that tax is owing, it *assesses* the tax by recording the amount on its own records. When it notifies the taxpayer of the assessment, that notice constitutes the *demand* described in I.R.C. §6321 and the tax lien comes into existence and relates back to the date and time of assessment.

The lien attaches to "all property and rights to property, whether real or personal, belonging to" the taxpayer. I.R.C. §6321. This is the ultimate floating lien; it reaches all property the debtor owns. But there are limits. Like a security interest that has attached under UCC §9-203 and has not yet been perfected under §9-308(a), this unperfected tax lien will be effective against the debtor, but not against third parties who acquire liens against or purchase the property.

2.   Perfection

The Federal Tax Lien Act does not use the word "perfection." Instead, it deems the federal tax lien not "valid" until the IRS files notice of its lien. I.R.C. §6323(a). I.R.C. §6323(f) defers to state law as to the system in which the IRS must file the notice. In response to that section, each state has enacted a law specifying the appropriate public record system. The following statute is typical:

New York Lien Law

(2015)

§240.   PLACE OF FILING NOTICES OF LIENS AND CERTIFICATES AND NOTICES AFFECTING SUCH LIENS

1. Notices of liens upon real property for taxes payable to the United States of America or otherwise created by federal law in favor of the United States of America or one or more of its instrumentalities, hereafter in this article referred to as "federal liens" and certificates and notices affecting such liens shall be filed in the office of the clerk of the county in which real property subject to any such lien is situated, except that if real property subject to any such lien is situated in the county of Kings, the county of Queens, the county of New York or the county of Bronx they shall be filed in the office of the city register of the city of New York in such county. If such property be situated in two or more counties, such notice or certificate shall be filed in the office of the clerk or the city register, as the case may be, in each of such counties.

2. Notices of federal liens upon tangible or intangible personal property and certificates and notices affecting such liens shall be filed as follows:

(a) If the person against whose interest the lien applies is a corporation or a partnership, as defined in the internal revenue laws of the United States, in the office of the secretary of state;

(b) In all other cases, in the office of the clerk of the county where the lienee, if a resident of the state, resides at the time of filing of the notice of lien, except that if such lienee resides at such time in the county of Kings, the county of Queens, the county of New York or the county of Bronx, the place for filing such liens shall be in the office of the city register of the city of New York in such county. . . .

Although the Federal Tax Lien Act (FTLA) does not use the term "perfected," the filing of a Notice of Tax Lien has essentially that effect. If a Notice of Tax Lien has not yet been filed when a debtor sells its property, grants a security interest in it, or loses possession to a sheriff under a writ of execution, the tax lien will not be valid against that competitor. If a Notice of Tax Lien has been filed before any of those events occur, the tax lien will be valid against that competitor. The Federal Tax Lien Act does not use the term "priority" either. Instead, it deems the tax lien "not valid" against a particular competing interest until notice of the lien is filed. Read literally, this language probably would not have integrated the federal tax lien into the state law system of priorities, but, fortunately, it has not been read literally. The admonition in §6323(a) that "the lien . . . shall not be valid against" certain competitors "until notice . . . has been filed" has been read to mean that the lien is subordinate to those competitors if those competitors perfect before the Notice of Tax Lien is filed.

The big picture here is that with regard to tax liens, the U.S. government participates in the perfection and priority game along with everybody else. Its tax liens prevail over the liens of others if the IRS files first, and loses to them if it does not. The IRS plays this game badly. It usually is slow to discover that taxes are owing and slow to file its Notice of Tax Lien when it does. But what is most interesting is that the IRS plays at all. The U.S. government could have enacted a statute giving federal tax liens priority over all other liens against the debtor's property. This is in fact what state governments have done with regard to property taxes. When a state property tax lien comes into existence under state law, it primes mortgages and other liens against the property.

Why didn't the federal government do the same for its tax liens? The answer to this question has two parts. First, the principal reason for not putting federal tax liens ahead of security interests and mortgages was a fear that doing so would deter needed commercial lending. State property taxes are relatively small in relation to the value of the property, and both the time of assessment and the amount of the taxes are fairly predictable. When such a lien arises and primes the mortgage lender, the mortgage lender can deal with it by paying the tax and adding it to the balance owing on the mortgage loan. Federal tax liens for payroll taxes are often large in relation to the value of the property and they can accumulate quickly and unpredictably. To give federal tax liens priority irrespective of when they arise would pose a much greater problem for secured lenders.

The second part of the answer is that the U.S. government may yet reconsider its decision to play in the perfection/priority game. In Canada, payroll taxes have priority over most security interests in personal property. For more than two decades, Canadian lenders have had strong incentives to monitor their debtors and make sure their debtors pay payroll taxes when due. The apparent success of the Canadian system may prompt reconsideration of the priority of tax liens in the United States.

While the U.S. government plays in the perfection/priority game essentially as it is defined by state law, the government brings its own set of rules. Those rules, most of which are contained in I.R.C. §6323, reconceptualize much of state law in ways disconcerting to those already familiar with Article 9. For example, I.R.C. §6323(h)(1) defines a security interest as existing only if it is perfected and only to the extent that the holder has "parted with money or money's worth." Thus, security interests that have attached and become enforceable under UCC §§9-203(a) and (b) may not yet exist for purposes of the Federal Tax Lien Act. (We will deal with this reconceptualization at length in the next assignment.) For now, the best way to cope with this and other inconsistencies in the perfection/priority system is what we call the "finger" method. When you are solving a problem, make sure your finger is on the governing rule (and, of course, that you read what your finger is on).

3. Remedies for Enforcement

The Federal Tax Lien Act provides the remedy for enforcement of federal tax liens. If the taxpayer does not pay the tax within ten days after notice and demand, the IRS can levy on the taxpayer's property. (The notice is notice that a levy is forthcoming, not merely a Notice of Tax Lien.) The IRS is not required to use the services of a sheriff or marshal to levy; IRS employees can perform the levy and, if necessary, sell the assets. The IRS can levy in either of two ways. The first is physically to seize property of the debtor. The second is to serve a notice of levy on a bank at which the debtor has an account or on some other third party who is in possession of the debtor's property. The third party must then remit the bank account or other property to the IRS or be liable for its value. Serving a notice of levy is easier and less complicated, which probably accounts for the fact that the IRS serves about two million notices of levy on third parties each year, but makes only about 500 physical seizures of property.

State exemption laws do not apply against the IRS; the Federal Tax Lien Act contains a set of exemptions from federal tax levies that are less favorable to debtors than the exemption laws of most states. (Here, too, the federal government brings its own rules to the game.) As soon as practicable after seizure, the IRS sells the property to the highest bidder by public auction or by public sale under sealed bids and applies the proceeds of sale to the tax debt. As you would expect, the tax sale is subject to prior liens, which often include security interests and mortgages. The buyer at the tax sale takes free of subordinate liens, which are discharged by the sale.

4.   *Maintaining Perfection of a Tax Lien*

I.R.C. §6323(g) establishes a "required refiling period" for a Notice of Tax Lien. The period is the one-year period ending 30 days after the expiration of ten years after the date of assessment of the tax. If the IRS fails to refile during the required refiling period, the effect is that the lien lapses. The IRS may be able to revive the lien by refiling after lapse, but the lien will then be subordinate to competing liens perfected against the collateral before the refiling. If the IRS does refile within the required periods, it can maintain the lien perpetually. (It is important to distinguish the tax lien from the underlying tax debt. If the statute of limitations runs on the underlying tax debt, the lien becomes ineffective even if the lien itself has not expired. The IRS may prevent the statute of limitations from running by taking certain actions, or the debtor may have taken some action that will toll the statute.) The requirement that the IRS must refile to keep its lien effective should seem familiar; it is essentially the scheme of Article 9 with regard to continuation and lapse, but with different time periods.

The Federal Tax Lien Act contains no provision analogous to UCC §9-507 regarding name changes and sales of collateral. But, as you can see from the following case, these issues occasionally arise.

In re LMS Holding Co.

50 F.3d 1526 (10th Cir. 1995)

LOGAN, CIRCUIT JUDGE.

The IRS perfected a notice of federal tax lien against MAKO, Inc. based on assessments for unpaid federal taxes of more than $330,000. MAKO later filed a petition for relief under Chapter 11 of the Bankruptcy Code. Pursuant to the MAKO plan of liquidation (MAKO Plan), RMC, an unrelated entity, acquired all of the assets of the MAKO bankruptcy estate and assumed all of MAKO's secured liabilities. The IRS consented to the liquidation plan and the parties agree that it retained its lien against the property securing the IRS claim. The IRS interests were represented through counsel during the administration of the MAKO bankruptcy. The bankruptcy court confirmed the MAKO plan in August 1989. The IRS never filed any federal tax lien notices in the name of RMC.

In September 1991 RMC, together with LMS Holding Company and Petroleum Marketing Company, filed Chapter 11 bankruptcy petitions. Thereafter the debtors jointly filed a complaint alleging they were entitled to avoid the federal tax lien on assets RMC acquired from MAKO.

The Bankruptcy Code provides that a trustee has the right "without regard to any knowledge of the trustee or of any creditor" to avoid "any obligation incurred by the debtor that is voidable by [a subsequent judgment lien creditor] or a bona fide purchaser of real property [who] has perfected such transfer at the time of the commencement of the case, whether or not such a purchaser exists." 11 U.S.C. §544(a). More specifically as to lien avoidance, 11 U.S.C. §545(2) provides that "[t]he trustee may avoid the fixing of a statutory lien on property of the debtor to the extent that such lien is not perfected or enforceable at the time of the commencement of the case against a bona fide purchaser that purchases such property at the time of the commencement of the case, whether or not such a purchaser exists." A debtor in possession in a Chapter 11 proceeding, as here, has essentially the same rights, powers and duties of a bankruptcy trustee. See 11 U.S.C. §1107(a). We must determine whether the federal tax lien was perfected as against a hypothetical bona fide purchaser at the time RMC filed for bankruptcy.

A federal tax lien arises when a person fails to pay assessed taxes; the amount due becomes a lien on "all property and rights to property" belonging to the person assessed. I.R.C. §6321. However, this lien is not "valid as against any purchaser . . . or judgment lien creditor until notice thereof which meets the requirements of subsection (f) has been filed by the Secretary." Id. §6323(a).

Subsection 6323(f)(3) provides that "[t]he form and content of the notice referred to in subsection (a) shall be prescribed by the Secretary. Such notice shall be valid notwithstanding any other provision of law regarding the form or content of a notice of lien." The regulations promulgated under this statute require that the notice of lien be filed on a Form 668 "Notice of Federal Lien under Internal Revenue Laws" and "identify the taxpayer, the tax liability giving rise to the lien, and the date the assessment arose." Treas. Reg. §301.6323(f)-1(d)(1) and (2).

As debtors acknowledge [in their brief], the filing of the tax lien notice naming MAKO as taxpayer perfected a lien against MAKO, and that lien "continued in the actual assets transferred by MAKO to RMC. As a result, the tax lien against MAKO followed the MAKO assets into the hands of RMC and was enforceable against RMC *prior to RMC's bankruptcy.*" But the bankruptcy and district courts determined that when debtors filed for bankruptcy the lien was not valid against a hypothetical bona fide purchaser from RMC. Those courts reasoned that when RMC assumed federal tax liabilities secured by the lien against MAKO, RMC became "the taxpayer"; that to comply with I.R.C. §6323(f) and the corresponding regulations, the IRS was required to refile or correct the lien notice by substituting "RMC" for "MAKO" as the taxpayer in order to preserve its priority.

RMC is not a new entity emerging from the bankruptcy of MAKO, analogous to a change of identity. Rather, RMC is "an unrelated third party entity," LMS Holding Co. v. Core-Mark Mid-Continent, Inc., 50 F.3d 1520, 1523 (10th Cir. 1995), to which the assets of MAKO were transferred. That RMC also assumed MAKO's liabilities does not make it "the taxpayer." An entity in RMC's position, purchasing another corporation's assets and assuming its liabilities, whether in a bankruptcy reorganization or otherwise, has long been characterized as the transferee and not the taxpayer.

Our conclusion that RMC is not the taxpayer, however, does not resolve the question of the need to refile. The regulations do not speak directly to the need to refile against the transferee in circumstances like that before us. The only provisions in §6323 that specifically reference refiling relate to time limits, requiring refiling essentially every eleven years. I.R.C. §6323(g). Nevertheless, Congress was concerned with the problem of notice to those who deal with debtors whose property is subject to the government's tax lien.

I.R.C. §6323(f)(4) answers the refiling question, we believe, in the context of tax liens against real estate. When the state maintains an adequate system for public indexing of federal tax liens, the bona fide purchaser of real estate prevails unless the notice of lien is "entered and recorded in [a public index at the place of filing] in such a manner that a reasonable inspection of the index will reveal the existence of the lien." *Id*. MAKO's ownership of the realty presumably was recorded. Thus, the government's tax lien filed against MAKO would show in any search of the chain of title by a person buying real property from MAKO's transferee, RMC. In those circumstances—because any purchaser would be considered to have notice of the unreleased tax lien against MAKO, RMC's predecessor in the title—§6323(f)(4) dictates that the government's lien would be valid against the debtor in possession of RMC's bankruptcy estate.

The Internal Revenue Code is less explicit as to refiling against a transferee when the lien is against personal property. But we believe §6323 provides a method of analysis that we can utilize to determine the refiling requirement. The relative priority of a federal lien for unpaid taxes is a matter of federal law. But I.R.C. §6323(h)(6) defines "purchaser" for purposes of federal tax lien avoidance as "a person who, for adequate and full consideration in money or money's worth, acquires an interest (other than a lien or security interest) in property which is valid *under local law* against subsequent purchasers without actual notice." (emphasis added). Thus, the federal law looks to state law to define the rights of a bona fide purchaser—the position occupied by a bankruptcy trustee or debtor in possession under Chapter 11.

Under the Uniform Commercial Code, adopted in Oklahoma, a lien creditor has priority over an unperfected secured creditor. [UCC §9-317(a)]. To acquire a perfected security interest the creditor must file a financing statement describing the collateral subject to the security interest and naming the debtor. A federal tax lien becomes a lien on all property of the debtor, so the property need not be described. But I.R.C. §6323(f)(1)(A)(ii) contemplates essentially the same kind of filing, under state law, to perfect the lien against a debtor's personal property. On the need to refile after a transfer of the property subject to the secured interest, [UCC §9-507(a)] states that "[a] filed financing statement remains effective with respect to collateral transferred by the debtor even though the secured party knows of or consents to the transfer." The official UCC Comment 3 to [that section] states the following: "[A]ny person searching the condition of the ownership of a debtor must make inquiry as to the debtor's source of title, and must search in the name of a former owner if circumstances seem to require it." Under this analysis a purchaser from RMC would have a duty to ask RMC's source of title—here MAKO—and search under MAKO's name for liens. Such a search would reveal the government's tax lien.

We have recently dealt with this issue in the instant bankruptcy proceedings, with respect to a nongovernment creditor. We held that the creditor's security interest remained perfected in collateral actually transferred to RMC under the MAKO plan, *LMS Holding Co.,* 50 F.3d at 1524, but that a new filing naming RMC would be required to establish the security interest in RMC's after-acquired property.

Consistent with *LMS Holding Co.,* we here hold that the government's tax lien remained perfected in the assets transferred to RMC from the MAKO bankruptcy, but that property acquired by [RMC] after the transfer would not be subject to the tax lien because the IRS did not refile against [RMC].

As *LMS Holding Company* illustrates, most of the same systems problems that arise with respect to Article 9 security interests also arise with respect to federal tax liens. To resolve the issue of whether the IRS must file against transferees, the *LMS* court borrows from Article 9. Similar perfection-maintenance problems arise regarding interstate movement. Article 9 includes several provisions that effectively give secured creditors four months or one year to react to a change in circumstances by refiling, but the Federal Tax Lien Act has no analogous provisions. The result is that the courts must decide what circumstances should require refiling to maintain protection and how long the IRS should have to refile.

In re Eschenbach

267 B.R. 921 (Bankr. N.D. Tex. 2001)

STEVEN A. FELSENTHAL, UNITED STATES BANKRUPTCY JUDGE.

On September 22, 1997, while the debtors lived in Martin County, Florida, the IRS filed a notice of federal tax lien in the Martin County courthouse. The notice of lien covers federal income taxes for 1994 and 1995 and applies to real and personal property.

Thereafter, the debtors moved to Tarrant County, Texas. On October 2, 2000, the debtors filed their petition for relief under Chapter 13 of the Bankruptcy Code. The IRS filed a proof of secured claim for unpaid 1995 taxes which, as of the petition date, totaled $5,906.12.

According to the debtors' schedules, they owned personal property on October 2, 2000, valued at greater than $5,906.12. Accordingly, the IRS asserts that it has a fully secured claim. However, the debtors contend that before they moved from Florida to Texas, they only owned personal property valued at $3,000.

On May 31, 2001, the debtors filed an objection to the IRS' proof of secured claim. The debtors stipulated that the lien covered all personal property that they owned in Florida and that the lien followed that property when they moved to Texas. But, the debtors contend that the lien does not cover the personal property that they acquired in Texas. Therefore, they maintain that the secured claim must be limited to the $3,000 of value of the property that they acquired while living in Florida, making the remainder of the claim unsecured.

As a result of this position, the parties agree that the court must decide whether a notice of federal tax lien for personal property, properly filed in the county where the taxpayer resided at the time the notice is filed, attaches to personal property acquired by the taxpayer after the taxpayer moves to a county in another state. If it does, then the IRS must be allowed its secured claim. However, if it does not, then the IRS would be allowed a secured claim of $3,000, with the balance of the claim allowed as unsecured.

If a person fails to pay their taxes, then the Internal Revenue Code imposes a lien for unpaid taxes upon the delinquent taxpayer's property. Under 26 U.S.C. §6321, a federal tax lien arises:

> If any person liable to pay any tax neglects or refuses to pay the same after demand, the amount (including any interest, additional amount, addition to tax, or assessable penalty, together with any costs that may accrue in addition thereto) shall be a lien in favor of the United States upon all property and rights to property, whether real or personal, belonging to such person.

The tax lien attaches to the taxpayer's property upon the filing of a notice of lien. 26 U.S.C. §6323(a). For a taxpayer's personal property, the Internal Revenue Code deems the property situated at the residence of the taxpayer at the time the notice of lien is filed. 26 U.S.C. §6323(f)(2)(B). The lien applies to all the taxpayer's property until either the taxpayer satisfies the liability or the statute of limitations on collection runs. 26 U.S.C. §6322.

The notice of federal tax lien must be filed in accordance with 26 U.S.C. §6323, which states that "the lien imposed by section 6321 shall not be valid . . . until notice thereof which meets the requirements of subsection (f) has been filed by the Secretary." Subsection (f) requires the IRS to file the notice of its lien according to laws of the state of the taxpayer's domicile. The Florida Uniform Federal Lien Registration Act requires that notices of federal tax liens for personal property be filed in the county where the taxpayer resides.

On September 22, 1997, the IRS filed its notice of federal tax lien in Martin County, Florida, where the debtors then resided. Consequently, under the Internal Revenue Code, from that time until the tax liability is paid, the lien attaches to all property belonging to the taxpayer, and all the property belonging to the taxpayer during that period of time is deemed situated in Martin County, Florida. Thus, wherever the taxpayer roams after September 27, 1997, the tax lien applies to his property until either the tax liability is paid or collection is barred by the statute of limitations, as if the taxpayer never left Martin County, Florida.

Accordingly, the United States Supreme Court has held that a federal tax lien attaches to any "property owned by the delinquent at any time during the life of the lien." Glass City Bank v. United States, 326 U.S. 265, 268-69 (1945). If a federal tax lien arises pursuant to §6321, then it attaches (and remains attached) to all property belonging to the debtor, including any after-acquired property, until paid. Additionally, once properly filed, the lien attaches to property no matter where it is located. Moreover, the lien remains valid even if the debtor leaves the residence. 26 U.S.C. §6323(f)(2)(B).

In this case, the debtors concede those points. But, they observe that relocation to a different state significantly changes the analysis. As previously stated, a federal tax lien follows the taxpayer and his property when the taxpayer relocates to a different state. However, to be effective against third parties, the Internal Revenue Code requires that notice of federal tax liens be filed as designated by the state of the taxpayer's residence. In this case, the debtors contend that if the taxpayer becomes a resident of a different state, then, to attach to property acquired in the new state, the IRS must file another notice of federal tax lien in the manner designated by the new state. The debtors argue that this interpretation of the law accords meaning to the requirement that the notice of federal tax liens for personal property be filed as designated by the several states and is consistent with lending practices under the Uniform Commercial Code.

The Internal Revenue Code does not require the IRS to file a tax lien in every county to which a taxpayer could carry personal property. See *Grand Prairie State*

Bank, 206 F.2d at 219. "To hold otherwise, would be to overlook the practical necessities of the situation and would require the Collector to file tax liens in every jurisdiction to which the taxpayers may at any time remove the property." *Id.* Similarly, by providing that the lien attaches to all property "belonging to" the taxpayer, 26 U.S.C. §6321, for the period until paid, 26 U.S.C. §6322, with the property deemed situated at the taxpayer's residence at the time the notice of lien is filed, 26 U.S.C. §6323(f)(2)(B), the Internal Revenue Code eliminates any need for the IRS to file tax liens in every jurisdiction to which a taxpayer may move and acquire new property. The IRS need not chase taxpayers, filing in every state to which the taxpayer moves. Taxpayers cannot pocket tax money, move to another state and acquire new property, thereby avoiding the IRS's lien. Moreover, the broad statutory language that appears in §6321 "reveals on its face that Congress meant to reach every interest in property that a taxpayer might have." See United States v. National Bank of Commerce, 472 U.S. 713, 720 (1985). In fact, "stronger language could hardly have been selected to reveal a purpose to assure the collection of taxes." Glass City Bank v. United States, 326 U.S. at 267.

The notice of tax lien filed September 27, 1997, captures all the debtors' personal property as if the debtors never left Martin County, Florida.

The Internal Revenue Code cannot be compared to the Uniform Commercial Code. Collection of taxes to finance the United States operates in a different sphere than perfection of security interests for commercial transactions. Besides, for registered organizations, recent revisions to the Uniform Commercial Code result in filing of financing statements in the place of incorporation, regardless of the location of the collateral. See, e.g., UCC §9-301, 307 (1998).

We find no fault with Judge Felsenthal's reading of the statutes. But we disagree with his assertion that collection of taxes "operates in a different sphere than perfection of security interests for commercial transactions." IRS liens encumber property and compete for priority just like any other liens. Searchers cannot discover liens like that against Eschenbach. If there are enough of them, these secret liens will interfere with commercial transactions.

B.   Competitions Involving Federal Tax Liens

The basic rule governing competition between federal tax liens and the rights of third parties is in I.R.C. §6323(a). That section provides that the tax lien "shall not be valid as against any purchaser, holder of a security interest, mechanic's lienor, or judgment lien creditor" until the IRS files a Notice of Tax Lien. The section is poorly drafted. Read literally, §6323(a) could yield a system in which tax liens had priority over nearly every other third-party interest. To illustrate the dangerous reading, assume that Debtor is the owner of Blackwidget and owes taxes, but the IRS has not yet filed a Notice of Tax Lien. Debtor borrows $60,000 from Firstbank and grants a security interest.

Firstbank perfects by filing. Charles Creditor, an unsecured creditor of Debtor, obtains a judgment and levies on Blackwidget. Debtor then sells Blackwidget to Bess Buyer for $40,000. She pays the purchase price and takes possession without knowledge of Debtor's problems with the IRS. The IRS then files a Notice of Tax Lien. Reading §6323(a) literally, the tax lien was not "valid" against Firstbank, Creditor, or Buyer *until* the IRS filed the Notice of Tax Lien. The clear implication is that the tax lien is valid against those competitors *after* it is filed. You already know, however, that interpretation is incorrect. To get the right answer from I.R.C. §6323(a), one must read into it something it does not say: Tax liens and third-party interests rank in the order in which they became "valid" within the meaning of the Federal Tax Lien Act. The idea of "first in time, first in right" is so basic that the drafters of I.R.C. §6323 did not even consider it necessary to mention.

What is it that each of these competitors must do for their interests to be valid within the meaning of the Federal Tax Lien Act? To put the question another way, what is it that the holder of the competing interest must do before the IRS files its Notice of Tax Lien to be valid and prevail over the tax lien?

1. Security Interest

With regard to security interests, the answer to this question is in I.R.C. §6323(h)(1), which defines "security interest." That section provides that a security interest "exists" only when (A) the property is in existence and the interest has become protected against a judgment lien under local law and (B) the holder has parted with the money or other value, the repayment of which is secured. In essence, an Article 9 security interest will satisfy this test when it is perfected with respect to the particular advance. The security interest will prevail over the tax lien if the security interest satisfies that test before the government files the Notice of Tax Lien. (The validity of the Article 9 security interest as to advances not made until after the filing of the Notice of Tax Lien is a subject dealt with in the next assignment.) With regard to a mortgage, the rule of §6323(h)(1) produces a somewhat surprising result. In most states, even an unrecorded mortgage has priority over a subsequent judgment lien. It follows that in most states a mortgage exists under §6323(h)(1) as soon as it is created — without recording — and so has priority over a subsequent tax lien, even though the tax lien is filed before the mortgage is recorded. In re Restivo Auto Body, Inc., 772 F.3d 168 (4th Cir. 2014).

2. Purchaser

To prevail over a tax lien, a purchaser must acquire its status as such before the government files notice of the tax lien. I.R.C. §6323(a). I.R.C. §6323(h)(6) defines "purchaser" as a person who, "for adequate and full consideration in money or money's worth," acquires an interest valid under local law (that is, state law) against a subsequent purchaser without actual notice of the interest. Thus, a purchase can prevail over the tax lien if, before the government files notice of the tax lien, the purchaser does whatever it must to prevail over a second, later purchaser of the same property who buys without actual notice of the would-be purchaser's interest. A first purchaser of real estate ordinarily will prevail over later purchasers if the first purchaser records its deed before the second purchaser contracts to purchase and pays value. It follows that a purchaser of real estate prevails over a federal tax lien if the purchaser records its deed before the IRS records its Notice of Tax Lien.

In some states, a purchaser of real estate who goes into possession but does not record prevails over a later purchaser who does not have actual notice of the sale. Thus, it has been held that "possession alone gives actual notice under Florida law, sufficient to defeat a subsequent federal tax lien." United States v. Pledger, 158 F. Supp. 612, 614 (N.D. Fla. 1958); Waldorff Insurance and Bonding, Inc. v. Elgin National Bank, 453 So. 2d 1383, 1385 (Fla. Dist. Ct. App. 1984).

In the opinion that follows, the court appears to have decided that the same rule should not apply to the purchase of an automobile.

Mayer-Dupree v. Internal Revenue Service

1993 U.S. App. LEXIS 24639 (10th Cir. 1993)

Deanell Reece Tacha, Circuit Judge.

Appellant challenges the dismissal on motion for summary judgment of her wrongful levy action under 26 U.S.C. §7426. The government seized a vehicle in 1991 in satisfaction of federal tax liens that accrued in 1985 and were noticed in 1988 and 1990. Appellant alleges that she purchased the vehicle from the delinquent taxpayer in 1986. Although she alleges that she received the certificate of title at that time, she did not register the title until after the government seized the vehicle. The district court dismissed her action. We affirm.

Under 26 U.S.C. §6323(a), a federal tax lien is not valid against a purchaser until the government files proper notice of the lien. Section 6323(h)(6) defines a purchaser as one who "acquires an interest (other than a lien or security interest) in property which is valid under local law against subsequent purchases without actual notice." We agree with the district court that appellant was not a purchaser because, under Colorado law, her failure to register the certificate of title as required by Colo. Rev. Stat. §42-6-109 (1984) rendered her interest in the vehicle invalid against a subsequent purchaser without notice.

Because appellant was not a purchaser, §6323(a) affords her no relief. We therefore AFFIRM for substantially the reasons given by the district court. The mandate shall issue forthwith.

———————————

As *Mayer-Dupree* illustrates, if local law requires the filing or recording of transfers of the particular type of personal property, the filing or recording is likely to be the act that protects the transferee against a tax lien later filed against the transferor. This will be true for sales of automobiles, aircraft, patents, trademarks, copyrights, accounts receivable, and chattel paper (remember

UCC §9-109(a)(3)). For most kinds of personal property, such filing or record-ing is not required. For them, the purchase is likely to be effective against later purchasers as soon as it is effective against the debtor. A purchase generally will be effective against the seller-debtor when the contract so provides. See UCC §2-401(1) ("Subject to these provisions and to the provisions of [Article 9], title to goods passes from the seller to the buyer in any manner and on any conditions explicitly agreed to between the parties."). UCC §2-403(2) is, how-ever, an important exception. Under that section, a purchaser who leaves the property purchased with a seller who deals in goods of the kind loses to a later buyer in the ordinary course of business. This purchaser could well lose to a later filed tax lien.

3. Judgment Lien Creditor

The Federal Tax Lien Act does not define "judgment lien creditor" or say when one comes into existence for purposes of I.R.C. §6323(a). The Supreme Court has, however, developed extensive case law on the issue.

United States v. McDermott

507 U.S. 447 (1993)

JUSTICE SCALIA delivered the opinion of the Court.

We granted certiorari to resolve the competing priorities of a federal tax lien and a private creditor's judgment lien as to a delinquent taxpayer's after-acquired real property.

I

On December 9, 1986 the United States assessed Mr. and Mrs. McDermott for unpaid federal taxes due for the tax years 1977 through 1981. Upon that assess-ment, the law created a lien in favor of the United States on all real and personal property belonging to the McDermotts, 26 U.S.C. §§6321 and 6322, including after-acquired property. Pursuant to 26 U.S.C. §6323(a), however, that lien could "not be valid as against any purchaser, holder of a security interest, mechanic's lienor, or *judgment lien creditor* until notice thereof . . . has been filed." (Emphasis added). The United States did not file this lien in the Salt Lake County Recorder's Office until September 9, 1987. Before that occurred, however—specifically, on July 6, 1987—Zions First National Bank, N. A., docketed with the Salt Lake County Clerk a state-court judgment it had won against the McDermotts. Under Utah law, that created a judgment lien on all of the McDermotts' real property in Salt Lake County, "owned . . . at the time or . . . thereafter acquired during the existence of said lien." Utah Code Ann. §78-22-1 (1953).

On September 23, 1987 the McDermotts acquired title to certain real property in Salt Lake County. To facilitate later sale of that property, the parties entered into an escrow agreement whereby the United States and the Bank released their claims to the real property itself but reserved their rights to the cash proceeds of the sale, based on their priorities in the property as of September 23, 1987. Pursuant to the escrow agreement, the McDermotts brought this interpleader.

II

Federal tax liens do not automatically have priority over all other liens. Absent provision to the contrary, priority for purposes of federal law is governed by the common-law principle that "the first in time is the first in right." United States v. New Britain, 347 U.S. 81, 85 (1954). For purposes of applying that doctrine in the present case—in which the competing state lien (that of a judgment creditor) benefits from the provision of §6323(a) that the federal lien shall "not be valid . . . until notice thereof . . . has been filed"—we must deem the United States' lien to have commenced no sooner than the filing of notice. As for the Bank's lien: our cases deem a competing state lien to be in existence for "first in time" purposes only when it has been "perfected" in the sense that "the identity of the lienor, *the property subject to the lien*, and the amount of the lien are established." *United States v. New Britain*, 347 U.S., at 84 (emphasis added).

The first question we must answer, then, is whether the Bank's judgment lien was perfected in this sense before the United States filed its tax lien on September 9, 1987. If so, that is the end of the matter; the Bank's lien prevails. The Court of Appeals was of the view that this question was answered (or rendered irrelevant) by our decision in United States v. Vermont, 377 U.S. 351 (1964), which it took to "stand for the proposition that a non-contingent lien on all of a person's real property, perfected prior to the federal tax lien, will take priority over the federal lien, regardless of whether after-acquired property is involved." That is too expansive a reading. Our opinion in *Vermont* gives no indication that the property at issue had become subject to the state lien only by application of an after-acquired-property clause to property that the debtor acquired after the federal lien arose. To the contrary, the opinion says that the state lien met (presumably at the critical time when the federal lien arose) "the test laid down in *New Britain* that 'the property subject to the lien [be] established.'" 377 U.S., at 358 (citation omitted). The argument of the United States that we rejected in *Vermont* was the contention that a state lien is not perfected within the meaning of *New Britain* if it "attaches to *all* of the taxpayer's property," rather than "to specifically identified portions of that property." 377 U.S., at 355 (emphasis added). We did not consider, and the facts as recited did not implicate, the quite different argument made by the United States in the present case: that a lien in after-acquired property is not "perfected" as to property yet to be acquired.

The Bank argues that, as of July 6, 1987, the date it docketed its judgment lien, the lien was "perfected as to all real property then and thereafter owned by" the McDermotts, since "nothing further was required of [the Bank] to attach the non-contingent lien on after-acquired property." That reflects an unusual notion of what it takes to "perfect" a lien. Under the Uniform Commercial Code, for example, a security interest in after-acquired property is generally not considered perfected when the financing statement is filed, but only when the security interest has attached to particular property upon the debtor's acquisition of that property.

[UCC §§9-203(a) and (b), 9-308(a)]. And attachment to particular property was also an element of what we meant by "perfection" in *New Britain*. See 347 U.S., at 84 ("when the property subject to the lien [is] established"); *id.*, at 86 ("the priority of each statutory lien contested here must depend on the time it attached to the property in question and became [no longer inchoate]"). The Bank concedes that its lien did not actually attach to the property at issue here until the McDermotts acquired rights in that property. Since that occurred after filing of the federal tax lien, the state lien was not first in time.

But that does not complete our inquiry: Though the state lien was not first in time, the federal tax lien was not necessarily first in time either. Like the state lien, it applied to the property at issue here by virtue of a (judicially inferred) after-acquired-property provision, which means that it did not attach until the same instant the state lien attached, viz., when the McDermotts acquired the property; and, like the state lien, it did not become "perfected" until that time. We think, however, that under the language of §6323(a) ("shall not be valid as against any . . . judgment lien creditor until notice . . . has been filed"), the filing of notice renders the federal tax lien extant for "first in time" priority purposes regardless of whether it has yet attached to identifiable property. That result is also indicated by the provision, two subsections later, which accords priority, even against filed federal tax liens, to security interests arising out of certain agreements, including "commercial transactions financing agreements," entered into before filing of the tax lien. 26 U.S.C. §6323(c)(1). That provision protects certain security interests that, like the after-acquired-property judgment lien here, will have been recorded before the filing of the tax lien, and will attach to the encumbered property after the filing of the tax lien, and simultaneously with the attachment of the tax lien (i.e., upon the debtor's acquisition of the subject property). According special priority to certain state security interests in these circumstances obviously presumes that otherwise the federal tax lien would prevail—i.e., that the federal tax lien is ordinarily dated, for purposes of "first in time" priority against §6323(a) competing interests, from the time of its filing, regardless of when it attaches to the subject property.

The Bank argues that "by common law, the first lien of record against a debtor's property has priority over those subsequently filed unless a lien-creating statute clearly shows or declares an intention to cause the statutory lien to override." Such a strong "first-to-record" presumption may be appropriate for simultaneously-perfected liens under ordinary statutes creating private liens, which ordinarily arise out of voluntary transactions. When two private lenders both exact from the same debtor security agreements with after-acquired-property clauses, the second lender knows, by reason of the earlier recording, that category of property will be subject to another claim, and if the remaining security is inadequate he may avoid the difficulty by declining to extend credit. The Government, by contrast, cannot indulge the luxury of declining to hold the taxpayer liable for his taxes; notice of a previously filed security agreement covering after-acquired property does not enable the Government to protect itself. A strong "first-to-record" presumption is particularly out of place under the present tax-lien statute, whose general rule is that the tax collector prevails even if he has not recorded at all. 26 U.S.C. §§6321 and 6322. Thus, while we would hardly proclaim the statutory meaning we have discerned in this opinion to be "clear," it is evident enough for the purpose at hand. The federal tax lien must be given priority.

The judgment of the Court of Appeals is reversed, and the case is remanded for further proceedings consistent with this opinion.

[Justices Thomas, Stevens, and O'Connor dissented.]

In this assignment, we have examined the race between the IRS and the holders of competing interests in situations where the first to come into existence will prevail. In the next assignment, we continue our examination of competitions involving federal tax liens by examining a number of interests that prevail over earlier-filed tax liens.

Problem Set 38

38.1.   Ronald Cheek was the hottest real estate developer in town, until it came to light how he was doing it. Ronald was selling multiple "first" mortgages on each of his properties, and forging title insurance policies to cover it up. Your law firm was the first to recover a money judgment against Cheek. The associate who worked the file before you recorded the $2,500,000 judgment in favor of Major Construction Company on May 5, 2004. The IRS filed a tax lien against Cheek on August 23, 2004, in the amount of $9,530,000. The IRS levied on three parcels of real property owned by Cheek on December 24, 2004. Cheek filed bankruptcy three days later. Subsequent investigation shows that the three parcels are the only property owned by Cheek that have value in excess of the mortgages against him. Cheek bought the Adams parcel in 2003; he bought the Baker parcel in June of 2004; and he inherited the Charlie parcel from his mother, who died in November 2004. Each of the parcels is worth $400,000 more than the mortgages. Who is entitled to that value? I.R.C. §6323(a); United States v. McDermott.

38.2.   Two years ago, Sally Deng opened a pretzel shop in a local mall, which she operates as a sole proprietorship. The business got off to a slow start; only in the past few months have revenues been sufficient to pay the bills. Even though Sally has been taking no salary from the business, she estimates that it lost $150,000 the first year and about $50,000 the second. She hopes that the flow of cash will reverse in the coming year and she will finally be able to get something for her efforts. In the meantime, Sally has been supporting both herself and her business with money from her divorce settlement and loans from friends and relatives. For the past three quarters, Sally has been filing payroll tax returns, but not sending the money. "I simply didn't have it," she says. She owes a total of $149,230. She received one notice of assessment about three months ago and another just a few days ago, but as yet has not received notice of the filing of a tax lien. Yesterday, there was a message on her answering machine from a Mr. Dobbins at the local office of the IRS. Sally has not yet returned the call. Sally (who is very well organized) has written the following list of questions for you:

a.   Does the IRS have a lien against her business? Her home (which is exempt from execution under state law)? Her two myna birds, which have a value of approximately $10,000? I.R.C. §§6321, 6322.

b.   What can the IRS do? What is it likely to do?

c.   Sally wants to sell one of the birds to her friend George for $5,000 to raise money to keep the business going. If George pays her the $5,000 and she gives him possession of the bird, the IRS can't take it back, can it? Does it matter whether George knows about the unpaid payroll taxes? I.R.C. §§6323(a) and (h)(6).

d.   Sally's mother, June, lent Sally $25,000 to make the payroll and pay some key suppliers two weeks ago. Sally told June that the other myna bird would serve as collateral for the loan. Sally wants to know how to arrange that and whether, once it is done, the IRS will be able to undo it. UCC §§1-204, 9-203(a), (b), 9-310(a), 9-317(a), 9-313(a); I.R.C. §§6323(a) and (h)(1).

38.3.   Sally, from Problem 38.2, lives in Wyoming County, New York, and her business is in neighboring Niagara County, New York. The only real estate she owns is her home in Wyoming County.

a.   Where should the IRS file its Notice of Tax Lien against Sally?

b.   Assume that instead of running her business as a sole proprietorship, Sally had incorporated it as "Sally Deng, Inc." The corporation owned the pretzel shop in Niagara County and also a second one in Erie, Pennsylvania, but owned no real property at either location. Sally ran the business from her office in the back of the Niagara County store. Under these circumstances, where should the IRS file its Notice of Tax Lien? I.R.C. §6323(f); New York Lien Law §240 (reproduced above in this assignment). You may assume for purposes of this problem that Pennsylvania has a statute identical in all relevant respects.

38.4.   Dan's only asset is a lunch wagon worth about $90,000. Dan grants a security interest in the wagon to Firstbank to secure a loan in the amount of $50,000, and Firstbank perfects. The IRS files a $45,000 tax lien against Dan. Dan sells the wagon to Betina, a buyer who does not check the records and does not have actual knowledge of either encumbrance. Neither secured party discovers the transfer or files against Betina. Eighteen months later, Betina files under Chapter 7 and you are appointed trustee. What do you do? UCC §9-507; I.R.C. §6323(a); Bankr. Code §544(a); United States v. LMS Holding Co., 50 F.3d 1526 (10th Cir. 1995).

Assignment 39: Competitions Involving Federal Tax Liens: Advanced Problems

In this assignment, we continue our examination of competitions involving federal tax liens. We focus on I.R.C. §6323(b), which contains a number of exceptions to the general rule of first in time, first in right. These are all exceptions that cut against the government; they apply to situations where the government has filed its tax lien first, and yet the Federal Tax Lien Act (FTLA) grants priority to a competitor whose interest arises later.

Nearly all of these exceptions seem to flow from a single motivation: the protection of commerce. (Well, okay, there is a bit of evidence that they are the direct result of lobbying by the interests involved.) The drafters seem to have assumed that debtors will continue to run their business and manage their financial affairs without disclosing the tax lien to the people with whom they deal. The drafters certainly did nothing to prevent that. Often, those continued operations and dealings help the debtor pay the outstanding taxes, and so are in the government's interest.

Although the Notice of Tax Lien is on the public record, many of the third parties who deal with these debtors will not actually know of the tax lien. To realize the extent of third-party ignorance, just consider how often you have dealt with people without first checking the public record to determine whether they had Notices of Tax Liens filed against them. One effect is that the government profits from the "errors" of those who do business without keeping an eye on the public record.

A. The Strange Metaphysics of the Internal Revenue Code

The provisions of the Federal Tax Lien Act may at the same time seem both strange and familiar. What is strange is the language and some of the concepts employed. Terms such as "security interest" and "purchaser" are assigned meanings slightly askew from those assigned in Article 9. The familiar concepts of "attachment" and "perfection" — or at least those words — are nowhere to be seen. Despite the differences in language and conceptualization, the Federal Tax Lien Act creates a world with familiar characters: the buyer in the ordinary course of business, the accounts and inventory financier, the construction lender, the mechanic's lien holder, and the holder of a property tax lien. There is a remarkable similarity in the level of clout these characters exercised in the other competitions we have studied and the level they exercise here against a federal tax lien.

This is probably no accident. As the 500-pound gorilla in the debtor-creditor game, the U.S. government insisted on describing the rules of that game in language of its own choosing and in a statutory scheme it has full power to amend. But that cannot change the fact that the menagerie of security interests, statutory liens, and judicial liens with which federal tax liens must compete exists and competes among themselves independent of the Federal Tax Lien Act. The United States can choose to insert its lien with any priority it likes, but it is beyond the federal government's power to alter the existing priorities among the other players or to make third parties do business without protection against unacceptable risks. If the Federal Tax Lien Act failed to recognize the existing hierarchy it would generate circular priorities and tangle up the system. Instead, the Federal Tax Lien Act reflects the system of perfection and priority that existed before the Act was adopted in 1966 and specifies the tax lien's priority in it.

While this preexisting system of perfection and priority based on the principle of "first in time, first in right" is in most respects consistent and coherent, it is not entirely so. As earlier assignments have indicated, the rules governing this system are made by different bodies and typically regulate competitions one by one. That is, they do not tell us the priority of *A* in relation to other liens. Instead, one rule tells us that *A* has priority over *B* and another, perhaps written and enacted by different bodies at different times, may tell us that *B* has priority over *C*. It is not safe to assume from these two rules that *A* will have priority over *C*: The rules may simply be inconsistent. The precision required of a lawyer called on to give advice, who virtually always is dealing in the particular, necessitates considering these competitions one at a time.

The rules governing priority between a federal tax lien and an ordinary Article 9 security interest provide an excellent example. These rules can be derived from I.R.C. §§6323(a), (d), and (h). Generally, the federal tax lien has priority if the IRS files a Notice of Tax Lien before the security interest comes into existence; otherwise, the security interest has priority over the federal tax lien. (In limited circumstances, the federal tax lien yields to a security interest that comes into existence before the 46th day after the IRS files the notice. More will follow on this point.)

I.R.C. §6323(h)(1) provides that a security interest comes into existence when it is protected by local law against a subsequent judgment lien, but it only comes into existence to the extent that the secured creditor has parted with money or money's worth. The first part of this test is a reference to UCC §§9-317(a) and 9-323(b), the sections that govern priority between a security interest and a judgment lien. In essence, a security interest is protected against a subsequent judgment lien under UCC §§9-317(a) when it is perfected or when the secured party has filed a financing statement and complied with the security agreement requirement of UCC §9-203(b)(3).

The second part of the I.R.C. §6323(h)(1) test as to when a security interest comes into existence differs from the UCC test in an important respect. The value requirement of UCC §9-203(b)(1) is met when the secured creditor parts with *anything*. Thus, a security interest can be perfected under Article 9 before the secured creditor has made the loan. The second part of the I.R.C. §6323(h)(1) test requires more: The security interest "exists" under that section only to the extent that the secured creditor has made the loan.

With such different metaphysics at work, one might assume that these two bodies of law were headed for inconsistent results — that, for example, a FTLA-designed security interest would be less powerful in competition with a tax lien than a UCC-designed security interest would be in competition with a judgment lien. In fact, as you will see in the next section, they reach remarkably similar results. We are unable to discern the purpose for which the drafters of the Federal Tax Lien Act redefined and reconceptualized the Article 9 security interest. Maybe it was a slow day in the drafting department.

B.   Protection of Those Who Lend After the Tax Lien Is Filed

1.   *The General Provision Regarding Future Advances, I.R.C. §6323(d)*

The virtual insignificance of the Federal Tax Lien Act redefinition and reconceptualization of the Article 9 security interest is illustrated in the rule protecting future advances made by secured creditors against federal tax liens. Assume that Firstbank takes a security interest in Debtor's Widgematic, files a financing statement, but makes no advance. At this point in time, Article 9 characterizes Firstbank's security interest very differently than does the Federal Tax Lien Act. Under Article 9, Firstbank's security interest may be both attached and perfected (if Firstbank has given "consideration sufficient to support a simple contract"). Under the Federal Tax Lien Act, Firstbank has no security interest at all. Article 9 encourages us to think of this security interest as having priority over one who might become a lien creditor; the Federal Tax Lien Act encourages us to think of this security interest as completely ineffective against a federal tax lien that might be filed. But, in reality, what either law says about this unfunded security interest makes no difference; a security interest can't compete with anyone until it is funded. As soon as this security interest is funded, the metaphysical differences between Article 9 and the Federal Tax Lien Act disappear.

To continue with the illustration, assume that the IRS files a Notice of Tax Lien and 30 days later Firstbank, unaware of the Notice, makes a $1,000 advance. Now the FTLA-defined security interest "exists." Despite the security interest's late arrival on the scene, I.R.C. §6323(d) gives it priority over the tax lien. It does so only to the extent that the security interest would be "protected under local law against a judgment lien arising, as of the time of tax lien filing, out of an unsecured obligation." Under these circumstances that would be to the full extent of the $1,000, UCC §9-323(b) would fully protect this security interest against a lien creditor who levied at the time of the filing of the tax lien. (The fact that UCC §9-323(b)'s 45-day protection is coextensive with that provided the holder of a security interest under §6323(d) is no coincidence. The drafters of the UCC designed §9-323(b) specifically to give secured creditors the full advantage available against tax liens under I.R.C. §6323(d). See Comment 4 to UCC §9-323.) Thus, once the FTLA-defined security interest is funded by a secured party who is unaware of the lien, it performs just as well against the tax lien as the UCC-defined security interest performed against the lien creditor. The difference in how this security interest was conceptualized under the UCC and the FTLA ends up making no difference in outcome.

2. Commercial Transactions Financing Agreements

I.R.C. §6323(c) offers somewhat incomplete protection to lenders secured by Article 9 floating liens against the sudden effects of tax lien filings. The protection I.R.C. §6323(c) offers, like the protection I.R.C. §6323(d) offers with regard to future advances, extends only to transactions occurring within 45 days after the tax lien filing. The 45-day period is, in essence, an opportunity for the lender to learn of the tax lien filing and react to it.

Much of the protection afforded secured creditors under I.R.C. §6323(c) would be available under I.R.C. §6323(d) anyway. Both give advances made by the lender within 45 days after the filing of the tax lien priority over the tax lien. But I.R.C. §6323(c) is both broader and narrower than I.R.C. §6323(d). The I.R.C. §6323(c) protection is narrower than I.R.C. §6323(d) in that the former applies only with respect to advances to be secured by "commercial financing security": accounts, inventory, chattel paper, and mortgage paper. I.R.C. §§6323(c)(2)(A) and (C). Subsection (d), by contrast, contains no limit as to the type of collateral involved.

Subsection (d) is narrower than (c) in that (d) protects only future advances; it does not protect the secured creditor's interest in after-acquired collateral. The subsection (c) protection of commercial transactions financing extends to collateral acquired by the debtor during the 45 days after the tax lien filing—apparently even to collateral the debtor acquires after the secured creditor learns of the tax lien filing. (Note the absence of an "actual notice or knowledge" limitation in I.R.C. §6323(c)(2)(B).) The need for protection of a security interest right in after-acquired property results from the Federal Tax Lien Act view that security interests exist only when "the property is in existence," I.R.C. §6323(h)(1), by which the drafters mean that the debtor has acquired it. This view, which you also saw reflected in *McDermott* in the previous assignment, is frequently referred to as the *choateness doctrine*.

How will the commercial financing lender learn of the tax lien in time to react? The Fifth Circuit addressed the issue in Texas Oil & Gas Corp. v. United States, 466 F.2d 1040 (5th Cir. 1972):

> Of course we realize that [§6323(c)] does not afford the protection that commercial lenders who deal with after-acquired property might prefer. As the law appears to stand, the commercial lender must check the applicable records every 45 days

or else seriously jeopardize his security under the varying degrees of rigor promulgated by the choateness doctrine. Even that 45-day grace period is probably of minimal efficacy. Commercial lenders might often be lulled into a false sense of security with debtors who are doing badly, for it might appear to the lender that such a debtor is unlikely to have any income to tax. Yet it is precisely in these circumstances that back taxes are likely to accrue. In addition, the lender would most likely not have the entire 45-day period in which to act unless he were lucky enough to discover the tax lien filing almost immediately after it was filed. Finally, there is often not a great deal that the lender can do to protect his advances even after he discovers the tax lien in time. Of course, he has little control over the actual receipt of after-acquired property by the taxpayer-debtor, which is usually subject to contracts and contingencies entirely within the authority of the taxpayer-debtor, and various third-parties. The lender can attempt to substitute other existing collateral for his interest in after-acquired property if the taxpayer-debtor has any substitutable assets and if there is sufficient time. But the whole genesis and historicity of section 6323(c) appears to have been to give only a slight handicap (45 days) to a private lien holder.

In In re Spearing Tool and Manufacturing Co., 412 F.3d 653 (6th Cir. 2005), a lender conducted searches at 45-day intervals, always searching in the correct name of the debtor. Those searches failed to discover the federal tax lien because the government filed against the debtor in a different name. The court nevertheless held the government's filing effective. (You have probably heard the expression "close enough for government work.") The holding in *Spearing Tool* leaves secured parties making future advances in a difficult situation. Even if they perform a complex, multiname search every 45 days, they still have no assurance they will not accidentally feed the government's lien.

3.   Real Property Construction or Improvement Financing

I.R.C. §6323(c) protects construction lenders against a tax lien filed during construction. Subsection (c) requires that the construction lender have entered into a contract to finance the construction prior to the filing of the tax lien. The protection afforded against the tax lien extends only to the real property improved.

The protection is not limited to advances made within 45 days of the filing of the tax lien. The only condition of protection is that the construction lender's priority must be protected under local law against a judgment lien arising as of the time of tax lien filing, out of an unsecured obligation. I.R.C. §6323(c)(1)(B). Protection extends to advances made more than 45 days after the filing of the tax lien and to those made after the construction lender knows of the tax lien. The rationale is that construction lenders cannot, as a practical matter, withdraw from a partially completed project. If they do, construction stops. The army of subcontractors, laborers, and suppliers painstakingly assembled by the contractor disperses, the property begins to deteriorate, legal claims are made that deter others from resuming construction, and the project gets a bad reputation that may carry through to its sale or leasing. Presumably, everyone with an interest in the construction project, including the IRS, will be better off if the construction lender continues to fund construction. While an argument like this can be made on behalf of one who makes advances to any business debtor after the filing of the tax lien, in the context of construction lending, the factual basis for the argument seems to be particularly widely accepted.

4. Obligatory Disbursement Agreements

I.R.C. §6323(c)(4) protects lenders who have agreed before the tax lien is filed to make disbursements that the lenders then make after the lien is filed. This is not, however, a general protection of such disbursements analogous to Article 9's protection of advances made "pursuant to commitment." As the tax regulations explain:

> (b) *Obligatory disbursement agreement.* For purposes of this section the term "obligatory disbursement agreement" means a written agreement, entered into by a person in the course of his trade or business, to make disbursements. An agreement is treated as an obligatory disbursement agreement only with respect to disbursements which are required to be made by reason of the intervention of the rights of a person other than the taxpayer. The obligation to pay must be conditioned upon an event beyond the control of the obligor. For example, the provisions of this section are applicable where an issuing bank obligates itself to honor drafts or other demands for payment on a letter of credit and a bank, in good faith, relies upon that letter of credit in making advances. The provisions of this section are also applicable, for example, where a bonding company obligates itself to make payments to indemnify against loss or liability and, under the terms of the bond, makes a payment with respect to a loss.

26 C.F.R. 301.6323(c)-3. The vast majority of advances made pursuant to commitment are not pursuant to obligatory disbursement agreements. It is nearly always the case that the loan commitment provides that when a tax lien is filed, the creditor is excused from making the promised advances. The unusual security agreements that do qualify as obligatory disbursement agreements are outside the scope of this assignment.

5. Statutory Liens

Statutory liens, you will recall, are liens that arise against specific property by operation of a statute. Statutes typically provide such liens for activities of a nature that they at least arguably tend to improve the value of the property against which the lien is granted.

I.R.C. §6323(b) grants some statutory liens priority over the federal tax lien, even when those statutory liens arise after the federal tax lien is filed. Among those granted priority are artisans' liens in favor of those who make repairs or improvements to personal property and retain possession of the property as security for their claims ((b)(5)), real property tax and special assessment liens ((b)(6)), mechanics' liens for improvements made to real property (although the Act limits them sharply to liens against the debtor's personal residence and to contracts not in excess of $1,000, (b)(7)), and attorneys' liens for fees against a judgment or settlement amount obtained by the attorney on behalf of a client ((b)(8)). Numerous other kinds of statutory liens are not recognized in I.R.C. §6323(b) and hence are subordinate to federal tax liens filed before they arise.

6. Purchase-Money Security Interests

Notice that there is no provision in I.R.C. §6323(b) protecting purchase-money security interests against earlier-filed tax liens. This was undoubtedly a mistake in drafting. The courts quickly read such a provision into I.R.C. §6323(b) and the IRS acquiesced. In the case that follows, the court explores the limits of the resulting protection.

The following case applied an earlier definition of "purchase-money security interest," but the key words of the definition remain the same.

First Interstate Bank of Utah, N.A. v. Internal Revenue Service

930 F.2d 1521 (10th Cir. 1991)

ALDISERT, CIRCUIT JUDGE.

This appeal requires us to interpret [UCC §§9-103(a) and (b)], which provides that:

> A security interest is a purchase money security interest to the extent that it is . . . taken by a person who by making advances or incurring an obligation gives value to enable the debtor to acquire rights in or the use of collateral if such value is in fact so used.

First Interstate Bank of Utah, N.A., the appellant, argues that it obtained a purchase money security interest in certain accounts receivable when it advanced funds to Olympus Glass Company enabling the debtor to complete performance of specified obligations. This question of statutory construction is a legal issue of first impression before this court. At issue here is whether the statute affords purchase money priority to First Interstate to preempt a tax lien previously asserted by the federal Government.

I

At a time when the debtor's assets were subject to a federal tax lien, First Interstate and Olympus Glass entered into a financing arrangement whereby the bank agreed to fund Olympus' performance of six glazing contracts. The bank paid the material and labor cost incurred by Olympus. After Olympus went into bankruptcy the question arose as to whether the tax lien was to be afforded the normal consequences of a lien filed prior in time to the extension of credit. While recognizing the existence of orthodox rules of lien priority, First Interstate relies upon a competing legal precept that a purchase money security interest has priority over a previously filed tax lien.

The general proposition is that a security interest based on the extension of purchase money defeats a previously filed federal tax lien. Slodov v. United States, 436 U.S. 238, 56 L. Ed. 2d 251, 98 S. Ct. 1778 (1978) ("The [Internal Revenue] Code and established decisional principles subordinate the tax lien, to certain perfected security interests in . . . collateral which is subject to a purchase-money mortgage regardless of whether the agreement was entered into before or after the filing of the tax lien."). Although a statement of this priority is not found in the express language of the Code, "the purchase-money mortgage priority is based upon recognition that the mortgagee's interest merely reflects his contribution of property to the taxpayer's estate and therefore does not prejudice creditors who are prior in time." Id. at 258 n.23.

The parties before us urge diametrically opposed interpretations of the UCC provision defining a purchase money security interest. First Interstate argues that the phrase, "a person who by making advances . . . to enable the debtor to acquire rights in or the use of collateral" brings it within the statutory definition when it extended money secured by accounts receivable. The Internal Revenue Service (IRS) contends that the money was extended to perform pre-existing contracts of the debtor and did not represent funds advanced to acquire property or rights in property.

II

Olympus is a glazing contractor and wholesale supplier of glass. On January 23, 1984, First Interstate extended to Olympus a $500,000 line of credit. Pursuant to this line of credit, Olympus drew down the entire amount. The line was secured by an Accounts Receivable and Inventory Security and Loan Agreement by which Olympus conveyed to First Interstate a security interest in all of Olympus' accounts (as defined in the agreement) "now existing or hereafter existing" and "all the proceeds of . . . the foregoing." The bank filed the UCC-1 financing statement with the Utah Secretary of State, thereby perfecting its security interest in the debtor's accounts and proceeds. On August 1, 1985, the IRS filed a Notice of Federal Tax Lien against the debtor in the amount of $57,147.94 for unpaid taxes withheld from the wages of the debtor's employees.

Several months later, First Interstate agreed to extend to the debtor a secured line of credit in the amount of $200,000, known as "[a] revolving loan." Pursuant to the agreement, signed on November 27, 1985, the loan was to be "secured by specifically assigned contracts." Borrowing was limited to the "amounts necessary for payment of direct labor expense and materials" and in no event was to "exceed 75% of the face value of the assigned contract." These advances were to be based on invoices for materials and appropriate records of labor expended on the contract, "with such invoices and records subject to Bank approval prior to disbursal of each advance." First Interstate signed a promissory note for the loan.

First Interstate did not file a UCC-1 financing statement in conjunction with the November Security Agreement; instead it relied on the financing statement accompanying the previous loan that it had filed on January 23, 1984, some twenty months earlier. The prior financing statement covered "all present and future accounts" of the debtor. Olympus used no source of financing other than the advances from First Interstate to perform the contracts.

On July 2, 1986, Olympus filed a voluntary Chapter 11 petition.

III

As was the task of the bankruptcy and district courts, our responsibility is to construe the security interest provision of [UCC §§9-103(a) and (b)]. Under the UCC and the Utah legislature's adoption of its key provisions, this purchase money security interest is generally manifested when taken or retained by the seller of collateral to secure all or part of its price. But such a security interest also may be created when a person gives value to enable a debtor to acquire rights in, or the use of collateral; this is the species of security interest asserted by First National Bank in these proceedings. New value may be given either in the form of advances or the incurring of an obligation. Such value must be used for this purpose in order to form the basis of this type of priority.

By definition, purchase money security interests are available to lenders as well as sellers. A lender may acquire it in collateral to be purchased with a loan provided the proceeds are in fact so used. This special category of security interest is entitled to special priority because it is considered an exception to the first-to-file rule of priority. Accordingly, such an interest takes priority over any pre-existing lien on the theory that because the lender has augmented the capital assets of the borrower, previous creditors are not prejudiced.

It is undisputed that First Interstate agreed to, and did, lend money to the debtor to fund the performance of specific, identified contracts. It is also undisputed that the UCC priority in question is given not only to lenders who permit a borrower to "acquire" collateral, but is conferred whenever the lender enables the borrower to "acquire rights in collateral." The debtor here already had acquired the collateral—the executory contracts—and thus the right to perform the contracts, and accordingly, the federal tax lien attached to these executory contracts. First Interstate anchors its claim on the basis that it advanced the funds that enabled the debtor to "acquire rights in [this] collateral" by converting contingent rights into matured rights.

IV

We return then to our task of statutory construction. Professor Grant Gilmore, a primary drafter of the UCC, has written that the purchase money security interest provision was narrowly constructed and that such an interest in intangibles would be the extraordinary situation. In describing what could or could not qualify under the statute, he stated:

> Farm products which are grown or raised by the debtor (such as crops or the increase of a herd of livestock) cannot become the subject matter of a purchase money security

interest, since the secured party's loan does not go directly into their purchase price. *Nor could such intangibles as accounts, contract rights,* chattel paper, or instruments normally be acquired by the debtor in a purchase money transaction.

Gilmore, The Purchase Money Priority, 76 Harv. L. Rev. 1333, 1385 (1963) (emphasis added).

A

It is clear that the drafters of the purchase money security interest provision in the UCC used precise and narrow language. First, the lender must have given "value" by making advances or incurring an obligation. Second, the value must have been "to enable the debtor to acquire rights in or the use of collateral." Third, such value must have been "in fact so used." [Comment 3 to UCC §9-103] tells us that this requirement excludes "any security interest taken as security for or in satisfaction of a pre-existing claim or antecedent debt."

Given this narrow construction, we must determine whether the interest in the case before us fits within these three requirements.

B

Clearly, the lender, First Interstate, gave value. The problem is with the second prong that requires that the value must have been given "to enable the debtor to acquire rights in or the use of collateral." Without surmounting this second requirement we cannot reach the third. We are assisted in our task by previous court decisions that have discussed whether contract rights qualify as "collateral" under this UCC provision.

In Northwestern Natl. Bank Southwest v. Lectro Systems, Inc., 262 N.W.2d 678 (Minn. 1977), the court faced the question of whether a "contract right" could be "collateral" under the second requirement. In *Lectro Systems*, the lender advanced money to subcontractors to enable them to complete their contract and took back a security interest in their contract right to payment. The lender claimed priority as a purchase money lender over a bank which had a prior perfected security interest in the contract right.

In rejecting the lender's claim, the court held that the loaned funds must be intended, and actually used, for the purchase of an identifiable asset and that "performance of a contract" is not such an asset.

C

At the risk of being guilty of *ad terrorem* discourse, we believe that First Interstate's argument proves too much. If accepted, it would make virtually any loan incurred in the course of fulfilling pre-existing business obligations a purchase money loan if it enabled the debtor to operate its business and generate a profit. The conceptual underpinning of our commercial purchase money security tradition with its concomitant priority attributes is that the extension of such funds reflects a contribution of property to the borrower's estate; accordingly, this extension does not prejudice creditors who are prior in time.

An important distinction exists between funds extended for asset acquisition and those extended for the ordinary operation of business. A bright-line demarcation must always exist between these two purposes. To accept the lender's contention in this case would be to blur, if not eliminate, that line.

V

Accordingly, we conclude that the right to perform the pre-existing executory contract in this case is not "collateral" or the "rights in collateral" within the requirements of the UCC

The court says that "[a]n important distinction exists between funds extended for asset acquisition and those extended for the ordinary operation of business." We don't find this distinction as important as the court does. Lending the debtor money to make its payroll enables the debtors to acquire an asset — it is just not quite as tangible an asset. The court continues that "[t]he conceptual underpinning of our commercial purchase money security tradition with its concomitant priority attributes is that the extension of such funds reflects a contribution of property to the borrower's estate; accordingly, this extension does not prejudice creditors who are prior in time." But doesn't providing money for "ordinary operation" do the same? For example, if a lender advances funds that a manufacturer uses to pay employees to turn raw materials into finished inventory, the advances may contribute value to the estate without prejudicing prior creditors. Unless the new money is *wasted* in operations, it should increase the value of the estate just as surely as money used to buy raw material. Funds extended for operations can disappear when operations are unprofitable. But so can funds extended for asset acquisition. For example, a retail store may buy inventory that does not appeal to its customers and find that it is ultimately of little or no value.

The decline does not detract from the argument in favor of purchase-money priority because the value of the priority shrinks with the value of the collateral. But neither does it detract from the argument in favor of purchase-money priority for contributions to "ordinary operations." If the debtor accepted First Interstate's loan proceeds, but did not manage to complete the contracts and thereby convert them to accounts, the value of First Interstate's purchase-money priority would shrink. If the debtor managed to complete the contracts using First Interstate's money, First Interstate contributed to the estate and, it seems to us, ought to have a purchase-money priority.

The distinction between lending to purchase the collateral and lending to keep the business going is made under Article 9 as well. Purchase-money protection under UCC §9-324(e) is afforded to the lender who assists with the purchase of assets; there is no corresponding protection of the lender who assists by financing continuing operations. We confess to much discomfort with the distinction.

Bankruptcy law resolves the same issue differently. If Olympus were in Chapter 11 and Olympus and First Interstate came to the court, hats in hands, to ask for permission to do specifically the deal they did in this case, the Bankruptcy Court would almost certainly approve the loan under Bankruptcy Code §364(d). The court would probably justify this priority in something like the same words the court used to justify the purchase-money priority in *First Interstate Bank*: "such funds reflect a contribution of property to the borrower's estate; accordingly, this extension does not prejudice creditors who are prior in time." This greater flexibility is one more advantage that the bankruptcy system can offer the struggling debtor who is in need of an infusion of new capital.

C. Nonadvances

Nonadvances are the interest, attorneys fees, and other expenses that may be incurred by a secured creditor in protecting and recovering its collateral and collecting the amount owing from the debtor. Nonadvances are analogous to future advances. The difference is that future advances result from a decision on the part of the lender; nonadvances just grow of their own accord. Nonadvances are a great favorite of both the UCC and the Bankruptcy Code, perhaps because they usually have in them a healthy component of attorneys fees and it is attorneys who design these systems. At least if they are provided for in the security agreement and are reasonable, nonadvances under a security agreement are equal in priority to the first advance. That enables these late-created charges to prevail over the intervening interests of secured creditors, lien creditors, and trustees in bankruptcy.

I.R.C. §6323(e) gives nonadvances equivalent protection against intervening tax liens. To illustrate, assume that on March 1, Firstbank lends $80,000 to Debtor, secured by an interest in Debtor's summer cottage, which is worth $100,000. The mortgage provides that in the event of default, Debtor will pay a higher "default rate" of interest, will pay Firstbank's reasonable attorneys fees incurred as a result of the default, will pay all expenses of insuring and preserving the property, and will pay any property tax liens or assessments levied against the property. On April 1, the IRS files a tax lien against Debtor for payroll taxes in the amount of $20,000. Having received no payments on the loan, Firstbank commences foreclosure against Debtor on May 1. On June 1, the city levies a $5,000 assessment against the property for emergency sewer repairs. Under local law, the assessment has priority over Firstbank's mortgage, so Firstbank pays the assessment to maintain its first position. On December 1, Firstbank completes the foreclosure and sells the property for $100,000. Firstbank pays its attorney $6,000 for the foreclosure and pays expenses of $3,000 for insurance, maintenance of the property, and other expenses of the legal proceeding and sale. As it is entitled to do under its contract with Debtor, Firstbank adds this $14,000 of expenditures to the amount of its mortgage, which has also increased by $2,000 as a result of accruing interest. The amount outstanding under the mortgage is now $96,000. Even though this $16,000 increase in Firstbank's mortgage occurred after the filing of the tax lien, it has priority over the tax lien. Firstbank gets $96,000 of the proceeds of the sale; the IRS gets only $4,000. To be a nonadvance is good.

Problem Set 39

39.1. In late July, Dawgs and More Dawgs (DAMD) applied to Bank One for a loan against its inventory of lawn dogs. Without committing to make the loan, on August 1, Bank One filed a financing statement against DAMD showing the lawn dogs as collateral. Also, in late July, DAMD applied for a similar loan from Bank Two. On August 5, Bank Two approved the loan and filed a financing statement against DAMD showing the lawn dogs as collateral. Bank Two and DAMD signed a security agreement on August 5 and Bank Two advanced funds to Debtor. The IRS filed a Notice of Tax Lien against DAMD on August 7 in the county records, the place specified by state law for the filing of tax liens. On August 10, Bank One received the report of their UCC search showing their financing statement to be in first position. They approved the loan to DAMD. Bank One and DAMD signed a security agreement, and Bank One advanced funds against the lawn dogs. As soon as the check from Bank One cleared, the owner of DAMD wired the Bank One loan proceeds to Freeport in the Bahamas, where they paused only long enough to join the proceeds from the Bank Two loan, and then continued on to places unknown. What are the relative priorities among Bank One, Bank Two, and the IRS in the lawn dogs? I.R.C. §§6321, 6322, 6323(a), (d), (h)(1); UCC §§9-317(a) and 9-323(b), 9-322(a). We suggest you solve the problem by breaking it into three parts: (1) priority between Bank One and the IRS, (2) priority between Bank Two and the IRS, and (3) priority between Bank One and Bank Two.

39.2. Tony Redding is the owner and operator of The Perfect Pet, a two-store chain that sells everything from kitty cats to boa constrictors. A variety of "non-recurring business setbacks" (as Tony calls them) have caused him to fall behind in his payroll tax deposits. Although he has been working with the IRS to make up the deficit, it has been going pretty slowly. The agent told him yesterday that the IRS will be filing a tax lien against Redding within a few days. Redding still believes in the business and wants to keep operating. "I've put my life into this business, and I'm going to fight it if there's any way I can." Redding is concerned about these situations:

a.   Will customers who buy pets from the store's inventory after the Notice is filed take free and clear of the IRS lien? I.R.C. §6323(b)(3).

b.   Tony needs to install a new fish tank that will cost $25,000. The seller of the tank will provide 100 percent financing and Tony will make payments over five years. For a number of reasons, Tony sees no way to get the deal done before the tax lien is filed. The seller will file a UCC-1, but probably won't do a search of the public record. I.R.C. §§6323(a) and (b); *First Interstate Bank*, above.

c.   Tony is worried about his employees. If he pays them with money on which the IRS has a lien, can the IRS take the money back? If the IRS levies on the day before payday, where do the employees stand?

d.   The business is financed with an inventory and accounts receivable loan from Glengary State Bank. Glengary lends 65 percent of the cost of inventory as The Perfect Pet receives it. The security interest contains the usual provisions regarding future advances and after-acquired property. Tony believes Glengary will work with him if the bank can. "They don't have much choice," he says. "I have $1,750,000 outstanding on the loan. In continued operations the collateral is worth that amount, but if this business closes, Glengary won't get $500,000 out of it." Can Glengary work with him without losing its priority over the tax lien? I.R.C. §§6323(c) and (d); *First Interstate Bank*, above.

e.   Can Tony keep going after the tax lien is filed?

39.3.   Your client, Wilmington State Bank (WSB), does a substantial amount of inventory and accounts receivable financing. Its contract with the debtor requires that the debtor notify WSB of any tax lien that arises. Not only do the bank's debtors not give the required notice, most of them actively conceal their failure to pay payroll taxes. WSB was recently burned in a situation where the tax lien was filed and 45 days went by without WSB learning of it. WSB continued to fund the loan and eventually lost nearly all of the remaining collateral to the tax lien. WSB asks what they should be doing to avoid recurrence of the problem in the future. What do you tell them? I.R.C. §6323(f); *Texas Oil & Gas Corp.*, above.

39.4.   Alecia Card (the client you were thinking of referring to a psychiatrist in Assignment 36) is back to see you. You know from reading the newspapers that she is now active in the local chapter of HALT, an antilawyer organization (the acronym stands for "Help Abolish Legal Tyranny"). "I'm not mad at you," she says "but we have to stop what lawyers and courts are doing to this country." Alecia has been researching tax liens and has a couple of questions. She has concluded that if she buys something at retail—a dress, a car, or a piano—she must never leave it in the possession of the seller for even a minute. "If there is a Notice of Tax Lien outstanding against the store, it will have priority over my purchase, *even if I paid for what I bought.*" In fact, Alecia won't let the store clerk wrap her packages after they ring up the sale; she grabs the items and stuffs them in the sack herself. Is Alecia right on the law? UCC §§2-403(2) and (3); I.R.C. §§6323(a), (b)(2), (b)(3), (b)(4), and (h)(6). Is she right to be upset?

39.5.   Alecia has another question. She shows you the following quotes from Davis v. Internal Revenue Service, 705 F. Supp. 446 (C.D. Ill. 1989):

> Under [§6323], as illustrated by its history, it is clear that Congress intended the IRS notice of tax lien to serve as notice to subsequent purchasers wherever possible. The sine qua non of §6323 is notice to subsequent takers of the existence of the IRS lien.

"Hypocrisy!" Alecia exclaims. "If I see a want ad for a used sailboat in the newspaper and want to buy it for the $30,000 the owner is asking, how am I supposed to know whether the owner has a tax lien against him?" Assume that the applicable tax lien filing statute is the same as the New York statute reproduced in Assignment 38 and that sailboats of the type Alecia is buying are covered by a certificate of title act. Explain to Alecia how this transaction is "supposed" to work in a world where there are tax liens. I.R.C. §§6323(a), 6323(b)(3), 6323(b)(4), 6323(f), 6323(h)(6).

Assignment 40: Why Secured Credit?

The idea that a debtor could grant a security interest in property while retaining possession of that property did not come easily to American law. In the earliest cases, such transfers were held to be a fraud on other creditors. For example, see Clow v. Woods, 5 Sergeant & Rawle 275, 9 Am. Dec. 346 (Sup. Ct. Pa. 1819). Even after the basic concept of security was accepted, grants of security interests in after-acquired property continued to be controversial. But with the widespread adoption of the Uniform Commercial Code in the 1960s, both concepts gained virtually full acceptance. The battle temporarily abated while the UCC was lauded as one of the greatest legislative accomplishments in history. If there were opponents of Article 9 during the 1970s, they left no written record.

The controversy reignited in the 1980s with the publication of an article by Professors Jackson and Kronman. Ironically, they were merely attempting to explain in passing what no one in their generation of scholars questioned.

Thomas H. Jackson and Anthony Kronman, Secured Financing and Priorities Among Creditors

88 Yale L.J. 1143, 1147-1148 (1979)

At first blush, it may seem unfair that a debtor should be allowed to make a private contract with one creditor that demotes the claims of other creditors from an initial position of parity to one of subordination. This thought may in turn suggest that debtors should be denied the power to prefer some creditors over others, and that all creditors should instead be required to share equally in the event of their common debtor's insolvency, each receiving a pro rata portion of his claim. The idea that all creditors should be treated equally, regardless of the private arrangements they may have made with their debtor, has played an important role in the evolution of the federal bankruptcy system. Reported case law is replete with references to the bankruptcy "principle" that "equality is equity."

Despite its apparent appeal, however, the principle of equal treatment has never succeeded in supplanting, even in the Bankruptcy Act itself, a basic recognition of the debtor's contractual power to prefer one creditor over another. When a debtor grants a security interest to one of his creditors, he increases the riskiness of other creditors' claims by reducing their expected value in bankruptcy. It is a fair assumption, however, that these other creditors will be aware of this risk and will insist on a premium for lending on an unsecured basis, will demand collateral (or some other form of protection) to secure their own claims, or will search for another borrower whose enterprise is less risky. In general, whatever level of risk he faces, if his transaction with the debtor is a voluntary one, a creditor may be expected to adjust his interest rate accordingly and to take whatever risk-reducing precautions he deems appropriate. Since creditors remain free to select their own debtors and to set the terms on which they will lend, there is no compelling argument based upon considerations of fairness for adopting one legal rule (debtors can rank creditor claims in whatever way they see fit) rather than another (all creditors must share equally in the event of bankruptcy).

Other scholars questioned Jackson and Kronman's explanation for the acceptance of secured credit and put forth their own. The following excerpt describes the early years of debate over what became known as the "puzzle of secured debt."

Robert E. Scott, A Relational Theory of Secured Financing

86 Colum. L. Rev. 901, 904-911 (1986)

A. THE SECURITY PUZZLE RECONSIDERED: THE COMPETING HYPOTHESES

1. The Zero-Sum Hypothesis—The conventional vision of secured credit assumes that security expands debtors' access to credit markets. This conception rests on the premise that security offers financing opportunities to high-risk debtors who would not otherwise qualify for credit. However, the insights of modern finance theory have seriously undermined the conventional wisdom.

Finance theory offers two complementary visions of the capital structure of the firm. The most provocative hypothesis traces its lineage to the Modigliani-Miller Irrelevance Theorem. Modigliani and Miller demonstrated that, under certain carefully specified assumptions, the value of a firm is independent of its capital structure. In essence, the Irrelevance Theorem holds that in perfectly functioning capital markets, absent taxes or bankruptcy costs, the particular mix of debt or equity held by a firm has no effect on the firm's value. Recently, legal scholars have begun to apply the insights of the Irrelevance Theorem to the debate over the function of secured debt. Alan Schwartz has shown that with homogeneous, risk-neutral creditors possessed of perfect information, a system of security operates as a zero sum game. Under these conditions, the benefits to one creditor by taking security are exactly offset by the increased cost imposed on an unsecured creditor whose claim to the debtor's asset pool has been correspondingly diminished. The "zero sum hypothesis" implies that the existing system of secured credit may operate as a net loss to debtors. Security interests are costly to create and administer. Moreover, if creditors are generally informed about credit risks, the reduction in interest charges that secured creditors are able to offer the debtor will be offset by more or less equivalent increases in interest charges by unsecured creditors. Thus, the debtor's total credit bill may well be larger under a system which permits security interests than in a world in which security is banned.

The zero-sum hypothesis searches for an explanation of secured financing through the systematic relaxation of its carefully articulated assumptions. Theorists have attempted explanations based on differing risk preferences of creditors or imperfections in the credit markets themselves. Thus, for example, in the real world of costly information, security may function as a means of signaling other creditors of the debtor's creditworthiness or, in the alternative, as a means of screening for eligible debtors. These explanations, however, are incomplete. They do not show convincingly why security is a preferable means of overcoming such informational barriers as compared to alternatives such as financial audits, the development of commercial reputation, or long term financial relationships.

Underlining the inadequacy of signaling or screening explanations is the possibility that information asymmetries explain the persistent use of secured credit. Assume that poorly informed creditors do not respond to the increased risk when others take security. In this case, security may persist not because of its socially beneficial effects, but because it permits informed creditors to capture wealth at the expense of other, uninformed creditors. Thus, firms may issue secured debt to protect themselves against informed creditors who expect it and to exploit uninformed creditors who neither expect it nor react to it. But such distributional explanations are inconsistent with the observed characteristics of credit markets. Specifically, distributional explanations predict that "firms will issue as much secured debt as possible; yet firms often borrow without security . . . many unsecured creditors appear well informed." As viewed through the lens of the zero sum hypothesis, therefore, the puzzle of security remains unresolved.

2. The Costly Contracting Hypothesis — The "costly contracting hypothesis" asserts that contractual mechanisms that control inevitable debtor-creditor conflicts can, in fact, increase the value of the firm.

Several legal theorists working in this tradition have attempted to explain secured credit as a means of controlling the risk of "asset substitutions." Thus, for example, after the credit contract is negotiated, a debtor may gamble with the creditor's money by substituting riskier business projects for the more conservative investments originally planned. Presumably, some creditors are better able to monitor the debtor for such misbehavior than are others. Jackson and Kronman have used a monitoring advantage theory to suggest that poorer monitors take security to focus their efforts at controlling asset substitutions, while the better monitors are able to lend unsecured and exploit their comparative monitoring advantage.

The Jackson and Kronman theory is an important and original contribution. However, the argument yields the counterintuitive conclusion that those creditors who are typically unsecured, such as trade creditors and employees, are better at monitoring against debtor misbehavior than are those typical secured parties such as banks and financial institutions. Moreover, the Jackson-Kronman model fails to account for the signaling effects of security. If some creditors take security to reduce the risks of misbehavior, it is because they regard monitoring the collateral as a good proxy for continued supervision of the entire enterprise. To the extent that a debtor's efforts to increase business risks—or otherwise to cheat on the agreement—require it to convert assets, a secured creditor who merely guards against substitution of its collateral has a monitoring advantage over the unsecured creditor who presumably must continue to police the debtor's activities more expansively. But if the continued viability of the collateral provides a signal to contract law or must explain why secured transactions differ from other transactions that the law respects.

———————

The debate over the appropriate division of assets between secured and unsecured creditors was an abstract affair, pitting archtypical "secured creditors" against archetypal "unsecured creditors." But, as virtually every discussion in this book has demonstrated, neither of those groups is monolithic. The category of "unsecured creditor" includes big banks that decided to make unsecured loans, trade creditors who made credit decisions that were part and parcel of their sales decisions, and utility companies that extended service at prices fixed without regard to creditworthiness, to mention but a few. They differ widely in their opportunity and ability to compete for priority. Some of those who end up with unsecured claims against a failing debtor never had the opportunity to refuse to extend credit. Tort victims cannot ask for financial references before they are injured. Environmental claimants, both governmental and civil, must advance funds to clean up toxic waste regardless of the balance sheet of the polluting company. The government cannot make an economically informed decision to withhold services from businesses who are not good credit risks.

Beginning in the mid-1980s, a number of commentators reached the conclusion that creditors who had no opportunity to bargain with the debtor for their status — including most kinds of tort creditors — should have priority over secured creditors. The following excerpt explains the economic rationale.

Lynn M. LoPucki, The Unsecured Creditor's Bargain

80 Va. L. Rev. 1887, 1896-1899, 1907-1914 (1994)

To reach the conclusion that involuntary creditors, including most kinds of tort creditors, should have priority over secured creditors on efficiency grounds we need only assume that the economy operates more efficiently when involuntary creditors are paid than when they are not. To understand why this is so, assume that a debtor has two creditors, one involuntary and one secured, and that the debtor's wealth is sufficient to pay either, but not both of them. If we view the competition between these two creditors ex post, that is, after both have extended credit, it appears not to matter which is paid. The aggregate loss to the economy is the same.

But if we view the competition ex ante, from the perspective of the two creditors before they extend credit, the superiority of the rule granting priority to involuntary creditors becomes apparent. In a world where involuntary creditors have priority, the secured creditor who can anticipate the priority contest can react to it by declining to extend credit beyond the debtor's ability to pay. On the facts assumed in the preceding paragraph, the secured creditor would not extend any credit, the involuntary creditor would be paid, and the aggregate loss to the economy would be zero.

In a world where secured creditors have priority, both these creditors would extend credit. The involuntary creditor would extend it because the involuntary creditor has no choice. The secured creditor would extend credit for the simple reason that it would be repaid. Because the debtor's wealth was assumed sufficient to pay only one creditor, the involuntary creditor would not be paid. The involuntary creditor's loss would be an aggregate loss to the economy.

In a very thoughtful, well-written article, Professor Shupack makes a variant of this argument. He notes that in a world where tort creditors had priority over secured creditors, secured creditors would condition their loans on the debtor's payment of a premium sufficient to compensate the secured creditors for their additional risk. He concludes, as I have, that the secured creditor suffers no loss.

He asserts, however, that the tort creditors will not necessarily be better off in the world where they have priority. His argument is one that others have made less formally, to justify the preferred status of secured creditors. It is that in the world where secured debt comes first and tort creditors take their leavings, entrepreneurs can borrow more money, there is more economic activity, the society is wealthier, and perhaps even the tort creditors themselves are better off.

To understand why neither tort creditors, nor the economy as a whole, are better off under current law than they would be in a tort-first regime, consider the following proof:

W = The wealth created by economic activity that will occur in a world where tort debt comes first

A = The added wealth created by activity that would not occur in a world where tort debt comes first but will occur in a world where secured debt comes first

T = The added uncompensated torts that would not occur in a world where tort debt comes first but will occur in a world where secured debt comes first

$$W \geq W + A - T$$

The left side of this inequality is total wealth in the tort-first world; the right side is total wealth in the secured-first world. The right side of this equation can be greater only if A is greater than T, that is, as Shupack asserts, the added activity A is greater than the tort loss resulting from that activity T. For A to be greater than T for the economy as a whole, A must be greater than T for at least some person in the economy. That is, there must be some person who would increase his or her wealth through expanded economic activity in the secured-first world over what it would have been in the tort-first world and whose increased wealth is greater than the expanded tort liability that results from the expanded economic activity. The existence of many such people seems unlikely. They would all be people who could have expanded their activity in the tort-first world, paid the tort liability with their added wealth, and had some left over.

In his comment, Professor Knippenberg notes that giving involuntary creditors priority over secured creditors may compel secured creditors "to become managers with or close monitors of" their borrowers. He would instead allow lenders to focus narrowly on being repaid and leave debtors to worry about the tort liability. The difficulty with such a division of labor is that there is no reliable way to bring

The thrust of this proposal is to permit a judgment lien creditor to attach up to twenty percent of the value of a debtor's assets without regard to outstanding security interests. The proposal permits secured creditors to marshal so that the lien creditor can be forced to satisfy itself first from unencumbered assets. If unencumbered assets are not available, however, the lien creditor can execute on property subject to a security interest and recover up to twenty percent of the value of the proceeds from the judicial sale. In order to avoid the problems of financing purchase money consumer sales, the proposal is limited to commercial loans. There is little evidence that the problem that prompts consideration of this proposal occurs in consumer settings.

During the past fifty years, Article 9 has shifted in practice from a statute that assured commercial creditors that they could reliably encumber some of the debtor's assets to a statute that permits secured creditors to take a first lien on virtually all of the debtor's assets. When the secured creditors encumber everything a debtor owns, the debtor's other creditors—particularly the trade creditors, the tort victims, employees, and the environmental claimants—are unable to reach the debtor's assets even when they can win a judgment against a debtor. The careful secured creditor with an interest in all the debtor's property is in the enviable position of not only creating a monopoly lending arrangement with the debtor, but also participating in the debtor's success (through continued interest payments) without suffering losses if the debtor fails (by taking all the hard assets of the business). This proposal requires that trade creditors, tort victims, employees, and other unsecured creditors who also contribute to the life of a business have some access to the assets of that business if it is unable or refuses to pay its debts.

The idea that there should be a limit to the reaches of secured credit is not new. Professor Grant Gilmore, the eminent Yale (and University of Chicago) professor who was the principal draftsman of the original Article 9, observed in his treatise:

> Considerations of policy and common sense suggest that there must be a limiting point somewhere. Borrowers should not be encouraged or allowed to hypothecate all that they may ever own in the indefinite future in favor of a creditor who is willing to make a risky loan now. . . . And ways should be found to penalize a lender who, after allowing his borrower to pile up an intolerable weight of debt, then claims all the assets of the insolvent estate, leaving nothing to satisfy other claims. [footnotes omitted]

1 Gilmore §7.12 at 248. Professor Gilmore used the approach of limiting the property to which the secured creditor would have access. Through the years, the restrictions on the kinds of property that could become collateral were eased. The current proposed revision of Article 9 eliminates most of the remaining limits.

The trend in the law of security interests toward encumbering all the property of the debtor caused Professor Gilmore to entitle his last law review article "Confessions of a Repentant Draftsman." He decried what had happened to Article 9: "[D]oes it make any sense to award everything to a secured party who stands idly by while a doomed enterprise goes down the slippery slope into bankruptcy?" 15 Ga. L. Rev. 605, 627 (1981). This proposal restores a balance among creditors by making a systematic set aside for unsecured creditors.

A set aside for unsecured creditors discourages asset-based lending to 100% value of the collateral. Would it therefore constrict commercial lending? That is a difficult question to answer. To the extent that much commercial lending is not based on the liquidation value of the assets, but is based instead on the ability to tie the debtor up and fence it off from other competing lenders, there would be no change in lending activity. To the extent that much commercial lending does not rely on the full liquidation value, but is based on significantly lower loan-to-value ratios, this proposal would not cause changes. To the extent that markets are rational, any constriction in the rights of secured creditors should be felt in offsetting benefits to unsecured creditors and might therefore be expected to produce more unsecured commercial debt as well as lower-cost trade debt.

But the proposal would have some important effects. If a business is viable only because the creditor can lend to 100% loan-to-value, thereby externalizing the risks of unpaid debt to the trade and tort creditors, this proposal would cause a constriction in credit. Even for creditors who currently lend on 90% or even 80% loan-to-value ratios, a proposal that permits unsecured creditors to take some collateral value might cause such creditors to re-adjust their percentages downward. In effect, this proposal would encourage some de-leveraging of American businesses, particularly of high-risk businesses.

The carve-out proposal was met by a storm of protest. Secured creditor advocates branded the attempt to limit priority "radical." The most frequently repeated argument was that without full priority for secured creditors, the total amount of credit available in the economy would decline sharply, injuring all businesses. Professor Warren responded:

Elizabeth Warren, Making Policy with Imperfect Information: The Article 9 Full Priority Debates

82 Cornell L. Rev. 101 (1997)

While there may be no way to test the credit-constriction assertion directly or to measure either the magnitude or the direction of the changes that would occur with partial priority, it is interesting to note how the assertion is treated as a debate-stopper. If credit is reduced, the assumption runs, both commercial lenders and their borrowers will be hurt, their potential trade creditors will be hurt, and even a robust economy will be threatened.

The argument proves too much. If the only test of any part of a commercial law system were whether it promoted or constricted credit, then our system would look very different. Why not return to the days of debt servitude? There were efficiency concerns about servitude, but the bottom line was that servitude made credit available to people who otherwise could not obtain it. Nonetheless, it was gone by the mid-1700s.

If the goal of a commercial law system is expansion of credit, then perhaps the revisions of Article 9 should reflect changes in medical technology since the 1960s. Why not permit security interests in body parts? Any debtor who promised her liver or her heart would surely have strong incentives to perform on the loan. It would be possible to restrict security interests to body parts that leave the debtor diminished but alive, such as offering a kidney, skin for a graft, a womb, or a cornea as collateral. It appears that the expansion of credit notion has not been embraced fully.

The idea here is not to give the current Article 9 drafters new ideas. Instead, the point is to note that even if a security device promotes lending, there may be reasons not to support it. Some of the reasons may be grounded in efficiency arguments. Some may be naked applications of paternalism. Some of the arguments may refer to community sensibilities and fairness that are hard to quantify in an equation full of sigmas and betas, but that have to do with our collective confidence in the commercial law system.

Even when the discussion is about nothing but money, the argument that full priority is justified whenever it promotes more lending still proves too much. The incursions on priority in tax law, in statutory liens, and in bankruptcy make clear that fostering as much lending as possible is not the only goal of any commercial law system. The question is always one of balance. Taxing authorities get priorities in part because of a judgment that a business that cannot meet its tax obligations should not be operating. Cattle feed suppliers get a priority in part because they add value in a way that makes it virtually impossible for them to take a protected interest through any other method. Employees may take priority because they are poor risk spreaders. And so on. Bankruptcy law takes precedence over contractual agreements in part because the rights of third parties to pro rata distribution at liquidation cannot be negotiated away without the consent of the losing parties.

The ultimate question is not whether a partial priority scheme might cause some constriction in lending. The empirical question remains open, although there are strong arguments both to refute and to support the idea that total credit available would remain the same. The real question is how the efficiency arguments, even if they were unambiguously true, stack up against other considerations.

Despite some popularity among academics and the adoption of a somewhat similar proposal in Germany and other countries, the "carve out" proposal, as it came to be called, failed to win favor either with practicing lawyers or members of the Article 9 Drafting Committee. As Professor Mooney has described it, the carve-out proposal "died for lack of a first" in the Drafting Committee.

While the debate over the appropriateness of the rules governing the priority of secured debt continues, commercial practices continue to evolve. In the article excerpted below, Professor LoPucki argues that with computerization of business practices and the increasingly strategic nature of legal practice, secured credit threatens to engulf the entire system of civil liability.

Lynn M. LoPucki, The Death of Liability
106 Yale L.J. 1 (1996)

The liability system works solely through the entry and enforcement of money judgments. Debtors can defeat it by rendering themselves judgment proof.

Judgment-proofing strategies are of four basic types: secured debt, third-party ownership, exemption, and foreign haven.

Secured debt strategies are the most complex and the most common of the judgment-proofing strategies. They are employed primarily by small, relatively uncreditworthy businesses, whose lenders insist on security interests. The debtor becomes judgment proof by incurring secured debts in amounts exceeding the liquidation values of the debtor's properties. Money judgments thereafter enforced against the debtor's properties are subordinate to the secured debt. Enforcement is by liquidation of the debtor's property. Pursuant to the principle of subordination, the proceeds of liquidation go first to pay the secured creditors. Because the proceeds are less than the secured debt, no balance remains to be paid to the holder of the money judgment. It follows that the holder of the money judgment cannot obtain full or even partial payment by exercising its legal remedies. The buyer at the sale of fully encumbered collateral will own the property and the judgment creditor will receive nothing.

Because it is costly and risky for a judgment creditor to liquidate the assets of its debtor and the judgment creditor recovers nothing anyway, judgment creditors who understand the system often give up without liquidating their debtors. They simply write off the debt. When judgment creditors and potential judgment creditors behave in this manner, their debtors can continue in business indefinitely without paying their debts.

Some judgment creditors will attempt to liquidate their debtors. Those debtors can still prevail by any of three strategies. First, the debtor who has the cooperation of a strategically placed secured creditor can enlist the secured creditor's help in blocking the judgment creditor's levy. In recent years, several courts have held that a secured creditor whose own debt is in default has the right to possession of its collateral and that the right primes even the right of a sheriff who would seize the property under a judgment creditor's writ of execution.

Second, the debtor may allow the sale to take place, but in some indirect manner become a purchaser at the sale. Sale of the property will move ownership to a new legal entity, leaving the debt behind in the old. For this strategy to succeed, the debtor must find a surrogate to purchase the property for it and must prevent the judgment creditor from purchasing at the sale. In the most common circumstance, where the debtor is itself a corporation, the surrogate may be another corporation created specifically for that purpose and owned by the owners of the debtor or its managers. The surrogate can then permit the debtor to continue using the property, as a gift or in return for periodic payment of rent.

In many circumstances, the strategy of stripping judgment liens from property through state court sales will not work. The sheriffs who conduct the sales may insist on interfering with the debtor's possession of the property and operation of the business between the time of the levy and the time the state court confirms the sale.

In those circumstances, debtors can employ a third and even more powerful strategy for defeating subordinate lien creditors. Under the principle of productive use, the bankruptcy court will permit a debtor to operate its business while attempting to sell it. Thus protected, the debtor can propose a plan of reorganization that provides for the sale of the property to the new entity owned by the insiders, for an amount modestly below market value. Provided that value is less than the amount of the prior liens, pursuant to the principle of subordination, the judgment creditor recovers nothing from the bankruptcy proceeding. Thus, Chapter 11 enables the debtor to strip from its property liabilities in excess of the property's value, even without the formality of a sale. It permits the debtor to do directly what it could do indirectly under state court or bankruptcy liquidation procedures. By confirmation of a Chapter 11 plan, the debtor can reduce its total debt to the value of its property and reschedule that debt for future payment. The owner-managers of a debtor corporation ordinarily can retain ownership and control through Chapter 11.

A debtor that enters Chapter 11 with secured debt exceeding the liquidation value of its collateral is likely to emerge with secured debt approximately equal to the value of that collateral. The effect is that the emerging debtor is also judgment proof. If it incurs post-bankruptcy liabilities, it can file another Chapter 11 case, and strip those liabilities from the assets. This judgment-proof structure can operate perpetually.

The secured debt strategy is a relatively recent phenomenon. It is effective only in a system that permits debtors to encumber all, or substantially all, of their assets.

In the parent-subsidiary strategy, the debtor isolates the most valuable assets of the business in an entity other than the one that conducts the liability-producing business activity. For example, assume that a large company (Operations, Inc.) sells its products on credit and then borrows from banks against its accounts receivable. To employ a secured debt strategy, the company would grant the banks a security interest in the accounts. To employ the parent-subsidiary strategy, the company incorporates a subsidiary (Finance, Inc.), and retains ownership of all the stock. As Operations sells its products, it creates accounts receivable. Operations sells the accounts to Finance, and distributes any proceeds beyond its immediate cash needs to its shareholders. Under the principle of transferability, both transfers become final as they occur, leaving Operations with minimal assets. Finance pays for the accounts by borrowing on an unsecured basis from a bank. If Operations sells defective products and incurs liability, its creditors eventually will obtain judgments against Operations. They can force the liquidation of Operations's assets, including its shares of stock in Finance. But in the ensuing liquidation of Finance, the bank will have priority over the judgment creditors. The bank claims the assets of Finance as an unsecured creditor while the judgment creditors claim them as a shareholder. Unsecured creditors are entitled to absolute priority over shareholders, so by the principle of subordination the bank prevails and the judgment creditors take nothing.

If the bank makes sure that Finance engages in no liability-generating activities, but is merely a borrower and a repository of accounts receivable, the bank assures itself of priority over any liability the business generates. That is precisely the result obtained through use of the secured debt strategy. But the parent-subsidiary strategy is an ownership strategy rather than a secured debt strategy because the bank defeats the judgment creditors by proving ownership by a separate entity rather than subordination to secured debt.

This parent-subsidiary ownership strategy is in wide use among the largest companies in America. Most large companies consist of numerous corporate entities. Limiting liability—that is, defeating part of it—is the principal reason for creating those entities.[2] But the parent-subsidiary strategy itself rarely renders companies entirely judgment proof. Alone, it defeats only liability in excess of the value of the assets of the operating company. Nevertheless, the parent-subsidiary strategy has had a major effect in the bankruptcy reorganizations of large, publicly held companies. Its use in combination with a secured debt strategy can defeat a company's liability entirely.

The parent-subsidiary strategy is vulnerable to legal attack. In theory, at least, courts can disregard a corporate entity if it is being used too aggressively to defeat liability. But the rhetoric of entity disregard far outstrips the reality. Overall, disregard of the entities that compose a corporate group remains very much the exception.[3]

Professor Ronald Mann argues that the same macro changes in the commercial environment referred to by Professor LoPucki are eroding the use of secured credit in small business lending and thereby solving the problem of secured credit in that arena.

Ronald J. Mann, The Role of Secured Credit in Small-Business Lending

86 Geo. L.J. 1 (1997)

[O]ne of the most prominent bank lending programs of the last few years is Wells Fargo's BusinessLine program, which offers unsecured debt to small businesses nationwide. Relying on publicly available credit information analogous to the information credit-card issuers use in pre-approving potential credit-card customers, Wells Fargo identifies large numbers of small businesses that are potential loan customers. It then sends unsolicited mailings to those businesses offering a hassle-free unsecured line of credit, ranging from $5,000 to $75,000, requiring only a one-page mail-in application. Because the borrower's signature on the application includes a promise to repay funds advanced under the line and a personal guaranty of that obligation, the signature on the application completes the

---

2. For example, the Eighth Circuit has written:

The doctrine of limited liability is intended precisely to protect a parent corporation whose subsidiary goes broke. That is the whole purpose of the doctrine, and those who have the right to decide such questions, that is, legislatures, believe that the doctrine, on the whole, is socially reasonable and useful. We think that the doctrine would largely be destroyed if a parent corporation could be held liable simply on the basis of errors in business judgment.

3. See, e.g., NLRB v. Fullerton Transfer & Storage Ltd., 910 F.2d 331, 336-39 (6th Cir. 1990) (upholding division of single business among three corporations—one to hire truck drivers, one to own trucks, and one to own real estate—and refusing to enforce NLRB back-pay order, obtained against corporation that hired drivers, against corporations that owned assets).

documentation process. There are no separate promissory notes, guaranties, loan agreements, or financing statements.

Those mailings have enabled the program to create a large portfolio that gives Wells Fargo a nationwide presence for its small-business lending program. Competing lenders (many of whom do require collateral) doubt Wells Fargo's ability to cut into their market share significantly, and are quick to point out that Wells Fargo's loans are significantly more expensive than more conventional, individually priced, small-business loans. However true those arguments may be, Wells Fargo clearly has tapped into a significant preference of many small-business owners. That program brought Wells Fargo substantially more than a billion dollars in new loans in 1995 and has brought its total portfolio of unsecured small-business loans up to about $4 billion. The fact is, many small-business owners are happy to pay more for money that comes with fewer strings attached.

Nor is it easy to dismiss Wells Fargo's program as an odd fad that will pass when cooler heads prevail. On the contrary, other major players recognizing the desire of borrowers for hassle-free lending are beginning to follow suit. Most prominently, two of the largest lenders in my sample—BankAmerica and Chase Manhattan—have altered their small-business lending programs to eliminate the use of collateral from large segments of that program. Most crucially, the borrowers eligible for those unsecured loans are selected not because they are the safest or most creditworthy borrowers in the portfolio. Rather, those programs extend unsecured loans to all borrowers in the portfolio whose loans are under $100,000. If that sounds like a small segment of the market, consider that it is more than half of BankAmerica's business banking portfolio, more than a billion dollars at that institution alone. Finally, even banks that typically take collateral on small business loans do make a substantial number of those loans without taking a lien.

The pattern of secured credit is not a simple one. Some banks' small-business loans are entirely or predominately secured. Other banks' small-business loans are entirely or predominately unsecured (at least for loans below $100,000). Still other banks have a mix of the two. One interpretation of the evidence would be a static one, that the relevant considerations are so closely balanced that there is little or nothing to choose between secured and unsecured transactions. Under that view, the choice between secured and unsecured credit matters so little that the choice of a particular bank can end up resting on the "philosophy" of that particular institution, with neither choice leading to a significant competitive disadvantage.

That interpretation, however, seems to me to ignore the dynamic character of the market. The small-business lending market is not some sleepy corner of the economy in which lending transactions are structured "the way we've always done it." This is an arena into which the largest financial institutions in our economy are throwing tremendous resources, motivated by the perception that technology provides an opportunity for profitable lending opportunities in areas banks historically have left underserved.

Two of the most powerful factors justifying the use of unsecured credit—declining constraints on future borrowing and advances in information technology—are factors that have changed dramatically during the last few decades and significantly during the last few years alone. Consider first the ability of secured credit to constrain future borrowing. The main source of funding that is defeating that use of secured credit is the credit card. Twenty-five years ago the credit-card market was in its infancy. Few individuals operating small businesses could have used credit cards to fund businesses with the tens of thousands of dollars of credit-card borrowing that has been thrust on any reasonably solvent individual during the last few years.

The story of information technology is the same. Twenty-five years ago it would have been completely impractical for banks to develop standardized scoring criteria for evaluating small-business loan applications. Only in the last few years have computers developed to the point where it is cost-effective for lenders to use credit-scoring and early-warning systems effectively. Indeed, even now it is clear that the costs of those technologies give the largest institutions a considerable advantage in their use. It takes a massive small-business portfolio to support a completely cutting-edge credit-scoring and early-warning system. Thus, although hundreds of banks are using credit scoring in some manner, only a handful of our banks have developed systems that reflect their own loan experience; the others rely on a standardized third-party scorecard developed from a sampling of several bank's portfolios. Similarly, I do not think it is a coincidence that the only institutions I interviewed with proprietary early-warning systems were Home Savings of America (the largest savings bank in the United States) and Chase Manhattan Corporation (perennially one of the largest banks in the United States).

Based on the rapid development of those factors, I prefer a dynamic interpretation of the mixed pattern of secured and unsecured credit. As I see it, only in the last few years has the comparative advantage passed from secured credit to unsecured credit. Under that perspective, the small-business bank lending market is in the middle of a shift of institutions, with secured credit quickly becoming the way of the past and unsecured credit quickly coming to dominance.

The declining trend in the use of secured debt in small business financing appears to have been matched by an opposite trend in lending to large, public companies. Andrew Wood reports an increase in the median level of secured debt for large public companies in bankruptcy from 23 percent of assets in 1997-99 to 41 percent of assets in 2009-10. Andrew A. Wood, *The Decline of Unsecured Creditor and Shareholder Recoveries in Large Public Company Bankruptcies*, 85 American Bankruptcy Law Journal. 429, 430-431 (2011).

Lynn M. LoPucki, Arvin I. Abraham, and Bernd P. Delahaye, Optimizing English and American Security Interests

88 Notre Dame L. Rev. 1785 (2013)

Security enjoys a highly privileged position in American law. A simple-sentence grant of a security interest, combined with the filing of notice in an obscure set of public records, will give the secured creditor's claim priority over employees' wage claims, child support obligations, tax claims, civil damage judgments, criminal fines and forfeitures, claims for unjust enrichment, and just about any other kind of debt imaginable.

Scholars have attempted to justify security on both contract and property theories. On the American side, Dean David Leebron best articulated the contract argument:

> The priority claim of a secured creditor rests almost entirely on principles of contract and notice. A persuasive theory of secured credit financing has been elusive, but the priority of a secured creditor over other financial creditors can be justified on the grounds that non-secured creditors grant a loan knowing that some assets are subject to security interests or could be subjected to security interests without their permission. If particular creditors will not tolerate other creditors having security interests in the borrower's assets, they can refuse to make a loan or make it only if the borrower agrees not to subject its assets to any security interests.[1]

Contract cannot, however, justify security because security agreements "[are] effective according to [their] terms . . . against purchasers of the collateral, and against creditors."[2] That includes purchasers and creditors who did not consent to the security agreement, had no way of knowing of its existence, or never chose to become creditors at all. Agreement is the essence of contract, but the affected purchasers and creditors have not agreed. As Professors Lynn LoPucki and Elizabeth Warren put it, "[s]ecurity is an agreement between A and B that C take nothing."

Other scholars attempt to justify security on property theories. For example, Professors Stephen Harris [sic] and Charles Mooney argued:

> It seems clear enough that security interests, under Article 9 and real estate law alike, are interests in property. The legal regime for security interests reflects property law functionally as well as doctrinally. We believe it follows that the law should honor the transfer or retention of security interests on the same normative grounds on which it respects the alienation of property generally.[3]

The property theory begins from the generally accepted premise that a building owner can, by conveying the building in an otherwise unobjectionable transaction, cut off the rights of the debtor's creditors to the building. By analogy, the property theory holds that by conveying the first $100,000 of the value of the building in return for a $100,000 loan, the owner should be able to cut off the rights of the debtor's other creditors to the first $100,000 of the value of the building. Frequent American literature references to security interests as "property" and English literature references to charges as "proprietary" are invocations of this theory.

A necessary implication of the property conveyance theory is that encumbered property has multiple owners. The secured creditor owns the value of the collateral up to the full amount of the debt. The debtor owns the value of the collateral in excess of the amount of the debt, the right to redeem the property by paying the debt, and the right to use the property in the interim.

The principal policy objections to security are that it is deceptive (the "Deception Problem") and that it distorts incentives for the management of property (the "Incentives Problem"). The essence of the Deception Problem is that debtors who

---

1. David W. Leebron, Limited Liability, Tort Victims, and Creditors, 91 Colum. L. Rev. 1565, 1646 (1991).

2. UCC §9-201(a)(2012).

3. Steven L. Harris & Charles W. Mooney, Jr., A Property-Based Theory of Security Interests: Taking Debtors' Choices Seriously, 80 Va. L. Rev. 2021, 2051 (1994).

have granted security interests appear to have wealth, but do not. The effect is to deceive third parties who extend credit without knowledge of the pre-existing security. The problem is generally referred to as "ostensible ownership" in the United States and as "false wealth" in England.

The Incentives Problem is most egregious and easiest to see when the amount of the secured debt equals or exceeds the value of the collateral. Consider, for example, a business that operates with one billion dollars in assets encumbered by one billion dollars in secured debt. As the property's owner, the debtor has the right to control its use. The debtor can engage in business activities that risk inflicting billions of dollars in damages on third parties. Those third parties have no remedy against the debtor, because the debtor owns no part of the value of its own assets. They have no remedy against the secured party because the secured party—switching its metaphorical role from "owner" to "creditor"—has priority over them. By shielding the debtor's property from the valid claims of third parties, security renders both "owners" judgment-proof and encourages the irresponsible management of wealth.

The view of secured credit we have presented in this book is not a flattering one. Secured credit is a deceptive, overly complicated, poorly implemented system for accomplishing goals that its proponents cannot quite explain. The premise of this system is that everybody knows certain things, when, in fact, few people do. The effect is to enable the sophisticated to take advantage of the unsophisticated and to blame the latter for their own losses.

The bewildering array of filing systems is growing in number and complexity. Their inaccuracy and inefficiency compel multiple filing and multiple searching. That has made secured credit a cash cow for strapped state and national governments. Those governments will not fix the filing systems because that would mean fewer filings and searches, which would lower government revenues. We believe that the secured credit system is badly in need of repair, if not exorcism.

Secured credit plays a central and unsettling role in the system of private property. No one can be secure in their property until they have classified that property and vetted it through the arcane secured credit system. To the extent that property is subject to liens, ownership may be illusory. The presence of, or potential for, liens affects criminal forfeiture, divorce settlement, the recoverability of tort damages, the enforcement of contract rights, the structure of intellectual property rights, the effectiveness of bankruptcy relief, and the effectiveness of government regulation. Secured credit potentially threatens every market transaction, including ordinary consumer purchases at the mall. Aside from ownership itself, secured credit is probably the most important legal institution in the economic system.

The very complexity and obscurity of secured credit make it an intellectually fascinating realm in which to practice law. Secured credit is an environment in which legal strategy flourishes, and lawyers can, for better or for worse, provide real value to their clients.

Problem Set 40

40.1.   Your long-time client and friend, Potsie Pottow is back. Potsie now works for Steady Hand, a venture capital firm that makes both loans and equity investments in high-tech start-up businesses. His client, Robert Alvin, is a geneticist who specializes in marketing "biological solutions" to diseases in plants, animals, and human beings. He identifies products developed in other countries and brings them to the United States for production and sales.

Alvin seeks $4 million in financing for three products he seeks to introduce. Because the safety of these products is unproven, liability insurance is unavailable. No established company will manufacture the products for Alvin, or even lease him a plant in which to do so. One million dollars of the financing he seeks will be invested in a plant, another million will go into inventory and equipment, a third will be paid to developers of the product for licensing fees (they want their money in advance), and the last $1 million will go for "soft costs" such as labor, start-up costs, and advertising. Each of the three products is alone capable of generating billions of dollars in profits (or in liability). The deal tentatively struck is that Steady Hand will receive 15 percent interest on the $4 million dollars while it remains outstanding and half the profits on these three products. Both parties are willing to talk about other structures, "so long as the bottom line stays about the same."

Potsie asks your advice on structuring the investment to minimize the risk to Steady Hand if one of the products should "blow up on us" — without, of course, limiting the profit potential. For the purpose of structuring the discussion, Potsie posits the following prospects for the business: It does three projects, two of which make a billion dollars each in profits and the third of which results in $3 billion in liabilities. What do you tell Potsie?

40.2.   In a parallel universe, you represent Alecia Card, who was severely injured by microbes released from the premises of Continental Magnatech Corporation, a corporation owned by Robert Alvin with financing from Steady Hand in accord with the scheme you came up with in Problem 40.1. Liability is clear. The doctors predict an extended agony followed by a horrible death, so the damages will likely be huge. Alecia is only the first of what are likely to be many victims of the microbe release over many years. Continental Magnatech Corporation (Magnatech) appears to own no assets of significant value. The manufacturing premises are leased from Shady Grove Leasing, Inc., a publicly-held company founded by Robert Alvin with investments from clients of Steady Hand. Magnatech had just commenced operations at the time of the release. Until then, Magnatech appeared to have great earning potential, but its operations have been suspended by state and federal authorities and it is not expected to reopen. Magnatech perfectly observed all corporate formalities. Other businesses owned by Alvin and various outside investors solicited by Steady Hand are producing and selling other products, and are expected to bring in billions of dollars in profits. Whom do you sue and on what theories? (We realize we have not given you the materials necessary to answer this question, but give it some thought in light of what you have learned in other courses in law school. As you think about it, keep in mind that (1) no court has ever pierced the veil of a publicly-held company, and (2) courts virtually never pierce the veil of a corporation that has observed corporate formalities.)

40.3.   For the past 14 years a member of your law firm, Shelley Kramer, has been doing the intellectual property work for Sigmet Electronics, a manufacturer of avionic components. Shelley bills Sigmet monthly. At any given time, Sigmet owes the firm about $20,000 to $50,000 for unbilled legal work and for legal work billed but not yet paid. This morning, while scanning recent UCC filings for another matter, you noticed a UCC filing against Sigmet as debtor and in favor of Portage State Bank. The filing is against "equipment, inventory, and accounts receivable." What are the implications of this filing for the firm? Are you relieved because Portage will now assist you in monitoring the debtor? Concerned? If so, what should you do? Should you be monitoring for UCC filings against all the firm's clients?

40.4.   As chair of the recently appointed National Secured Credit Review Commission, your job is to decide whether to recommend federal legislation to replace Article 9 and, if so, what that legislation should provide. How do you rank the following options going in and how do you respond to the arguments noted?

a.   *Retain Article 9 in basically its current state.* If you choose this option, how do you respond to the arguments that (1) secured credit encourages excessive lending by making it possible to finance even bad businesses; (2) secured credit facilitates judgment proofing, which eventually will destroy the liability system; and (3) secured credit is unfair to trade creditors and buyers of collateral because it is fundamentally deceptive?

b.   *Give nonconsensual tort creditors and/or small wage claims priority over secured creditors under federal law.* If you choose this option, how do you respond to the argument that every secured lender will be at the mercy of runaway juries in tort cases, leading them to cut back on the amounts they lend, and ultimately leading to a slowing of the economy?

c.   *Adopt the Warren carve-out proposal, in its current form or some closely related form, under federal law.* If you choose this option, how do you respond to the arguments that (1) granting a security interest harms unsecured creditors no more than selling property or paying one creditor in preference to another; (2) lenders will cut back on the amounts they lend, leading to a slowing of the economy; and (3) the 20 percent carve-out won't benefit general unsecured creditors significantly because most of the money will go to bankruptcy lawyers and other creditors with priority under Bankruptcy Code §507(a)?

d.   *Adopt solution b or c, above, but do it through uniform state law, rather than federal law.* If you choose this option, how do you deal with the problem of particular states giving absolute priority to secured creditors in order to attract business?

Table of Cases

Italics indicate principal cases.

Table of Statutes

Code of Federal Regulations

Internal Revenue Code (I.R.C.)

Uniform Motor Vehicle Certificate of Title Act

Index

Alphabetization is letter-by-letter. References are to page numbers.